Contents

P9-DED-326

Regional Map Contents

Grand Bahama
(pp102–3)

Abacos
(p147)

Berry
Islands
(p133)

Biminis
(p126)

Eleuthera
(pp176–7)

Andros
(p136)

New
Providence
(pp64–5)

Cat Island
(p209)

San Salvador
(p216)

Exumas
(p193)

Long Island
(p223)

Crooked &
Acklins Islands &
Long Cay
(p230)

Inaguas &
Mayaguana
(p233)

Caicos Islands
(p241)

Turks Islands
(p259)

Highlights

CHRISTOPHER P BAKER

Pink Sands Beach (p178), Harbour Island,
is the perfect place for a romantic stroll

Wild bottlenose dolphins (p169)

CHRISTOPHER P BAKER

Quaint clapboard houses and picket fences line the
streets of New Plymouth, Green Turtle Cay (p169)

Dance to the *goombay* drumbeat of Junkanoo (p33) midsummer or Boxing Day carnival

JEFF GREENBERG

MICHAEL LAWRENCE

Turtle Cove possesses the world's largest and deepest blue hole (660ft; p228), leading to a vast underwater cavern

Iconic Grace Bay Beach (p242) is aquamarine bliss

GREG JOHNSTO

An inquisitive iguana at Allan's Cays (p80)

GREG JOHNSTON

One of the historic buildings on Bay St (p63), reflecting Nassau's colonial days

CHRISTOPHER P BAKE

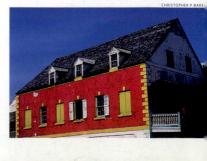

GREG JOHNSTON

Sea kayaking at sunset (p109)

A horse-drawn surrey in front of a Loyalist's home at elegant Eleuthera Point (p191)

GREG JOHNSTON

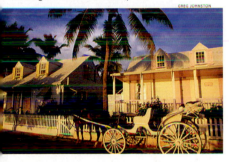

DAVE LEWIS

Sail boats ready to be launched into picturesque Grace Bay (p246)

A local woman from Cat Island (p209) displays straw-work for sale outside her home

GREG JOHNSTON

CHRISTOPHER P BAKER

Mt Alvernia Hermitage (p210) on Cat Island

One of the spectacular dive sites located at Grand Bahama (p106)

MICHAEL LAWRENCE

LEE FOSTER

The West Indian flamingo, leggy super-model of the bird world (p236)

Scintillating Nassau Harbour at dusk (p63)

CHRISTOPHER P BA

The Author

JILL KIRBY

Having been lucky enough to travel through the Caribbean Islands by fishing boat and ferry, Jill has also taken time over the years to dance at the 'Sunsplash' Reggae Festival in Jamaica, bask on Barbados beaches over Christmas and dive during New Year in St Vincent and the Grenadines, with a little bit of partying along the way. Now living in Australia, Jill jumped at the chance to return to her Caribbean and West Indian adventures. As a journalist and freelance writer Jill also provided the Bahamas, Turks and Caicos chapters for Lonely Planet's *Caribbean Islands*.

My Favorite Trip

The following fought off some tough competition:

Best sights? The Gothic churches of Long Island's Clarence Town (p227), pretty Hope Town (p155) on Elbow Cay and Provo's stunning Chalk Sound National Park (p245).

Best adventures? Swimming with affable wild pigs off the coast of Major Cay (p206), houseboating the other 364 Exuma Cays (p203) and kayaking through Lucayan National Park (p118) in Grand Bahama.

Best diving? Handfeeding wild stingrays at Green Turtle Cay (p167), meeting wild dolphins in North Bimini (p129), cuddling divers' pet groupers off Grand Turk (p263) and watching Salt Cay's (p267) humpback whales.

Best place for beach bumming? Overall, Eleuthera (p178) – you can't beat pink-sand beaches at sunset.

Best fun? A karaoke night in Provo (p249) and a Sunday church service anywhere, for the music and sheer exuberance.

CONTRIBUTING AUTHORS

Jean-Bernard Carillet prepared the Diving chapter (p45). Having been born with restless feet and equally restless fins, Jean-Bernard's journeys have taken him to the ultimate dive destinations in the world, which include French Polynesia, New Caledonia, Egypt and the Caribbean. A more recent addition to this list is his foray into the Seine River in Paris, where he dived with a team of professional firemen. As a dive instructor and incorrigible traveler, Jean-Bernard has written extensively for various French publications, including *Plongeurs International* magazine. Other Lonely Planet titles that he has coordinated and co-authored include two Diving & Snorkeling guides: *Tahiti & French Polynesia* and *The Red Sea*.

LONELY PLANET AUTHORS

Why is our travel information the best in the world? It's simple: our authors are independent, dedicated travelers. They don't research using just the Internet or phone, and they don't take freebies in exchange for positive coverage. They travel widely, to all the popular spots and off the beaten track. They personally visit thousands of hotels, restaurants, cafés, bars, galleries, palaces, museums and more – and they take pride in getting all the details right, and telling it how it is. For more, see the authors section on www.lonelyplanet.com.

Dr David Goldberg, MD wrote the Health chapter (p296). David completed his training in internal medicine and infectious diseases at Columbia Presbyterian Medical Center in New York City, where he has also served as voluntary faculty. He is an infectious diseases specialist in Scarsdale, New York, and is the editor-in-chief of the website www.mdtravelhealth.com.

LAST EDITION
Christopher P Baker wrote the previous two editions of *Bahamas, Turks & Caicos*.

Getting Started

Your visit to the Bahamas and Turks and Caicos will benefit from a bit of preplanning. It's not particularly difficult to get to the region or to navigate your way around, but a little forethought will save you money as accommodations, travel and eating costs can be high. If you're after a get-away-from-it-all experience it's wise to avoid costly stays in Nassau between flights. See the island chapters and Transportation on p287 for more suggestions and local airline information.

See Accommodations on p270 for some suggestions on how to save money on accommodation.

WHEN TO GO
The Bahamas and Turks and Caicos enjoy approximately 320 sunny days a year. During winter (December to April), temperatures average 70°F to 78°F, while in summer (mid-April to mid-December) a range of 80°F to 90°F is the norm. Winter is the best time to visit as the weather is balmy and there are fewer mosquitoes. Humidity in the northern islands is relatively high year-round, but lower in the southern islands. The rainy season extends from late May to November, with the hurricane season occurring toward the end of this period – from September through November.

See Climate Charts (p277) for more information.

The peak holiday season typically runs from mid-December to mid-April, and at this time hotel prices are highest. Some hotels are booked solid around Christmas and Easter; it's especially advisable to plan ahead if you want to visit during these periods.

COSTS & MONEY
The Bahamian dollar is linked one-to-one with the US dollar, and the Turks and Caicos has the US dollar as its official currency, so all prices in this guide are in US dollars. A midrange traveler visiting during peak season and budgeting on accommodations and two meals a day should expect to spend from $120 to $200 per day. If you're traveling on a budget you can get by on $105 to $120 per day, while those wanting to stay in top-end accommodations will pay upward of $200 each day. On top of

---

DON'T LEAVE HOME WITHOUT...

■ Photographic equipment and film as these are pricey in the Bahamas and Turks and Caicos.

■ Proof of ownership of laptops and computer equipment to show customs officials.

■ Your patience, if flying with Bahamasair across the region.

■ A healthy liver and a bottle opener – there are some fabulous local beers!

■ An empty suitcase in which to gather some duty-free goodies and original vibrant artworks.

■ Your manners, which will be held in very high esteem across the islands.

■ A balance of priorities for any vegetarians and vegans who will enjoy much here, but not the cuisine.

■ Diapers, tampons and teabags as these can be hard to find and expensive to buy in the outer islands.

■ Condoms, especially as AIDS is a growing concern in the Bahamas.

these prices you will also need to budget in bottled water, all drinks, activities and travel to your costs.

Even if you prefer to use cash, credit cards are required by airlines and most lodgings as a form of security (with the paperwork torn-up upon payment). Travelers checks are accepted in many places, but the further off-the-beaten track you are, the more cash is preferred.

TRAVEL LITERATURE

There are heaps of good books that will provide insight into the history, culture and lifestyle of the Bahamas and Turks and Caicos. Below is a selection of these.

- *Bahama Saga: the Epic Story of the Bahama Island* by Peter Barratt is a well-researched, very digestible 'factional' novel that details the history of the Bahamas.
- *Isles of Eden* by Harvey Lloyd is a splendid coffee-table book about life in the southern Family Islands. This book has some super photos.
- *Tale from Margaritaville: Fictional Facts & Factual Fictions* by Jimmy Buffett. He is better known as a singer-songwriter, and he clearly adores the Bahamas; this collection of short stories affectionately depicts island life.
- *Don't Stop the Carnival* by Herman Wouk is a funny romp about a New York publicist who gives it all up to open a hotel on a fictitious Caribbean isle. The book was made into a musical by Jimmy Buffett in the '90s.
- *Islands in the Stream* by Ernest Hemingway provides a fictitious but accurate look at the Biminis and island life, as well as his own bohemian ways during WWII. Not one of his best, but an interesting read nevertheless.
- *'Who Let the Dog Out?' Dottie's Story* by Carole Hughes tells the tale about a Dalmatian born in Green Turtle Cay who heads off to explore the world. This one is for the kiddies, and is lots of fun.
- *Once Below a Time: Bahamian Stories* by Telcine Turner's is an illustrated collection of short stories for children. Youngsters might also enjoy *Climbing Clouds: Stories & Poems from the Bahamas,* which is also edited by Turner.

"...catch the island's biggest and best festivals: Boxing Day's Junkanoo... and any of the island's regattas."

INTERNET RESOURCES

See also Tourist Information on p285.

Abacos Islands (www.go-abacos.com) The official website has good practical information.

Bahamas Ministry of Tourism (www.bahamas.com) The official tourism site is a useful place to start researching your trip.

Bahamas Out Islands Promotion Board (www.bahama-out-islands.com) Information about the Family Islands, including a listing of events.

Grand Bahama Island Tourism Board (www.grand-bahama.com) Another good official site, with useful regional information.

Lonely Planet (www.lonelyplanet.com) With postcards from other travelers and the Thorn Tree bulletin board.

Provo.net (www.provo.net) Providenciales (known as 'Provo'), the main gateway to the Turks and Caicos Islands.

Turks & Caicos Islands Tourist Board (www.turksandcaicostourism.com) The official site of these islands has much practical information.

FESTIVALS & EVENTS

If possible, try to catch the island's biggest and best festivals: Boxing Day's Junkanoo, summer's *goombay* celebrations, and any of the island's

---

CONDUCT IN THE BAHAMAS & TURKS & CAICOS ISLANDS

People are courteous and conservative on the islands, and it takes very little to open the door to their welcoming and friendly ways.

- Always greet people with a smile, and, when driving on the outer islands, with a wave.
- When greeting someone, ask about their welfare before addressing any business.
- Wait in lines or queues to be served.
- Tip around 15% in bars, restaurants and cafés.
- Dress formally for church and smartly for any evening entertainment.
- Cover up swimming gear and bare bods when heading for town.

---

regattas. For more information on these and other festivals in the region see the island chapters and the Directory on p279.

RESPONSIBLE TRAVEL

The Bahamas and Turks and Caicos are promoting care for their environment; here's how to help.

- Don't touch or stand on coral. Coral is extremely sensitive and can be killed by touch. Snorkelers, divers, fishing fans and boaters should be especially careful.
- Don't buy products made from endangered species, such as anything made from coral or conch shell. Some of these are killed to make trinkets for tourists, so please shop with a conscience.
- Don't eat meals using endangered species. Whatever the tourist dollar will buy, the poacher will supply. Still widely eaten across the islands, grouper and conch fall into these categories.
- Keep to the footpaths. When you're hiking, always follow designated trails. The breeding grounds of animals and habitats of plants are easily destroyed by walkers who stray off the beaten path.
- Discourage littering. Forget about social protocols – if you see other travelers throw their litter on the ground or stick their cigarette butts in the sand, please do something about it. If they're bigger than you, pick up their rubbish. Otherwise, tell them to put it in the trash themselves.

Itineraries
CLASSIC ROUTES

BAHAMAS HIGHLIGHTS
One to Two Months

The Bahamas'
870-mile run is
a waterbaby's
delight: snorkel,
dive or enjoy the
shallows off tiny
islands dotted
with cute churches
and lively bars.
Jump on a water
taxi, ferry or plane
for your next
deserted beach.

Spend three days in **Nassau** (p63) sightseeing before taking a three-day trip to Alice Town in **North Bimini** (p127). There, go bonefishing or snorkel the mystical Bimini Road, and raise a glass at **Hemingway's haunts** (p131).

Make your way to **Grand Bahama** (p106) for glorious beach bumming, trips to see **dolphins** (p107) and kayaking in **Lucayan National Park** (p118). Fly to Abaco's Treasure Cay and enjoy the exquisite **Treasure Cay Beach** (p165). Take a ferry from **Marsh Harbour** (p148) to friendly **Green Turtle Cay** (p171) for a Goombay Smash, and to **Elbow Cay** (p155) to wander Hope Town's streets.

Having returned to Nassau, catch a fast ferry to see the beautiful people on **Harbour Island** (p175), and enjoy the rosy hue of **Pink Sands Beach** (p178) at sunset. Then catch a ferry and hire a car so you can delight in the beaches and Duck Inn at Governor's Harbour in **Eleuthera** (p187). Fly via Nassau to George Town in **Great Exuma** (p193) to sleep under the stars in a **houseboat** (p198). Visit **Stocking Island** (p200) and snorkel at **Thunderball Grotto** (p206). Then fly onto pretty **Long Island** (p222). Once there, drive to the striking churches of **Clarence Town** (p227) and the world's deepest blue hole at **Turtle Cove** (p228). Dive from **Shark Reef** (p226) and at **Guana Key beach** (p226).

TURKS & CAICOS TRANQUIL TOP SPOTS   Three Weeks to Two Months

Fly into friendly **Providenciales** (p242) for a few days' bumming around on delightful **Grace Bay Beach** (p242) and nights' playing at the surrounding bars and restaurants. Hire a car to visit some sights such as the stunning **Chalk Sound National Park** (p245) and the western hills. Then sign up for fantastic boat excursions to **Little Water Cay** (p252) to meet friendly iguanas, **French Cay** (p252) for a dive with gentle stingrays, or **Pine Cay** (p252) for an unforgettable dive or two or to bask in the light of glowworms.

Take a flight directly to **North Caicos** (p253) and spend a few days cycling along the paved roads, enjoying the scenery of this island's lush vegetation. Make sure you visit the **Wades Green Plantation ruins** (p254), the magnificent, leggy flamingos at **Flamingo Pond** (p254) and **Three Mary Cays National Park** (p242), which is also a flamingo sanctuary, for a snorkel. Hikers should then fly to the **Middle Caicos Reserve & Trail System** (p255), where the unspoilt beauty of pine forests and freshwater lakes, and the adorable lovely cottages of Middle Caicos can be enjoyed.

Divers and those who appreciate the quiet life should fly from North Caicos to **Grand Turk** (p260) for a few relaxing days. Wander the quiet beaches and streets of **Cockburn Town** (p261) and spend the evenings at friendly local bars, such as the **Sand Bar** (p265), or take night dives to the famous and fabulous reef wall, where the coral glows as though it has gemstones encrusted in it. Make sure you don't miss diving at **Macdonalds** (p263), which is frequented by groupers and angelfish, or near the 18th-century shipwreck at **Salt Cay** (p266). Here, the land holds relics of the 'white-gold' trade and the seas envelope birthing **humpback whales** (p268).

Start with some partying, then move across the 95 miles of this route for some beach living and exhilarating encounters in the ocean's coral 'cities'. On these islands time ticks by slowly. The soothing seas and gentle folk will entice you to slow down, unfold and really blossom.

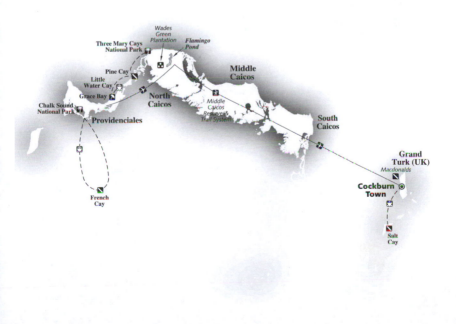

ROADS LESS TRAVELED

OUT ISLAND ADVENTURES   Two Months

Travel the untrod-
den 2390-mile
route through this
region, detouring
to many cays that
surround each
island group.
Journey by boat for
watery adventures,
by land to mark
your footprints in
pristine earth and
sand, or by air to
give yourself the
time you will need
to traverse each of
these places.

For explorers, the vast but relatively undeveloped **Andros** (p135) will surely appeal. Smothered in pine forests, thick undergrowth and wetlands, the **Bluff** (p144) on South Andros has a palm-lined sandy hideaway. **Central Andros** (p138) has waterways and caves.

Culture vultures may want to focus on the African heritage of the Bahamas, still found in **Cat Island's** (p209) plantation and church ruins as well as in the mysticism of **obeah** (p212). You're able to canoe around quiet **Turtle Cove** (p210) and find a hermit's work at **Mt Alvernia Hermitage** (p210). **San Salvador** (p215) is a tiny spot where bush medicine and old plantation ruins prevail, and the diving is stunning. Remote and un-spoiled, the **Crooked Island District** (p229) offers a remote natural setting with a few splendid beaches, bat caves, birds (especially flamingos) and nesting turtles. **Mayaguana** (p237) is one of the least developed Bahamian islands, as is **West Caicos** (p251), known for fantastic diving, popula-tions of iguanas and flamingos and isolated beaches. Finally, head for semiarid, scrub-covered **Great Inagua** (p235). Nature rules here, with a turtle reserve at Union Creek and the famous **Bahamas National Trust Park** (p237), where a hike takes you into the heart of one of the world's largest flocks of flamingos. A tour through the reservoirs of **Morton Salt Works** (p237), north of Matthew Town, will also put you in touch with the region's past.

TAILORED TRIPS

DIVING & SNORKELING

You can't beat diving or snorkeling with whales, which, in season, is best from **Salt Cay** (p266) in the Turks and Caicos. At **Grand Turk** (p263) there's also a myriad of great dive sites that are home to dozing turtles, grinning moray eels and giant groupers. Snorkelers will love **Gibb's Cay** (p263), where southern stingrays flutter. You can venture to **South Caicos** (p256) for massive schools of eagle rays, and on to Providenciales' host of snorkeling spots, beginning in **Grace Bay** (p242). Divers make a beeline for **French Cay** (p252), where hawksbill turtles roam, and the marine life–rich

Northwest Point Marine National Park (p245). At **West Caicos** (p251) snorkelers and divers can see pelagics, corals and neon-colored fish.

If you're looking for top spots in the Bahamas, dive the deepest blue hole at **Long Island** (p222) and the fantastic wall-dive sites off **San Salvador** (p215), and enjoy the caverns, blue holes and coral reefs in the **Exuma Cays Land & Sea Park** (p204). Also visit the many wrecks off **New Providence** (p79), the **Andros** (p135) barrier reef, and possible remnants of Atlantis at the **Biminis** (p126), where you can also swim with wild Atlantic spotted dolphins. Adventurous types can socialize with sharks at **Walker's Cay** (p151), and with glamorous people at **Eleuthera** (p175).

BEAUTIFUL BALMY BEACHES

For lounging at the dreamiest stretches of sugar-soft sand and sparkling turquoise seas in the region, here are some beaches to tempt you. Grand Bahama's 8-acre stretch **Lucaya Beach** (p106) is loved by families, and is perfect for water sports, or you could try the soft sands of quiet **Churchill Beach** (p106).

The Abacos cays hold the award for several of the most beautiful beaches of this region, with Treasure Cay's gorgeous turquoise and white crescent, **Treasure Cay Beach** (p165), and pretty Elbow Cay's equally tantalizing **Hope Town Beach** (p158). Next is Paradise Island's amusement-filled **Cabbage Beach** (p79) with its snowy-white sand, followed by Eleuthera's famous rosy **Pink Sands Beach** (p178) on Harbour Island and the endless drifts of East Point's

Lighthouse Beach (p191). Exuma has the stunning beaches of **Exuma Cays Land & Sea Park** (p204) and the miles of talcum-powder fine **Stocking Island Beach** (p200), site of the world's best beach bar right at the water's edge. Long Island has the well-protected **Guana Key Beach** (p226), facing jade-colored seas, and secret stunner **Gordon's Beach** (p231). Everyone loves the tiny **Caicos Cays** (p246), Provo's 5-mile-long, iconic **Grace Bay Beach** (p242) with its extraordinary aquamarine waters and Grand Turk's pine-shaded **Governor's Beach** (p263), which is also a popular site for locals enjoying picnics and partying.

Snapshot

'No Toilet Paper at Nassau International Airport!' screamed the headline in the *Confidential Source*. The real story here wasn't just uncomfortable tourists, but another example of the inefficient, government-owned airport system and debt-ridden airline, Bahamasair, that drives Bahamians mad. Sit for a day in the airport when there are no announcements telling people where their plane, crew or luggage is, and you will understand why this is one of the many topics that get locals fired up.

Another issue is crime control. Although violent crime in the Bahamas is still comparatively rare, numbers of domestic, sexual and gun-related attacks are rising. One former cabinet minister's suggested solution to sexual attacks was chemical castration of rapists, in response to the physical castration advocated by the Bahamian Democratic Movement. Talk radio went bananas.

The continuing involvement of Bahamians in the cocaine trade also worries many. In May 2004 US authorities picked up Bahamians in possession of $100 million of cocaine, and in the following month a cocaine-smuggling ring of 15 Bahamians and 21 Colombians was broken.

The Family Islands continue repairing villages and infrastructure damaged by 2004's powerful hurricanes. Meanwhile in Nassau, the hot topic is whether judging processes for the popular Junkanoo festival's parade competition could be improved, after the bitterness of 2004's results.

There are a number of issues that the Bahamas and Turks and Caicos share. The depletion of the region's conch and grouper stocks is a major concern in all fishing villages. Locals wonder whether a two-month fishing ban on grouper by the Bahamian government is enough, and, if so, how fishermen are to survive during this time.

Development issues also abound. When the Bahamian prime minister signed an agreement in June 2004 for a Bimini Bay property development on top of reclaimed wetlands, many Bahamians were appalled. Not only could this construction swamp the tiny island, it could also obliterate important bird-breeding grounds. Other announcements in 2004 suggest that northern Grand Bahama may become the site of the world's largest resort.

Meanwhile in Grand Turk, angry rumors persist that an international cruise ship, with government permission, is about to sequester the island's most attractive and popular beach for its passengers. Likewise, developers can now build seven-story buildings around the rim of the island's most important public beach, Grace Bay Beach, where Provo Belongers (locals) are definitely not made welcome.

Bickering also continues within Turks and Caicos political circles about the best way to proceed toward the country's right to self-determination and full independence. Turks and Caicos is a British crown colony; a British governor takes responsibility for the country's internal security and external affairs, as well as certain judicial matters. Local self-government is administered by the 13-member Legislative Council, an elected body headed by the chief minister (appointed by the governor).

As politicians nitpick details of the outdated 1988 constitution, such as changing the chief minister's title to 'premier,' locals believe they are not addressing the fundamental question, namely whether Turks and Caicos people actually want independence at all. Debates in bars therefore continue to ask, 'Do we trust our politician's ability to run an economically successful, honest and democratic government?'

FAST FACTS

Population Bahamas/Turks & Caicos: 301,790/20,556

GDP per capita (purchasing power parity): $5.495 billion/$216 million

Inflation: 1.2%/4.0%

Number of islands: 700 (around 40 inhabited)/49 (9 inhabited)

Number of cellular phones: 121,800/1700

History
THE BAHAMAS

The peaceful Lucayans knew a good spot when they found one. This tribe of Arawak Indians paddled into the Bahamas' glistening seas at the turn of the 9th century. They decided to stay and became the country's first inhabitants.

Living primarily off the sea, they evolved skills as potters, carvers and boat-builders, and they spun and wove cotton into clothing and hammocks, which they traded with neighbors. The Lucayans, however, had no conception of the wheel and no written language, and they did not use beasts of burden or metals.

Religion played a central role in Arawak life. They worshiped various gods who were thought to control the rain, sun, wind, and hurricanes. The little that remains of their culture is limited to pottery shards, petroglyphs, and English words such as 'canoe,' 'cannibal,' 'hammock,' 'hurricane,' and 'tobacco.'

This website examines the history, navigation and landfall in the Bahamas of Christopher Columbus; www1.minn .net/~keithp

COLUMBUS & THE SPANISH

Native Americans had occupied the Bahamas for at least 500 years by the time Christopher Columbus first sighted the New World on October 12, 1492, during the first of his four voyages to find a westward route to the East Indies.

The expedition had sailed west and after 33 days and more than 3000 miles, the shout of 'Tierra!' went up and an island gleamed in the moonlight. Columbus planted the Spanish flag on an island he named San Salvador. From here, the fleet sailed south to Santa María de la Concepción, then west to a large island he named Fernandina. Turning southeast, they touched at a fourth island, christened Isabela, then sailed southwest to today's Ragged Island Range.

Columbus and his fellow expeditionaries were underwritten by monarchs and merchants whose interest was economic. Gold, or at least the thought of it, filled the sails. The Spaniards did not linger in these barren coral islands. The Indians told Columbus that gold might be found in Cubanacan (middle Cuba), which he translated as 'Kublai Khan.'

Until his death, Columbus was convinced that these islands were the easternmost outposts of Asia. Since he had traveled west to reach them, he named them the West Indies.

There has been much speculation over the decades as to which island Columbus actually landed on first. One of the explorer's biographers believed it to be San Salvador. A National Geographic Society study has convincingly proposed Samana Cay as the first landfall.

As the search for gold dominated all adventurers' priorities it was no surprise that the Spanish returned in 1495, and started shipping out enslaved Lucayan Indians from the Bahamas to work their gold seams in Hispaniola.

Buccaneers of America is John Esquemeling's eyewitness account of the extermination of the Lucayans. It was first published in 1684.

TIMELINE	900s	1492
	The Arawaks arrive in the Bahamas and Turks and Caicos from South America	Christopher Columbus sets sight and foot onto the New World

---

WHAT'S IN A NAME?

'Cay' (pronounced 'key') is an English term meaning 'small island.' The word, however, comes from 'cairi,' the Lucayan word for 'island.' Hence the names given to individual islands depended upon who was doing the naming, not their size. While Harbour Island is a mere 1 sq mile for example, Rum Cay has an area of 30 sq miles.

Siboney Indians were the earliest settlers of the Grand Bahama eventually superseded by the Lucayans; www .interknowledge .com/grandbahama /gbhistory01.htm

The Indians were worked to death. Those who resisted perished by the sword, the rest by European diseases or mass suicide. Within 25 years the entire Lucayan population of 50,000 was gone. The Spaniards then casually sailed away, leaving the island chain devoid of human life.

PIRATES EXPELLED – COMMERCE RESTORED

Tales of Spanish treasure lured pirates and other adventurers to the islands, such as Francis Drake and Walter Raleigh, who operated with the sanction of Queen Elizabeth I. San Salvador became the base for Raleigh's colony at Roanoke Island, England's first settlement in America. Charles Town was then founded by the British in 1666 (renamed Nassau in 1695 in honor of William III, formerly Prince of Orange-Nassau).

During the 17th century, England was constantly at war with France or Spain. Since the Royal Navy couldn't effectively patrol the Caribbean, the crown sponsored privateers to capture enemy vessels and plunder foreign cities. A combination of absentee landlords and the growing number of ruffian residents meant that the city descended into the hands of pirates such as Henry Jennings and 'Blackbeard' (Edward Teach), who terrorized his victims by wearing flaming fuses in his matted beard and hair. Blackbeard took over New Providence, establishing a lawless city that in 1666 was lined with brothels and taverns.

For details on the ships and crews that have sailed the Caribbean over the ages, try www.angel fire.com/realm3/carib beantales/ships.html

Spain, of course, was outraged, especially since it still claimed title over the Bahamas and on at least four occasions attacked and razed Charles Town. In 1718 Governor Woodes Rogers (himself a former privateer) was appointed by the British king to finally suppress piracy. Rogers arrived with three warships and issued the king's ultimatum to pirates: 'death or pardon'. He described his own tenure: *Expulsis Piratis – Restituta Commercia* (Pirates Expelled – Commerce Restored), words that still adorn the official seal of the Bahamas.

The Department of Archives in the Bahamas is the primary repository of the history of the Bahamas and holds records dating back to the 17th century; www .bahamasnationalarchives .bs/index.html

Yet in 1850 as much as half of the islands' population were still making a livelihood from wrecking – as did the government, which took 15% customs duty on the proceeds of sales from salvaged goods.

THOSE DAMNED YANKEES

The Bahamas lay close to the North American colonies, and the outbreak of the American Revolution in 1775 put the Bahamas in the firing line. Not for the last time, the American Navy fell upon Nassau, intent on capturing arms and explosives (the first-ever foreign invasion by US forces). The Yankees occupied Nassau, carousing for two weeks before sailing away.

In 1782 a joint Spanish–French–US force again took advantage of England's weakened position to capture the city. Spain declared possession of the Bahamas and then made life intolerable for the city's inhabitants.

1678

Bermudian salt traders clear land in the Turks and Caicos and create *salinas* (salt-drying pans)

1700s

Pirates establish bases on Grand Bahama

Andrew Deveaux, a Loyalist, recaptured the Bahamas for England a year later with 200 pro-British mercenaries. The Spaniards watched from afar as longboats ferried soldiers ashore. As the landing point was hidden from view, the soldiers stood up for the journey to shore and then the same men lay out of sight for the journey back to the ship, repeatedly. Thus the Spaniards gained the impression that thousands of troops were landing. The Spaniards packed their belongings and set sail for Cuba. The Treaty of Versailles formally ceded the Bahamas to England from Spain.

Following the American Revolution, more than 8000 Loyalists and their slaves resettled in the Bahamian islands between 1783 and 1785, tripling the existing population. They introduced two things that would profoundly shape the islands' future: cotton and slaves, but the land was ill-suited to cotton. Then in 1807 the British banned slave trading, and brought their liberated 'cargoes' to the Bahamas. The abolition of slavery in 1834 and transition to a free society went smoothly, but a white elite minority of merchants and administrators now ruled over an ill-represented black majority, a state of affairs that would last for more than a century.

The US Civil War (1861–65) gave the Bahamas another economic boost and the Bahamas became the major trading center for the blockaded South. Ships such as the *Ballymena* became infamous blockade-runners, running supplies to the South and returning with holds full of cotton. Author Margaret Mitchell, in *Gone with the Wind*, presents Rhett Butler as a well-known figure in Nassau, where he loaded his schooner with luxuries for the Confederacy.

But the end of hostilities burst Nassau's bubble again, and the ensuing decades witnessed an exodus of migrant labor to the US.

By the turn of the century, Florida was a tourist hot spot and the Bahamas were catching the spin-off.

A RUM DEAL

The islands were again granted divine deliverance in the 1920s with Prohibition, which forbade the sale of alcohol in the US. The Nassau waterfront soon resembled a vast rum warehouse. Millions of gallons of alcohol were whisked across the water to Florida or New Jersey's Rum Row. Construction boomed and the islands' first casino opened, attracting gamblers and gangsters alongside a potpourri of the rich and famous. However the repeal of Prohibition again burst Nassau's bubble, the Depression followed, and the Bahamas hit skid row.

During WWII the islands served as a base for Allied air and sea power. Exhausted GIs came to the islands to recuperate and were joined by wealthy Canadians and Americans wanting some winter sun.

INDEPENDENCE 'SOON COME'

The decision to promote tourism coincided with the arrival of the jet age and the Cuban Revolution in 1959. During the 1950s, Havana was the mecca for American tourists. When Fidel Castro spun Cuba into Soviet orbit in 1961, the subsequent US embargo forced revelers to seek their pleasures elsewhere, and Nassau became the new hot spot.

The Bahamas was redefined as a corporate tax haven, aided by statutes modeled on Switzerland's secrecy laws. Tourism and finance bloomed.

The Story of The Bahamas by Paul Albury and *A History of the Bahamas* by Michael Craton (San Salvador Press) both give a good general overview of Bahamian history.

These books by Gail Saunders trace the trauma of the slave era; *Bahamian Loyalists and Their Slaves* and *Slavery in the Bahamas*.

The most famous example for a foreigner's view of the Bahamas is *Out Island Doctor* by Evans Cottman, a Yankee teacher who fell for Crooked and Acklin Islands in the 1940s.

1718	1760
The Bahamian nation's motto; Pirates Expelled—Commerce Restored is coined	Governor William Shirley, former governor of Massachusetts, drains swamps, surveys the land and lays Nassau's streets

A RIGHT ROYAL RENEGADE

In 1940 the Duke and Duchess of Windsor arrived as governor and governess. Formerly King Edward VIII of England, the duke abdicated the throne in 1936 to marry an American divorcee; Wallis Simpson, 'the woman I love.' The couple ensured that the rich and famous poured into Nassau in postwar years, and set the trend for the ruling Brits and their romances to hit the headlines…

Edward, who had suffered great humiliation in Britain, proved as controversial in the Bahamas as he had at home. Some claim that he made strides to right the colony's backward and racist politics. Others believe he endorsed the corrupt ways of the 'Bay Street Boys,' an oligarchy of white lawyers and merchants that dominated the islands' assembly for many years.

It is argued that the duke was sent to the Bahamas as a punishment. Other evidence suggests that on the eve of WWII, the Nazis were planning to kidnap the duke – who had settled in the south of France – and restore him to the throne as a puppet after Hitler's forces had conquered Great Britain. Edward had shown sympathies toward Nazism. Winston Churchill, the prime minister, urged King George VI to send his brother to the Bahamas to place him out of harm's way.

Nonetheless, the duke was beloved by many, Blacks and Whites alike, and became the topic of several endearing songs and poems.

For a look at the Duke of Windsor's highly controversial time in the Bahamas, see *The King Over the Water* by Michael Pye and *The Duke of Windsor's War* by Michael Bloch.

The upturn in fortunes coincided with (and perhaps helped spark) the evolution of party politics and festering ethnic tensions, as the white elite and a growing black middle class reaped profits from the boom.

Only a small number of black representatives (mostly wealthy black businessmen) sat in the assembly, which remained dominated by the Bay Street Boys, descendants of the white Loyalists and British appointees. Middle-class Blacks' aspirations for representation coalesced with the pent-up frustrations of their brethren who remained impoverished.

In 1953 a local firebrand named Lynden Pindling formed the Progressive Liberal Party (PLP) to seek justice for the nation's majority at the ballot box. In 1963 the tensions bubbled up into a violent national strike supported by the PLP. A new constitution, proposed by Britain, was drawn up with the aim of creating a more representative legislature and providing for internal self-government. The UBP, led by white Bahamian Roland Symonette, gained power in national elections by a slender majority, and Symonette became premier. The close race allowed for white dominance to be somewhat diluted, but black aspirations had barely been appeased, particularly since voting was restricted to male property owners, a provision overwhelmingly favoring whites.

20,000 Leagues under the Sea by Universal/Williamson in 1916 was the first underwater motion picture ever made, and it was shot in the Bahamas.

Pindling and his party followers refused to recognize the parliamentary speaker's authority. In 1967 the PLP finally boycotted Parliament altogether, but not before winning an elimination of the property-ownership qualification. A new election was held, and Pindling's PLP came to power, a position it would maintain for the next 25 years.

On July 10, 1973, the Bahamian islands officially became a new nation, The Commonwealth of The Bahamas, ending 325 years of British rule.

THE COMMONWEALTH & COLOMBIANS

Pindling initially continued the progressive economic policies first adopted by his predecessors, based on tourism and finance. However,

1775	1843
The American Revolution starts an exodus of Loyalists and their slaves to the region	The British abolish slavery and freed slaves establish villages

foreign-owned development interests enjoyed preferential treatments and when his government tried to redress these problems the economy stalled.

Kickbacks to government members had become a staple of political life by the early 1980s and the Bahamas' hundreds of islands, marinas, and airstrips had become the frontline staging post for narcotics en route to the US. Bahamians from all walks of life made hay on the trade, and the government seemed disinclined to crack down on it.

In 1984 it was suggested by an American television program that Colombian drug barons had corrupted the government at its highest levels, and the country's drug-heavy reputation tarnished its image abroad. Pindling and his ministers were accused of involvement in drug trafficking. A Bahamian royal commission found against several ministers but Pindling was cleared. However the report noted that his expenditure was eight times his declared income.

Captain Leonard M Thompson's autobiographical *I Wanted Wings* is a splendid introduction to Loyalist Bahamian history and ways.

The country's drug-heavy reputation tarnished its repuation abroad. Tourism and financial investment declined, so the government belatedly launched a crackdown led by the US Drug Enforcement Agency (US DEA).

The electorate had become frustrated and voted in a conservative and business-orientated government, the FNM, in 1992. Lynden Pindling died in August 2000.

BAHAMAS TODAY

Announcements in 2004 that the American government may reduce funding of the successful joint anti-drug-trafficking campaign (OPBAT) 'Operation Bahamas Turks & Caicos' caused some concerns that drug trafficking could once again get out of hand. The *Tribune*, for example, revisited the days when Colombian drug traffickers rained money down on celebrating Bahamians from planes as thanks for their cooperation and even a clergyman argued that 'principles don't put bread on the table.'

Drug trafficking through the Bahamas to the US and Europe is still very much alive, although concerted Bahamian and US DEA efforts have curtailed much activity. In 2003 and 2004 the Bahamian police announced a number of arrests on Grand Bahama in connection with millions of dollars' worth of smuggled cocaine. The US Attorney-General in 2004 also announced arrests of Bahamians in Eleuthera, the Biminis and New Providence during the cracking of a Colombian-led drug-trafficking network.

WAS THE BIRTH OF TOURISM THE DEATH OF HIM...?

It was clear in the slump that followed the end of WWII that the Bahamas' future lay in the still-embryonic tourism industry. Canadian entrepreneur and philanthropist Sir Harry Oakes, who owned one-third of New Providence and built the Cable Beach Golf Course, the Bahamas Country Club, and much of the tourist infrastructure, had lain the foundation.

Oakes' brutal murder in his bed on July 7, 1943, and the subsequent trial of his son-in-law, Duke Alfred de Marigny, reverberated around the world as 'The Crime of the Century.' The son-in-law was acquitted, the Bahamas was put on the international map once again and the case remains unsolved.

1920	1958
Prohibition opens the door to the Bahamas first American tourists	Exuma Cays Land & Sea Park becomes the first marine fishery reserve in the world

In August 1999 Hurricane Dennis raked the Abacos and Grand Bahama. A month later, Hurricane Floyd – a 600-mile-wide whopper – pounded Cat, San Salvador, Abaco and Eleuthera with winds up to 155 mph. In 2004 two more hurricanes, Frances and Jeanne, hit these same islands along with Grand Bahama in quick succession. Massive flooding and the destruction of many buildings again hit the villages and tourism industry of these already-struggling islands.

The Bimini Museum has a website that covers local history and events; www.bimini-museum.org

Despite these blows, Prime Minister Perry Christie and the ruling Progressive Liberal Party can celebrate that the Bahamas per-capita disposable income is around $16,700, one of the highest in the region. The economy has also flourished, thanks to its stable political climate, liberal laws designed to attract investment, and, undoubtedly, its proximity to North America.

One of the country's assets is its large, skilled, well-educated workforce, 10% of which is employed in banking and insurance industries.

Another one third is employed by the government. The wealth is concentrated in Nassau however, so there are plenty of pockets of poverty, especially in the Family Islands, where unemployment is high and much of the local economy operates on a barter basis. Thousands of Bahamians earn their income as itinerant vendors.

Tourism alone accounts for more than 60% of GDP and directly or indirectly employs half of the archipelago's labor force. Despite a slowdown in the tourism sector in 2001 following 11 September, tourist arrivals in 2003 were 4.6 million, the highest number in the Caribbean. Americans now make-up of over 80% of the Bahamian visitors, no wonder the pizzas are so good!

A TAX SHELTER IN THE SUN

The Bahamas is one of the world's premier tax-free havens and financial services are the second-most important sector of the Bahamian economy, accounting for about 15% of GDP. Incentives offered to investors attract millions of dollars every year.

The Bahamas levies no taxes on personal or corporate income, capital gains, dividends, interest, royalties, sales, estates, inheritances, or payrolls. The repatriation of foreign investment funds, foreign assets and dividends, and profits arising from investments is permitted tax-free.

The system primarily serves as a tax-planning haven and place of asset security; financial records cannot be subpoenaed or released. Although the FNM government made sweeping changes in banking laws to help the US DEA and the US Internal Revenue Service combat money laundering (Bahamian-held assets are no longer secure from US federal agencies), in 2000 the 26-country International Financial Action Task Force named the Bahamas among a 'black list' of 15 nations failing to cooperate in the fight against money laundering.

Still one of the world's principal international financial and insurance centers, Nassau claimed in 2003 that 284 institutions from the Bahamas, US, Canada, UK, South America, Central America, Asia and Europe were licensed to do business within or from the Bahamas. Financial services annually contributed about 15% of the GDP, paying $196.5 million in 2003 for salaries and wages to employees who are nearly 94% Bahamian.

However a number of international banks and other financial institutions have withdrawn from the country, whether this is down to changes in the laws protecting client confidentiality from DEA investigations or not, is of much speculation within the country's electronic and print media.

1960s	1962
Grand Turk's 'white gold' salt export industry collapses	John Glenn splashes down from space, just off Grand Turk

TURKS & CAICOS

Recent discoveries of Indian artifacts on Grand Turk have shown that the islands evolved much the same indigenous culture as did their northern neighbors. A ball court similar to those of the far more advanced Maya culture in Central America has been found on Middle Caicos. Locals even claim that the islands were Christopher Columbus' first landfall in 1492 (much-disputed by historians).

The island group was also a pawn in the power struggles between the French, Spaniards, and British and remained virtually uninhabited until 1678, when a group of Bermudians settled and began to extract salt and timber. Salt traders cleared the land and created the *salinas* (salt-drying pans) that still exist on several islands. Most of the salt went aboard swift sloops to supply the cod-fishing industries of New England and Canada's Maritime Provinces. Salt remained the backbone of the British crown colony until the 1950s, when the industry collapsed.

As with the Bahamas, the islands became a base for notorious pirates, who were not averse to sacking the wealthy salt merchants' homes. Some people claim that piracy accounts for the islands' name: 'Turks' for the name of a group of Mediterranean pirates and 'Caicos' for the name of the boats. ('Baloney!' say others: 'Turks' refers to the species of native cactus whose scarlet blossom resembles a Turkish fez; 'cayos' is for the Spanish word for 'tiny isles.')

Following the American Revolution, waves of colonial Loyalists arrived with their slaves to build plantations. By 1820 the cotton crop had failed and the planters sailed off leaving many slaves behind who then also became salt rakers. A whaling industry (now defunct) was established in the mid-19th century.

FROM WWII TO SATELLITE TV

Although the US military built airstrips here during WWII, the islands were still British, classified as part of the UK's Jamaican colony until 1962, when they were then annexed to the Bahamas. The Governor of the Bahamas oversaw the island's affairs from 1965 to 1973, when the Turks and Caicos became a separate crown colony of Great Britain.

Meanwhile, the doors to tourism really began to open; Count Ferdinand Czernin, son of the last prime minister of the Austro-Hungarian Empire, ferreted out a tiny dot on the map – Pine Cay, northeast of Provo – on which he planned an exotic resort. After his death, this became the exclusive Meridian Club, a prize-winning resort still frequented by the sophisticated elite. Then in 1984 Club Med opened its doors on Provo, and the Turks and Caicos started to boom. In the blink of an eye, the islands, which had had no electricity, acquired satellite TV.

LIVING TODAY

Today the finance, tourism and fishing industries generate most private-sector income. The Turks and Caicos are a tax-free offshore finance center, offering services such as company formation, offshore insurance, banking, trusts, and limited partnerships. Still, the industry is a mere

Did you know that in the 2004 Olympics Bahamian sprinter Tonique Williams-Darling won the gold medal in the women's 400m final and Debbie Ferguson won bronze for the women's 200m final in Athens.

Did you know that some rock carvings in Sapodilla Bay, Caicos date back to 1844 and record the names of ship-wrecked sailors who found themselves on this island?

Turks Islands Landfall by HE Sadler is an illustrated, large-format text regaling the history of the Turks and Caicos.

1973	1984
The Bahamas achieves independence and becomes the Commonwealth of the Bahamas	Club Med opens in Providenciales and tourism starts to boom in the Turks and Caicos

minnow compared to that of the Bahamas, and you will no doubt be astonished to discover that Grand Turk, the much-hyped financial center, is just a dusty backwater in the sun.

Most capital goods and food for domestic consumption are imported from Haiti and the US, along with some human traffic. Whereas many of the Haitians are en route to the US as illegal immigrants, more than half of the 93,000 visitors in the late 1990s were American tourists. However, tourism fell by 6% in 2002, and in 2005 the per capita GDP was estimated at a low $9,600.

Major sources of government revenue include fees from offshore financial activities and customs receipts. Still, income from tourism and offshore investment is not yet sufficient for the islands to survive without British aid. Practically all consumer goods and foodstuffs are imported. Agriculture is limited to small family gardens and teeny farms. The islands' most important exports are conch and lobster (about 750,000lb annually). Commemorative coins and souvenir-issue stamps bring in considerable revenue.

With the Turks and Caicos covered by the US-funded anti-drug trafficking operation (OPBAT), some individuals within the country are believed to continue to derive revenue from the international drugs trade.

Although independence was agreed upon for 1982, the policy was reversed and the islands remain a British crown colony, while the existing constitution dates from 1988. A governor from the UK acts as the Queen's representative, with responsibility for internal security, external affairs, and certain judicial matters, also presiding over the Executive Council of Ministers.

Local self-government is administered by the 13-member Legislative Council, an elected body headed by the chief minister (appointed by the governor) and empowered to enact local statutes and run the show on a daily basis, with a good deal of power to determine the islands' future.

Relations between the islanders and British-appointed governors have been strained since 1996 when incumbent Governor Martin Bourke's comments suggesting that government and police corruption had turned the islands into a haven for drug trafficking appeared in the Offshore Finance Annual, and opponents accused him of harming investment. Growing opposition threatened to spill over into civil unrest and the Brits sent over a warship and trained policeman. In the end there was no revolt, but the issue created resurgence in calls for independence that still continue today. Mr Richard Tauwhare was named as Governor of the Turks and Caicos, effective July 2005.

1996	**2004**
A British warship arrives in the Turks and Caicos, after the British Governor claims the islands were a haven for drug smugglers	Hurricanes Frances and Jeanne lash the islands and the Bahamas win their first individual track Olympic gold medal

The Culture

THE NATIONAL PSYCHE
The Bahamas

Contemporary Bahamian culture revolves around the family, the church and the sea. However the proximity of North America and cable TV has had a profound influence on contemporary life and material values, although many British traditions, courtesies and attitudes remain.

As with any society there are some lovely ironies. For example, although investors are encouraged to build casino complexes on Bahamian soil, gambling is outlawed for Bahamian nationals! Even better, these casinos are then staffed by trained Bahamian croupiers.

A very low crime rate and an extremely welcoming people illustrates the strength of a cohesive community led by overt Christian beliefs. However in 2004 a cruise ship carrying gay passengers and their families planned to dock in Nassau. This resulted in outrage expressed both in the media and on the streets, with protesters calling for bans to stop the ship docking. Another example of this very un-Christian intolerance is the discrimination against Haitian immigrants. Spirit beliefs, held over from slave days, are a mix of African and Christian religions. These are still important to many Bahamians and are presented in many daily rituals (see p32).

In Nassau and Freeport, most working people are employed in banking, tourism or government work and live a nine-to-five lifestyle. The maturation of the banking and finance industries has fostered the growth of a large professional class, many of whom have become extremely wealthy.

The folks of the Out Islands – the Family Islanders – are altogether more at ease as well as more traditional. The practice of obeah, bush medicine, and folkloric songs and tales still infuse their daily lives.

Tourism has barely touched many islands and poverty sits hand-in-hand with undeveloped local economies. Despite many expat billionaires hidden away on these cays, many people live a hand-to-mouth existence alleviated by the government's social security system, fishing, catching conch and lobster, and raising corn, bananas and other crops for the kitchen.

Turks & Caicos

The islands have their own identity, but are as devoutly religious as their northern neighbors. This doesn't stop some from having a tipple on Sunday, when the pubs (strictly speaking) aren't serving.

Turks and Caicos islanders ('Belongers') are descendants from the early Bermudian settlers, Loyalist settlers, slave settlers and salt rakers. Many resident expats, notably Brits, are employed in the hospitality and finance industries, having escaped the cities and miserable weather of Europe. Others are 'retirement-aged swashbucklers' or those avoiding open conversations about their origins!

More recently, hundreds of Haitians have fled their impoverished island and landed in the Turks and Caicos, many on their way to Miami. Some residents and Belongers, as with the Bahamians, resent the Haitians' intrusion into the islands' scarce economic resources.

POPULATION

Around 80% of the Bahamian population is urban, with nearly two-thirds of residents living in Nassau (212,432) and around 47,000 in Grand Bahama. The remainder of the population is scattered among about a

Bahamians and Turks and Caicos Islanders drive on the left and enjoy the odd roundabout or two. As they say: the left side is the right side, the right side is suicide!

Speed 2 Cruise Control with a bomb on board, and *The Loveboat Reunion*, by Aaron Spelling, with several blonde bombshells on board, were both shot in the Bahamas, and should stand as a warning that you can never rely on the brochures when booking your next cruise…

Water and Light by Stephen Harrigan is a splendid memoir by a Texan who 'followed his bliss' and spent several months diving off Grand Turk.

dozen Family Islands; predominantly the Abacos, Andros, Eleuthera and a few dozen offshore cays. The islands tend to be less populated as you move south, and the southern islands are suffering significant declines in population.

The Bahamas prides itself on its harmonious race relations. Indeed, the islands are refreshingly free of racial tensions, and class divisions are markedly less related to color than on many neighboring islands. Everyone can socialize together. The most virulent prejudice, among both black and white Bahamians, is against Haitians, a recent immigrant underclass.

Most Haitians are illegal immigrants seeking a better life whom the Bahamian government has tried to repatriate without success. Haitians perform menial tasks, farm labor and domestic work and are frequently exploited at below-minimum wages. A Human Rights Watch report also revealed that 90% of prisoners in the Bahamas are Haitians.

Other immigrants come from the Dominican Republic and Jamaica, or are of Asian or Hispanic descent. There are no descendants of the indigenous Lucayans. But around Red Bay (Andros), you may note the distinct features of Seminole Indians, whose forefathers fled Florida and settled here two centuries ago.

> Did you know that actor Sidney Poitier is the current Bahamian Ambassador to Japan?

Bahamian Lineage

About 85% of the population is Black, with ancestry traced to slaves brought from the Carolinas. They in turn were drawn predominantly from West African tribes such as the House, Ibo, Mandingo and Yoruba.

The Bahamas' black population has grown out of several events. When Loyalists arrived in the islands, they brought with them their most trusted and able slaves. In other cases, slave traders called into Nassau en route to other destinations and sold Africans to local slaveholders.

Scores of free Blacks also fled the United States for the islands, where many became large landholders (often slave-owners themselves) and prominent citizens. Additionally, thousands of runaways and Blacks liberated from slave ships by the British also landed in the islands as free people.

Whites constitute 12% of the population; most are of British and to a lesser degree American, Irish and Greek descent. Outside Nassau, most Whites are centered in a few settlements where they are a conspicuous majority: Marsh Harbour, Cherokee Sound, Treasure Cay, Green Turtle

> Did you know that the Bahamas levies no taxes on personal or corporate income, capital gains, dividends, interest, royalties, sales, inheritances or payrolls?

BUSH MEDICINE *Christopher P Baker*

Traditional folk healing is still alive, especially in the Family Islands, where locals have a suspicion of doctors and cling to folk remedies. Bush-medicine healers, often respected obeah practitioners, rely on native herbs, which they mix into concoctions, or potents, using recipes that have been handed down through many generations.

The sovereign ingredient is *cerasee (Momordica charantia)*, an orange-fruited vine credited with resolving every imaginable human ailment. Aloe is also used for curing many ills, from sunburn to insect bites, while breadfruit leaves are said to cure high blood pressure.

However, not all cures use berries and leaves. For example, 'goat nanny' (goat droppings) is said to cure whooping cough, while congested air passages are cured by pouring 'chamber lye' on the head. This golden liquid is named for the pot into which a person relieves himself at night when not blessed with an indoor toilet.

There are a couple of grand 'Bush Medicine' walks to be taken in the Grand Bahamas (see p103) and in George Town in the Exumas (see p197) which will give you a few more tips. As will *Bush Medicine in the Bahamas* by Leslie Higgs which provides recipes for curing everything from warts to a broken heart.

Cay, Great Guana Cay, Elbow Cay and Man O' War Cay (Abacos); and Spanish Wells and Harbour Island (Eleuthera).

Most Whites in these settlements can claim descent from the earliest English settlers, Loyalists who fled the American Revolution. Others claim descent from Southerners escaping the US Civil War. A few like to claim ancestry from the English ruling elite. A far greater number are descended from pirates and vagabonds.

Nassau's white community remains somewhat clannish and dominates the upper echelons of economic life. Every Loyalist descendant and other Caucasian born in the islands is known as a 'Conchy Joe,' identifiable by their distinctive features: usually blue or green eyes, freckled skin and blondish hair.

Then there are the thousands of part-time and full-time residents – predominantly wealthy North Americans, who have escaped from the prying eyes of the world.

If you want to check out any lineage that you may share with the peoples of the Bahamas and Turks and Caicos, check out this website and its comprehensive links at www.genforum.genealogy.com/bahamas

RELIGION

Christianity is a powerful and conservative force in the Bahamas and Turks and Caicos Islands, with the overwhelming majority of islanders devout believers who profess to live by the word of God. Virtually every taxi driver has a Bible at hand, as do many office workers. State functions and the school day begin with prayers. Church affairs make headline news, while major international events are relegated to the inside pages. Every political speech is peppered with biblical quotations and is considerate of the Church's position on social issues.

The Bahamian nation claims the greatest number of churches per capita in the world. The vast majority of the populace are mainstreamers; Baptists (35%), Anglican/Episcopalian (15%) and Catholic (14%). The official state religion is the Anglican Church, although some Christian priests hedge their bets and mix a little good-willed obeah into their practice (see p212).

When the British abolished slavery in 1834, many of the emancipated former slaves were bequeathed land by their former owners.

Every island is a veritable jumble of chapels and churches, usually Baptist revival centers, referred to as 'jumper churches' by locals – with every conceivable body in the world represented (as with the Feed My Sheep Church of God). Often you'll see as many as a dozen churches in settlements with barely 200 people. Most of these churches are maintained with much love and money the congregation can ill-afford. Fundamentalists have made serious inroads in recent years often through cable TV, while some Family Islands have been won over by a single church (Seventh-Day Adventists, for example, predominate on Crooked Island).

Sundays really are blessed days, when businesses outside main tourist centers are closed. Less so with the Turks and Caicos islanders, but Bahamians normally dress-up to show respect even if they are working (as with Nassau's taxi drivers) and the churches are a vision of glamour. Hats and heels are *de rigeur* for women, along with suits and ties for the men. Little girls are resplendent in white dresses and their brothers immaculate in shirt and trousers, both impatiently waiting their freedom.

Gospel choirs across the region take their work seriously, with uplifting and joyous sounds wafting out of halls and churches throughout the week, in preparation for Sunday's list of lengthy services.

For a hilarious look at what it means to be a Conchy Joe, see Patricia Glinton-Meicholas' *How to Be a True-True Bahamian*.

Funerals

Some of the most important events on a Bahamian family calendar are funerals. The national newspapers dedicate a huge percentage of space to announcing deaths and funerals (weddings get little play) while radio programs are frequently interrupted by death and funeral announcements.

> **SPIRIT BELIEFS** *Christopher P Baker*
>
> Despite the force of Christianity in society, many Bahamians and Turks and Caicos islanders still keep spirit beliefs held over from slave days, when African religions melded with Christianity. Rooted in the animist beliefs of West Africa (animism has nothing to do with animal spirits; the name is derived from the Latin word *anima*, meaning 'soul'), they are based on the tenet that the spiritual and temporal worlds are a unified whole.
>
> A core belief is that spirits live independently of the human or animal body and can inhabit inanimate objects. They can communicate directly with humans and are usually morally neutral; it is the service to which humans call them that determines whether they will be a force of good or evil. Cantankerous, onerous people beget evil 'sperrids'; kind and thoughtful people beget good spirits. Spirits particularly like to live in silk cotton trees, of which many Bahamians are extremely wary.
>
> Spirits reveal themselves on a whim; not being able to see them doesn't mean they aren't there. Many Bahamians believe that if you take the 'bibby' (mucus) from a dog's or horse's eye and put it in your own, you can actually see a spirit.
>
> All kinds of practices have evolved to guard against evil spirits. Even physicians are known to tie a black cord around a newborn baby's wrists to guard against evil spirits. A Bible is often placed at the head of a sleeping child for the same reason. And if this fails, a Bahamian may attempt to dispel a malicious spirit by marking Xs all around and repeating the all-powerful phrase, 'Ten, ten, the Bible ten.'
>
> To discover more about these customs, see the boxed text 'Obeah' – the practice of African witchcraft (p212), and pick up *Ten, Ten, the Bible Ten: Obeah in the Bahamas* by Timothy McCartney.

Bahamian funerals are big events. On the Family Islands and cays, businesses close, residents dress in mourning for the passing of the funereal cortege and children play a doleful dirge at the head of the procession.

ARTS

The Cocaine Wars by Paul Eddy, Hugo Sabogal and Sara Walden covers drug trafficking in the Bahamas and is an interesting read.

Relative to its neighbors, the Bahamas' intellectual tradition is comparatively weak and, for a capital city, Nassau has been surprisingly unsophisticated in the visual and performance arts. That has certainly been changing however, especially in music and art, and with the opening of the National Gallery in Nassau, displays of really impressive works are gaining their rightful place in Bahamian society.

Literature

While the Bahamas has produced no writer of world renown, the nation does have its literati. Few, however, are known even within the Caribbean region.

Bahamian Anthology (published by the College of The Bahamas) is a selection of poetry, stories and plays by Bahamian writers. In a similar poetic vein, try *Bahamas: In a White Coming On* by Dennis Ryan.

Author Ian Fleming, famous for his James Bond novels, was so taken with the Bahamas that he set several of his books here.

However, the Bahamas has been the setting for work of more notable, non-Bahamian writers. Ernest Hemingway's *Islands in the Stream* is a fictitious but accurate look at the Biminis' history and his own brutish ways during WWII.

Robert Wilder's *Wind from the Carolinas* is a historical novel that tells of the settlement of the Bahamas in the form of a generational saga. And Barbara Whitnell's *The Salt Rakers* follows suit.

A more contemporary romp is Herman Wouk's *Don't Stop the Carnival*, the tale of a publicist who gives it all up to open a hotel on a fictitious Caribbean isle.

FOLK TALES & CHILDREN'S STORIES

Several books trace the evolution and meaning of Bahamian folktales, including *Bahamian Lore: Folk Tales and Songs* by Robert Curry. Patricia Glinton-Meicholas is another name to look out for, this prolific writer has a real panache in bringing oral histories and folk tales to life.

An Evenin' in Guanima: A Treasury of Folktales from The Bahamas by Patricia Glinton-Meicholas is a great introduction to the Bahamas.

Telcine Turner's *Once Below a Time: Bahamian Stories* is an illustrated collection of short stories for children. Likewise, youngsters might enjoy *Climbing Clouds: Stories & Poems from The Bahamas*, also edited by Turner, and *Who Let the Dog Out? (Dottie's Story)* by Carole Hughes, a story about a Dalmatian born into Green Turtle Cay who heads off to explore the world.

Oscar-winning Sidney Poitier tells of his upbringing on Cat Island in his autobiographies, *This Life* and *The Measure of a Man*.

Music

From hotel beach parties to the raw-sound-system dance clubs of Over-the-Hill, Nassau's poorer quarter, the Bahamas reverberates to the soul-riveting sounds of calypso, soca, reggae and its own distinctive music, which echoes African rhythms and synthesizes Caribbean calypso, soca and English folk songs into its *goombay* beat.

GOOMBAY

This type of music – the name comes from an African word for 'rhythm' – derives its melody from a guitar, piano or horn instrument accompanied by any combination of goatskin *goombay* drums, maracas, rhythm (or click) sticks, rattles, conch-shell horns, fifes and flutes, and cowbells to add a uniquely Bahamian *kalik-kalik-kalik* sound. It's typified by a fast-paced, sustained, infectious melody. *Goombay* is to the Bahamas what reggae is to Jamaica and is most on display during Christmas and midsummer Junkanoo celebrations.

The Bahamas Concert Orchestra website is www.geocities.com /bahamasconcert orchestra/index.html.

Goombay draws on a heritage of folk music introduced by African slaves from North America, Jamaica and other neighboring islands. Particularly important are the 'talking drums,' once used to pass along information, and folk songs developed in the cane fields to ease the backbreaking labor. Over generations, European elements, such as the French quadrille introduced by planters, were absorbed as well, creating a unique style.

OTHER BAHAMIAN STYLES

The Bahamas' down-home, working-class music is rake 'n' scrape, usually featuring a guitar, an accordion, shakers made from the pods of poinciana trees and other makeshift instruments, such as a saw played with a screwdriver.

Rake 'n' scrape music can be heard at local bars throughout the islands, and is a highlight of many festivals such as Family Island regattas. Grand Turk has a fabulous annual festival when these musicians gather from across the Turks and Caicos region to display and enjoy their talents.

Junkanoo: Festival of the Bahamas by Clement Bethel examines the history of this fabulous Bahamian festival.

Spirituals were brought to the islands by Southern Loyalists' slaves, then adapted to incorporate purely Bahamian 'call and answer' techniques, rhyming exchanges of voices. Bahamian folk music is rooted in spiritual and gospel hymns often performed in 'rhymin' style. Androsian folk-singer Joseph Spence was the islands' master of folk and blues.

Dance hall, a kind of Caribbean rap and the in-vogue working-class music of the formerly British Caribbean islands, has evolved its own style in the Bahamas, where it is known as 'chatting.' It is performed entirely in

The official Junkanoo
website is www
.junkanoo.com.

local dialect. The music has its origins in US urban ghettos of the 1990s, and usually has a monotonous yet fast-paced, compulsive beat, often with vocals added to the rhythms. It is most often performed by local DJs with their own mobile discos.

Architecture

The islands have their own architectural styles reflecting the influences of early Bermudian settlers and US Loyalists. Most plantation and government buildings were built of local sandstone and limestone, as were the homes of the wealthy. The stones were fixed and finished by mortar and plaster containing lime produced by burning conch shells. Being thick – sometimes as much as 3ft – these massive walls became temperature sinks, keeping the building relatively cool even during the heat of midday.

The Hermit of Cat Island,
by Peter F Anson, tells
the fascinating story of
Father Jerome, the hermit
architect who blessed Cat
and Long Islands with
splendid churches. These
miniature Gothic build-
ings are everywhere.

On many islands, wooden houses are more prevalent. On Eleuthera and the Loyalist Cays of the Abacos, a distinctive style evolved that has been likened to that of Cape Cod in Massachusetts. The most splendid examples are in Dunmore Town and Spanish Wells (Eleuthera) and in Hope Town, New Plymouth and Man O' War Cay (Abacos). The Bahamian clapboard house has been widely copied throughout the Caribbean and in the Turks and Caicos a uniquely Bermudian influence has been at work. Often the houses are made of ship-timber driftwood and planking, the framework filled with cemented rubble rock and finished in plaster.

Smaller wooden homes in the Bahamas were elevated atop a masonry ground floor, with balconies supported by stilts or masonry pillars. Not

JUMPING AT JUNKANOO

You feel the music before you see it...a frenzied barrage of whistles and horns overriding the cowbells, the rumble of drums and the joyful blasts of conch shells. Then the costumed revelers stream into view, whirling and gyrating like a kaleidoscope in rhythm with the cacophony. This is Junkanoo, the national festival of the Bahamas – its equivalent of Carnaval or Mardi Gras – and it is a mass of energy, color and partying that starts in the twilight hours of Boxing Day.

The name, pronounced *junk-uh-NOO*, is thought to come from a West African term for 'deadly sorcerer.' Others say the festival is named for John Canoe, the tribal leader who demanded that his enslaved people be allowed to enjoy a festivity. With its origins in West African secret societies, the parade evolved on the plantations of the British Caribbean among slaves who were forbidden to observe their sacred rites. The all-male cast of masqueraders hid their identity, following West African mask-wearing tradition.

At first Junkanoos were suppressed by the Bahamian colonial government, which feared they might get out of hand and lead to slave uprisings. Later, planters encouraged them. Creole elements found their way into the ceremony, along with British Morris dancing, polkas and reels. On Jamaica and other islands, Junkanoo was suppressed to extinction, but in the Bahamas it became an integral part of the culture.

Junkanoo is fiercely competitive and many marchers belong to 'shacks,' groups who vie to produce the best performance, costume, dancing and music. The most elaborately costumed performers are one-person parade floats whose costume can weigh over 200lb, and depict exotic scenes adorned with a myriad of glittering beads, foils and rhinestones. Many spend a year planning their costumes, keeping their designs a carefully guarded secret.

The energy of this carnival is that of a joyous and frenetic explosion. In Nassau the first 'rush,' as the parade is known, occurs on Boxing Day (December 26); the second happens on New Year's Day and the third in summer, when the shacks go over their game plans. Head for the Fish Frys if you won't be there for the festival, this is where the shacks rehearse their dances and the music for the big nights. Thursday nights are practice night in Grand Bahama. In the Family Islands the summer 'rushes' are on different days to Nassau. Parades start around 3am and finish by noon in time for a big lunch.

only did this allow airflow beneath the living quarters, it also kept them above water level in the event of a hurricane surge.

The Family Islands are also peppered with tiny square stone buildings – 'slave homes' – that have survived decay and natural disasters. Many are still inhabited. Each is the size of a pillbox, with a steep-angled, four-sided roof and an open kitchen in back, but no toilet. Communal outhouses (they, too, still stand) were built along the shore, where one would make a deposit straight into the sea.

Paint finishes were produced from linseed oil, wood spirits, or turpentine derived from pine and mixed with ochre, sienna, and other mineral or organic pigments: iron oxides for barn red, copper oxides for green, cobalt for blue, and zinc for white. The last two were expensive, and a white house with blue shutters became a true status symbol.

Two common features on historic buildings are steep-pitched roofs and an absence of roof overhangs. Designed to reduce wind resistance during hurricanes, the steep pitch aids in rigidity and also prevents airfoil uplift (the process that 'lifts' an aircraft off the ground) when strong winds blow across it. The lack of overhang prevents the wind from peeling back the roof. Those shady verandas you see everywhere are invariably separate 'sacrificial' extensions to the roofs, designed so that the wind may tear them away without taking the roofs as well.

A splendid book on visual arts is *Bahamian Art* by Patricia Glinton-Meicholas, Charles Huggins and Basil Smith.

Visual Arts
THE BAHAMAS
The so-called father of Bahamian art is Amos Ferguson, the foremost folk artist. Ferguson is intensely spiritual. His naive, palette-bright canvases focus upon religion, history, nature and folklore, or 'ol' story.' Ferguson began making bird figurines, tumblers and jars for the tourist trade. You can see a permanent collection of his works in the Pompey Museum in Nassau.

Brent Malone, Max Taylor, Rolph Harris and Alton Roland Lowe – the Bahamas' artist laureate for more than three decades – are also all writ large in the Bahamian art world.

The oils of Alton Lowe, a seventh-generation Loyalist Abaconian, are much sought after by blue bloods and corporations. While Eddie Minnis, also cartoonist, songwriter and musician is inspired by his devotion to the church of Jehovah's Witnesses. His limited-edition prints are popular, and his original oils, works of intricate detail and vibrant color (he paints less than a dozen per year), command thousands of dollars.

The islands' plastic arts (ceramics, sculpture, painting, woodcarving and textiles) have been late in flowering, and with the exception of straw-work, the crafts industry is relatively undeveloped. It has been influenced in recent years by the influx of Haitians, who have inspired intuitive hardwood carvings, often brightly painted and highlighted by pointillist dots.

Bahamian indigenous artist Amos Ferguson defines his love of the islands in *Under the Sunday Tree: Paintings by Mr Amos Ferguson*, with poems by Eloise Greenfield.

TURKS & CAICOS
Though slow to develop, the arts scene in the Turks and Caicos has begun to blossom. Traditional music, folklore and sisal weaving evolved during colonial days and have been maintained to this day.

The local art scene is dominated by the Haitian community who paint delightful oil and acrylic illustrations of village life back home. Many of these artworks are of the vividly colored naif style, which has inspired some plagiarism to benefit from the Haitians' popularity. Look for galleries and stores that sell signed paintings, these originals are still a steal, ranging from around $18 to $200.

The stunning National Art Gallery of the Bahamas, housed in Lord Dunmore's old house, now has a website at www.nagb.org.bs.

However, Turks and Caicos Belongers artistry is also well represented. Much of the work is inspired by the islands' scenery, bird and marine life, with rich colors redolent of the Caribbean. A thriving art scene has also attracted expat artists from around the globe whose work should not be dismissed lightly.

Some roadside stalls sell decorative metal tapestries, designed as wall hangings. These are cut from old car wrecks, painted and varnished and illustrate underwater scenes as well as Turks and Caicos island life. These works are clever, witty and mostly small enough to fit in a suitcase. Go shop!

Artist on His Island: A Study of Self-Reliance by Randolph W Johnston, tells of his and his family's lives in the Abacos.

The Bamboo Gallery, in Provo, promotes the work of local artists, including Dwight Outten, from Middle Caicos, whom some people consider the leading artist in the islands. Another family member, Phillip Outten, a Rastafarian, produces acrylic works (some in gay primary colors, others more somber) inspired, he says, by his meditations and 'concept of daily reality.'

The North Caicos Art Society in Whitby (North Caicos) sponsors local art, emphasizing silkscreen painting. Lookout for Anna Bourne, one of many expat artists who now lives on Provo and paints on silk with French dyes.

The shopping section in Provo profiles a few really talented local artists and details galleries (p250).

Environment

If you're keen to get close to nature, you'll find plenty to keep you enthralled in the Bahamas and Turks and Caicos. You'll also be doing the islands a good turn, with nature tourism one of the most practical ways to save wild places and their inhabitants from erosive exploitation. The Bahamas and Turks and Caicos governments take their role as guardians of their ecology seriously and work in cooperation with several worldwide conservation bodies. Both nations have designated large areas of land and sea as national parks.

If you love whales, find out more about them on this site dedicated to the whales of the Bahamas www.rockisland .com/%7eorcasurv /bcruisgd.htm.

BAHAMAS

The Bahamas archipelago sits atop, and is formed by, one of the greatest masses of limestone in the world: a reef-shelf of solid sea fossils 20,000ft thick, rising sheer-sided from the seabed. The result of nearly 150 million years' deposits, the islands as we know them today began to take their present form only about 500,000 years ago.

THE LAND

The mostly linear islands are strewn in a general northwest–southeast array. Several – Great Abaco, Eleuthera, Long Island, Andros – are as much as 100 miles long. Few, however, are more than a few miles wide. All are low lying, the terrain either pancake-flat or gently undulating. Cat Island's Mt Alvernia, the highest point in the Bahamas, is only 206ft above sea level.

These shores are lined virtually their entire lengths by white- or pinkish-sand beaches – about 2200 miles in all – shelving into turquoise shallows.

Most islands have barrier reefs along the length of their eastern shores, anywhere from 200yd to 2 miles out, that offer protection from Atlantic waves.

For a general overview, *Caribbean Flora* by C Dennis Adams has detailed descriptions of individual species, accompanied by illustrations.

Blue Holes

The islands are pocked by giant sinkholes – water-filled, often fathomless circular pits that open to underground and submarine caves and descend as far as 600ft.

Unique creatures have evolved to exist solely within the gloom of the underwater caverns, including blind, pigmentless fish. Local lore attributes deadly mermaids, mermen and sea monsters to many of the holes.

WILDLIFE

Apart from the cute curly tailed lizards darting around everywhere, a number of iguanas can be found on Bahamian cays. Unfortunately development hasn't been good for them, and most species are now endangered. Animal lovers will also enjoy seeing the wandering bands of donkeys, horses and chickens.

Virtually every island is a bird watcher's haven, with accessible vegetation and a variety of habitats for migrating and resident populations.

After the Sunset (2004) had Pierce Brosnan, Woody Harrelson and Salma Hayek swanning around the shores of Eleuthera while involved in a big heist: a retiring thief's parting shot.

Animals

The archipelago has only 13 native land mammal species, 12 of them are bats. All are endangered. The most common is the leaf-nosed bat. Bats

---

BIG BLOWS

The hurricane season in the Bahamas, like that of the US east coast, is from June to November, with most activity occurring in August and September. The Turks and Caicos are luckily out of the main hurricane paths.

Hurricanes that hit the Bahamas form off the coast of Africa and whip in a westerly direction across the Atlantic. The first stage of a hurricane's approach is called a tropical disturbance. The next stage is a tropical depression. When winds exceed 40mph, the system is upgraded to a tropical storm and is usually accompanied by heavy rains. The system is called a hurricane if wind speed exceeds 75mph and intensifies around a low-pressure center called the eye of the storm.

The strength of a hurricane is rated from one to five. The strongest and rarest hurricanes, the Category-5 monsters, pack winds that exceed 155mph. Hurricanes travel at varying speeds, from as little as 6mph to more than 31mph.

If you are caught by an approaching hurricane, follow local warnings. Hotels are typically of concrete and steel construction capable of withstanding strong winds. If you have an oceanfront room relocate inland.

In August, 1999, Hurricane Dennis raked the Abacos and Grand Bahama. A month later, Hurricane Floyd, a 600-mile-wide whopper, pounded Cat, San Salvador, Abaco and Eleuthera with winds up to 155 mph. In late 2004 two more hurricanes, Frances and Jeanne, hit these same islands along with Grand Bahama in quick succession. Massive flooding and the destruction of many buildings again hit villages and the tourism industry. Luckily, few lives were lost.

For warnings, check the USA National Hurricane Center's **Tropical Prediction Center** (www .nhc.noaa.gov).

---

consume large amounts of insects, especially mosquitoes, and act as important seed dispersers and pollinators for flora.

The only native terrestrial mammal is the endangered hutia, a cat-size brown rodent akin to a guinea pig; a small population lives on a small cay in the Exumas.

The human population on Mayaguana is out-numbered five to one by wild horses and burros.

Wild boar roam the backcountry on larger islands. You might be surprised to find North American raccoons on Grand Bahama. They were introduced during Prohibition (popular pets among Yankee bootleggers).

Iguanas are shy and harmless vegetarians that have been virtually eradicated by humans, feral dogs and cats, and now inhabit some outlying isles and are protected.

Many Bahamian islands have endemic species of reptiles, such as Cat Island, home to the Cat Island terrapin. Great Inagua also has its own terrapin.

There are frogs, too, including the Cuban tree frog, whose mucus is poisonous.

A useful book is Birds of New Providence and the Bahama Islands by PGC Brudenell-Bruce. Also try Natives of the Bahamas: A Guide to Vegetation and Birds of Grand Bahama, a nifty pocket-size booklet by Erika Moultrie.

BIRDS

Bird-watchers exalt in the Bahamas' 300 recorded species of birds. Only a few are endemic, including the Bahama swallow, endangered Bahama parrot and the Bahama woodstar hummingbird, which weighs less than a US nickel.

The West Indian (Caribbean) flamingo, which is the national bird, inhabits Crooked Island, Long Cay and Great Inagua, a sanctuary with over 50,000 birds.

From September through May, the forests swarm with visitors. Vireos, flycatchers, thrushes and plovers visit, migrating between summer and winter habitats. Bird-watchers also can spot Bahama whistling ducks, guinea fowl, quails, snipes, coots, herons and gallinules in the wetlands.

The pinelands of the northern Bahamas support a wide variety of resident summer nesters, plus migratory songbirds in winter.

The red-tailed hawk is one of several birds of prey commonly seen soaring high overhead, as is the jet-black turkey vulture, unmistakable with its undertaker's plumage and bald red head. The beautiful and diminutive osprey and kestrel prefer to spy from atop telegraph poles.

The islands are also home to the burrowing owl and the barn owl. Both are protected species.

MARINE LIFE

Different sources claim that the Bahamas has between 900 and 2700 sq miles of coral reef. What is certain is that there are countless species of fish inhabiting these coasts, such as bonito, inflatable porcupine fish, three species of stingrays, moray eel, lobsters, parrotfish, sharks, kingfish, groupers, barracudas, jewelfish and deep-blue Creole wrasse.

Many dive outfitters offer trips to encounter wild stingrays. Up to 5ft across, stingrays are quite gentle and will take food from your hand.

Humpback whales pass through the waters windward of the Bahamas and blue whales are also frequently sighted. Atlantic bottlenose dolphins frequent these waters, as do the less often seen Atlantic spotted dolphins.

Three species of marine turtles – green, loggerhead and, more rarely, hawksbill – use the islands' beaches as nest sites. Turtles migrate thousands of miles to nest and lay their eggs here, as they have for at least 150 million years. Unfortunately these gentle creatures are endangered, yet still hunted.

> The 287-sq-mile national park on Inagua protects the world's largest breeding colony of West Indian flamingos.

Plants

The Bahamas thin, rocky soil, underlain by limestone, is not conducive to lush vegetation. Nonetheless, the islands together boast more than 1370 species of trees and plants, including 121 endemics, such as Bahamian mahogany and Bahamian pine.

Lignum vitae, the national tree – which you may recognize by its clusters of dark-blue blooms – has the heaviest timber of all known woods and is much in demand among carvers (its bark, gum, fruit, leaves and blossoms also serve useful purposes, including medicines for gout and syphilis).

The waxy branches of the candlewood tree, another endemic species, were once lit as torches by Lucayan Indians.

NATIONAL PARKS

The Bahamas has 22 national parks, reserves and protected areas which include large sections of the barrier reef.

The parks are used for both scientific research and for protecting endangered species, and are maintained by the **Bahamas National Trust** (BNT; ☎ 242-393-1317; bnt@batelnet.bs; The Retreat, Village Rd, Nassau). Notably, the 175-sq-mile Exuma Cays Land & Sea Park was created in 1958 as the first marine fishery reserve in the world. The park now teems with prehistoric life forms, coral reefs, turtles, fish and endangered rock iguanas and hutias.

The following boxed text does not include all the Wild Bird Reserves, obtainable from the **Department of Agriculture** (☎ 242-325-7413; fax 242-325-3960; Levy Bldg, E Bay St, Nassau).

> *Flipper* (1996) brought us a fresh (and tuna-free) version of the old TV series. A young boy and dolphin become pals and once again save the day, showing the Bahamian seas in all their glory.

ENVIRONMENTAL ISSUES

Outside of the national park system, inappropriate development, pollution and overexploitation increasingly threaten wildlife and marine resources. Although the Bahamas was the first Caribbean nation to outlaw

WILDLIFE PRESERVES IN THE BAHAMAS

Park	Features	Activities	Location	Page
Abaco National Park	20,500 acres; endangered Bahama parrot	hiking, bird-watching		p165
Black Sound Cay National Reserve	small mangrove island; wintering habitat for waterfowl & avifauna	walking, bird-watching	Abaco; adjacent Green Turtle Cay	
Pelican Cays Land & Sea Park	2100 acres; extensive coral reefs, undersea caves, abundant terrestrial plant & animal life	yachting, snorkeling, diving, bird-watching	Abaco	p160
Tilloo Cay National Reserve	20-acre area of pristine wilderness; vital nesting site for tropical birds	hiking, bird-watching	Abaco; between Marsh Harbour & Pelican Cays	p160
North Bight, Fresh Creek, Blanket Sound, Young Sound & Staniard Creek	initial stages of designation	yachting, snorkeling, diving, bird-watching	Andros	p140
Conception Island National Park	temporary station for migrating birds & nesting green turtles	yachting, snorkeling, diving, bird-watching	between Long Island and San Salvador	p220
Crab Cay & Mamma Rhoda Cay	wild bird reserves	walking, bird-watching	Berry Islands	
Exuma Cays Land & Sea Park	176 sq miles; world's first marine fishery reserve (1958); coral reefs, turtles, fish, endangered rock iguanas & hutias	yachting, snorkeling, diving, hiking	Exuma Cays	p204
Moriah Harbour Cay	beaches, sand dunes & mangrove creeks; gull-billed terns, least terns, nighthawks, ospreys & oystercatchers	yachting, snorkeling, diving, hiking, bird-watching	between Great and Little Exuma	p205
Peterson Cay National Park	1½-acre cay & surrounding coral gardens	yachting, snorkeling, diving, hiking	Grand Bahama	p118

long-line fishing as a threat to the marine ecology, the islands' stocks of grouper, spiny lobster, turtle and conch all face the consequences of over-fishing.

Commercial poaching, mostly by Cuban-Americans from Florida in the west and by Dominicans in the east, has also been a significant problem. From the late 1970s the problem stirred several island communities to establish their own nongovernmental reserves. The conch has been listed by the **Convention on International Trade in Endangered Species** (CITES; www.cites.org) as 'commercially threatened' since 1994, and the Bahamas' groupers are now considered as being at the same risk. In early 2005 Bahamian fishermen were complaining that international poachers were fishing the stock during the ban. It should be added that it was still possible to find locally caught grouper in the Bahamas at this time. See the boxed text on p89.

Coral reefs have also experienced damage by anchors, careless divers and snorkelers as well as by Bahamian fishermen. The biggest culprit, however, is Mother Nature: hurricanes cause as much devastation as a minor war.

As someone new (or not so new) to diving or snorkeling, why not learn how to avoid damaging the reefs that sustain the marine life? Have a look at www.breef.org.

Park	Features	Activities	Location	Page
Lucayan National Park	world's longest known underwater cave & cavern system; mangrove wetland; birds	yachting, snorkeling, diving, hiking, bird-watching	Grand Bahama	p101
Rand Memorial Nature Center	100-acre site & BNT HQ; captive flamingo flock, native boa constrictors & curly tailed lizards	hiking, bird-watching	Grand Bahama	p103
Walker's Cay Marine Park	tropical fish, marine predators & underwater cathedrals	yachting, snorkeling, diving, hiking	Grand Bahama	p101
Bahamas National Trust Park	287 sq miles; world's largest breeding colony of West Indian flamingos	bird-watching tours organized through Nassau's BNT office	Great Inagua	p237
Union Creek Reserve	7 sq miles; tidal creek & marine turtle research facility	tours organized through Nassau's BNT office	Great Inagua	p18
Little Inagua	no freshwater or habitation, with undisturbed biodiversity	contact BNT for access	Little Inagua	p237
Little Island, Goat Cay	wild bird reserves	walking, bird-watching	Little San Salvador & adjacent cay	p214
Bonefish Pond National Park	1800 acres; marine nursery for fish, crawfish, conch, waterfowl & flora	yachting, snorkeling, diving, bird-watching	New Providence	
Harrold & Wilson Ponds	250 acres; 100 avian species including herons, egrets & cormorants	hiking, bird-watching	New Providence	p63
Primeval Forest	hardwood forest supports diverse plant species & features	hiking	New Providence	
Retreat	11 acres; very large collection of palms & tropical plants; BNT HQ	hiking	New Providence	p63

TURKS & CAICOS

The islands are predominantly semi-arid, notably Salt Cay and much of South Caicos and Grand Turk, which were denuded of vegetation to dissuade rainfall during the heyday of the salt industry. The larger, middle islands of North, Middle and East Caicos are lusher, with creeks, sand flats, lagoons and marshy wetlands. Most of the sandy beaches – some of the finest on the planet – are on the north and west shores, facing the open ocean.

More than 30 protected areas have been set aside to conserve delicate ecosystems and wildlife habitats.

WILDLIFE
Animals
There are almost as many donkeys, wild horses and cattle as humans, though they stay in the wilds.

The Turks and Caicos Islands – Beautiful by Nature by Julia and Phil Davies is a lovely illustrated introduction to the islands.

Iguanas once inhabited much of the Turks and Caicos until they lost their lives to introduced dogs and cats and their habitats to development. Now Little Water Cay, Fort George Cay and Ambergris Cays are all protected iguana reserves.

The Turks and Caicos rock iguana is monogamous over its 40-year life-span.

BIRDS
The vast wetlands in the southern portions of the Caicos and numerous uninhabited cays make perfect nesting sites for seabirds. More than 175 species have been sighted, of which 78 are migratory land birds. Ospreys are numerous and easily spotted, as are sparrow hawks and barn owls. Flamingos – once numerous throughout the chain – are now limited to West, North and South Caicos, where you may also see Cuban herons.

Frigate birds are more commonly seen here than in the Bahamas. The most important nesting site is Vine Point (Middle Caicos), but they also nest on Penniston Cay (near Grand Turk) and other islands. Many cays are important nesting sites for sooty and roseate terns, Audubon's shearwaters and brown noddy terns.

MARINE LIFE
A flourishing population of bottlenose dolphins lives in these waters. Some 7000 North Atlantic humpback whales use the Turks Island Passage and the Mouchoir Banks, south of Grand Turk, as their winter

WILDLIFE PRESERVES IN TURKS & CAICOS

Park	Features	Activities	Location	Page
West Caicos Marine National Park	coral reefs	yachting, diving, snorkeling	West Caicos	p242
Lake Catherine Nature Reserve	breeding grounds of flamingos, osprey & waterbirds	hiking, bird-watching	West Caicos	p242
Northwest Point Marine National Park	elkhorn coral; inland saline ponds attract roseate spoonbills & other waterfowl	wall diving, hiking, bird-watching	Providenciales, Caicos	p245
Chalk Sound National Park	a cay-studded lagoon	snorkeling, swimming	Providenciales, Caicos	p245
Princess Alexandra National Park	the shore and offshore reefs along Grace Bay & the cays northeast of Provo	snorkeling, diving, yachting, hiking	Providenciales, Caicos	p242
Ramsar Site	marsh & intertidal wetlands; breeding site & nursery for waterfowl, lobster, conch & fish	hiking, bird-watching, snorkeling, diving	North, Middle & East Caicos	p242
Three Mary Cays National Park	seabird nesting site	hiking, bird-watching	North Caicos	p242
East Bay Islands National Park	numerous small cays off North Caicos, favored sites for seabirds	hiking, bird-watching, snorkeling, yachting, diving	North Caicos	p242
Conch Bar Caves National Park	an extensive cave system, some with lagoons & most with colonies of bats & Indian petroglyphs	hiking, bat-watching, swimming, historical site viewing	Middle Caicos	p255
Middle Caicos Reserve & Trail System	beaches, freshwater lakes & pine forests are accessed by 10 miles of trails inside the Ramsar site	hiking, bird-watching, swimming	Middle Caicos	p255

breeding grounds between January and March. Manta rays are commonly seen during the spring plankton blooms off Grand Turk and West Caicos.

The waters are favored by four species of turtle; hawksbills (an internationally endangered species, although sadly not recognized in this region), greens, Loggerheads and occasionally leatherbacks.

Plants

Unique to the islands is the Turk's Head cactus, which you'll see on the national flag. It's easily recognizable: a short, stubby cactus topped by a red flower shaped like a fez. Aloe and sisal are also common.

Wild orchids bloom in winter. The bougainvillea, the magnificent royal poinciana and the casuarina are common introduced species.

Trees that bear fruits include the pigeon plum (good for making jams), passion flower, genip (known in the Florida Keys as 'Spanish lime') and wild dilly, whose gummy fruit is favored by iguanas (humans prefer its domesticated cousin, which produces chicle, once the main ingredient in chewing gum).

Listen to the dolphins chatting to each other, and follow links to a heap of dolphin sites and pictures at http://neptune .atlantis-intl.com /dolphins/sounds.html.

FLOWERING VARIETIES

Flowers abound every month of the year. In spring, all the islands are ablaze with the orange blossoms of the croton and the dramatic vermilion

Park	Features	Activities	Location	Page
Vine Point & Ocean Hole Nature Reserve	vast intertidal swamplands along the south shore, a frigate-bird breeding colony & a huge blue hole	hiking, bird-watching, snorkeling	Middle Caicos	p255
Admiral Cockburn Land & Sea Park	scrub-covered shore & offshore coral reefs off western South Caicos	hiking, snorkeling, yachting, diving	South Caicos	p242
Belle Sound & Admiral Cockburn Cays Nature Reserve	mangroves & bonefish flats west of South Caicos	hiking, bird-watching	South Caicos	p257
Columbus Landfall National Park	western shore & coral reefs off Cockburn Town; the ocean deep begins within 400yd of shore	hiking, bird-watching, snorkeling, yachting, diving	Grand Turk	p259
South Creek National Park	mangroves & wetlands along the island's south shore, home to migrating shorebirds & waders	hiking, bird-watching, snorkeling, yachting, diving	Grand Turk	p259
Grand Turk Cays Land & Sea Park	comprises tiny cays – Gibb's, Penniston, Long & Martin Alonza Pinzon – off the southeast shore; important nesting sites for seabirds, with abundant iguanas & Turk's Head cactus	hiking, bird-watching, flora & fauna spotting, snorkeling, yachting, diving	Grand Turk	p266

of the *Spathodea*, known locally as the 'Jesus Christ tree' because it blooms blood-red at Easter. It is commonly found outside churches.

The long, thin, twirled leaves of the sisal (which rattles in the wind and is therefore also known as mother-in-law's tongue) are used for weaving.

Many plants have long been used for bush medicines. Five-finger (also known as chicken-toe), for example, is used to make a tea that relieves body aches. The aromatic leaves of white sage are used as a salve for chicken pox and measles, and wild guava is used to treat diabetes.

NATIONAL PARKS

The Turks and Caicos Pocket Guide, edited by Julia Blake, is a handy encyclopedia full of facts and figures.

Native flora and fauna are protected within 33 areas set aside as national parks, nature reserves, sanctuaries and sites of historical interest under the aegis of Turks and Caicos Islands National Parks, which administers 23 national parks and nature reserves. More information can be sought from the **Department of Environment & Coastal Resources** (Grand Turk ☎ 649-946-2855; ccr@tciway.tc; Providenciales ☎ 649-946-4017; South Caicos ☎ /fax 649-946-3306).

Turks & Caicos National Trust (TCNT; ☎ 649-941-5710; tc.nattrust@tciway.tc; PO Box 540, Providenciales) is a nongovernmental organization dedicated to the preservation of the cultural, natural and historical heritage of the islands. The Trust has established three underwater snorkeling trails: two off Provo (Smith's and Bight Reefs) and another off Grand Turk. It has initiated countrywide studies of bird populations, and in 1999 gained international funding to manage the Ramsar wetlands in North, Middle and East Caicos.

Diving   Jean-Bernard Carillet

Be prepared to run out of superlatives. When it comes to providing enjoyable, enthralling diving for the experienced and novices alike, the Bahamas has no peer. Its great success as a diving mecca is due primarily to the unbeatable repertoire of diving adventures it offers. Pristine reefs, shipwrecks, blue holes, vertigo-inducing drop-offs, colorful tropical fish, rays, sharks and dolphins are the reality of diving here. Where else in the world can you join a shark feed, then go mingle with dolphins, visit movie-set shipwrecks, descend along bottomless walls and explore a mysterious blue hole – all in the same area? Added bonuses include state-of-the-art dive operations and warm turquoise waters year-round. In this fantasyland of colors, textures and shapes, several weeks would not exhaust the opportunities for adventure and discovery.

DIVING CONDITIONS
There are consistently optimal diving conditions throughout the year. Gin-clear visibility is the norm – it runs to 100ft and more – although the occasional winds can roil the waters. The lack of pollution and run-off is a definite bonus. Current conditions vary, but are generally imperceptible to mild.

During the coolest months (December through April), water temperatures are usually between 72°F and 76°F. Summer water temperatures range from a balmy 78°F to 84°F. You won't need anything more than a 3mm wetsuit.

MARINE LIFE
The Bahamas is one of the richest marine realms in the Caribbean. Its warm tropical waters hold one of the greatest varieties of sea life found in the region. Dream of encountering the big stuff? You can mingle with Caribbean reef sharks and nurse sharks, barracuda, bottlenose dolphins and spotted dolphins. Prefer smaller, Technicolor critters? You'll spot loads of reef fish, including angelfish, snapper, jacks, grunts, parrotfish, lobsters, cardinal fish, damselfish, Nassau groupers, stingrays and moray eels. Want to see invertebrates? The vertical walls drip with gorgonians, hard corals, sponges and crinoids, combining to create a vivid and sensual tapestry.

'When it comes to providing enjoyable, enthralling diving...the Bahamas has no peer.'

DIVE SITES IN THE BAHAMAS

The following descriptions are by no means exhaustive. For a detailed guide of the Bahamas' underwater possibilities, see Lonely Planet's *Diving & Snorkeling Bahamas*.

NEW PROVIDENCE
The strength of New Providence is the sheer variety of attractions, including superb shipwrecks, breathtaking walls along the Tongue of the Ocean, a varied topography and healthy coral gardens. But what makes it so unique is the shark diving. Divers from all over the world come here to experience a fantastic adrenaline rush at Shark Wall and Shark Arena, two feeding spots south of the island. On a coral rubble patch, in less than 65ft, the divers form a semicircle a few meters away from the feeders to watch the show. And what a show! Wearing a helmet and steel

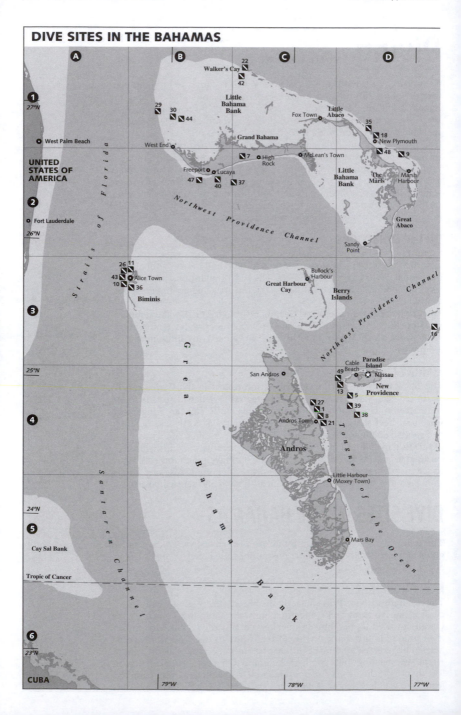

DIVE SITES IN THE BAHAMAS

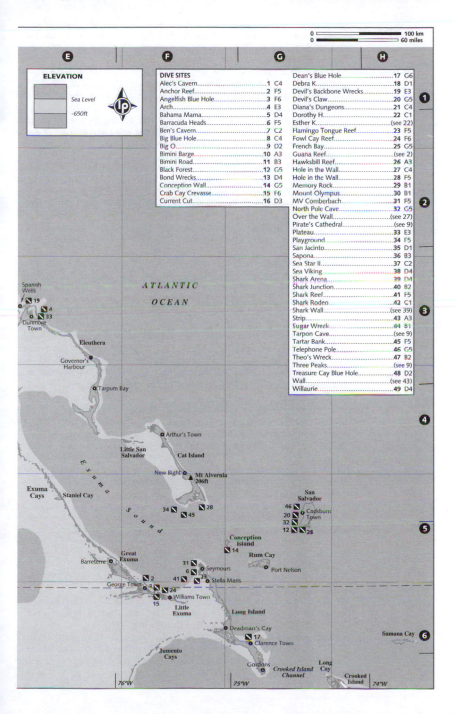

0 _____ 100 km
0 _____ 60 miles

E   **F**   **G**   **H**

ELEVATION

Sea Level

-650ft

DIVE SITES

Alec's Cavern	1	C4
Anchor Reef	2	F5
Angelfish Blue Hole	3	F6
Arch	4	E3
Bahama Mama	5	D4
Barracuda Heads	6	F5
Ben's Cavern	7	C2
Big Blue Hole	8	C4
Big O	9	D2
Bimini Barge	10	A3
Bimini Road	11	B3
Black Forest	12	G5
Bond Wrecks	13	D4
Conception Wall	14	G5
Crab Cay Crevasse	15	F6
Current Cut	16	D3

Dean's Blue Hole	17	G6
Debra K	18	D1
Devil's Backbone Wrecks	19	E3
Devil's Claw	20	G5
Diana's Dungeons	21	C4
Dorothy H	22	C1
Esther K	(see 22)	
Flamingo Tongue Reef	23	F5
Fowl Cay Reef	24	F6
French Bay	25	G5
Guana Reef	(see 2)	
Hawksbill Reef	26	A3
Hole in the Wall	27	C4
Hole in the Wall	28	F5
Memory Rock	29	B1
Mount Olympus	30	B1
MV Comberbach	31	F5
North Pole Cave	32	G5
Over the Wall	(see 27)	
Pirate's Cathedral	(see 9)	
Plateau	33	E3
Playground	34	F5
San Jacinto	35	D1
Sapona	36	B3
Sea Star II	37	C2
Sea Viking	38	D4
Shark Arena	39	D4
Shark Junction	40	B2
Shark Reef	41	F5
Shark Rodeo	42	C1
Shark Wall	(see 39)	
Strip	43	A3
Sugar Wreck	44	B1
Tarpon Cave	(see 9)	
Tartar Bank	45	F5
Telephone Pole	46	G5
Theo's Wreck	47	B2
Three Peaks	(see 9)	
Treasure Cay Blue Hole	48	D2
Wall	(see 43)	
Willaurie	49	D4

ATLANTIC OCEAN

Spanish Wells

19

4

33

Dunmore Town

Eleuthera

Governor's Harbour

Tarpum Bay

Arthur's Town

Little San Salvador

Cat Island

New Bight

Mr Alvernia 206ft

Exuma Cays

Staniel Cay

34   45   28

San Salvador

46
20
32
12   25

Cockburn Town

Conception Island

14

Rum Cay

Port Nelson

Great Exuma

31
6
41   23

Seymours

Stella Maris

Barreterre

George Town

2
3
24

15

Williams Town

Little Exuma

Long Island

Deadman's Cay

17

Clarence Town

Samana Cay

Jumento Cays

Gordons

Crooked Island Channel

Long Cay

Crooked Island

76°W   75°W   74°W

gloves and using a pole spear, the feeders dip into a box and pull out a hunk of fish. In a few seconds they are surrounded by a dense cloud of Caribbean reef sharks, along with nurse sharks. The scene is awesome: the sharks tear hunks off the bait, ripping it away with a shake of the head. The divers are motionless, within touching distance of the sharks. After 15 minutes of intense activity, the remains are tossed aside and the dive continues at a calmer pace.

Need a less challenging site? Check out the numerous wrecks around the island. The Bond Wrecks are probably the most appealing. The site earned its name from the wrecks' roles in James Bond '007' films. They feature a tug that sits upright on a sandy bottom in about 45ft, and a nearby mock fighter plane that has disintegrated. You'll swim around and inside the ribs of the mock-up, festooned with soft and hard corals, all with vivid hues. Other recommended wrecks include the massive Willaurie, draped with corals and glowing sponges, in about 60ft, the 110ft Bahama Mama, which was scuttled in 1995, and the Sea Viking, another vessel still in good shape, on the edge of the drop-off. The abundant fish life around the wrecks is a bonus. All of them are accessible to novice divers.

'...sharks tear hunks off the bait, ripping it away with a shake of the head.'

GRAND BAHAMA

Like New Providence, Grand Bahama boasts an exceptional diversity of underwater wonders. The island is world famous for its Dolphin Experience programs offered by the Underwater Explorers Society (UNEXSO; p107). Divers can interact with tame bottlenose dolphins in the open ocean, in a fascinating – though artificial – show conducted by dolphin trainers. Divers are positioned on the seafloor while two semicaptive dolphins glide over and play with them, under the guidance of the trainer. Take your regulator out of your mouth and these graceful cetaceans will expect a kiss! Some divers find it fun, while others are much more skeptical about this circuslike performance and prefer real encounters in the wild.

Grand Bahama is also blessed with first-rate shipwrecks. The photogenic Theo's Wreck is a long-standing favorite. She rests on her port side at a depth of 110ft. Divers can penetrate the engine rooms and cargo holes. Another prime wreck is the Sea Star II, a large vessel scuttled in 2002. She is starting to be encrusted by invertebrates, and can be entered as well. In less than 20ft, the scattered remnants of Sugar Wreck are not exactly impressive but they host a profusion of fish life, including nurse sharks, moray eels, turtles, groupers and barracuda.

Mount Olympus and Memory Rock rank among the most spectacular sites, and for good reason. On the eastern edge of the Gulf Stream, far from the island, they boast a dramatic seascape. Memory Rock is a superb wall dive, sporting a dazzling array of sponges, corals and gorgonians. The frequent occurrence of pelagics also spices up the diving. Mount Olympus is a very atmospheric site, featuring a series of prominent, mountainlike coral boulders laced with sand valleys and gullies. The area shelters an underwater Eden of lush coral growth and copious fish life. If you're lucky, you'll spot hammerheads.

Inland, experienced divers might want to dive at Ben's Cavern, which sits within the boundaries of Lucayan National Park. The vast cave is decorated with huge stalactites and stalagmites.

In the mood for a thrill-packed dive? Try Shark Junction, another shark dive. Here, the feeders wear chain mail shark suits and lead an exceptional show. They can literally place sharks in a trance, stroking their snouts and holding the predators' heads in their laps for several seconds. Visiting divers are thus given a chance to approach a shark very closely.

> **BLUE HOLES**
>
> Blue holes are the result of changing sea levels and chemical reactions (the limestone platforms are dissolved by the combination of fresh water and carbon dioxide). The Bahamas, and especially Andros, are famous for their numerous, massive and mysterious blue holes that form a fantastic playground for divers. They vary in shape and size, but many blue holes lead into elaborate cavern systems. The opening resembles a large, deep-blue disk.

ANDROS

A mere 20-minute plane hop from Grand Bahama opens up a whole new world of diving. Andros is one of the most intriguing islands in the Bahamas, with a sense of frontier diving. Dive Andros Wall and you'll understand why. This awesome drop-off plummets down 6000ft into the Tongue of the Ocean. It is adorned with sponges, sea whips and gorgonians, and riddled with overhangs, chimneys, arches and caverns, such as those in Diana's Dungeons, Alec's Cavern, Hole in the Wall and Over the Wall, four fantastic sites at the edge of the wall. Keep your eyes peeled for big pelagics. There are also numerous shallow reef dives in the area.

Another attraction is the presence of oceanic and inland blue holes. Over the years Andros has become the epitome of blue hole diving. While inland blue holes are for highly trained specialty divers only, there are some exceptional oceanic blue holes that are perfectly suitable for novice and intermediate divers. Consider the Big Blue Hole that originated from a collapse of the sea wall. This magical site features an enormous cavern system endowed with huge tunnels, boulders and other massive geological structures. You'll feel like you're floating in a lunar landscape. Unforgettable.

'Andros is one of the most intriguing islands in the Bahamas, with a sense of frontier diving.'

CAT ISLAND

Less-visited Cat Island is a true gem with numerous untouched sites for those willing to venture away from the tourist areas. The dramatic seascape is the main drawcard, with an outstanding vertical wall that borders the south end of the island. It is peppered with numerous chasms, coral canyons, sandy valleys, gullies, faults and swim-throughs. Pelagics, especially sharks, regularly patrol the area. There are also elaborate shallow reefs and coral gardens inside the reef. Recommended sites include Hole in the Wall, an L-shaped channel in the wall, teeming with snappers, groupers, jacks and lots of soft and hard corals; the Trench, an impressive groove in the reef, with an exit over the vertical wall; the Playground, at the tip of Devil's Point, a varied site with a prolific fish life, including turtles, jacks, groupers, lobsters, squirrelfish and nurse sharks hanging under ledges. Tartar Bank, an offshore pinnacle three miles from the coast, deserves special attention: the site's near-constant current attracts plenty of schooling fish, along with nurse sharks and turtles.

BIMINIS

The Biminis are famous for the Wild Dolphin Excursions offered by Bill & Nowdla Keefe's Bimini Undersea dive center (p129). The experience differs completely from the Dolphin Encounter programs in Grand Bahama. Here it's much more spontaneous. You'll snorkel with a pod of wild Atlantic spotted dolphins in their natural habitat on a flat northeast of the island – it requires a 1½-hour boat trip from the marina. While the encounter is not exactly guaranteed, Bill & Nowdla Keefe's Bimini Undersea claims a success rate of 80%. On a safe, sandy bottom less than

33ft deep, the graceful creatures gently frolic with the snorkelers. The dolphins are never forced to do anything they don't want to, and they are never rewarded with food. Don't miss this exhilarating excursion, it's sheer delight.

Diving in the Biminis is not limited to dolphin encounters. Wreck buffs will explore the Bimini Barge, a magnificent barge sitting upright in about 90ft near the edge of the drop-off, and the Sapona, which sits half in and half out of the water and is surrounded by a smorgasbord of reef fish. Both are decorated with a kaleidoscope of delightful corals and sponges.

Experienced divers won't miss the Wall, a sensational, high-voltage drift dive in the nutrient-rich Gulf Stream, over the edge of the continental shelf. Here you never know what you're going to see. Other favorites include the Strip, a colorful night dive along a strip of reef surrounded by sand, Hawksbill Reef and Bimini Road, an unusual site with a double line of large, neat square slabs, said to be the remnants of the legendary civilization of Atlantis.

SAN SALVADOR

'San Sal' boasts world-class wall-diving. Look at a topographic map and you'll see why. The island is an exposed seamount, surrounded by walls that tumble vertically to several thousand feet. Its isolation and the depth of the surrounding water make it a magnet for both pelagic and reef species, including big numbers of friendly groupers and passing hammerheads. There are also big cave and tunnel formations. Most dive sites are scattered along the west coast, sheltered from the prevailing winds. Don't think this is all challenging diving, however. You don't need to go deep – the wall starts at just 50ft or so. The local dive center, Riding Rock Resort & Marina (p218) uses at least 20 dive sites. Don't miss Devil's Claw, Telephone Pole, Doolittle's Grotto, North Pole Cave, Black Forest and French Bay.

THE EXUMAS

If you want relaxed diving, the Exumas will appeal to you. There are some excellent reef dives off George Town, near Stocking Island – ask for Guana Reef, Fowl Cay Reef or Anchor Reef, ablaze with colorful life. The barrier reef is in pristine condition and you'll have the sites to yourself. Another

---

CLOSE ENCOUNTERS WITH SHARKS AND DOLPHINS

The Bahamas was one of the very first places where the art of shark diving was refined. Shark feeding started in the '70s in Long Island and has now reached a very commercial level. Divers from all over the globe come to the 'shark-diving capital of the world' to sample the thrill of a lifetime. Whether or not these artificial encounters are a good idea is open to debate. On the one hand, it undeniably disrupts natural behavior patterns. Sharks that grow dependent on 'free lunches' may unlearn vital survival skills. Some have developed dangerous Pavlovian responses to the sound of revving boat motors. On the other hand, it is undoubtedly spectacular and it has been conducted without any accident so far. Some experts we met, including people from **BREEF** (Bahamas Reef Environment Educational Foundation; ☎ 242 362-6477; www.breef.org) and Dr Samuel Gruber, a marine biologist based in the Biminis, think that these well-choreographed performances have educational virtues and are a good way to raise awareness among divers. In other words, a diver who has viewed this often-misunderstood creature up close becomes an instant shark lover. These encounters have done a lot to restore a positive image of these denizens of the deep.

And what about dolphin encounters? Again, the big dolphin business might make you feel uncomfortable, and for good reason. But underwater your suspicions will be dissipated: interacting with wild dolphins in the open ocean is an extraordinary experience.

highlight is the numerous caves and blue holes that are hollowed out in the reef. They are far less intimidating than those at Andros and are a perfect introduction to blue hole diving. You'll explore the nooks and crannies of Crab Cay Crevasse, a very atmospheric blue hole, divable only at outgoing tide, and Angelfish Blue Hole, with an O-shaped entryway in about 25ft. Look for the resident lobsters, grunts, angelfish and nurse sharks.

WALKER'S CAY

Walker's Cay's main claim to fame is Shark Rodeo, a bewildering shark gathering that will enthrall even the most blasé divers – expect more than 100 sharks at a time. Guests are positioned on the seabed while bait made of frozen fish scraps – commonly referred to as a 'chumsicle' – is lowered in the midwater. It attracts dozens of sharks that hurl themselves onto the offerings. What's astonishing is the variety of species that congregate around this free snack; you'll see the usual bulky Caribbean reef sharks and nurse sharks, plus bull, blacktip and lemon sharks. Sometimes a hammerhead joins the fray. If you feel comfortable, you can swim around with the swirling predators. A truly memorable experience.

The dive menu also includes two wrecks, the *Esther K* and the *Dorothy H.* These 100ft tugboats were scuttled as artificial reefs. They rest upright on a sandy bottom in about 100ft and are home to a variety of reef species.

LONG ISLAND

Relaxed, unhurried Long Island offers superb dive sites off its northwestern tip. There are some outstanding reefs with thriving fish life, and a not-to-be-missed wreck, MV *Comberbach*, a 103ft steel freighter scuttled in 1986 and resting upright in 100ft. Since then it has become nicely encrusted and has attracted a host of colorful species, including amberjacks, groupers and parrotfish. Inside you'll find a broken van. Another Long Island perennial favorite is Barracuda Heads. Imagine a vast, sandy expanse studded with a jumble of large coral heads, with the usual species of multicolored reef fish fluttering about. Big barracuda also patrol the area. Further south, Flamingo Tongue Reef is also well worth it, with a similar setting.

If you're after something more thrilling, you'll find Shark Reef very rewarding. This is a very special shark feed. Divers kneel on the sandy seabed in about 40ft, then a bucket of chum is released from the stern of the dive boat. A gang of Caribbean reef sharks will immediately dart to the scene, vying for the free meal. The frenzy is quite intimidating but when the bucket is empty the sharks usually leave the area. The dive continues across the reef. Dean's Blue Hole is another fave. It's the largest blue hole in the Bahamas and is accessible from shore.

Long Island is also a good base for day trips to Conception Island, an uninhabited island and a national nature reserve 15 miles to the north. It features an absolutely pristine wall, densely carpeted with massive sponges and lush corals. For sheer beauty and plenty of fish life, this protected sanctuary is hard to rival.

'For sheer beauty and plenty of fish life, this protected sanctuary is hard to rival.'

ABACOS

Abacos is a diver's treat, with a good mix of caves, reef dives, wrecks and inland holes. Of particular interest is the *San Jacinto*, which sank in 1865. Her remains are strewn on a gentle slope in less than 50ft. You'll see its big boilers, engine, propeller, stern and other structures. There's abundant fish life hanging around, including schools of grunts, snapper, goatfish, groupers and spotted eels. Further south, the *Debra K* is another fish haven, at about 45ft. It's also broken up, but is very atmospheric.

There are some excellent reef dives near Great Guana Cay, including Three Peaks, Big O, Cathedral and Tarpon Cave. They feature an intricate cave system, with fissures and chimneys, in about 30ft. You shouldn't feel apprehensive, because sunbeams shine through skylights in the caves. The caverns, nooks and crannies are worth close inspection since they are packed with groupers, silversides, lobsters, snapper and jacks. Outside, you'll probably come across huge tarpon and big barracuda.

Seasoned divers will take to Treasure Cay Blue Hole, a fantastic inland blue hole, accessible by car from Marsh Harbour. The profile is a bit intimidating – there's a sulfur layer between 45ft to 60ft that prevents light from penetrating further. A strong flashlight is needed, and there's a rope to help the descent.

ELEUTHERA

Eleuthera offers a wide range of diving experiences, ranging from wall diving to drift dives and wreck dives. Most sites are located in the north, out of Harbour Island. If you want a thrilling ride, try Current Cut, a narrow channel between the western tip of North Eleuthera and Current Island. During tidal exchange, divers are sucked into the pass and propelled through the funnel by the powerful current. For about 10 minutes, you'll feel as though you're gliding, accompanied by a procession of fish, both reef species and pelagics. The ride of a lifetime!

> '...you'll feel as though you're gliding, accompanied by a procession of fish, both reef species and pelagics.'

Wreck enthusiasts will enjoy Devil's Backbone Wrecks. The treacherous Devil's Backbone reef has snared many vessels, such as the Cienfuegos, a 292ft American steamship that ran aground on the reef in 1895, the Potato & Onion Wreck and the Carnarvon, another freighter. They are mostly dismembered but some of their structures are still recognizable.

Other must-see dives include the Plateau, the Arch, the Grotto and the Blow Hole. As their names suggest, they boast a dramatic topography, with canyons, grooves, ledges, tunnels and crevices, all harboring large and small tropical fish.

DIVE CENTERS

FACILITIES & COSTS

The Bahamas' dive centers offer a whole range of services and products, such as introductory dives (for children aged six years and over, and adults), night dives, exploratory dives, specialty dives (such as blue holes, drift dives, Nitrox dives) and certification programs (usually PADI or NAUI).

While most dive shops are owned and operated independently of the island hotels, you may be able to book a dive package that includes both diving and lodging at a reputable hotel or resort. Generally, dive operations provide transfers to and from hotels.

An introductory dive, including equipment, will cost about $90. A single dive, with only a tank and weights supplied, runs from $35 to $45, and much more for a specialty dive (such as shark dives or dolphin dives). If you need to rent equipment as well, expect to pay an extra $15 to $20 per dive. There are usually two-, five- and 10-dive packages, which are much cheaper. An Open Water certification course will set you back about $380.

CHOOSING A DIVE CENTER

Good news – there's a plethora of full-service, professional dive operations in the Bahamas. All of them are affiliated to one or more professional certifying agencies (PADI, NAUI, CMAS). You can expect well-maintained

---

RESPONSIBLE DIVING

The Bahamas islands are ecologically vulnerable. By following these guidelines while diving, you can help preserve the ecology and beauty of the reefs:

- Encourage dive operators in their efforts to establish permanent moorings at appropriate dive sites.
- Practice and maintain proper buoyancy control.
- Avoid touching living marine organisms with your body and equipment.
- Take great care in underwater caves, as your air bubbles can damage fragile organisms.
- Minimize your disturbance of marine animals.
- Take home all your trash and any litter you may find as well.
- Never stand on corals, even if they look solid and robust.

---

and cutting-edge equipment, top-notch facilities and friendly, knowledge-able staff. But like a hotel or a restaurant, each diving center has its own style. Some people may suit the personalized attention and family-like atmosphere of a smaller outfit, while others will prefer the logistics and the structured professionalism of a larger center. Do your research and opt for the one that best suits your expectations. Check the Bahamas Diving Association website www.bahamasdiving.com for more information.

New Providence
Bahamas Divers (☎ 242-393-5644, 800-398-3483; www.bahamasdivers.com)
Dive Dive Dive (☎ 800-368-3483; www.divedivedive.com)
Nassau Scuba Centre (☎ 242-362-1964, 800-805-5485; www.divenassau.com)
Stuart Cove's Aqua Adventures (☎ 800-879-9832, 954-524-5755; www.stuartcove.com)

Grand Bahama
Grand Bahama Scuba (☎ 242-373-6775; www.grandbahamascuba.com)
Sunn Odyssey Divers (☎ 242-373-4014; www.sunnodysseydivers.com)
Underwater Explorers Society, UNEXSO (☎ 242-373-1244, 800-992-3483; www.unexso.com)
Viva Diving (☎ 242-373-4000; www.vivaresorts.com)
Xanadu Undersea Adventures (☎ 800-327-8150; 242-352-3811; www.nealwatson.com /freeport.html)

Abacos
Abaco Dive Adventures (☎ 242-367-2963; www.abacodiveadventures.com)
Brendal's Dive Center (☎ 242-365-4441; www.brendal.com)
Dive Abaco (☎ 800-247-5338, 242-367-2787; www.diveabaco.com)
Dive Guana (☎ 242-365-5178; www.diveguana.com)
Treasure Divers (☎ 242- 365-8465, 800-327-1584; www.treasure-divers.com)

Biminis
Bill & Nowdla Keefe's Bimini Undersea (☎ 242-347-3089, 800-348-4644; www.bimini undersea.com)
Scuba Bimini Dive Centre (☎ 954-524-6090, 800-848-4073, 242-347-444; www.scubabimini.com)

Long Island
Cape Santa Maria Beach Resort (☎ 242-338-5273, 800-663-7090; www.capesantamaria.com)
Reel Divers (☎ 242-338-0011; www.reeldivers.com)
Stella Maris Resort Club (☎ 242-338-2051, 800-426-0466; www.stellamarisresort.com)

LIVE-ABOARDS

Several live-aboards ply the waters of the Bahamas, with usually weeklong itineraries. A live-aboard dive trip is recommended for those looking to experience unchartered and uncrowded dive sites beyond the reach of land-based dive operations. Each vessel has its own itinerary but most of them stage shark dives and dolphin dives. The following vessels leave from Miami, Fort Lauderdale or Nassau.

Aqua Cat (www.aquacatcruises.com)
Blackbeard's Cruises (www.blackbeard-cruises.com)
Bottom Time Adventures (www.bottomtimeadventures.com)
Dream Too (www.dolphindreamteam.com)
Nekton Diving Cruises (www.nektoncruises.com)
Ocean Explorer (www.oceanexplorerinc.com)

Andros
Small Hope Bay Lodge (☎ 800-223-6961, 242-368-2014; www.smallhope.com)

Cat Island
Hawk's Nest Resort & Marina (☎ 242-342-7050, 800-688-4752; www.hawks-nest.com)
Hotel Greenwood Beach Resort (☎ 242-342-3053; www.greenwoodbeachresort.net)

Eleuthera
Ocean Fox (☎ 242-333-2323, 877-252-3594; www.oceanfox.com)
Valentine's Dive Center (☎ 242-333-2080; www.valentinesdive.com)

Exuma
Exuma Scuba Adventures (☎ 242-336-2893; www.exumascuba.com)

San Salvador
Club Med Columbus Isle (☎ 242-331-2000; www.clubmed.com)
Riding Rock Resort & Marina (☎ 800-272-1492, 242-331-2631; www.ridingrock.com)

DIVING IN THE TURKS & CAICOS

It's more or less the same story below the waterline. Though less charismatic and less varied than the Bahamas, the Turks and Caicos offer premier dive sites. Here, you can expect magnificent reefs, dramatic walls and an abundance of marine life, including wild dolphins, sharks, rays and even humpback whales during winter months in Salt Cay. Most of the dive sites are wall dives on the protected sides of the islands. Here's a list of the main dive outfits:

Big Blue Unlimited (☎ 649-946-5034; Providenciales; www.bigblue.tc)
Blue Water Divers (☎ 649-946-2432; Grand Turk; www.grandturkscuba.com)
Caicos Adventures (☎ 649-941-3346; Providenciales; www.caicosadventures.tc)
Dive Provo (☎ 649-946-5029; Providenciales; www.diveprovo.com)
Flamingo Divers (☎ 649-946-4193; Providenciales; www.flamingodivers.com)
J&B Tours (☎ 649-946-5047; Providenciales; www.jbtours.com)
O2 Technical Diving (☎ 649-941-3499; Providenciales; www.o2technicaldiving.com)
Ocean Vibes Scuba & Watersports (☎ 649-231-6636; Providenciales; www.oceanvibes.com)
Provo Turtle Divers (☎ 649-946-4232; Providenciales; www.provoturtledivers.com)
Salt Cay Divers (☎ 649-946-6906; Salt Cay; www.saltcaydivers.tc)
Silver Deep (☎ 649-946-5612; Providenciales; www.silverdeep.com)
South Caicos Ocean Haven (☎ 649-946-3444; South Caicos)

Food & Drink

The cuisine of the Bahamas and Turks and Caicos Islands is influence by the surrounding ocean, with fish and shellfish appearing as the main ingredient in many dishes across the region. Cultural influences are also distinctive. From the African slaves came spices such as chili peppers as well as the side dishes of johnnycakes – sweetbreads or drop-scones made with shortening – and peas 'n' rice. English settlers brought in stews, roasts, pies and the ubiquitous macaroni cheese, while US fast-food dishes, such as burgers (albeit with an island slant) are also hugely popular.

There isn't great variety in the sometimes bland dishes prepared across the islands. However a distinctive French flavor is emerging in the Turks and Caicos which helps to give their cuisine a distinctive edge.

Multi-Oscar-winning *Silence of the Lambs* by Orion Pictures (1991) did a lot for promoting Bahamian cooking. The famous scene where Hannibal tells Clarice that he's having a friend for dinner was shot in the Bahamas.

STAPLES & SPECIALTIES

With little agriculture or production in the region, most Bahamians and Turks and Caicos islanders rely mainly on imported fruit, vegetables, meat and general foodstuffs for their consumption and for supplying the tourists. Conch and grouper, free-range chickens and eggs are examples of the few locally provided proteins.

Rice (imported) is the dietary staple, usually eaten with peas, such as red beans, pigeon peas, or lima beans. Another favorite is grits (ground corn), also usually mixed with peas. Peas also find their way into hearty soups along with okra, meats, and vegetables. Potato salad sometimes takes the place of rice.

Breakfasts tend toward US style, with grits the staple. A local breakfast favorite is grits served with either tuna, corned beef or eggs.

Jaws: the Revenge by Universal Pictures (1987) had scenes shot in the Bahamas. Guess what? There's a hungry shark out there who fancies something other than conch burgers...

Fruit & Vegetables

At one time rare and exotic fruits were synonymous with the Bahamas, most notably pineapple, which during the 19th century enjoyed a worldwide

---

JOHNNYCAKE

Look out for johnnycake, sweet bread that is served hot with creamy butter. This is the bread eaten for breakfast on all regional islands. It is heavier and sweeter than most breads, but when served hot with fresh butter, there is nothing better. Don't even bother adding jam or marmalade. You can make your own with these ingredients:

- ¾ cup vegetable shortening
- 6 cups plain flour
- a generous pinch of salt
- 1–3 tbs sugar
- 2 cups water

Mix the shortening and flour with a dough knife until there is a lumpy consistency throughout. Stir in the salt and sugar, then add the water a little bit at a time until the dough is the proper consistency for regular bread. Knead it for about 10 minutes, until it's smooth, and plop it into a greased bread pan. Bake at 350°F (180°C) until it is tawny and crusty. Serve it right away, plain or with butter.

TRAVEL YOUR TASTEBUDS

Souse is a regional favorite. There are many different ways of preparing it, but the end result is generally a sort of stew with a thick gravy. Fish is the usual main ingredient, but souses can also be made with conch, chicken, meat or tongue.

Those with delicate stomachs should avoid meat souse; mutton boiled in saltwater, along with tongue, trotters, anything else lying around that is also grey and wobbly, and cooked with lime juice and pepper.

reputation. Only minuscule quantities are produced today, but look for the Eleutheran sugar loaf or Spanish scarlet varieties, considered especially delicious.

Hurricanes have destroyed many small plantations, but there are still fruits and vegetables to be found including green and yellow bananas, plantains and thyme (one of most popular herbs in Bahamian and indeed, Caribbean cooking), tomatoes (crushed and bottled or fresh), Irish potatoes, chunks of cassava, plums, mangoes, a hot variety of chili called finger pepper, onions, sweet peppers, regular limes and the more tart key limes.

Roadside shacks also proffer papayas and pineapples. Also look out for the less well-known but equally enjoyable jujubes, star apples, pigeon plums, Surinam cherries, sapodillas, or soursops.

The conch, a staple protein in the islands, is an endangered species. See the boxed text, p89.

Seafood

Conch, crab, grouper, jack, shrimp, snapper, turbot, and tuna are all daily staples of Bahamian cooking, often cooked with carrot, cassava, cucumber, grits, guinea corn, okra, plantain, and wild spinach. Lobsters (crawfish) are other favorites, though being pricey they are not as important a staple as you may imagine.

The region's favorite fish is grouper, a mild-flavored white fish, often served poached, grilled, or steamed in a mildly spiced sauce. It's often eaten as 'grouper fingers' – thin, battered strips that are deep fried.

A popular breakfast dish is boil' fish, a bouillabaisse of grouper boiled with salt pork, onion, potato, and seasonings. It is generally served with grits or johnnycakes. If you want to try a johnnycake recipe, see the boxed text, p55.

Bahamas Cookery: Cindy's Treasures by Cindy Williams is a great collection of the simple regional delicacies – such as moist pineapple cake and guava duff with rum-cream sauce.

Everybody consumes conch (pronounced 'conk'); every home, restaurant and roadside takeout has it on the menu. This tough snail-like mollusk is served pounded, minced, and frittered; marinated and grilled; raw as a ceviche or conch salad (which is diced with onions, celery, pepper and cucumber then soaked in lime juice); as a chowder or 'soused' (stewed); 'scorched' (scored in a salad); and 'cracked' (battered and deep fried).

These days fishermen bemoan the difficulty of finding conch and grouper; it's much more difficult than it used to be, and everyone agrees that over-fishing is the culprit.

When it comes to meat, chicken is the most popular. In some places, you can't throw a rock without hitting a place that serves fried chicken and greasy chips. 'Mutton' – frequently seen on menus – can be goat or lamb and is frequently served curried.

The trademark Bahamian dessert is duff or guava duff, a fruit-filled jelly pudding served with sauce made of sugar, egg, butter and rum. It can be steamed, baked or even boiled. Another yummy favorite is coconut tart, a thin baked pie with a sweetened shredded coconut filling.

Check out Nassau Memories by Debby Nash. Successful Bahamian restaurants are profiled along with their signature dishes as a memento of the Bahamas.

Colonial cultural hangovers are often retained on menus in tourist spots as well as in residential suburbs. Regular dishes include steak and kidney pudding, bangers and mash, and shepherd's pie, while main courses across the region are served with a choice of coleslaw and macaroni and cheese. This is not, it must be stated, the same sort of macaroni and cheese that comes in a box with a foil-lined package of powdered cheese product. This is the genuine thing, baked in the oven and packed so tightly that it can be cut into slabs and served in the same style as lasagne.

It is virtually impossible to avoid dishes without some fried ingredient or carbohydrate. This means that healthy eating is not easy or cheap.

Turks & Caicos Specialties

As in the Bahamas, conch, lobster, soft-shell crab and fresh fish (often blackened with Cajun seasoning) are favorites in Turks and Caicos, along with spicy Jamaican jerk chicken.

Food in this region is generally a lot healthier and uses more fresh fruits, such as sapodillas and sugar apples, and vegetables.

A lot of foods are imported from Haiti rather than the US, which may help to make healthy eating more affordable than in the Bahamas.

The cooking is also more sophisticated; there's less fried-food and it has distinctive French influences.

Red Cross Cookbook (published by the Red Cross) is a fund raiser sold in the Turks and Caicos. It is a fabulous collection of the whole region's recipes and a bargain for $10.

DRINKS

The Bahamian beer Kalik is fantastic; golden bubbles and a sharp flavor. The national Bahamian cocktail could be the Goombay Smash, a lethally easy-to-drink fruit juice and rum cocktail (see also the boxed text, p171), although the Bahama Mama is probably one of the better known rum cocktails, with a coffee liqueur thrown in for good measure.

The infamous rum that bottoms up local cocktails is simply called 151, as it is 151% proof. There is an excellent range of duty-free quality rums available in Nassau, including the Bacardi line, which can also be bought at their factory on New Providence (see p99). Flavored rums are also popular and include coconut, banana, mango and pineapple rum, and the best local brand for these is Ricardo.

Wine is widely sold, but costly. Be aware that some bottles will have been exposed to the heat. Wine connoisseurs should head to Graycliff in Nassau; its owner, Enrico Garzaroli, claims the largest wine collection in the Caribbean, with some rare vintages offered at over $10,000.

Many restaurants in the Bahamas and Turks and Caicos serve the old colonial favorites of 'bangers and mash' and 'steak and kidney pudding'?

BAHAMA MAMA

Here are the makings of a classic Bahamian cocktail.

- ½ fl oz (15ml) dark rum
- ½ fl oz (15ml) coconut liqueur
- ¼ fl oz (8ml) 151%-proof rum
- ¼ fl oz (8ml) coffee liqueur
- ½ lemon, juice
- 4 fl oz (120ml) pineapple juice

Combine the ingredients and pour over ice. Garnish with a cherry. Skol! Slàinte! Cheers!

BAHAMAS & TURKS & CAICOS TOP FIVE

- **Club Caribe** (Churchill Beach, Grand Bahama, p114) Sit on the deck and look out over the wide, blue ocean. Bahamians gather here for great peppery fish salads, chilled cocktails and live music.
- **Chez Pierre Bahamas** (Simms Beach, Long Island; p225) Fall asleep following a delicious pasta dinner in your wooden hut on stilts overlooking the sea and deserted beach.
- **Chat n Chill Bar & Grill** (Stocking Island; Exumas; p200) Specializing in Island Daiquiris and yummy grilled barbecues; call for a pick-up from George Town dock, and rejoice in *the* perfect beach bar!
- **Tiki Hut** (Providenciales, Caicos; p248) A good place for breakfast, but an even better place for Wednesday night's $10 barbecue; a 13-year tradition that packs out the place.
- **Grace's Cottage** (Providenciales, Caicos; p249) Dine under the stars in a garden sprinkled with flowering shrubs, where chocolate soufflé is always on the menu and the white linen is always crisp.

More people drink wine informally in the Turks and Caicos than in the Bahamas, and the local brew is a full-flavored Turks Head beer. There is also some delicious rum on the market, such as the black and spicy Gosling, which makes potent cocktails.

CELEBRATIONS

West Indian families are usually enormous and widely dispersed. Despite the distance, families remain incredibly close and when the whole crew gets together every few years, it is a major production that usually takes place over several days. These reunions often happen during events such as island regattas, sporting competitions and Christmas. Needless to say, the familiar recipes are popular at these reunions, with families sitting down to souse and 'boil' fish, myriad conch dishes and the winning favorite; fried chicken with peas 'n' rice.

Throughout the predominantly Christian Caribbean, Christmas is the most important culinary celebration of the year, followed closely by New Year's Eve – often celebrated with parties in which the centerpiece may well be a roasting pig. In fact, in many places, celebrating and feasting stretches from Christmas Eve through to New Year's Day.

And then there's Junkanoo, a celebration in which the entire Bahamian population heads out into the streets for a huge, nonstop party.

WHERE TO EAT & DRINK

There's a full gamut of restaurant types, from funky seafood shacks and burger joints to ritzy restaurants with candelabras. Restaurants range from wildly expensive (the norm) to humble roadside stands where you can eat simple Bahamian fare from $6. Small hole-in-the-wall restaurants often serve fabulous local food; don't be put off by their often basic appearance.

Larger resorts have a choice of restaurants, with one always serving buffets. The ultradeluxe hotels have restaurants that are among the best on the islands, but they can't replicate the taste and atmosphere of small, locally run eateries.

Some all-inclusive resorts that are otherwise only for guests sell evening passes that allow you to eat and drink in their restaurants, bars, and nightclubs for a single fee. Hotels may also offer bargain-priced 'Dine-Around' programs, sometimes included in the hotel rate.

The wonderful woman who invented the Goombay Smash cocktail was a teetotaler.

You can buy a rum so flammable that it has been banned from aircraft.

Many of the restaurants geared to the tourist trade are overpriced. Groceries are also expensive; canned and packaged goods are imported and cost up to three times what you might pay at home.

Most settlements have either a makeshift market – where fishermen filet and sell their fresh catches of dolphin (the fish), grouper, conch, and lobster (in season) – or a cache in someone's home. With the exception of Nassau, it's often difficult to find fresh fruits, vegetables, and spices at markets and roadside stalls.

Quick Eats

Bahamians have taken to processed snack foods in a massive way, and even the most faraway location is sure to have a local shack selling snacks, from candy bars to cookies and other packaged snack foods. Nassau and Freeport also have dozens of name-brand fast-food outlets in their midst.

Beware! Very few food outlets open on Sundays outside of tourist centers.

VEGETARIANS & VEGANS

There's no easy way to say this, but vegetarians will find it tough going in the Bahamas and Turks and Caicos, while vegans will find the only way to eat is by buying their own groceries.

The concept of not eating meat or animal products is understood but too rarely experienced to be catered for; nevertheless, there is normally at least one vegetarian dish on a restaurant menu. Off the main islands, dairy foods are the most accessible form of protein and can be eaten with restaurant-staple side dishes of peas 'n' rice, macaroni cheese, plantains and coleslaw.

With so many hotel rooms now fitted with fridges it is possible to keep a stock of fruit and vegetables (when you can find them!) to balance the diet a bit.

All supermarkets stock a range of tinned beans and seeds, while the main islands' supermarkets in the Turks and Caicos also stock some soy meals and tofu.

EATING WITH KIDS

Generally all the island communities are very family oriented, and this includes restaurants and cafés. However, you will rarely see islanders' children out for late dinner, and if you do, they are very well-behaved and do not freely run around.

Let the cooks know if you don't want any sauces on your children's food. Islanders love very hot pepper and chili sauces as well as lime juice on their food. This may cause you a few pangs, and test your little ones'

How do you imbibe this wonderful liquor using other means than a glass? *Cooking with Caribbean Rum* by Laurel-Ann Morley has the answers.

www.swagga.com /drinks.htm is the virtual doorway to a teetotaler's Caribbean paradise. Learn how to make everything from seamoss drinks to soursop punch.

DOS & DON'TS

- Do tip 15% with a smile at all restaurants and bars.
- Do stand in line or wait your turn to be served.
- Do take a small gift when dining at someone's home.
- Don't smoke indoors at restaurants.
- Don't take children to bars.
- Don't assume drinking alcohol is the norm, many islanders are teetotalers.

delicate systems. Also, be aware that conch salads are normally made with raw mollusk.

HABITS & CUSTOMS

The cultural habits of the English and North Americans are similar to those of the Bahamians, and Turks and Caicos Islanders; many travelers will find their eating and drinking customs easily translate to this region. Most people eat three meals a day, and many workers buy takeouts from roadside stalls for picnic lunches. Courtesy is very important across the islands, as is respect for those serving in eateries and bars.

Bahamas

DENNIS JOHNSON

New Providence

Most visitors to New Providence stay within the heady triangle of charming, colonial downtown Nassau, Cable Beach's fun-filled beachside resorts, and the all-pervasive excitement of the Atlantis water and casino complex on adjoining Paradise Island. Nassau is so geared to the tourist that the 'real' island takes some seeking out. Yet it lies close at hand.

The narrow streets of downtown Nassau spill over with busy residents, hedonistic holiday-makers and shopping cruise-ship passengers. By strolling down to Potter's Cay when fishing boats return laden with glistening fish, you can experience an aspect of Bahamian life that hasn't changed much since the 1800s. Or to enjoy a real Bahamian community experience, attend an exuberant church service or wander amid the *goombay* dancers and the bustle of Arawak Cay, where multicolored shacks sell beer and hot, crispy pieces of fried fish. Quiet communities and fishing villages dot the coastline, where friendly artists display their vivid wares and Bahamians chat while children play on undisturbed beaches after school.

Most of the interior of the island is marshy, with large lakes and dense scrub forest, but it is enjoyed by bird-watchers. Here, serene Lake Nancy is edged by grandiose homes that are only outshone by billionaires' dwellings in the secured settlements on the western coast.

Two-thirds of the nation's population live on this 21 mile-long isle, mostly within Nassau. Although the turquoise seas and white, sugar-soft sands of Cable and Cabbage Beaches are renowned, other idyllic spots include uninhabited cays, perfect for day trips. Locals relish the pretty western and southern beaches, where the snorkeling and diving are superb.

HIGHLIGHTS

- Shop till you drop at the duty-free shops along lively Nassau's **Bay St** (p95) and around **Rawson Sq** (p72), brimming with historic buildings and bustle

- Head for Paradise Island to visit **Atlantis'** (p78) incredible waterpark and aquarium, and then sunbathe and people-watch on the stunning white sands of adjacent **Cabbage Beach** (p79)

- Sip a golden Kalik (locally brewed beer) and dance to the drums of **Junkanoo's** (p83) midsummer or Boxing Day carnival

- Take an exhilarating **powerboat adventure** (p80) to the idyllic Exuma Cays or the pink sands of Eleuthera

- Explore the underwater reefs and cays off the **southwestern** and **northern beaches** (p79) and meet some neon-colored fish

Underwater Reefs & Cays

Paradise Island

Nassau

Underwater Reefs & Cays

- TELEPHONE CODE: 242 | - POPULATION: 228,329 | - AREA: 80 SQ MILES

National Parks

Harrold and Wilson Ponds are perfect for a spot of hiking or bird-watching, with over a hundred listed bird species including herons, egrets and cormorants to be viewed here.

The Retreat (p74) is tucked away in the center of Nassau, and has a vast collection of palms and tropical plants plus the Bahamas National Trust (BNT; p74). Enjoy a stroll through the garden's 11 acres and collect some detailed information on regional sites of interest.

Bird-watchers should head for the reserves of Paradise Island, Cable Beach Golf Course, the caves, Lakeview, Red Sound, Twin Lakes, Westward Villas, Lake Cunningham, Waterloo, Adelaide Creek, Goulding Cay, Prospect Ridge, Waterworks and Skyline Heights. For the details on where to find these and other Wild Bird Reserves contact the **Department of Agriculture** (☎ 242-325-7413; fax 242-325-3960; Levy Bldg, E Bay St, Nassau, New Providence).

Other national parks are listed on p39.

Getting There & Away

Most travelers to New Providence and the Bahamas fly into Nassau International Airport, which lies 8 miles west of town. Others arrive at Nassau's Prince George Wharf on international cruise ships or on private boats.

Getting Around

You can easily navigate your way around downtown Nassau and Cable Beach by foot. They are joined by a regular stream of jitney buses (private minibuses), which also run around the island, making exploration pretty easy.

Pedestrians can either take the regular ferries between Prince George Wharf and Paradise Island or walk across the Paradise Island bridges to or from downtown. Keep in mind that there is a walk of almost a mile from the bridges into Nassau's tourism center.

Car-rental agencies are located at the airport and in all tourism areas, as are scooter-hire operators.

There are tons of tourism and dive operators who visit surrounding cays and other Bahamian islands, as do mail boats and Bahamas Ferries services.

NASSAU

pop 227,936

Modern Nassau is not such a far cry from the rowdy town that once harbored pirates, stockade runners and prohibition-avoiding party crowds. It's still a lively place fueled by commerce and rum, but more legitimate. The small, historic downtown core is a charming mix of narrow streets, grand sugar-pink neocolonial government buildings, and old wooden and limestone buildings, which are dignified in their faded grandeur.

But downtown is more than a pretty snapshot. It is also a hub of commerce and government, policed by immaculately dressed and starched police officers. Bankers in pinstriped shirts dodge between tourists to reach a myriad of international banks, intent on manipulating billions of dollars to make the wealthy wealthier in this offshore banking haven.

The waterfront and Bay St shops (the heart of downtown) are packed with tax-free sparkling emeralds, spiced rums and elegant silk clothing. Here cafés serve chattering tourists fueled by multicolored cocktails, while vast cruise liners loom nearby, disgorging their hordes which swamp Nassau's identity, but also her cash registers.

Jitney buses run constantly to the soft sands of Cable Beach and adjacent hotels while taxis honk for those heading to Paradise Island. Here the concrete cladding of ritzy resorts covers the land and almost dwarfs the snowy-white sands of Cabbage Beach.

Low-income and middle-class residential suburbs extend inland for miles. Government ministries, modern shopping malls and colleges all lie south of downtown, along with Over-the-Hill, which is bordered by East St and Blue Hill Rd to the east and west, and Prospect Ridge and Blue Hill Heights to the north and south. This African-Bahamian enclave contains both colorful family homes and an edgier and messier picture of Nassau's less affluent and contented residents.

HISTORY

The island's colorful early history is steeped in rum-running and roguery. Nassau (initially known as Charles Town) was established in 1666, her dirt streets pounded by pirates and wreckers, and lined with brothels

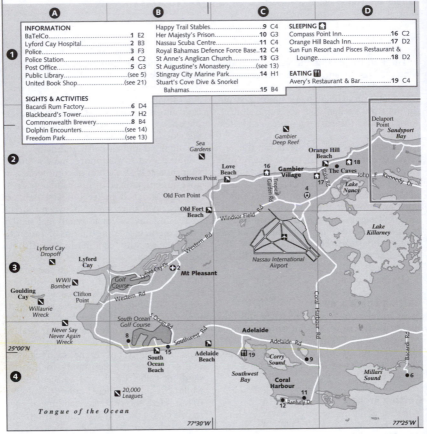

NEW PROVIDENCE

A	**B**	**C**	**D**

INFORMATION
BaTelCo...................................**1** E2
Lyford Cay Hospital...................**2** B3
Police.......................................**3** F3
Police Station...........................**4** C2
Post Office................................**5** G3
Public Library........................(see 5)
United Book Shop...............(see 21)

SIGHTS & ACTIVITIES
Bacardi Rum Factory.................**6** D4
Blackbeard's Tower....................**7** H2
Commonwealth Brewery.............**8** B4
Dolphin Encounters................(see 14)
Freedom Park.......................(see 13)

Happy Trail Stables....................**9** C4
Her Majesty's Prison.................**10** G3
Nassau Scuba Centre................**11** C4
Royal Bahamas Defence Force Base.**12** C4
St Anne's Anglican Church.........**13** G3
St Augustine's Monastery.........(see 13)
Stingray City Marine Park..........**14** H1
Stuart's Cove Dive & Snorkel
  Bahamas...............................**15** B4

SLEEPING
Compass Point Inn....................**16** C2
Orange Hill Beach Inn...............**17** D2
Sun Fun Resort and Pisces Restaurant &
  Lounge.................................**18** D2

EATING
Avery's Restaurant & Bar...........**19** C4

and taverns for 'common cheats, thieves, and lewd persons.' Fed up with relentless attacks by Charles Town's pirates on their ships, the Spaniards attacked the town in 1684, followed by an assault by a combined Spanish and French force in 1703, which didn't help the city's development much either.

Fifteen years later the pirates were ousted by the British but by the middle of the 18th century Nassau still simply consisted of a church, jail, courthouse plus an Assembly House on Bay St. In the 1760s Governor William Shirley, who had been a governor of Massachusetts, brought a Yankee sense of order and ingenuity to help create a *real* city. The swamps were drained, the land was surveyed, and tidy new streets were laid.

The American Revolution boosted the city's fortunes, as citizens took to running the English blockade and a flood of entrepreneurial loyalist refugees arrived. In 1787 the haughty and inept Earl of Dunmore arrived as governor of the Bahamas, despite disgracing himself in the posts of governor of New York and Virginia and being accused of a reprehensible private life. Dunmore's legacy is evident today in several fine buildings. These include Fort Charlotte (p75) and Fort Fincastle (p73). The governor was saved from the axe for his extravagance and stupidity by the outbreak of Britain's war with France in 1793.

0 ———————— 4 km
0 ———————— 2 miles

Northeast Providence Channel

Salt Cay ● 14
Blue Lagoon

Long Cay

See Paradise Island Map (p77)

See Nassau Map (pp66–7)

Paradise Island

Sun Cay

25°05'N

Discovery Island

See Cable Beach Map (p76)

Crystal Cay

Saunders Beach Arawak Cay Nassau Harbour

W Bay St

Potter's Cay

Athol I

Goodman's Bay Cable Beach

W Bay St

Nassau

East St

Market St

Village Rd

Montagu Bay

Great Bahama Bank

Lake Cunningham

Faith Ave

Wulff Rd

20

Lost Ocean Hole

Oakes Field Airfield

Robinson Rd
Independence Dr

22

21

Prince Charles Ave

5

7

Bernard Rd

Fox Hill

13

Eastern Rd

East End Point

Harrold Rd

Blue Hill Heights

Harrold Pond

Soldier Rd

23

Wilson Pond

East End Lighthouse

Blue Hill Rd

Gladstone Rd

Fire Trail Rd

Golf Course Rd

East St

Fox Hill Rd

10

Yamacraw Hill Rd

Culbert's Bay

Yamacraw Beach

Carmichael Rd

S Beach Rd

Carmichael Village

Cow Pen Rd

Harbour Rd

South Beach

Great Bahama Bank

77°20'W

Bonefish Pond

SHOPPING		
Bonneville Bones	(see 21)
Brass & Leather Shops	(see 21)
Mall at Marathon	21 G3
Towne Centre Mall	22 F3

ENTERTAINMENT		
Galleria Cinema 11	(see 21)
Galleria Cinemas 6	20 E2

TRANSPORT		
Gas Station	23 F3
Gas Station	24 E2

By the late 18th century Nassau had settled into a slow-paced, glamorous era in which the well-to-do lived graciously and were serviced by slaves who resided in Over-the-Hill shanties. Following the abolition of the slave trade by the Brits in 1807, numerous public edifices and sites, such as the Queen's Staircase, were constructed using the manual labor of former slaves.

The American Civil War and Prohibition further enhanced Nassau's fortunes; many fine hotels and homes were erected on the proceeds from blockade- and rum-running. The 'winter season' of visiting socialites set the pattern for the Bahamian peak tourism season.

ORIENTATION

Historic downtown Nassau is 10 blocks long and four blocks wide and faces north toward Paradise Island and Nassau Harbour. The town rises south to Prospect Ridge, a steep limestone scarp that parallels the entire north shore about a half-mile inland. A second, higher ridge – Blue Hill Heights – rises to 120ft and runs east–west along Nassau's southern border, 3 miles inland. The major residential areas lie between the ridges.

The main thoroughfare through town is Bay St, which runs east to the Paradise Island Exit Bridge; beyond, it follows the windward shore as Eastern Rd. West of downtown, Bay St becomes W Bay St, and runs to Cable Beach. From here, continue on this road (which changes names several times) to complete a loop of the island via Lyford Cay, Adelaide and Carmichael Village. At Fox Hill join Eastern Rd to get back into town.

Downtown, Bay St is one-way, from west to east. The main westbound thoroughfare

downtown is Shirley St, which runs from Eastern Rd.

Paradise Island is 4 miles long and a half-mile wide, tapering to the west. It is divided in two by a narrow man-made waterway linking Nassau Harbour to the Atlantis marina. Two road bridges (one to enter and the other to exit the island) link

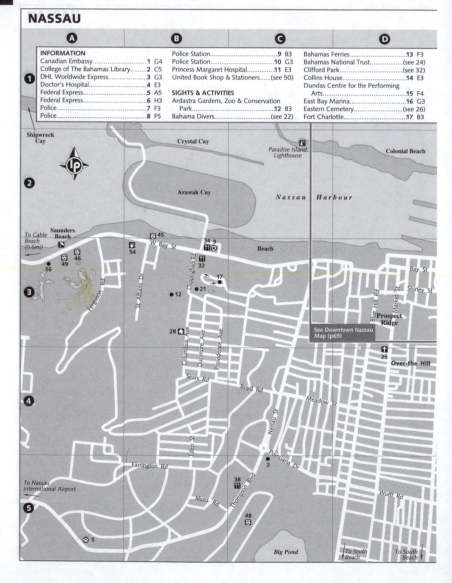

NASSAU

INFORMATION		
Canadian Embassy...........................**1** G4	Police Station...................................**9** B3	Bahamas Ferries.............................**13** F3
College of The Bahamas Library....**2** C5	Police Station.................................**10** G3	Bahamas National Trust................(see 24)
DHL Worldwide Express...................**3** G3	Princess Margaret Hospital.............**11** E3	Clifford Park..................................(see 32)
Doctor's Hospital............................**4** E3	United Book Shop & Stationers......(see 50)	Collins House...................................**14** E3
Federal Express...............................**5** A5		Dundas Centre for the Performing
Federal Express...............................**6** H3	**SIGHTS & ACTIVITIES**	Arts...**15** F4
Police...**7** F3	Ardastra Gardens, Zoo & Conservation	East Bay Marina..............................**16** G3
Police...**8** F5	Park..**12** B3	Eastern Cemetery..........................(see 26)
	Bahama Divers................................(see 22)	Fort Charlotte.................................**17** B3

Shipwreck Cay

Crystal Cay

Paradise Island Lighthouse

Colonial Beach

Arawak Cay

Nassau Harbour

To Cable Beach (0.6mi)

Saunders Beach

W. Bay St

Beach

Bay St

Shirley St

Blue Hill Rd

Market St

Prospect Ridge

St Albans Dr

Ferguson Rd

Chippingham Rd

Columbus Ave

Dunmore Ave

Providence Ave

See Downtown Nassau Map (p69)

Over-the-Hill

Sears Rd

Boyd Rd

Meadow St

Nassau St

Eden St

Poinciana Dr

Farrington Rd

To Nassau International Airport

Thompson Blvd

Moss Rd

Wulff Rd

Big Pond

To South Beach

To South Beach

Paradise Island to New Providence. Both bridges have pedestrian walkways.

See p96 for information on getting to/from the airport.

Maps

Stores and hotels have the free tourist *Bahamas Trailblazer Map* and *Super Map*.

INFORMATION
Bookstores

Several stores on Bay St stock a wide range of magazines, newspapers and books.
Island Shop (Map p69; ☎ 242-322-4183; fax 242-322-8470; 2nd fl, cnr Bay & Frederick Sts, Nassau) Sells a good collection of Bahamian literature, maps, nautical handbooks and Lonely Planet guides.

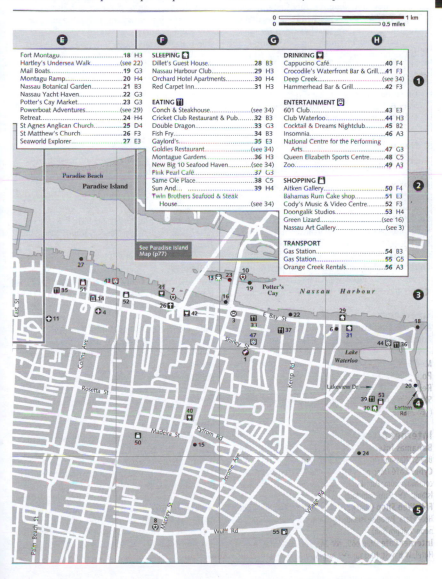

Fort Montagu.....................**18** H3		
Hartley's Undersea Walk.............(see 22)		
Mail Boats.......................**19** G3		
Montagu Ramp..................**20** H4		
Nassau Botanical Garden..........**21** B3		
Nassau Yacht Haven..............**22** G3		
Potter's Cay Market...............**23** G3		
Powerboat Adventures...........(see 29)		
Retreat.........................**24** H4		
St Agnes Anglican Church........**25** D4		
St Matthew's Church.............**26** F3		
Seaworld Explorer...............**27** E3		

SLEEPING 🏠
Dillet's Guest House...............**28** B3
Nassau Harbour Club.............**29** H3
Orchard Hotel Apartments.........**30** H4
Red Carpet Inn...................**31** H3

EATING 🍴
Conch & Steakhouse.............(see 34)
Cricket Club Restaurant & Pub......**32** B3
Double Dragon..................**33** G3
Fish Fry........................**34** B3
Gaylord's......................**35** E3
Goldies Restaurant..............(see 34)
Montague Gardens..............**36** H3
New Big 10 Seafood Haven.......(see 34)
Pink Pearl Café..................**37** G3
Same Ole Place.................**38** C5
Sun And.......................**39** H4
Twin Brothers Seafood & Steak House................(see 34)

DRINKING 🍷
Cappucino Café.................**40** F4
Crocodile's Waterfront Bar & Grill....**41** F3
Deep Creek.....................(see 34)
Hammerhead Bar & Grill.........**42** F3

ENTERTAINMENT 🎭
601 Club.......................**43** E3
Club Waterloo..................**44** H3
Cocktail & Dreams Nightclub.....**45** B2
Insomnia......................**46** A3
National Centre for the Performing Arts........................**47** G3
Queen Elizabeth Sports Centre....**48** C5
Zoo...........................**49** A3

SHOPPING 🛍
Aitken Gallery..................**50** F4
Bahamas Rum Cake shop.........**51** E3
Cody's Music & Video Centre.......**52** F3
Doongalik Studios...............**53** H4
Green Lizard...................(see 16)
Nassau Art Gallery...............(see 3)

TRANSPORT
Gas Station.....................**54** B3
Gas Station.....................**55** G5
Orange Creek Rentals............**56** A3

NASSAU IN...

Two days

Start your day with a Bahamian breakfast at **Café Skan's** (p88) followed by a stroll through historic downtown, past the huge floating cities docked in port, and the **Pompey Museum** (p72) before jumping on a **jitney bus** (private minibus; p97) to explore the island.

Then laze on **Cable Beach** (p75), sipping a rum cocktail at sunset before relaxing into the Italian ambience of nearby **Capriccio Ristorante** (p91) for a creamy pasta.

The next day, shop for duty-free goodies along **Bay St** (p95). Salute the marching flamingos and snoozing iguanas of **Ardastra Gardens, Zoo & Conservation Park** (p75) before heading off to the southwestern beaches (p98) for lunch at Avery's and a snorkel.

Treat yourself to fine wine and dining at the **Humidor Restaurant** (p90), followed by a Cuban cigar and the nightspots of **Paradise Island** (p93).

Four days

Go scuba diving or have a fun day trip **snorkeling** (p80) at Rose Island, take a walk around the leafy **Retreat** (p74) or **Nassau Botanical Garden** (p75) and have a look at the vibrant artworks found in Nassau's studios and elegant **National Art Gallery of the Bahamas** (p71).

One week

Add a **fast ferry** (p80) ride to Eleuthera's pink-sand beaches, an **island adventure** (p80) trip to the Exuma Cays, a **diving** or **fishing expedition** (p79) to the Abacos or Biminis, and some rum-tasting at the **Bacardi Rum Factory** (p99).

United Book Shop (Map pp64-5; ☎ 242-393-6166; Mall at Marathon, Robinson & Marathon Rds, Nassau) A wide selection of children's books and novels are stocked here.

United Book Shops & Stationers (Map pp66-7; ☎ 242-322-8597; Palmdale Shopping Centre, Madeira St, Nassau) Stocks a fairly comprehensive variety of novels.

Emergency
Air Sea Rescue Association (☎ 242-325-8864)
Ambulance (☎ 242-322-2221, 911)
Fire (☎ 242-302-8404, 911)
Med-Evac (☎ 242-322-2881)
Police (☎ 242-322-4444, 911; E Hill St)
Red Cross (☎ 242-323-7370)
State Care Medical & Emergency Centre (☎ 242-328-5596)

Internet Access
Bahamas Internet Café (Map p69; ☎ 242-325-7458; Bay St, Nassau; 9am-5pm Mon-Sat)
Cyber Café (Map p77; ☎ 242-363-1253; cybercafé3@coralwave.com; Paradise Island Shopping Centre, Paradise Island; 9am-6pm Mon-Sat)
FML Web Shop (Map p77; ☎ 242-363-2241; Hurricane Hole Plaza, Paradise Island; 7am-7:30pm Mon-Sat, noon-7:30pm Sun)
Internet Café (Map p69; ☎ 242-323-1000; West Bay Hotel, W Bay St, Nassau; 9am-5pm Mon-Sat)

Tech Shop (Map p76; ☎ 242-327-0081; W Bay St, Cable Beach; 9am-7pm Mon-Sat, 10am-6:30pm Sat, 11am-4pm Sun)

Libraries
The Historical Library & Museum (p73) is a public library dedicated mostly to works of popular fiction. It also houses a small museum.
College of The Bahamas Library (Map pp66-7; ☎ 242-323-8552; Poinciana Dr, Nassau; 8am-9pm Mon-Fri plus 9am-5pm Sat Oct-Jun) The largest collection of books in Nassau.
Public library Blue Hill Rd (Map pp64-5; ☎ 242-322-1056); Fox Hill (Map pp64-5; ☎ 242-324-1458); Mackey St (☎ 242-322-1096)

Media
Apart from the daily and weekly newspapers listed in the boxed text on p271, there are two monthly tourist papers, *What's On* and *Tourist News*. These are available free in hotel lobbies, stores and tourist information booths. They include feature articles, a calendar of events, and discount coupons. *What-to-do: Where to shop, dine, stay, play, invest* is available free at tourist bureaus and most hotel lobbies. It has a good shopping section.

DOWNTOWN NASSAU

0 ———————————— 400 m
0 ———————————— 0.2 miles

A   **B**   **C**   **D**

① ② ③ ④ ⑤ ⑥

INFORMATION
ATM	**1** C5
ATM	(see 13)
Bahamas Internet Café	**2** D5
Bahamas Ministry of Tourism Information Booth	**3** D4
BaTelCo	**4** D5
British High Commission	**5** D5
Destinations	**6** C5
Internet Café	**7** A5
Island Shop	(see 67)
Main Post Office	**8** C6
Police Headquarters	**9** D5
Police Station	**10** D5
Police Station	**11** A5
Police Station	**12** D5
Public Toilets	**13** D6
Royal Bank of Canada	**14** C5
Royal Bank of Canada	**15** C6
Scotiabank	**16** B5
Scotiabank	**17** B5
Scotiabank ATM	**18** C5
US Embassy & Consulate	**19** B5

SIGHTS & ACTIVITIES
Bahamas Historical Society Museum	**20** D5
Balcony House	**21** C5
Central Bank of the Bahamas Annex	**22** C5
Christ Church Anglican Cathedral	**23** B5
Cumberland House	**24** B5
Deanery	**25** B5
Devonshire House	**26** B5
Dunmore House	**27** A5
Fort Fincastle	**28** D6
Government House	**29** B6
Graycliff Cigar Co	(see 64)
Greek Orthodox Church of the Annunciation	**30** B5
Gregory Arch	**31** C6
Historical Library & Museum	**32** D5
Horse-Drawn Surreys	**33** D4
Jacaranda	**34** C6

Junkanoo Expo	(see 3)
Masonic Temple	**35** C5
Ministry of Foreign Affairs	**36** C6
National Art Gallery of the Bahamas	(see 27)
Pirates of Nassau Museum	**37** B5
Pompey Museum	**38** B5
Queen Victoria Statue	**39** D5
St Andrews Presbyterian Kirk	**40** C5
St Francis Xavier Cathedral	**41** A5
St Mary's Church	**42** A5
Seaworld Explorer Office	**43** D5
Statue of Christopher Columbus	**44** B5
Supreme Court	**45** D5
Trinity Methodist Church	**46** C5
Water Tower	**47** D6
Welcome Centre	(see 3)

SLEEPING
British Colonial Hilton Nassau	**48** B5
Buena Vista Restaurant & Hotel	**49** A6
El Greco	**50** A5
Grand Central Hotel	**51** D5
Graycliff Hotel & Restaurant	**52** B6
Holiday Inn Junkanoo Beach Hotel	**53** A5
Mignon Guest House	**54** C5
Quality Inn	**55** A5
Towne Hotel	**56** B5

EATING
Bahamian Kitchen, Restaurant & Bar	**57** C5
Brussels Brasserie	**58** C5
Café Matisse	**59** D5
Café Skan's	**60** C5
Chez Willie	**61** A5
Conch Fritters Bar & Grill	**62** C5
Green Shutters Restaurant & Pub	**63** C6
Humidor Restaurant	**64**
Imperial Cafeteria & Take-Away	**65** B5
Mama Lyddie's Place	**66** C6
Sbarro's	**67** C5

DRINKING
Dockside Sports Bar & Grill	**68** C5
Drop-Off	**69** D5
Rumours	**70** C5

ENTERTAINMENT
Blue Note Club	(see 48)
Fluid Lounge & Nightclub	**71** C5

SHOPPING
Balmain Antiques & Gallery	(see 80)
Bay	(see 68)
Brass & Leather	**72** C5
Coin of the Realm	**73** C5
Coles of Nassau	**74** C5
Colombian Emeralds	**75** C5
Gucci	**76** D5
John Bull	(see 83)
Kennedy Gallery	**77** C5
Linen Shop	(see 67)
Marlborough Antiques	**78** B5
Perfume Shop	(see 67)
Philatelic Bureau	(see 8)
Pipe of Peace	**79** C5
Prince George Plaza	(see 68)
Pyrroms	(see 75)
Solomon's Mines	**80** C5

TRANSPORT
Avis	**81** B5
Bus Stop to Cable Beach & west	**82** B5
Buses to Cable Beach & West	**83** C5
Buses to Paradise Islands & East	**84** C5
Dollar	(see 48)
Ferries to Paradise Island	**85** D4
Knowles Scooter Rentals	(see 3)
Water Taxis to Paradise Island	**86** C4

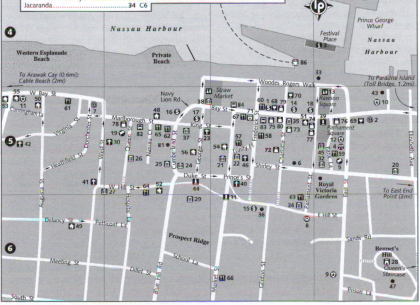

Medical Services

Pharmacies exist in all shopping malls, but mainly keep standard shop hours.

Cable Beach Medical Centre (Map p76; ☎ 242-327-2886; W Bay St, Cable Beach) Outside Sandals Royal Bahamian.

Doctor's Hospital (Map pp66-7; ☎ 242-322-8411, 242-302 4600; Shirley St at Collins Ave) Privately owned full-service hospital east of Princess Margaret Hospital; provides emergency services and acute care.

Princess Margaret Hospital (Map pp66-7; ☎ 242-322-2861; Elizabeth Ave at Sands Rd) This government-run, full-service hospital is the island's main facility, providing emergency services and acute care.

Money

There are plenty of banks clustered around Rawson Sq and Bay St. ATMs dispensing US and Bahamian dollars can be easily found throughout Nassau. The Rawson Sq branch of Scotiabank has an ATM.

Commonwealth Bank (Map p76; ☎ 242-327-8441; W Bay St, Cable Beach)

Destinations (Map p69; ☎ 242-322-2931; 303 Shirley St, Nassau) Represents American Express.

First Caribbean International Bank (Map p76; W Bay St, Cable Beach) Opposite Sandals Royal Bahamian.

Royal Bank of Canada Cable Beach (Map p76; ☎ 242-327-6077; W Bay St) Downtown Nassau (Map p69; ☎ 242-322-8700; E Hill St; ☎ 242-356-8500; W Bay St)

Scotiabank Cable Beach (Map p76; ☎ 242-327-7380; Cecil Wallace Whitfield Centre, W Bay St); Downtown Nassau (Map p69; ☎ 242-356-1400; Rawson Sq, Nassau) The Cable Beach branch is opposite Nassau Beach Hotel.

Western Union (Map p76; ☎ 242-394-1429; W Bay St, Cable Beach)

Post

DHL Worldwide Express (Map pp66-7; ☎ 242-394-4040; E Bay St, Nassau)

FedEx (Map pp66-7; ☎ 242-322-5656; www.fedex .com; EE McKay Plaza, Thompson Blvd, Nassau)

Main post office (Map pp66-7; ☎ 242-322-3025; E Hill St at Parliament St, Nassau; ⏰ 8:30am-5:30pm Mon-Fri, to 12:30pm Sat)

Telephone

BaTelCo East St (Map pp66-7; ☎ 242-323-6414; ⏰ 7am-10pm); John F Kennedy Dr (Map pp64-5; ☎ 242-323-4911; ⏰ 7am-10pm) Has public phone booths for international calls. The East St branch is a half-block south of Bay St.

Toilets

There are public toilets on Bay St (on the west side of the Straw Market) and on the north side of Rawson Sq. Apart from those two, public toilets are as rare as hen's teeth. Just pop in and use the facilities at big hotels as everyone else does!

Tourist Information

Bahamas Ministry of Tourism information centers are based at the airport and the Welcome Centre in downtown Nassau. Information can also be obtained from websites listed on p285.

Bahamas Ministry of Tourism (Map pp64-5; ☎ 242-377-6806; Nassau International Airport; ⏰ 9am-5pm Mon-Fri) In the arrivals area.

Festival Place (Map p69; ☎ 242-323-3182; fax 322 7680; Welcome Centre, Prince George Wharf; ⏰ 9am-5pm Mon-Fri) Open on Saturday and Sunday if cruise ship is in port.

DANGERS & ANNOYANCES

Avoid Over-the-Hill at night; this area suffers from violence. Also use caution by day, as the area's down-at-the-heels quality is aggravated by the presence of 'Joneses' (drug users). You should also avoid walking alone downtown at night; stick to well-lit main streets.

SIGHTS

Even if you are short on time, it's worth seeing Nassau's attractive historical sights, many of which can be found downtown and around W Hill St and E Hill St. Art fans should also head to these locations and to Village Rd for the galleries, while those itching for sand and sea should go to Cable Beach, the southern beaches and Paradise Island. On the way to Cable Beach, families may want to stop downtown and west of downtown for fun museums and some wildlife, but don't miss Atlantis on Paradise Island!

Downtown Nassau

The heart of downtown Nassau is a compact and colorful historic area with many well-preserved 18th- and 19th-century buildings.

Before embarking on a walking tour of downtown, get yourself a copy of *Nassau's Historic Buildings* by C Sieghbert Russell, available at the Bahamas Historical Society Museum (p73).

MARLBOROUGH STREET & W BAY STREET

Much of the north side of Marlborough St, once occupied by Fort Nassau, is taken up by the British Colonial Hilton (p86), fronted by a statue dedicated to Governor Woodes Rogers, plus a rusty anchor and cannon. Remnants of the old walls can be seen on the hotel grounds.

Marlborough St runs east into King St, which parallels Bay St for two blocks. The heart of Nassau's financial affairs is concentrated between Cumberland and Market Sts. Several old cut-stone buildings here are now fine restaurants.

Queen St, which ascends south from Marlborough St, is lined with fine balconied colonial homes, particularly **Devonshire House** (Map p69). Two blocks east, **Cumberland House** (Map p69) and the **Deanery** (Map p69) are described as 'the quintessential trademark of colonial Bahamian architecture.'

At Marlborough St's west end, it becomes Virginia St. Prim 1868 **St Mary's Church** (Map p69) could have fallen out of a postcard depicting the English countryside. The junction of Marlborough and West Sts has several fine old balconied houses.

Nassau has a large Greek community which is served by the Kurikon, also called the **Greek Orthodox Church of the Annunciation** (Map p69). Erected in 1932 the church is one block south of the Marlborough and West Sts junction. It's intimate and beautiful within, with an exquisite gilt chandelier.

The interactive **Pirates of Nassau Museum** (Map p69; ☎ 242-356-3759; pirates@bahamas.net.bs; King St; adult/child $12/6; 9am-6pm Mon-Fri, 8:30am-noon Sat) is hugely popular, with life-size re-creations of pirate life, including a twilit quayside replete with all the sounds of the era, and a cutaway of the pirate ship *Revenge*. Beware Blackbeard and his ferocious Amazon, Anne Bonney! Stop for a break and drink at the adjacent Pirate's Pub.

The striking 1753 **Christ Church Anglican Cathedral** (Map p69; King St) nearby has a splendid wood-beamed roof, stained glass and pendulous Spanish-style chandeliers. The current structure is the fourth version. The original church was destroyed in 1684 by the Spaniards. Its successors were leveled during the French-Spanish invasion in 1703 and by the ravages of weather and termites.

W & E HILL STREETS

These two streets run parallel to Nassau Harbour and are joined by Duke St, running east to west. They're lined with important historical buildings, including **Jacaranda** (Map p69), previously home to the duke of Windsor.

The 1885 **St Francis Xavier Cathedral** (Map p69; cnr W Hill St & West St) has a long, slender nave topped by a bell tower, illuminated within at night. Many prominent Protestants of the time resented the incursion of the Catholics and ascribed to the hands of God the bolt of lightning that struck the church during construction, killing a workman and doing significant damage.

The huge three-story balconied **Dunmore House** (Map p69) was built by the disreputable Lord Dunmore after his arrival as governor in 1787. This stunning yellow-and-white mansion now houses the **National Art Gallery of the Bahamas** (☎ 242-328-5800; info@nagb.org.bs; admission adult/child $3/2; 11am-4pm Tue-Sat). Different exhibitions display a wealth of Bahamian art that traverses many eras, but it's always vibrant. Don't miss the extraordinary sculptures in the gardens.

The beautiful **Graycliff Hotel & Restaurant** (see the boxed text, p86) was built partly on the ruins of the oldest church in the Bahamas, erected in 1694 but destroyed by the Spaniards in 1703. It became a hostelry in 1844 and later passed into the hands of the Earl and Countess of Dudley, whose guests included Sir Winston Churchill. Today it is one of the city's finest hotels and restaurants, redolent with faded charm, antiques and original Cuban art.

Two doors down and part of the same property is **Graycliff Cigar Co** (Map p69; ☎ 242-322-2795; W Hill St; admission free; 9am-5pm Mon-Fri), staffed by 20 Cuban cigar rollers under the tutelage of Avelino Lara, former head of the El Laguito factory in Havana, and former personal roller for Fidel Castro. Visitors are always courteously welcomed.

GOVERNMENT HOUSE

The vast cotton-candy pink Georgian structure commanding the city from atop Mt Fitzwilliam, just south of W Hill St, is the **official residence** (Map p69) of the Bahamas' governor-general. The original home was built in 1737 by Governor Fitzwilliam but was destroyed by a hurricane in 1929. The current building was completed in 1932, and the lavish decorations date from the Duke of Windsor's time as governor in the 1940s. Visitors can walk the grounds for a close look at the building, but must be accompanied by the guards. Twice a month, you can 'have a cuppa' with the governor-general's wife (contact the Bahamas Ministry of Tourism on ☎ 242-322-7500 or visit the website www.bahamas.com) or watch the changing of the guard. This British tradition of pomp and ceremony includes a performance of the Royal Bahamas Police Force Band, and occurs at 10am twice a month; call ☎ 242-322-2020 to confirm date and time.

A **statue of Christopher Columbus** (Map p69) stands on the steps overlooking Duke St. It was designed by US writer Washington Irving, who dressed the 15th-century Genoese explorer in the garb of Irving's day.

Gregory Arch (Map p69), a stone arch topped with iron railings, spans Market St at the east end of Government House grounds, and informally delineates downtown Nassau and Over-the-Hill.

Handsome **St Andrews Presbyterian Kirk** (Map p69), below Government House on Prices and Market Sts, owes its existence to a loyalist who settled in Nassau at the end of the American Revolution. In 1798 he established the St Andrew's Society, comprising 55 Scots, to 'cultivate good understanding and social intercourse.' The Freemasons laid the cornerstone in 1810, and the church has since undergone many architectural changes.

East of Gregory Arch is where the **Ministry of Foreign Affairs** (Map p69) is located, a beautiful pink Georgian edifice fronted by a cannon. Outside you'll see a modern purple sculpture *El Vigía* (The Lookout) – by Mexican sculptor Sebastian. It was a gift from the Mexican government for the 1992 quincentennial of Columbus' landing.

BAY STREET

This is the heart of the duty-free shopping district. Two impressive buildings are the Royal Bank of Canada (1919) and the 1885 **Masonic Temple** (Map p69).

The Bahamas' history is told through displays at the small **Pompey Museum** (Map p69; ☎ 242-326-2566; Vendue House; adult/child $5/1; 9:30am-4:30pm Mon-Wed, Fri & Sat, noon-4pm Sun). The building was once a slave-auction site, and the museum is named in memory of a slave who led a rebellion on Exuma in 1830. The exhibits include artifacts, straw-work, historical documents, and drawings tracing events from the Lucayan period (the

Lucayans were a tribe of Arawak Indians who arrived in the Bahamas near the turn of the 9th century) to the bootlegging era. Upstairs is a permanent exhibit of vibrant naïf paintings by noted artist Amos Ferguson.

Life at the west end of Bay St is dominated by what is said to be the world's largest **Straw Market**. Some 160 vendors set up stalls daily to sell everything from straw-work to T-shirts, woodcarvings, shell souvenirs and other island handicrafts, all decorated with brightly colored motifs. You can watch craftspeople whittling wood or weaving straw.

A restored two-story 18th-century merchant's home, **Balcony House** (Map p69; ☎ 242-302-2621; Market St; admission by donation; 10am-4:30pm Mon, Wed & Fri, to 1pm Thu & Sat), a few blocks off Bay St, was named for its prominent balcony supported by wooden knee braces. The original slave kitchen remains, as does the staircase, taken from a sailing ship. It is now a local history museum.

RAWSON SQUARE

The heart of town for tourists is Rawson Sq, on the south side of Bay St. It's a natural place to begin a tour of downtown Nassau. Guided walking tours also begin here (see p83). Nearby is a life-size bronze statue, **Bahamian Woman**, which honors the role of women during 'years of adversity.' She holds a small child. In the center of the square is a **bust of Sir Milo Butler**, the first governor-general of the independent nation, and a fountain pool with leaping bronze dolphins.

PARLIAMENT SQUARE

The area immediately south of Rawson Sq on Bay St is known as Parliament Sq. On three sides of the square nestle three pink-and-white Georgian neoclassical buildings (1805–1813) that house the offices of the leader of the opposition (on the left), the Assembly House (right), and the Senate (facing Bay St). In their midst sits the 1905 **Queen Victoria statue** (Map p69), whose presence reflects still-held allegiances.

You can peek inside the House of Assembly to watch proceedings when it's in session. Make such arrangements at the **House Office of the Clerk of Courts** (☎ 242-322-7500). Note its green carpet, symbolizing the English meadow where King John was forced to sign the Magna Carta in 1215.

The Senate also has a visitors' gallery, with tickets given out free on a first-come, first-served basis.

Immediately south of Parliament Sq, between Parliament St and Bank Lane, is the **Supreme Court** (Map p69), a Georgian edifice where bewigged judges perform their duties.

A few yards further north is the small Garden of Remembrance, with a **cenotaph** (Map p69) honoring Bahamian soldiers who died in the two world wars. Also note the plaque to four members of the Royal Bahamas Defence Force killed in 1980 when their patrol vessel, *Flamingo*, was attacked by Cuban MiGs.

PRINCE GEORGE WHARF

The historic cruise-ship wharf, north of Rawson Sq and Bay St, is the gateway to Nassau for 1.4 million visitors a year!

The wharf is fronted by bustling **Woodes Rogers Walk** (Map p69), lined with souvenir stalls, fast-food outlets and a canopied stand where **horse-drawn surreys** (Map p69) await customers. The drivers will take you around the historical landmarks of the Bay St area. The rides begin and end at the Welcome Centre, Woodes Rogers Walk, Prince George Wharf. A 30-minute ride costs approximately $10/5 per adult/child. Negotiate a price before climbing aboard if you want to hire a surrey for longer, and to avoid jammed streets only take the rides when the cruise ships are not in town. Ferries to Paradise Island also leave from Woodes Rogers Walk.

The old wharfside customs building today houses the **Welcome Centre** containing visitor information, a few pricy craft stalls, as well as the **Junkanoo Expo** (Map p69; ☎ 242-356-2731; adult/child $1/0.50; ☼ 9am-5pm Mon-Fri, 9am-5pm Sat & Sun when cruise liners are in dock), with its decidedly patchy display of some costumes and paraphernalia that make up the colorful and high-spirited street extravaganza of Junkanoo (see the boxed text, p34).

SHIRLEY STREET

The delightful **Trinity Methodist Church** (Map p69), at the west end of Shirley St, was originally planned for a congregation of 800 people. Alas, the four carpenters sent from Scotland all succumbed to yellow fever, and a more modest church was built in 1861. It had been open only a year when it was blown down by a hurricane. The current church dates from 1869 and was significantly repaired following damage in the 1928 hurricane.

With its old prison cells now crammed with books and dusty periodicals, the unusual octagonal 1790 **Historical Library & Museum** (Map p69; ☎ 242-322-4907; Parliament & Bank Lane; admission free; ☼ 10am-8pm Mon-Thu, to 5pm Fri, to 4pm Sat) was originally a jail (the dungeon still exists below ground). Convicts gave way to books in 1873. Note the amazing model of *Arethusa*, the rum-running schooner of Captain Bill McCoy. A museum on the 2nd floor, dedicated to the peaceful Lucayan Indians, has a motley collection of artifacts, including bones, a few old maps, engravings, photographs, shells, stamps and old parchments.

The **Bahamas Historical Society Museum** (Map p69; ☎ 242-322-4231; Shirley St at Elizabeth Ave; adult/child $1/0.50; ☼ 10am-1pm Mon, to 4pm Tue-Fri, to noon Sat) has a modest miscellany of artifacts and documents tracing the islands' history from Lucayan times to the contemporary era. It's worth the admission merely to admire the beautiful model of the Spanish galleon *Santa Luceno*.

Collins House (Map pp66–7), an attractive two-story property built in 1929 and later used as a school, began housing the Ministry of Education & Culture in 1971.

BENNET'S HILL

At the south end of Elizabeth Ave, a passage and 90ft-deep gorge in Prospect Ridge lead to Fort Fincastle and a water tower. The passageway was cut from solid limestone by slaves, beginning in the 1790s, with the intent of constructing a roadway through Prospect Ridge. Emancipation was proclaimed before it could be finished.

The **Queen's Staircase** (Map p69), also known as the '66 Steps,' leads up to the tiny 1793 **Fort Fincastle** (Map p69), built by Lord Dunmore. Why it was whimsically built in the shape of a paddle-wheel steamer isn't clear. The fort faces east and was intended to guard 'all the Town and the Road to the Eastward.'

The **Water Tower** (Map p69; ☎ 242-322-2442; admission $0.50; ☼ 8am-5pm) behind the fort was erected in 1928 to maintain water pressure on the island. It is 126ft tall and provides a marvelous panoramic view of Nassau. You can walk up the narrow, winding staircase – there are 216 steps (or take the elevator).

OVER-THE-HILL

This area began as a settlement for free Blacks and slaves liberated from slave ships after 1807 by the British Navy. After emancipation in 1834, the area – comprising the villages of Grants Town and Bains Town and, further east, Fox Hill – expanded. Most inhabitants were destitute and lived in squalor.

The historic 1847 **Wesley Methodist Church** (Map p69) on Market St and the 1846 **St Agnes Anglican Church** (Map pp66–7) on Cockburn St are both worth a visit. Much caution is needed in this area and it should be avoided at night, as drug users and pushers are unfortunately quite discernible.

East of Downtown
EASTERN CEMETERY

Near the juncture of Bay and Dowdeswell Sts, this grassy **cemetery** (Map pp66–7) holds the remains of pirates and other rascals executed during the past three centuries. The tumbledown tombs are above ground. Behind is the 1802 **St Matthew's Church** (Map pp66–7). The cemetery to the west of the churchyard also dates back to the 1800s.

POTTER'S CAY

The liveliest **market** (Map pp66–7) in town sits beneath the Paradise Island Exit Bridge, where fishing boats from the Family Islands arrive daily carrying the sea's harvest, as well as fruit, herbs, biting pepper sauces and vegetables. Piles of glistening conch, crab, jack, mackerel and spiny lobster are sold alive, dead, dried or filleted, along with, more distressingly, dismembered turtles.

Nevertheless it is a great place to hang out and watch the pandemonium whenever a boat returns.

The mail boats serving the Family Islands also berth here.

VILLAGE ROAD

The **Retreat** (Map pp66–7; ☎ 242-393-1317; fax 242-393-4978; The Retreat, Village Rd; admission $3; ☉ 9am-5pm Mon-Fri) is an 11-acre garden which claims to have one of the largest private collections of palms in the world (176 species representing more than half of all known genera of palms). The **Bahamas National Trust** (Map pp66–7; ☎ 242-393-1317; fax 242-393-4978; The

Retreat, Village Rd; admission $3; ☉ 9am-5pm Mon-Fri) is located here. The star of the show was a rare and awesome Ceylonese talipot palm that expended all its energy in 1986 on a once-in-a-lifetime bloom and then died. Other specimens include hardwoods such as mahogany. Native orchids grace the trunks, and splendid ferns nestle in the limestone holes in which the palms are planted. Take a tour or stroll in this peaceful place.

Alongside working artists flaunting their creative skills, **Doongalik Studios** (Map pp66–7; ☎ 242-393-6640; www.doongalikstudios.com; 18 Village Rd; admission free; ☉ 9am-5pm Mon-Fri) serves as a gallery for exuberant Bahamian fine art, Junkanoo crafts, T-shirts and rainbow-hued furniture. The entrance is guarded by three larger-than-life statues, and a bush garden to the rear features native trees and plants.

FORT MONTAGU

There's not much to draw you to this diminutive **fort** (Map pp66–7), though the place is intact and the cannon in situ. The oldest of Nassau's remaining strongholds, it was built in 1741 to guard the eastern approach to Nassau Harbour. It never fired its cannon in anger. The surrounding park is enjoyed by football-playing Bahamians and occasional market stalls.

EASTERN ROAD

A shoreline park south of Fort Montagu is lined with palms and casuarina trees. Nearby **Montagu Ramp** (Map pp66–7) is the site where locals bring fish and conch ashore to clean and sell. You'll smell it well before you see it!

Sitting atop the ridge 2 miles south of Fort Montagu is **Blackbeard's Tower** (Map pp64–5), a semiderelict cut-stone tower that, according to local lore, was built by Edward Teach – 'Blackbeard' – as a lookout tower. Historians point out that it was actually built in the late 18th century, long after the infamous pirate had been killed. The view is good but the place isn't worth the journey in its own right. To reach it, you go up an unmarked path next to a green-and-white house called 'Tower Leigh,' 400yd south of Fox Hill Rd.

This windward shore is quite scenic towards the **East End Lighthouse** (Map pp64–5) at the easternmost point of New Providence. Just south is **Yamacraw Beach** (Map pp64–5), where the road turns west and heads inland via a middle-class residential area, ending at **Her Majesty's Prison** (Map pp64–5).

FOX HILL

This settlement for freed slaves began life in the 18th century as Creek Village. During the 1900s, Robert Sandilands, chief justice of the Bahamas, bought much of the area and distributed land grants to Blacks for £10 or the equivalent in labor. The recipients named their settlement after their benefactor.

Freedom Park (Map pp64–5), at the juncture of Fox Hill Rd and Bernard Rd, is the center of town and the setting each year for Emancipation Day celebrations in the first week of August.

Other highlights include the 1867 **St Anne's Anglican Church** (Map pp64–5) and the fortresslike **St Augustine's Monastery** (Map pp64–5; ☎ 242-364-1331; admission by donation), atop a rocky perch on Bernard Rd. This working monastery was designed by Father Jerome, the itinerant architect-cleric who blessed Cat and Long Islands with beautiful Gothic churches (see the Father Jerome boxed text, p211). The imposing building dates from 1947 and is still used by Benedictine monks, who give guided tours that offer a fascinating glimpse of monastic life. A college run by the monks is attached. Phone ahead to enquire about opening hours.

West of Downtown

About a half-mile from the British Colonial Hilton, you'll see remains of a battery of cannons on the harborside, immediately next to the road. A cricket ground, **Clifford Park** (Haynes' Oval; Map pp66–7;), is to the south; it's the site of the annual Independence Day festivities on July 10.

At the entrance to **Arawak Cay** (Map pp66–7) is a very lively village of small bars, and fresh-fish and conch stalls, as well as Bahamian takeouts housed in multicolored shacks. Lunchtime fish sales and weekend-long Fish Frys are high-spirited occasions worthy of a smoky fritter, chat and rum or two! Junkanoo 'shacks' practise their music and choreographed dance moves here throughout the year.

Fort Charlotte (Map pp66–7; ☎ 242-322-7500; admission free; ⏰ 8am-4pm), the largest in the Bahamas, was built between 1787 and 1790

to guard the west entrance to Nassau Harbour. Sitting on the ridge above Clifford Park, it is intact and today is painted white. The deep moat and exterior walls were cut from solid rock and the walls buttressed by cedars. Lord Dunmore estimated its cost as a 'trifling' £4000 and, to ensure the approval of the crown, proposed to name it Charlotte, after the consort of King George III. Within a year Dunmore had exceeded all resources. Reluctantly the English War Office forwarded the extra £17,846 required to complete the fort. Dunmore's folly was ill-conceived, with the troops' barracks erected directly in the line of fire! Today its moat, dungeon, underground tunnels and bombproof chambers make an intriguing excursion, enhanced by a re-creation of a torture chamber. Tours are led by guides in period costume who expect a tip.

Nassau Botanical Garden (Map pp66–7; ☎ 242-323-5975; adult/child $1/0.50; ⏰ 8am-4pm Mon-Fri, 9am-4pm Sat & Sun) was constructed in 1951 on the site of an old rock quarry. The 26 acres contains more than 600 species of tropical plants, many indigenous, plus lily ponds, grottoes and a waterfall fountain donated by the government of China.

The well-stocked **Ardastra Gardens, Zoo & Conservation Park** (Map pp66–7; ☎ 242-323-5806; fax 242-323-7232; Chippingham Rd; adult/child $12/6; ⏰ 9am-5pm) has a few placid iguanas and around 50 species of animals, birds and reptiles from around the world. Indigenous species of flora and fauna include hutias (similar to guinea pigs), snakes and the endangered Bahama parrot, which, uniquely, is bred in captivity here. The zoo also has a large collection of nonnative species, including monkeys and caimans, and sleek cats such as jaguars and ocelots. The undisputed highlight, however, is the small army of West Indian flamingos trained to strut their stuff on voice command at 11am, 2pm and 4pm daily (except Sunday, when they have the day off). Facilities include a snack bar and toilets.

Cable Beach

A long, curved white-sand beach and sparkling turquoise sea is linked to downtown Nassau by a 3-mile long stretch of coastline. The beach is named for the undersea telegraphic cable laid from Florida in 1892 that came ashore here. Cable Beach's resorts seem to have derived from the Floridian peninsula

NEW PROVIDENCE

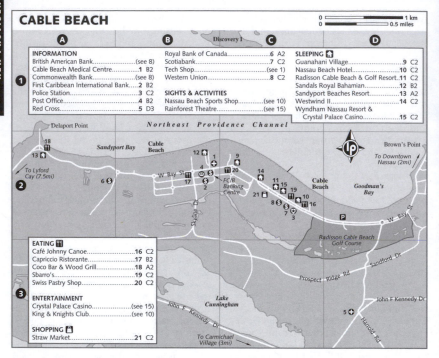

CABLE BEACH

0 _____ 1 km
0 _____ 0.5 miles

INFORMATION
British American Bank.....................(see 8)
Cable Beach Medical Centre.............1 B2
Commonwealth Bank.....................(see 8)
First Caribbean International Bank.....2 B2
Police Station.........................3 C2
Post Office............................4 B2
Red Cross..............................5 D3

Royal Bank of Canada....................6 A2
Scotiabank.............................7 C2
Tech Shop.............................(see 1)
Western Union...........................8 C2

SIGHTS & ACTIVITIES
Nassau Beach Sports Shop.............(see 10)
Rainforest Theatre...................(see 15)

SLEEPING
Guanahani Village.......................9 C2
Nassau Beach Hotel....................10 C2
Radisson Cable Beach & Golf Resort..11 C2
Sandals Royal Bahamian................12 B2
Sandyport Beaches Resort.............13 A2
Westwind II...........................14 C2
Wyndham Nassau Resort &
   Crystal Palace Casino................15 C2

EATING
Café Johnny Canoe......................16 C2
Capriccio Ristorante...................17 B2
Coco Bar & Wood Grill..................18 A2
Sbarro's...............................19 C2
Swiss Pastry Shop......................20 C2

ENTERTAINMENT
Crystal Palace Casino..................(see 15)
King & Knights Club....................(see 10)

SHOPPING
Straw Market...........................21 C2

as well. Beloved by families seeking simple seaside pleasures, the hotels also have bars, clubs, casinos and many eateries.

One mile east of Cable Beach is tiny **Saunders Beach**, popular with locals at lunchtime (they sit in their cars, munching cracked conch). At Delaport Point is the waterfront residential and resort development of Sandyport (p87).

For a break, you can head out to **Discovery Island** (Map p76), a small cay – formerly Balmoral Island – about a mile offshore from Cable Beach. Now leased by the Sandals chain but open to nonguests, it has its own beach, an atmospheric restaurant, and a lively bar with swim-up pool and Jacuzzi.

Free ferries run regularly from Sandals Royal Bahamian (for guests only). Ferries also operate from the pier between the Radisson and Marriott Wyndham Nassau Resort hotels on a regular basis, charging $10 round-trip.

Paradise Island

This island lies almost shouting distance across the harbor from Nassau, to which it is linked by two great arcing bridges and regular ferry services. The whole island appears to be man-made; an endless array of ritzy resorts, stacked cheek to cheek, that loom over the land and line the island's gorgeous beaches, almost without a pause. Parking is at a premium, and the public beaches on Paradise Island are becoming increasingly difficult to access, unless you are a guest at the resorts or pay out for a 'day ticket' (to utilize a hotel's facilities). But for those seeking an idyllic island holiday with serene seas and empty beaches, or more of a Bahamian-style experience, this is not the place for you.

Yet this Bahamian playground understandably appeals to many who want an easy all-inclusive holiday with some sand and sea thrown in for good measure. Families, casino-lovers and nightclubbers particularly enjoy the resorts' facilities, especially the amazing Waterscape, casino and social amenities of Atlantis (p78).

In 1939 Dr Axel Wenner-Gren, a wealthy Swedish industrialist, developed his 'Shangri-La' on adjacent 'Hog Island,' now the tourist mecca of Paradise Island. His ostentatious binge resulted in the creation of the sweeping 35-acre **Versailles Gardens** (Map p77), stepped in tiers and lined with classical statues depicting the millionaire's heroes. They span the ages: Hercules, Napoleon Bonaparte and Franklin D Roosevelt to name a few. Equally wealthy Huntington Hartford II then bought and remodeled the property as an exclusive golf resort and marina, simultaneously persuading the Bahamians to rename the island 'Paradise Island.' At the crest of the gardens is **Cloisters**, (Map p77), a romantic gazebo where weddings are often held. This genuine 14th-century cloister was purchased by newspaper magnate William Randolph Hearst from an Augustine estate in France.

The first bridge between Paradise Island and Nassau was built in 1967, followed by a casino and the arrival of Donald Trump and Merv Griffin, who built further resorts.

Billionaire Sol Kerzner's South African company Sun International, having bought and demolished many competing small and traditional hotels, now owns most of the island in the guise of the vast and expanding Atlantis complex (supposedly the largest employer in the Bahamas after the Bahamian government). The Atlantis project included massive private home development for the superrich (Oprah Winfrey and Michael Jordan are reputed to have bought homes in the woodlands behind Cabbage Beach). A second bridge was built in 1998 to

PARADISE ISLAND

0 ————————— 600 m
0 ————————— 0.4 miles

INFORMATION	
Cyber Café.................................1 B4	
FMI Web Shop........................(see 4)	
Piranha Club..........................(see 15)	
Police Station.............................2 B4	

SIGHTS & ACTIVITIES	
Cloisters...............................(see 5)	
Excursion Boat Dock................(see 21)	
Flying Cloud Snorkeling Trips.........(see 21)	
Hurricane Hole Marina...................3 B4	
Hurricane Hole Plaza......................4 B4	
Versailles Gardens..........................5 C4	
Waterscape...................................6 B3	

SLEEPING	
Atlantis Resort & Casino....................7 B3	
Comfort Suites................................8 B3	
Ocean Club.....................................9 C3	
Paradise Harbour Club & Marina......10 D4	
Sunshine Paradise Suites................11 C4	

EATING	
Blue Marlin.................................(see 4)	
Columbus Tavern Restaurant........12 D4	
News Café.................................(see 4)	
Paradise Supermarket & Deli..........13 B4	

DRINKING	
Green Parrot Bar & Grill...................14 B4	

ENTERTAINMENT	
Atlantis Resort & Casino................15 B3	
Bahama Mama Mia...........................(see 4)	
Dragons Lounge & Dance Club......(see 15)	
Joker's Wild................................(see 15)	
Oasis Lounge...............................(see 20)	
Plato's Lounge.............................(see 15)	

SHOPPING	
Bahamas Craft Center....................16 B4	
Havana Humidor.........................(see 15)	

TRANSPORT	
Avis..17 B4	
Budget...18 B4	
Chalk's Ocean Airways..................19 A4	
Club Land'Or...............................20 B3	
Ferries to/from Nassau..................21 B4	

Porkfish Rocks

Northeast Providence Channel

Hog Point

Paradise Beach

Pirate's Cove

Cabbage Beach

Paradise Lake

Atlantis

Paradise Beach Dr

Scotiabank (ATM)

Ferry

Nassau Harbour

First Caribbean Intl Bank (ATM)

To Downtown Nassau (1.2mi); Cable Beach (2.5mi)

Bay St

Potter's Cay

To East End Point (2.5mi)

Casino Dr

Paradise Island Dr

Ridge Rd

Bayview La

New Paradise Island Bridge (toll)

Paradise Island Exit Bridge

Harbour Rd

Cloister Dr

Ocean Club Dr

Ocean Ridge Dr

Ocean Club Golf Course

Nassau Harbour

handle the increased traffic and Sol Kerzner's eye has turned west to Cable Beach, where existing resorts tremble with fear.

ATLANTIS

No trip would be complete for families, or even big kids, without a visit to Atlantis' 34-acre (and growing) **Waterscape** (Map p77; ☎ 242-363-3000, ext 28; www.atlantis.com; Atlantis Resort; guided walking tours nonguests $25; ☯ tours 9am-5pm). It claims to be the world's largest open-air aquarium and has a whole host of lagoons and is home to 200 species of marine life.

Sun International remade the Paradise Island Resort & Casino as the Atlantis at a cost of $850 million (only the initial expenditure). It now has waterfalls and the quarter-mile 'Lazy River Ride' for tubing, plus six exhibit lagoons filled with live coral, more than 14,000 fish and heaps of other sea life. It's best viewed from a 100ft-long underwater Plexiglas walkway or from other subaqueous tunnels surrounded by massive aquariums.

The waterscape is centered on The Dig, a full-size depiction of the ruins of Atlantis, linked by interconnecting passageways; and a Mayan temple with six water slides, one of which – the Leap of Faith – sends brave

vacationers through a Plexiglas tube that plummets down through the Predator Lagoon full of sharks. The best time to check out Waterscape is at feeding times; check at reception. Tours depart from the Coral Towers Lobby. A new marine park, mini-zoo and dolphin-channel were under construction at the time of research.

BEACHES
Downtown Nassau

Western Esplanade Beach (Map p69), on W Bay St, is downtown Nassau's only beach and stretches west from the British Colonial Hilton Hotel (which has its own private beach). It has limited attractions and no facilities, but is within minutes of downtown restaurants and hotels.

Cable Beach

Saunders Beach is tiny, and sits between Cable Beach and downtown. Local families head there at weekends, although there are no facilities.

The most beautiful beach on the main island, **Cable Beach** (Map p76), is about 2 miles long and has plenty of water sports and activities. Hotels, restaurants, and bars line the beach.

CONFETTI & SAND

OK, who hasn't dreamt of mother-in-law- and hassle-free nuptials, where you and your beloved are alone on an idyllic island beach with a backdrop of astonishing turquoise seas? Where simple white cotton clothes and a garland of wild flowers mark the occasion, and the pastor blesses you with a smile and a reasonable invoice?

The Bahamas is a popular destination for honeymooners, many of whom also tie the knot in these gorgeous islands. The Bahamians make it easy for nonnationals to meet their requirements, and it is possible to marry with just a 24-hour wait.

You can even get married underwater, provided you and your spouse-to-be are certified divers and can blow the right-sounding bubbles. Maybe you just make the thumb & finger 'OK' sign? Get out your waterproof mascara and contact **Underwater Explorers Society** (UNEXSO; ☎ 242-373-1244; www.unexso.com; UNEXSO, Port Lucaya Marina, Freeport) in Grand Bahama.

Marriage licenses cost $100 and can be obtained from the **Registrar General's Office** (☎ 242-326-5371, 242-328-7810; Rodney E Bain Bldg, Parliament St, Nassau). You'll need photo identification, proof of citizenship, proof of status if divorced or widowed, and to swear an oath of eligibility before a notary of the Bahamas. No blood test is required. Anyone under 18 years of age requires notarized parental consent.

If you want help with the event, contact the **Bahamas Ministry of Tourism** (☎ 242-302-2034; www.bahamas.com), who have a division specifically for all the dewy-eyed romantics out there. It can put you in touch with local wedding consultants, photographers and ministers. Most major hotels and tour operators can also make arrangements; they usually ask couples to send notarized copies of required documents at least one month in advance. Major resorts also have special honeymoon packages and can make wedding arrangements at your behest.

Paradise Island

Cabbage Beach (Map p77) is a stunner that stretches 2 miles along the north shore, with plenty of activities and water sports. Several resorts have facilities at the west end.

Pirate's Cove (Map p77) nestles in its own cove west of Atlantis. It has no facilities.

Another beauty, **Paradise Beach** (Map p77) curves gently along the northwest shore of the island; it is very lonesome to the west. The resorts have their own facilities, but nonguests pay for privileges.

Snorkeler's Cove Beach (Map p77) lays east of Cabbage Beach and is favored by day-trippers on picnicking and snorkeling excursions from Nassau.

ACTIVITIES

Look out for the free monthly *What's On* guide, which can be found in most hotel lobbies and outside many retail outlets. The guide details a lot of upcoming events and sporting matches as well as containing discount coupons for plenty of tourist activities.

Diving & Snorkeling

New Providence offers superb diving close to its shores, including fantastic wall and wreck dives. The most noted sites lie off the southwest coast between Coral Harbour and Lyford Cay, as well as north of Paradise Island.

At **Anchor** a coral head pokes out of a wall 60ft below the surface, and teems with fish life. At **School House**, another favorite snorkeling and diving spot, there are endless varieties of coral at depths that rarely exceed 20ft. Fish life ranges from blennies and gobies to schooling yellowtail.

Divers love the **Lost Blue Hole.** This vertical cavern gapes in 30ft of water on a sand bottom is frequented by nurse sharks and stingrays. The cave bells out to 200ft and deeper. There's a lobster-filled cavern at 80ft. **Oasis Wall**, a deep dive just off Old Fort Beach, is known for reef corals all the way down to 200ft. There's plenty of lobster and pelagics too.

The spectacular dive site, **Razorback** is named for the arcing ridge of coral-covered limestone that rises from a sand bottom before plummeting into the Tongue of the Ocean. The reef is a menagerie of fish, and the wall attracts hammerhead sharks.

Equally spectacular is the **Valley**, a path leads you through a labyrinth of coral and marine life to the Tongue of the Ocean, just over the ridge.

Professional Association of Diving Instructors (PADI) certification courses, as well as snorkeling trips, equipment hire and hotel transfers, are offered by all the following operators.

One of the Bahamas best and largest outfits, **Stuart Cove's Dive & Snorkel Bahamas** (Map pp64-5; ☎ 242-362-4171; www.stuartcove.com; Southwest Rd) offers a mass of diving, PADI certification and snorkeling choices, including a bone-rattling shark wall and shark-feeding dives ($135); a two-tank dive trip ($88); and 'wall-flying' (a two-tank underwater scooter adventure that is as good as it sounds!; $135). Snorkeling trips are available (adult/child $48/24) and you can even pilot your own Scenic Underwater Bubble (SUB), a scooter with air wheels and a giant plastic bubble that envelops your shoulders and head ($135).

A good bunch of pros, **Bahama Divers** (Map pp66-7; ☎ 242-393-5644; www.bahamadivers.com; E Bay St, Nassau) has a variety of trips, including some to the Lost Blue Hole (famous for its sharks and schools of stingrays) and wrecks. A three-hour learn-to-dive course can be taken prior to PADI certification courses (PADI course $449). A two-tank dive trip costs $130 and half-day snorkeling trips are also available ($30).

Nassau Scuba Centre (☎ 242-362-1964; www.dive nassau.com; Coral Harbour) is another excellent outfit. They also offer two-tank dives ($90), night dives ($65), trips to the walls and drop-offs and the separate shark-feeding dives ($135). And if that is not enough for you (eek), try the shark suit adventure ($425). A range of PADI diver and diving instructor training courses are also on offer, including one that teaches you how to feed sharks while wearing a chainmail suit…

Sportfishing & Boat Charters

For general information about sailing and chartering boats see p273. Nassau is a great base for sportfishing, with superb sites just 20 minutes away. Charters can be arranged at most major hotels or by calling a charter company. The following recommended companies mainly offer sportfishing, but will also happily take you exploring, diving

NEW PROVIDENCE

BLUE LAGOON

Several uninhabited cays are sprinkled northeast of New Providence, together with **Blue Lagoon** (Map pp64-5) on Salt Cay, which is featured on several day cruises. It's a 30-minute ride to the lagoon. Here you can create your own desert-island fantasy. Choose from snorkeling, parasailing, volleyball or even a dolphin encounter. There are nature walks, changing rooms, restrooms, showers and 250 hammocks slung between palms. Please be aware that the stingrays and dolphins on this island are captive. See the boxed text on opposite.

Not included in your tour price is the Lagoon's **Stingray City Marine Park** (Map pp64-5; ☎ 242-363-3333; www.nassaucruisesbahamas.com; admission $55), where you can swim or snorkel in 12ft of water with captive rays.

The movies *Zeus & Roxanne*, *Splash* and *Flipper* were filmed at this 2-sq-mile private cay and featured the aquatic dolphin stars Jake, MacGyver and Fatman.

You can take a half-day trip to Blue Lagoon with **Dolphin Encounters** (Map pp64-5; ☎ 242-363-1003; www.dolphinencounters.com; Blue Lagoon Island) from Paradise Island. The choices include either a 30-minute swim ($165) or a waist-deep standing encounter ($85) with these captive mammals. These hugely popular trips depart the ferry terminal four times daily from the base of Paradise Island Exit Bridge.

A full-day excursion to Blue Lagoon with **Nassau Cruises** (☎ 242-363-3333; www.nassaucruises bahamas.com) costs $65, and includes hotel transfers, unlimited water sports and lunch.

and snorkeling. They charge two to six people from $400 to $500 per half-day, $700 or $1000 per day.

Born Free Charter Service (☎ 242-393-4144; www.bornfreefishing.com)

Brown's Charter (☎ 242-324-2061; www.browns charter.com)

Chubasco Charters (☎ 242-324-3474; www.chubasco charters.com)

Coral Reef Boat Rentals (☎ 242-327-2098; Sandy Port) Rents out small speedboats from $250/400 per half/full day.

Paradise Island Charters (☎ 242-363-4458; www.paradise-island-charters.com)

Boat Excursions

Dozens of day trips are offered, with options for snorkeling, diving, beach and island visits, partying, sunset and dinner cruises, and anything else you can think of! A few vessels depart the Nassau waterfront; most depart the dock immediately west of the Paradise Island Exit Bridge.

Apart from the public fast ferry, **Bahamas Ferries** (Map pp66-7; ☎ 242-323-2166; www.baha masferries.com; Potter's Cay, Nassau; adult/child $159/99) also operates the great value 'Harbour Island Day Away' excursion to wonderful Eleuthera. It departs daily from Potter's Cay, takes two hours each way and includes a tour of pretty Harbour Island, a great lunch and refreshments on the idyllic Pink Sands Beach. This is a simple decision – go!

Powerboat Adventures (Map pp66-7; ☎ 242-393-7116; www.powerboatadventures.com; Nassau; adult/child $190/130) take you on a thrilling power-boat trip which zips you from Nassau to the Exuma Cays in an hour. The first stop is Allan's Cays to say hi to some iguana families, then it is time for drift snorkeling, before heading to Ship Channel Cay for a nature hike. The excursion also includes shark feeding, snorkeling with stingrays, a barbecue lunch and plenty of rum swizzles.

Island World Adventures (☎ 242-363-3333; www.islandworldadventures.com; Nassau; adult/child $175/120) has daylong excursions on a high-powered speedboat to Saddleback Cay, in the Exumas. There's great snorkeling and seven private beaches to wander. Trips include lunch, an open bar, snorkeling gear and a stop at lovely Leaf Cay to commune with iguanas.

Nassau Cruises (☎ 242-363-3333; www.nassau cruisesbahamas.com) offers a 'Historical Harbour Cruise' around Paradise Island, passing the East End Lighthouse, Arawak Cay, pirate homes and other sites, tracing the Bahamas' colorful past. The trips depart daily, take about 90 minutes and cost around $40.

A day of fun is on offer with **Flying Cloud Catamaran Cruises** (Map p77; ☎ 242-363-4430; flyingcloud@coralwave.com; Paradise Island Ferry Terminal; adult/child $90/45), with a catamaran cruise, snorkeling around lovely little Rose Island and a chance to snooze in a hammock after a beach BBQ lunch with wine; perfect.

UNDERWATER EXCURSIONS

For those who don't want to get wet, **Seaworld Explorer** (Map pp66-7; ☎ 242-356-2548; shorex@batelnet.bs; adult/child $22/10) departs from John Alfred Wharf off Bay St, and has an office in the city. This 45-passenger semisubmarine with a window-lined hull takes a great 90-minute daily excursion above the fish-filled coral reefs of the Sea Gardens Marine Park, off the north shore.

Hartley's Undersea Walk (Map pp66-7; ☎ 242-393-8234/7569; www.underseawalk.com; adult $125) is a daily 3½-hour cruise that includes an escorted undersea adventure; you don't need snorkeling or diving experience to wear a roomy brass helmet with large glass windows for all-around viewing. Trips depart from Nassau Yacht Haven.

Water Sports

Most resort hotels either include water sports in their rates or offer them as optional extras. On offer are nearly every kind of beach and water activity, including parasailing, water-skiing and windsurfing.

Nassau Beach Sports Shop (Map p76; ☎ 242-327-7711, ext 6590; Nassau Beach Hotel, W Bay St, Cable Beach; ☐ 9am-5pm) rents sailboards for $20 per hour, and has equipment for a plethora of other sports.

ARE DOLPHIN ENCOUNTERS KILLING DOLPHINS?

Dolphin encounters are a popular attraction in the Bahamas and elsewhere, but they are not without controversy. Many scientists and conservation groups maintain that dolphin encounters harm the very creatures that we are all so enamored with. It appears that it is not so much the encounter, but the location and context of the meeting that can do so much damage to these graceful, playful and ultimately, wild animals.

One thing is clear: dolphin encounters that take place within enclosed environments such as pools and lagoons mean that those dolphins have been taken traumatically from their environment, their family pod and a natural way of life.

The US National Marine Fisheries Service has kept an inventory of captive marine mammals since 1972, which reports the births, deaths and migrations of each creature. In 2004 the South Florida *Sun Sentinel* (see below) ran a series of articles analyzing these figures. The conclusion: that captivity considerably shortens the life expectancy of dolphins, whales and sea lions.

The following figures from different sources are believed to be a pretty accurate reflection of the effects of captivity upon dolphins.

- The maximum life expectancy of a dolphin in the wild is around 40 to 50 years.
- The average life expectancy of a dolphin in captivity is 5 to 10 years.
- Stress of confinement results in behavioral abnormalities, illness, lowered resistance to disease and early death.

If you want the joy of meeting a dolphin, there are outfits that will take you to see, swim and dive with wild dolphins in their environment, out in the ocean. See p125 for details. Across the world, sanctuaries look after injured dolphins and would also welcome your visits. For further information, check out the following organizations:

- **Captivity Stinks Organisation** (www.captivitystinks.org) Records how long dolphins live at individual parks around the world.
- **Earthwatch Institute** (www.earthwatch.org/expedselect.html) and **Ecotourism Lindblad Expeditions** (www.expeditions.com) can organize volunteering with dolphin-trips.
- **Whale & Dolphin Conservation Society** (www.wdcs.org) Strongly advocates the removal of dolphins from theme parks.
- **NOAA, National Marine Fisheries Service** (www.nmfs.noaa.gov) Produces US Marine Mammal Inventory Reports and keeps comprehensive records of captive mammals in the US.
- **Sun Sentinel** (www.sun-sentinel.com) Check out this South Florida US newspaper's archives for its May 2004 stories entitled 'Marine Attractions Below the Surface.'

Water sports are available at all the resorts along Paradise and Cabbage Beaches on Paradise Island. Most of the motorized sports are operated by local entrepreneurs. Typical prices include $50 for 30 minutes' jet-skiing, $30 per person for a 15-minute banana-boat fun ride, and $45 to $60 for parasailing.

Tennis, Racquetball & Squash
Dozens of hotels have tennis courts, some of which are open to nonguests for a fee. **Radisson Cable Beach Golf Course** (Map p76; ☎ 242-327-6000; W Bay St, Cable Beach) has tennis, squash and racquetball courts that are open to nonguests for $10 per person, per day (racquet hire is $5). Night court hire is also possible.

Golf
New Providence has three great golf courses open to the public, including Paradise Island's Ocean Club Golf Course (p88).

The challenging 7-acre **Radisson Cable Beach Golf Course** (Map p76; ☎ 242-327-6000; www .radisson-cablebeach.com; Cable Beach) is the oldest in the Bahamas, but has been recently redesigned. Once managed by golfing supremo Arnold Palmer, it charges a $140 green fee ($100 for nine holes) and rates include a golf cart.

Another excellent course, the South Ocean Golf Course (p98) is at New Providence's western tip, and was closed for a face-lift at the time of research.

Running
Fitness fanatics can run the shaded jogging trail that snakes along the central median of W Bay St, a 1½-mile-long path from Sandals Royal Bahamian to the Cable Beach Golf Course.

The **Nassau Hash House Harriers** (Brian Crick ☎ 242-325-2831; www.nassauhash.com) have an organized run that lasts around 40 minutes each Monday (April to October) or Sunday (November to March).

Bird-Watching
The **Bahamas National Trust** (Map pp66-7; ☎ 242-393-1317; fax 242-393-4978; Village Rd, Nassau; ☼ 9am-5pm Mon-Fri) regularly offers guided bird-watching walks.

Also contact the **Bahamas Ornothology Group** (☎ 242-393-1317) for news on further bird-watching activities.

Horseback Riding
Take a trot on a trail with the horses of **Happy Trails Stables** (Map pp64-5; ☎ 242-362-1820; Coral Harbour, Southern Beaches; $90; ☼ Mon-Sat). Ninety-minute rides take in the woodland and beach scenery of the southern coastlands, and transfers are also provided.

For further horseback-riding options, also see Earth Village (opposite).

NASSAU FOR CHILDREN
The following are some ideas for things that children, and their parents, might enjoy doing while in Nassau.

- Take a tour of the amazing 34-acre Waterscape at the Atlantis resort (p78), where a whole host of lagoons are home to over 200 species of marine life, including sharks.
- Sit and wave at people from your horse-drawn surrey (p73).
- Gawp at the huge diamante-studded and rainbow-colored costumes of the Junkanoo carnival at the Junkanoo Expo (p73).
- Salute a marching flamingo, yawn at a dozing iguana, cluck at a Bahama parrot and smile at a big cat at Ardastra Gardens, Zoo & Conservation Park (p75).
- Walk past a bunch of wicked and wanton buccaneers and their pirate ship at the brilliant interactive Pirates of Nassau Museum (p71).
- Ride in a glass-hulled semisubmarine with Seaworld Explorer (p81).
- Swim or snorkel in 12ft of water with gentle captive rays in Blue Lagoon's Stingray City Marine Park (see the boxed text, p80).
- Mingle with a captive dolphin at Blue Lagoon's Dolphin Encounters (see the boxed text, p80).

Cable Beach and Paradise Beach are both lined with operators offering water-sports activities and equipment for hire. Beachside resorts usually have their own facilities which are open to nonguests upon the purchase of a day ticket.

For more information on traveling with children in the Bahamas, see p276.

TOURS
Nearly all hotels have tour desks that will offer a selection of choices and make all bookings on your behalf. Also refer to the

recommended boat excursions that are listed on p80.

Many taxi drivers will offer tours of the island and/or Nassau. Negotiate prices carefully prior to commencing any trips. It may well be cheaper to hire a car and take yourself to any spots of interest.

Nassau's quaint horse-drawn surreys (p73) are a great way to explore downtown Nassau at an easy pace.

Earth Village (☎ 242-356-2274, 242-434-8981; tkmiller@coralwave.com; ☺ Mon-Sat) Offers something off the beaten track. Enjoy exploring the island's center and coppice forests either on a guided walking tour (adult/child $50/15), horseback ride (adult/child $90/50) or through a special bird-watching experience (adult/child $60/20). This 155 acres of protected territory for birds encompasses water ponds teeming with fish, windmills and wooden bridges providing access to historical ruins; perfect for nature lovers (adult/child $75/45).

Majestic Tours (☎ 242-322-2606; www.majesticholidays.com; $35) Runs a number of air-conditioned bus tours including the extended City & Country Tour, which incorporates the city and environs, such as Forts Fincastle and Charlotte, the Queen's Staircase, plus Government House and Ardastra Gardens, Zoo & Conservation Park. The company offers a good-value deal on three tours for $110 (City & Country; Robinson Crusoe – snorkeling and lunch on a deserted cay; and a dinner-cruise with buffet and a DJ). Majestic Tours also have a range of land- and water-based tours.

Nassau Walking Tour (☎ 242-325 8687, 242-328 8687; tour $10; ☺ tours 10am & 2pm Mon-Sat) Departs twice daily from the bust of Sir Milo Butler in Rawson Sq (the guides wear blue batik waistcoats), and covers all the major points of historical interest in downtown Nassau. This is a great way to find your way around as well as learning all the salient bits of Nassau's past. Take a hat and some water; this 90-minute walk covers a fair bit of ground.

FESTIVALS & EVENTS

Major Bahamian Festivals, such as Boxing Day's brilliant Junkanoo, are listed on p279. For more on local events and festival dates, contact the **Bahamas Ministry of Tourism** (☎ 242-302-5000; www.bahamas.com) information booths at the Welcome Centre or at the airport.

One of two great events full of colonial tradition is the **Opening of Parliament**, a colorful, formal occasion featuring the Royal Bahamas Police Force Band marching in pith helmets, starched white tunics and leopard-skin shawls. The governor-general delivers a speech on behalf of Her Majesty, to whom the gathered officials swear allegiance.

Pageantry also marks the **Opening of the Supreme Court Sessions** in January, April, July, and October. Lawyers and judges in full regalia march to Christ Church Anglican Cathedral for a service, followed by an inspection of the guard of honor. Music and even more pageantry are provided by the police force band.

The following are a few other fun-filled local proceedings.

JANUARY
Classic Cars Race Lovers of flashy vintage cars should head to Nassau for this four-day, midmonth festival when rare Ferraris, Jaguars and other classics dating back to the 1920s gear up for a race along Cable Beach.

FEBRUARY
International Food Fair Local Bahamian fare comes to the streets of Nassau, with cookouts and competitions highlighting the bounty of the sea and land.
People of the Bahamas Annual Archives Exhibition Held in Nassau, the exhibition features exhibits showcasing the contributions of various ethnic groups to the historical and cultural development of the nation.

APRIL
Snipe Winter Sailing Championship Draws homemade boats to race one another in Montagu Bay; contact Royal Nassau Sailing Club (☎ 242-393-0145) for details.

JUNE
Caribbean Muzik Fest This will make you shake something! Move to reggae, soca, calypso and dance hall at the Queen Elizabeth Sports Centre until dawn.
Goombay Summer Festival Nassau hosts a midyear Junkanoo, with round-the-clock festivities for summertime visitors.

AUGUST
Emancipation Day Held the first Monday in August to commemorate the emancipation of slaves in 1834. A highlight is an early-morning 'Junkanoo Rush' at 4am in Fox Hill.
Fox Hill Day Celebration Held a week after Emancipation Day, this celebration recalls the day on which residents of Fox Hill learned of emancipation.

Miss Bahamas Contest More than 10 finalists vie for the coveted Miss Bahamas title in a gala evening featuring star-spangled entertainment. It's held midmonth in Nassau. The winner represents the Bahamas in the Miss Universe contest.

SEPTEMBER
Bahamas Atlantis Superboat Challenge Life is never so fast in Nassau as in late September, when this annual professional powerboat race is held. Forty or more teams compete in boats that are to smaller speedboats what dragsters are to the family sedan.

Summer Madness Revue A satirical review at the Dundas Centre for the Performing Arts looks at local politics.

OCTOBER
Great Bahamas Seafood Festival The Arawak Cay Seafood Market in Nassau is the setting for this annual four-day culinary and cultural extravaganza, featuring concerts, Junkanoo and plenty of food.

International Cultural Weekend Bahamians celebrate unity among the many nationalities residing in the islands with a midmonth weekend of float parades, food fests, arts and crafts displays, and concerts; held in Nassau.

International Mixed Championship Golf Tournament This is a weeklong 54-hole event for amateurs, traditionally held at the Ocean Club Golf Course (p88).

NOVEMBER
Guy Fawkes Night On November 5, Bahamians celebrate retribution for the Gunpowder Plot of 1605, when Catholic plotters tried to blow up the Houses of Parliament in London, by lighting bonfires and burning the lead villain, Guy Fawkes, in effigy, accompanied by fireworks and a nighttime parade.

Christmas Jollification An arts and crafts bonanza at The Retreat (p74) with food, drink, kids and music, as well as a lot of fun.

Thanksgiving Ball This black-tie do at the British Colonial Hilton Nassau (p86) is a long-established traditional fundraiser for the Bahamas Humane Society. Anyone who is anyone is seen here.

DECEMBER
Police Band Annual Christmas & Classical Concert The Royal Bahamas Police Force Band performs holiday classics at the Atlantis resort on Paradise Island, with accomplished local musicians assisting in the festivities.

Junior Junkanoo Parade A fabulous taste of things to come with some serious competitors, beating drums and wonderful images.

SLEEPING
Visitors of all budgets tend to agree, New Providence in particular, and the Bahamas

---

GAY & LESBIAN NASSAU

The pink dollar is not welcomed by many Bahamians, and there are few public illustrations of support for a Bahamian gay and lesbian population across the islands, unless individuals openly support the political pressure group Rainbow Alliance. Sadly, although Bahamians are generally an extremely tolerant and friendly people, the pervasiveness of fundamentalist religious beliefs has fostered an ugly bigotry and intolerance of progressive lifestyles, particularly towards gays and lesbians.

Most Bahamian gays are still deeply in the closet, and the nation has draconian laws against homosexual activity, which is punishable by prison terms. Laws are strictly enforced and public expressions of affection between gays will bring trouble.

In 1998 a group of religious bigots called Save the Bahamas made waves when it angrily protested against the arrival of a gay charter-cruise. The group compounded the negative press by also protesting against the arrival of the company Holland America's *Veendam,* which they mistakenly believed was chartered by a gay group, causing Bahamian Prime Minister Hubert Ingraham to issue a public apology.

This remonstration was then followed up by a preemptive protest against the docking of the *Norwegian Dawn,* a gay family cruise backed by American comedian and actor Rosie O'Donnell, in July 2004. By the actual date of the cruise ship's arrival, the previously vocal protestors were greatly reduced in number, but among them were the Bahamian gay rights group Rainbow Alliance, who bravely met and welcomed the cruise ship's gay and lesbian passengers.

According to the former group Bahamian Gays & Lesbians Against Discrimination, Club Med, Super Club Breezes, and Atlantis resorts are gay-friendly, but Sandals Royal Bahamian forbids same-sex couples.

Rainbow Alliance (☎ 242-328-1816), the aforementioned political pressure group, is a good point of contact for assistance and advice in planning a trip. Try also the website www.bahamasuncensored.com for some information on gay issues.

overall, has surprisingly expensive accommodations. Many hotels are obviously overpriced. These places provide meanly equipped or tatty rooms, but charge the same rates as the hotels that work hard to maintain good standards and offer a variety of guest facilities. Even some charming, modern and well-facilitated lodgings tend to push the line between 'reasonable' and 'over-the-top' rates. However, most accommodations share one thing in common; additional room and guest charges that can push the daily rate up by 20% to 30%.

But don't despair; with a bit of easy planning, there are ways to find reduced rates (up to 60 per cent), at all budget levels. Many hotel websites offer lower rates not available through tour operators. See p270 for more information.

Downtown Nassau

In general, downtown Nassau hotels tend to be smaller and cheaper than those in Cable Beach. Paradise Island resorts top the scale, both in terms of luxury and rates. It is strongly rumored that many Cable Beach hotels and adjacent businesses are to be demolished for another vast Paradise Island–style Atlantis and casino complex, which probably means a price hike in Cable Beach, so make hay while the sun shines.

BUDGET

Mignon Guest House (Map p69; ☎ 242-322-4771; 12 Market St; s/d $40/45; ✕ 🕾) This neat, clean and comfortable guesthouse is situated in the heart of downtown and is a veritable bargain; prices have not changed over the years, and are inclusive of taxes. If the aging hosts are a bit inflexible, they are refreshingly not driven by money, and the security is good. There are six small rooms, with fans, TV and central air-conditioning, that share a toilet and bathroom. Guests also have access to a small kitchen, fridge and microwave.

Buena Vista Restaurant & Hotel (Map p69; ☎ 242-322-2811; stanbv2000@yahoo.com; Delancy St; r $50; P ✕ 🕾) This faded old mansion, acclaimed for its restaurant (p90) of the same name, still has much charm, and some great-value lodgings upstairs. The rooms have en suites, and are clean and furnished with some lovely antique furniture, they also have TV, radio and direct-line phones. The rates are inclusive of all charges and it

is only a 10-minute walk into town or to the city beach.

Towne Hotel (Map p69; ☎ 242-322-8450; www .townehotel.com; 40 George St; r $70; ✕ 🕾) This hotel offers 46 small, well-lit rooms, but they have been cheaply refurbished. However, the rooms appear to be clean, and the location is good. Each room has a fan, king-size bed, and small bathroom. There is a nice downstairs bar and small dining area, where the house parrots natter away with an American accent.

Grand Central Hotel (Map p69; ☎ 242-322-8356; www.grand-central-hotel.com; Bay & Parliament Sts; r $70; 🕾) If you can cope with gloomy rooms, try this small, well-located hotel. The rooms are certainly better than the lobby would suggest, and they are very clean. Despite dowdy orange-and-brown decor, each room has its own bathroom, TV, air-con and phone. Overpriced but negotiable, the rates are inclusive of all charges.

MIDRANGE

Holiday Inn Junkanoo Beach Hotel (Map p69; ☎ 242-356-0000; www.basshotels.com/holiday-inn; W Bay St at Nassau St; r $135; P ✕ 🕾 🖳 🖭) Although things can be a little haphazard occasionally (the booking system can fail, and the fittings in refurbished rooms are sometimes not what they should be), this hotel has the best facilities of the midrange hotels in Nassau. Rooms are clean, light and comfortable, and are decorated in bright tropical pastels. Each has a balcony, TV, safe, fridge, data port, hairdryer, iron and coffeemaker. Rooms have en suites, and the beds are firm and spacious. The hotel has a guest laundry, gym, shop, business services, restaurant as well as a bar.

Quality Inn (Map p69; ☎ 242-322-1515; www.quality inn.com; cnr W Bay & Nassau Sts; r $90; P ✕ 🕾 🖭) This shiny new hotel sits next door to the Holiday Inn Junkanoo, and all rooms face the sea, some with better views than others. The cheerfully decorated rooms are nearly as well equipped as their neighbor's (unfortunately no fridge though), which will attract a similar business client as well as midrange travelers. Mind you, there are no hotel facilities, such as laundries, a restaurant or Internet connections, and the pool is tiny.

El Greco (Map p69; ☎ 242-325-1121; fax 242-325-1124; cnr W Bay & Augusta Sts; s/d $90/110; P ✕ 🕾 🖭) At the west end of downtown, this compact family-run hotel, enhanced by Spanish decor, surrounds a small courtyard with pool and bougainvillea. The rooms can be gloomy, the fittings ramshackle and the facilities limited, but the location and security are good, and rates are inclusive of all charges. Rooms come with phone, fan and TV. Upstairs rooms are larger, have balconies and a little more light.

TOP END

British Colonial Hilton Nassau (Map p69; ☎ 242-322-9036; www.hiltoncaribbean.com/nassau; 1 Bay St; s/d $230/240; P ⊠ ⊗ ▣ ▨) This massive grande dame of a hotel, built in 1922, is a Bahamian institution and was a location for two James Bond movies. The rooms have elegant, contemporary decor and modern amenities, with marble-lined bathrooms and a surfeit of mahogany. Or maybe you'd enjoy the 'Double-O Suite,' stocked with James Bond movies and decorated with Bond posters on the walls? There's a choice of restaurants as well as bars offering live music, big US sports games on TV, and dancing and entertainment. Other facilities include a swimming pool, tennis courts and some water sports. The rooms have their own climate control, Internet connections and video games – something to please everyone. The small private beach doesn't get washed by the sea but it does face the cruise-ships dock, and offers some amazing sights.

East of Downtown

Red Carpet Inn (Map pp66-7; ☎ 242-393-7981; www.redcarpetinnbahamas.com; E Bay St; r $106; P ⊠ ⊗ ▨) A contemporary 40-room hotel with adequate but plain rooms, this is a quiet and simple place, taxes are included and the security is good. The rooms are clean, with double beds, fridges, microwaves, safes, TV and phone. Some have a kitchenette. There's also a restaurant and guest laundry.

Nassau Harbour Club (Map pp66-7; ☎ 242-393-0771; nch@batelnet.bs; E Bay St; r $90; ⊠ ⊗ ▨) Popular with yachties and spring-breakers, this place overlooks the marina and has a pool and sundeck suspended over the water. The rooms are appealing if a little bare. The Dockside Bar & Grill, downstairs, and another on-site restaurant add to the party atmosphere. Each room has a TV and phone.

Orchard Hotel Apartments (Map pp66-7; ☎ 242-393-1297; fax 242-394-3562; Village Rd; studios $95, standard/superior cottages from $130; ⊗ ▨) Fourteen pink cottages are tucked away in quiet, lush grounds centered on a small pool. A little worn around the edges, each is pleasantly furnished and has air-con, TV and a small kitchen.

West of Downtown

Dillet's Guest House (Map pp66-7; ☎ 242-325-1133; fax 242-325-7183; Columbus Ave at Strachan St; s/d incl continental breakfast $85/135; ⊠ ⊗ ▣ ▨) One of Nassau's true gems, this family-run B&B is a great place to experience some Bahamian hospitality. A row of tall palms guides you up the path to the 1920s-era home, with rocking chairs on the veranda, hammocks in the garden, wicker furniture, original art and squawking parakeets. All the comfortable rooms have cable TV and some have kitchenettes. Dinners are available on request. Care is definitely required in this area at night.

Cable Beach

There are some great family-friendly resorts along this beach. Most offer tons of daytime and evening activities, water sports and restaurants. Parents will also be grateful for in-house bars and restaurants as well as baby-sitting services and laundry facilities. Many resort hotels also offer some good-value packages.

MIDRANGE

Radisson Cable Beach & Golf Resort (Map p76; 242-327-6000; www.radisson.com; W Bay St; r $165; P ⊠ ⊠ ⊠) This large resort has spacious ocean-view rooms, all with balcony, over-looking an exquisitely landscaped 25,000 sq ft courtyard with three large pools, cascading falls, whirlpool spas, outdoor dining and shady palms. The resort offers six restaurants, 'Camp Junkanoo' – an extensive supervised program for kids – and after-dark activities for teens. Guests can also take part in tennis, golf, racquetball, squash and water sports.

Nassau Beach Hotel (Map p76; ☎ 242-327-7711; www.nassaubeachhotel.com; W Bay St; r $150; P ⊠ ⊠ ⊠) This older, traditional hotel was featured in two James Bond movies many years ago. All the rooms are admirable, but those in the east wing are spacious and nicely furnished. There's a small shopping arcade and several dining options, including Café Johnny Canoe (p91). Flood-lit tennis courts and water sports are offered.

Guanahani Village (Map p76; ☎ 242-327-0688; www.guanahanivillage.com; 8-person units from $415) These garden and oceanfront rental units in three-story townhouses are attractive and great-value.

TOP END

Westwind II (Map p76; ☎ 242-327-7211; ww11club@ batelnet.bs; W Bay St; d $210; ⊠ ⊠) This intimate resort is immediately west of the Radisson. A small number of well-maintained, self-contained, two-bedroom air-con villas are centered on lush grounds with tennis courts and pools. Dinghy boats as well as snorkeling are on offer. Each unit has satellite TV and a fully furnished kitchen and there is easy access to the beach from the grounds.

Wyndham Nassau Resort & Crystal Palace Casino (Map p76; ☎ 242-327-6200; www.wyndham nassauresort.com; W Bay St; r $199; P ⊠ ⊠ ⊠) This outwardly gaudy resort has tasteful, contemporary and comfortable rooms. Fun-lovers will revel in the Crystal Palace

Casino, a cabaret nightclub, golf course, tennis and squash courts, shopping plaza and several bars and restaurants. The hotel also has a kids club, with supervised activities and theme days. The landscaped beachfront courtyard has a 100ft waterslide, Jacuzzi and swim-up bar – what else do you need?

Sandals Royal Bahamian (Map p76; ☎ 242-327-6400; www.sandals.com; W Bay St; d $645-925; P ⊠ ⊠ ⊡ ⊠) Minimum stays of two days are required at this all-inclusive hotel, which is recommended for those couples who like to party. No children or singles are permitted at this award-winning flagship of the renowned Sandals hotel chain. The property extends over 13 landscaped acres and includes a private beach with water sports and full-service spa.

Sandyport

Sandyport Beaches Resort (Map p76; ☎ 242-327-4279; www.sandyport.com; W Bay St; d $100, town-houses $210; P ⊠ ⊠ ⊠) This snazzy new residential-resort complex at the west end of Cable Beach has a marina, fitness center, tennis courts and church to keep you toned, spiritually and physically. Airy, modern and well-equipped rooms and townhouses offer good value with weekly and monthly deals. Townhouse rates are for two adults and two children. The gardens are still a building site but the beach is just across the road.

Sun Fun Resort (Map pp64-5; ☎ 242-327-8827; www.sunfunbahamas.com; W Bay St; r per week $800; P ⊠ ⊠ ⊠) Although 'resort' is stretching it a bit, this small hotel's rooms are clean and nice, if a tad small, and come equipped with telephone, satellite TV and a balcony that overlooks the pool or the ocean. The in-house Pisces Restaurant & Lounge serves a range of Bahamian and seafood dishes as well as tropical drinks.

Paradise Island

This is a fairly ritzy place, make no mistake. The beaches are lined with big hotels that offer all facilities, luxuries and activities. There is fun to be had, but at a price. At the time of writing several of the island's former hotels were being replaced with new resorts.

MIDRANGE

Sunshine Paradise Suites (Map p77; ☎ 242-363-3955; Paradise Island Dr; r $145; ⊠ ⊠) These 16

self-contained apartment suites are very good value, if a little spartan and short on furniture! However, they are clean, spacious and sit in the center of the island. Rates are for four people, and weekly and monthly rates are also good. All units come with TV and a fully fitted kitchen.

Paradise Harbour Club & Marina (Map p77; ☎ 242-363-2992; www.phc-bahamas.com; Paradise Island Dr; $150; P ⊠ ⊠ ⊠) At the east end of Paradise Island Dr, this is a small, attractive Swiss-run property in a marina setting. An eclectic collection of buildings contain spacious and clean rooms, with large kitchens and contemporary decor. There's no beach at hand, but the splendid Columbus Tavern Restaurant (p92) is here, and the small pool has a water cascade.

TOP END

Atlantis (Map p77; ☎ 242-363-3000, ext 28; www.atlantis.com; r $350; P ⊠ ⊠ ⊠ ⊠) Merge Disneyland and Sea World and you have a bustling mega-resort unlike any hotel this side of Vegas. This 24-story resort's rooms all boast balconies and mod cons. Atlantis also has 11 swimming areas, a 7-acre snorkeling lagoon, six-story water slides, 35 specialty restaurants, numerous bars and an entertainment complex with a 50,000 sq ft casino, and cabaret and other shows. There's also exercise and sports facilities, a full-service spa, a shopping plaza, a Discovery Channel Camp for kids and Club Rush for teens. Phew! The resort offers special package rates and the off-peak rates make staying here a more feasible option.

Ocean Club (Map p77; ☎ 242-363-2501; www.oneandonlyoceanclub.com; Paradise Island Dr; r $695; P ⊠ ⊠ ⊠ ⊠). This exquisite colonial property exudes European elegance, serenity and class. A large garden fronts the ocean and a wonderful and peaceful beach, while the central building contains an elegant library, small bar and dining areas. Crystal and silver sparkle on linen-draped tables around a courtyard dining area, and a children's club offers a full day of activities. Rooms, cottages and villas are capacious, with private verandas, large marble bathrooms, elegant bygone-era decor and state-of-the-art amenities. A Bermudan-style bar, nine tennis courts plus the nearby Ocean Club Golf Course are open to guests, as are the Atlantis facilities.

Comfort Suites (Map p77; ☎ 242-363-3680; www.comfortsuites.com; Casino Dr; r incl breakfast $215-275; P ⊠ ⊠ ⊠) This large, efficient hotel is nicely furnished and the attractive rooms are well equipped with king-size beds, a sitting area with sofa bed, cable TV, minibar, hairdryer and safe. There is a great pool and deck area containing a swim-up bar. What makes this hotel really impressive is that guests have free access to all Atlantis facilities, and that children (under 18) who share their parents' room stay for free.

EATING

Nassau's eateries run the gamut from colorful local establishments serving down-home Bahamian dishes to chic restaurants offering world-class gourmet fare.

The resort hotels contain a plethora of good restaurants and more informal eateries, as do the lively Arawak Cay's Fish Fry (p91) and Potter's Cay market (p74).

Downtown Nassau
Budget

Imperial Cafeteria & Take-Away (Map p69; ☎ 242-322-4522; Marlborough St; mains $5-10; ☽ breakfast, lunch & dinner) Ignore the yellow Formica, this is consistently the best-value takeout food in Nassau, beloved of many Bahamians and guests of the lordly British Colonial Hilton opposite. Simple fast-food cooked well; the fish is fresh, light and crispy, the burgers are tasty and the $3 breakfasts are filling.

Bahamian Kitchen, Restaurant & Bar (Map p69; ☎ 242-325-0702; Trinity Place; mains $10-18; ☽ lunch & dinner Mon-Fri) *The* place for traditional Bahamian dishes, specializing in seafood dishes from S15, but also serving salads, curried, steamed and broiled meats, and BBQ chicken and ribs. Most customers choose the day's specials while enjoying a chilled beer.

Café Skan's (Map p69; ☎ 242-322-2486; Bay St at Frederick St; mains $12-20; ☽ breakfast, lunch & dinner) The Bahamian and American breakfasts are very popular and getting a table can be a squeeze; it's chock-full of breakfasting businessmen and police officers – you can't go wrong with those references.

Also recommended for tasty and quick food:

Conch Fritters Bar & Grill (Map p69; ☎ 242-323-8778; Marlborough St; mains $9-16; ☽ lunch & dinner) Specializes in conch dishes and burgers.

GROUPER & CONCH; DISTINCT FLAVORS OR EXTINCT SPECIES?

With conch and grouper on every restaurant menu across the isles, you are not going to be able to avoid a very difficult moral decision; should you eat what are rapidly declining species in this region? It is your choice of course, but international and local research all says the same thing: grouper and conch populations in the Bahamas and Turks and Caicos region are fast approaching the point of no return.

Grouper populations have collapsed in most of the Caribbean, and the Nassau grouper is now classified as an endangered species in many areas. The Bahamian grouper catch in 2001 was less than half a million pounds, about a third of the 1999 catch. And recent surveys of discarded conch shells show that 75% of those taken for food and tourism are undersized.

The cause for the decline is pretty obvious; over-fishing at the worst possible times. Bahamian groupers are being fished en masse as they group together to spawn, while conch are being harvested before they can breed.

The Queen conch *(Strombus gigas)* is a large marine snail with a spectacular pink shell that grazes on sea grasses and lives for 20 years. The primary source of protein for islanders, it is widely sought after for its sweet, white meat, which tastes somewhat like a rubbery scallop.

Groupers are very slow-growing fish, and some species of grouper live to be over 120 years old. The fish like to breed in groups of thousands at a full moon during the months of November to February. Fishermen have been deliberately targeting these fish at this time with big nets and satellite navigation equipment. To put it into perspective, a similar practice in Bermuda resulted in a 95% decline in the population. Evidence shows that the fish and conch do not repopulate locations even if they are protected.

Following the collapse of the conch populations in parts of the Caribbean, Florida and Bermuda, the Nassau grouper and conch have been protected from all fishing in Florida for around 25 years. But both species are rarely seen.

Groups such as the **Bahamas Reef Environment Educational Foundation** (☎ 242-362-6477; www.breef.org; 24b Wulff Rd, W Bay St, Nassau) have been virtually begging the Bahamian government to take swift and decisive action as follows:

■ Establish marine reserves to protect conch populations, which will also benefit grouper (and other species such as crawfish).

■ Set up a four-month total ban (from November to February inclusive) on fishing grouper; this is, they say, the most critical action required.

■ Police the marine reserves and the seasonal ban on grouper fishing to prevent both local fishermen and international poachers ignoring these edicts.

The Bahamian government instigated a one-month ban on fishing grouper during January 2004, and a two-month ban during January and February 2005, but this is not perceived to be enough to save the species in the long run.

Likewise, in 1992 the Convention on International Trade in Endangered Species listed the conch one category below threatened status, yet these creatures are still exported across the Caribbean to other regions where the fishing of them has been banned. Contact CITES (www.cites.org) for more information.

So perhaps you fancy pizza or chicken for supper after all?

Sbarro's (Map p69; ☎ 242-356-0800; Bay St; mains $5-12; ☽ lunch & dinner) Very popular with Bahamian workers and cruise-ship passengers for its yummy pizza slices, pastas and hot Bahamian lunches.

MIDRANGE
Brussels Brasserie (Map p69; ☎ 242-326-4523; Maritime House, Frederick St; mains $22-28; ☽ lunch Mon-Fri)

This licensed and intimate restaurant is authentically Belgian, from the gleaming wood and mirrored walls to the great menu. Delicate crepes, steak and omelette dishes are listed alongside the monthly special of steamed mussels and Belgian frites. A long-luncher's paradise; don't miss out on the wonderful chocolate-orange crepes.

THE AUTHOR'S CHOICE

Café Matisse (Map p69; ☎ 242-356-7012; Bank Lane, Nassau; mains $18-24; ⦿ lunch & dinner Tue-Sat) A comfortable restaurant with great atmosphere and excellent food that is reasonably priced – what more could you ask for? The decor combines leopard-skin fabrics, rich hardwoods, bare limestone walls and Matisse prints. However, regulars prefer a bottle of wine and lunch alfresco, under the dappled shade of the courtyard's trees. The menu displays Italian flair and tasty vegetarian choices with homemade pastas that melt in the mouth and pizzas with pizzazz. The service is exemplary and friendly. This is real understated class.

Green Shutters Restaurant & Pub (Map p69; ☎ 242-322-3701; 48 Parliament St; mains $8-25; ⦿ lunch daily, dinner Mon-Sat) You'd swear you were in old country England; this intimate pub has authentic beamed ceilings, leather chairs and a polished wooden bar serving ploughman's platters and bangers and mash with pints of best Bitter and draught ales. The dining room offers good fish and beef dishes as well as live music at weekends; do make reservations beforehand. Cheers!

Chez Willie (Map p69; ☎ 242-322-5364; W Bay St; mains $14-30; ⦿ lunch & dinner Mon-Sat, brunch Sun) The coy statues that surround this place usher you into a little courtyard where you can dine alfresco or indoors. The menu covers French and Bahamian cuisines. Dishes include pumpkin soup and blackened swordfish, although they love doing fancy things with lobster, cream and puff pastry too. Smart dress required.

Gaylord's (Map pp66-7; ☎ 242-356-3004; Dowdeswell St; mains $8-25; ⦿ lunch Mon-Fri, dinner daily) The Indian cuisine is excellent, and vegetarians will also rejoice in a rare choice of dishes. Creamy masalas and kormas, spicy tandooris and *bhunas* and more are consumed to a backdrop of gentle, classical music on the small veranda or in the dining room.

TOP END

Graycliff Hotel & Restaurant (Map p69; ☎ 242-322-2796; www.graycliff.com; W Hill St, Nassau; r $290; Ⓟ Ⓧ Ⓧ ⬜ Ⓡ) has mains for $30 to $45 and is open for lunch from Monday to Friday

and for dinner daily. The French-inspired cuisine here is superb, as is the signature dish of Lobster Graycliff. The wine cellar with its hundreds of thousands of bottles, including some rare dusty gems worth thousands of dollars, claims to be the largest collection in the Caribbean region. There is no better selection of fine Cuban cigars with which to end the evening. Jacket and tie are required. See the boxed text on p86.

Buena Vista Restaurant & Hotel (Map p69; ☎ 242-322-2811; stanbv2000@yahoo.com; Delancy St; r $50; Ⓟ Ⓧ Ⓧ)p85) has mains for $34 to $40 and is open for dinner. There's an aura of faded but comfortable elegance in this mansion and grounds, which is the backdrop to a creative and unpretentious menu. The French and Italian cuisine includes dishes such as snapper sautéed with almonds, sirloin or filet mignon with cream, brandy and peppercorns.

Humidor Restaurant (Map p69; ☎ 242-322-2796, ext 301; mains $22-35; ⦿ lunch & dinner, closed Sun) Next door to Graycliff Hotel & Restaurant is this elegant bistro. A Grand Award Winner in *Wine Spectator*, it serves California-Caribbean fare under the baton of a master chef. Typical dishes include seafood in a large scallop shell and pasta in saffron cream sauce with mussels and roasted bell peppers. The adjacent lounge is awash in Cuban art.

East of Downtown

Pinder's Place, at Potter's Cay Market (p74), is a simple stall under the Paradise Island Exit Bridge. However, the place is packed to the brim at night with diners who love the conch dishes here as well as the exuberant Bahamian atmosphere. Open till late, but watch yourself at night.

Double Dragon (Map pp66-7; ☎ 242-393-5718; Bridge Plaza; mains $8-15; ⦿ lunch Mon-Fri, dinner Thu-Sun) This cheap and cheerful Chinese eatery is at the foot of the Paradise Island Exit Bridge.

Pink Pearl Café (Map pp66-7; ☎ 242-394-6413; E Bay St; ⦿ lunch & dinner, closed Sun) A consistently top-notch restaurant, its setting is a cool two-story house with polished wood floors, vibrant contemporary artworks and a wrap-around, breeze-swept deck. The service is grand, as is the delicious food. Appetizers include roasted peppers, spinach and *cho-cho* (crispy beef in a garlic sauce), and such mouthwatering entrees as ginger chicken and guava-glazed pork. Don't miss out on the lemon-scented cake or the lively jazz nights at weekends.

Montagu Gardens (Map pp66–7; ☎ 242-394-6347; E Bay St; mains $15-26; ☻ lunch & dinner Mon-Sat) For surf 'n' turf, head to this casually elegant place located in an old Bahamian home, with gardens, on Lake Waterloo. The somewhat flat atmosphere is, however, up-lifted with live music on Friday evenings, and reasonably priced meals include flame-grilled and blackened entrees and specials such as snapper cooked with wine, butter and capers. These continental dishes are served alongside steaks, seafood, ribs, lamb dishes and burgers. Smart dress is required.

Sun And… (Map pp66–7; ☎ 242-393-1205; Lakeview Dr; mains $36-42; ☻ dinner Tue-Sat) An acclaimed option is the oddly named and, some might say, teeny-bit pretentious restaurant that vets its customers before allowing them to enter the converted home on a cul-de-sac off the east end of Shirley St. Yet the highly acclaimed menu offers wonderful French cuisine as well as Bahamian dishes with a French twist. Steak and stone crabs are the house specialties and the baked Alaska and soufflé desserts are equally renowned. Reservations and extremely smart dress are required.

West of Downtown

Fish Fry (Map pp66–7; ☎ 242-328-5033; W Bay St, Arawak Cay) This is the place to be on weekends. A number of small huts and established restaurants serve hot food and drinks to a backdrop of Caribbean music. Some local favorites include **Goldie's Restaurant** (Map pp66–7), **New Big 10 Seafood Haven** (Map pp66–7; ☎ 242-322-5344; ☻ lunch & dinner Tue-Sun), **Conch & Steakhouse** (Map pp66–7), **Twin Brothers Seafood & Steak House** (Map pp66–7; ☎ 242-328-5033; ☻ lunch & dinner Tue-Sun) and **Deep Creek** (Map pp66–7) bar. Early evenings here are busy with all age groups, but take care as it can get a bit feral later on. The Great Bahamas Seafood Festival (p84) is also held here each October.

Cricket Club Restaurant & Pub (Map pp66–7; ☎ 242-326-4720; W Bay St; mains $8-15; ☻ lunch & dinner) Homesick male Brits ahoy! Come here for a bellyful of shepherd's pie, bangers and mash, and Courage or Fosters beer, at the same time you're being intellectually stimulated by the accompanying soccer,

cricket and rugby games on satellite TV. It's opposite Arawak Cay.

Coco Bar & Wood Grill (Map p76; ☎ 242-327-4287; W Bay St, Sandyport; mains $12-26; ☻ breakfast, lunch & dinner) Sitting adjacent to Sandyport Bridge, this packed eatery brims with chatter and the aroma of wonderful wood-fired dishes and the best pizzas for miles. Just a gem on all levels.

Cable Beach

Capriccio Ristorante (Map p76; ☎ 242-327-8547; cnr W Bay St & Skyline Dr, Cable Beach; mains $14-23; ☻ lunch & dinner Mon-Sat, dinner Sun & public holidays) Head here for a cosy ambiance enhanced by classical music and friendly Italian hosts. A choice of dishes to please all includes wonderfully luscious pastas, such as fettuccine with rosé and mushrooms. The attention to detail also makes this place a true and consistent star. The coffee is a joy alone – aromatic, rich and authentically Italian – and the baguettes are a crisp and refreshing change to some of the soggy bread found locally.

Café Johnny Canoe (Map p76; ☎ 242-327-3373; W Bay St, Cable Beach; mains $8-20; ☻ breakfast, lunch & dinner) This popular café and bar adjoins the Nassau Beach Hotel. It has a rustic yet atmospheric outside deck (lit up at night by Christmas lights) and a brightly colored air-conditioned interior. It serves mainly US-style burgers, ribs and chops, and Bahamian fish dishes. The cocktails are bucket-sized, and happy hour starts at 4pm. There's also a Junkanoo performance on Friday evening.

Swiss Pastry Shop (Map p76; ☎ 242-327-7601; W Bay St, Cable Beach; pastries $3-6; ☻ 9am-6pm Mon-Sat) This shop near Sandals Royal Bahamian is one of the few places to find cheap beef patties. It also serves yummy brownies and some very ornamental cakes.

Sbarro's (Map p76; ☎ 242-327-3076; W Bay St, Cable Beach; mains $5-12; ☻ lunch & dinner) This is the place to fill up on cheap, tasty pizza, calzone, salads or American-Italian fare. Sbarro's also offers daily Italian and Bahamian specials.

Paradise Island

There are few budget options here, and most eateries are contained within the various hotel resorts.

News Café (Map p77; ☎ 242-363-4684; Hurricane Hole Plaza; mains $8-18; ☻ breakfast, lunch & dinner) Homesick Americans will love this delight-ful deli; there's indoor or patio dining, an all-American menu of deli sandwiches, burgers, salad platters, delicious coffee and popular breakfasts, and American newspapers are on sale as well as a range of magazines.

Blue Marlin (Map p77; ☎ 242-363-2660; Hurricane Hole Plaza; mains $26-35; ☻ lunch & dinner) Come here for dinner and a show. Mains include creamy and spicy dishes such as the yummy Eleuthera coconut chicken. The show includes calypso music, a steel band and some Junkanoo fun.

Columbus Tavern Restaurant (Map p77; ☎ 242-363-2992; Paradise Island Dr; mains $14-34; ☻ lunch & dinner) This place exudes a maritime air. It offers a popular mix of French and Swiss specialties, such as stuffed escargots in shells, roast duck *à l'orange* and sirloin steak.

You can purchase groceries at the **Paradise Supermarket & Deli** (Map p77; ☎ 242-363-1056; Harbour Rd).

Over the Hill
Same Ole Place (Map pp66-7; ☎ 242-322-1311; Thompson Blvd; mains $5-12; ☻ lunch & dinner) This place in the Oakes Field area serves okra soup, crawfish and pork chops, drawing locals ranging from the hoi polloi to Prime Minister Hubert Ingraham.

Mamma Lyddie's Place (Map pp66-7; ☎ 242-328-6849; Market St; mains $8-18; ☻ breakfast, lunch & dinner Mon-Sat) This cheerful place sells johnnycakes (sweet bread that is served hot with creamy butter) and guava duff (a fruit-filled jelly pudding served with sauce made of sugar, egg, butter and rum), as well as truly fabulous side dishes, in particular the macaroni cheese, plantain, and peas 'n' rice.

DRINKING
Most bars in Nassau bill themselves either as English-style pubs or US-style sports bars (or 'satellite lounges,' so named for their satellite TVs). Many resort hotels have at least one such bar, as well as more sophisticated lounge bars where music plays in the background to the low-key chatter of groups of groomed cocktail drinkers.

You will not experience the local color by playing the tourist, however. For that, you need to hang out at satellite lounges. Although middle-class locals tend toward the same places as out-of-towners, there are plenty of funky watering holes where the activities center on downing beers and

playing dominoes. Most have a TV and pool table.

Downtown Nassau
Good coffee shops or wine bars are rare, as most people use hotel lounges to dither, gossip, people-watch and sup their caffeine and alcohol.

Rumours (Map p69; ☎ 242-323-2925; Charlotte St) Tucked away in a little house in the center of town, this wine bar services a lot of local business types and those who want a quiet drink away from the hustle and bustle.

Drop-Off (Map p69; ☎ 242-322-3444; Bay St) This slightly sleazy but atmospheric basement bar and dance club attracts a mix of locals and staff from the cruise ships, as well as Boddington's draft ale fans. It starts to get jam packed after midnight, especially on weekends when the ships are in port. Check out the aquarium and see if the fish will perform for you after you've had a draft or two. Drop-off is near East St.

East of Downtown
Cappucino Café (Map pp66-7; ☎ 242-394-6332; Mackey St; mains $5-8; ☻ breakfast & lunch) This small place gets packed out by a lunch crowd desperate to get their teeth into the light lunches which include yummy tuna melts and desserts. The great coffee might also have something to do with its popularity.

Crocodiles Waterfront Bar & Grill (Map pp66-7; ☎ 242-323-3341; E Bay St, Paradise Island Bridge; ☻ noon-late) Although this place is more an eatery than a bar, many people also come here for the great atmosphere and rum cocktails at sunset.

Dockside Sports Bar & Grill (Map p69; ☎ 242-393-0771; E Bay St, Nassau; ☻ noon-late) This bar is teeming with life at the weekends, and with yachties at festival times.

Hammerhead Bar & Grill (Map pp66-7; ☎ 242-393-5625; E Bay St; ☻ noon-late) This small bar has a three-hour happy hour from 4pm and carries the subtle advertising line 'get hammered at hammerheads.' You will find the bar between the two Paradise Island bridges.

West of Downtown
Fish Fry (p91), kicks off at weekends and a number of bars serve golden beer and rum cocktails while rocking to reggae and Junkanoo music; check out the life at Deep Creek bar. The area can get a bit wild later

on, but the early evenings here are lively with all age groups, and the police do keep an eye on things.

Paradise Island
Green Parrot Bar & Grill (Map p77; ☎ 242-363-3633; Hurricane Hole Marina, Paradise Island; ☯ noon-midnight) One of the few bars on the island outside the hotel complexes. Live music on Saturday and Sunday evenings helps add to this place's popularity.

ENTERTAINMENT
Downtown Nassau is strangely dead at night, once the day's business is put to bed. Cruise-ship passengers return to their ships and the Christian community, including the Bahamas Christian Council, have influenced the decision to centralize nightspots around a couple of areas. See the media section p68 for details on the nightlife.

Anyone who wants to party should head for the tourist nightspots of Cable Beach and Paradise Island. Here you can party and swill at will!

At the opposite end of the spectrum, afternoon-tea parties are hosted regularly at Government House, which forms part of the People-to-People program, designed to put tourists in closer contact with Bahamians. This highly recommended and free program also runs on many of the Family Islands. Contact the **Bahamas Ministry of Tourism** (☎ 242-302-2000; www.bahamas.com) for more details.

Nightclubs
There are numerous clubs that come and go, but the following are staunch favorites. Promotion nights normally mean free entry. It is also worth checking on dress codes and which nights the clubs open. Some clubs only open at weekends in quieter periods but then party nightly during the peak times of spring break, Easter, Christmas and New Year.

Several resort hotels have their own dance clubs, too, including Sandals Royal Bahamian, which is private. Nonguests can buy an evening pass to the resort's own club, Breezes, and the Fanta-Z Disco at the Radisson Cable Beach (p87) is open to all comers.

Fluid Lounge & Nightclub (Map p69; ☎ 242-356-4691; Bay St, Nassau; admission $5-25; ☯ from 9pm Tue-Sun) Two dance floors and a mix of hip-hop,

R&B and karaoke keep this place popular. Dress and minimum age requirements may apply. There is free entry for women until 11pm and tourists with a taxi-driver pass can get in for $5.

601 Club (Map pp66-7; ☎ 242-322-3041; 601 Bay St, Nassau; admission $5-30; ☯ Fri-Sun) This club on the east end of downtown is the snazziest place. Dress and minimum age requirements may apply. There is free entry for women until 11pm and tourists with a taxi-driver pass can get in for $5.

Club Waterloo (Map pp66-7; ☎ 242-393-7324; E Bay St, Nassau; admission $5-30; ☯ 9pm-4am) Near Fort Montagu, this indoor/outdoor club is still going strong after seven years, and is popular with Bahamians and holidaymakers of most ages. American spring break college students also head here. The old colonial building contains a number of bars, and separate dance areas that host live rock-and-roll bands and play hip-hop and reggae. Wednesday's 'happy hour' continues until midnight.

Insomnia (Map pp66-7; ☎ 242-322-7664; W Bay St, Nassau; admission $25; ☯ from 10pm Thu-Sun) Fans of reggae, soca, calypso and Bahamian music head to Insomnia. Admission charges can vary, check ahead.

Cocktail & Dreams Nightclub (Map pp66-7; ☎ 242-328-3745; W Bay St, Nassau; admission $20; ☯ from 9pm Tue-Sun) This indoor/outdoor venue has a dance-hall vibe and a DJ, and is popular with tourists, visitors and local crowds. On Thursdays they play 'old school' reggae, and on Wednesdays most drinks are half price.

Zoo (Map pp66-7; ☎ 242-322-7195; W Bay St, Saunders Beach; admission $20-40; ☯ Thu-Sat) The dance club of choice is near Saunders Beach, though it was in the process of reopening with a new name and management at the time of research. Admission prices may change, but previously some Cable Beach hotel guests gained free entry with hotel ID. This ultramodern club has a number of different bars, a ground-floor late-night eatery, and plays house, techno, R&B and reggae music to a pretty cool crowd.

Dragons Lounge & Dance Club (Map p77; ☎ 242-363-2400; Atlantis Resort, Paradise Island; admission $30; ☯ from 9pm till late) Atlantis' hot, high-tech nightclub is part of the casino complex and is hugely popular with locals as well as tourists. Entry is free to hotel guests.

Live Music

Many restaurants and bars rock it up at the weekends; check the local tourist newspapers for a calendar of events, but it's also worth asking hotel and restaurant staff as not everything is listed.

Arawak Cay (p75) is always lively at weekends, especially as it draws close to Junkanoo times. Many bands and dancers practice their routines for the Junkanoo parades at the Fish Fry. It is great fun to watch performers from competing 'shacks' or groups and comment on their performances along with the crowd.

The classy Pink Pearl Café (p90) keeps its hungry diners coming back for more with some great jazz music that adds to the night's entertainment. Yet, it also hosts R&B, headliner names and jam sessions. Call for details about who's playing.

For rake 'n' scrape music on Sunday evenings, check out Same Ole Place (p92). It guarantees a warm welcome and a richly rewarding experience.

Blue Note Club (Map p69; ☎ 242-322-3301; British Colonial Hilton, Bay St, Nassau) Has regular free jazz nights. There's some other really great live music in the hotel's other bars and lounges.

Most Paradise Island hotels have bars playing live music, including a fistful of options at Atlantis: **Plato's Lounge** (Map p77; ☎ 242-363-3000; www.atlantis.com), with candlelight and a pianist, and the **Piranha Club** (Map p77; ☎ 242-363-3000; www.atlantis.com), where you can watch the eponymous fish through Plexiglas. A crooner sings nightly at the **Oasis Lounge** (Map p77; ☎ 242-363-3000; www.atlantis .com) of Club Land'Or. And live musicians perform at **Bahama Mama Mia** (Map p77; ☎ 242-363-2660; Paradise Island) located in Hurricane Hole Marina.

Casinos & Floorshows

Wyndham Nassau Resort & Crystal Palace Casino (p87) The casino at the Wyndham Nassau Resort in Cable Beach is vast and is open to anyone over 21 years of age. The tables and poker machines are open 24 hours and tuition is given to anyone wanting to learn how to throw away their money. The 800-seat **Rainforest Theatre** (Map p76; ☎ 242-327-6200; www.wyndhamnassauresort.com; Wyndham Nassau Resort & Crystal Palace Casino, W Bay St, Cable Beach; admission $25) hosts Las Vegas–style revues such as the 'Magical Voyage' show, which blends

comedy, dance and magic acts. The show changes themes regularly.

Atlantis Resort & Casino (Map p77; ☎ 242-363-2400; www.atlantis.com; Atlantis Resort, Paradise Island; admission free; ☼ 10am-4am) This enormous casino links to the resort's restaurants. Poker machines are rattling 24 hours a day amid tables offering every conceivable means of losing your money or watching others get poorer. Also in the Atlantis resort, **Joker's Wild** (Map p77; ☎ 242-363-3000; www.atlantis.com; Atlantis Resort, Paradise Island; admission price varies; ☼ 9:30pm Tue-Sun) hosts Bahamian and international acts who enjoy their gigs tremendously.

King & Knights Club (Map p76; ☎ 242-327-7711; www.nassaubeachhotel.com; Nassau Beach Hotel, W Bay St, Cable Beach; admission $25) This club offers a Bahamian dance show that includes traditional rake 'n' scrape music, limbo, a fire dance and Junkanoo music.

Cinemas

Matinee prices at these cinemas are slightly cheaper (adult/child $6/2.50).

Galleria Cinemas 11 (Map pp64-5; ☎ 242-380-3549; Mall at Marathon, Prince Charles Ave & Marathon Rd, Nassau) An 11-screen theater with super-surround sound that has day and evening shows (adult/child $7/3.50).

Galleria 6 (Map pp64-5; ☎ 242-380-3549; RND Plaza, John F Kennedy Dr, Nassau) This six-screen multiplex also has matinees and evening shows (adult/child $7/3.50).

Theater

Dundas Centre for the Performing Arts (Map pp66-7; ☎ 242-393-3728; fax 242-394-7179; Mackey St, Nassau; admission $10-20) This is Nassau's most valued venue, hosting plays, dances, revues, musicals and (occasionally) ballets.

National Centre for the Performing Arts (Map pp66-7; ☎ 242-301-0600; Shirley St, Nassau) This 600-seat center hosts large-scale performances and international productions. Look out for 'Summer Madness,' when popular local theatrical troupes address contemporary issues in Bahamian society. The excellent National Youth Choir, who have recorded eight CDs, hold an annual concert here in late April or early May. Performances by the National Dance Company, Nassau Amateur Operatic Society, Chamber Singers, and Diocesan Chorale are also a fabulous treat.

Spectator Sports

Check the weekend papers for matches that may be of interest. The following are two key match venues.

Clifford Park (Map pp66-7; ☎ 242-322-1875/3622; W Bay St, Nassau; free admission) Cricket is played on weekends from March to December at this park below Fort Charlotte, where informal soccer matches also occur.

Queen Elizabeth Sports Centre (Map pp66-7; ☎ 242-323-5163; Over-the-Hill off Thompson Blvd, Oakes Field, Nassau) The center has track and field and softball stadiums, plus netball courts. The swimming pool and cycling tracks attract amateur and professional athletes. Baseball games are hosted here for the Little League and Pony League Baseball Diamonds.

SHOPPING

Bay St is lined with arcades (such as Prince George Plaza; Map p69) and duty-free stores selling everything from Swiss watches and nugget-sized Colombian emeralds to Milanese fashions and spicy rums. The side streets are favored by stores selling leather goods, artwork and collectibles. Upscale resorts also have duty-free jewelry and gift stores. The largest are the 'malls' in the Radisson Cable Beach & Golf Resort (p87) and Wyndham Nassau Resort & Crystal Palace Casino (opposite).

It is worth checking out comparative prices at home before visiting the Bahamas. Also look out for special deals and coupons in the free *What-to-do* tourist booklets, available from any shop or hotel lobby.

Most Bahamians shop for major items in Miami, but use the shopping malls in the residential areas south of downtown for the weekly shop and other incidentals. The largest, with 70 stores, is the **Mall at Marathon** (Map pp64-5; ☎ 242-393-4043; Marathon & Robinson Rds); you can take the shuttle that leaves from outside KFC on Woodes Rogers Walk for $1 one-way. The **Towne Centre Mall** (Map pp64-5; ☎ 242-326-6992; Blue Hill Rd & Independence Dr) is another multilevel mall.

Antiques

Marlborough Antiques (Map p69; ☎ 242-328-0502; Marlborough St, Nassau) A wide range includes items with a nautical theme. Prices are high!

Balmain Antiques & Gallery (Map p69; ☎ 242-323-7421; 2nd fl, Mason's Bldg, Bay & Charlotte Sts, Nassau) For antique maps and etchings.

Arts & Crafts

Galleries abound, as do souvenir shops selling cheap original or hand-copied oil and acrylic Haitian paintings from as little as $15. Many of the straw items are imported from Asia. The vendors expect you to bargain the price down by about 10%, but don't be too miserly!

Aitken Gallery (Map pp66-7; ☎ 242-328-7065; Madeira St, Nassau; ☉ 9am-5pm Mon-Sat) This Palmdale district gallery promotes paint and photographic works.

Balmain Gallery (Map p69; ☎ 242-323-7662; Bay St at Charlotte St, Nassau; ☉ 9:30am-5:30pm Mon-Sat) A mix of maps, antique prints, coins, postage stamps, lead soldiers, and oil and watercolor paintings.

Central Bank of the Bahamas Annex (Map p69; ☎ 242-322-2130; Trinity Pl & Frederick St, Nassau; ☉ 9:30am-4:30pm Mon-Fri) Monthly exhibitions of classic and contemporary Bahamian artists.

Doongalik Studios (Map pp66-7; ☎ 242-393-6640; dstudios@bahamas.net.bs; 18 Village Rd, Nassau; ☉ 9am-5pm Mon-Fri) For vibrant Junkanoo-inspired paintings, masks, crafts and T-shirts.

Kennedy Gallery (Map p69; ☎ 242-325-7662; http://mymurphys.com/kennedy/; Parliament St, Nassau; ☉ 9am-5pm Mon-Sat) Paintings, sculptures, ceramics, wind chimes and other works from both established and emerging artists, includes children's art.

Nassau Art Gallery (Map pp66-7; ☎ 242-393-1482; fax 242-393-1483; East Bay Shopping Centre, E Bay St, Nassau; ☉ 9am-5pm Mon-Sat) Just east of the Paradise Island Exit Bridge, this long-established gallery has a good selection of works.

Straw Market Cable Beach (Map p76; W Bay St); Nassau (Map p69; Bay St) The market near Prince George Wharf is a veritable Bahamian souk, bustling with vendors selling T-shirts, wood carvings, and straw baskets, mats, dolls, hats and other items. You'll also find a large straw and crafts market across from the Radisson Cable Beach.

Bahamas Rum Cake Shop (Map pp66-7; ☎ 242-322-3444; Bay St, Nassau; cakes $6; ☉ 7am-5pm Mon-Fri, 9am-noon some Saturdays) Tourist shops sell these buttery delights in fancy sealed tins for around $20. Buy and eat a warm one right now or take it home; they also sell the fancy tinned version.

Green Lizard (Map p69; ☎ 242-323-8076; Bay St, Nassau) A diverse range of island-made items is offered, with items including crafts made of straw, handprinted Androsia batiks and sarongs, plus guava jams, pepper sauces and even Haitian artworks and hammocks.

Cigars

Premium Cuban cigars can be bought for a song in Nassau, but remember, Uncle Sam prohibits US citizens from importing them. The good news is that Graycliff's cigars are not made with Cuban tobacco so *are* permitted into the US by customs.

Pipe of Peace (Map p69; ☎ 242-322-3908; Bay St at Charlotte St) Has a fine selection of Cuban cigars.

Havana Humidor (Map p77; ☎ 242-363-5809; Crystal Court, Atlantis, Paradise Island) A sizeable collection of Cuban cigars; includes rolling demonstrations.

Graycliff Cigar Co (p71) is also worth checking out. Castro's own cigar-roller oversees fellow Cubans hand-rolling these award-winning cigars

Clothing

You'll find T-shirts and resort wear at all the resort boutiques and in dozens of stores downtown. Several stores also sell simple clothes made from Androsia batiks. There are few bargains on high-fashion clothing.

Bonneville Bones (Map pp64-5; ☎ 242-394-2746; Mall at Marathon) This store sells elegant designer garb for men.

Brass & Leather Shops Charlotte St (Map p69, ☎ 242-322-3806); Mall at Marathon (Map pp64-5; ☎ 242-394-5676) All-leather goods and clothes.

Coles of Nassau (Map p69; ☎ 242-322-8393; Parliament St at Bay St, Nassau) These stores sell designer fashions such as Calvin Klein, Vittadini and Mondi.

The Bay (Map p69; ☎ 242-356-3918; Prince George Plaza, Bay St, Nassau) This store stocks elegant designer duds.

Gucci (Map p69; ☎ 242-325-0561; Saffrey Sq, Nassau) This store off Bay St sells the well-known brand.

Jewelry, Perfume & Collectibles

Coin of the Realm (Map p69; ☎ 242-322-4497; Charlotte St, Nassau) Bahamian coins, stamps and semiprecious stones.

Colombian Emeralds (Map p69; ☎ 242-322-2230; Bay St, Nassau) Bright sparkling emeralds and much more at this chain store.

John Bull (Map p69; ☎ 242-322-4252, Bay St, Nassau) All the big names are here, such as Cartier

and Tiffany & Co, as well as all the classic perfumes.

Solomon's Mines (Map p69; ☎ 242-356-4362; Bay St, Nassau) This chain sells jewels and watches.

Linen Shop (Map p69; ☎ 242-322-4266; Bay St at Frederick St, Nassau) Stocks…yep linen!

Perfume Shop (Map p69; ☎ 242-322-2375; Bay St at Frederick St, Nassau) A vast collection of designer sniffs.

Philatelic bureau (Map p69; ☎ 242-322-3344; E Hill St at Parliament St, Nassau) The main post office sells collectible stamps.

Music

Cody's Music & Video Centre (Map pp66-7; ☎ 242-323-8215; fax 242-323-2408; E Bay & Armstrong Sts, Nassau) Carries a large stock of Bahamian and Caribbean music.

Pyfroms (Map p69; ☎ 242-322-2603; Bay St) Head here if you want to take a Junkanoo drum or some CDs home.

GETTING THERE & AWAY

For information on international flights to the Bahamas and Nassau please refer to p288. For travel information between Nassau and other Bahamian islands, please refer to those destinations.

To reach Paradise Island, there are flights operated by **Chalk's Ocean Airways** (OP; ☎ 1-800-424-2557, 242-363-3114; www.flychalks.com; hubs Paradise Island Nassau & Fort Lauderdale), which uses the seaplane landing.

GETTING AROUND
TO/FROM THE AIRPORT

Nassau International Airport (NAS; Map pp64-5; ☎ 242-377-7281) lies 5 miles west of the city.

There are no buses to or from the airport, as the taxi-drivers' union has things sewn up. A few hotels do provide shuttle services, and taxis also line the forecourts of hotels and the area outside the arrivals lounge of the airport. Call the day ahead to book a **taxi** (☎ 242-323-5111/4555). Rates are fixed by the government and displayed at the airport on the wall by the taxi-rank; all destination rates are for two people with standard luggage, while each additional person costs $3.

One-way rates to/from the airport are as follows: Cable Beach $15; downtown Nassau and Prince George Wharf $22; and Paradise Island $27.

Taxi sightseeing rates are usually in the vicinity of $50 per hour, which makes car hire a very attractive option!

Bicycle

Ask at your hotel; most either have bicycles for hire, or can arrange their availability (from $10 per day).

On Paradise Island you can rent bicycles from Club Land'Or ($10 daily) and at Pirate's Cove (around $20 per day). They're single-gear beach cruisers with back-pedal brakes, but the island is flat and bicycling should prove no hardship given the short distances.

Boat

A two-level ferry departs Nassau for Paradise Island from the cruise dock ($3 per person) every 30 minutes, 9:30am to 6pm, departing when full. It deposits passengers at the ferry terminal just west of the Paradise Island Exit Bridge; ferries for Nassau depart here on a regular basis. You'll see the signs or be hustled aboard by touts.

Water taxis also ply the same route between 8am and 6pm, but leave Nassau from Woodes Rogers Walk. They will drop you at any of the Paradise Island wharves upon request.

Car & Scooter

You really don't need a car to explore Nassau, Cable Beach and Paradise Island or to get to their beaches.

However if you intend to explore New Providence, it's worth saving the taxi fare to and from Nassau by hiring a car at the airport. Collision-damage waiver insurance

costs $15 a day. For information on road rules, see p294.

The following companies have rental booths at the airport. (Dollar are the cheapest from around $80 per 24 hours).

Avis Airport (☎ 242-377-7121); Cable Beach (☎ 242-322-2889); Paradise Island (☎ 242-363-2061)
Budget Airport (☎ 242-377-7405); Paradise Island (Map p77; ☎ 242-363-3095)
Dollar Airport (☎ 242-377-8300); Nassau (Map p69; ☎ 242-325-3716; British Colonial Hilton Nassau, 1 Bay St)
Hertz Airport (☎ 242-377-8684)

Several local companies also rent cars that are cheaper, from about $55 daily. Ask your hotel to suggest a company or try **Orange Creek Rentals** (Map pp66-7; ☎ 242-323-4967, 800-891-7655; fax 242-356-5005; W Bay St, Nassau).

Scooters are widely available and can be found outside most major hotels. They cost $50 a day.

Knowles Scooter Rentals (Map p69; ☎ 242-322-3415; Welcome Centre, Festival Pl, Nassau) rents scooters for $30/45 per half-day/day.

You can rent scooters from $40 to $50 daily from Club Land'Or and from rental agencies at Pirate's Cove.

Public Transportation

Nassau and New Providence are well served by jitney buses, which run constantly from 6am to 8pm, although there are no fixed schedules. No buses run to Paradise Island.

All jitney buses depart downtown from Frederick St at Bay St and at designated bus stops. Destinations are clearly marked on the buses, which can be waved down. Likewise to request a stop anywhere when you're onboard, simply ask the driver.

The standard fare is $1 (children $0.75), paid to the driver upon exiting the bus.

Bus Number	Destination
No6	South New Providence
Nos10 & 10A	Cable Beach & Sandy Point
No38	Cable Beach & Prince George Wharf via Over-the-Hill
Nos24 & 30	New Paradise Island Bridge

While there's no bus service to Paradise Island, you can catch Bus 24 or 30 from Frederick St in downtown Nassau to the New Paradise Island Bridge, and then walk over to the island.

SCAM ALERT!

Some taxi drivers may try to charge the third or fourth person the same rate as for two people, or try to charge additional rates for luggage once you reach your destination. Don't agree to these blatant scams – the drivers normally will back down.

On the rare occasion they don't back off, take their license number and report them the next day (☎ 242-323-5111/4555). Most drivers are good folk who are appalled at this sort of behavior.

The 'Casino Express,' operated by Atlantis, runs a clockwise route throughout the day and early evening on Paradise Island, picking up and dropping off passengers at major hotels; the fare is $1 for nonguests of Atlantis.

Western Transportation runs hourly buses from downtown Nassau (opposite the British Colonial Hilton) to Lyford, South Ocean and Compass Point ($2 one way). In the evenings buses only depart from town at 9pm and midnight.

Free shuttle buses run between the Cable Beach hotels from 6pm to 2am.

AROUND NASSAU

WEST NEW PROVIDENCE

Running west from Cable Beach on the island's north shore, W Bay St offers a beautiful drive. The area is favored by the wealthy, who live in upscale homes atop the ridge.

Sights & Activities

One-and-a-half miles west of Delaport Point you'll pass the **Caves**, just east of Blake Rd. This large cavern system once sheltered Lucayan Indians. Just west is **Orange Hill Beach**, shaded by sea grapes and palms. It is undeveloped, except for the Orange Hill Beach Inn (right) hidden on the bluff overlooking the beach, and very popular with Bahamian families.

West of Compass Point is **Love Beach**, a small, little-used beach near Gambier Village. It's known for its snorkeling. Beyond Love Beach, the road turns inland and curls past the small settlement of Mt Pleasant and around **Lyford Cay**, a sprawling walled estate of manicured, tree-lined streets and canals framed by glorious multimillion dollar mansions. Here billionaires and celebrities – Sean Connery for one – protect themselves from the world.

Beyond the Commonwealth Brewery you'll pass the **South Ocean Golf Course** (☎ 242-362-4391, ext 6687; South Ocean Rd, West Providence) and a 5-mile-long beach lining Southwest Bay.

Sleeping & Eating

Compass Point Inn (☎ 242-327-4500; fax 242-327-3299; W Bay St, Gambier Village; r $410, mains $12-35; ☺ breakfast, lunch & dinner; ⓟ ✖ ✖ ▯ ▮) For

pure rock-star fun, stay, eat and drink at recording genius Chris Blackwell's former joint. Although this inn was likely to be resold at the time of research, it was once beloved by musicians recording at Compass Point Studios across the road, as well as by celebs like Naomi Campbell and Cindy Crawford. The octagonal clapboard cottages (some on stilts) boast large windows, cute porches, conical beamed ceilings and rustic yet tasteful furnishings, and edge up to the turquoise sea. The beachside restaurant is known for its wonderful breakfast dishes, such as coconut French toast and hickory-smoked salmon, as well as their lunch and dinner menus. The bar (open noon until late) attracts locals in the know, with an extended happy hour from 4pm to 7pm. Live music adds to the fun on weekends.

Orange Hill Beach Inn (☎ 242-327-7157; orange hil@batelnet.bs; W Bay St, Orange Hill; d $130, mains $15 to $25; ⓟ ✖ ✖ ▮) This casual family-run place, on the bluff overlooking Orange Hill Beach, is preferred for overnights in transit between islands, and offers airport drop-offs. The uninspiring rooms have contemporary furniture, refrigerators, microwaves and toasters. A simple traditional and burger dinner menu changes daily and there's also a bar.

SOUTH NEW PROVIDENCE

Most of this region is backed by mangroves, swampy wetlands and brine pools, parts of which have been used for years as rubbish dumps. Curiously, dozens of minor Christian bodies have erected their little churches along these roads.

On the southwest side of the island, **South Ocean Beach** is narrow, secluded, several miles long, and trodden by very few people. You'll find great scuba-diving offshore.

Adelaide

Adelaide is a quiet village whose nostalgic lifestyle revolves around fishing. Visually it isn't noteworthy, but it is about as close as you can get to traditional life on the island. Seventeen miles southwest of Nassau on a spit of land jutting into a navigable creek rich in conch, fish and lobster, the village dates back to 1832 when it was founded for slaves freed from a Portuguese slave trader,

A hurricane in 1926 wrecked the harbor. In 1990 the Bahamas National Trust initiated a plan to restore Adelaide Creek, and an army of volunteers and schoolchildren from across New Providence showed up to lend a hand. Donations flooded in to replace the causeways with bridges. Finally, on Earth Day the creek's mouth was reopened and a tidal creek was reborn. Almost immediately marine life returned: crabs, shads and even bonefish. Today baby tiger sharks, barracudas, snappers, lobsters and vast armadas of other young fish journey in and out.

The village is fronted by narrow, white-sand **Adelaide Beach**, extending between South Ocean and the village. Fishing boats are drawn up on the beach, and the wharf is lively at sunset when the day's work is done.

For yummy seafood and rum drinks, loiter at **Avery's Restaurant & Bar** (☎ 242-362-1547; Adelaide Village; mains $10-20; ⊙ lunch & dinner), a very popular little restaurant and bar.

Coral Harbour

Coral Harbour Rd leads south to this residential marina community. Several dive and sportfishing operators are based here (see p79), and there's a small beach. The road turns west along the shore, becoming Ranfurly Dr, and dead-ends at the base of the Royal Bahamas Defence Force.

After Fidel Castro's expropriation of the Bacardi family's rum factories during the Cuban Revolution, the family set up its business in other locales, including this site east of Coral Harbour. The **Bacardi Rum Factory** (☎ 242-362-1412; cnr Bacardi & Carmichael Rds; ⊙ tours 10am-3pm Mon-Thu) produces Bacardi rum (the family successfully sued the Castro regime for the Bacardi title) from sugar imported from other Caribbean islands. The free 30-minute guided tours are for eight people or more, but you can hang around in the pavilion, sampling free drinks in the hope that other visitors achieve a quorum.

Grand Bahama

This island is for those who love to spend their days immersed in nature, and then relish the pleasures of a lively bar, good restaurant and comfortable hotel at night. It is also a cheaper and less frenetic place to be than New Providence, despite being the Bahamas second-most popular stop.

The flat, narrow 85 mile-long island is blanketed by miles of upright Cuban pines and dwarf palms and the glorious Lucayan National Park. Grand Bahama's south shore is edged with sugar-white beaches and the warm aquamarine sea. Turtles occasionally emerge from these waters to nest at Gold Rock Creek, Hawksbill Creek and High Rock.

The north shore's mangrove and wetland habitats host colorful birdlife and raccoons meander in the undergrowth. A bracelet of cays to the east is home to the island's fishing industry and villages.

Little curly-tailed lizards are everywhere, scurrying across the sands and pavements of the hotels, golf courses and marinas that are concentrated around Freeport and Lucaya.

The small bars and restaurants of these tourism centers resound with chatter and laughter in the evenings, while strollers choose to enjoy the stars. At weekends *goombay* and reggae rhythms take over Count Basie Plaza, and the adjacent lively market stalls abound with colorful clothing and woven accessories.

Families will appreciate the affordable resorts that provide a heap of beachside and indoor activities for children. The scuba-diving is also fabulous, including opportunities to dive with wild dolphins, while some great ecotours take you kayaking, bicycling and snorkeling through a range of habitats, including the stunning marine parks.

HIGHLIGHTS

- **Kayak** (p109) through mangrove forests, find the world's longest underground cavern and snorkel with fish in Lucayan National Park
- Lounge on the deck of Churchill Beach's **Club Caribe** (p114), toasting the ocean with a cold beer, before the fun of the Friday night pig roast begins
- Gallop on **horseback** (p108) along a deserted southern beach at sunset
- Watch Freeport's **Conchman Triathlon** (p110) competitors strain their way to glory
- Dive in the company of **wild dolphins** (p107) around coral reefs

- TELEPHONE CODE: 242
- POPULATION: 49,566
- AREA: 530 SQ MILES

History

Juan Ponce de León visited Grand Bahama in 1513 while searching for the Fountain of Youth, and pirates marauded their way around the island during the 17th and 18th centuries. The islanders benefited from the pirates' spoils, and briefly from acting as a supply depot for the Confederacy during the US Civil War. Another prosperous time came when Grand Bahama acted as a staging post for rumrunners during Prohibition.

For many decades the islanders then lived meagerly from the proceeds of lumbering, fishing and diving for sponges, until the 1950s when American Wallace Groves and Brit Sir Charles Hayward developed the area. This turned a vast, uninhabited area into a town known as Freeport, complete with an airport and a port with an oil-bunkering storage complex that would prove a bonanza for the Bahamas. (Oil is still purchased, stored and resold to the US at a handsome profit.)

The British crown then granted permission for these men to buy and develop a further 150,000 acres of the island's middle section, which led to the destruction of the remaining West Indian and British architecture. Initial plans for tourism floundered, and Freeport was then (optimistically) promoted as an offshore financial and high-technology industrial center.

The city is still overseen by the Grand Bahama Port Authority, or 'The Port,' set up by Groves. It maintains strict zoning laws, assesses all business licenses, and has the same defining role in matters of commercial probity as the Christian Council has in Nassau.

In 1996 a development group, Sun & Sea Estates, began a major redevelopment project in Lucaya. The five-year, $290 million multiresort project has integrated existing hotels with new hotels, vacation clubs, restaurants, shops, theme parks, a new golf course and golf school, and a marina.

Many hoped that this massive investment would do for Grand Bahama what the Atlantis resort (p78) did for Paradise Island. It is certainly successful. However, hurricanes such as Frances and Jeanne in 2004, badly damaged residential communities, nature reserves and woodlands, as well as many hotels, and certainly dampened the island's hopes.

National Parks

Grand Bahama has some of the country's best parks, which are perfect for those interested in hiking, biking and kayaking, as well as those wanting to sunbathe, stroll and lounge in the shallows! For more information see p39.

Lucayan National Park (p118) contains the world's longest known underwater cave and cavern system, with caves that are habitats for rare underground crustaceans and migratory bats, and mangrove wetlands.

Peterson Cay National Park (p118) is a one to 1½-acre cay that has a striking coral garden.

Another ocean delight is **Walker's Cay** (p173), where several dive operators from Grand Bahama venture to, while the 100-acre **Rand Memorial Nature Centre** (p103) has distinctive flora and fauna.

Dangers & Annoyances

Be careful downtown near Winn Dixie Plaza in Freeport and at Pinder's Point and Eight Mile at night. There have been issues with street lighting in some of these areas since the 2004 hurricanes, and there have been some reports of drug-related violence.

Getting There & Away

Most travelers to Grand Bahama fly into Freeport International Airport, 2 miles north of Freeport, or arrive at Freeport Harbour on the weekly mail boat from Nassau, a fast ferry from Florida or an international cruise ship.

Getting Around

You'll need your own transport if you want to explore the island outside of Freeport or Lucaya, although these two centers are linked by a regular stream of jitney buses. Car rental agencies are located at the airport, and boats can also be easily hired.

FREEPORT & LUCAYA

pop 46,535

Freeport has the characteristic wide, grid-style streets and simple modern buildings of a planned city, but sadly no real community feeling or defined center. Downtown has only a few shops, banks and businesses. Consequently many tourists (wrongly) believe that Freeport's center is around the International Bazaar and Crowne Plaza Resort & Casino Complex, where the hotels are based.

GRAND BAHAMA

GRAND BAHAMA

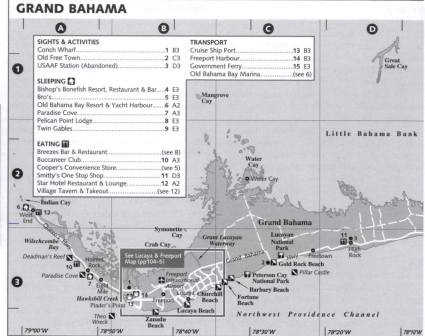

SIGHTS & ACTIVITIES	TRANSPORT
Conch Wharf..................................1 B3	Cruise Ship Port..........................13 B3
Old Free Town..............................2 C3	Freeport Harbour.........................14 B3
USAAF Station (Abandoned)...........3 D3	Government Ferry.........................15 E3
	Old Bahama Bay Marina..............(see 6)
SLEEPING
Bishop's Bonefish Resort, Restaurant & Bar....4 E3
Bro's...5 E3
Old Bahama Bay Resort & Yacht Harbour.......6 A2
Paradise Cove................................7 A3
Pelican Point Lodge........................8 E3
Twin Gables...................................9 E3
EATING
Breezes Bar & Restaurant...............(see 8)
Buccaneer Club.............................10 A3
Cooper's Convenience Store...........(see 5)
Smitty's One Stop Shop..................11 D3
Star Hotel Restaurant & Lounge......12 A2
Village Tavern & Takeout................(see 12)

Lucaya is welldesigned and is a nicer option for those on holiday. It is antiseptic, but there is a great stretch of beach and it is possible to walk easily and safely to surrounding bars, hotels and restaurants. Although Freeport has marginally cheaper accommodation, the facilities in Lucaya are more centralized and offer more choice.

Orientation
Freeport's town center lies 1 mile north of the International Bazaar between West Mall and East Mall Dr. At its heart is **Winn Dixie Plaza**, but the hotels are located a mile south of downtown, centered on Ranfurly Circle and the International Bazaar.

E Sunrise Hwy runs from Ranfurly Circle in Freeport towards Lucaya, where Seahorse Rd turns off to the heart of the Lucaya hotel district. Taino, Churchill, and Fortune Beaches extend east from Lucaya. The Grand Bahama Hwy will take you to the east end of the island and McLean's Town. Queen's Hwy will take you to the West End of Grand Bahama.

Complimentary copies of the *Grand Bahamas Trailblazer Map* are obtainable from most hotel lobbies and tourist retail outlets.

Information
BOOKSTORES & LIBRARIES
Charles Hayward Library (Map pp104-5; ☎ 242-352-7048; E Mall Dr, Freeport)
H&L Bookstore (Map pp104-5; ☎ 242-373-8947; Pt Lucaya Marketplace & Village)

EMERGENCY
Ambulance (☎ 242-352-2689, 911)
Emergency (☎ 911)
Police (☎ 911)

INTERNET ACCESS
Log on Cyber Café (Map pp104-5; ☎ 242-559-0111; Pt Lucaya Marketplace & Village; per 15min $5; ☻ 9am-10pm) For long-distance calls and Internet – although rates are expensive.

MEDICAL SERVICES
LMR Drugs (Map pp104-5; ☎ 242-352-7327; 1 W Mall Dr, Freeport; ☻ 8am-9pm Mon-Sat)

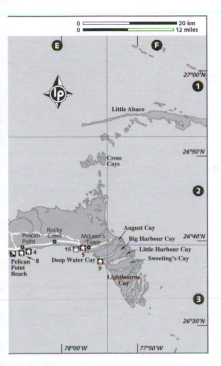

GRAND BAHAMA

Lucayan Medical Centre East (Map pp104-5; ☎ 242-373-7400; E Sunrise Hwy, Lucaya)
Lucayan Medical Centre West (Map pp104-5; ☎ 242-352-7288; Adventurers Way, Freeport)
Rand Memorial Hospital (Map pp104-5; ☎ 242-352-6735; E Atlantic Dr, Freeport)
Sunrise Medical Centre & Hospital (Map pp104-5; ☎ 242-373-3333; E Sunrise Hwy, Lucaya)

MONEY
Bank of the Bahamas (Map pp104-5; ☎ 242-352-7483; cnr Bank Lane & Woodstock St, Freeport)
British American Bank (Map pp104-5; ☎ 242-352-6676; East Mall Dr, Freeport)
First Caribbean International Bank (Map pp104-5; ☎ 242-352-6651; E Mall Dr, Freeport)
Royal Bank of Canada (Map pp104–5; ☎ 242-352-6631; cnr E Mall Dr & Explorers Way, Freeport)
Scotiabank (Map pp104-5; ☎ 242-352-6774; Regent Centre, Freeport)
Western Union (Map pp104-5; ☎ 242-352-6676) Based at the British American Bank.

POST
Post office (Map pp104-5; ☎ 242-352-9371; Explorers Way, Freeport)

FedEx (Map pp104-5; ☎ 242-352-3402; www.fedex.com; Seventeen Plaza, cnr Bank Lane & Explorers Way, Freeport)

TELEPHONE
BaTelCo (Map pp104-5; ☎ 242-352-6220; Pioneer's Way, Freeport) Offers telephone and fax services.

TOURIST INFORMATION
Newspapers such as the daily *Freeport News* (published Monday to Saturday in the afternoons) and the monthly *Freeport Times* are both worth checking out for arts and entertainment information as well as any upcoming sporting events.

What-to-do in Freeport/Lucaya, Grand Bahama is full of handy information and discount coupons, while *Island Magazine* provides information on shopping, dining, and entertainment. *Discover Port Lucaya* has a map of Port Lucaya and discount coupons. All are free publications and can be located in hotel lobbies and tourism outlets.

Also visit the following for information on local events and activities.
Grand Bahama Island Tourism Board (www.grand-bahama.com) Main Office (Map pp104-5; ☎ 242-325-8356); Tourism Booth (Map pp104-5; ☎ 242-352-8356; International Bazaar, Freeport)
Tourism Booth, Freeport International Airport (Map pp104-5; ☎ 242-352-2052)

Sights
INTERNATIONAL BAZAAR
This small, overrated **marketplace** (Map pp104-5; Freeport) lies beyond the Japanese *torii* (gates) on the northwest side of Ranfurly Circle. Ignore the hype; this is not a center of life and activity. There is a small number of tourist shops worth browsing and some very disappointing eateries. Some of the businesses open daily, but others open only when a cruise ship is in town.

RAND MEMORIAL NATURE CENTRE
This headquarters of the Bahamas National Trust is a rewarding 100-acre nature retreat. In 1969 the **centre** (Map pp104-5; ☎ 242-352-5438; East Settlers Way, Freeport; adult/child $5/3; ☺ 9am-4pm Mon-Fri, 9am-1pm Sat) was established as a living memorial to Freeport philanthropist James Rand. There are more than 130 native plant species including a number of weird and wonderful orchids and a native coppice that has grown here since before the time of Columbus.

FREEPORT & LUCAYA

INFORMATION
Bank of the Bahamas.......................1	B2
BaTelCo.......................................2	A3
British American Bank......................3	B2
Charles Hayward Library...................4	B3
Federal Express..............................5	A2
First Caribbean International Bank......6	B3
Grand Bahama Island Tourism Board..(see 7)	
International Bazaar: Info & Eating....7	A5
LMR Drugs...................................8	A2
Log on Cyber Café....................(see 66)	
Lucayan Medical Centre East.............9	E4
Lucayan Medical Centre West..........10	A3
Police..11	A5
Police Station..............................12	A3

Police Station..............................13	G5
Post Office.................................14	A2
Rand Memorial Hospital.................15	B2
Royal Bank of Canada....................16	B2
Scotiabank.................................17	A2
Sunrise Medical Centre..................18	D4
Tourist Information.......................19	D3
Western Union.........................(see 3)	

SIGHTS & ACTIVITIES
Caribbean Divers......................(see 32)	
Dolphin Experience...................(see 37)	
Grand Bahama Brewing Company...20	D4
Hydroflora Gardens......................21	D4
Isle of Capri Casino...................(see 42)	

Lucayan Marina Village..................22	H5
Nautical Adventures..................(see 77)	
Parrot Jungle's Garden of the Grove..23	H3
Pinetree Stables...........................24	E4
Pirates of The Bahamas Beach	
Theme Park.............................25	H5
Regency Theatre..........................26	C4
RND Cinemas..............................27	B4
UNEXSO....................................28	G5
Water World...............................29	D4
Watersports................................30	G5
Xanadu Undersea Adventures.........31	D5

SLEEPING
Bell Channel Inn...........................32	G5
Best Western Castaways Resort.......33	B4
Coral Beach Hotel.........................34	E5
Crowne Plaza Golf Resort & Casino..35	A5
Crowne Plaza Golf Resort & Casino..36	A5
Flamingo Bay Yacht Club And	
Marina...................................37	G4
Island Palm Resort.......................38	B2
Island Seas Resort........................39	E5
Lakeview Manor Club....................40	C4
Ocean Reef Yacht Club & Resort.....41	E5
Our Lucayan Beach & Golf Resort....42	G5
Pelican Bay at Lucaya....................43	G5
Port Lucaya Resort & Yacht Club.....44	G5
Royal Islander Hotel......................45	B5
Running Mon Resort & Marina........46	D5
Taino Beach Resort & Marina..........47	H5

It's worth making a reservation for a guided tour along the half-mile trail that meanders through numerous acres of coppice and pine trees. The tour highlights bush medicine plants, and heads towards a relatively small flock of striding West Indian flamingos. Interestingly, a small indigenous fish, the Bahamian gambusia, keeps the flamingos' pond-water free of mosquito larvae.

Rand is a gathering spot for the endangered Bahama parrot, Cuban emerald hummingbirds, the tiny yet stunning parula, and Antillean peewees. Also spotted are red-tailed hawks, great blue herons, egrets, kingfishers and ospreys.

GRAND BAHAMA

Raccoons and red-eared turtles also call this park home, as do butterflies, tree frogs, some harmless snakes and the curly-tailed lizards that nervously rush everywhere. There's also a replica of a Lucayan village and a gift shop. Guided walks are available at 10am Monday to Friday; bookings required.

HYDROFLORA GARDENS
These landscaped **gardens** (Map pp104-5; ☎ 242-352-6052; cnr East Beach Dr at E Sunrise Hwy, Freeport; adult/child $3/1.50; 🕙 9am-4pm) abounds in shrubs, tropical fruit trees, and fragrant foliage. Highlights include a rock garden, bush medicine plants and a hydroponics garden. Call ahead if you want to take a guided tour ($6).

GRAND BAHAMA

PORT LUCAYA MARKETPLACE & VILLAGE
This **village** (Map pp104–5) is an attractive, low-key waterfront shopping, dining and entertainment precinct that is opposite Our Lucayan Beach & Golf Resort (p111). It is much more appealing than the International Bazaar; at its heart beats Count Basie Sq, where everyone from church choirs to Junkanoo bands performs at weekends and on public holidays.

PARROT JUNGLE'S GARDEN OF THE GROVE
This 12-acre lush **garden** (Map pp104-5; ☎ 242-373-5668; www.gardenofthegroves.com; Midshipman Rd & Magellan Dr, Freeport; adult/child $10/7; 🕐 9am-4pm) had been closed for renovations, so check ahead for updated opening times. There are thousands of species of semitropical plants, a 400ft-long (122m-long) fern gully and a hanging garden, as well as four waterfalls cascading into a placid lake that is ringed with tropical foliage. For children, the highlight is a petting zoo with African pygmy goats, Bahamian raccoons and cuddly Vietnamese pot-bellied pigs as well as caged parrots and flamingos.

The gardens contain a peaceful hillside chapel (used for wedding parties), scenic trails and an on-site café.

GRAND BAHAMA BREWING COMPANY
The island's only **brewery** (Map pp104-5; ☎ 242-351-5191; Logwood Rd, Freeport; 🕐 Mon-Fri) welcomes visitors during business hours to try and buy their Hammerhead Amber Ale and Stout and Lucayan lagers.

BEACHES
The island has gorgeous beaches that suit all moods and tastes. Most of the beaches close to Freeport and Lucaya can be reached via hotel courtesy buses or on foot. To go further afield you will need your own transport or to take an organized tour, but it will be well worth it. The beaches outside the main tourist centers, such as the stunning Gold Rock Beach at Lucayan National Park, are superb and offer tranquility as well as azure seas and white-sand beaches.

Xanadu Beach (Map pp104–5) is a white-sand beach at the southern end of the Mall, and is the most accessible beach from downtown. It extends westward about a half-mile and although not one of Grand Bahama's most lavish beaches, it is great for a day of

sunning or splashing around in the shallows. The beach is dominated by the Xanadu Beach Resort & Marina (p112); a snack bar opens and water sports are on offer when the resort is busy or over the Christmas and Easter breaks. A dive operation is conveniently located onsite.

Silver Point Beach (Map pp104–5) is a narrow stretch of beach east of Xanadu Beach. (They are separated by two marina channels and Silver Point Beach can be accessed from Beachway Dr.) There are a few hawkers, which can be off-putting, but the shallow waters are popular with families and water sports are available year-round. The Island Seas Resort (p112) stands at the eastern end, beside another harbor channel separating Silver Point Beach from Lucaya Beach.

Stunning **Lucaya Beach** (Map pp104–5) runs from the marina to Bell Channel, at the mouth of the Port Lucaya Harbour. There are a long stretch of white sand, water sports and a beach bar (adjacent to the Our Lucayan Beach & Golf Resort) that also whips up burgers and snacks. The central part of the beach doesn't have as many resort guests and is great for a stroll. The beach can also be accessed from various suburban roads.

East of Bell Channel lays the long and languorous **Taino Beach** (Map pp104–5) with talcum-powder sand and occasional water sports, as well as the Taino Beach Resort (p112) condos. Most of the year there are few people here, making it even more attractive to those who prefer solitude. To the north of the beach is the waterfront residential community of **Smith's Point**.

Two of the most gorgeous beaches, **Churchill** and **Fortune** (Map pp104–5), extend several miles east of Taino Beach, separated by Sanctuary Bay, a marina complex lined with the holiday homes of the well-heeled. The Viva Wyndham Fortuna Beach (p112) sits behind Fortune Beach but there is plenty of space for all to enjoy the beauty of these beaches.

Farther east, beyond the Grand Lucayan Waterway, is secluded and **Barbary Beach** (Map pp102–3). Each spring its shoreline bursts into bloom with white spider lilies.

Activities
DIVING & SNORKELING
The diving here is considered some of the best in the Bahamas. As well as the dolphin,

shark and cave dives, wreck-dive fans will
love the thrill of swimming through *Theo*, a
240ft-long sunken freighter, where you can
safely wiggle through the hold and engine
room, and visit the friendly resident moray
eels. Other enjoyable wrecks include two
Spanish galleons, the *Santa Gertrude* and
San Ignacio, which ran aground in 1682 off
the south shore near present-day Lucaya.

Another popular dive spot is East End
Paradise, an underwater coral range.

All dive operators offer snorkel trips that
include transportation (adult/child $45/30).
Some of the more popular and established
dive and snorkel operators include:
Underwater Explorers Society, UNEXSO (Map
pp104-5; ☎ 242-373-1244; www.unexso.com; Pt
Lucaya Marina) Offers facilities for those wanting to
qualify as scuba divers. They also have a full range of dive
programs, including a two-tank dive for $70; equipment
hire is $43. A four-hour learning to dive course ($90) is
available as well as specialist dives with wild dolphins
and sharks. Reservations are required.
Xanadu Undersea Adventures (Map pp104–5;
☎ 242-352-3811; www.xanadudive.com; Xanadu
Beach & Marina, Freeport) Offers two-tank dives ($70),
night dives ($55) and PADI certification courses ($450).
There are reduced rates if you buy a minimum of 10
dives (which can be shared amongst divers).
Caribbean Divers (Map pp104–5; ☎ 242-373-9111;
Bell Channel Inn, Pt Lucaya Marina) Runs NAUI certification
courses ($350) and offers various dive options including
two-tank dives ($65) and night dives ($70).
Pat & Diane Fantasia Tours (☎ 242-373-8681;
www.snorkelingbahamas.com; adult/child $35/18) Offers
two-hour snorkeling and fish-feeding trips to shallow coral
reefs on their Snorkeling Sea Safari. The trip on their 72ft
catamaran, which has an in-built 30ft waterslide and a
20ft rock-climbing wall is great fun.
Reef Tours (☎ 242-373-5880; www.bahamasvg
.com/reeftours) Offers snorkeling and fish-feeding tours
(adult/child $35/16) and a fabulous sailing and snorkel
tour (adult/child $45/25).
Paradise Cove (☎ 242-349-2677; www.deadmansreef
.com) There is a vibrant reef in the shallows just off the cove
here. Unless you're staying at the resort (p120), pay your access fee ($3), hire your snorkel gear ($10 per day) and jump
in. Guided snorkeling tours are also available and include
snorkel hire, lunch and transportation (adult/child $35/23).

Cave Diving
Experienced divers can check out Ben's
Cave, part of Lucayan National Park, by
following cables through 7 miles of underwater caves. A permit must first be obtained

from **Underwater Explorers Society, UNEXSO** (Map
pp104-5; ☎ 242-373-1244; www.unexso.com; Pt Lucaya
Marina).

DOLPHIN & SHARK ENCOUNTERS
There are some great options here for encounters with dolphins that live in a lagoon,
but also swim freely in the ocean. The Close
Encounter trip run by UNEXSO (adult/
child aged 4 and under $75/free) is great for
nondivers and children, who receive an educational lecture and then stand waist-deep
in a sheltered lagoon, where they meet dolphins well-accustomed to humans.

You can swim in the lagoon with the
dolphins ($170), while on a full-day Open
Ocean Dolphin Experience ($200) you will
learn how to interact with dolphins from
the lagoon using hand signals, but in the
outer ocean.

A Dolphin Dive trip ($160) involves en-
joying these creatures' company in the outer
ocean. All of these are hugely popular activities and advance bookings are required.

Adrenaline junkies will jump at the
chance to dive among feeding Caribbean
reef sharks at Shark Junction. Two divers
armed with sticks are on hand to ward off
wayward sharks. A cameraperson will record
your experience on video for an extra fee.
The dive adds $40 to normal dive rates and
reservations are necessary.

BONEFISHING & SPORTFISHING
The Gulf Stream, off the west coast of Grand
Bahama, teems with game fish. The Northwest Providence Channel drops to 2000ft
just 400yd off the south shore, where snapper and barracuda are prevalent. And bonefishing (half-/full-day $250/350) is superb
on the flats of the Little Bahama Bank to the
north and east of the island.

Deep-sea fishing per person costs around
$70 to $90 per half-day. **Night Hawk Fishing**
(Map pp104-5; ☎ 242-373-7226; Pt Lucaya Marina) offers half-day charter fishing trips from $65.
Other chapter operators include:
HG Forbes Charters & Tours (p109; ☎ 242-352-9311;
bahamas@forbescharter.com)
Nautical Adventures (Map pp104-5; ☎ 242-373-
7180; Port Lucaya Marina)
Reef Tours (☎ 242-373-5880; www.bahamasvg
.com/reeftours)
Running Mon Marina (Map pp104–5; ☎ 242-352-
6834; close to Xanadu Beach)

BOAT EXCURSIONS

There is a range of different trips offering underwater sightseeing, beach parties, on-board dining, dancing and partying.

Most hotels have booking desks for these tours. If your hotel doesn't, walk into the nearest one and book from there. Transfers are usually provided. If your time on the island is limited, see opposite as some operators combine land and water excursions.

Pat & Diane Fantasia Tours (☎ 242-373-8681; www.snorkelingbahamas.com) run snorkeling trips as well as a Steak & Lobster Cruise (adult/child $70/45), an adults-only Mango Tango Evening Cruise ($35), and a Deserted Island & Beach Party trip (adult/child $70/40) where you head off to the marine park at Peterson Cay for snorkeling and then on to private beaches for swimming, sunning, lunch and drinks.

Reef Tours (☎ 242-373-5880; www.bahamasvg .com/reeftours) has a Sunset Bar Sailing Cruise ($40) and a glass-bottomed boat tour, where a diver feeds fish underwater for your benefit (adult/child $25/15). Fish-feeding is also on offer (adult/child $45/30).

Superior Watersports (☎ 242-373-7863) runs two very popular party tours on board the *Bahama Mama*. The Robinson Crusoe Beach Party includes a 1½-hour snorkeling trip followed by lunch, drinks and beach games on a deserted beach (adult/child $60/40) and the Bahama Mama Booze Cruise which is a drink and dance party (hot and cold hors d'oeuvres, and all the Bahama Mama cocktails and wine you can drink) held on Tuesday, Thursday and Saturday ($30). Dinner cruises with limbo dancing (adult/child $70/45) and sunset dinner cruises ($40) are also on offer.

Seaworld Explorer (☎ 242-373-7863; adult/child $40/25) offers a two-hour trip on a glass-bottomed boat which saves your hairdo and brings you closer to the marine world.

WATER SPORTS

Most resort hotels rent snorkel gear ($10), sea kayaks ($20), Sunfish dinghies ($20) and equipment for other water sports. Independent concessions on most beaches offer parasailing ($60), banana boat rides (adult/child $15/10), waterskiing ($40) and windsurfing ($30).

Ocean Motion (☎ 242-374-2425; oceanltd@batelnet .bs; Our Lucayan Beach & Golf Resort, Lucaya) has virtually every water sport under the sun, including water trampolines (half-day $10), and also rents out boats (half-/full-day $130/260).

Paradise Watersports (☎ 242-373-4001; pwsports@ batelnet.bs; Island Seas Beach & Viva Wyndham Fortuna Beach) has water sports including waverunners ($60 per 30 min).

Sea Affairs Watersports (☎ 242-352-9311; Xanadu Beach Resort & Marina) rents out glass-bottomed kayaks ($20 per day).

GOLF

The island has five championship courses, and all clubs rent equipment and carts.

The Emerald & Ruby Golf Courses are part of the Crowne Plaza Golf Resort & Casino (p110) and Royal Oasis complex, which was undergoing extensive renovations during 2005. Green fees are $95 for 18 holes.

Fortune Hills Golf & Country Club (Map pp104-5; ☎ 242-373-4500; E Sunrise Hwy, Freeport) is popular with beginners. Games cost $70.

Our Lucayan Beach & Golf Resort (Map pp104-5; ☎ 242-373-1066; Balao & Midshipman Rds, Lucaya) contains plenty of water hazards. The Butch Harmon School of Golf is based here. Harmon, an ex-PGA touring pro, was credited with modifying Tiger Wood's game. Green fees are $120.

Reef Golf Course (Map pp104-5; ☎ 242-373-2002; Seahorse Rd) is the island's largest course at 6920yd. Games are $120.

HORSEBACK RIDING

There are some grand places on the island to take a horse for a gallop, and both experienced and amateur riders are welcomed by operators.

Pinetree Stables (Map pp104-5; ☎ 242-373-3600; www.pinetree-stables.com; Beachway Dr; $75) takes two-hour horseback rides, where you gallop through pine forests, along the southern shore and through the shallows.

Trikk Pony Adventures (☎ 242-374-4449; leo@ trikkpony.com) offers free transportation for its 1½-hour beach horseback rides ($75). The operators say you will get wet when riding through the surf. For those inclined to make the most of these glorious romantic sunsets, horses can also be provided for weddings.

TENNIS

Most resorts have tennis courts and will rent out courts and equipment to 'walk-ins' and guests. Typical hourly fees are $10 to $20 or $20 to $28 for night play.

Our Lucayan Beach & Golf Resort (Map pp104-5; ☎ 242-373-1333; www.ourlucaya.com; Seahorse Rd, Lucaya) Has grass, hard and clay courts that are lit at night.

Crowne Plaza Golf Resort & Casino (Map pp104-5; ☎ 242-350-7000; www.theroyaloasis.com; W Mall Dr & W Atlantic Av, Freeport) Several hard courts are lit at night.

Xanadu Beach Resort & Marina (Map pp104-5; ☎ 242-352-6783; www.xanadubeachhotel.com) Will also hire out their hard courts to nonguests.

Tours

One way of seeing the sights would be to book a taxi through the **Grand Bahama Taxi Union** (☎ 242-352-7858/7101). Expect to pay about $50 per hour.

CITY TOURS & FURTHER AFIELD

All the hotels can book you onto city bus tours (adult/child $25/18). These will generally take you to Freeport's International Bazaar (p103), liquor stores as well as the Parrot Jungle's Garden of the Groves (p106). Entry fees are included in the price.

HG Forbes Charter & Tours (☎ 242-352-9311; bahamas@forbescharter.com) offers the Super Combination Tour (adult/child $35/25), a similar tour to the East End that also takes in Millionaire Row and the home of Count Basie, as well as the West End Tour that includes Eight Mile Rock and covers local history and folklore (adult/child $40/30).

Capron's Charter & Tours (☎ 242-352-9262; caproncharters@hotmail.com) also tours Freeport's sights and markets in a Super Combination Tour (adult/child $35/25) and the Lucayan National Park in the East End Experience (adult/child $35/25). Tours also explore the bush medicine plants and fauna of Rand Memorial Nature Centre (adult/child $35/25).

NATURE TOURS

East End Adventures (☎ 242-373-6662; www.bahamasecotours.com) offers Blue Hole Snorkeling Safari (adult/child $85/35). Several spectacular snorkeling sites are visited by speedboat and on foot, including a blue hole and blue-hole lagoon. Lunch is provided. Their Out Island Cultural Safari Tour ($110) is an adults-only day that includes hiking, snorkeling and cay-hopping.

Kayak Nature Tours (☎ 242-373-2485; www.grandbahamanaturetours.com) leads sea kayaking tours from Freeport into Lucayan National Park, also biking tours ($80) and kayaking/snorkeling trips ($70). These trips relish the natural quiet and splendor of the park and its many scaled, furry and feathered inhabitants. The certified and trainee guides really know their stuff.

Lucayan National Park & Cave Tour (☎ 242-373-7863; adult/child $40/30) has experienced guides to take you to the caves where Lucayan Indians once lived in part of the world's longest underground cavern, and to introduce you to the birds and wildlife of this glorious 42-acre park.

PEOPLE TO PEOPLE

The Bahamas Ministry of Tourism's 'People to People' program puts you in touch with locals who share their visitors' interests or professions. Call the **Grand Bahama Island Tourism Board** (Map pp104-5; ☎ 242-325-8044; www.grand-bahama.com; International Bazaar, Freeport) for information.

Festivals & Events

For information on these events and many others, contact the Grand Bahama Island Tourism Board (see p103).

JANUARY

New Year's Day Junkanoo Parade The flamboyant music, dancing and costumes of Boxing Day's Junkanoo are publicly judged and awarded, with much crowd support and hollering.

MARCH

Annual Easter Rugby Festival Join in with the Freeport Rugby Club supporters to cheer on their star players.

JUNE

Sailing Regatta A huge three days full of self-made boats, racing, and much hollering and onshore partying.
Bahamas Heritage Festival Music, the arts and the island's history are all celebrated this month.

JULY

Sweeting's Cay Homecoming A grand event with live bands, cultural performances, kid's activities, and plenty of food and drinks.

AUGUST

Bernie Butler BASRA Marathon Swim A 2-mile ocean marathon race, starting off Lucaya Beach.
Emancipation Day These public holiday and associated celebrations mark the abolition of slavery.

SEPTEMBER
Small Boat Tournament A four-day fishing tournament, which sets off from Port Lucaya Marina, features small boats and massive fish.
Grand Bahama Island Jazz, R&B Festival Two days of local and international artists keep it cool.
Latin Jazz Festival Three days of local and international artists make it hot.

OCTOBER
Kalik Junkanoo Rushout Held at Taino Beach, where Junkanoo shacks compete for the Best Music title.
Red Rose Ball A fundraising black-tie event with proceeds dedicated to those living with HIV/AIDS.
Halloween Party Count Basie Sq is the setting for children aged 12 and under to wreak havoc with games, music, a haunted house and a costume competition.

NOVEMBER
Bahamas Wahoo Fishing Championship Season-opening tournament for this celebrated national competition starts from Port Lucaya Marina.
Mini Cricket Festival Involves local and international teams at the Lucayan Cricket Club.
Grand Bahama Conchman Triathlon (www.conchman.com) Amateur athletes are tested to the limit with a ½-mile swim, 20-mile bike ride, and 3½-mile run. Exhausted just reading about this one? Then just watch with a coconut ice cream and your feet up.

DECEMBER
Festival Noel The Rand Memorial Nature Centre party has fine wine, art and crafts, food, live music, face painting, pony rides and a visit from Santa.
Junkanoo Boxing Day Parade A highlight of the social calendar, the parade kicks off at 5am with costumed revelers and a cacophony of sounds. The build up to this starts the January before, with practices downtown near the post office.
Port Lucaya New Year's Eve Celebration Put on your dancing shoes for non-stop dancing in between the drinking and the fireworks.

Sleeping
Budget hotel options are not impossible to find as nearly all accommodations here offer great specials that make a holiday much more affordable than Nassau, even in peak season.

Another very good budget and midrange option is apartment rentals. These can be great value, with studio units for two people renting from $85/450 per night/week from mid-December to mid-April. The apartments are generally bright and light with wicker furniture and all the mod-cons including fully-equipped kitchens. One- and two-bedroom apartments can sleep from two to six people.

Try contacting **Thompsons Real Estate** (☎ 242-373-9050; www.thompsonsrealestate.com; Freeport) which rent out a range of apartments from studios to two-bed units (mainly around Lucaya).

Many hotels in Grand Bahama also contain privately-owned condos that they rent out (on behalf of the owners), alongside their usual hotel rooms. These condos have the advantage of well-equipped kitchens and more privacy, yet guests can still use the hotel facilities.

Expect to pay additional taxes and service charges on all accommodations (see p270).

FREEPORT
Island Palm Resort (Map pp104-5; ☎ 242-352-6648; ispalm@batelnet.bs; cnr Explorers Way & E Mall Dr; r $70; P ⊠ ✖ ⊒ ⊠) Let's just say that 'resort' is an exaggeration, and that there are some dingy rooms. There is a small pool, it's very cheap (ongoing Internet specials in peak season bring daily room rates down to $56), and a free daily bus takes guests to beaches and into town. The Safari Restaurant & Nightclub keeps the motel lively at night, but good security stops things from getting too rowdy.

Crowne Plaza Golf Resort & Casino (Map pp104-5; ☎ 242-350-7000; www.theroyaloasis.com; Mall Dr & W Atlantic Av; r $100; P ⊠ ✖ ⊒ ⊠) The resort at the Royal Oasis complex carried out pretty extensive hurricane repairs and renovations in 2005 to comprehensively update this vast, lush resort. Cleverly designed as a family-friendly complex, it has pools and waterslides, tropical gardens, tennis courts, a gym, a spa, indoor and outdoor games, watersports, and a new beach lagoon and water park. Seven restaurants include the children-only Odie (where kids can be left to eat with free hotel supervision for an hour), the Fat Cat Beach Club (☺ 9am-9pm, for kids aged three years and over) and baby-sitting facilities (from $20). Golf fans are well taken care of with two championship 18-hole courses, and those inclined can enjoy the casino's temptations. Revelers will relish the Tonic nightclub and for the simple hedonists, surely a swim-up pool bar and a steady stream of multihued cocktails will suffice? Accommodation is in two separate locations; the Crowne Plaza Tower adjacent to the casino contains more luxurious rooms with bright comfortable and classical furnishings, while the self-contained Crowne Plaza Country Club is next to the gardens. Rooms here are decorated with lively tropical decor and cool tiled floors, and are arranged in a circle around a splendid water park. All rooms have TV, fridge and coffee-making facilities.

Best Western Castaways Resort (Map pp104-5; ☎ 242-352-6682; www.castaways-resort.com; E Mall Dr; r $110; P ⊠ ⊠ ⊡ ⊡) This new hotel is spotless and offers large, light and comfortably furnished modern rooms with cable TV and balconies. Facilities include a reasonably priced restaurant and full-sized pool. It's only a five-minute walk to the casino complex and courtesy buses go to two beaches. Security is great and so are the staff.

Lakeview Manor Club (Map pp104-5; ☎ 242-352-9789; lakeview@coralwave.com; adjacent to Ruby Golf Course; r $100; P ⊠ ⊠ ⊡) Well-maintained studio ($85), one-bed ($100) and two-bed ($115) rental apartments are available here. All units have great weekly rates, fully-equipped kitchens, comfortable furnishings and cable TV. Guest facilities include spacious grounds, a generous-sized pool, an on-site laundry, complimentary town and beach buses, baby-sitting services and some poolside social activities.

Royal Islander Hotel (Map pp104-5; ☎ 242-351-6000; www.royalislanderhotel.com; E Mall Dr; r $124; ⊠ ⊠ ⊡) This attractive two-story property is centered on a courtyard with a pool and shady palms. It's a few minutes' walk to the casino complex and rooms are large, cheerfully furnished with bright prints and there's heaps of light. Rooms come with an in-room safe, cable TV and phone, but unfortunately no tea- or coffee-making facilities. There's also a Jacuzzi, restaurant and children's playground.

LUCAYA
Bell Channel Inn (Map pp104-5; ☎ 242-373-1053; www.bahamasvg.com; King's Rd, Pt Lucaya Marina; r $80; P ⊠ ⊠ ⊡) All taxes and service charges are included in the rates for these lodgings situated off Jolly Roger Dr on the east side of Bell Channel and Port Lucaya Marina. Older rooms have dated facilities, but all rooms overlook the marina and are only

THE AUTHOR'S CHOICE
Our Lucaya Beach & Golf Resort (Map pp104-5; ☎ 242-373-2396; www.ourlucaya.com; Seahorse Rd, Lucaya; r $320; P ⊠ ⊠ ⊡ ⊡) Incorporating two main accommodations; the Westin and less expensive Sheraton hotels, this attractive open complex is brilliant for both couples and families who want everything within easy reach.

The resort sits on 7 acres of public beachfront, and incorporates numerous restaurants, bars (with dance floors), casino, three great swimming pools with slides totaling 50,000 sq ft (4645 sq meter), kids' facilities, the Port Lucaya Marketplace & Village promenade of boutiques, cafés, bars and shops, and two 18-hole golf courses, all linked by a ¾-mile boardwalk.

Special deals bring rates down to as low as $200 in peak season. If this place suits your bank balance, gambling mother-in-law, golf-fanatic partner and kids who are attention-span challenged, you should book soon.

a 10-minute walk to Port Lucaya Marketplace & Village or 15-minute walk to Lucaya Beach. Facilities include a restaurant and on-site dive operation.

Port Lucaya Resort & Yacht Club (Map pp104-5; ☎ 242-373-6618; www.portlucayaresort.com; Bell Channel Rd, Pt Lucaya Marina; r $100; P ⊠ ⊠ ⊡) This lodging wins the prize for the best location for the most reasonable rates in Lucaya. Although 'resort' is an optimistic description, 10 two-story units encircle a lawn and a full-sized pool with Jacuzzi. The rooms are light, spacious and spotless, all of them have patios or balconies. Some look out over the full-service marina. Adjacent to Port Lucaya's Marketplace & Village's plaza of bars and restaurants, it is a five-minute walk across the road to the Our Lucaya Beach & Golf Resort and that lovely beach.

Coral Beach Hotel (Map pp104-5; ☎ 242-373-2468; www.bahamasvg.com/coralbeach; Royal Palm Way; r $110; P ⊠ ⊠ ⊡) The neat little units at this high-rise condo are a great and affordable beachfront option (rates are inclusive of taxes and charges). Although the building can get warm in the hotter months, individual units do have air-con and there is a small pool onsite. It is about a 20-minute walk to Port Lucaya Marketplace & Village. Balconies overlook the gardens and private parking facilities. Popular with retired couples, this is not suitable for children or party animals!

Pelican Bay at Lucaya (Map pp104-5; ☎ 242-373-9550; www.pelicanbayhotel.com; Pt Lucaya Marina; r $165; P ⊠ ⊠ 🖳 🖳) This award-winning boutique hotel is pretty luxurious, and it's a five-minute walk to Port Lucaya Marketplace & Village. Although part of the Our Lucayan Beach & Golf Resort, it maintains its distance and intimacy. The contemporary but soothing rooms are excellent, and are equipped with TV, phone, safe, refrigerator, coffee machine and private balcony. Hotel guests can use their own small on-site pool and bar, hot tub and restaurant as well as all of the resort's facilities.

THE BEACHES

Island Seas Resort (Map pp104-5; ☎ 242-373-1271; iseas@batelnet.bs; 123 Silver Point Dr, Silver Point Beach; r $120-220; P ⊠ ⊠ 🖳) Tucked away on its own, this intimate resort sits on a small beach and is highly popular with families. One- and two-bedroom self-contained units surround Coconuts Grog and Grub Bar (their beachside bar) and facilities include a pool with swim-up bar, plus tennis court, shuffleboard court and water sports. A complimentary bus runs into town.

Running Mon Resort & Marina (Map pp104-5; ☎ 242-352-6834; www.running-mon-bahamas.com; 208 Kelly Court, near Xanadu Beach; r $100; P ⊠ ⊠ 🖳) Although this place is a good hike to the beach or town, it is attractive, peaceful and good value. Additionally, free transport is offered to Xanadu Beach (a 20-minute walk) and Freeport. The marina-view rooms have colorful floral furnishings, TV, fridge and safe. There is also the popular Mainsail Restaurant & Bar, a children's playground, dive shop, deep-sea fishing charters, tennis courts and a swimming pool.

Taino Beach Resort & Marina (Map pp104-5; ☎ 242-373-4677; Jolly Roger Dr, Taino Beach; r weekly $850) Located at the far west end of Taino Beach, near Port Lucaya, these beachside condos and their *Pirates of the Bahamas* theme park were badly damaged during the 2004 hurricanes and were still undergoing renovations at the time of research. Popular with families, the self-contained apartments have good-value weekly rates.

Flamingo Bay Yacht Club & Marina (Map pp104-5; ☎ 242-373-4677; www.flamingobayhotel.com; Port Lucaya

Marina; P ⊠ ⊠ 🖳) The sibling to Taino Beach Resort & Marina, these lodgings sit across the marina from Taino Beach. Rooms come with microwaves, coffeemakers and toasters, and all have balconies. The rooms are small but nice, with simple decor. However the lodgings feel tired and the staff are not as helpful as they could be. Hourly water taxis will take you across to Taino Beach.

Xanadu Beach Resort & Marina (Map pp104-5; ☎ 242-352-6783; www.xanadubeachhotel.com; Xanadu Beach; r $145; P ⊠ ⊠ 🖳) This high-rise and isolated hotel looks over small Xanadu Beach and all the rooms have private balconies. The hotel obviously was once grand, (Howard Hughes locked himself up complete with his toenail and urine collections on the 12th and 13th floors for two years until his death in 1976.) However the hotel is now faded and its staff are not exactly enthusiastic. The rooms are spacious and comfortably furnished, rates are negotiable and there are tennis courts and water sports, plus an on-site dive shop and a fully serviced marina.

Ocean Reef Yacht Club & Resort (Map pp104-5; ☎ 242-373-4662; www.oryc.com; Bahamas Reef Blvd off Coral Rd, nr Silver Point Beach; r $260; P ⊠ ⊠ 🖳) Boaters love this quiet and tucked-away club that has rows of townhouses and suites with Jacuzzis that sits alongside the marina. The grounds and lodgings are wellmaintained, the rooms are attractive and comfortable, and the facilities are very nice. There are two swimming pools, one with a swim-up bar (that also serves hot snacks), hot tubs, a guest laundry and complimentary buses to town and the beach as part of the package.

Viva Wyndham Fortuna Beach (Map pp104-5; ☎ 242-373-4000; www.vivaresorts.com; Fortune Beach; d/q $180/130; P ⊠ ⊠ 🖳 🖳) This sprawling resort is not flashy and some of the facilities are a bit dated, but it has a large pool and sun deck and backs onto its best feature, a really beautiful section of beach. Packages can be inclusive of meals and there are tons of family activities; dance lessons, volleyball, bingo, karaoke, table tennis, and a good kids' club that runs a minidisco each evening for the children before a nightly show.

Eating & Drinking

Hotels tend to have at least one in-house café or restaurant, while resorts offer a choice of casual and formal dining rooms and bars which are always open to non-guests.

There are a heap of informal places to eat in the Port Lucaya Marketplace & Village; on Thursday nights and at weekends the atmosphere is enlivened by the plaza's live music and DJ nights.

FREEPORT

Gelati Silvano's (Map pp104–5; 242-352-5110; Ranfurly Circle, E Mall Dr at E Sunrise Hwy; mains $9-18; lunch & dinner, closed Mon) Making the best coffee and homemade gelati in town, this elegant and cheerful restaurant also serves a good plate of pasta. Dishes such as beef with mushrooms and white-wine sauce, and vegetarian lasagna keep the locals happy.

Islander's Roost (Map pp104–5; 242-352-5110; Ranfurly Circle, E Mall Dr at E Sunrise Hwy; mains $28-42; lunch & dinner, closed Sun) Adjoining Silvano's, this lofty restaurant is a steak-lover's paradise and vegetarian's nightmare. Large portions of beef in different satisfying guises are accompanied by live entertainment on most nights.

Geneva's Place (Map pp104–5; 242-352-5085; cnr E Mall Dr & Kipling Lane; mains $5-10; breakfast & lunch) For good Bahamian food, this is the place. The fish, peas 'n' rice are great and the guava duff (sweet dumpling with guava purée) is virtually drowned in a milky rum sauce.

Pepperpot (Map pp104–5; 242-373-7655; 8 E Sunrise Hwy; mains $6; breakfast, lunch & dinner) This takeout reputedly serves the island's best peas 'n' rice and fried chicken. Stopping here at night is not recommended, though.

The **International Bazaar** (see p103) has more than a dozen places to eat; but most are highly forgettable. The following are popular for quick meals.

Zorba's (Map pp104–5; 242-352-4185; International Bazaar; mains $5-12; breakfast & lunch) The sibling to Zorba's in Port Lucaya Marketplace & Village, you will see a steady stream of working Bahamians come here for their breakfast and lunchtime takeouts. This is the Bazaar's best grub; try the authentic Greek salads and breakfast omelettes for simple but good food.

Le Rendezvous (Map pp104–5; 242-352-9610; International Bazaar; mains $10-20; breakfast, lunch & dinner) Opening when the cruise ships are in port, this outdoor restaurant has breakfast specials from $3 along with a range of

good-value ethnic meals. Dishes include a range of savory and sweet soups. The aromatic onion with melted cheese and chilled mango soup (made with cream, rum, ginger and nutmeg) are both delicious.

Cafe Michel's (Map pp104–5; 242-352-2191; International Bazaar; mains $9-20; breakfast, lunch & dinner) This alfresco café opens every day, serving an ambitious range of Bahamian and American dishes from black-bean soup to cheeseburgers, steak and some upmarket seafood dishes. The food here is pretty ordinary, but it is popular with many visitors seeking a quick bite to eat.

Also recommended for its European cuisine is **Ruby Swiss** (Map pp104–5; 242-352-8507; cnr W Sunrise Hwy & W Atlantic Dr; mains $18-30; lunch & dinner). For a drink and to watch some sport, try the **Red Dog Sports Bar** (242-352-2700) or have an old-fashioned drink and a chat the **Prince of Wales Lounge** (242-352-2700), both located in the **Pub on the Mall** (Map pp104–5; 242-352-5110; Ranfurly Circus, W Sunrise Hwy).

The **Western Bakery** and **Produce Market** (Map pp104–5) at Winn Dixie Plaza are good for bread and groceries.

LUCAYA

All the following eateries and bars are located in the **Port Lucaya Marketplace & Village** (see p106). Count Basie Sq sits in the middle of this plaza and hosts a stage for live performers. There is a great atmosphere at the square's surrounding small bars where people perch on bar stools to sip cold beers and exotic cocktails or wander into one of the neighboring eateries for a range of ethnic dishes.

Zorba's (Map pp104–5; 242-373-6137; mains $8-15; breakfast, lunch & dinner) Enjoy your meal alfresco beneath a canopy of grapevines and pink bougainvillea. Tasty, reasonably priced breakfasts and Greek cuisine, such as moussaka and Greek salad for $10, are drawcards.

Luciano's (Map pp104–5; 242-373-9100; mains $20-40; lunch & dinner, closed Sun) Specializing in Italian and French fare, this food is simply delicious. Try any of the day's specials and seafood dishes. Also enjoy the balcony's harbor and plaza views with a predinner drink.

Pisces Seafood Restaurant (Map pp104–5; 242-373-5192; mains $18-35; dinner till late, closed Sun) Wonderful things are done with seafood,

GRAND BAHAMA

pasta, garlic, butter and cream at this small and charming restaurant. Pizzas add to the fattening and thoroughly wicked options presented here.

Caribbean Cafe (Map pp104–5; ☎ 242-373-5866; mains $6-18; ☯ breakfast, lunch & dinner) A pleasant, clean and cheerful little place, this café is wellsuited for breakfasts, salads and a sandwich.

Also recommended for food or pre-dinner drinks, these bars are all open for lunch and dinner:

Rum Runners (Map pp104–5; ☎ 242-373-7233) Has ice-cold Red Stripe beer and friendly chatter.

Happy Bar & Lounge (Map pp104–5; ☎ 242-373-6852) A sports bar with a large-screen TV that shows all the big games.

Shenanigan's Irish Pub (Map pp104–5; ☎ 242-373-4734) Serves Guinness.

Pub at Lucaya (☎ 242-373-8450) The place for Brits and lovers of great pub grub.

THE BEACHES

The beachside hotels and resorts listed in Sleeping (p110) all have bars, most of them beachside, that will happily indulge you with fruity rum cocktails or an icy, golden beer. Most of these bars also serve snacks.

Coconuts Beach Restaurant & Bar (Map pp104-5; ☎ 242-373-1271; Island Seas Resort, Silver Point Beach) This popular poolside bar has a happy hour nightly from 4pm and serves a range of fried goodies, perfect to eat with sandy fingers and a cold drink.

Stoned Crab (Map pp104-5; ☎ 242-373-1442; Taino Beach; mains $22-30; ☯ dinner) This classic two-story restaurant overlooks the sea and beach and serves its specialty to many amateur gourmands, namely the seafood platter: lobster, crab, mahi-mahi and shrimp. Crab-cake appetizers are also yum. Seafood dishes dominate the menu and guarantee a full house, so book ahead.

Tranquillity Shores (Map pp104-5; ☎ 242-374-4460; Taino Beach; mains $6-10; ☯ lunch Sun-Thu, dinner Fri & Sat) An all-timber beachfront bar is enhanced by nets and driftwood and a mix of visitors and locals keen to enjoy the party atmosphere on weekends. Situated next to the Stoned Crab, many head to this bar for predinner drinks, or stop for a Bigmouth Burger and chilled Kalik beer after an energetic day on the beach. It's open until late on Fridays and Saturday nights.

THE AUTHOR'S CHOICE

Club Caribe (Map pp104-5; ☎ 242-373-6866; Mather Town off Midshipman Rd, Churchill Beach; mains $8-12; ☯ 11am-6pm Sun & Tue, 11am-10pm Wed-Sat) As soon as you walk onto their wooden deck with a chilled beer in hand and look out over the wide, blue ocean and deserted beach, you'll understand this recommendation.

Hidden away from the madding crowds, this restaurant/bar is simple, homely and a marvelously friendly place to hang out. Bahamians gather here for great peppery fish salads and Friday night pig roasts, as well as live Bahamian music on Friday and Saturday nights (hotel transfers are provided). Whether you're here for a long tasty lunch, convivial dinner or a rum-fueled celebration of the sunset, you won't be disappointed with the ambience, food or surroundings.

Entertainment

The resorts offer in-house entertainment and shows as well as live music and plenty of opportunities to trip the light fantastic. Hotels also host frequent beach parties, which include bonfires and BBQs (remember your mosquito repellent).

Many of the evening boat excursions (see p108) are tremendous fun, providing liberal drinks, liberating music and lithe limbo dancers; a great way to spend an evening or two.

NIGHTCLUBS

Amnesia (Map pp104-5; ☎ 242-351-2582; E Mall Dr, Freeport; ☯ 9pm-late Thu, Fri & Sat) This tropical-themed nightclub has a state-of-the-art lighting and sound system, and the nights blend reggae, soca, *goombay* and hip-hop. Hours and admission fees vary so check beforehand (if you can remember!).

Prop Club Beach Bar & Restaurant (Map pp104-5; ☎ 242-373-1333; Our Lucayan Beach & Golf Resort, Lucaya; ☯ till late) The TV screens attract the boys for the big American sports games, but the dance floor takes pride of place for either nights of entertainment or live music. Karaoke nights are de rigueur for the more extroverted, and the glass walls lift up to expose a sand volleyball court.

Safari Lounge Dance Club & Restaurant (Map pp104-5; ☎ 242-352-6648; Island Palm Resort, Explorers

Way at E Mall Dr, Freeport; ⊗ 9pm-late Thu, Fri & Sat) Locals head here at the weekends for *goombay* and hip-hop. Admission prices vary (some nights are free), so check beforehand. Take care when leaving the hotel, although security guards do patrol the parking lot.

LIVE MUSIC
Port Lucaya Marketplace & Village (Map pp104-5; ☎ 242-373-8446; www.portlucaya.com) This place hosts live music from Thursday to Sunday. It has a great open-air setting with a stage and dance floor, as well as a plethora of surrounding bars and cafés. Head there for some rake 'n' scrape, quadrille dancing and general fun.

Illusion's Jazz Club (Map pp104-5; ☎ 242-373-8576; 2 & 9 Pt Lucaya Marketplace & Village; admission $15; ⊗ Sat & Sun till late) Live jazz is played twice weekly depending upon the season.

CASINOS & FLOORSHOWS
The two main casinos also host shows and entertainment.

Crowne Plaza Golf Resort & Casino (see p110) A Las Vegas–style sports book, slot machines and table games here cover a huge 28,000 sq ft space. A twice-weekly floor show and fine dining add to the entertainment.

Isle of Capri Casino (Map pp104-5; ☎ 242-373-2396; www.ourlucaya.com; Our Lucayan Beach & Golf Resort, Seahorse Rd, Lucaya) This 19,000 sq ft (1765 sq meter) casino has 400 slot machines, 21 game tables and a racing sports book.

THEATER
From September to June **Freeport Players Guild** (☎ 242-373-3718) and **Grand Bahamas Players** (☎ 242-557-6997, 242-352-9851) both appear in plays, musicals and comedies at the **Regency Theatre** (Map pp104-5; ☎ 242-352-5533; Regency Park, Freeport).

CINEMAS
RND Cinemas (Map pp104-5; ☎ 242-351-3456; RND Plaza, E Atlantic Dr, Freeport; admission $10) This five-screen cinema shows mainstream hits.

Shopping
The duty-free shopping fans head to the International Bazaar (p103) and Port Lucaya Marketplace & Village (p106) for their jewelry and perfume. It is worth bringing a price-comparison list from home when considering purchasing these goods.

Some of the resort wear and batik prints are worth a look too, but you will find that prices can vary quite considerably between the Freeport and Port Lucaya markets, where it is acceptable to haggle the prices down by about 10% to 15%.

ARTWORKS
Many artworks are small enough to pack into a suitcase. Check out the African-style wooden carvings and some simple but colorful Haitian and Haitian-style oil and acrylic paintings that are sold from around $15 unframed. A bargain gift or souvenir!
Bahamian Tings (Map pp104-5; ☎ 242-352-9550; 15 Poplar Cres, Freeport) Sells Bahamian craftworks.
Flovin Gallery International Bazaar (Map pp104-5; ☎ 242-352-7564); Port Lucaya Marketplace & Village (Map pp104-5; ☎ 242-373-8388) Exhibits include original paintings and artworks.
Leo's Art Gallery (Map pp104-5; ☎ 242-373-1758; Pt Lucaya Marketplace & Village) Leo paints vibrant and rich portrayals of Caribbean living in Haitian-style.

MARKETS & STALLS
Duty-free shopping is best conducted in the two main markets, the International Bazaar (p103) and the Port Lucaya Marketplace & Village (p106), which should cover all your needs for luxury goods. *What-to-do in Freeport/Lucaya* lists major stores and has maps of the International Bazaar and Port Lucaya Marketplace & Village. The other markets listed sell mainly souvenirs, woven straw-work, craftworks and clothing.

Locals do their shopping downtown at malls such as The Towne Centre and Churchill Square, while visitors enjoy the following markets:

- **Goombay Gardens** (Map pp104-5; Freeport) This collection of market stalls sells ethnic jewelry, straw-work, craftworks and T-shirts. It is worth the short walk west of the International Bazaar.
- **Port Lucaya Straw Market** (Map pp104-5; Seahorse Dr, Lucaya) These stalls both west and east of the Port Lucaya Marketplace & Village sell clothing, T-shirts and crafts including straw-work.

Tiffographs (Map pp104-5; ☎ 242-373-6662; Pt Lucaya Marketplace & Village)Has displays of batik paintings & prints.

CIGARS

Cuban cigars are a great buy. Most quality gift shops sell Cohibas (the Rolls Royce of cigars), Montecristos, and other notable brands at 50% or more off black-market prices in the US. We recommend **Smoker's World** (Map pp104-5; ☎ 242-351-6899; International Bazaar, Freeport).

CLOTHING & CLOTH

If you're into striking textiles, try these places.

Androsia (Map pp104-5; ☎ 242-373-8387; Pt Lucaya Marketplace & Village) Sells batik clothing and cloth.

Far East Traders (Map pp104–5; ☎ 242-352-9280; International Bazaar, Freeport) For embroidered linens, silk pajamas and clothing.

Leather Shop International Bazaar (Map pp104–5; ☎ 242-352-5491); Port Lucaya Marketplace & Village (Map pp104-5; ☎ 242-373-2323) Sells leather clothes, shoes and handbags.

Linens of Lucaya (Map pp104-5; ☎ 242-373-8697; Pt Lucaya Marketplace & Village) Sells hand-embroidered materials.

Nautica Boutique (Map pp104-5; ☎ 242-373-8642; Pt Lucaya Marketplace & Village) Sells resort wear, silk paintings and custom-made crafts with a nautical theme.

Needful Tings (Map pp104-5; ☎ 242-373-3450; Pt Lucaya Marketplace & Village) Sells resort wear and swimwear.

CRYSTAL & COLLECTABLES

The Bahamas is renowned for some of its collectible stamps.

Bahamas Coin & Stamp Ltd (Map pp104-5; ☎ 242-352-8989; International Bazaar, Freeport) Sells coins from ancient Rome, Spanish galleons, the USA & UK.

Island Galleria International Bazaar (Map pp104–5; ☎ 242-352-8194); Port Lucaya Marketplace & Village (Map pp104-5; ☎ 242-373-4512) This is the store for crystal and fine porcelain.

Plaka (Map pp104–5; ☎ 242-352-5932; International Bazaar, Freeport) Sells items from Greece.

JEWELRY

Watches and gems are top of most visitors' shopping lists.

Colombian Emeralds International International Bazaar (Map pp104-5; ☎ 242-352-5464); Port Lucaya Marketplace & Village (Map pp104-5; ☎ 242-373-8400) A chainstore specializing in watches and gems.

Goldylocks Jewelry International Bazaar (Map pp104-5; ☎ 242-352-3872); Port Lucaya Marketplace & Village (Map pp104-5; ☎ 242-373-5920) Has Bahamian jewelry.

Jeweler's Warehouse (Map pp104-5; ☎ 242-373-8400; Pt Lucaya Marketplace & Village) Has watches and trinkets.

Jewellery Box (Map pp104-5; ☎ 242-373-8319; Pt Lucaya Marketplace & Village) Gold, silver and gems for all.

Paradise Jewels (Map pp104–5; ☎ 242-351-1392; International Bazaar, Freeport) A range of gems and gold on offer.

MUSIC

Buck's Record Gallery (Map pp104-5; ☎ 242-352-5170; Churchill St, Freeport) Downtown on Pioneers Way near E Mall Dr or at the International Airport, Buck's is one place for serious music buffs to build up their collections of Bahamas and Caribbean music.

Intercity Music (Map pp104-5; ☎ 242-352-8820; Pt Lucaya Marketplace & Village) Another outlet that is well-established, it sells *goombay*, reggae and soca, including some local recordings.

PERFUME

Perfume Factory (Map pp104-5; ☎ 242-352-9391; International Bazaar, Freeport) Adjacent to the Bazaar's parking lot, this shop allows you to mix, bottle, and name your own fragrance ($30 for one-ounce spray) using the six Fragrances of the Bahamas. Every bottle of Sand perfume for men has real Bahamian sand; each bottle of Pink Pearl contains several conch-shell pearls.

Also recommended:

Les Parisiennes (Map pp104-5; ☎ 242-373-2974; Pt Lucaya Marketplace & Village)

Parfum de Paris International Bazaar (Map pp104-5; ☎ 242-352-5923); Port Lucaya Marketplace & Village (Map pp104-5; ☎ 242-373-8403)

STRAW-WORK & TRADITIONAL ITEMS

There are several straw markets behind the International Bazaar that sell woven-straw crafts, as well as T-shirts, carvings, and ethnic jewelry. Look for Bahamian wood-carvings, especially the simple yet dramatic works by Michael Hoyte which are often hewn from ebony driftwood washed ashore from Africa.

Solomon's Food Court (Map pp104-5; ☎ 242-352-9681; Cedar St, Freeport) For Bahamian sauces and preserves, specialty oils, and other culinary items, head towards the International Bazaar and you'll find it.

Getting There & Away
AIR
Freeport International Airport (FPO; Map pp104–5; ☎ 242-352-6020) lies 2 miles north of Freeport. For international flights to Grand Bahama and the Bahamas see p288.

The following airlines fly between Grand Bahama and other Bahamian islands.
Bahamasair (UP; www.bahamasair.com) Freeport (☎ 242-352-8341); Moss Town, George Town, Exuma (☎ 242-345-0035); Nassau (☎ 242-377-5505) Hub Nassau.
Major's Airlines Bahamas (☎ 242-352-5778; www.thebahamasguide.com/majorair) Hub Grand Bahama.
Flamingo Air (☎ 242-351-4963) Hub Nassau.

Quoted fares are one-way:

Route	Price	Frequency
Freeport–Nassau	$85	6 daily
Freeport–Marsh Harbour, Abaco	$85	1 daily
Freeport–San Andros, Andros	$150	2 weekly
Freeport–Fresh Creek, Andros	$150	2 weekly
Freeport–Mangrove Cay	$150	2 weekly
Freeport–Congo Town	$150	2 weekly
Freeport–Bimini	$65	1 daily
Freeport–Governors Harbour	$135	2 weekly
Freeport–Nth Eleuthera	$135	2 weekly

BOAT
Mail Boat
Contact the **Dockmaster's Office** (Map pp102–3; ☎ 242-393-1064) located at Potter's Cay in Nassau or **Freeport Harbour** (Map pp104–5; ☎ 242-352-9651) to confirm departure schedules, and for transport operators, and contact and fare details.

Marcella III ($50 one way, 12 hours, one weekly) sails on Wednesday for Freeport from Nassau. It docks half a mile east of the Cruise Ship Port.

Marinas
If traveling in your own boat, you must clear customs and immigration at Lucayan Marina Village, Port Lucaya Marina, or Running Mon Marina.

You'll need to call ahead to arrange clearance with **Customs** (☎ 242-352-7361) and **Immigration** (☎ 242-352-9338).

All marinas provide electricity & freshwater hookups.
Lucayan Marina Village (Map pp104–5; ☎ 242-373-8888; www.lucayanmarinavillage.com; Pt Lucaya Marketplace & Village) Located on the north side of Port Lucaya,

facilities include 150 slips, fuel and accommodations. A ferry to Port Lucaya is free to guests.
Ocean Reef Yacht Club (Map pp104–5; ☎ 242-272-4661; www.oryc.com; Silver Point Beach) Has accommodations, over 55 slips and free buses to town.
Old Bahama Bay Resort & Marina (see p120) Has 70 slips and there are fuel, shower and laundry facilities.
Port Lucaya Marina & Yacht Club (Map pp104–5; ☎ 242-373-9090; www.portlucaya.com; Pt Lucaya Marketplace & Village) Off Seahorse Rd, this modern marina has 150 slips and accommodations.
Running Mon Marina (Map pp104–5; ☎ 242-352-6834; www.running-mon-bahamas.com; Kelly Ct at the foot of the Mall, Freeport) Has 70 slips, fuel, accommodations, a boat-lift, laundry and showers.
Xanadu Beach Resort & Marina (Map pp104–5; ☎ 242-352-6783; Sunken Treasure Dr, Freeport) Has 75 slips and accommodation facilities next to Xanadu Beach.

Getting Around
AIR
To/From the Airport
Freeport International Airport (Map pp104–5; ☎ 242-352-6020) lies 2 miles north of Freeport. There's no bus service to or from the airport. However, car rental booths are based in the arrivals hall and taxis meet each flight. Displayed fares are set by the government.

Taxi rides for two people to/from the airport to Freeport are $11 and $19 to/from Lucaya. Each additional passenger costs $3.

BOAT
Cruise ships dock at **Freeport Harbour** (Map pp104–5; ☎ 242-352-9651). Taxis meet all cruise ships and charge $16 to Freeport and $24 to Lucaya.

McLeans Town to Sweeting's Cay (East End) has a free government **ferry** (Map pp102–3) which runs twice daily.

CAR & SCOOTER HIRE
The following companies have car-rental agencies at the airport. The local companies are cheaper than the internationals, and daily car hire is from $60. Collision waiver insurance is about $15 a day.
Avis (☎ 242-352-7666)
Brad$ (☎ 242-352-7930)
Dollar (☎ 242-352-9325)
Hertz (☎ 242-352-9277)
KSR Rent A Car (☎ 242-351-5737)

You can rent a scooter in the parking lot in front of the Port Lucaya Resort & Yacht

GRAND BAHAMA

Club (p111) for $40 a day, plus a hefty cash deposit.

BUS

The eastern end of the island is known as the East End and the western end of the island is known as the West End. A handful of private minibuses operate as 'public buses' on assigned routes from the bus depot downtown at Winn Dixie Plaza, traveling as far afield as West End and McLean's Town. Buses are frequent and depart when the driver decides he has enough passengers. The bus stop in Freeport is at the parking area behind the International Bazaar, and the bus stop in Lucaya is on Seahorse Dr, 400yd west of the Port Lucaya Marketplace & Village.

Timetables can be obtained from the **Grand Bahama Island Tourism Board** (p103).

Fares from Freetown include Port Lucaya Marketplace & Village ($1), East End ($8, twice daily) and West End ($4, twice daily). Buses will occasionally drop you in taxi-designated city areas for $2.

Free shuttles also run between the most downtown hotels, the beach and town.

TAXI

You'll find taxis at the airport and major hotels. Fares are fixed by the government for short distances. Bonded taxis (with white license plates) can't go outside the tax-free zone. You can call for a radio-dispatched taxi from **Freeport Taxi** (☎ 242-352-6666) or **Grand Bahama Taxi Union** (☎ 242-352-7101).

EAST OF FREEPORT

East of the Grand Lucayan Waterway (a 7½-mile canal), the Grand Bahama Hwy runs parallel to the shore to East End. Side roads lead to the south shore's talcum-powder soft beaches.

Water Cay

This tiny, simple settlement is on the cay of that name, 2 miles off the north shore. The community relies on fishing and is as unspoiled as things get on Grand Bahama. You can catch a boat from Hawksbill Creek or the Grand Lucayan Waterway or drive the dirt road from the Grand Bahama Hwy to the north shore dock, where you might be able to hire a local's boat to Water Cay.

Peterson Cay National Park

This 1½-acre park is the only cay on Grand Bahama's south shore. It is one of the Family Islands' most heavily used getaway spots, busy with locals' boats on weekends. Coral reefs provide splendid snorkeling and diving. You can hire a boat from any marina in Freeport and Lucaya or take an organized snorkeling excursion (see p106).

Old Free Town

The settlement of Old Free Town, 3 miles east of the Grand Lucayan Waterway, was forcibly abandoned in the 1960s when the Port Authority acquired the land. There are several blue holes (subaqueous caves) in the surrounding swamp, notably **Mermaid's Lair** and **Owl Hole**. Stalactites dangle from the roof of the bowl. And owls have nested on the sill as long as residents can remember – the blue holes are well hidden, so ask a local for directions!

Lucayan National Park

This 40-acre park is the Grand Bahama's finest treasure. It is divided in half by the Grand Bahama Hwy. On the north side, trails lead from the parking lot onto a limestone plateau riddled with caves that open to the longest known underwater cave system in the world, with over 6 charted miles of tunnels. From here you can follow steps down to viewing platforms in **Ben's Cave** and **Burial Mound Cave**, which have formed blue holes. These blue holes will fill with fish if you sprinkle the surface with bread. Colonies of bats use Ben's Cave as a nursery in summer, where a unique class of opaque blind crustacean, *Speleonectes lucayensis*, that resembles a swimming centipede also resides. In 1986 four skeletons of indigenous Lucayans were found in what appeared to be an ancient cemetery on the floor of one cave.

Creek Trail (330yd) and **Mangrove Swamp Trail** (480yd) form a loop on the southern side of the park and pass through three signed shoreline ecosystems. The trails head first through miniature woodlands with ming, cedar, mahogany, and poisonwood, cinnecord, cabbage palms, and agaves, which produce towering yellow flowers favored by insects and hummingbirds. Their low branches are festooned with orchids and bromeliads.

Between this area and the shore lie mangroves, where raccoons and land crabs roam under the watchful eyes of ospreys, herons and waterfowl. **Gold Rock Creek** is the home to snapper, barracuda, manta ray and crabs. Passages lead underground between the creek and the Lucayan Caves so that ocean fish are often seen in the blue holes north of the road.

Trails are marked through the beachside whiteland coppice of giant poisonwood and pigeon plum trees, frequented by woodpeckers ('peckerwoods' in local parlance).

Both trails spill out onto the secluded and beautiful white-rippled sands of **Gold Rock Beach**, fringed by dunes fixed by coco plum, sea grape, spider lily and casuarina trees. Named for the small rock that lies 200yd offshore, this is one of the island's most stunning beaches.

Bring all water and food with you and don't forget your bug spray. The park is open daily year-round, although Ben's Cave is closed in June and July to protect the birthing bats. For more information contact the **Bahamas National Trust** (Map pp104-5; ☎ 242-352-5438; Rand Memorial Nature Centre, E Settlers Way, Freeport).

You can take a jitney bus from Winn Dixie Plaza in downtown Freeport to reach the park. The jitney buses ($8 one-way, twice daily) pass by the park en route to McLean's Town. Check with the Grand Bahama Island Tourism Board (p103) for updated schedules.

However a number of operators organize tours (p109) and activities (p106) that explore the park on foot, horse, bike, kayak and boat.

Cave diving is allowed only by special permit under the supervision of UNEXSO in Port Lucaya (see p107).

Lucayan National Park to McLean's Town

The route to McLean's Town (population 3744) is normally taken by those seeking a boat ride to Sweeting's Cay, Lightbourne and Deep Water Cays for snorkeling or the excellent bonefishing.

On the way you will pass sleepy **Freetown** and **High Rock** settlements. About 10 miles east, beyond the Burma Oil Depot (with a harbor facility for the world's largest supertankers), is **Pelican Point Beach** and **Rocky Creek**, which harbors another blue hole.

McLean's Town residents live off their conch and lobster fishing, and some also act as bonefishing guides.

Deep Water Cay attracts fishing fans while **Sweeting's Cay** (population 483) holds a small fishing village and some visitors' accommodations. **Lightbourne Cay** has a lovely beach and shallows that are a snorkeler's dream.

Captain Phil & Mel's Bonefishing Guide Service (Map pp102-3; ☎ 242-353-3960; www.bahamasbonefishing.net; half-/full-day $250/350) provides transport to and from Freeport.

SLEEPING & EATING
Bishop's Bonefish Resort, Restaurant & Bar (Map pp102-3; ☎ 242-353-5485; www.gbweekly.com/bishopsbonefish; High Rock Beach; r $85; P X X) Eight light and bright motel-style rooms are set on the beach, each with a fridge. An on-site bar and popular local restaurant serve Bahamian dishes and burgers, and the owner can also organize bonefishing trips.

Pelican Point Lodge (Map pp102-3; ☎ 242-353-6064; r $80; P X X) These three beachside units have kitchenettes. A small bar and restaurant **Breezes Bar & Restaurant** is attached.

Twin Gables (Map pp102-3; ☎ 242-373-6662; eastend safari@yahoo.com; Sweeting's Cay; r $140; X) Three rooms in this waterside villa come fitted with TV and fridges. The nearby **Seaside Fig Tree** (mains $7-15) offers meals and drinks all day.

Bro's (Map pp102-3; ☎ 242-353-3440; McLean's Town; r $50; P X) This mint-green, three-story building on the left as you enter town has a choice of clean but very basic rooms, some with air-con.

Smitty's One Stop Shop (Map pp102-3; ☎ 242-353-4242; Bevans Town) About 5 miles east of Lucayan National Park, Smitty's serves burgers and basic fare (mains $6-10); sells gasoline and has a general store.

You can buy groceries at the **Cooper's Convenience Store**, a tiny hut in the middle of McLean's Town.

GETTING THERE & AROUND
A minibus operates twice daily from Winn Dixie Plaza in downtown Freeport.

East End Adventures (p109) also takes in McLean's Town on its day trip to Sweeting's Cay.

Water taxis operate between McLean's Town and the cays. Rates are negotiable.

WEST OF FREEPORT

This peninsula is separated from the 'mainland' by Freeport Harbour Channel and the surrounding industry. Already pretty poor, the area was further devastated by the 2004 hurricanes and is in the process of recovering.

The highlight here is **Paradise Cove** and the pristine **Deadman's Reef** which can be reached by simply walking off the beach.

Hawksbill Creek to West End

The channel opens to **Hawksbill Creek**, named for the once-common marine turtles that now infrequently come ashore. Fishermen bring their catch ashore here to the **Conch Wharf**; and huge shell mounds line the road.

The rough and poorer suburb of **Eight Mile** lies west of the channel and should be avoided after dark, along with the area that stretches west to Holmes Rock. Nearby are several 'boiling holes' (subterranean water-filled holes that bubble under the tides' pressure).

There's good diving and snorkeling offshore, especially from **Paradise Cove** (☎ 242-349-2677; pcove@batelnet.bs; Paradise Cove; r per night/per week $100/625; P X X). Definitely the bargain of the week, this handful of small apartments sits on secluded Coral Beach and has the most amazing sea views at a very reasonable weekly rent! Fully-equipped, the apartments come with all linen, including beach towels. The attractive furnishings are simple and there is a bar on site that makes killer piña coladas. What else do you need?

Farther up the road is the atmospheric **Buccaneer Club** (Map pp102-3; ☎ 242-349-3794; mains $10-35), centered on a magnificent Old World stone-and-timber restaurant festooned with polished driftwood and nautical regalia. You can also dine on traditional seafood dishes, rack of lamb and broiled lobster outside on a patio shaded by palms.

Jitney buses run several times a day from Winn Dixie Plaza in Freeport to Eight Mile and Holmes Rock ($4). Excursions are also offered from Freeport/Lucaya (see p109).

West End

This fishing village, 25 miles west of Freeport, was a sleepy haven of tumbledown shacks, half-sunken boats and piles of sun-bleached conch shells before the decimating 2004 hurricanes which swooped over Grand Bahama from this end of the island. Rebuilding the community will take some time.

Once the center of activity on the island, Prohibition rumrunners dominated the area and yachters with sterling surnames like Kennedy, DuPont or Hearst were callers to the Grand Bahama Resort & Country Club.

The village was also known for the stone-and-wood **Mary Magdalene Church** (1893), which has three small yet beautiful stained-glass windows in contemporary style.

SLEEPING & EATING

Old Bahama Bay Resort & Marina (Map pp102-3; ☎ 242-346-6500; www.oldbahamabay.com; Bayshore Rd; r $275; P X X) The luxurious Bahamian-style cottages are part of an upmarket 150-acre resort that is full of boaters. Classic darkwood and comfortable furnishings in the open-suite rooms incorporate all mod-cons including bars and DVD/CD-players, coffeemakers and fridges. Private porches complete the spacious and luxurious feel of this attractive and low-key resort. Facilities include walking and snorkeling trails, a vast heated swimming pool with massage jets, tennis courts, a gym, spa, dive shop, helipad and well-equipped marina.

Star Hotel Restaurant & Lounge (Map pp102-3; ☎ 242-346-6207; Bayshore Rd; mains $7-18; ☼ lunch & dinner) This weather-worn, two-story old clapboard hotel now serves simple but hugely popular Bahamian fare. Weekends here are party time, with live music and late nights on offer.

Village Tavern & Takeout (Map pp102-3; ☎ 242-346-6102; Bank Lane off Bayshore Rd; mains $6-12; ☼ breakfast, lunch & dinner) They serve traditional Bahamian breakfasts and fried and souse (stew) meals at this small place.

GETTING THERE & AWAY

A jitney bus ($4 one-way) runs several times daily from Freeport's International Bazaar and Port Lucaya Marketplace & Village.

The marina at Old Bahama Bay Resort & Marina attracts many boaters.

Several tour operators include West End in their sightseeing excursions (see p109).

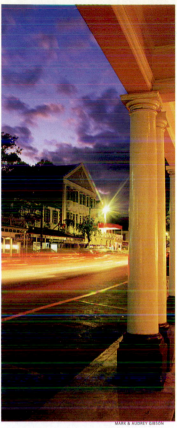

Bright lights in downtown Nassau (p63)

MARK & AUDREY GIBSON

Adrenaline junkies can mingle with reef sharks off Grand Bahama (p107)

STEVE SIMONSEN

Scuba-diving lesson at one of Paradise Island's resorts (p76)

DENNIS JOHNSON

Cottages adorned in the festive colors of Junkanoo at Compass Point, near Nassau (p98)

CHRISTOPHER P BAKER

Port Lucaya Marketplace & Village (p106) is a jovial place to unwind on the waterfront

Has Dr Who arrived? An English telephone booth in Lucaya (p101)

Traversing a lush waterway in spectacular Lucayan National Park (p118)

A tropical mural at one of Marsh Harbour's resorts (p148), reflecting the nearby underwater world

Sunset over tranquil Cat Island (p209)

The simple beauty of St Peter's Catholic Church, Clarence Town (p228)

An iguana welcomes arrivals on Allan's Cays (p203)

MICHAEL LAWRENCE

A local shares his fishing techniques,
Grand Turk (p260)

Divers at Northwest Point (p245), Providenciales

MICHAEL LAW

One of the many exquisite inlets that lead to inviting turquoise waters, Grand Turk (p261)

JIM

Biminis, Berry Islands & Andros

These three island groups on the western side of the Bahamas make up a little piece of heaven for anglers, divers and explorers.

Just 50 miles east of Miami (the city's glow can be seen at night) and 120 miles northwest of Nassau, the Biminis, or 'islands in the stream,' were made famous by Ernest Hemingway in his novel of that name. The Gulf Stream brings marlin close to shore, making sportfishing visitors an economic mainstay of the islands. Hemingway fished, fought and caroused in the Biminis during the mid-1930s, and became the first vice president of the International Game Fishing Association (IGFA), which heralded the start of modern-day game fishing around the world. Since then, four out of the six IGFA world records have been made in Bimini waters.

Divers can enjoy the company of rare Atlantic spotted dolphins here, while at Andros, the vast 140-mile-long barrier reef lies a couple of miles offshore. The Great Bahama Bank's scary 6000ft drop-off in the Tongue of the Ocean canyon harbors some amazing marine life.

On Andros, bird-watchers, hikers and those who want the untrodden path have 2300 sq miles of wilderness to explore, while anglers can head to the island's bights or boneflats.

The Berry Islands sit closest to Nassau, on a plateau rising between the Northwest Providence Channel (to the north) and the Tongue of the Ocean (to the south). There, birds outnumber humans, and it's possible to find a deserted cay where your cares will disperse in the wind.

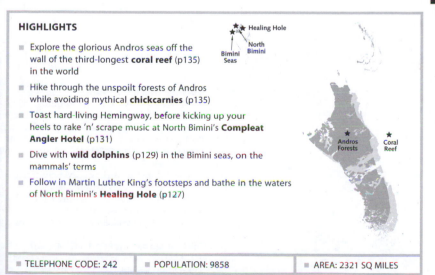

HIGHLIGHTS

- Explore the glorious Andros seas off the wall of the third-longest **coral reef** (p135) in the world
- Hike through the unspoilt forests of Andros while avoiding mythical **chickcarnies** (p135)
- Toast hard-living Hemingway, before kicking up your heels to rake 'n' scrape music at North Bimini's **Compleat Angler Hotel** (p131)
- Dive with **wild dolphins** (p129) in the Bimini seas, on the mammals' terms
- Follow in Martin Luther King's footsteps and bathe in the waters of North Bimini's **Healing Hole** (p127)

■ TELEPHONE CODE: 242   ■ POPULATION: 9858   ■ AREA: 2321 SQ MILES

BIMINIS

pop 1736

Big-game fishing devotees in the know have headed to North and South Bimini for decades, and are a mainstay of the local economy, as are the less-welcome rowdy US college students living large during spring break.

Scuba divers are also lured to these small islands' sunken Spanish galleons and the wreck of a WWI freighter. Then there's the underwater Bimini Road, claimed to be part of the lost city of Atlantis; the famous Bimini Wall, plummeting over 4000ft; and a unique opportunity to dive with wild Atlantic spotted dolphins in the open ocean.

There is a lot of mystery on these 9 sq miles of land: the Healing Hole and Memory Ledge in particular are immersed in it. And for more earthly pursuits, there are Hemingway's still-great haunts; this man certainly knew his bars!

North Bimini's unpretentious Alice Town is the center of activity, with the most beautiful beach in Bimini Bay, while the less-

developed South Bimini has long been favored by Americans, who fly or boat in to their weekend island homes.

History

Pirates like Henry Morgan thought the Biminis a splendid lair from which to pounce on treasure fleets, while the five founding families here in 1835 were licensed wreckers – 'rescuing' ships and their cargoes. Later Biminites tried the more honest occupation of sponging, which thrived until a decimating blight in the 1930s. Prohibition in the 1920s boosted the Biminis' economy (if not reputation) when Alice Town became the export capital for illegal Scotch whisky runs into the US.

Ernest Hemingway (see the boxed text, p129) briefly made the Biminis his summer home. Other infamous visitors included Howard Hughes, Richard Nixon and Adam Clayton Powell Jr (New York congressman and Harlem preacher), who arrived with his mistress. Back in 1987, US presidential contender Gary Hart's aspirations were sunk when he was spotted here cavorting with a woman who was not his wife – on a yacht appropriately named *Monkey Business*!

In ensuing decades the Biminis became a major stopover for drug shipments. The work of the US and Bahamian authorities continues; in June 2004 the US attorney general announced the smashing of an international cocaine-trafficking network, in which Bahamians were arrested in the Biminis, New Providence and Eleuthera.

The Biminis have been featured in films such as *Cocoon* and *Silence of the Lambs*.

Getting There & Around

Most visitors fly into the Biminis, while others arrive by mail boat. The Biminis are served by two airports: **Bimini Seaplane Landing** (NSB) at Alice Town, North Bimini, and **South Bimini Airport** (BIM; ☎ 242-347-3101) on South Bimini.

The following airlines fly between the Biminis and other Bahamian islands.
Bahamasair (UP; ☎ 242-377-5505, Freeport ☎ 242-352-8341; www.bahamasair.com; hubs Nassau & Freeport) Includes some flights to the Berry Islands, but schedules are variable.

Chalk's Ocean Airways (OP; ☎ 1-800-424-2557, 242-363-3114; www.flychalks.com; hubs Paradise Island Nassau & Fort Lauderdale) Uses the seaplane landing.

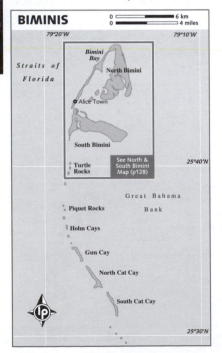

BIMINIS

0 —————— 6 km
0 —————— 4 miles

79°20'W   79°10'W

Straits of Florida

Bimini Bay

North Bimini

Alice Town

South Bimini

Turtle Rocks

See North & South Bimini Map (p128)

25°40'N

Great Bahama Bank

Piquet Rocks

Holm Cays

Gun Cay

North Cat Cay

South Cat Cay

25°30'N

Major's Air Services (☎ 242-352-5778; www.thebaha
masguide.com/majorair; hubs Grand Bahama & Eleuthera)
Tropical Diversions Air (US ☎ 954-921-9084;
www.tropicaldiversions.com/air-charter.htm) Flies from
Fort Lauderdale on charter only.
Western Air (☎ 242-329-4000; fax 242-329-3167; hubs
Andros & Nassau)

One-way fares include South Bimini Airport flights to Nassau ($65, twice daily) and
South Bimini Airport flights to Freeport
($70, once daily).

With only one compact settlement on
North Bimini, feet are the main transportation for getting around, although bicycles
and golf carts are easily hired for longer
excursions.

NORTH BIMINI

This skinny island stretches for almost 7
miles before fanning out into a quilt work
of mangrove swamps and fishing flats. A
narrow sliver of lovely white sand, shaded
by palm and pine trees, colors the edge
of the eastern ocean shore. The beaches
are generally prettier to the north, with
the most beautiful being Bimini Bay, but
take your mosquito spray along.

The only settlement is unassuming Alice
Town (population 950), at the south end of
the island. King's Hwy, the main street, runs
along the inner shore, while Queen's Hwy,
a one-lane concrete path, runs along the
western shore. The suburb where Biminites
mainly live is Bailey Town, which merges
into Porgy Bay (or 'Poggy Bay'). You can
continue north along the dirt road that
leads to Bimini Bay and beyond.

Information

There are public telephone booths all along
King's Hwy. A small library is opposite the
customs building at the mail-boat dock.
Bahamas Ministry of Tourism (☎ 242-347-3529;
fax 242-347-3530; Government Bldg, King's Hwy, Alice
Town; 🕙 9am-5:30pm Mon-Fri)
BaTelCo (☎ 242-347-3311; King's Hwy, Alice Town)
Sells phone cards.
Government Medical Clinic (☎ 242-347-2210;
King's Hwy, Alice Town)
Police (☎ 242-347-3144, 919; King's Hwy, Alice Town)
Post office (☎ 242-347-3546; Government Bldg, King's
Hwy, Alice Town)
Royal Bank of Canada (☎ 242-347-3031; King's Hwy,
Alice Town; 🕙 9am-3pm Mon, Wed & Fri)

Sights

The one-room **Bimini Museum** (☎ 242-347-3038;
King's Hwy; admission $2; 🕙 9am-9pm Mon-Sat, noon-
9pm Sun), above the library opposite the straw
market (customs building), tells the island's
history through videos and photos, and has
sections on fishing legends, Hemingway,
and sporting figures.

No visit to the Biminis is complete without raising a drink at the famous Compleat
Angler Hotel, where Hemingway duked it
out with all comers every Sunday in a ring
he made (he had a standing offer to pay $100
to any resident of the Biminis who could
punch him out). This lounge is now the **Ernest Hemingway Museum**, complete with black-
and-white photos of Hemingway that recall
his time here (1935–1937).

Local lore attributes the inspiration for
Martin Luther King Jr's 'I Have a Dream'
speech to the mystical effect of the **Healing
Hole**, south of Easter Cay. The great man
bathed in this freshwater sulfur spring
shortly before speaking those memorable
words. Many visitors here experience an
enigmatic calming sensation.

Several restaurants, such as Captain Bob's
(p131), have photographic **Fishing Halls of
Fame** celebrating those who've made the islands' angling heritage an international draw.
Dozens of photos and other memorabilia
recall celebrities and commoners who have
pulled prize-winning fish from the drink.

Ask a local to point out **Memory Ledge**. It
is claimed that if you lie down here, you'll
be flooded with flashbacks.

The ridge above **Spook Hill**, a cemetery at
the east end of Porgy Bay, drops to a **beach**
popular with locals on weekends for picnics. It's a great spot for enjoying sunsets.

Activities
DIVING & SNORKELING

Some grand dive sites include the Bimini
Barge, where the 270ft *Sapona* wreck lies
75yd from the Gulf Stream drop-off, and
where prolific reef life and pelagic big boys
roam. You can't miss Bimini Road, where
1000ft-long underwater formations resemble the Incas' hand-hewn blocks and are
claimed as 'The Lost Outpost of Atlantis.'
(The discovery in 1977 of 500ft-long sand
mounds shaped as a shark, a square, a cat
and a seahorse in the eastern part of Bimini
added fuel to the Atlantis fire).

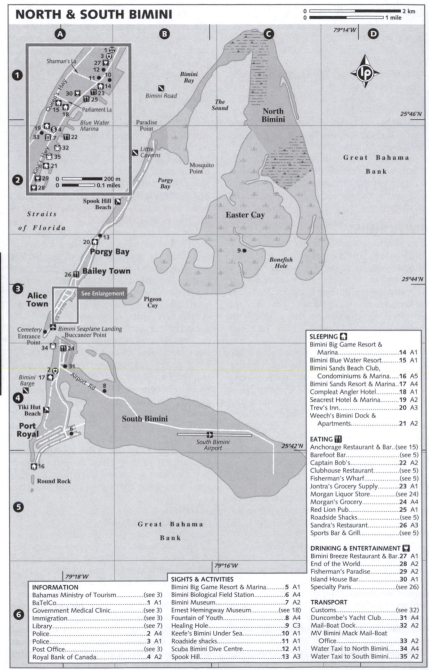

NORTH & SOUTH BIMINI

BIMINIS, BERRY ISLANDS & ANDROS

INFORMATION
Bahamas Ministry of Tourism...............(see 3)
BaTelCo...1 A1
Government Medical Clinic...................(see 3)
Immigration...................................(see 3)
Library..(see 7)
Police...2 A4
Police...3 A1
Post Office....................................(see 3)
Royal Bank of Canada...........................4 A2

SIGHTS & ACTIVITIES
Bimini Big Game Resort & Marina...........5 A1
Bimini Biological Field Station...............6 A4
Bimini Museum.................................7 A2
Ernest Hemingway Museum.................(see 18)
Fountain of Youth..............................8 A4
Healing Hole.....................................9 C3
Keefe's Bimini Under Sea.....................10 A1
Roadside shacks................................11 A1
Scuba Bimini Dive Centre.....................12 A1
Spook Hill......................................13 A3

SLEEPING 🏠
Bimini Big Game Resort &
  Marina..14 A1
Bimini Blue Water Resort........15 A1
Bimini Sands Beach Club,
  Condominiums & Marina.........16 A5
Bimini Sands Resort & Marina.....17 A4
Compleat Angler Hotel............18 A1
Seacrest Hotel & Marina..........19 A2
Trev's Inn......................20 A3
Weech's Bimini Dock &
  Apartments....................21 A2

EATING 🍴
Anchorage Restaurant & Bar..(see 15)
Barefoot Bar....................(see 5)
Captain Bob's....................22 A2
Clubhouse Restaurant............(see 5)
Fisherman's Wharf...............(see 5)
Jontra's Grocery Supply.........23 A1
Morgan Liquor Store............(see 24)
Morgan's Grocery................24 A1
Red Lion Pub....................25 A1
Roadside Shacks.................(see 5)
Sandra's Restaurant.............26 A3
Sports Bar & Grill..............(see 5)

DRINKING & ENTERTAINMENT 📺
Bimini Breeze Restaurant & Bar..27 A1
End of the World................28 A2
Fisherman's Paradise............29 A2
Island House Bar................30 A1
Specialty Paris................(see 26)

TRANSPORT
Customs........................(see 32)
Duncombe's Yacht Club..........31 A4
Mail-Boat Dock.................32 A2
MV Bimini Mack Mail-Boat
  Office.........................33 A1
Water Taxi to North Bimini.....34 A1
Water Taxi to South Bimini.....35 A2

HEMINGWAY AND THE BIMINIS

Ernest Hemingway put the Biminis on the map when he briefly made them his summer home during the mid-1930s, and later featured the islands in his best-selling novel *Islands in the Stream* (published in 1970, nine years after his death).

One of the greatest American writers of the 20th century, Hemingway was born in 1899 in Oak Park, Illinois. His spare, stylized realism – which he attributed to his background as a newspaper reporter – revolutionized modern literature, and he was awarded both the Pulitzer and Nobel Prizes for Literature during his lifetime.

Hemingway based much of his fiction on his adventurous and troubled life, including his traumatic experiences as an ambulance driver during WWI. In 1918 Hemingway was severely wounded in a mortar attack in Italy; although his legs were riddled with shrapnel, he reportedly carried a wounded soldier to safety. The horror of the war and his relationship with his nurse while recuperating in Milan formed the basis of his antiwar novel *A Farewell to Arms* (1929). His short story *Soldier's Home* tells of a soldier returning home to a family and town that doesn't comprehend what he's been through.

In 1921 Hemingway was sent to Paris as a correspondent for the *Toronto Star Weekly*. There he was introduced to such literary greats as Ezra Pound, James Joyce and Gertrude Stein, and wrote some of his most important novels. Hemingway later moved to Key West, where he developed a passion for big-game fishing, a sport he pursued in the Biminis and later made the topic of *The Old Man and the Sea* (1953). In the Biminis, Hemingway was legendary for winning fishing tournaments and unofficial boxing matches, and for nights of drunken debauchery.

It's been suggested that his father's depression and eventual suicide in 1928 influenced not only Hemingway's own psychological well-being but also his manic pursuit of love, alcohol and life. Hemingway had four wives and many mistresses, and actively pursued some nerve-racking adventures. These included hunting big game in Africa in 1933 and covering the Spanish Civil War in 1937; his experiences there resulted in the evocative *For Whom the Bell Tolls* (1940). Following the Spanish Civil War, Hemingway moved to Cuba, where he spent the early part of WWII hunting for German submarines along the coast, an activity also pursued by the protagonist of *Islands in the Stream*. Hemingway then traveled to Europe to cover the end of WWII, and was there for the liberation of Paris.

Hemingway's escapades were eventually curtailed by the severe injuries he received in one of two plane crashes during a trip to Africa in 1954 – he was so badly hurt that he was unable to collect his 1954 Nobel Prize. By this stage, his deteriorating health had affected his writing, leaving Hemingway suicidal and drinking up to a quart of liquor a day. In desperation his fourth wife organized electroshock therapy to treat his depression. When these 'therapies' erased many of his extraordinary memories, Hemingway finally gave up the fight. On July 2, 1961, Ernest 'Papa' Hemingway followed his father's lead; he took a 12-gauge shotgun and shot himself in the head.

But despite his tragic end, Hemingway's legacy is very much alive in his body of writing, his lasting influence on literature, and – in the Biminis and elsewhere – in his many former haunts, such as the Compleat Angler Hotel (p131), which now houses the Ernest Hemingway Museum. The Bimini Museum (p127) also has a section on Hemingway.

Hawksbill Reef is home to lobsters and reef fish; Little Caverns has mountainous coral formations that rise from a sandy bottom at 65ft; and at the Wall, a popular drift site at 130ft along the continental shelf, the Gulf Stream carries you. Beyond, the abyss drops to 2000ft.

Snorkelers should head for the Bimini Shoreline, where coral and rock formations are smothered by sponges, Eagle Ray Run, where these graceful stingrays fly and LaChance Rocks, with its many marine critters. Also try Turtle Rocks, where there are plenty of coral, fish and turtles, and the highlight, Stingray Hole, where friendly rays glide around waiting to be hand-fed.

Bill & Nowdla Keefe's Bimini Undersea (242-347-3089; www.biminiundersea.com; Bimini Big Game Resort & Marina, Queen's Hwy, Alice Town) offers two-tank dives ($90) and snorkel trips (adult/child $40/20). Their tremendous 'Wild Dolphin Excursions' (adult/child $120/100) leave the dolphins completely in charge, and encounters last about an hour. They also run diving and accommodation packages, which can include videos and night dives.

The **Scuba Bimini Dive Centre** (☎ 242-347-4444; www.scubabimini.com; South Bimini Yacht Club, King's Hwy, Alice Town) offers one-tank dives for $50, two-tank dives for $80 and three-tank dives for $100 (gear is extra). Snorkeling trips are $30. They will also organize wild dolphin observation and interaction for $119 per person with accommodation (based on double occupancy).

Enjoy leisurely diving excursions with **K&B EZ Dive** (☎ 242-347-4071; www.knbezdive.com; Bimini), which offers one-tank dives for $50, spearfishing ($150 per half day; bring your own mask, fins and snorkel), snorkeling ($35) and beach picnics ($125 per person). Learn to use the Hawaiian sling to catch a lobster or visit Honeymoon Harbour for a cookout.

BONEFISHING & SPORTFISHING

What drew Hemingway more than half a century ago still draws people today – the famous big fish. The catch of the day in winter months is wahoo. All manner of other game fish – tuna, sailfish, mako shark, barracuda and, above all, blue marlin and other billfish that put up a bruising battle – are caught year-round. The hot spots are Bimini Road, off Paradise Point; just off Bimini Bay's Three Sisters Rock; and off Great Isaac, 15 miles north. Those bonefishing fans who prefer smaller fry such as snapper and grunt look east to the Biminis flats.

Typical fishing charter fees are $400 to $500 for a half day and $800 to $900 per full day. Marinas in North and South Bimini offer charters, bonefishing and deep-sea adventures including **Bimini Big Game Resort & Marina** (☎ 242-347-3391; www.biminibiggame.com; King's Hwy) and **Bimini Blue Water Resort** (☎ 242-347-3166; fax 242-347-3293; King's Hwy).

Also contact these excellent guides:
Bonefish Ansil Saunders (☎ 242-347-2178) The world champ. Charges around $300/600 per half/full day.
Bonefish 'Ebbie' David (☎ 242-347-2053; shannys home@msn.com) Runs bonefishing trips ($250/400 per half/full day for two people).
Captain Jerome's Deep Sea Fishing (☎ 242-347-2081; www.biminifishing.com) Fishing for 25 years, he charges $550/900 for half-/full-day trips, and runs shark trips all year round, hunting lemon, hammerhead and black tip sharks.

BIMINIS FISHING TOURNAMENTS

Month	Tournament
Feb	Hemingway Championship
	Midwinter Wahoo
Mar	Bacardi Billfish Tournament
May	Billfish Championship
	Bimini Beach Blue Marlin Rendezvous
	Memorial Day Weekend Tournament
Jun	Big Five Club Tournament
Jul	Fourth of July Tournament
Aug	Junior Anglers Tournament
Sep	BOAT Tournament
Nov	All Wahoo Tournament

Tours
Bonefish Ansil Saunders (☎ 242-347-2178) Runs tours that take in the Bonefish Hole, Healing Hole, East Point, Creeks (mangroves) and Bimini Bay. Maximum of four people for $125.
Bonefish 'Ebbie' David (☎ 242-347-2053; shannys home@msn.com) As well as fishing trips, he runs the Healing Hole Tour, with a half-hour in the pool for $35 per person, and a maximum of 17 people.

Festivals & Events
The Biminis' party-hearty islanders put on a **Junkanoo** extraordinaire each Boxing Day and New Year's Day, and on July 10 in celebration of **Bahamian Independence**. There's also a festive, despite being early, 5am **Christmas Day parade**.

The **Bimini Regatta Blast** at the end of March features live reggae and other bands. The **Bimini Festival** in mid-May features a sportfishing tourney and cookouts.

The Biminis welcome yachters in the annual **Bahamas Boating Flings** each June through mid-August, when first-time boaters arrive en masse from Fort Lauderdale.

Sleeping
All the hotels in Alice Town are strung along King's Hwy. Hotel rooms are usually sold out during big fishing tournaments.

Compleat Angler Hotel (☎ 242-347-3122; fax 242-347-3293; King's Hwy, Alice Town; r $90; P ⊠ ✖) For atmosphere, the best bar in town and a look at Hemingway's old hangout, take a room and a drink here. Mr Hemingway's snoring could be heard from Room 1; you may prefer a sea view. Character-laden rooms are wood paneled and imbued with the spirit of bar tales and Bahamas living. Weekly live music makes the joint jump.

Seacrest Hotel & Marina (☎ 242-347-3071; www .seacrestbimini.com; King's Hwy, Alice Town; r standard/ dockside $100/125; P ⊠ ☒) Take a third-floor room for views over the marina in this pleasant, modern and friendly place. Room facilities include cable TV and a fridge. The beach is 30yd away.

Weech's Bimini Dock & Apartments (☎ 242-347-3028; fax 242-347-3508; King's Hwy, Alice Town; r $125; P ☒) For an atmosphere that is friendly and welcoming, this is the place. Airy and clean rooms overlook the marina.

Bimini Blue Water Resort (☎ 242-347-3166; blue waterresort@boipb.com; King's Hwy, Alice Town; r standard/ suite $90/190, Blue Marlin cottage $285; P ⊠ ☒ ☒) This resort has a full-service marina, restaurant and bar. Choose from the three-bed Blue Marlin cottage (Hemingway's home away from home), rooms in the more atmospheric older building or cheaper, motel-type rooms. A variety of water-based activities is offered, including sportfishing.

Bimini Big Game Resort & Marina (☎ 242-347-3391; www.biminibiggame.com; King's Hwy; r $185, cottages $225, penthouses $325; P ⊠ ☒ ☒) A favorite of anglers and yachters, with a large, fully equipped marina. Charter boats are available, as are bonefishing and deep-sea adventures.

Trev's Inn (☎ 242-347-2452; www.trevinn.com; Porgy Bay; r $80, additional person $15; P ☒) Basic but clean and tidy rooms.

Eating

Most hotels and pubs around town offer meals.

Captain Bob's (☎ 242-347-3260; Blue Harbour Marina, Alice Town; breakfast $10; ☺ breakfast & lunch Wed-Mon) Bahamians pack in here early for scrumptious corned-beef hash with eggs, as well as French toast and omelettes.

Anchorage Restaurant & Bar (☎ 242-347-3166; Bimini Blue Water Resort, King's Hwy, Alice Town; mains $12-30; ☺ breakfast, lunch & dinner Wed-Mon) Good, reasonably priced Bahamian food includes burgers, salads and tasty seafood dishes.

Red Lion Pub (☎ 242-347-3259; King's Hwy, Alice Town; mains $10-23; ☺ dinner Tue-Sun) This intimate place prepares succulent seafood (fish and lobster) and meat dishes, followed by yummy lime pie and banana cream pie.

Clubhouse Restaurant (☎ 242-347-3391; Bimini Big Game Resort & Marina, King's Hwy; mains $15-30; ☺ dinner Wed-Mon) For something different

and tasty, head here. Try the spicy Bahamian gumbo, pepper pot stew, Asian-style dishes or smoked game fish. Reservations are recommended.

Sandra's Restaurant (☎ 242-347-2336; Bailey Town; mains $6-19; ☺ lunch & dinner) This nice little place has lunch and dinner specials daily, ranging from chicken snacks to stuffed lobster. There's also a bar and lounge.

The following are all based at Bimini Big Game Resort & Marina (left): **Fisherman's Wharf** (mains from $12; ☺ lunch & dinner), with a large menu of seafood and steaks and an extensive wine list; the **Barefoot Bar** (☺ lunch & dinner), serving snacks; and **Sports Bar & Grill** (☺ lunch & dinner), which has three satellite TVs and features Bahamian and US dishes as well as pizza. You can buy the Biminis' exquisite, renowned homemade white bread and confections at roadside shacks opposite the resort. Try coconut candy, raisin bread and delicious banana cake.

Head to **Jontra's Grocery Supply** (☎ 242-347-3401; Alice Town) or **Bimini Food Supply** (☎ 242-347-2305; Bailey Town) for groceries.

Entertainment

Compleat Angler Hotel (☎ 242-347-3122; fax 242-347-3293; King's Hwy, Alice Town; ☺ 11am-1am) The larger-than-life hotel where Ernest Hemingway hung his hat is still the center of action more than 50 years later, drawing colorful, offbeat characters. It's the place to be when the calypso band strikes up and the dance floor begins to cook. The band plays three to seven nights a week December to April, and Wednesday night and weekends the rest of the year. One of the rooms holds the original bar, fashioned from prohibition-era rum kegs.

End of the World (☎ 242-347-3277; Alice Town) The health authorities had the original shack condemned, and it's been replaced with a modern wooden unit. But the floor is still covered in sand, dogs wander in and out, and you can add your scrawl to the graffiti-covered walls. It closes at 3am.

Dancing also takes place on weekends at **Fisherman's Paradise**.

Also try the **Island House Bar** (☎ 242-347-2439), opposite the Red Lion Pub, and nearby **Bimini Breeze Restaurant & Bar** (☎ 242-347-3419; Alice Town).

In Bailey Town check out the upstairs bar known as the Specialty Paris (there's no sign), opposite the Anglican Church, where a rake 'n' scrape band play occasionally.

Getting There & Away

AIR

Refer to p288 for information on international flights to the Bahamas and p126 for information on getting to the Biminis.

BOAT

Call the **Dockmaster's Office** (☎ 242-394-1237) in Nassau and check the website of the **Bahamas Ministry of Tourism** (www.bahamas.com) for the latest schedules and prices.

MV Bimini Mack mail boat ($45, 12 hours) departs Nassau for Bimini, Cat Cay and Chubb Cay on Thursday, returning on Monday.

Marina

Boaters and pilots arriving from abroad must clear **Immigration** (☎ 242-347-3446; Government Bldg, King's Hwy) and **Customs** (☎ 242-347-3100; by the mail-boat dock) in Alice Town.

Bimini Big Game Resort & Marina (p131) has around a hundred slips and full-service facilities. Bimini Sands Beach Club, Condominiums & Marina (right) on South Bimini also has a full-service marina.

Getting Around

Most places are within walking distance. However, golf carts can be hired at the marinas in North and South Bimini for $65 per day.

Water taxis between North and South Bimini depart near the Bimini mail-boat dock; the trip costs $5 one way.

SOUTH BIMINI

Less-developed South Bimini has long been a weekend hideaway for wealthy expats, but has also maintained large areas of mangroves, tropical hardwood forest and saltwater pools. This tiny 5-mile-long isle is therefore still popular with waterfowl, who head for Duck Lake, their winter getaway.

A paved road leads from the water-taxi dock on the northwest tip to the airport. A dirt road loops around the west and south shores, connecting with Airport Rd.

There is a public phone booth located at the Bimini Sands Beach Club, Condominiums & Marina along with the **police** (☎ 242-347-3424, 919).

Sights & Activities

Ponce de Leon's mythical **Fountain of Youth** is said to be 2 miles southeast of the water-taxi berth on Airport Rd. Look for the sign amid the undergrowth to the side of the road. It's actually a natural, 18-inch-wide hole (often dry) in the limestone, surrounded by a crumbling wall.

The remains of the **Sapona**, a concrete ship, lie half submerged offshore, 4 miles south of South Bimini. It was built by Henry Ford during WWI. During prohibition it was anchored here and turned into a private club – a favored haunt of the rum-runners.

Officially named the **Bimini Biological Field Station** (Dr Samuel H Gruber in the US ☎ 305-274-0628; www.miami.edu/sharklab/index.html; VHF Channel 88), this 'Shark Laboratory' east of Port Royal researches the lemon shark, one of the 13 shark species common hereabouts. Visitors are welcome. There are no sharks here, however.

Tiki Hut Beach is a lovely 2-mile strip of white sand on the west shore. Snorkeling is best close to **Corner Reef**, half a mile south of Tiki Hut Beach, where spotted eagle rays and grunts can be seen close to shore, and tiny caves and rocks are home to lobsters, octopus and crabs. Snorkelers should also try **Buccaneer Point**, at the north end of the beach, but beware of strong currents. An **airplane** forced down by the US Drug Enforcement Administration lies just offshore.

The Bimini Sands Beach Club, Condominiums & Marina charters sportsfishing boats and skippers, and can suggest guides.

Rodney Rolle (VHF Channel 68) rents sea kayaks for $25/40 per half/full day.

Sleeping & Eating

Bimini Sands Beach Club, Condominiums & Marina (☎ 242-347-4500; www.biminisands.com; r $175, units $250-385; P ⊠ ⊠ ⊠) One of two types of accommodation at this resort, the attractive motel-style lodgings here are popular with scuba divers. Rooms are bright and comfortable and offer either sea or marina views. The spacious and light-filled one- and two-bedroom units have either a marina or an ocean view, and are well fitted with large kitchens. There's a restaurant and bar, and facilities at the sibling Beach Club are open to guests. Water taxis run day and night to Alice Town. A two-night minimum applies.

You can stock up on drinks and snacks at Morgan's Grocery or Morgan's Liquor Store, the only stores on the island; they're near Duncombe's Yacht Club.

Getting There & Around
Refer to p126 for additional information on travel to and from these islands.

The Bimini Airport is 3½ miles east of the ferry dock.

BICYCLES, BOAT & KAYAK
Bimini Sands Beach Club, Condominiums & Marina rents bikes for $15 per day, an 18ft boat for $120 per day, and single/double kayaks for $25/35 per day.

MARINA
Please contact **Immigration** (☎ 242-347-3447) and **Customs** (☎ 242-347-3101) when arriving at the island.

Bimini Sands Beach Club, Condominiums & Marina (opposite) has a 150-slip full-service marina.

WATER TAXI & TAXI
TSL Water Taxi and PHK Water Taxi run water-taxi services ($5) between North Bimini and South Bimini, leaving from the water-taxi dock on the northwest tip.

Minibus taxis wait at the South Bimini wharf for the water taxis.

NORTH CAT CAY
Ten miles south of South Bimini, North Cat Cay is a private island run as an exclusive, members-only club, beloved by magnates, Hollywood stars and the late former US president Richard Nixon. Nonmembers are restricted to the marina area. For information on membership, call the **Cat Cay Yacht Club & Marina** (☎ 242-347-3565; www.catcayclub.com).

The medical clinic is open 10am to noon daily. The staff are available at other times for emergencies.

The marina has grocery and liquor stores.

BERRY ISLANDS

pop 742
Despite being so close to New Providence, these solitary islands and cays receive few mainstream visitors. There is a much greater population of birds than humans,

and it is quite possible to find a tiny cay where you can be alone – provided you have your own boat.

The 30 mostly uninhabited islands and cays of the Berry Islands only make up 12 sq miles of land, but span a distance of about 25 miles across the ocean. The largest and most important island is Great Harbour Cay, a 10-mile-long, mile-wide island of scrub-covered rolling terrain. Chub Cay, renowned among the wealthy elite, also attracts those who enjoy game fishing and boating. Several other cays are privately owned, such as Bond's Cay, where a private bird sanctuary is maintained, and Cistern Cay, a stone's throw northwest of Great Harbour Cay.

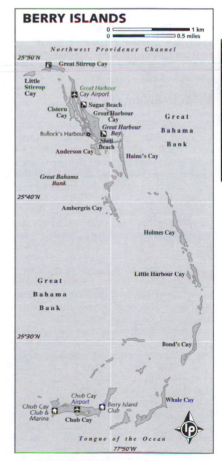

BERRY ISLANDS

History

In the 1960s Douglas Fairbanks Jr and others among the US social elite took Great Harbour Cay to their hearts. The Great Harbour Cay Club was formed, nine rippling fairways were sculpted on the rises falling down to the sea, and marinas were built and lined with luxury waterfront homes. Jet-setters flocked to these shores, including Brigitte Bardot, Cary Grant and members of the Rockefeller clan (mobster Meyer Lansky also had a stake). However, the troubled club was closed and ransacked in the '70s.

Since then the island has mostly kept its own counsel. Occasional visitors arrive to restock their boats and join the locals in fishing expeditions.

Getting There & Around

Most visitors arrive at Great Harbour Cay either by charter plane, private boat or mail boat. You can get around mainly on foot, or rent a bicycle or scooter.

GREAT HARBOUR CAY

pop 370

This is the main center of the islands, where most islanders live and where most visitors will find company, lodgings and food. Great Harbour Marina is built on a narrow channel south of Bullock's Harbour and is entered via a slender cut with cliffs to each side.

The island's main attraction is the 8-mile-long white-sand beach along the eastern shore, where the warm shallows are every shade of green. The beach is formed by two great scallops: Sugar Beach to the north and Great Harbour Bay to the south. A few dozen expats have houses along the shore. Great Harbour Bay runs south to Shell Beach and a reef (exposed at low tide) that is good for finding sand dollars.

Birds prefer the mangroves, flats and salt pools on the west of the island, where herons and egrets hunch and watch for their lunch. Most of the interior is smothered in thatch palm, scrub and casuarinas, and snakes and butterflies abound. There are vast flats for bonefishing. Great Harbour Dr runs the length of the east coast.

The island's annual Homecoming Regatta is held each August, with plenty of home cooking, live music and fun.

Information

BaTelCo (☎ 242-367-8199; Bullock's Harbour)
Medical clinic (☎ 242-367-8400; Bullock's Harbour; ◔ 9am-2pm Mon-Fri)
Police (☎ 919, 242-367-8344; Bullock's Harbour)
Post office (☎ 242-367-8293; Bullock's Harbour; ◔ 9am-5:30pm Mon-Fri) Has a public telephone kiosk.

Activities

There are good dive and snorkel sites northeast of Great Harbour Cay. The Berries are also superb for fishing. Permits are required for sportfishing boats.

Happy People's Gift Shop & Rentals (☎ 242-367-8117; Great Harbour Marina; ◔ 8am-5pm) rents snorkel gear for $10 per day, and a 15ft bonefishing skiff for $85/105 per half/full day. It also rents fishing rods for $15 and sells tackle.

Bonefishing guides can be hired through the marinas. Rates are around $250/375 per half/full day, including boat charter for bonefishing, and $375/550 per half/full day for deep-sea fishing. Try **Percy Darville** (☎ 242-367-8119; Great Harbour Yacht Club & Marina).

Sleeping & Eating

Some private homes will rent out rooms, so just ask around.

Ogburn's Conch Villa (☎ 877-669-5275; www.a1 vacations.com; villas per week $900; ✕ ✕) This ocean-front villa in Great Harbour Cay sleeps six, and has a fab wraparound balcony perfect for a sunset tipple. This super place is modern, and kids will love the loft rooms.

Tropical Diversions Resort at Great Harbour Cay (☎ 954-921-9084; www.tropicaldiversions.com/great -harbour-cay.htm; d $135-195, villas $494-630; ℗ ✕ ✕ ✕) This resort provides two-bedroom, two-story townhouses with patios and decks overlooking the marina, with private docks below. All of the rooms are splendidly decorated and have a TV, a washing machine and a full kitchen. It also has studio units and beach villas. Daily maid service is included with villa rentals.

Wharf (☎ 242-367-8762; mains $7-20; ◔ breakfast, lunch & dinner Wed-Mon) This place overlooking the marina serves hearty US-style and Bahamian breakfasts. Also head here for salads, soups and burgers and a wide-ranging dinner menu including seafood starters and pizza.

Tamboo Dinner Club (☎ 242-367-8203; Great Harbour Marina; mains $25-50; ◔ Wed & Sat) Dress up and book ahead to eat at this elegant club along with the expats. The menu includes boned duck, Bahamian-style spicy chicken and seafood. Booking is compulsory.

Watergate Bar & Restaurant (☎ 242-367-8177; mains $8-14; ☺ breakfast & lunch) Try this place, opposite the school, for huge servings of pork chops, peas 'n' rice and potato salad. It's a gas at lunchtime when the schoolkids pour in for their takeout lunches.

Mama & Papa T's Beach Club (☺ breakfast, lunch & snacks until 3pm) For a beer and burger try this eatery on the beach facing Great Harbour Bay.

You can buy groceries and general goods at the **Marina Store** (☎ 242-367-8768), and there are plenty of other small grocery stores.

Try Roberts Disco & Lounge for evening activities.

Getting There & Away
AIR
Refer to p288 for information on international flights to the Bahamas and p126 for details on getting to the Biminis.

The Berry Islands are served by two airports: Great Harbour Cay Airport, based on Great Harbour Cay; and Chub Cay Airport, at Chub Cay. The one-way fare from Great Harbour to Nassau is $70.

BOAT
Call the **Dockmaster's Office** (☎ 242-394-1237) in Nassau and check the website of the **Bahamas Ministry of Tourism** (www.bahamas.com) for the latest schedules and prices.

The following mail boats are available:
MV Bimini Mack Departs Nassau for Chub Cay, Bimini and Cat Cay on Thursday ($45, 12 hours), returning Monday.
MV Captain Gurth Deane Departs from Nassau for Bullock's Harbour ($45, seven hours) on Friday, returning Sunday.

Marina
Boaters and pilots arriving from abroad must clear **Immigration** (☎ 242-367-8112) and **Customs** (☎ 242-367-8566) at Great Harbour Cay.
Berry Island Club (☎ 800-933-3533; VHF Channel 16; Frazzer's Cay) Provides eight moorings and 10 slips, and has a restaurant and bar.
Great Harbour Cay Yacht Club & Marina (☎ 242-367-8076; VHF Channels 16 & 68) Has 86 slips and full services.

Getting Around
Happy People's Gift Shop & Rentals (☎ 242-367-8117; Great Harbour Marina; ☺ 8am-5pm) rents bicycles ($20 per day), scooters ($50 per day)

and Suzuki jeeps ($65 per day). Deposits are required and weekly rates are available.

CHUB CAY
The southernmost isle in the chain, this little place has been popular over the years with all sorts of moneyed folk who like to fish, from Texan businessmen to Quincy Jones and Bill Cosby.

The 4-mile-long Chub Cay sits at the edge of the Tongue of the Ocean and offers fabulous wall-diving. One of the best sites is **Mama Rhoda Rock**, protected by the Bahamas National Trust and known for its moray eels, lobsters and yellow trumpetfish, as well as healthy staghorn and elkhorn coral. There's a shipwreck with cannon nearby. Divers will require their own gear.

Favored by boaters and sportfishing fans, **Chub Cay Club & Marina** (☎ 242-325-1490; www.chubcay.com; ☒ ☒ ☒) offers a range of comfortable rooms and three-bed villas on the beach. The club's amenities include tennis courts, diving and fishing trips. At the time of writing this exclusive club was closed for extensive renovations; it's due to reopen in March 2006. The historic two-story **Berry Island Club** (☎ 800-993-3533; VHF Channel 68; Frazer's Cay; r $130; ☒ ☒) on Frazer's Hog Cay has nicely appointed rooms over the stone-and-timber clubhouse; one room has a four-poster bed. Its restaurant has a fine reputation among sailors and its charming little bar also draws mariners.

Refer left for information on travel to the Berry Islands.

ANDROS

pop 7380
Andros is the largest island in the Bahamas, a whopping 2300 sq miles, and has been barely touched by the tourist dollar. It actually comprises three main islands separated by enormous bights, or sounds, that are up to 25 miles across and spotted with numerous cays. Divers and bonefishing fans go mad for Andros' seas, which offer some of the best diving and bonefishing in the Bahamas.

It is bounded on one side by the Great Bahama Bank, an underwater plateau that is about as shallow as the island is high. A 140-mile-long coral reef lies a few hundred yards to 2 miles off the east shore (surpassed

ANDROS

0 _____ 30 km
0 _____ 20 miles

Northeast Providence Channel

Morgan's Bluff
19
10
Lowe Sound
31
Red Bay
9
23
Nicholl's Town
Conch Sound
Conch Sound
37
San Andros
San Andros
Airport
44
32
Mastic Point
36
25°00'N

Great Bahama Bank

North Andros

Stafford Creek
6
Blanket Sound
Stafford Ck

Staniard Creek
25
5
Love Hill
Beach
Love Hill
43
15
8
Calabash Bay
Fresh Ck
13
18
2
30
7
Andros Town & Coakley Town
Andros Town
Airport
Somerset Beach

Bowen Sound

Central Andros

Tongue of the Ocean

24°30'N

Cargill Creek
20
14
Cargill Ck
27
Behring Point
34

North Bight

Great Bahama Bank

Wood Cay

Big Wood Cay

Little Harbour
(Moxey Town)
3
24
33
11
39
Mangrove
Cay
Airport
26
28
Lisbon Creek
42
41
21
Drigg's Hill

Middle Bight

Mangrove Cay

Congo Town
Airport
35
40
Congo Town

South Bight

The Bluff
High Rock

South Andros

Kemp's Bay
4
9
24°00'N
22
12
Deep Creek
16
Deep Ck
Little Creek
17
38
12
Mars Bay

78°30'W
78°00'W
77°30'W

INFORMATION
Andromed Medical Centre......1 B1
Bahamas Ministry of Tourism....2 C2
Bank of the Bahamas
International........................3 D4
Bank of the Bahamas
International........................4 D5
BaTelCo................................5 C2
BaTelCo.............................(see 3)
BaTelCo.............................(see 1)
Canadian Imperial Bank.......(see 1)
Government Medical Clinic....6 C2
Government Medical Clinic...(see 2)
Government Medical Clinic...(see 1)
Government Clinic...............(see 3)
Police...............................(see 2)
Police...............................(see 1)
Police...............................(see 4)
Police...............................(see 3)
Post Office........................(see 2)
Post Office........................(see 1)
Post Office........................(see 3)
Saunder's Drugs and Notions..(see 3)
Scotiabank.........................(see 1)

SIGHTS & ACTIVITIES
AUTEC.................................7 C3
Captain Bill's Blue Hole.........8 C2
Charlie's Blue Hole................9 B1
Henry Morgan's Cave...........10 B1
Seascape Divers...................11 D4
Stargate Blue Hole...............12 D6
Twin Lakes.........................13 C2

SLEEPING
Andros Island Bonefishing
Club................................14 D3
Androsia Ltd........................15 C2
Bair Bahamas Guest House....16 D5
Bonefish Beach Club.............17 D6
Chickcarnie's Hotel..............18 C2
Coakley House...................(see 15)
Conch Sound Resort Inn.......19 B1
Creekside Lodge..................20 C3
Emerald Palms Resort...........21 D4
George's Point Villas...........(see 18)
Glato's Apartments..............22 D5
Green Windows Inn..............23 C1
Hellen's Motel Complex........24 D4
Kamalame Cay Villas............25 C2
Lighthouse Yacht Club &
Marina...........................(see 18)
Mangrove Cay Club.............(see 24)
Mangrove Cay Inn...............26 D4
Moxey's Guest House & Bonefish
Lodge............................(see 24)
Nottage's Cottages...............27 C3
Point of View Villas.............(see 18)
Seascape Inn.....................(see 18)
Skinny's Landmark Motel......(see 18)
Small Hope Bay Lodge.........(see 15)
Taimo Resort......................28 C4
Tranquility Hill Fishing Lodge..29 C3

EATING
Adderley's Bargain Mart........30 C3
Big J's on the Bay Restaurant &
Bar..................................31 B1
Brinka's Hallelujah Corner......32 B1
Cargill Creek Convenience
Store.............................(see 20)
Dianne Cash.....................(see 3)
Fish Fry...........................(see 1)
Fisherman's Paradise.........(see 38)
Hank's Place, Restaurant &
Bar...............................(see 30)
McPhee's Food & Variety
Store...............................33 D4
Pineyard Discount Centre....(see 32)
Sea View Restaurant & Bar.....34 D3
Square Deal Restaurant 35 D5
Stacey's Restaurant & Lounge..(see 33)

DRINKING
Bluebird Club......................(see 35)
Flamingo Club....................(see 35)
Rubber Tree Bar..................36 C1
Twilight Zone....................(see 31)
Woody's Beach Club..............37 C1

ENTERTAINMENT
Cabana Beach Bar..................38 D6
Donny's Sugar Sweet Lounge..(see 30)
Happy Three Soca Club..........39 D4
Leadon's Creek Side Lounge &
Disco...............................(see 20)
Lewis' Restaurant & Bar........(see 38)

SHOPPING
Gibson's Straw Market...........40 D5
Wendy's Craft Centre...........(see 21)

TRANSPORT
Basil Martin.......................(see 37)
Ferry Dock & Mail-Boat Dock..41 D4
Ferry Dock & Mail-Boat Dock..42 D4
Gas Station.........................43 C2
Gordon Gaitor Car Rental.......44 B1

BIMINIS, BERRY ISLANDS & ANDROS

in length only by Australia's Great Barrier Reef and the Reef off the Caribbean Coast of Central America). Beyond it, barely two miles from shore, the plateau drops off to a very dark 6000ft in the Tongue of the Ocean canyon.

Andros is akin to a tremendous 100-mile-long and 45-mile-wide jigsaw puzzle, divided by countless creeks, lakes, palm savannas and eerie primal forests of mahogany, pine and palmetto, as well as vast mangrove swamps. This probably helps explain why it has so far escaped the commercial development of Nassau, just 25 miles away.

Various Bahamian settlements sprawl along Queen's Hwy on the east coast, separated by an immensity of scrub and forest filled with wildlife. Unfortunately much of this fauna is hunted; wild boar in particular, but also dove, duck, quail and white-crowned pigeons (the latter are slaughtered each spring). During late spring and early summer, giant land crabs cross the road en masse for a paroxysm of mating and egg laying, though many end up in Androsian cooking pots. The skies are also busy; patrolled by turkey buzzards and shrieking ospreys. Or is that the mythical and evil chickcarnies (see the boxed text, p139) you can hear…?

History

The wild island became a refuge for both Seminole Indians and runaway slaves fleeing Florida during colonial days. A community of their descendants still exists in Red Bay on the northwest coast.

Andros' renowned sponge beds, west of the island, supported much of the population in the late 19th and early 20th centuries, until a mysterious blight in 1938. Some believe that the island was named by Greek spongers for the Mediterranean island of Andros. A few locals still make a living sponging (see the boxed text, below), but most earn a living from fishing. The famous Androsian sloops, however, have been replaced by fiberglass outboards.

Dangers & Annoyances

A word of warning, especially for hikers and bird-watchers; the gargantuan forests, marshlands and scrublands are also used by Bahamians hunting wild boar and birds, so be careful.

Also come well prepared for the aggressive horsefly (or 'doctor fly,' because its bite hurts like a syringe) and clouds of mosquitoes.

Getting There & Away

Many visitors arrive in Andros by plane. There are four regional airports, however,

BIMINIS, BERRY ISLANDS & ANDROS

SPONGERS

The sponges that made this island so famous lie in water or mudflats so shallow that they can be pried from the coral with rods.

The sponge is a marine animal composed mainly of microscopic calcareous rods, stars and hooks held in place by elastic fibers. Nourishment is extracted from water via a vast network of pores and canals. Although they don't have hearts or brains, sponges produce sperm and eggs. There are various species, including the supersoft 'velvet' or wool sponge, and the 'hardhead,' so durable that it has many industrial uses.

Sponging in the Bahamas began in earnest in 1841 after a Frenchman, Gustave Renouard, was shipwrecked here and discovered superior sponges to the Mediterranean varieties. Greek deep-sea sponge divers left their homeland to make their money from the Bahamian seabed, using glass-bottom buckets and a hooked pole. (Today spongers dive with snorkel or scuba gear. They also slice the sponges at the base, leaving the root to regenerate). Ashore, the sponges were beaten to death and put in shallow-water 'kraals' to allow the flesh to rot and decompose. Then they were rinsed, pounded to a pleasing fluffiness, and strung up to dry before being shipped for sale at the Greek Sponge Exchange in Nassau.

At the close of the 19th century, 500 schooners and sloops and 2800 smaller vessels were working the sponge beds, and in the peak year of 1917, 1½ million lb of sponges were exported. 'The Mud,' an extensive 140-mile-long, 40-mile-wide shoal off Andros, was a major source of income for sponge divers. Sponging was the chief source of livelihood on all the Bahamian islands until 1938, when a fungal blight killed the sponges overnight.

so be sure to fly to the correct one for wherever you intend to stay. You can also catch a fast ferry (car and passenger) or mail boat to the islands.

Getting Around
This is a tough place to get around. Car rentals are mainly organized on an informal ad hoc basis. This means that you may not get a rental unless you book ahead, and even then it won't be guaranteed. Taxis also run on an informal basis, and can be very expensive.

Getting between the islands that make up Andros is only possible by flight or coordinating mail-boat schedules, though a small passenger ferry runs between Lisbon Creek and Drigg's Hill in South Andros.

NORTH & CENTRAL ANDROS
Technically one island, North and Central Andros are the largest of the three islands that make up Andros (North Andros lies north of Stafford Creek and Central Andros lies to the south). Much of the island is smothered in pine forests that have twice been logged – first to provide pit props for English coal mines and later for Chicago newspapers. The island's exotic hardwoods, mahogany and lignum vitae (sometimes called 'sailor's cure' because its sap provided a cure for syphilis in the 19th century), for example, are long gone, but the logging tracks remain. It's the most popular of the Andros islands, and visitors here enjoy great diving, fine beaches and bonefishing.

For information on getting to and from North and Central Andros, see p142.

Nicholl's Town Area
A small sleepy center, Nicholl's Town (population 270) has small stores, a supermarket, a gas station, a Georgian-style government building and equally endearing, more venerable colonial-era buildings at its heart.

Fishing boats line the shore and palms fringe the beach. Behind which the town's

---

TIMES THEY ARE A-CHANGIN'
Take note! The peak holiday time in Andros (February 20 to April 23) is different to the rest of the Bahamas. This coincides with the peak bonefishing season through March and April.

---

houses and shacks dot along the roads, with US-model cars rusting on their front lawns.

To head south, follow the road via the little fishing village of Lowe Sound, and then pass Conch Sound to Mastic Point. This small commercial harbor dates from 1781, and is the place to hunt down *goombay* music. Much of the land inland around San Andros is intensively farmed for citrus, potatoes, tomatoes and other produce.

INFORMATION
Banks open Monday and Wednesday, but the hours across the whole island are erratic.
Andromed Medical Centre (☎ 242-329-2171; Queen's Hwy, Nicholl's Town).
BaTelCo (☎ 242-329-2131)
Canadian Imperial Bank (☎ 242-329-2164)
Government Medical Clinic (☎ 242-329-2399; Nicholl's Town)
Police (☎ 919, Nicholl's Town ☎ 242-329-2353, Lowe Sound ☎ 242-329-7095)
Post office (☎ 242-329-2034; Nicholl's Town)
Scotiabank (☎ 242-329-2700)

SIGHTS
There's a nice beach west of **Morgan's Bluff**, and a wharf where tankers and barges take on 6 million gallons of water daily for New Providence. The water is drawn from a massive reservoir north of San Andros that is fed by a vast underground aquifer.

If you believe local lore, Henry Morgan, the wily Welsh pirate, hid his treasure in a cave – **Henry Morgan's Cave** – about 30yd from the road (it's well signed). Bring a flashlight.

Scuba divers who first explored **Charlie's Blue Hole** (refer to the boxed text, opposite) were quite astonished to find sharks swimming in the narrow caverns. There is a sign off Queen's Hwy.

Another blue hole, **Benjamin's Blue Hole**, boasts fabulous underwater stalactites and stalagmites.

ACTIVITIES
Rates are around $250/375 per half day/day for bonefishing, $250/420 per half day/day for reef fishing and $300/500 for deep-sea fishing. The following are recommended bonefishing guides:
Arthur Russell (☎ 242-329-2484; Nicholl's Town)
Bonefish Andros (☎ 303-338-8540; www.bonefish andros.com; Stafford Creek) Bonefishing packages are $1095 per person for three nights' accommodation, meals

BEWARE THE CHICKCARNIES AND LUSCA'S LAIR

To you or me, the cheeky chickcarnie is a product of local imagination. But to the Androsians, the devil-in-disguise is as real as the nose on your face.

Chickcarnies are a strange hybrid of man and bird; red-eyed, three-fingered, owl-like elves with beards and feathered scalps that supposedly live atop cotton or pine trees and hang by their tails. They wreak mayhem on whoever disturbs them, screech like the damned and are quite vain. Additionally, if you don't show them the proper respect, your punishment could be pretty severe. Local opinion is that if you happen upon one, it is wisest to strip down to your underwear; it shows that you have nothing to hide (though this advice does sound a bit like a leg-pull for credulous visitors!).

At the end of the 19th century, when sisal growers were thriving, young Neville Chamberlain (British prime minister 1937–40) and his father ran a 4000-acre sisal plantation, **Twin Lakes Farm**, 16 miles inland up Fresh Creek, but the enterprise failed. Locals firmly believe this happened because the Chamberlains disturbed the chickcarnies, who caused Neville no end of grief – not least the Munich Pact (the treaty signed between Chamberlain, Daladier, Hitler and Mussolini in 1938, which resulted in the annexation of Czechoslovakia). Twin Lakes now lies in ruins, but the two blue holes that gave the plantation its name can still be accessed by a rough, overgrown track.

Don't miss the **Chickcarnie Festival**, held in October at Fresh Creek, North Andros, which celebrates and respects these creatures.

Meanwhile **Charlie's Blue Hole**, near Nicholl's Town, is renowned for its 'boil,' a whirlpool caused when water is sucked out to sea through subterranean passages. Any boats that happen to be on the surface can be pulled underwater. Several boats have been lost this way, adding to the local legend of the monstrous octopus, Lusca, in residence here. Scuba divers have not yet discovered this vile leggy monster, or maybe we just didn't hear them scream…

BIMINIS, BERRY ISLANDS & ANDROS

and two days' fishing with guides. Weeklong packages are $2615 per person.

Neville 'Uncle JT' Dean (☎ 242-329-7629; Lowe Sound)

SLEEPING & EATING

Credit cards may not be accepted at some lodgings, so check when booking.

Conch Sound Resort Inn (☎ 242-329-2060; conch soundresort@yahoo.com; Conch Sound; d/ste $85/190; P ⊠ ⊠) The motel-style lodgings are surrounded by pine forests (good for hiking), with the beach a free 10-minute shuttle away. Pleasant but modest rooms have satellite TV, while simple units have kitchens. Meals are served at the relaxing restaurant and bar. Fishing and other activities can be arranged.

Green Windows Inn (☎ 242-329-2194; fax 242-329-2016; Nicholl's Town; r $80; P ⊠ ⊠) This charming green-roofed inn and guest restaurant is set in a tropical garden with orchids and fruit trees, a 10-minute walk from the beach. Rooms come with satellite TV. Bicycle and car rentals and scuba diving are offered, and babysitting and bonefishing trips can be arranged.

Big J's on the Bay Restaurant & Bar (☎ 242-369-1954; Lowe Sound; mains $8-22; ☽ breakfast, lunch & dinner) Here you can munch on home-style Bahamian dishes and seafood, watch a game in the satellite lounge and sip a beer or two.

You can stock up at the **Pineyard Discount Centre** (☎ 242-329-4595; San Andros) on the main road south of Nicholl's Town, next to which a stall called Brinka's Hallelujah Corner serves real Bahamian fare at its finest.

DRINKING

For bars try the **Twilight Zone** (Mastic Point; ☽ 9pm-late), **Woody's Beach Club** (☎ 242-329-3454; Mastic Point) and nearby **Rubber Tree Bar**, where dominoes is the name of the game.

For real atmosphere, however, enjoy fresh fish and a rum cocktail or Kalik beer at the Fish Fry on the beach in Nicholl's Town.

GETTING THERE & AROUND

For information on flights, boats and ferries, see p142.

You can rent cars from around $70 per day and there's a gas station at the entrance to Nicholl's Town.

Basil Martin (☎ 242-329-3169; Mastic Point)
Gordon Gaitor Car Rental (☎ 242-329-3043; San Andros)

Red Bay

The descendants of the Seminole Indians and runaway slaves who fled Florida in the 17th and 18th centuries live at this down-at-the-heels settlement on the west coast of Andros. A few locals earn an income from weaving, using practices passed down from Seminole forebears. Handwoven, watertight straw baskets are sold, along with others interwoven with locally made batik fabrics.

Stafford Creek Area

The southern road from Nicholl's Town cuts inland through pine forest before heading south. It then turns east and leaps over the mouth of Stafford Creek. On the northern side of the bridge is the disheveled village of **Staniard Creek**, which sits on the southern end of a cay. A really lovely 2-mile-long beach forms the eastern shore, with swaying palm trees and enticing tranquility.

For medical services try the **Government Medical Clinic** (☎ 242-368-6238).

Kamalame Cay Villas (☎ 242-368-6281; www.ka malame.com; r marina/beach $560/650; P ⊠ ⊠ ⊠), tucked away at the north end of Staniard Creek, has thoroughly luxurious rental villas where you will want for nothing. Big and beautiful rooms are furnished with polished antiques, while your watery requirements are met by the azure sea, the marina and water sports. Rates include all meals, house wines and liquor.

Fresh Creek Area

pop 2456

Andros Town and Coakley Town make up the Fresh Creek township and are the crossroads of Central Andros, lying about 30 miles south of Nicholl's Town. A giant plastic crab greets visitors at Coakley Town on the north side of the creek; the hamlet of Andros Town is on the south side. Fresh Creek itself extends into the inland depths of Andros. This is an area popular with divers and anglers, many of whom head here for the facilities at Small Hope Bay Lodge.

INFORMATION

Bahamas Ministry of Tourism (☎ 242-368-2286; Andros Town)
BaTelCo (☎ 242-368-2521)
Government Medical Clinic (☎ 242-368-2038)
On the north side of the Fresh Creek Bridge.
Police (☎ 242-368-2626, 919; Coakley Town)

Post office (☎ 242-368-2012; Coakley Town)
Royal Bank of Canada (☎ 242-368-2071; ⊗ 9:30am-3:30pm Wed)

SIGHTS

The jointly run US-UK navies' **Atlantic Undersea Test & Evaluation Center** (Autec) antisubmarine warfare testing facility is a mile south of town and strictly off limits; the same goes for the waters up to 2 miles offshore.

Somerset Beach is 2 miles south of town, and when the tide recedes, the miles-long beach is extremely deep and splendid. Wading birds patrol the shore, and you can admire the sand dollars at low tide.

The famous Androsia batiks of **Androsia Ltd** (☎ 242-368-2020; www.androsia.com; ⊗ 9am-4pm Mon-Fri, 8am-1pm Sat) are sold throughout the Bahamas. Melding age-old wax techniques and island motifs, workers create a wide range of clothing out of four types of natural fabrics. A guide will show you around and there's a factory outlet.

Calabash Bay is a small coastal settlement, which gains a certain charm from its several churches and the flats that are picked at by herons when the tide is out. An apocryphal story has Henry Morgan and Blackbeard together here with a cache of treasure. The two rogues rowed ashore with six sailors, buried the loot and then killed the witnesses. As they were rowing back, one of the two supposedly said 'There's small hope that'll ever be found.' Hence the bay's alternative name, **Small Hope Bay**.

The Small Hope Bay settlement merges into the **Love Hill** settlement, where a side road just north of the gas station reaches pleasant **Love Hill Beach**. Nearby, **Captain Bill's Blue Hole**, amid pine forests, is popular with divers. There's a ladder and a rope swing for would-be Tarzans. Twin Lakes Farm (see the boxed text, p139) and the two blue holes that gave the plantation its name are also nearby.

ACTIVITIES
Diving & Snorkeling

For some fabulous dive sites, try the following: the Barge, where a wreck lies 70ft below the surface and is now a home to large groupers; the Black Forest, with its crop of three dozen black coral trees; the deep Blue Hole, where large rays and sharks often gather; and the *Potomac*, a 345ft British tanker that sank in 1929.

Expert divers may venture to Alex & Cara Caverns, descending 90ft on the edge of the Tongue of the Ocean, and to Over the Wall, which begins at 80ft and plunges another 100ft at the edge of the Tongue of the Ocean. The Tongue itself drops another 6000ft.

Snorkelers should seek out the Solarium, shallow flats favored by lobsters and stingrays; Red Shoal, for schooling grunts and elkhorn reef; and China Point, where blue tangs and sergeant majors frolic. Also try the Compressor, where, yes, a compressor has metamorphosed into a reef; Central Park, with acres of corals; and Trumpet Reef, home to brittle stars and spiny urchins.

The only operator is Small Hope Bay Lodge, highly acclaimed by divers, which offers a whole range of specialist and basic one-/two-tank dives ($50/70) and night and shark dives ($60/85), as well as snorkeling trips ($25). Divers should ask about blue-hole dives and wall dives to 185 feet.

Bonefishing & Sportfishing

Small Hope Bay Lodge and Coakley House offer bonefishing ($250/375 per half/full day; add $40 for fishing North Bight or Stafford Creek), reef fishing ($250/420 per half/full day) and deep-sea fishing ($300/500 per half/full day).

Lighthouse Yacht Club & Marina also has bonefishing ($250/300 per half/full day).

TOURS

The Small Hope Bay Lodge offers some great bird-watching treks with ornithologists. Check what is planned closer to the time of your visit.

SLEEPING

Credit cards may not be accepted by guesthouses or some smaller lodgings; check when booking.

Skinny's Landmark Motel (☎ 242-368-2082; Coakley Town; r $70; P ⊠ 🏠) This no-frills place has simply furnished, pine-walled rooms above a lively restaurant and bar. The rooms have TVs, and balconies overlooking the village. Skinny's wife, Carmetta, brews up a mean hot-pepper sauce to enliven her traditional-style dishes at their restaurant and bar.

Lighthouse Yacht Club & Marina (☎ 242-368-2305; www.androslighthouse.com; r $120, villas $140; P ⊠ 🏠 🛥) Named for the neighboring

107-year-old lighthouse, these nicely furnished modern rooms and villas, replete with fridges and balconies, are often enjoyed by yachties. A spacious, elegant restaurant and bar serves seafood, Bahamian dishes and great buffet breakfasts. Breakfast and dinner packages for guests are $40 per person. Facilities include a games room, bicycle rentals, tennis courts and fishing charters.

Small Hope Bay Lodge (☎ 242-368-2014; www .smallhope.com; Calabash Bay; r $209; P ⊠) Families and anglers head to this cozy, informal dive resort made out of coral rock and pine. A central lodge strewn with couches and throw pillows incorporates a library, games room, music, and a bar hewn from half a boat. All rooms and cottages look out onto the beach, and have king-size beds, screened windows and Androsia batik fabrics. Fine US-style breakfasts, pig-roast barbecues and buffets are served on a tree-shaded patio by the beach. Restaurant reservations are essential for nonguests. They will host weddings ($500) for those taken by the moment.

The following we also recommended.
Coakley House (☎ 242-368-2013; www.smallhope .com/CH; Calabash Bay; r night/week $300/1750; P ⊠ 🏠) A large three-bedroom villa.
George's Point Villas (☎ 242-368-2238; www .georgespoint.com; Fresh Creek; nightly/weekly $95/600; P ⊠ 🏠) Waterside (perfect for spotting dolphins) and spacious.
Point of View Villas (☎ 242-368-2750; fax 242-368-2761; Fresh Creek; r $300; P ⊠ 🏠 🛥) A little village complex of two-bed cottages, which also has a great little restaurant.

EATING & DRINKING

Hank's Place Restaurant & Bar (☎ 242-368-2447; Fresh Creek; mains $10-22; ⏰ lunch & dinner) For inexpensive but good food head to Hank's, where a shady deck overhanging the creek is the prime spot to munch buffalo wings, baked snapper or lobster washed down with the house drink, a lethal cocktail called the Hanky Panky. Look out for weekend fish fries and roasts.

Donny's Sugar Sweet Lounge (☎ 242-368-2080) This is the place to drink and dance despite the less than glamorous surroundings. Who cares, it gets packed at weekends with some hot music and cold beers.

Chickcharnie's Hotel (☎ 242-368-2026; Coakley Town; mains $8-18; ⏰ lunch & dinner) Try this place for simple and tasty Bahamian dishes, served in the dining room which overlooks the creek. They also have a grocery store.

Square Deal Restaurant (☎ 242-368-2593) Serves simple Bahamian fare.

Captain Crunch Fish Fry (Calabash Bay) Should be visited for the name alone.

Adderley's Bargain Mart (☎ 242-368-2201) For fruit and veggies; it's by the lighthouse.

GETTING THERE & AWAY
Air
Refer to p288 for information on international flights to the Bahamas.

Andros is served by four airports:

Andros Town Airport (ASD; ☎ 242-368-2030) Three miles south of Fresh Creek.

Congo Town Airport (TZN; ☎ 242-369-2640) Four miles north of Congo Town.

Mangrove Cay Airport (MAY; ☎ 242-369-0083) Sits on Mangrove Cay.

San Andros Airport (SAQ; ☎ 242-329-4224) About 10 miles south of Nicholl's Town.

Flights between these airports are $30 one way and depart twice weekly.

The following airlines fly between Andros and other Bahamian islands:

Bahamasair (UP; Andros ☎ 242-377-5505, Freeport ☎ 242-352-8341; www.bahamasair.com; hubs Nassau & Freeport)

Major's Air Services (☎ 242-352-5778; www.the bahamasguide.com/majorair; hubs Grand Bahama & Eleuthera)

Western Air (☎ 242-329-4000; fax 242-329-3167; hubs Andros & Nassau)

The following fares are one way.

Route	Price	Frequency
Andros Town–Freeport	$150	2 weekly
Andros Town–Nassau	$68	2 daily
Congo Town–Freeport	$150	2 weekly
Congo Town–Nassau	$68	2 daily
San Andros–Freeport	$150	2 weekly
San Andros–Nassau	$68	2 daily
South Andros–Freeport	$150	2 weekly
South Andros–Nassau	$68	2 daily

Boat
Call the **Dockmaster's Office** (☎ 242-394-1237) and check the website of the **Bahamas Ministry of Tourism** (www.bahamas.com) for the latest schedules and prices.

The following mail boats are available for travel:

MV Lisa JIII Departs Nassau for Morgan's Bluff and Nicholl's Town ($30, six hours) on Wednesday, returning Tuesday.

MV Lady D Departs Nassau for Fresh Creek ($35, 5½ hours) on Tuesday, returning on Sunday.

MV Mangrove Cay Express Departs Nassau for Drigg's Hill, Mangrove Cay and Cargill Creek ($30, 5½ hours) on Thursday, returning on Tuesday.

MV Captain Moxey Departs Nassau for Kemp's Bay, Long Bay and the Bluff ($35, 7½ hours) on Monday, returning Wednesday.

Ferry
Bahamas Ferries (☎ 242-323-2166, 242-323-2168; www.bahamasferries.com; child/adult/car $20/35/140) operates a car-and-passenger ferry service from Nassau to Morgan's Bluff (2½ hours) on Monday and Saturday, and to Fresh Creek on Wednesday, Friday and Sunday.

GETTING AROUND
The Mastic Point harbor is clogged by sunken boats and is not recommended for private boaters.

The Lighthouse Yacht Club & Marina (p141) has 18 slips for vessels.

You can rent a car for $80 to $90 per day (plus $200 deposit) from several places. There's an Esso gas station in Love Hill, and gas pumps on Edgecomb's St in Calabash Bay. **AMKLCO** (☎ 242-368-2056) garage also rents cars.

When booking accommodations ask about taxis, as they run on an informal basis. However, be warned: the drivers can be a little greedy as there are no formalized rate structures.

Cargill Creek Area
You are now in supreme bonefishing territory; anglers, polish your rod and head onwards. **Cargill Creek** opens westward into the expansive flats of both the North and Middle Bights. Queen's Hwy continues south approximately 2 miles to **Behring Point**, which is located on top of a bluff overlooking the mouth of North Bight. North Bight separates the island from Mangrove Cay.

Contact Tranquillity Hill Fishing Lodge and Nottage's Cottages, which will put you in touch with some excellent bonefishing guides working out of Cargill Creek and Behring Point.

SLEEPING

The lodgings are designed for anglers seeking bonefishing packages, not romantic beachy getaways.

Andros Island Bonefishing Club (☎ 242-368-5167; www.androsbonefishing.com; Cargill Creek; P ⊠ ⋈) Small wood and concrete bungalows each have a fridge and private bathroom. They lie just 100yd away from a productive wadable flat with bonefish. Seven- and three-night packages (single/double $1540/2240) include all meals and transfers.

Tranquility Hill Fishing Lodge (☎ /fax 242-368-4132; www.tranquilityhill.com; Behring Point; s/d $175/320; P ⊠ ⋈) It may look blocky from the outside, but its interiors are clean and bright and all rooms have TV. Rates include all meals. Fishing packages are offered.

Also recommended:

Creekside Lodge (☎ 242-368-5395; Cargill Creek; s/d $185/320; P ⊠ ⋈)

Nottage's Cottages (☎ 242-368-4297; bigcharlie andros@yahoo.com; Charlie's Haven; s/d $180/345) Upgraded in 2004.

EATING & DRINKING

You can dine and drink at any of the fishing lodges.

Sea View Restaurant & Bar (☎ 242-368-4005; Behring's Point) Locals frequent this place, 100yd south of the Cargill Creek Bridge.

Leadon's Creek Side Lounge & Disco (☎ 242-368-4167; Cargill Creek) Open till around 3am on weekends, head here for some classic Bahamian artists and rake 'n' scrape bands like Kelly & the Boys.

Cargill Creek Convenience Store (☎ 242-368-5221) Buy groceries here.

SOUTH ANDROS

Virtually bypassed by tourists, South Andros has superb bonefishing and some beautiful beaches. Look out for Androsian iguanas, which can grow to 5ft in length and dwell in scattered coppices.

Most locals reside on lobstering, crabbing or sponging, but pockets of poverty do exist. Sir Lynden Pindling (the 'fallen' former Bahamian prime minister) hails from here (see p24).

Refer opposite for information on travel to Mangrove Cay and South Andros. For getting around, ask about taxis or possible car hire when booking accommodation. A cash deposit for rentals will be required.

Mangrove Cay

The cay makes up northern South Andros. A narrow but lovely beach stretches out along the eastern shore, and at least 23 blue holes await exploration. Little Harbour or 'Moxey Town' is the (only) center and was blessed with electricity in 1989.

Andros' southernmost airport is at Mangrove Cay.

INFORMATION

Banks open on Monday and Wednesday, but the hours are erratic.

Bank of the Bahamas International (☎ 242-369-0502)

BaTelCo (☎ 242-369-0131)

Government Medical Clinic (☎ 242-369-0089)

Police (☎ 242-369-0083)

Post office (☎ 242-369-0494)

Saunder's Drugs & Notions (☎ 242-369-0312)

SIGHTS & ACTIVITIES

Lynward Saunders (☎ 242-369-0414) will show you how sponges are cleaned and dried and made ready for export.

There is no shortage of bonefishing guides who will charge around $350 per day for two people. On Mangrove Cay, try **Ralph Moxey** (☎ 242-369-0218) or 'Bonefish' John (ask around, everyone knows him).

Seascape Divers at Seascape Inn rents scuba equipment and offers Professional Association of Diving Instructors (PADI) instruction (prices on application).

SLEEPING & EATING

Seascape Inn (☎ /fax 242-369-0342; www.seascapeinn .com; standard/superior cabanas incl breakfast $135/145; P ⊠) Right on the beach, 2 miles south of Little Harbour, these attractive and simply furnished off-ground cabanas come with private decks, ceiling fans and beach views. Hammocks encourage lounging, while free bicycle and kayak trips are on offer, and quotes for diving and bonefishing can be given. There's a lofty all-timber restaurant and bar on tall stilts, with a TV, dartboard and stereo. On Sunday a Fish Fry is hosted. Breakfast is included in the rates.

Moxey's Guest House & Bonefish Lodge (☎ 242-369-0023; fax 242-369-0726; r $90; P ⊠ ⋈) Dating from the 1930s, this attractive two-story yellow and white stuccoed lodge sits directly on the water in Little Harbour. A vast and generous almond tree shades the front, and the rooms are modestly yet attractively furnished. There's a delightful dining room and a splendid and popular bar. Packages are on offer.

Mangrove Cay Inn (☎ 242-369-0069; fax 242-369-0014; r $110; P X X) This place is set amid lawns about 200yd from a beach, and there are three blue holes nearby. Bicycle and snorkel-gear rentals, a guest laundry and a bar with an electric piano are on offer. Credit cards are not accepted.

Taimo Resort (☎ 242-357-2489; http://www.tiamo resorts.com/; r $380; X X) This award-winning and solar-powered resort has ecofriendly beachside bungalows for adults.

Hellen's Motel Complex (☎ /fax 242-369-0033; s/d $70/85; P X X) Small, clean rooms.

Mangrove Cay Club (☎ 242-369-0731; www .mangrovecayclub.com; P X X) For dedicated bonefishing fans. Three- and seven-night packages are offered (for the latter, single/ double $4995/6380).

Stacey's Restaurant & Lounge (☎ 242-369-0161) Bahamian dishes include fish and grits or chips.

Dianne Cash (☎ 242-369-0430) For great sides and peas 'n' rice, head here; she has a small place a mile south of the Seascape Inn.

You can buy groceries at McPhee's Food & Variety Store, opposite Seascape Inn.

ENTERTAINMENT
Happy Three Soca Club (☎ 242-369-0030; Grants) Has live soca music, dancing and a pool table.

Drigg's Hill to Congo Town
Visitors to South Andros proper will land at Congo Town airport, 3 miles south of Drigg's Hill, a scrawny hamlet facing Mangrove Cay across South Bight at the northern tip of the island. The equally diminutive settlement of Congo Town, also known as Long Bay, is 2 miles south of the airport.

Stanley 'Jolly Boy' Forbes (☎ 242-369-4767) will take you bonefishing for $375 per day for two people.

Emerald Palms Resort (see following) can organize a guide for **walking tours** to the blue hole and swampland. It takes about two hours.

The only true beach resort on Andros, the rooms at **Emerald Palms Resort** (☎ 242-369-2713; www.emerald-palms.com; r $195; P X X) are small but quite nicely furnished. An elegant dining room opens to the pool and the

beach, where buffets are hosted. Hammocks are strung between palms. Bonefishing, diving, snorkeling and excursions are offered. A MAP (breakfast, lunch and dinner) plan costs $70 daily and ocean-view lodgings start at $495.

Four hundred yards south of the resort, **Square Deal Restaurant** (☎ 242-368-6050) serves Bahamian meals, as do the Bluebird Club and **Flamingo Club** (☎ 242-369-2671; Drigg's Hill). Both clubs have pool tables and host local nightlife.

For shopping, try **Gibson's Straw Market** (Congo Town). You can buy homemade jewelry crafted from shells at **Wendy's Craft Center** (Drigg's Hill), opposite the BaTelCo office.

A small government-run passenger ferry runs from Lisbon Creek to Drigg's Hill.

The Bluff & High Rock
Three miles south of Congo Town, The Bluff is the largest and most orderly settlement on the island. The village extends south to the suburb of High Rock, a disorderly place atop a limestone bluff overlooking fabulously blue flats. Two narrow yet beautiful beaches run north and south.

Kemp's Bay to Mars Bay
Five miles south of High Rock, Kemp's Bay is a small yet lively center of action, with the island's high school and a concentration of services.

Tinker's Rock, a mile offshore, is favored by fishermen. Catches are shipped aboard the weekly mail boat to the Nassau market.

The road continues south through the tiny settlement of **Pleasant Bay** and onto Mars Bay. This colorful seaside settlement has quaint wooden and emancipation-era stone houses painted in bright pastels. You may see old ladies weaving straw, and fishermen scaling their catch down by the wharf, where a grand old Androsian schooner lies beached.

Stargate Blue Hole, looking like a country pond, is actually the local harbor! It descends to about 300ft, with galleries of stalactites and stalagmites.

Based in Kemp Bay, there is the **Bank of the Bahamas International** (☎ 242-369-1787) and **police** (☎ 242-368-4733, 919).

SLEEPING & EATING
This area is truly for anglers, exemplified in the accommodation choices and packages.

Glato's Apartments (☎ 242-369-4669; www.island aze.com/glatos; Johnson's Bay; r $80; P ⊠ ⊠) Four hundred yards north of the bridge over Deep Creek, this two-story guesthouse is simple but modern, surrounded by lawns and within yards of the ocean. Fishing packages for three days are $1500 and the owners adhere to a strict catch and release policy for fish.

Bair Bahamas Guest House (☎ /fax 242-369-4518; P ⊠ ⊠) For a more intimate experience, head to Little Creek and check in at this charming, strawberry-pink three-bedroom guesthouse with TV lounge and meals, including fabulous coconut shrimp and key lime pie. Bonefishing packages are $580 per person per day.

Bonefish Beach Club (☎ 242-369-1608; fax 242-369-1934; r $75; P ⊠ ⊠) This place to stay is also recommended, with six-night fishing packages at $3175/4600 per single/double.

Grab a Bahamian snack in Mars Bay at **Fisherman's Paradise**. **Lewis' Restaurant & Bar** offers barbecues and dances on weekends, as does the **Cabana Beach Bar**. On weekends head for the Fish Fry north of town at Smith Hill beachfront.

A minibus from Drigg's Hill occasionally stops at Kemp's Bay.

Abacos

Yachting and the Abacos go together like wind and sail; the chain is known as 'The Sailing Capital of the World.' Visitors hire boats to wander the boomerang-shaped chain that has 130-mile-long Abaco, the nation's third-largest settlement, and many smaller cays stretching 200 miles from Walker's Cay in the northwest to Cherokee Sound in the southeast.

Most folks live in Abaco's Marsh Harbour, a quiet working town with a small tourist center, or on the Loyalist Cays of Elbow, Man O' War, Great Guana and Green Turtle. Tight-knit families and expats live in colourful gingerbread houses adorned with white fascia, and painted flowers, fish and turtles. Their bloomfilled gardens are framed by picket fences which line the narrow streets where cars are banned and people go about their day on foot, golf cart or bicycle. The cays vary in size and character, but all have glorious white-sand beaches and little cottages to rent, so that you can happily play at island living.

Coral-reef gardens beckon; walk off village beaches like Great Guana Cay for easy snorkeling, head to deeper waters for fabulous sportfishing, and experience the marine marvels of Fowl Cay National Reserve among special diving sites.

The inshore waters of the Sea of Abaco are also home to bottlenose dolphins. There is Abacos National Park, made for hikers and bird-watchers seeking endangered Bahama parrots, plus the exuberant onshore fun of sailing regattas and summer *goombay* festivities.

HIGHLIGHTS

- Snorkel or dive with stingrays, angelfish and flounder at **Pelican Cays Land & Sea Park** (p160), followed with a cold beer at nearby **Pete's Pub & Gallery** (p164)

- Whiz down Elbow Cay's length on a golf cart and stroll pretty **Hope Town** (p155)

- Lounge in the brilliant azure seas off the dazzling white crescent of **Treasure Cay Beach** (p165), one of the world's top 10 beaches

- Hire a boat and head for **Tilloo Cay** (p160) to spot the rare and beautiful tropicbird

- Sip a rum-laced Goombay Smash in the affable and tiny **Miss Emily's Blue Bee Bar** (p171) on Green Turtle Cay

Green Turtle Cay ★
Treasure Cay Beach ★
Hope Town ★
Tilloo Cay ★
Pelican Cays Land & ★ Sea Park

■ TELEPHONE CODE: 242   ■ POPULATION: 14,815   ■ AREA: 650 SQ MILES

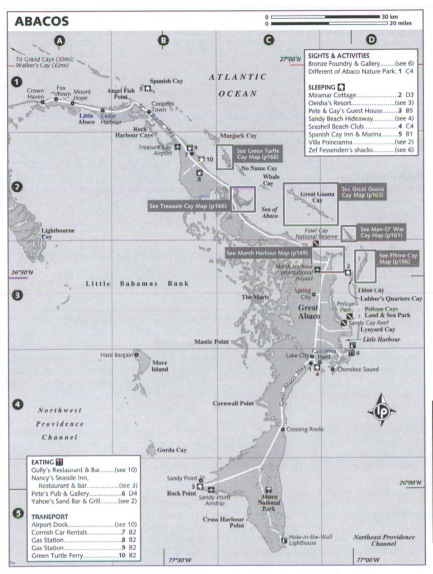

ABACOS

Scale: 0 — 30 km / 0 — 20 miles

SIGHTS & ACTIVITIES
Bronze Foundry & Gallery........(see 6)
Different of Abaco Nature Park..**1** C4

SLEEPING
Miramar Cottage......................**2** D3
Oeisha's Resort.......................(see 3)
Pete & Gay's Guest House......**3** B5
Sandy Beach Hideaway...........(see 4)
Seashell Beach Club................**4** C4
Spanish Cay Inn & Marina......**5** B1
Villa Poincianna....................(see 2)
Zef Fessenden's shacks...........(see 6)

EATING
Gully's Restaurant & Bar........(see 10)
Nancy's Seaside Inn,
   Restaurant & Bar.................(see 3)
Pete's Pub & Gallery...............**6** D4
Yahoe's Sand Bar & Grill.........(see 2)

TRANSPORT
Airport Dock.........................(see 10)
Cornish Car Rentals................**7** B2
Gas Station............................**8** B2
Gas Station............................**9** B2
Green Turtle Ferry.................**10** B2

Map labels: Spanish Cay, Angel Fish Point, Cooper's Town, Crown Haven, Fox Town, Mount Hope, Little Abaco, Cedar Harbour, Rock Harbour Cays, Manjack Cay, No Name Cay, Whale Cay, Great Guana Cay, Treasure Cay Airport, Lightbourne Cay, Little Bahamas Bank, Sea of Abaco, Fowl Cay National Reserve, Marsh Harbour International Airport, Spring City, The Marls, Great Abaco, Tilloo Cay, Lubber's Quarters Cay, Pelican Park, Pelican Cays Land & Sea Park, Sandy Cay Reef, Lynyard Cay, Little Harbour, Mastic Point, Hard Bargain, More Island, Lake City, Casuarina Point, Cherokee Sound, Northwest Providence Channel, Cornwall Point, Crossing Rocks, Gorda Cay, Sandy Point, Rock Point, Sandy Point Airstrip, Abaco National Park, Cross Harbour Point, Hole-in-the-Wall Lighthouse, Northeast Providence Channel. See Green Turtle Cay Map (p168), See Treasure Cay Map (p166), See Great Guana Cay Map (p163), See Man-O'-War Cay Map (p161), See Marsh Harbour Map (p149), See Elbow Cay Map (p156). ATLANTIC OCEAN. To Grand Cays (30mi); Walker's Cay (32mi). 27°00'N, 26°30'N, 26°00'N, 77°30'W, 77°00'W.

History

After decimating the Lucayan Indian population on 'Habacoa,' early Spanish explorers moved on to more fruitful lands. It was not until the American Revolution, when numerous loyalists left the newly independent USA in the 1700s and settled in the Abacos, that a thriving population began.

Their names linger on today in quaint communities whose residents cherish their past and independence. On the eve of independence in 1972, Loyalist Abaconians petitioned the Queen to be made a British crown colony, separate from the Bahamas. Upon refusal, some even contemplated a revolution. Each cay still follows its own

Protestant church, but the islanders share a strong Christian ethic.

The Loyalist settlers were mostly merchants and craftspeople involved in trading, boatbuilding and salvaging shipwrecks, and they became relatively wealthy.

This island group was severely affected by Hurricane Floyd in 1999 and Jeanne and Frances in 2004. However, rebuilding began immediately after the hurricanes passed, although roads remain potholed and many outlying villages still bear visible damage.

National Parks

Most of Abaco is smothered with scrub and pine forest, good for bird-watching and nature hikes and popular with locals hunting wild boar.

Off the west shore of central Great Abaco is a vast wetlands area, the Marls, which provides a vital nursery for young fish and invertebrates, plus an important habitat for ducks, egrets and herons.

The Abacos has four national parks, notably Pelican Cays Land & Sea Park (p160), which preserves the barrier islands and coral reefs south of Tilloo Cay; also Tilloo Cay National Reserve (p39); the 20,500-acre Abaco National Park (p165), which protects the native habitat of the endangered Bahama parrot and other wildlife; and Black Sound Cay National Reserve (p39), which has mangrove habitats loved by birds.

Getting There & Away

Most travelers to the Abacos fly into Marsh Harbour's International Airport, about 3 miles southeast of Marsh Harbour; others arrive on their own boats, or on the weekly mail boat from Nassau.

Getting Around

You'll need your own transport if you want to explore the main island outside of Marsh Harbour, where a car-, bicycle- and motorbike-rental agency is fortunately based (see p155). An excellent ferry service links the mainland and the major cays, while boats can also be easily hired to explore further afield. Golf carts are used on all inhabited cays.

MARSH HARBOUR
pop 5314

This quiet town has worked hard to establish itself as a small tourism and boating

centre for visitors to the Abacos. Despite a fairly unsophisticated demeanor and outer pockets of obvious poverty, the town is a pleasant enough gateway to the island's eclectic and charming set of cays.

Many expats have settled here. The wealthiest have their homes along Pelican Shores Rd; at Eastern Shores, lined with beaches and shady casuarinas; and on Sugar Loaf Cay. By contrast, African-Bahamian residents are found northwest of Marsh Harbour in Dundas Town, a tumbledown suburb with a high crime rate (at least by Bahamian standards).

Marsh Harbour, long-reliant on sponging, fishing and shipbuilding, boomed in the mid-'80s, thanks to drug money and, more recently, because of tourism. Boating is still hugely important to the local economy, as is the steady stream of visiting yachties.

A number of hurricanes have knocked the town back over the years, most recently in 2004, taking out necessary visitor infrastructure such as marinas and boat yards; these are yet again being rebuilt.

Orientation

Marsh Harbour is situated on a peninsula just off the Great Abaco Hwy, the main road running part of the length of Great Abaco.

At the southern edge of town, at the junction with SC Bootle Hwy, Great Abaco Hwy becomes Don McKay Blvd, which leads past the clinic, post office and leading stores to Queen Elizabeth Dr, in the heart of town.

SC Bootle Hwy leads northwest to Treasure Cay.

Queen Elizabeth Dr runs through Marsh Harbour's tourist area, heading west to Dundas Town and east towards Bay St. Bay St leads past the Abaco Beach Resort and ends at Albury's Ferry Dock.

Information
BOOKSTORES
Solomon's Supercenter (Map pp150-1; ☎ 242-367-2602; off Queens Elizabeth Dr; ◷ 8am-6pm Mon-Sat, to 2pm Sun) Sells a few novels.

EMERGENCY
Emergency (☎ 919, 911)
Police (Map p149; ☎ 242-367-3500; Dundas Town Rd)

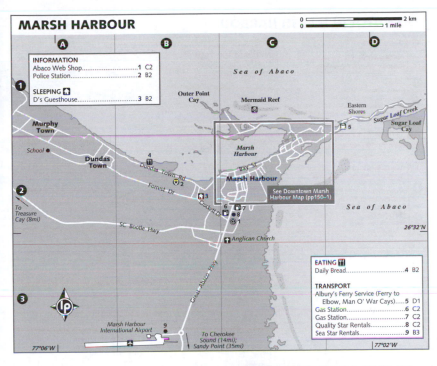

MARSH HARBOUR

INFORMATION
Abaco Web Shop.............................1 C2
Police Station.................................2 B2

SLEEPING
D's Guesthouse...............................3 B2

EATING
Daily Bread.....................................4 B2

TRANSPORT
Albury's Ferry Service (Ferry to
   Elbow, Man O' War Cays).....5 D1
Gas Station....................................6 C2
Gas Station....................................7 C2
Quality Star Rentals.......................8 C2
Sea Star Rentals.............................9 B3

INTERNET ACCESS

Abaco Web Shop (Map p149; ☎ 242-367-0116; Great Abaco Hwy; per 30min $5; ✆ 8am-7pm Mon-Sat, 4-7pm Sun)

Out Island Inter.net (Map p150-1; ☎ 242-367-3006; accounts@abacoinet.com; Queen Elizabeth Dr; per 20min $5; ✆ 9am-5pm Mon-Fri) It stays open later on some Friday evenings and from 9am to 2pm some Saturdays.

INTERNET RESOURCES

www.abacolife.com The online version of local magazine *Abaco Life*.

www.go-abacos.com The official Abaco website with good practical information.

www.oii.net Contains boat-rental, accommodations and restaurant information.

MEDIA

Abaconian (www.abaconian.com) The island's monthly newspaper.

Abaco Journal (http://oii.net/journal) A monthly news journal.

Abaco Life (www.abacolife.com; $2) A quarterly island magazine carrying information of interest to residents and travelers.

Radio Abaco (☎ 242-367-2935; fax 242-367-4531) The station broadcasts on 93.5FM.

MEDICAL SERVICES

Family Medical Centre (Map p150-1; ☎ 242-367-2295, after hr 242-359-6569; Don McKay Blvd; ✆ 9am-5pm Mon-Fri, to noon Sat)

Greater Abaco Dental Clinic (Map pp150-1; ☎ 242-367-4070; Don McKay Blvd)

Love's Pharmacy (Map pp150-1; ☎ 242-367-3292; fax 242-367-3292; Don McKay Blvd; ✆ 8:30am-5pm Mon-Fri)

MONEY

All the listed banks have ATMs.

Commonwealth Bank (Map pp150-1; ☎ 242-367-2370; fax 242-367-2372; Queen Elizabeth Dr; ✆ 8:30am-3pm Mon-Thu, to 4:30pm Fri)

First Caribbean International Bank (Map pp150-1; ☎ 242-367-2166; fax 242-367-2156; Don McKay Blvd; ✆ 9:30am-3pm Mon-Thu, to 4:30pm Fri)

Royal Bank of Canada (Map pp150-1; ☎ 242-367-2420; Don McKay Blvd; ✆ 9:30am-3pm Mon-Thu, to 4:30pm Fri)

Scotiabank (Map pp150-1; ☎ 242-367-2142; fax 242-367-2565; Don McKay Blvd; ✆ 9:30am-3pm Mon-Thu, to 4:30pm Fri)

DOWNTOWN MARSH HARBOUR

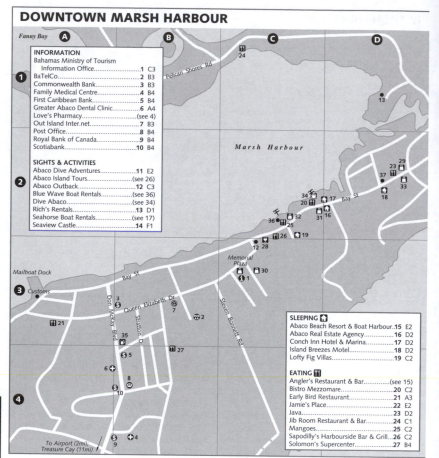

INFORMATION
Bahamas Ministry of Tourism
  Information Office..........................1 C3
BaTelCo...2 B3
Commonwealth Bank.........................3 B3
Family Medical Centre.......................4 B4
First Caribbean Bank..........................5 B4
Greater Abaco Dental Clinic...............6 A4
Love's Pharmacy...........................(see 4)
Out Island Inter.net..........................7 B3
Post Office..8 B4
Royal Bank of Canada.......................9 B4
Scotiabank.......................................10 B4

SIGHTS & ACTIVITIES
Abaco Dive Adventures...................11 E2
Abaco Island Tours......................(see 26)
Abaco Outback................................12 C3
Blue Wave Boat Rentals..............(see 36)
Dive Abaco...................................(see 36)
Rich's Rentals..................................13 D1
Seahorse Boat Rentals................(see 17)
Seaview Castle.................................14 F1

SLEEPING
Abaco Beach Resort & Boat Harbour..15 E2
Abaco Real Estate Agency.................16 D2
Conch Inn Hotel & Marina................17 D2
Island Breezes Motel.........................18 D2
Lofty Fig Villas.................................19 C2

EATING
Angler's Restaurant & Bar..............(see 15)
Bistro Mezzomare............................20 C2
Early Bird Restaurant........................21 A3
Jamie's Place....................................22 E2
Java...23 D2
Jib Room Restaurant & Bar...............24 C1
Mangoes..25 C2
Sapodilly's Harbourside Bar & Grill...26 C2
Solomon's Supercenter.....................27 B4

POST
Post office (Map pp150–1; ☎ 242-367-2571; Don McKay Blvd)

TELEPHONE
Public telephone booths are located in several places downtown. There's also a booth just outside the office of **BaTelCo** (Map pp150–1; ☎ 242-367-2200).

TOURIST INFORMATION
Ministry of Tourism (www.go-abacos.com) Very useful website for details on entertainment, special events and accommodations.
Abaco Tourist Office (Map pp150–1; ☎ 242-367-3067; fax 242-367-3068; Memorial Plaza, Queen Elizabeth Dr; ☼ 9am-5:30pm Mon-Fri)

Sights
Marsh Harbour is a little lacking in terms of sights. On a hill east of town, the canary yellow **Seaview Castle** (Map pp150–1) overlooks Marsh Harbour. It was once the home of Evans Cottman, author of *Out Island Doctor*. A good mile from the town, it is not open to the public.

Activities
Although there are few boat tours on offer from Marsh Harbour, local ferries are excellent, making it easy to visit different cays and their idiosyncratic dive and snorkel sites.

There are also a large number of rental boats available.

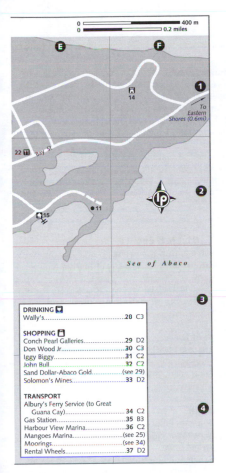

DIVING & SNORKELING

There are some tremendous and easy snorkeling sites to enjoy in the Abacos. **Sandy Cay Reef** in Pelican Cays Land & Sea Park is renowned for its population of spotted eagle rays and huge stingrays, **Fowl Cay Reef** in Fowl Cay National Reserve for friendly groupers, and **Pelican Park** in Pelican Cays Land & Sea Park for eagle rays and sea turtles.

A huge variety of dive sites take in wrecks, walls, caverns and coral kingdoms, including **Bonita Wreck**, a WWII wreck populated by groupers that like to be hand-fed; **Cathedral**, a swim-through cavern with rays and parrotfish; and **Tarpon Cave**, a 50ft drop-off with smiling moray eels.

Dive operators also offer snorkel trips ($50).

Abaco Dive Adventures (Map pp150-1; ☎ 242-367-2963; www.abacodiveadventures.com; Abaco Beach Resort, Bay St) has two-tank dives ($110), twilight and night dives ($126), and Sandy Point wall and reef dives with lunch ($189). Cave dives ($210) include Nitrox for decompression.

Dive Abaco (Map pp150-1; ☎ 242-367-2787; www.diveabaco.com; Conch Inn Hotel & Marina, Bay St) offers two-tank dives ($90) and two-tank shark dives ($115) with tank refills ($50).

SPORTFISHING

The average price for bonefishing commences at around $250/400 per half-/full-day excursion.

JR's Bonefish (☎ 242-366-3058; www.jrsbonefishabaco.com; Casuarina Point) takes in three major fishing locations on its trips, and recommends bringing rare Crazy Charlies or Small Hermit Crab flies with you to the Bahamas.

Justin Sands Bonefishing (☎ 242-367-3526; www.bahamasvg.com/justfish.html; Marsh Harbour) is run by Cpt Justin Sands, a past Abaco Bonefish Champion, which means he knows where to find the slippery critters you desire.

Errol H Thurston Jnr (☎ 242-375-9910; loverboylilt@hotmail), or 'Loverboy,' will take you deepwater, shallow-water and shark fishing (and hold off on the romancing).

BOAT & KAYAKING EXCURSIONS

Dive Abaco (Map pp150-1; ☎ 242-367-2787; www.diveabaco.com; Conch Inn Hotel & Marina, Bay St; cruise $25) welcomes you to gaze at Abaco's spectacular sunsets on a cruise; rum and fruit punches intensify the sensual pleasure. Minimum numbers apply.

Abaco Outback (Map pp150-1; ☎ 242-367-5358; VHF Channel 16; www.abacooutback.com; Bay St; trips from $95) proffers relaxing half- and full-day kayak trips to serene spots where you can snorkel off deserted beaches looking for sea turtles, explore tangled mangroves, spot wild orchids and learn about native plants.

BOAT RENTALS

Sailboats and motorboats can be rented at most marinas. Demand often exceeds supply, so make reservations early! These operators can be reached on VHF Channel 16. Rates do not include fuel and gas for cooking, but boats are provided with

ABACOS

THE BAHAMAS BILLFISH CHAMPIONSHIP

This renowned annual sportfishing competition tours the Family Islands and attracts hundreds of international and national teams.

The championship started in 1968 as an informal contest, set up by regular competitors in individual Bimini, Cat Cay, Chub Cay and Walker's Cay challenges. Since 1973 the Bahamas Billfish Championship has run consecutive yearly competitions including as many as six tournaments covering Bimini, the Berry Islands, the Abacos, Cat Cay, Paradise Island and North Eleuthera.

Running for over 30 years, the Bahamas Billfish Championship runs through April to the end of June. Anglers can fish any or all, the tournaments with cumulative points determining the overall Bahamas Billfish Champions.

In 2005 the Abacos leg of the tournament included several top sportfishing spots off south Abaco, Spanish Cay, central Abaco, Treasure Cay and Boat Harbour on the mainland.

Registration costs $1000, and entry to each tournament is $1500. Contact the **organizers** (☎ 954-920-5577; www.bahamasbillfish.com; 2 Oakwood Blvd, Suite 195, Hollywood, fl 33020, USA) in the US for more information.

---

communication and safety equipment. Local weather reports can be heard on FM radio 93.5 and VHF marine channel 68.

Blue Wave Boat Rentals (Map pp150-1; ☎ 242-367-3910; www.bluewaverentals.com; Harbour View Marina) charges $150/375/700 per day/three days/week for a 21ft Dusky, a favored family craft. They also have 26ft Paramounts for $200/525/950 per day/three days/week.

Seahorse Boat Rentals (Map pp150-1; ☎ 242-367-2513; www.seahorseboatrentals.com; Abaco Beach Resort, Bay St) will rent a 15ft Boston Whaler for $130/560 per day/week or a 20-footer for $190/910 per day/week. It also has a 26-footer for hire at $275/1295 per day/week.

Rich's Rentals (Map pp150-1; ☎ 242-367-2742; fax 242-367-2682; off Pelican Shore's Rd, Marsh Harbour) charges $100/270/595 per day/three days/week for a 21-footer and $150/380/850 per day/three days/week for a 26ft boat.

Tours

Abaco Outback (Map pp150-1; ☎ 242-367-5358; VHF Channel 16; www.abacooutback.com; Bay St) has off-road cycling through pine forests ($70); hikes to the southernmost point of Great Abaco and a blue hole ($95) or nature walks in search of the native Bahama parrot ($60).

Abaco Island Tours (Map pp150-1; ☎ 242-367-2936; www.abacoislandtours.com; Sapodilly's Harbour-side Bar & Grill, Bay St) has day tours to Marsh Harbour ($19) and various cays including Elbow and Man O' War Cay ($38) with a stop at the Albury Brothers boat-building facility. Diving, kayaking and snorkeling activities can also be organized.

Festivals & Events

Check out the www.go-abacos.com website or **Bahamas Ministry of Tourism** (Map pp150-1; ☎ 242-367-3067; www.bahamas.com; Memorial Plaza, Queen Elizabeth Dr; ☼ 9am-5:30pm Mon-Fri) for up-to-date information on these and many other events.

FEBRUARY

Abaco Art Festival Showcases a range of Bahamian artists and their colorful subjects.

Great Abaco Triathlon Tests the mettle of teeth-gritting competitors in Marsh Harbour.

APRIL

Bahamas Billfish South Abaco Championship (www.bahamasbillfish.com) Five days of chasing fish and a record or two.

Bahamas White Marlin Open Abaco (☎ 242-367-2158) Another fishy record-chaser.

Abaco Anglers Fishing Tournament Yup, another one for fishing-fans!

JUNE

Goombay Summer Festival Party, party, party at Marsh Harbour's Junkanoo Rush, which runs through July as well.

Little Abaco Homecoming Welcomes locals back with celebrations.

Bahamas Billfish South Abaco Championship Stage 4 (www.bahamasbillfish.com) Six days of chasing Stage 4's record at Treasure Cay.

JULY

Abaco Regatta (www.rtia.net) Held over a week, this great regatta commences with the 'cheeseburger in paradise' pre-race party; festivities really jump off after the final chew.

Sleeping

There are some great rental units and cottages on the island cays, where many visitors head after a quick stop in Marsh Harbour. As well as the accommodations listed in this guide, try contacting **Abaco Real Estate Agency** (Map pp150-1; ☎ 242-367-2719; www.abacobahamas.com; Bay St) or visit www.abacovacations.com.

Island Breezes Motel (Map pp150-1; ☎ 242-367-3776; fax 242-367-4179; E Bay St; r $90; P ✕ ✕) This small roadside property with eight modestly furnished rooms is a five-minute walk to the town's small tourist center. The location makes it a good budget option and rates include taxes.

D's Guesthouse (Map p149; ☎ 242-367-3980, 242-554-8212; Forest Dr; r incl taxes $75; ✕ ✕) On the west edge of town, the four one-bedroom units here have simple and plain furnishings with TV, refrigerator, microwave oven and coffeepot. The place is well maintained, but take care after dark in this neighborhood.

Lofty Fig Villas (Map pp150-1; ☎ 242-367-2681; loftyfig@mymailstation.com; Bay St; r $110; P ✕ ✕ ✕) These six canary yellow units sit very conveniently in the middle of town and are a two-minute walk from the Conch Inn Hotel & Marina and adjacent to a number of eateries and bars. Surrounding a small pool, the cottages need a little TLC, but are light and pleasantly decorated in tropical colors, and come with kitchenettes and fridges.

Conch Inn Hotel & Marina (Map pp150-1; ☎ 242-367-4000; www.go-abacos.com/conchinn; Bay St; r $130; ✕ ✕ ✕) Also right in the center of the town's restaurant and bar area, this busy but informal marina complex is popular with yachties and local expats. Newly renovated, the smallish but comfortable rooms come with cable TV and a small patio. There is a good restaurant on site, along with a lively and convivial bar, and small freshwater pool.

Abaco Beach Resort & Boat Harbour (Map pp150-1; ☎ 242-367-2158; www.abacoresort.com; Bay St; r $205; P ✕ ✕ ✕) This large resort has a Hawaiian feel, with tall palms and a small beach, while fishing tournaments keep the place busy. Rooms are smallish, but furnished with rich tropical colors and solid wood furniture; dehumidifiers and balconies help on sultry nights. There is also a kiddies' pool, tennis courts and dive shop, plus the Angler's Inn (p154).

Eating & Drinking

There's a good selection of cafés and bars across the Abacos, while Marsh Harbour restaurants also host regular musical bashes.

BUDGET

Daily Bread (Map p149; Dundas Town Rd; mains $5-8; ☼ dinner Mon-Sat) Next to the Kingdom Wash launderette in Dundas Town, this place is named in honor of Christian gods, who have certainly blessed these cooks. Here you will find the best ribs in town (try the Kingdom Ribs and fried rice combo) and the honey-garlic wings are also lip-smackingly good.

Early Bird Restaurant (Map pp150-1; ☎ 242-367-5310; Unit 6, Queen Elizabeth Dr; mains $3-8; ☼ breakfast, lunch & dinner Mon-Sat) It opens early for workers heading to the ferries and businesspeople heading off to the airport. Tuna, corned beef or sardines with grits is the dish of choice.

Java (Map pp150-1; ☎ 242-367-5523; Bay St; mains $4-6; ☼ 8am-5pm Mon-Fri, 9am-noon Sat) A nice little café serving scrumptious sugar-crusted donuts, cinnamon buns and great coffee. As you sip away, enjoy the decorative, bright and colorful paintings, artworks and quilts, and the relaxed atmosphere.

MIDRANGE

Jamie's Place (Map pp150-1; ☎ 242-367-2880; Bay St; mains $7-18; ☼ breakfast, lunch & dinner) This spotless, light and cheerful family joint serves takeaways and luscious homemade ice creams. A mix of American and Bahamian dishes includes 'scram' eggs and pancakes, fish dishes, a refreshing tropical salad of lettuce, pineapple, grapes and crushed walnuts, and great veggie omelettes.

Sapodilly's Harbourside Bar & Grill (Map pp150-1; ☎ 242-367-3498; Bay St; mains $12-25; ☼ lunch & dinner) The tree-shaded deck welcomes drinkers and diners throughout the day. Great burgers and crunchy fish appetizers satisfy, as do the pastas and fish dinners. A pool table and two-for-one cocktails during happy hour bring in the customers, as does the live calypso on Friday and Saturday nights.

Bistro Mezzomare (Map pp150-1; ☎ 242-367-4444; Conch Inn Hotel & Marina, Bay St; mains $8-25; ☼ breakfast, lunch & dinner) For lunch, grab a tasty Angus beef burger topped with bacon, onions and cheese. The chef's dinner specials include grilled chicken with sun-dried tomatoes and

ABACOS

basil, plates of fettucine with marinara sauce, and seafood sautéed in a garlic, white wine and light tomato sauce. Yum.

Jib Room Restaurant & Bar (Map pp150-1; ☎ 242-367-2700; Marsh Harbour Marina, Pelican Shore's Rd; mains $10-20; ☣ lunch daily, dinner Wed & Sat) This very casual waterside place has BBQ nights with live music and dancing. There are rib BBQs on Wednesday and steak BBQs on Saturday.

Wally's (Map pp150-1; ☎ 242-367-2074; Bay St; mains $11-25; ☣ lunch Mon-Sat, dinner Fri & Sat) Head here for live music on weekends and Wally's Special, the lethal house cocktail.

TOP END

Angler's Inn (Map pp150-1; ☎ 242-367-2158, US ☎ 800-468-4799; Abaco Beach Resort & Boat Harbour, Bay St; mains $20-35; ☣ breakfast, lunch & dinner Mon-Sat) This elegant waterside restaurant serves fine food. Try the superb island seafood cake, grilled shrimp garnished with avocado chutney and red curry sauce, or delicate coconut mango shrimp. The resort bar hosts music many nights in the holiday season.

Mangoes (Map pp150-1; ☎ 242-367-2366; Bay St; mains $18-25; ☣ lunch & dinner) International dishes with a Bahamian twist are served on a shaded deck overlooking the marina. Fish and mango combinations are delicious, and desserts are simply wicked – a favorite among Bahamians and anyone with taste buds. Hurricane Libby is the house cocktail. There is live music a couple of nights a week.

Solomon's Supercenter (Map pp150-1; ☎ 242-367-2602; off Queens Elizabeth Dr; ☣ 8am-6pm Mon-Sat, to 2pm Sun) This is an excellent supermarket and general store, certainly the best on the Abacos. Even vegetarians crying out for protein will find a few soya dishes.

Shopping

Conch Pearl Galleries (Map pp150-1; ☎ 242-367-0137; Royal Harbour Village, Bay St) Enjoy Bahamian and resident artists' works depicting nature, fauna and seascapes in acrylics and oils.

Don Wood Jr (Map pp150-1; ☎ 242-367-3681; adjacent to Memorial Plaza) Self-proclaimed 'Carver, Sailor, Rum Barrel Bailer,' Don sculpts wood, gold and other metals into furniture, earrings and desktop ornaments such as turtles and swordfish. He often works outside his shack, with his four-legged pal alongside, and enjoys a chat.

Iggy Biggy (Map pp150-1; ☎ 242-367-3596; Bay St) Across from the Conch Inn Hotel &

Marina, this Bahamian chain sells resort clothing, T-shirts, gifts, jewelry and island music.

For duty-free watches, jewelry, china and crystal, try **Solomon's Mines** (Map pp150-1; ☎ 242-367-3191) and for handcrafted jewelry try **Sand Dollar-Abaco Gold** (Map pp150-1; ☎ 242-367-4405), both outside the entrance to the Abaco Beach Resort, or **John Bull** (Map pp150-1; ☎ 242-367-2473; Bay St).

Getting There & Away

AIR

For information on international flights to the Abacos and the Bahamas see p288.

Marsh Harbour International Airport (MHH; Map p149; ☎ 242-367-3039) is located 3 miles northeast of Marsh Harbour.

The following airlines fly between the Abacos and other Bahamian islands.

Abaco Air (☎ 242-367-2267; www.abacoaviationcentre.com/abacoair; hub Marsh Harbour) Flies between the Abacos, Nassau and North Eleuthera.

Bahamasair (airline code UP; ☎ 242-367-2039; www.bahamasair.com; hubs Nassau & Freeport) The main airline flying within the Bahamas.

Cat Island Air (☎ 242-377-3318; fax 242-377-3723; hub Nassau) Flies between the Abaco cays and Marsh Harbour.

Cherokee Air (☎ 242-367-3450; www.cherokeeair.com; hub Marsh Harbour) Flies between the Abacos and North Eleuthera.

Major's Air Services (☎ 242-352-5778; www.thebahamasguide.com/majorair; hub Grand Bahama) Flies between Freeport, Marsh Harbour, Bimini, Andros and Eleuthera.

Southern Air Charters (☎ 242-367-2498; Nassau; www.southernaircharter.com; hub Nassau) Flies between Nassau, the Exumas and Marsh Harbour.

Quoted fares are one-way.

Route	Price	Frequency
Marsh Harbour–Freeport	$85	1 daily
Marsh Harbour–Moore Island (Abacos)	$42	3 weekly
Marsh Harbour–Nassau	$81	several daily
Marsh Harbour–North Eleuthera	$90	2 weekly
Marsh Harbour–Treasure Cay (in the Abacos)	$35	2 daily
Treasure Cay (in the Abacos)–Nassau	$81	several daily
Treasure Cay (in the Abacos)–Freeport	$85	1 daily

ABACOS

BOAT

Mail Boat

Contact the **Dockmaster's Office** (☎ 242-393-1064) at Potter's Cay in Nassau to confirm schedules, and for further contact and fare details. *Captain Gurth Dean* sails weekly from Nassau to Marsh Harbour ($45 one-way, 12 hours).

Ferry

Pinder's Ferry sets off twice daily from McLean's Town, Grand Bahama, for Crown Haven, Abaco (adult/child $80/40 round-trip, one hour).

Albury's Ferry Service (☎ 242-367-0290; www.oii .net/alburysferry; adult/child $20/10 round-trip) Operates scheduled daily water taxis to Elbow (Hope Town; adult/child one-way $15/7.50), Man O' War (adult/child one way $12/6) and Great Guana Cays (adult/child one-way $15/7.50). The dock for Elbow and Man O' War services is at the east end of Bay St (Map p149); the dock for Great Guana Cay (Map pp150–1) services is at the Conch Inn Hotel & Marina. Private charters are also available.

Bahamas Ferries (☎ 242-323-2166; www.bahamasfer ries.com; Nassau; $90 round-trip) These good-value fast ferries make the trip from Nassau to Sandy Point twice weekly.

MARINAS

All the following marinas can supply electricity and water.

Abaco Beach Resort & Boat Harbour (p153) Offers daily ($1.75 per foot) and long-term ($1 per foot for 61 days and over) dockage. The resort's full marina, accommodations and dining facilities are available with their 200 slips.

Harbour View Marina (Map pp150-1; ☎ 242-367-3910; troy@bluewaverentals.com; Marsh Harbour) Had 68 slips and is also fairly central to the tourist area. Due to hurricane damage this marina was being completely rebuilt at the time of research.

Mangoes Marina (Map pp150-1; ☎ 242-376-4255; Marsh Harbour) Adjacent to the Moorings, this marina has 30 slips, and restaurant and bar facilities.

Moorings (Map pp150-1; ☎ 242-367-4000; www.the moorings.com; Conch Inn Hotel & Marina, Marsh Harbour) Is central to the tourist area and has 80 slips. Accommodations, laundry, cable TV connections and provisions are also available.

Getting Around

Rental Wheels (Map pp150-1; ☎ 242-367-4643; VHF Channel 16; www.rentalwheels.com; Bay St; ☼ 8am-5pm Mon-Fri, 9am-1pm Sat & Sun) are located in the tourist center. It's the only outfit open on Sundays. Bicycles are $10/45 per day/week, motorbikes are $45/200 and cars are $65/300.

Sea Star Rentals (Map p149; ☎ 242-367-4887; Marsh Harbour International Airport; ☼ 8:30am-5pm Mon-Sat) has handy premises at the airport, and rents cars from $65 per day.

Quality Star Rentals (Map p149; ☎ 242-367-2979; fax 242-367-2977; Don McKay Blvd; ☼ 7am-7pm Mon-Thu, to 8pm Fri & Sat) rents cars from $65/325 per day/week and vans from $75/375.

Taxi fares are pre-established. A ride between Marsh Harbour's airport and most hotels costs $10 for two people. Taxis run up and down Marsh Harbour and are easy to flag down.

LOYALIST CAYS

East of Marsh Harbour lie three Loyalist Cays: Elbow, Man O' War and Great Guana. The fourth Loyalist Cay, Green Turtle, lies miles to their northwest (see p167).

Elbow Cay

pop 310

Picturesque **Hope Town** will welcome your arrival on Elbow Cay with its 120ft-high red-and-white-ringed lighthouse, set on the eastern slope of a splendid harbor. As you approach the docks, an entrancing toy-town collection of immaculate white and pastel-colored cottages will come into view. Tiny gardens full of bougainvillea and flowering shrubs spill their blossoms over picket fences and walls, and pedestrians stroll along the two narrow lanes that encircle the village.

Lying 6 miles east of Marsh Harbour, this 5-mile-long island mostly relies on low-key tourism for its income. Hope Town's council is responsible for the conservative but charming community by maintaining strict building and business codes, and banning cars in the village. The hamlet was founded in 1785 by Loyalists from South Carolina whose blond, blue-eyed descendants still live here, interacting, but not intermarrying, with African-Abaconians.

A blight in 1938 ruined the island's sponge bed industry, but some locals still make a living from boatbuilding and fishing.

In July Hope Town hosts Regatta Week, a lively mix of sailing races and land-based festivities.

INFORMATION

There's a meager visitors' information board in the peppermint green building facing the Government Dock on Bay St.

ABACOS

ELBOW CAY

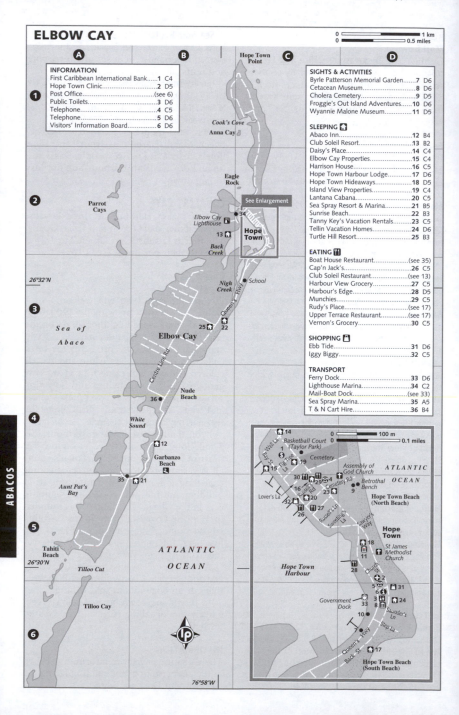

0 ———————— 1 km
0 ———————— 0.5 miles

INFORMATION
First Caribbean International Bank......**1** C4	
Hope Town Clinic...........................**2** D5	
Post Office....................................(see 6)	
Public Toilets...............................**3** D6	
Telephone....................................**4** C5	
Telephone....................................**5** D6	
Visitors' Information Board...............**6** D6	

SIGHTS & ACTIVITIES
Byrle Patterson Memorial Garden.......**7** D6	
Cetacean Museum.........................**8** D6	
Cholera Cemetery.........................**9** D5	
Froggie's Out Island Adventures.....**10** D6	
Wyannie Malone Museum..............**11** D5	

SLEEPING
Abaco Inn...................................**12** B4	
Club Soleil Resort.......................**13** B2	
Daisy's Place.............................**14** C4	
Elbow Cay Properties...................**15** C4	
Harrison House..........................**16** C5	
Hope Town Harbour Lodge............**17** D6	
Hope Town Hideaways..................**18** D5	
Island View Properties................**19** C4	
Lantana Cabana..........................**20** C5	
Sea Spray Resort & Marina............**21** B5	
Sunrise Beach............................**22** B3	
Tanny Key's Vacation Rentals.........**23** C5	
Tellin Vacation Homes..................**24** C5	
Turtle Hill Resort........................**25** B3	

EATING
Boat House Restaurant................(see 35)	
Cap'n Jack's...............................**26** C5	
Club Soleil Restaurant.................(see 13)	
Harbour View Grocery..................**27** C5	
Harbour's Edge...........................**28** D5	
Munchies...................................**29** C5	
Rudy's Place..............................(see 17)	
Upper Terrace Restaurant.............(see 17)	
Vernon's Grocery........................**30** C5	

SHOPPING
Ebb Tide....................................**31** D6	
Iggy Biggy.................................**32** C5	

TRANSPORT
Ferry Dock.................................**33** D6	
Lighthouse Marina.......................**34** C2	
Mail-Boat Dock..........................(see 33)	
Sea Spray Marina........................**35** A5	
T & N Cart Hire..........................**36** B4	

Hope Town Point

Cook's Cove

Anna Cay

Parrot Cays

Eagle Rock

See Enlargement

Elbow Cay Lighthouse

Hope Town

Back Creek

26°32'N

Sea of Abaco

Nigh Creek

School

Elbow Cay

Centre Line Rd

Nude Beach

White Sound

Garbanzo Beach

Aunt Pat's Bay

Tahiti Beach
26°30'N

Tilloo Cut

ATLANTIC OCEAN

Tilloo Cay

76°58'W

0 ———————— 100 m
0 ———————— 0.1 miles

Basketball Court (Taylor Park)

Cemetery

Fig Tree La

Assembly of God Church

ATLANTIC OCEAN

Betrothal Bench

Cemetery Rd

Lover's La

Hope Town Beach (North Beach)

Sawyer's Way

Sweeting's La

Ruder's La

Hope Town

St James Methodist Church

Hope Town Harbour

Church St

Government Dock

Saunder's Ln

Step La

Queen's Hwy

Back St

Hope Town Beach (South Beach)

ABACOS

Public telephone booths can be found in central areas, including near the Government Dock, and public toilets are located opposite the Government Dock.

First Caribbean International Bank (☎ 242-366-0295; Fig Tree Lane; 🕑 10am-2pm Tue)

Hope Town Clinic (☎ 242-366-0108; Queen's Hwy)

Police (☎ 919, 911; ☎ 242-367-3500; VHF Channel 16; Dundas Town Rd, Marsh Harbour)

Post office (☎ 242-366-0098; Queen's Hwy) Above tourist information opposite the dock.

SIGHTS

Hope Town is dominated by the historic, candy-striped **Elbow Cay Lighthouse** (🕑 8am-4pm Mon-Fri, 8am-noon Sat). It was built in 1863 despite active opposition from local wreckers fearful of the lighthouse's effects on their profiteering. One hundred steps lead to the kerosene mantle and magnifier that still provide illumination today, and offer fabulous views. Ask the ferry operator to drop you at the lighthouse, and catch the next mainland ferry by waving to the captain from the dock.

The splendid little **Wyannie Malone Museum** (Bay St; 🕑 10am-12:30pm Mon-Sat) has an eclectic collection that includes genealogical information pertaining to loyalist settlers and Lucayan Indians.

The tiny **Byrle Patterson Memorial Garden** has two bronze sculptures of dolphins and a seagull shaded by pine trees.

Cholera Cemetery (Cemetery Rd) graves recall the cholera epidemic that swept through Hope Town in 1850, claiming one-third of the population. Note the weathered Betrothal Bench at the crest of the hill. Cemetery Rd is off Back St.

The tiny **Cetacean Museum** (admission free), in the old peppermint green building facing the Government Dock on Bay St, has a few whale bones, charts, a fine mural and a map showing sightings of whales in Bahamian waters. Eleven species have been sighted in recent years in and around Elbow Cay.

South of Hope Town, Queen's Hwy continues south along a narrow peninsula between the ocean and **White Sound**, a shallow, mangrove-lined bay with the Sea Spray Resort & Marina at its southern end.

The road continues to **Tahiti Beach**, which extends as a sandbar along the peninsula and is backed by an extensive palm grove. Marine turtles still come ashore to nest on the champagne-colored beach.

ACTIVITIES
Diving & Snorkeling

The reefs off the Atlantic side of the cay are excellent for diving and snorkeling. The waters near Hope Town and the northern tip of the cay are calmer and are easily reached by swimming from shore. Staghorn, elkhorn, star and brain coral are abundant.

Froggies Out Island Adventures (☎ 242-366-0431; www.froggiesabaco.com), down the narrow cove south of the harbor, offers one-/two-tank dives for $100/110. It also provides snorkeling excursions ($40/50 per half-/full-day; children are $15 less).

Sea Spray Resort & Marina (p159) runs snorkel trips and rents snorkel gear for $10 per day.

Bonefishing & Sportfishing

Elbow Cay's weeklong, family-oriented **Abaco Anglers Tournament** (☎ 242-366-0004) in mid-April requires little gear and welcomes all participants, children included. If you enter the bonefishing category, beware – Maitland Lowe has won every year since 1972!

Bonefishing guides will charge from $350/600 per half-/full-day.

A Salt Weapon (☎ 242-366-0245; www.asaltweapon charters.com) offers a 31ft Bertram rigged and ready to go on deep-sea fishing charters ($380/580 per half-/full day).

Sea Spray Resort & Marina (p159) offers reef, deep and bonefishing.

Lighthouse Marina (p160) sells bait and rents out fishing rods.

Boat Excursions

Froggies Out Island Adventures (☎ 242-366-0431; www.froggiesabaco.com) Offers full-day excursions to Great Guana Cay with snorkeling at Fowl Cay. It also has trips to Little Harbour with snorkeling at Sandy Cay ($70), and snorkeling and diving trips (see above).

Abaco Multihull Charters (☎ 242-366-0552; abaco multihull@oii.net) runs two-hour sunset cruises ($75) and sailing lessons ($25 per hour). They also rent 30ft catamarans ($225/350 per half-/full-day with captain) and 25ft boats ($225/125 with/without captain).

Boat & Dinghy Rentals

Abaco Bahamas Charters (☎ 242-366-0151; www.abacocharters.com) rents sailboats from $1925 per week. Alternatively, it hires out a 37ft catamaran for $3950 per week.

Abaco Dingy Rentals (☎ 242-366-0309; 2surfers@ coralwave.com) rents dinghies from $20/100 per hour/day, with a three-hour minimum.

Surfing

The offshore waters boast at least six good surfing breaks on the south Atlantic shore, especially in winter months. The Bahamas' top surfing is at the reef off Garbanzo Beach, 2 miles south of Hope Town. Bring your own gear.

SLEEPING

Several agents rent out a number of properties both in Hope Town and elsewhere on the cay. These rentals are great value for all sized wallets, and range in size and location.

Try **Elbow Cay Properties** (☎ 242-366-0569; www.elbowcayrentals.com; Bay St), who list a variety of cottages and villas from $600 to $7000 per week. **Tanny Key's Vacation Rentals** (☎ 242-366-0053; www.tannykey.com; Back St, Hope Town) has houses all over the island from about $900 to $2,000 per week for one or two people. **Hope Town Hideaways** (☎ 242-366-0024; www.hope town.com; Porpoise Pl, Hope Town) and **Island View Properties** (☎ 242-366-0601; classicmarine77@hotmail .com; ⏰ 8am-6pm Mon-Sat; Fig Tree Lane, Hope Town) are also worth a call. Some of the agents' properties are listed in the next section.

Hope Town

Daisy's Place (☎ 242-366-0569; Well Lane; per week $800; ✗ ▨) This cute, light one-bedroom waterfront cottage at the harbor's edge has a nice-sized porch with great views, and is a stroll away from the town beach. Also great value is Upsy Daisy, the 2nd-floor apartment, also with fabulous views ($875 per week). Contact Elbow Cay Properties (above).

Hope Harbour Town Lodge (☎ 242-366-0095; www.hopetownlodge.com; Queens Hwy; r $135; Ⓟ ✗ ▨ ▣) Atop a bluff at the south end of Hope Town, this lodge's hammocks gently sway under coconut trees overlooking Atlantic Ocean. There is a choice between lovely oceanfront cottages with kitchenette ($225) that spill down the garden toward the beach, or some bright and welcoming rooms in the main building, many with harbor views. Facilities include a splendid restaurant and bar, a small freshwater pool and sundeck, and water sports. Bicycle and boat rentals – including powerboats – are offered, plus snorkel gear.

Harrison House (☎ 242-366-0569; www.elbowcay rentals.com; Elbow Cay Properties; per week $1000; ✗ ▨) This is a great-value and comfortable house in the center of town, with a large deck and porch swing, and a grassed garden where kids can kick up their heels. The house has a lovely wooden interior, three bedrooms, and is a few minutes' walk to everything.

Club Soleil Resort (☎ 242-366-003; www.clubsoleil .com; Western Waterfront; r $140; ✗ ▨ ▣) These seven hacienda-style units have a tranquil location across the harbor. The rooms come with balconies and all mod cons. There's also a great fish restaurant, freshwater pool, complimentary boat service, and a bar where you can sip the house special, the Tropical Shock (you're warned!). Access is only by boat.

Tellin Vacation Homes (☎ 242-366-0053; fax 203-227-6898; www.hopetownvillas.com; Bay St; cottages from $1300 per week; ✗ ▨) Three gorgeous adjacent cottages have benefited from the love and paintwork of the artistically inclined owners. Blue-and-white one-bedroom Sunrise Tellin sits on the beach, with pink curtains and a pretty garden where even the garbage cans are painted with flowers! Bay St Tellin ($1800 per week) sits across the road, and cute Tellin Guest Cottage is closest to the sea, perfect for a lovey-dovey couple.

Sunrise Beach (☎ 242-366-0024; per week $2200; ✗ ▨) This three-bedroom cottage with exquisite decor in West Indian style and romantic net-draped four-poster beds is another super place. The backyard is the beach, and there's also a barbecue, cable TV and stereo. Contact Hope Town Hideaways (left).

Lantana Cabana (☎ 242-366-0053; fax 242-366-0051; cottage $1400; ✗ ▨) Another lovely historic cottage with four bedrooms that overlooks the harbor from the 2nd floor. Contact Tanny Key's Vacation Rentals (left).

South of Hope Town

Abaco Inn (☎ 242-366-0133, US ☎ 1-800-468-8799; www.abacoinn.net; Queen's Hwy; r $126; Ⓟ ✗ ▨ ▣) Two miles southwest of Hope Town, these great-value and super ocean-side lodgings sit shaded by palm trees, and crown a bluff between two lovely beaches at the narrowest point of the island. A lively bar serves pub grub.

Turtle Hill Resort (☎ 242-366-0557; www.turtlehill .com; Queen's Hwy; r for 1-4 persons per day/week $340/1850; Ⓟ ✗ ▨ ▣) Fresh and clean with mainly white decor and tiled floors, these four luxury villas come with kitchen, barbecue and cable TV. Some have rooftop sea views, and all are a short walk to a great beach.

Sea Spray Resort & Marina (☎ 242-366-0065; www .seasprayresort.com; White Sound; r $1500; P ⊠ ⊠ ⊠) These two- and three-bedroom modern properties have great marina or beach views and spacious rooms, but small kitchens. Facilities include a barbecue, and the clubhouse has a pool table and TV. Free Sunfish sailing is offered, and surfboards, sailboards, bicycles and snorkel gear are available for rent. There's a free shuttle to Hope Town; water taxis take 20 minutes.

EATING & DRINKING
Hope Town
Munchies (☎ 242-366-0423; Back St; mains $4-10; ☻ breakfast, lunch & dinner Mon-Sat) Good-value, casual snack meals such as burgers, pasties and deli sandwiches can be ordered here. A small shaded patio provides some seating.

Cap'n Jack's (☎ 242-366-0247; Bay St; mains $6-15; ☻ breakfast, lunch & dinner Mon-Sat) The best breakfasts in town, with waffles and tasty omelettes. This is a nice harborfront spot, and a very popular local bar with live music midweek and at weekends. Try the bar's Jack Hammer (copious rum, vodka and Tia Maria), guaranteed to get you jiving.

Harbour's Edge (☎ 242-366-0087; fax 242-366-0292; Queens Hwy; mains $8-25; ☻ lunch & dinner Wed-Mon) The deck here stretches out over the water with excellent views of the lighthouse and harbor, perfect for lingering sundowner drinks and meals. The Over the Edge cocktail (Matusalem rum, banana rum and fruit juices) was the result of a three-week taste testing.

Club Soleil Restaurant (☎ 242-366-003; Western Harbourfront; mains $18-30; ☻ breakfast, lunch & dinner Fri-Wed) This alfresco and indoor waterfront restaurant serves everything from burgers to fish and steak dishes with French influences. If you book in advance the owners will dispatch a water taxi to pick you up and drop you off.

Upper Terrace Restaurant (☎ 242-366-0095; Hope Town Harbour Lodge, Queens' Hwy; mains $28-35; ☻ dinner) For a great formal dinner, enjoy juicy salads and dishes like blackened fish; chicken marinated in coconut rum; shrimp-and-coconut-battered lobster; and creamy mango and guava cheesecake.

Rudy's Place (☎ 242-366-0062; Hope Town Harbour Lodge; mains $23-35; ☻ dinner Mon-Sat, closed Sep & Oct)

Has Bahamian food swathed with French style and sauces.

Harbour View Grocery (☎ 242-366-0033; Bay St; ☻ 9am-5pm Mon-Sat, 10am-3pm Sun) and **Vernon's Grocery** (☎ 242-366-0037; Bay St; ☻ 8am-6pm Mon-Fri, to 7pm Sat) both sell fresh produce and groceries.

South of Hope Town
Abaco Inn (opposite) has mains from $11 and is open breakfast, lunch and dinner. It offers an eclectic menu including vegetarian meals, but has a heavy slant toward Bahamian seafood. Reservations are required.

Boat House Restaurant (left) Eat alfresco, and munch on great blackened-fish burgers with sides of coleslaw, or rice and peas, Caesar salad and entrees (from filet mignon to seafood primavera). There's a regular barbecue with live DJ and weekly live music.

SHOPPING
Ebb Tide (☎ 242-366-0088; Back St, Hope Town) Original watercolors and prints painted by local artists and some handmade gold jewelry are sold here. Also on offer are some Androsia batiks and locally made spices and preserves.

Iggy Biggy (☎ 242-366-0354; Bay St, Hope Town; ☻ 9:30am-5:30pm) This clothing store sells some funky resort wear and handmade gifts.

GETTING THERE & AWAY
The mail boat *Captain Gurth Dean* sails to Hope Town from Nassau weekly. See p155 for information.

Albury's Ferry Service (☎ 242-367-3147; www .oii.net/alburysferry/; Marsh Harbour; adult/child $15/7.50) operates water taxis from Marsh Harbour to Elbow Cay at 7:15am, 9am, 10:30am, noon, 2pm, 3:30pm, 4pm and 5:45pm daily. Additionally, it runs at 9pm and 10:45pm on Friday and Saturday evenings. The boats depart Elbow Cay at 8am, 9:45am, 11:30am, 1:30pm, 3pm, 4pm and 5pm daily, and also 6:15pm, 9:45pm and 11:30pm on Friday and Saturday evenings. The ferry will stop at the lighthouse, and all docks and marinas on Elbow Cay, including many hotels. Albury's can also provide charters to Green Turtle Cay.

A water taxi runs from Man O' War Cay to Hope Town at 7:30am daily, returning at 4:30pm. The taxi pilot will drop you off and pick you up at specific docks as requested.

ABACOS

Marinas

Lighthouse Marina (☎ 242-366-0154; VHF Channel 16; Western Harbourfront) offer dockage ($1.75 to $2.50 per foot) at one of their slips in the harbor. It has a nice setting right in township and has an off-license and small shop.

Sea Spray Resort & Marina (p159) has a 24-slip, full-service marina exclusively for the use of guests at the Sea Spray Resort. It offers daily transient dockage ($1.20 per foot) and long-term dockage ($0.75 per foot on a daily basis). Electricity and water is extra.

GETTING AROUND

You can walk or bicycle everywhere in Hope Town. Cars and golf carts are banned along Bay St but can be hired at the ferry dock (Government Dock) to explore the rest of the island.

Island Cart Rentals (☎ 242-366-0448; VHP Channel 16; www.islandcartrentals.com; Hope Town; ☾ Mon-Sat) have 20 carts at $45/270 per day/week.

T & N Cart Hire (☎ 242-366-0199; fax 242-366-0393; Centre Line Rd; ☾ Mon-Thu) also offers carts from $45 per day and will deliver to your accommodation or to the ferry landing.

Lubber's Quarters Cay

This 300-acre private island lies between Marsh Harbour and Elbow Cay. It's perfect for secluded beaches and nature trails. There are few lodgings, no roads, cars or stores.

The modern, spacious **Villa Poincianna** (Map p147; US ☎ 815-399-4068; www.poincianna.com; cottage for 2/4/6 persons $950/1100/1250; ☷) sits just 50ft from the shore.

Miramar Cottage (Map p147; cottage $800) is a simple two-bedroom lodging that requires a boat for access. Contact Abaco Real Estate Agency (p158).

The popular **Yahoe's Sand Bar & Grill** (Map p147; ☎ 242-366-3110; VHF Channel 16; mains $10-18) has new-moon parties, and serves burgers, pasta and seafood dishes.

Tilloo Cay

This 5-mile-long cay, spitting distance south of Elbow Cay, is renowned for its bonefishing flats. The 20-acres of pristine wilderness is a vital nesting site for seabirds, including the rare and beautiful tropicbird.

Pelican Cays Land & Sea Park

This 2,100-acre park protects the half-dozen tiny Pelican Cays, south of Tilloo, and their surrounding waters and fringing reef. The park is centered around **Sandy Cay Underwater National Sea Park**, which has great snorkeling. The cays are nesting sites for bridled, sooty and least terns. The park also boasts shallow coral gardens and underwater caves that abound with marine life.

Man O' War Cay

pop 306

This thin little island is imbued with a highly conformist and proud 'Conchy Joe' Loyalist culture (see p30). Almost as powerful is the 200-year-old boat-building industry that still thrives today.

Lying 3 miles northwest of Elbow Cay, most of this cay's income is derived from the sea. Fishermen use homemade fiberglass boats or 12-foot wooden crawfish boats to collect their catch; dozens of these sailing dinghies date back half a century and are still in perfect shape.

The cay's boatyards have a long-held reputation of employing black laborers, mostly 'Bahaitians' (Haitians born in the Bahamas), who are also employed as domestic help but who are obliged to leave the island by nightfall. This Bible-steeped, white-only island lifestyle also prohibits the sale of liquor (bring your own) and prefers residents and visitors to dress conservatively.

The wreck of the USS *Adirondack*, which went down in 1862, lies offshore in 40ft of water and attracts many divers, who head over for the day, as do most visitors.

INFORMATION

There are public phones, and two banks: the **First Caribbean International Bank** (☎ 242-352-9365; ☾ 9:30am-1pm Fri) and the **Royal Bank of Canada** (☎ 242-365-6323; ☾ 10am-2pm Thu).

SIGHTS & ACTIVITIES

A hand carved sign on the waterfront points the way to **Joe Albury's Studio** (☎ 242-365-6082), Man O' War's finest boatbuilder. Joe crafted traditional Bahamian sailboats with a purist's passion, just as his great-great-great-uncle Billie Bo did 150 years ago. Beautiful model boats now dominate the studio, along with local artisans' works.

Albury's Sail Shop (☎ 242-365-6014), on the waterfront, no longer makes sails but has continued manufacturing all manner of things from cast-off sail material, such as

MAN O' WAR CAY

INFORMATION
First Caribbean International
Bank.................................**1** C2
Royal Bank of Canada.........**2** C1

SIGHTS & ACTIVITIES
Albury's Sail Shop................**3** B1
Joe Albury's Studio..............**4** C1
Man O' War Marina Dive
Shop...............................**5** C2

SLEEPING 🏠
Schooner's Landing Resort....**6** B2

EATING 🍴
Albury's Harbour Store.........**7** C1
Hibiscus Cafe......................**8** C1
Man O' War Grocery............**9** C1
Mary's Corner Store............**10** C1
Pavilion Restaurant.............**11** C2

TRANSPORT
Albury's Ferry Dock............**12** C2
Man O' War Marina...........**13** C2
Water Taxi Dock..............(see 12)

jackets and duffle bags. Some fashion items using Androsia batiks are also sold.

Man O' War Marina Dive Shop (☎ 242-365-6013) rents equipment (except regulators) and provides air fills but does not offer dives. You can rent snorkel gear for $10 per day. It also offers kayak and bicycle rentals.

SLEEPING & EATING

Schooner's Landing Resort (☎ 242-365-6072; www .schoonerslanding.com; r $280; 🅿 🅿) Five two-bedroom town houses with full kitchen overlook the sea from their tranquil position northeast of town. The houses come with TV/VCR, private patio, dockage, plus laundry, bar and barbecue pit. Beaches lie a stone's throw in either direction.

Hibiscus Cafe (☎ 242-365-6380; mains $8-14; 🍽 lunch Mon-Sat, dinner Thu-Sat) Indoor dining is based around Bahamian cuisine and burgers.

Pavilion Restaurant (☎ 242-365-6185; mains $5-24; 🍽 lunch & dinner Mon-Sat, closed Aug 15-Sep 30) This waterfront eatery serves hot Bahamian dishes, with roasts, barbecues and steaks on weekends.

Albury's Harbour Store is a fully stocked groceries. You can also pick up groceries at **Man O' War Grocery** and **Mary's Corner Store**.

GETTING THERE & AROUND

Albury's Ferry Service (☎ 242-367-3147; www.oii .net/alburysferry/; Marsh Harbour; adult/child one-way $12/6) operates scheduled daily water taxis from Marsh Harbour to Man O' War Cay at

10:30am, 12:15pm, 2:30pm, 4pm and 5:30pm daily (the 12:15 and 2:30pm ferries don't operate on Sunday). Return service departs Man O' War at 8am, 11:30am, 1:30pm and 3:15pm (there are no 11:30am or 3:15pm services on Sunday). Charters are available to outlying cays.

Water taxis also run from Man O'War to Great Guana Cay at 7:30am and 3:30pm Friday; and from Man O' War to Elbow Cay at 7:30am, returning at 4:30pm. They leave from the same dock as the ferry to Marsh Harbour.

Facilities for boaters include the 60-slip **Man O' War Marina** (☎ 242-365-6008), complete with kiddies' playground, boat rentals and water sports.

Ask at businesses in Man O' War town about renting a golf cart.

Great Guana Cay
pop 134
This 6-mile-long cay lying 8 miles north of Marsh Harbour is the least developed of the Loyalist Cays, with a tiny, unsophisticated fishing village that concentrates on lobstering for an income.

A weathered old sign on the cay welcomes visitors with 'It's Better in the Bahamas, but…It's Gooder in Guana.' It is hard to argue with that statement when you see the spectacular 5-mile-long beach with soft, pure-white sand that runs the length of the Atlantic shore.

Just southeast of Great Guana Cay is the wondrous Fowl Cay Reef Reserve, a national underwater sea park which protects a stunning coral reef and seabirds' shore-based nesting sites. There is also fabulous snorkeling off the town beach in front of Nipper's Beach Bar & Grill.

Small pockets of strewn rubbish and the occasional unfriendly local do detract somewhat from the charm of nature's gifts here, as do the clouds of vicious mosquitoes that hover over the island's center. Come prepared with bug spray and you will love the quiet and unspoilt nature of this little island.

July's Regatta Week features sailing races and festivities on Great Guana and other towns and cays.

INFORMATION
A post office with varied opening hours sits on the harborside. A part-time police office

shares the same tiny cement building. The **emergency** (☎ 911, 919) numbers for the cays are the same. A public phone box also sits on the waterfront.

ACTIVITIES
Great Guana has superb snorkeling inside the reef along its windward shore and some excellent diving and bonefishing. Troy Albury is 'the main man' for many visitors' needs. He runs the friendly dive shop, and hires out a ton of gear for different activities, as well as looking after some decent accommodation.

Dive Guana (☎ 242-365-5178; VHF Channel 16; www.diveguana.com; Fishers Bay) offers two-tank dives ($80) and snorkeling trips ($40) to the fabulous Fowl Cay and the northern end of island. Ask about visiting the divers' favourite 'pet' fish, Gilly the 70lb black grouper and Charlie the reef shark. Also call here for bikes ($12 per hour), kayaks ($12 per hour), fishing rods ($7 per day) and boat hire: a 23ft Robalo ($140 per day) and a 21ft Angler ($130 per day).

Henry Sands (☎ 242-365-5140) operates as a bonefishing guide.

SLEEPING
Guana Seaside Village (☎ 242-365-5106; www.guana seaside.com; Crossing Bay; d $130; P X X R) Both hotel units and a variety of separate wooden cottages sit right on beach. These were being repaired at the time of research. The hotel provides complimentary water gear (snorkel equipment, sea kayaks, paddle-boats) and has a poolside bar and grill, and a restaurant.

Harbour View Haven (☎ 242-365-5028; www .guanacayvillas.com; Great Guana Cay Villas; r $130-145; X X R) In the village, this very well-maintained place has a choice of lovely spacious rooms with shared balcony. It also has good weekly rates and equally tasteful sibling apartments for rent.

Guana Beach Resort (☎ 242-365-5133; VHF Channel 16; www.guanabeachresort.com; d/q $1000/1500; P X X R) These gorgeous beachside rooms and two-bedroom units are spacious, cool and airy, and furnished with beautiful handmade Balinese four-poster beds and love seats. Kitchens have toasters, microwaves and fridges. Adjacent to the public dock, there is a beachside bar, sundeck and hammocks, and volleyball and water sports on offer.

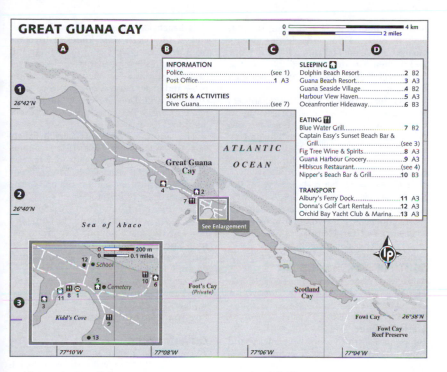

GREAT GUANA CAY

0 — 4 km
0 — 2 miles

INFORMATION
Police...(see 1)
Post Office..**1** A3

SIGHTS & ACTIVITIES
Dive Guana..(see 7)

SLEEPING
Dolphin Beach Resort..............................**2** B2
Guana Beach Resort................................**3** A3
Guana Seaside Village.............................**4** B2
Harbour View Haven................................**5** A3
Oceanfrontier Hideaway...........................**6** B3

EATING
Blue Water Grill......................................**7** B2
Captain Easy's Sunset Beach Bar &
  Grill..(see 3)
Fig Tree Wine & Spirits.............................**8** A3
Guana Harbour Grocery...........................**9** A3
Hibiscus Restaurant................................(see 4)
Nipper's Beach Bar & Grill......................**10** B3

TRANSPORT
Albury's Ferry Dock................................**11** A3
Donna's Golf Cart Rentals.......................**12** A3
Orchid Bay Yacht Club & Marina.............**13** A3

ATLANTIC OCEAN

Great Guana Cay

Sea of Abaco

Foot's Cay (Private)

Scotland Cay

Fowl Cay

Fowl Cay Reef Preserve

See Enlargement

School
Cemetery
Kidd's Cove

26°42'N
26°40'N
26°38'N

77°10'W   77°08'W   77°06'W   77°04'W

0 — 200 m
0 — 0.1 miles

Also recommended:

Dolphin Beach Resort (☎ 242-365-5137, US ☎ 1-800-222-2646; www.dolphinbeachresort .com; r per day/week $190/1330, cottages per day/week $276/1932 plus per child $15; P X X Q) Tucked away, this place has super and cheerful private villas.

Oceanfrontier Hideaway (Canada ☎ 519-389-4846; www.oceanfrontier.com; d $200/1200 per day/week; P X X Q) Beachfront log cabins.

EATING & DRINKING

Hibiscus Restaurant (☎ 242-367-3498; Guana Seaside Village; mains $8-22; ☺ breakfast, lunch & dinner) A Bahamian and American menu includes kids' menu, charbroiled steak and deli sandwiches. This beachside eatery is neat and clean, and has a shady garden with palm trees.

Captain Easy's Sunset Beach Bar & Grill (☎ 242-365-5133; Guana Beach Resort; mains $7-13; ☺ lunch & dinner) Seafood, steaks, pastas and island-style, hickory-smoked barbecue buffets are all great choices at this atmospheric little waterside bar at the harbor.

Blue Water Grill (☎ 242-365-5230; mains $12-27; ☺ lunch & dinner Wed-Mon) This classy bar and spacious restaurant gleams with polished wood, while huge windows overlook their deck and sea views. Italian and Bahamian dishes are interspersed with prime rib nights, which makes this a perfect place for a romantic meal or long lunch on the deck.

Nipper's Beach Bar & Grill (☎ 242-365-5143; VHF Channel 16; mains $10-24; ☺ lunch & dinner) Rely on the free rides from the harbor to get here; it is quite a hike to this well-known beachside bar. A late-middle-aged crowd of locals and visitors enjoy drinking here during the day, while visitors drift in at night and for the Sunday afternoon pig roasts.

For groceries, try **Guana Harbour Grocery** (☎ 242-365-5067). **Fig Tree Wine & Spirits** (☎ 242-365-5058; mains $16-20; ☺ breakfast & lunch) is a one-stop shop for drinks, cigarettes and groceries.

Orchid Bay Yacht Club & Marina (p164) offers lunch ($10 to $14), such as tasty grilled jerk chicken and catch-of-the-day sandwiches (with blackened, grilled or fried fish).

GETTING THERE & AROUND

Albury's Ferry Service (☎ 242-367-3147; www.oii .net/alburysferry/; Marsh Harbour; adult/child one-way $15/7.50) operates scheduled daily ferries from

ABACOS

Marsh Harbour at 6:45am, 10:30am 1:30pm, 3:30pm and 5:45pm. The ferries depart Guana Cay at 8am, 11:30am, 2:30pm, 4:45pm and 6:30pm. Charters are available and the ferries will drop off or pick up at locations upon request.

Green Turtle Ferry (☎ 242-365-8749; Mariner's Cove, Treasure Cay) travels from Treasure Cay to Guana Cay at 10am and 3pm, going onto Green Turtle Cay, and departs Guana Cay for Green Turtle Cay at 11am and 4pm Wednesday and Friday to Monday ($8/15 one-way/return).

Orchid Bay Yacht Club & Marina (☎ 242-365-5175; www.orchidbay.net) has 32 slips, a laundry, showers, telephone and Internet service, pool, tennis court, restaurant and bar.

Donna's Golf Cart Rentals (☎ 242-365-5195) charges $40 per day for golf carts.

SOUTH OF MARSH HARBOUR

The Great Abaco Hwy runs from Marsh Harbour to Sandy Point, at the southwestern end of the island.

Little Harbour

Be prepared from some very rocky and roughly hewn roads to get down to the beach at Little Harbour. To reach the jewel in the crown, Pete's Pub, abandon your car at the beach and walk across the sands toward an icy-cold beer and gorgeous views of this lovely bay, popular with yachters and turtles.

The perfectly sheltered crescent bay is held in the cusp of crumbling limestone cliffs and a kerosene-lantern lighthouse looms over the holiday 'shacks' of wealthy American expats. You can climb to the top for a view of the waves running in toward the reef and the wreck of the *Anne Bonney*.

Zef Fessenden's Shacks (Map p147; US ☎ 813-495-0222, 1-845-679-5334; r per week $425) Zef can offer you a choice of accommodations: a house overlooking the ocean on one side of the bluff ($675 per week), and a tiny little A-shaped shack (ideal for one or two small, and romantically inclined, people) in this quiet little bay on the other. Both places are fairly basic, with no electricity, but have gas cookers and lamps, beds and outdoor showers. They are right on the beach in stunning settings, just a hop, skip and jump away from Pete's Pub.

Pete's Pub & Gallery (Map p147; ☎ 242-366-3503; www.petespub.com; mains $8-18; ☯ lunch & dinner)

This beachside bar and grill at the north end of the beach were knocked together from driftwood, with sand for a floor and T-shirts and ships' pendants for decor. You can sip grog at a bar shaped like a ship's prow and order burgers or a barbecue from the open grill. Don't miss the famous 'Pete's Pub Pig & Pea Party' (pig roast) every Saturday.

The adjoining **Bronze Foundry & Gallery** (Map p147; ☯ 10am-noon & 2-4pm Mon-Sat) contains some marine sculptures and gold jewelry as well as some remarkable bronze castings; the Vatican museum owns one of the pieces, *St Peter Fisher of Men*.

The turnoff from Great Abaco Hwy is 15 miles south of Marsh Harbour and leads to Cherokee Sound. Two miles before Cherokee Sound, a turnoff leads to Little Harbour via a very rough dirt road; you're warned!

Froggies Out Island Adventures (p157) offers excursions to Little Harbour.

Albury's Ferry Service (☎ 242-365-6010) may take you from Marsh Harbour.

Casuarina Point

The small, pin-neat village of **Cherokee Sound** (population 122), 25 miles south of Marsh Harbour, sits at the end of a peninsula jutting out into its namesake sound, and surrounded by mangrove shores and miles of turquoise flats. The fishing village of **Casuarina Point**, with a beautiful beach, lies on the west side of Cherokee Sound.

Different of Abaco Nature Park (Map p147; ☎ 242-366-2150; www.differentofabaco.com; r $125-200; ☯ call ahead for access; P ⊠ ☺), immediately west of Casuarina Point, is a run-down natural-adventure park where you can go bird-watching, boar- and flamingo-spotting and hiking in the extensive mangroves and pine forests. Different of Abaco also owns **Seashell Beach Club**, with modest, meagerly appointed rooms with high ceilings, fans and oceanfront verandas.

Sandy Beach Hideaway (Map p147; ☎ 242-367-2655; kopet@aol.com; Casuarina Point; per week from $1400; P ⊠ ☺) This attractive, fully contained three-bedroom house is in a fantastic location on a nice family beach with shallow waters and a sheltered bay. A modern open-plan design with church-style roof, fans and blinds keep it cool, while a balcony and deck have terrific views.

Sandy Point

South of **Crossing Rocks**, a forlorn fishing village 40 miles south of Marsh Harbour, the Great Abaco Hwy sweeps southwest through vast acres of pineland and ends at Sandy Point, a picturesque fishing community backed by a coconut-palm plantation.

Twenty miles northwest of Sandy Point, **More Island** is the only inhabited island off the west coast of the Abaco mainland. The settlements of **Hard Bargain** and the **Bight** have a long fishing tradition and a wild, rustic spirit.

Oeisha's Resort (Map p147; ☎ 242-366-4139; fax 242-366-4493; r $70; P X R) sits between the airstrip and village, and has a restaurant that doubles as a dance club.

Pete & Gay's Guest House (Map p147; ☎ 242-366-4119; fax 242-366-4007; r $70; P X R), at the head of the dock, has rooms with TV and also serves meals.

The other eatery and bar of choice is **Nancy's Seaside Inn, Restaurant & Bar** (Map p147; ☎ 242-366-4120).

A taxi from Marsh Harbour to Sandy Point costs $140.

Bahamas Ferries (Map p147; ☎ 242-323-2166; www.bahamasferries.com; Nassau) makes the trip from Nassau to Sandy Point twice weekly ($90 round-trip, four hours).

Captain Gurth Dean (Map p147; ☎ 242-393-1064) mail boat sails from Nassau to Sandy Point weekly ($30 one-way, 11 hours), also stopping at More Island.

Abaco National Park

The 32-sq-mile park was established in 1994 to protect the major habitat of the endangered Bahama parrot. About 1500 parrots now live here along with some wild pigs and stunning orchids.

There's also an extensive limestone cave system to explore (the local parrot population is unique – the birds nest in holes in the limestone rocks), plus hiking trails, lonesome beaches, and incredibly wild and spectacular scenery along the Atlantic shore. A turnoff for the park is signed 10 miles south of Crossing Rocks.

The dramatic headland at the southern tip of the island is dominated by red-and-white-hooped **Hole-in-the-Wall Lighthouse**, reached by a horrendously potholed and tortuous road that adds to the sense of separation from civilization. The mosquitoes are very active here, so if you want to climb the lighthouse for the view, make sure you come prepared!

NORTHWEST OF MARSH HARBOUR
Treasure Cay

Treasure Cay, which lies 17 miles north of Marsh Harbour, is not a true cay but a narrow peninsula that has secreted away one of the Bahamas most idyllic and captivating beaches, Treasure Cay Beach. A 4-mile-long crescent of sugar-soft white sand appears to melt into a vast expanse of glittering jewel-like waters that extend to the horizon. Docile rays glide through the turquoise shallows and seabirds echo their movements across the sky. Voted one of the world's top 10 beaches, this treasure is protected by a ring of palm trees, although some private houses and condos have crept alongside the perimeter.

Treasure Cay still has an island feel about it, attracting a retired expat community that inhabit condos and play golf or indulge their boating hobbies at the one hotel's marina.

INFORMATION

Most facilities exist here. For emergencies call the **police** (☎ 242-365-8048, 919, 911; VHF Channel 19), while **Corbett Medical Centre** (☎ 242-365-8288; Wilson Ronald M Dr) also has a minor **Emergency Medical Clinic** (☎ 242-375-8882).

The **Royal Bank of Canada** (☎ 242-365-8119; 9:30am-2pm Mon, Tue & Thu) has an ATM. Public telephone booths can be found north of shopping complex where the **post office** (☎ 242-365-8230; 9am-5pm Mon-Fri) is based.

SIGHTS & ACTIVITIES

Anything to do with that compelling azure sea must be taken advantage of! There's good bonefishing in the shallow waters on the south side of the peninsula. Treasure Cay Hotel Resort & Marina (p167) can organize sportfishing trips (from $375/500 per half-/full-day charter).

Treasure Divers (☎ 242-365-8465; VHF Channel 16; www.treasure-divers.com; Treasure Cay Hotel Resort & Marina) offer two-tank dives ($80), night dives ($85) and blue-hole dives ($85). Snorkeling is $35. They also rent gear, mask and snorkel ($8), fins ($8) and fishing rods ($10).

Rich's Boat Rentals (☎ 242-365-8582; VHF Channel 16) provides 21ft Paramount boats ($100/270/595 per day/three days/week) and 26ft

ABACOS

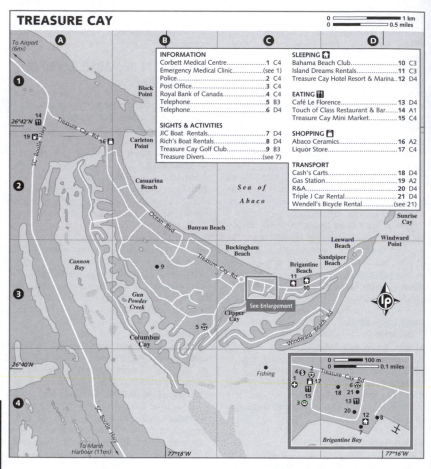

TREASURE CAY

INFORMATION
Corbett Medical Centre.....................1 C4
Emergency Medical Clinic.............(see 1)
Police..2 C4
Post Office.....................................3 C4
Royal Bank of Canada.....................4 C4
Telephone......................................5 B3
Telephone......................................6 D4

SIGHTS & ACTIVITIES
JIC Boat Rentals.............................7 D4
Rich's Boat Rentals..........................8 D4
Treasure Cay Golf Club....................9 B3
Treasure Divers............................(see 7)

SLEEPING
Bahama Beach Club.......................10 C3
Island Dreams Rentals....................11 C3
Treasure Cay Hotel Resort & Marina..12 D4

EATING
Café Le Florence............................13 D4
Touch of Class Restaurant & Bar......14 A1
Treasure Cay Mini Market..............15 C4

SHOPPING
Abaco Ceramics.............................16 A2
Liquor Store..................................17 C4

TRANSPORT
Cash's Carts...................................18 D4
Gas Station....................................19 A2
R&A..20 D4
Triple J Car Rental.........................21 D4
Wendell's Bicycle Rental..............(see 21)

Paramount boats ($150/380/850 per day/
three days/week).

JIC Boat Rentals (☎ 242-365-8465; VHF Channel
16) provides a 24ft Angler ($150/390/840
per day/three days/week) for rent and con-
ducts guided tours as well as fishing trips to
Shell Island, Great Guana Cay, Green Turtle Cay and New Plymouth (prices upon
application).

Treasure Cay Golf Club (☎ 242-365-8045; Treasure Cay Rd; green fees $85) is a 6985yd, 18-hole
golf course that has a reputation for its
narrow fairways. They have cheaper rates
for Treasure Cay Hotel Resort & Marina
guests. It is possible to rent golf carts and
tennis courts are also available ($20 per
hour).

FESTIVALS & EVENTS

In May the **Annual Bahamian Arts & Crafts Show**
is held here as part of the long-running
Treasure Cay Billfish Tournament (☎ 242-365-
8578; www.treasurecayfishing.com), held in June (see
the boxed text, p152). Another popular
event is December's **Treasure Cay Golf Championship** (☎ 242-365-8578; www.treasurecay.com).

SLEEPING & EATING

Rentals are available from **Island Dreams Rentals** (☎ 242-365-8507; www.islanddreamrentals.com;
Treasure Cay Rd; d $250; P X X X X). It has a
variety of good-quality accommodations
for rent, including two-bedroom beach villas, townhouses ($300) and three-bedroom
houses ($400).

Treasure Cay Hotel Resort & Marina (☎ 242-365-8578; www.treasurecay.com; Treasure Cay Rd; r $170; P ✗ ✗ ✗) Pleasant two-story buildings house spacious, light and airy rooms (deluxe suites are $315) and two-bedroom fully furnished condos. Rooms are furnished with floral prints, wicker furniture and balconies, as well as coffeemakers There is also Spinnakers Restaurant, Coco Beach Bar and the Tipsy Seagull Outdoor Bar. Golf and diving packages are available.

Bahama Beach Club (☎ 242-365-8500; www.bahamabeachclub.com; Treasure Cay Rd; d $350; P ✗ ✗ ✗) These super pale-pink two-story condos sit on the beach and offer spacious and light living areas and fully equipped kitchens (four to six people $400). There's a three-night minimum stay, but it may take longer to drag yourself away from the balconies' sea views. A perfect spot.

Banyan Beach Club (☎ 242-365-8111; www.banyanbeach.com; Treasure Cay Rd) Was closed for renovation at the time of research (due to the 2004 hurricanes), but should be checked out for the stunning beachfront location alone.

Touch of Class Restaurant & Bar (☎ 242-365-8195; SC Bootle Hwy; mains $15-30; ☻ dinner) On the highway 100yd south of the turnoff for Treasure Cay, this popular and pleasant place serves Bahamian dishes, a great range of turf 'n' surf plates and lobster.

Cafe Le Florence (☎ 242-367-2570; shopping center; ☻ 7am-6pm) A sticky, spicy and warm cinnamon roll creates queues at this small café and takeaway. Fresh bread, pies and cakes also run out of the door.

Gully's Restaurant & Bar (Airport Ferry Dock; mains $5-10; ☻ breakfast & lunch Mon-Sat) Don't miss the Fish Fry on Sundays, or the grilled red fish (snapper) and lobster. Burgers and other snacks are also available.

Treasure Cay Mini Market (☎ 242-365-8350; shopping center; ☻ 8am-6pm Mon-Sat, 9am-1pm Sun) This very good supermarket is well stocked, and considerately has an adjacent liquor store.

SHOPPING
Abaco Ceramics (☎ 242-365-8489; Treasure Cay Rd; ☻ 9am-4pm Mon-Fri) Handmade and hand-painted kitchenware and adornments are manufactured and sold here.

The gift shop at the marina sells Abaco gold jewelry and resort wear.

GETTING THERE & AROUND
For information on traveling to the Abacos and flights between the Abacos and Bahamian islands please refer to p154.

Air
Treasure Cay International Airport (airport code TCB) is located 15 miles north of town. A taxi to/from the airport to Treasure Cay for two people is $14. To catch a taxi, there is the **Airport Taxi Stand** (☎ 242-365-8661).

Bicycle, Scooter & Car
Cars rent from $80 per day, and bicycles from $10 per day. Weekly rentals should be cheaper. Most rental companies close on Sundays (except R&A, which is open daily).
Cornish Car Rentals (☎ 242-365-8623)
R&A (☎ 242-365-8475; VHF Channel 16; ☻ daily) Rent motor scooters ($31/44 per three hours/day).
Triple J Car Rental (☎ 242-365-8761)
Wendell's Bicycle Rentals (☎ 242-365-8687)

Boat
Captain Gurth Dean sails from Nassau to Treasure Cay weekly (see Marsh Harbour, p155).

Treasure Cay Hotel Resort & Marina (left) has 150 slips, and provides dockage $1.10/0.75 for transient/long-term stays. Cable TV and all facilities are available, including dining and accommodations.

Golf Carts
Cash's Carts (☎ 242-365-8771; shopping center; ☻ 8am-5pm) rents golf carts for $25/40/245 per half-day/day/week. Use the radio if they are not there.

Taxi
A taxi to/from the ferry dock from Treasure Cay is $14. Call **Hart's Taxi Service** (☎ 242-365-8572; VHF Channel 6).

Green Turtle Cay
pop 461
This gorgeous island has it all, and it is still enough off the beaten track to give you an authentic Family Island experience. It's 8 miles north of Treasure Cay and the northernmost of the four Loyalist Cays. The shores are lined with magnificent white-sand beaches, and reefs call to divers, snorkelers and the loggerhead turtles that still crawl ashore to nest.

GREEN TURTLE CAY

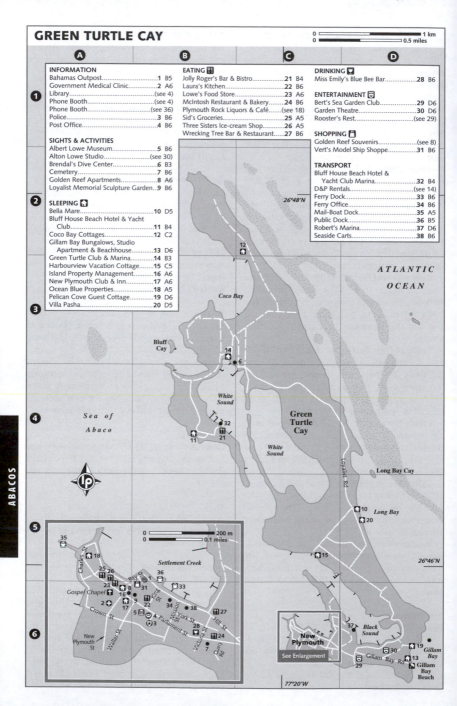

0 _____ 1 km
0 _____ 0.5 miles

INFORMATION
Bahamas Outpost.......................1 B5
Government Medical Clinic..........2 A6
Library.......................................(see 4)
Phone Booth..............................(see 4)
Phone Booth............................(see 36)
Police..3 B6
Post Office.................................4 B6

SIGHTS & ACTIVITIES
Albert Lowe Museum.................5 B6
Alton Lowe Studio..................(see 30)
Brendal's Dive Center.................6 B3
Cemetery....................................7 B6
Golden Reef Apartments............8 A6
Loyalist Memorial Sculpture Garden..9 B6

SLEEPING
Bella Mare...............................10 D5
Bluff House Beach Hotel & Yacht
  Club.....................................11 B4
Coco Bay Cottages...................12 C2
Gillam Bay Bungalows, Studio
  Apartment & Beachhouse........13 D6
Green Turtle Club & Marina......14 B3
Harbourview Vacation Cottage...15 C5
Island Property Management......16 A6
New Plymouth Club & Inn..........17 A6
Ocean Blue Properties...............18 A6
Pelican Cove Guest Cottage......19 D6
Villa Pasha...............................20 D5

EATING
Jolly Roger's Bar & Bistro..........21 B4
Laura's Kitchen........................22 B6
Lowe's Food Store....................23 A6
McIntosh Restaurant & Bakery...24 B6
Plymouth Rock Liquors & Café....(see 18)
Sid's Groceries.........................25 A5
Three Sisters Ice-cream Shop......26 A5
Wrecking Tree Bar & Restaurant...27 B6

DRINKING
Miss Emily's Blue Bee Bar..........28 B6

ENTERTAINMENT
Bert's Sea Garden Club..............29 D6
Garden Theatre.......................30 D6
Rooster's Rest........................(see 29)

SHOPPING
Golden Reef Souvenirs.............(see 8)
Vert's Model Ship Shoppe.........31 B6

TRANSPORT
Bluff House Beach Hotel &
  Yacht Club Marina................32 B4
D&P Rentals...........................(see 14)
Ferry Dock..............................33 B6
Ferry Office.............................34 B6
Mail-Boat Dock.......................35 A5
Public Dock............................36 B5
Robert's Marina......................37 D6
Seaside Carts.........................38 B6

ATLANTIC
OCEAN

26°48'N

Coco Bay

Bluff
Cay

White
Sound

Sea of
Abaco

Green
Turtle
Cay

White
Sound

Long Bay Cay

Long Bay

26°46'N

Settlement Creek

Gospel Chapel

New
Plymouth
St

Crown St

New
Plymouth

See Enlargement

Black
Sound

Gillam
Bay

Gillam
Bay
Beach

Gillam Bay Rd

77°20'W

0 _____ 200 m
0 _____ 0.1 miles

ABACOS

New Plymouth, the island's town, is a pretty, amiable and historic place, with neat little streets and pastel-colored cottages with carefully tendered gardens. Spirited churches exhale the songs of tuneful congregations on Sundays (listen to the exuberant meetings at the daffodil-yellow Gospel Chapel and charismatic tiny bars jump to rake 'n' scrape bands.

The three-masted schooner that sailed into these sun-dappled waters in 1783 carried 500 New Yorkers (mostly Irish Protestants whose property had been confiscated by the victorious colonials). During the 19th century, the town they founded grew to be the second-largest city in the Bahamas, and it remains a charming place. Many locals gain their income by fishing for conch and lobster. Loyalist descendants won't sell town property to out-of-towners, although some rich expats live elsewhere on the island.

INFORMATION

For emergencies contact the **police** (☎ 242-365-4450, 911) who are adjacent to the **post office** (☎ 242-365-4242) in the old pink-and-white building on Parliament St.

For communications, phone booths are in several locales, including outside the library and by the ferry dock. The library, adjoining the post office, has a good array of novels and general reference titles. Books are borrowed on the honor system. **Bahamas Outpost** (☎ 242-365-4695; bahamaoutpost@cocotels.net; Bay St, New Plymouth; ⏰ 9am-4:30pm Mon-Fri, 9am-noon Sat) has Internet access. **Government Medical Clinic** (☎ 242-365-4028; New Plymouth St, New Plymouth).

SIGHTS

The 1826 **Albert Lowe Museum** (☎ 242-365-4095; Parliament & King Sts, Loyalist Rd, New Plymouth; admission $6; ⏰ 9am-noon & 1-4pm Mon-Fri) is housed in a building (1826) that has served as headquarters for the US consul and as home to Neville Chamberlain before he became prime minister of England. The museum was founded in 1976 by the nation's most prominent artist, Alton Roland Lowe, who has dedicated most of his adult life to preserving the long-neglected history of his native Abacos.

Albert Lowe Studio (☎ 242-365-4094; Black Sound; ⏰ Mon-Sat Jul & Dec or by appointment) belongs to the nation's artist laureate, and he is certainly the Bahama's most successful (his works are sought after by monarchs, prime ministers and others with heaps of cash to spare). There's no sign. Look for the tall white gates set back from the road and the white, pink and peppermint green house amid trees on the hill above.

Vert's Model Ship Shoppe (☎ 242-365-4170; vertsmodels@hotmail.com; Bay St, New Plymouth; ⏰ Mon-Fri) is a small place owned by Alton Lowe's brother Vert. He makes intricate model sailing ships, a genius he picked up from his father, a master model-boat builder. You are welcome to watch him conjuring miniature sailing vessels from redwood, spruce and fir.

Loyalist Memorial Sculpture Garden (Parliament St, New Plymouth) features 25 bronze busts of notable loyalists and slaves from all the Bahamian islands, arranged in the shape of the Union Jack. Two loyalist women – one black, one white – stand as the centerpiece atop a coral platform.

The 200-year-old bones of Loyalist ancestors lie in a wee **cemetery** at the east end of Parliament St. Descendants of the long-deceased still adorn the graves with flowers and wreaths.

The handsome **Gillam Bay Beach** lies a half-mile east of town and lines a glorious 2-mile wide bay.

White Sound is a deep bay protected by a bluff-faced peninsula – the setting for a notably affluent community of expats. Pre-Columbian Lucayan artifacts have been found on the bluff. It's located 2 miles north of New Plymouth,

Dirt roads lead north from White Sound to the wild Atlantic shore and **Coco Bay**, with a lovely crescent of powder-soft sand.

ACTIVITIES
Diving & Snorkeling

Brendal's Dive Center (☎ 242-365-4411; VHF Channel 16; www.brendal.com; White Sound) This excellent diving outfit offers two-tank dives ($82), night dives ($72) and snorkel trips ($52). Ask about meeting the divers' wild 'pets': groupers Junkanoo and Calypso, who cuddle up like dogs, and Goombay the grinning green moray eel. Dolphin encounters are instigated by the dolphins. Specialty trips include diving and hand-feeding a family of wild stingrays ($95, including fresh seafood picnic). There's also a snorkel reef trip and wild dolphin encounter with lunch ($75) or a Guana Cay trip to Nipper's Beach Bar ($75). You can rent all kayaks, bicycles, diving

ABACOS

and snorkeling equipment here, including underwater camera and video gear.

Boat Excursions & Rentals

The Green Turtle Club & Marina (right) offers island cruises to guests.

Brendal's Dive Center (p169) offers day-long sailing cruises with beach cookout and punch on Manjack or No Name Cays. Other options include snorkeling, hand-feeding stingrays, diving for lobster, hiking, and shelling (prices on application). Glass-bottomed boat excursions to the reef are $75; snorkeling gear is extra.

Lincoln Jones (☎ 242-365-4223) runs fishing and snorkel trips with beach picnics and cookouts ($75/45 per adult/child).

Boat rentals range from $80 to $150 per day. Weekly rates are better.

Donny's Boat Rentals (☎ 242-365-4119)
Reef Rentals (☎ 242-365-4145)

Bonefishing & Sportfishing

A 1035lb blue marlin was caught in 1998 in one of the Abaco tournaments held annually (the Green Turtle Club & Marina hosts the annual billfishing tournament in May). Typical bonefishing rates are $250/400 per half-/full-day.

Joe Sawyer (☎ 242-365-4173) Has 45 years of bone-fishing experience.

Rick Sawyer (☎ 242-365-4261) A reef and bonefishing guide.

Ronnie Sawyer (☎ 242-365-4070) A bonefishing guide profiled in the media.

FESTIVALS & EVENTS

Green Turtle Cay's traditional **Junkanoo** parades, held on Boxing Day and New Year's Day, attract scores of visitors. In the weeks leading up to Junkanoo, visit Corporal Hubert James Smith (Corporal 'Smitty'), the undisputed king of costuming, and watch him make his magical suits. You can find him at Miss Emily's Blue Bee Bar (opposite).

The **Bluff House Fishing Tournament** in May is a winner, but the annual highlight is **Regatta Week**, held each July, beginning with sailing races and festivities at Green Turtle Cay, followed by the same at Great Guana Cay, Marsh Harbour, Man O' War Cay, Elbow Cay and, again, Marsh Harbour.

During the last week in December, the **Christmas Concert Under the Stars** is held at the Garden Theatre (p172). **An Evening of Music &**

Comedy is traditionally held here in January. Call **Ivy Roberts** (☎ 242-365-4094) or **Alton Lowe** (☎ 242-365-4264).

Also in December, during **Plymouth Historical Weekend**, Green Turtle residents celebrate their loyalist heritage with cultural events and barbecues.

SLEEPING

For some super vacation rentals contact **Island Property Management** (☎ 242-365-4047; ipm@batelnet.bs; Parliament St, New Plymouth) and **Ocean Blue Properties** (☎ 242-365-4636; www.oceanblueproperties.com; Parliament St, New Plymouth).

New Plymouth

Golden Reef Apartments (☎ 242-365-4055; harmony@batelnet.bs; Parliament St, New Plymouth; apt per week $1200; ⊠ ⊠) A peppermint green building on the main street in the centre of town contains this 2nd-floor, two-bedroom apartment. The attractive decor of pale wood, white tile, rattan furniture and breezy ceiling fans lends a cool tropical feel to the place, and a spacious veranda overlooks the street below.

New Plymouth Club & Inn (☎ 242-365-4161; fax 242-365-4138; Parliament St, New Plymouth; s/d/tr $100/130/195; P ⊠ ⊠ ☒) This place, set among quaint cloistered gardens, has 19th-century colonial charm. It also has a restaurant (see opposite).

Gillam Bay Beach

The following great properties all sit on a lovely hidden-away beach, found down the end of a forested road. They can be rented from **Ocean Blue Properties** (above). Choose from the cute **Gillam Bay Bungalows** (2-4 persons per week $950), **Gillam Bay Studio Apartment** (d per week $1250) or **Gillam Bay Beachhouse** (2-6 persons per week $2500) which all sit on the beachside.

Also recommended is the one-bedroom **Pelican Cove Guest Cottage** (d $650).

Black Sound Harbour

Harbourview Vacation Cottage (☎ 242-365-4120; marilyn@oii.net; Black Sound; per week $1250; P ⊠ ☒) This blue-and-white two-bedroom cottage is a great family rental with a good-size garden and screened deck.

White Sound & Coco Bay

Green Turtle Club & Marina (☎ 242-365-4271, US ☎ 800-688-4752; www.greenturtleclub.com; White Sound; r per day/week $195/1070; P ⊠ ☒ ☒) This

THE GOOMBAY SMASH: THE BIRTH OF A CLASSIC COCKTAIL

Miss Emily, a Christian teetotaler who passed away in March 1997, came up with the seductively lethal trademark drink of **Miss Emily's Blue Bee Bar** (☎ 242-365-4181; Victoria St; ☣ noon-10pm) when she was 'fooling around' with mixes about 20 years ago. This mix of rums and fruit juices is now as famous across the Bahamas and the world as the Bahama Mama cocktail. However, only family members are entrusted with the original cocktail's recipe – a still closely guarded secret. If you have enjoyed the inferior versions of the Goombay Smash, try one here and you will be very happy indeed!

The bar is now run by her charming daughter, Violet, who still brews the secret recipe at home in plastic jugs. The simple wooden hut has only rustic seating, and decor is provided by a large portrait of the kindly-looking Miss Emily (who should be toasted with respect), business cards festooning the walls, T-shirts hanging from the ceiling, and all manner of scribbles from happy customers. Yacht pennants from around the world also indicate the fame that this modest blue bar (named after a tiny fish) has justifiably gained.

The friendly mood of the bar is only heightened when the music gets going. Junkanoo kicks off here, as do many celebrations. By the way, the record number of Goombay Smashes consumed in one night is a whopping 23; the man was taken home in a wheelbarrow.

---

hugely popular and good-value place gets booked out well in advance. Rooms have attractive tropical decor and pine decks. Facilities include an English pub–style lounge, and a restaurant offering candlelit dining. Activities include fishing and diving. Excursions are offered.

Coco Bay Cottages (☎ 242-365-5464; www.coco baycottages.com; Coco Bay; d per day/week $250/1500; P ☒ ☒) Secluded and fabulous with miles of beach.

Bluff House Beach Hotel & Yacht Club (☎ 242-365-4247; www.bluffhouse.com; White Sound; d per night/week $180/800; P ☒ ☒ ☒) These light and immaculate modern two-story villas are spaced across a low hillside and have balconies facing the sea and a private beach to share. A minimum three-night stay is required. An elegant bar and restaurant serves lunch and formal dinners, and has a predinner cocktail hour which is included in the price ($40).

Long Bay Beach

Bella Mare (☎ 242-287-3849; www.bellamaregreen turtle.com; Long Bay; r 1-8 persons $5000, 9-10 persons $5500; P ☒ ☒) The modern beachside Bella Mare has huge glass windows and a deck; perfect for families.

Villa Pasha (☎ 242-287-3849; www.bellamare greenturtle.com; Long Bay; villa for 1-4 persons $5500, 9-10 persons $6500; P ☒ ☒) Next door to the Bella Mare is the immaculate Villa Pasha, with a coat of arms on their golf cart and a chandelier in the living room.

EATING & DRINKING

Along with some excellent hotel dining and bars, the island is not short of places to eat and drink.

McIntosh Restaurant & Bakery (☎ 242-365-4625; Parliament St, New Plymouth; mains $5-11; ☣ breakfast, lunch & dinner) American breakfasts and local fare for lunch and dinner are served here, where you also can buy carrot cake and homemade desserts. For luscious, creamy homemade ice cream, head to the adjoining Three Sisters Ice-cream Shop.

Plymouth Rock Liquors & Café (☎ 242-365-4234; Parliament & Charles Sts, New Plymouth; ☣ lunch & dinner) Sandwiches and soups and 70-odd options of rum will keep you occupied. If not, the gallery of extensive local art certainly will!

Laura's Kitchen (☎ 242-365-4287; King St, New Plymouth; mains $6-12; ☣ lunch & dinner) The Bahamian fare is simple but good. The lunch menu includes a tuna sandwich, Bahamian platters and burgers.

Wrecking Tree Bar & Restaurant (☎ 242-365-8635; Hill St, New Plymouth; mains $6-15; ☣ breakfast, lunch & dinner Mon-Sat) The site where 19th-century wreckers brought their ungodly salvage is now a grand place for breakfast, or a beer and fried fish or chicken lunch.

You can buy groceries at **Lowe's Food Store** (☎ 242-365-4243; Parliament St, New Plymouth) and **Sid's Groceries** (☎ 242-365-4055; Parliament St; New Plymouth).

New Plymouth Club & Inn (opposite) serves dinner ($25 to $33) in the cozy lounge-cum-dining room, with jazz and classical

ABACOS

music and soft candlelight adding to the romance. Dinner is with reservations.

The attractive, busy and upmarket restaurant at the Green Turtle Club & Marina (p170) overlooks the marina and water. Try dishes such as the succulent coconut-cooked shrimp or Asian-spiced duck breast with raspberry drizzle (mains $27 to $30). A log fire is lit on cool winter evenings. It's open for breakfast, lunch and dinner but dinner is only with reservations.

Bluff House Beach Hotel & Yacht Club (☎ 242-365-4247, US ☎ 800-688-4752; White Sound; mains $15-25; ☺ lunch & dinner) Jolly Roger's Bar & Bistro is popular for the reggae, lively bar staff, American and Bahamian food (mains $8-15), frozen daiquiris and Vern's famous Tranquil Turtle (more like crawling-on-your-knees-turtle), to be sipped on the wooden deck.

ENTERTAINMENT

Rooster's Rest (☎ 242-365-4066; Gilliam Bay Rd, New Plymouth) The Gully Roosters perform rake 'n' scrape calypso and soca music here on Friday and Saturday nights.

You can play pool next door at **Bert's Sea Garden Club** (Gilliam Bay Rd, New Plymouth), where Bert Reckley serves a house concoction of coconut, rum and milk.

The Gully Roosters also perform at Bluff House (above) on Thursday night, and at the Green Turtle Club (see p170) on Wednesday night.

On Thursday night there's a beach barbecue with live bands and Junkanoo mini-events at Bluff House (p172). Live music is also offered on Tuesday.

The open-air **Garden Theatre** (Black Sound), adjacent to the Alton Lowe Studio, hosts comedy, and musical and theatrical concerts throughout the year.

SHOPPING

Model boats at Vert's Model Ship Shoppe (p169) are not cheap, beginning at over $100. A 26-inch one-master costs about $600. For two- or three-masted ships up to 5ft long, expect to pay $1200 to $2500.

Golden Reef Souvenirs (☎ 242-365-4511; Parliament Rd, New Plymouth) They sell handmade gold jewelry, resort wear and other souvenirs.

Also look for paintings by Alton Lowe, sold at the gallery next to the Albert Lowe Museum (p169). You might see some of his works displayed at the Ocean Blue Gallery in the Plymouth Rock Liquors & Café (p171), where over 50 artists are represented by prints, oils and watercolors. Other gems include stained-glass work by Rome Heyer.

GETTING THERE & AWAY

Green Turtle Ferry (☎ 242-365-4166; VHF Channel 16, Airport Ferry Dock; $8/14 single/return) departs from Green Turtle Cay for Treasure Cay at 8am, 9am, 11am, noon, 1:30pm, 3pm and 4:30pm. The ferries return at 8:30am, 10:30am, 11:30am, 1:30pm, 2:30pm, 3:30pm, 4:30pm and 5pm.

The ferries will drop you at White Sound for an extra $2. The skipper will also drop you off at the dock nearest your hotel or radio ahead so that your rental's caretaker will be waiting for you. Ferries also operate on demand, at extra cost, for people with flights; call ahead.

Mail boat *Captain Gurth Dean* calls in once a week from Nassau; see p155.

Green Turtle Cay is a Port of Entry for the Bahamas; **Customs & Immigration** (☎ 242-365-4077) is on Parliament St, in New Plymouth. Black Sound is considered a hurricane shelter.

Bluff House Beach Hotel & Yacht Club (☎ 242-365-4247; VHF Channel 16; www.bluffhouse.com; White Sound) has 45 slips and there is transient/monthly dockage on offer for $1.15/0.85 per foot. It provides electricity, water and laundry.

Green Turtle Club & Marina (p170) has 40 slips offering dockage and providing electricity, water and laundry facilities.

Robert's Marina (☎ 242-365-4249; Black Sound) has a full-service marina.

GETTING AROUND

The preferred mode of transportation is the golf cart. Carts can be ordered by getting the ferry captain to call ahead on VHF.

D & P Rentals (☎ 242-365-4655; VHF Channel 16; dmcintosh@oii.net; Green Turtle Marina, White Sound; ☺ 8am-5pm) rent gas or electric carts for $25/50/240 per half-day/day/week and scooters for $50 per day.

Seaside Carts (☎ 242-365-5497; VHF Channel 16; seasidecarts@hotmail.com; Bay St, New Plymouth) meets the ferries and rent carts for $25/50/230 per half-day/day/week.

Brendal's Dive Centre (p169) rents out bicycles ($12) and kayaks ($10 per hour).

Spanish Cay

On your way to Spanish Cay you will pass **Cooper's Town**, a center for commercial citrus farms. Spanish Cay, a 3-mile-long sliver of land 3 miles off the northern tip of Great Abaco, was once owned by Queen Elizabeth II. Four beautiful beaches line the eastern shore. Most of its 185 acres are covered in palm groves and tropical forest, with a few homes of the international gentry hidden in their midst.

Spanish Cay Inn & Marina (Map p147; ☎ 242-365-0083; www.spanishcay.com; r $150; P ⊠ ⊠ ⊠) This small luxury resort used to host the Dallas Cowboys. It has light and comfortable two-room suites, condos and villas. Facilities include a waterfront restaurant, tennis courts, and a whirlpool with a nearby bar. Golf carts are available, as are boats for fishing or diving. The marina offers 82 slips and full facilities.

Spanish Cay has a 5000ft airstrip for guests arriving by private plane.

A water taxi runs from the Government Dock at Cooper's Town.

Little Abaco

Great Abaco finishes 5 miles northwest of Cooper's Town at Angel Fish Point, where SC Bootle Hwy swings west over a bridge onto Little Abaco island.

The population lives in four small and relatively poor settlements: Cedar Harbour, Mount Hope, Fox Town and Crown Haven. There's a post office, small hotel and police station in Fox Town. There are a few modest beaches and the bonefishing on the south side of the island is said to be excellent.

NORTHWEST CAYS
Grand Cay
pop 435

Near the top of the Abacos chain, Grand Cay is divided into the larger, box-shaped, virtually uninhabited isle of that name and, to its east, Little Grand Cay and Mermaid Cay, both with small settlements. There are several beaches; the most spectacular is Wells Bay, which runs the 2-mile west shore of Grand Cay. The bonefishing here is superb.

Walker's Cay

This tiny rocky cay sits right at the northern end of the Abacos chain. It is fringed by a barrier reef that offers spectacular diving, often in less than 30ft of water. Highlights include old wrecks, including a WWII relic; Jeanette's Reef, boasting a large population of eels; caverns full of silver minnows; and Travel Agent Reef, a beautiful coral garden ideal for snorkelers and novice divers.

Walker's Cay Hotel & Marina (☎ 242-353-1264; www.walkerscay.com; d/ste $170/335; ⊠ ⊠ ⊠) has been a firm favorite with fishermen since the 1930s, and is operated by staff who boat in each day. Other than visitors, the cay's residents consist of scurrying, curly-tailed lizards and seabirds, including sooty terns and frigates. Two restaurants and bars offer enough steak and fish to keep everyone happily fed. Attractive rooms have private terraces. Facilities include two swimming pools (one freshwater, the other saltwater) and a Jacuzzi, plus stores, a volleyball court, a tennis court and water sports, including diving.

An airstrip welcomes chartered planes from Florida and elsewhere, while the marina has 75 slips and full facilities.

ABACOS

Eleuthera

When it comes to wishing for the archetypal 'idyllic island,' it is impossible to think past the delicate pink-sand beaches and sparkling turquoise seas of tranquil Eleuthera. On the east coast, dramatic cliffs, sheltered coves and offshore coral reefs add to this vivid panorama.

However, barely 50 miles east of Nassau, Eleuthera's infamous Devil's Backbone reef has claimed plenty of ill-fated ships over the centuries. Although divers explore these evocative remains, many other vessels still wait to be found. The hurricanes of 1992, 1999 and 2004 have also whacked many villages across the main island.

The Queen's Hwy runs the length of this fashionably thin 100-mile-long island, making exploration easy, while the Bight of Eleuthera to the west is a vast expanse of shallow scalloped waters where bonefish hunters await their prey.

The high-speed ferry service makes Nassau accessible and day-trippers can visit the haunt of the rich, famous and beautiful – Harbour Island, coined the prettiest Caribbean island. It still has an attractive Bahamian character, despite the laconic wealth displayed by visitors and expats. An indescribably lovely coral pink beach runs along the windward shore, and breakers are stopped by coral reefs, guaranteeing superb bathing and snorkeling.

While hotels on these isles cater for the seriously wealthy, boutique hotels and self-contained accommodations make these rosy beaches and warm azure waters accessible to us all.

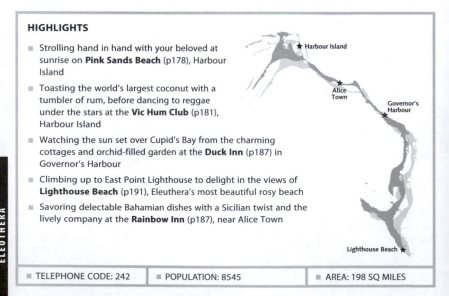

HIGHLIGHTS

- Strolling hand in hand with your beloved at sunrise on **Pink Sands Beach** (p178), Harbour Island
- Toasting the world's largest coconut with a tumbler of rum, before dancing to reggae under the stars at the **Vic Hum Club** (p181), Harbour Island
- Watching the sun set over Cupid's Bay from the charming cottages and orchid-filled garden at the **Duck Inn** (p187) in Governor's Harbour
- Climbing up to East Point Lighthouse to delight in the views of **Lighthouse Beach** (p191), Eleuthera's most beautiful rosy beach
- Savoring delectable Bahamian dishes with a Sicilian twist and the lively company at the **Rainbow Inn** (p187), near Alice Town

★ Harbour Island

★ Alice Town

Governor's Harbour

Lighthouse Beach ★

| ■ TELEPHONE CODE: 242 | ■ POPULATION: 8545 | ■ AREA: 198 SQ MILES |

History

The name 'Eleuthera' comes from the Greek word *eleutheros,* meaning freedom (the Lucayans who originally settled the island called their home 'Cigatoo'). In 1648, English refugees fleeing religious persecution in Bermuda during the English Civil War era landed in Eleuthera after the Devil's Backbone reef ripped open their boats. They were later joined by Loyalists, who brought their slaves and founded new settlements.

Massive pineapple exports in the late 1800s and early 1900s were replaced with less intensive farming crops. Abandoned silos recall the thriving cattle and chicken industries that evolved in the 1950s. Alas, following independence the government bought out the farmers, and within a short period of time the farms were derelict. Since then, with the exception of Harbour Island, tourism on Eleuthera has also withered and many once-fashionable resort hotels are now closed. St Georges Island's Spanish Wells, however, has a thriving lobster industry.

Hurricane Andrew knocked the socks off much of North Eleuthera in 1992, and Hurricane Floyd hit the island with a right hook in 1999. The 2004 hurricanes also added to the general damage sustained by the infrastructure and many villages.

Getting There & Away

Most travelers to Eleuthera fly into Governor's Harbour Airport or North Eleuthera International Airport (if they are heading to Harbour Island). Others take the twice-weekly fast ferry from Nassau. A number of day trips to the cays from Nassau on super-zippy powerboats are also very popular. Cheaper but slow mail boats and expensive private boat charters round out the options.

Getting Around

You'll need your own transport if you want to explore Eleuthera outside of Governor's Harbour or Harbour Island. Fortunately, car-rental agencies can be found at the airport and through accommodations. If you fly in, you'll have to catch a ferry or water taxi to Harbour Island where bicycles or golf carts are the modus operandi; they're easily rented at the dock.

NORTH ELEUTHERA

Eleuthera is neatly divided by a tendril-thin strip of land called The Glass Window, one-quarter of the way down the island. Immediately north, the isle broadens out in a rough triangle with Current Island to the west. To the east, Harbour Island and neighboring cays enclose a vast harbor. North Eleuthera includes Governor's Harbour.

HARBOUR ISLAND
pop 1523

It is hard to live up to the accolade of being the prettiest island in the Caribbean, but 'Briland,' as it is known, is especially charming. The lovely little pastel-colored cottages with their tiny and immaculate gardens, the narrow streets hung with vibrant garlands and that indescribably beautiful coral pink beach running the length of the windward shore are all simply entrancing. Although many Eleutherans shudder at the island's tourism, for visitors it is an entrancing mix of Old World Bahamas and island living at a very comfortable level, all underscored by the undeniable charm and friendliness of the Brilanders.

Harbour Island discreetly houses well-known Bahamian artist Eddie Minnis, singer Jimmy Buffett, Aussie supermodel Elle Macpherson and many other celebrities.

Quaint **Dunmore Town**, on the harbor side, harks back 300 years. The town was laid out in 1791 by Lord Dunmore, governor of the Bahamas (1787–96), who had a summer residence here. Maybe the clip-clop of hooves has been replaced with the whir of golf carts, but the daily pace has not changed much. Once a noted shipyard and a sugar-refining center from which a rum-making tradition evolved, today most adults are employed at the hotels or in fishing.

The Bahamas Billfish Championship regularly heads this way around May (see boxed text, p152).

Orientation

The ferry alights on the corner of Bay and Church Sts. Church St and other streets rise gently inland to Dunmore St. The resorts run along Pink Sands Beach, to the east.

Colebrook St runs south to a private residential estate, while Bay St extends north to Nesbit St at the northern end of the town.

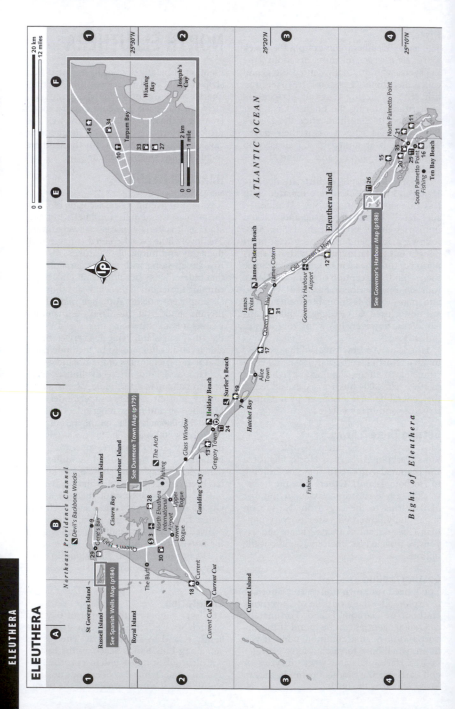

ELEUTHERA

ELEUTHERA

Map labels

Windermere Island
Savannah Sound
Queen's Hwy
Savannah Sound
Fishing
22
See Enlargement
Half Sound
Fishing
Tarpum Bay
Fishing
Rock Sound
Cape Eleuthera
Eleuthera Island
Rock Sound Airport
Rock Sound
4
32
1
5
Jacks Bay
Cotton Bay Golf Club
Cotton Bay
6
Wemyss Bight
Queen's Hwy
Greencastle
Waterford
Davis Harbour
23
The Village
Deep Creek
Millars
Bannerman
Lighthouse Beach
Eleuthera Point
Lighthouse Bay
East Point Lighthouse
Exuma Sound

24°40'N
25°00'N
24°50'N
76°10'W
76°20'W
76°30'W
76°40'W
76°50'W

ELEUTHERA

INFORMATION

Government Medical Clinic	1 E7
Government Medical Clinic	(see 2)
Police	2 C2
Police	(see 1)
Post Office	(see 2)
Scotiabank	3 B2
Scotiabank	4 E6

SIGHTS & ACTIVITIES

Bahamas Out-Island Adventures	(see 19)
Blow Hole	5 E7
Cotton Bay Club (Closed)	6 E7
Hatchet Bay Cave	7 C3
Ocean Hole	8 F7
Preacher's Cave	9 B1
St Columbus Church	10 E1

SLEEPING

Bahama Sands Real Estate	11 F4
Cocodimama Charming Resort	12 D3
Cove Eleuthera	13 C2
Ingraham's Beach Inn	14 F1
Palmetto Point Lighthouse	15 E4
Palmetto Shores Vacation Villas	16 E4
Rainbow Inn	17 D3
Sammy's Place	(see 32)
Sandcastle Apartments	18 A2
Surfer's Haven	19 C3
Tropical Dreams Motel Resort	20 E4
Unique Village Resort Hotel	21 F4
Windermere Island Club (Closed)	22 F5

EATING

Big Rock General Store	(see 31)
D & N Pizza	23 E7
Dolcevita Restaurant & Lounge	(see 17)
Down Home Pizza	(see 32)
Elvina's Bar & Restaurant	24 C2
Haven Bakery	(see 32)
Juneek's Savoury Snacks	(see 31)
Marketplace Supermarket	(see 32)
Mate & Jenny's Restaurant & Bar	25 E4
Mery's Bakery	(see 19)
Palm Garden Restaurant & Bar	(see 32)
Thompson's Bakery	(see 24)
Tippy's Bar & Beach Restaurant	26 E4

DRINKING

Corner Bar	(see 24)

SHOPPING

Island Made Gift Shop	(see 2)
Tarpum Bay Shopping Centre	27 E2

TRANSPORT

Ferry Dock (Ferry to Harbour Island)	28 B2
Ferry Dock (Ferry to Spanish Wells)	29 B1
Gas Station	30 B2
Gas Station	31 D3
Gas Station	32 E6
Gas Station	33 E2
Gas Station	34 F1
Gas Station	35 E4

Information

Public telephone booths sit along Bay St.

Bahamas Ministry of Tourism (☎ 242-333-2621; Dunmore St; 🕑 9am-5:30pm Mon-Fri)

BaTelCo (☎ 242-333-2648; Colebrook St)

Harbour Island Medical Clinic (☎ 242-333-2227; Church St; 🕑 9am-5pm Mon-Fri, to noon Sat)

Harbourside Pharmacy (☎ 242-363-2514; Bay St) Also sells papers, including the *New York Times*.

Police (☎ 242-332-2111, 919; Goal Lane)

Post office (☎ 242-332-2215; Goal Lane)

Red Apple Internet Lounge (☎ 242-333-2750; Colebrook St; per 20 min $10; 🕑 9am-7pm Mon-Sat) South of the center.

Royal Bank of Canada (☎ 242-333-2250; Murray St; 🕑 9am-1pm Mon-Fri) The only bank here.

Sights & Activities

One of the finest examples of loyalist architecture is the **Loyalist Cottage** (1797) on Bay St. The 1843 **Wesley Methodist Church** (cnr Dumore & Chapel Sts), with beautiful hardwood pews and a huge model sailing ship that honors the seafaring tradition of the Brilanders, is close to the 1768 **St John's Anglican Church** (Dunmore St). St John's, near Church St, is claimed to be the oldest church in the Bahamas.

Also worth a visit are the ancient graves at the **cemetery** on Chapel St. Bahamians give it a wide berth at night, being fearful of spirits. The handsome 1913 **Commissioner's Residence** sits on Goal Lane at Colebrook St.

There's a bizarre collection of **international license plates** and **driftwood signs** painted with humorous limericks and aphorisms on Dunmore St, opposite the Royal Palm Hotel.

Cannons can be seen at the southern end of Bay St. Named **Roundheads**, this now overgrown 17th-century battery was built by the English to defend the island.

No exaggeration, the wide and stunning length of **Pink Sands Beach** is really pink; a faint blush by day, turning a rosy red when fired by the dawn or sunset. The sea is great for swimming and snorkeling, while nearby hotels have public bars and restaurants. It's perfect for self-indulgent beach bumming.

DIVING & SNORKELING

Fish have long been protected off Harbour Island, where groupers are so tame that they will nuzzle divers, hoping to be fed. The island is surrounded by superb dive sites, highlighted by the **Devil's Backbone**, with more than 3 miles of pristine reefs littered with ancient wrecks. Among them are **Cienfuegos**, a cruise ship, and the **Potato & Onion**, a massive 19th-century wreck just 15ft down. Dive operators also head for the **Arch**, where sharks, rays and schools of jacks swim through a coral archway which begins at 75ft, and **Current Cut**, where you're whipped along at speeds of up to 10 knots, in depths down to 65ft. Here coral walls encourage voluminous sea life.

Snorkelers also have a lot of choice: **Bird Cay** has large populations of conch and fish; **Blue Hole's** cavern features a low-lying reef; **Gaulding's Cay** is where soft coral, sea anemone and bonefish abound across a large area; **Oleander Reef**, which is close to shore, has a tremendous variety of tropical fish; and **Paradise Beach's** barrier-reef system has heaps of coral and fish species. Moreover, **Pineapple Rock's** shipwreck, now claimed by myriad tropical fish, is great, as is **Seafan Gardens**, where Gorgonians await, along with Baron, the friendly barracuda.

Dive prices here soar considerably with equipment rental costs included. The following companies rent snorkel gear for $10 and provide snorkeling trips for approximately $30.

Valentine's Dive Center (☎ 242-333-2080; www .valentinesdive.com; Bay St) offers two-tank ($65) and one-tank night dives ($60). All-day dive excursions ($115) and reef-running underwater scooters ($125) are also to be enjoyed. Fishing fans can also charter boats (per half-day/day $400/650). Deep-sea fishing is also offered ($575/775 per half-day/day).

Romora Bay Dive Shop (☎ 242-333-2325; Queen's Hwy), south of the center, has two-tank dives ($110), twilight and night dives ($126), Sandy Point wall and reef dives with lunch ($189) and cave diving including Nitrox for decompression. It also rents Sunfish and sailboards ($20/60 per hour/day).

Ocean Fox Divers (☎ 242-333-2323; www.oceanfox .com; Harbour Island Marina), south of the center, is a small outfit that caters for up to six on its 34ft-custom dive boat. It also has two-tank dives ($105), one-tank night dives ($90), dive tours to Grouper Hole ($65) and Current Cut & Wreck dives ($125). It also has deep-sea fishing ($525/895 per half-/full-day).

BONEFISHING & SPORTFISHING

Fishing guides and boats cost around $250 to $350 per half-day and $400 to $600 per

DUNMORE TOWN

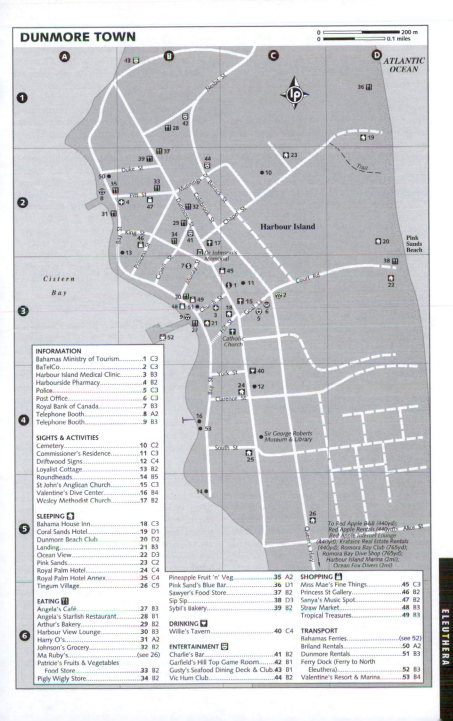

0 ————————— 200 m
0 ————————— 0.1 miles

ATLANTIC OCEAN

Harbour Island

Pink Sands Beach

Cistern Bay

Dr Johnson's Memorial

Catholic Church

Sir George Roberts Museum & Library

To Red Apple B&B (440yd);
Red Apple Rentals (440yd); Alice St
Red Apple Internet Lounge
(440yd); Kratains Real Estate Rentals
(440yd); Romora Bay Club (765yd);
Romora Bay Dive Shop (765yd);
Harbour Island Marina (2mi);
Ocean Fox Divers (2mi)

INFORMATION
Bahamas Ministry of Tourism.............1 C3
BaTelCo..2 C3
Harbour Island Medical Clinic...........3 B3
Harbourside Pharmacy......................4 B2
Police..5 C3
Post Office...6 C3
Royal Bank of Canada.......................7 B3
Telephone Booth.................................8 A2
Telephone Booth.................................9 B3

SIGHTS & ACTIVITIES
Cemetery..10 C2
Commissioner's Residence...............11 C3
Driftwood Signs.................................12 C4
Loyalist Cottage.................................13 A2
Roundheads..14 B5
St John's Anglican Church................15 C3
Valentine's Dive Center....................16 B4
Wesley Methodist Church................17 B2

SLEEPING
Bahama House Inn..............................18 C3
Coral Sands Hotel..............................19 D1
Dunmore Beach Club........................20 D2
Landing...21 B3
Ocean View..22 D3
Pink Sands..23 C2
Royal Palm Hotel...............................24 C4
Royal Palm Hotel Annex...................25 C4
Tingum Village...................................26 C5

EATING
Angela's Café.....................................27 B3
Angela's Starfish Restaurant.............28 B1
Arthur's Bakery..................................29 B2
Harbour View Lounge.......................30 B3
Harry O's..31 A2
Johnson's Grocery..............................32 B3
Ma Ruby's.....................................(see 26)
Patricie's Fruits & Vegetables
   Food Store......................................33 B2
Pigly Wigly Store...............................34 B2

Pineapple Fruit 'n' Veg.....................35 A2
Pink Sand's Blue Bar.........................36 D1
Sawyer's Food Store..........................37 B2
Sip Sip..38 D3
Sybil's Bakery.....................................39 B2

DRINKING
Willie's Tavern...................................40 C4

ENTERTAINMENT
Charlie's Bar.......................................41 B2
Garfield's Hill Top Game Room........42 B1
Gusty's Seafood Dining Deck & Club.43 B1
Vic Hum Club.....................................44 B2

SHOPPING
Miss Mae's Fine Things.....................45 C3
Princess St Gallery............................46 B2
Sanya's Music Spot...........................47 B2
Straw Market......................................48 B3
Tropical Treasures.............................49 B3

TRANSPORT
Bahamas Ferries...........................(see 52)
Briland Rentals..................................50 A2
Dunmore Rentals..............................51 B3
Ferry Dock (Ferry to North
   Eleuthera).......................................52 B3
Valentine's Resort & Marina.............53 B4

ELEUTHERA

full-day. See p178 for alternative arrangements.

Bonefish Stuart (☎ 242-333-2072)
Maxwell Higgs (☎ 242-333-2323)
Patrick Roberts (☎ 242-333-3014)

OTHER ACTIVITIES

Horseback riding on Pink Sands Beach is around $20 per half-hour; wave down the gent strolling the sands with his untethered four-legged friends or call on ☎ 242-333-2317. **Ron & Cleotis** (☎ 242-333-2317) also offer horseback riding. Ask about rates.

Bicycles can be rented ($30 per day) from **Michaels Cycles** (☎ 242-2384).

Kayaks are rented ($25 per hour) from Dunmore Beach Club (right).

Sleeping

There are some great-value rental and self-contained places listed on the island. Contact **Bahama Sands Real Estate** (Map pp176-7; ☎ 242-332-2662) and **Krataios Real Estate Rentals** (☎ 242-333-2750; www.redapple.bb.com; Queen's Hwy).

MIDRANGE

Bahama House Inn (☎ 242-333-2201; www.bahama houseinn.com; cnr Dunmore & Hill Sts; r $140; ✗ ✗) This super and spacious B&B is a charming and subtly restored colonial home. Outdoor decking connects cool and comfortable living, dining and library/lounge areas, while bedrooms are furnished with eclectic colonial furniture, some with draped four-poster beds. En-suite rooms overlook a large garden and patio deck, just made for a quiet read and a glass of chilled rum and pineapple juice. A studio apartment is also offered. No children under 12 are allowed.

Landing (☎ 242-333-2707; landinghl@aol.com; Bay St; r $155; P ✗ ✗) This lovely old colonial building (circa 1899) on the waterfront in town has a few rooms with creaky polished wooden floors, and four-poster beds made up with crisp white cotton sheets. A library, TV lounge and lovely back garden are open to guests, and a popular restaurant (reservations required) serves classic dinners.

Tingum Village (☎ /fax 242-333-2161; Queen's Hwy; r/ste $115/125, ste with Jacuzzi $175; P ✗ ✗) This pleasant and friendly place has a choice of spick-and-span rooms and suites, all furnished with Bahamian cane and handmade wooden furniture (suites have kitchen and Jacuzzi). The on-site restaurant and bar (Ma

Ruby's; opposite) open on to a pleasant garden. A path leads from the garden over hill to the beach, probably a 10-minute walk away.

Red Apple B&B (☎ 242-333-2750; www.redapplebb .com; Queen's Hwy; r per night/week $129/903; P ✗ ✗ 🖳) These fabulous self-contained units are great value and very tastefully decorated. Light wood and white surrounds are the setting for large and comfortable one- and two-bedroom apartments. Large bathrooms and useful kitchens are also well maintained. The friendly owners, Rosita and Joseph Roberts, also rent golf carts and offer bonefishing expeditions.

Royal Palm Hotel (☎ 242-333-2738; www.royal palmhotel.com; Clarence St; r $97-120; P ✗ ✗) This small and modern motel-style lodging is very popular with divers. Spotless rooms are tiled in white and are simply but comfortably furnished. This nice, attractive part of town is more Bahamian in character and very good value.

TOP END

Coral Sands Hotel (☎ 242-333-2350; pamela@coral sands.com; Chapel St; r $235; P ✗ ✗ 🖳) This classy and intimate beach resort extends over 14 acres. Rooms blend Caribbean colors, wicker furniture and artwork to create a homey feel; oceanfront rooms have French doors opening to balconies, while a library, games room, tennis court and water sports are all on site. Bicycles, scooters and golf carts are also available for rent.

Dunmore Beach Club (☎ 242-333-2200; www .dunmorebeach.com; Court Rd; r $499; P ✗ ✗ 🖳) An unpretentious, friendly but elegant place with warmly hued and comfy rooms, and units scattered back from the beach. Options include deluxe room/ocean house ($579/1600), and all rates include meals, served on a deck overlooking the beach. There's a handsome clubhouse with bar and lounge, complete with fireplace, and a highly rated restaurant requiring men to wear jackets and ties at dinner.

Pink Sands (☎ 242-333-2030; www.islandoutpost .com/pinksands/; Chapel St; r $655; P ✗ ✗ 🖳 🖳) Just made for its exotic and wealthy rock-star and super-model clientele, this place has to be seen (and lunch must be eaten on the Blue Bar's patio overlooking Pink Sands Beach). Stone floors and Moroccan furnishings are used in secluded luxurious cottages, dotted throughout a tropical garden. Cottages contain a full sound and TV system, wet bar, private patio and exotic bathrooms. Rates include full breakfast and dinner in the exotically splendid Moroccan lounge bar.

Ocean View (☎ 242-333-2276; fax 242-333-2459; Court Rd; r $250-375; P X X) A beautifully yet eclectically decorated nine-bedroom mansion where all rooms have ocean views.

Romora Bay Club (☎ 242-333-2325; www.romora bay.com; Queen's Hwy; r per night/week $370/2100; P X X ☎) This place south of town faces west, with self-contained cottages spilling down through riotously colorful gardens to wooden sun decks, a Jacuzzi and nice little pool with sea views. Rates include breakfast and dinner.

Eating & Drinking

You won't go hungry and thirsty here!

Some super classic meals with a twist are served at the Landing (opposite), such as rack of lamb with mint sauce, pomegranates, green beans and mashed potatoes, or fragrant chicken curry with fried plantain and all the trimmings. Specialty pastas include *capellini* with lobster, chili and lime. The desserts are to die for! Mains are $30 to $38. It's open for dinner from Thursday to Tuesday, and lunch on Sunday; reservations are suggested.

Arthur's Bakery (☎ 242-333-2285; arthursbakery@ yahoo.com; Crown St) You can buy fresh herb bread, scrumptious pastries, croissants and pies at this family bakery.

Angela's Cafe (Bay St) This café is no more than a little outdoor stall across from The Landing. The women cook fabulous crispy fritters and chicken wings (two for $4), along with slices of moist coconut cake.

Angela's Starfish Restaurant (☎ 242-333-2253; Nesbit St; mains $5-12; lunch & dinner) Bahamian food is served in this nice little place with an outside garden and very friendly owners. Popular dishes include burgers and pork, and rice and peas.

Harbour View Lounge (☎ 242-333-2031; Bay St; mains $15-36; lunch & dinner Tue-Sun) The cosy pink-and-mint-green restaurant has a nice casual indoor restaurant and outdoor deck; ideal for lounging and watching people stroll along the waterfront. Meals are pricey, but tasty. Try the grilled fish with spicy sauces and curried pumpkin soup.

Ma Ruby's (☎ 242-333-2161; Tingum Village, Queens Hwy; mains $10-20; lunch & dinner) Serving Bahamian dishes, the outdoor/indoor café and

bar are bright and airy with upbeat decor. Ma Ruby's 'Cheeseburgers in Paradise' are featured in Jimmy Buffett's *Parrot Head Handbook*.

Sip Sip (☎ 242-333-3316; Pink Sands Beach; mains $14-21; lunch) This hugely popular place has grand sea views and attracts young trendies with lots of shiny flicked hair, designer shades and golf carts with go-faster stripes. The lime green house is easy to spot, and serves drinks, salads and burgers.

Pink Sand's Blue Bar (☎ 242-333-2030; Chapel St; mains $20-30; lunch & dinner) A must for lunch, overlooking Pink Sands Beach. À la carte lunches for all-comers, with chicken tikka, spring rolls, jerked chicken Caesar salad and super grilled-fish burgers. The fresh-fruit cocktails are luscious and unmissable, as is the view from the patio.

Charlie's Bar (Dunmore St; mains $8-14; breakfast, lunch & dinner) This friendly bar is quite elegant, serves bar meals and a great selection of rums.

Willie's Tavern (☎ 242-333-2121; Dunmore St) Another popular, down-to-earth bar with a lofty ceiling festooned with fishing nets. It has a pool table and sports on TV.

A number of grocery stores include **Johnson Grocery** (☎ 242-333-2279; Dunmore St); **Patricie's Fruits & Vegetables Food Store** (☎ 242-333-2289; Pitt St), just north of the village center; **Sawyer's Food Store** (☎ 242-333-2356; Dunmore St); **Pigly Wigly Store** (☎ 242-333-2120; King St); **Pineapple Fruit 'n' Veg** (☎ 242-333-2454; Bay St); and **Sybil's Bakery** (cnr Duke & Dunmore Sts). **Harry O's**, a stall north on Bay St, serves all manner of burgers and fried chicken.

Entertainment

Vic Hum Club (☎ 242-333-2161; Barrack & Munnings Sts; 11am-late) This funky and sometimes fiery locale has a fine collection of rums, a checkerboard court that doubles as a dance floor, busy pool table and live reggae music from performers like Maxi Priest or the bar's own Paddy 'Big Bird' Lewis. Most importantly the world's largest coconut sits behind the bar. The place can get rowdy, fights often break out, and the owner has a running battle with locals who don't like the noise. Here's a promise, you won't suffer from ennui here.

Then there's **Gusty's Seafood Dining Deck & Club**, at the north end of town, which claims to be Jimmy Buffett's original 'Margaritaville' and where the musician has been known to

ELEUTHERA

jam. Nearby, **Garfield's Hill Top Game Room** has video-game machines.

The bar at Pink Sands (p180) offers up-scale ambience and some grand people-watching opportunities (count the number of air kisses in one evening). There's riffs off the Island Records label on the sound system (Mr Blackwell of Island Records is the owner of this place).

The Harbour View Lounge (p181) has live music and a dance club on weekends.

Shopping

There's a waterfront straw market facing Sugar Mill Gifts. You can buy newspapers, batteries and Cuban cigars at **Tropical Treasures** on the waterfront. And **Sanya's Music Spot** sells tapes and CDs of island music.

Princess St Gallery (☎ 242-333-2788; Princess St) Local artists are represented here, along with Bahamian star-dauber Eddie Minnis. Works include original oils, acrylics and prints, hand-colored maps, antique prints and driftwood paintings.

Kevin Cooper (☎ 242-334-2478) A local man and modest artist who really appreciates the glorious colors of his surroundings, Kevin is one of a few artists selling their afford-able wares near the ferry dock (outside The Landing).

Miss Mae's Fine Things (Dunmore St) You wouldn't guess from the name or the flow-ered sign, but this store sells sophisticated designer resort wear; lots of cream linen and light cotton clothes.

Getting There & Away

AIR

Most flights arrive at **North Eleuthera International Airport** (ELH; ☎ 242-335-1242), located in North Eleuthera, at the top end of the mainland, or at **Governor's Harbour Airport** (☎ 242-332-2321), halfway down the island. Some also fly to **Rock Sound Airport** (☎ 242-334-2177) down south.

For international flights to the Bahamas and Eleuthera please refer to p288.

These airlines fly between the Bahamian islands and Eleuthera:

Abaco Air (☎ 242-367-2266; www.abacoaviationcentre .com/abacoair) Hub Marsh Harbour, Abaco.

Bahamasair (UP; ☎ 242-377-5505; www.bahamasair .com) Hubs Nassau & Freeport.

Cherokee Air (☎ 242-367-3450; www.cherokeeair .com) Hubs Marsh Harbour, Abaco.

Major's Air Services (☎ 242-352-5778; www.the bahamasguide.com/majorair) Hubs Grand Bahama and Eleuthera.

Southern Air (Nassau ☎ 242-377-2014; www.southern aircharter.com) Hub Nassau.

Quoted fares are one-way.

Route	Price	Frequency
Governor's Harbour–Freeport, Grand Bahama	$135	2 weekly
Governor's Harbour–Nassau	$70	3 daily
Governor's Harbour–North Eleuthera	$30	3 daily
North Eleuthera–Freeport, Grand Bahama	$135	2 weekly
North Eleuthera–Marsh Harbour, Abaco	$90	once daily
North Eleuthera–Nassau	$70	3 daily
Rock Sound–Nassau	$70	2 daily

BOAT

Also see p80 for daily boat excursions to Eleuthera and Harbour Island from Nassau.

Ferry

Bahamas Ferries (☎ 242-323-2166, 242-322-8185; www.bahamasferries.com; Potters Cay, Nassau) offers a daily fast luxury passenger catamaran, the *Bo Hengy*, from Nassau to Harbour Island, North Eleuthera and Spanish Wells ($128 return). The ferry leaves Nassau at 8am and there's an extra sailing on Fridays at 1:30pm. The trip takes two hours each way. Daily excursions from Nassau to Harbour Island are also offered, which include tours and a grand picnic lunch at Pink Sands Beach.

Mail Boat

These leave from Potter's Cay dock in Nassau; please call the **Dockmaster's Office** (☎ 242-393-1064) for further details on these schedules. One-way fares are from $30.

Eleuthera Express Departs Nassau for Governor's Harbour and Spanish Wells on Monday and Thursday.

MV Bahamas Daybreak III Departs Nassau for Rock Sound, South Eleuthera, on Monday, and the Bluff and Harbour Island on Thursday.

MV Current Pride Departs Nassau for Current, Lower Bogue, Upper Bogue and Hatchet Bay every Thursday.

Marinas

Valentine's Resort & Marina (☎ 242-333-2142; VHF Channel 16; info@valentinesresort.com; Bay St, Eleuthera) Offers transient/long-term dockage and has all facilities.

Harbour Island Marina (☎ 242-333-2427; VHF Channel 16; www.harbourislandmarina.com; Queen's Hwy, Eleuthera) Has 35 slips and offers transient/long-term dockage. It's south of town.

Getting Around

This information is solely for Harbour Island.

Flights arrive at **North Eleuthera International Airport** (☎ 242-335-1242), at the top end of the mainland. Taxis from the airport to the dock are $4 per person.

The dock for ferries to Harbour Island is 2 miles east of North Eleuthera International Airport.

Water taxis also operate from North Eleuthera to the ferry dock, Harbour Island ($5 one way).

Briland Rentals (☎ 242-333-2342; Bay St) rents bikes from $20 per day.

Everyone walks or uses a bicycle or golf cart if staying awhile. You can rent carts from taxi drivers and rental agencies who are based at the dock for $40 to $50 per day. Try **Dunmore Rentals** (☎ 242-332-3372; Bay St) or **Red Apple Rentals** (☎ /fax 242-333-2750; Queen's Hwy), which are located south of the center.

On Harbour Island taxis are slightly pricier than elsewhere in Eleuthera.
Big M Taxi Service (☎ 242-333-2285)
Percival Johnson (☎ 242-333-2174; Taxi 3)
Reggie & Jena's Taxi (☎ 242-333-2116)

SPANISH WELLS

pop 1631

The first thing that may unnerve you when heading for Spanish Wells on the early morning ferry is that the younger men getting on the boat may be swaying a little under an alcoholic cloud. The second thing that you may notice is that your smiles and 'good day' wishes are deliberately ignored by fellow passengers and the ferry operators. Mainland Bahamians will warn you that the islanders here do not want tourism on their island, and may not give you much of a welcome. It is unfair to say that all islanders here will react this way, but do be prepared for some frosty stares and displays of passive hostility. It may well even suit you if you want a quiet holiday!

St Georges Island only lies 1 mile offshore from Gene's Bay. The village of Spanish Wells dominates the island and dates back to the days of the Eleutheran Adventurers.

The deeply religious and mainly white population follows an alcohol-free, ordered and reticent lifestyle. Generations of isolation have concentrated the gene pool, reflected in traits much of the population shares, another slightly unnerving characteristic of this place. It seems as if half of the island is named Pinder. Many of the neat and pretty little houses are over 200 years old, and display handmade quilts for sale. Fishing and diving fans will enjoy these pristine waters and a beautiful beach rims the north shore.

Lobstering is its major trade and the source of phenomenal incomes (the locals are among the wealthiest of all Bahamians). Fishermen operate from state-of-the-art trawlers and go out as far as 250 miles for a month at a time. When the 'boys' are away the town is deathly still.

Information

For emergencies contact the **police** (☎ 242-333-4030, 919; Main St) or **Spanish Wells Clinic** (☎ 242-333-4064; Adventurer's Ave). The **Royal Bank of Canada** (☎ 242-333-4131; Main St; 9am-3pm Mon, to 1pm Tue-Thu, to 4:30pm Fri) has an ATM. The **post office** (☎ 242-333-5254; Main St) is also central; telephone boxes can be found here.

Sights & Activities

The island's history is told at **Spanish Wells Museum** (☎ 242-333-4710; Main St; 10am-noon & 1-3pm Mon-Sat), which contains a motley collection of photos and bric-a-brac. It's next to the Islander Shop (the owner will open up for you).

Manual's Dive Station (☎ 242-333-4495; fax 242-333-4622; Mickey & Karen Pinder sign on Main St) is a hardware store that also rents out some dive equipment. It may be wise to call ahead to see if they stock your requirements, as there is not a great range of gear available.

Spanish Wells Pilot Service (☎ 242-333-4427; VHF Channel 16) offers fishing, snorkeling and boat rentals; prices upon application.

Sleeping & Eating

Adventurers Resort (☎ 242-333-4883; mapeleaf@ batelnet.bs; Adventurer's Ave; r $80; P) Carpeted one- and two-bedroom motel-style rooms are pleasantly, if modestly, furnished. Some have kitchenettes, and there are eateries within a short drive or walk. This L-shaped block has two stories that surround a small green. The beach is half a mile away.

ELEUTHERA

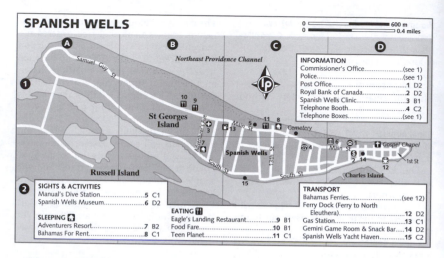

SPANISH WELLS

0 ——————— 600 m
0 ——————— 0.4 miles

INFORMATION
Commissioner's Office..................(see 1)
Police...................................(see 1)
Post Office..............................1 D2
Royal Bank of Canada....................2 D2
Spanish Wells Clinic.....................3 B1
Telephone Booth..........................4 C2
Telephone Boxes.........................(see 1)

SIGHTS & ACTIVITIES
Manual's Dive Station.....................5 C1
Spanish Wells Museum....................6 D2

SLEEPING
Adventurers Resort......................7 B2
Bahamas For Rent.......................8 C1

EATING
Eagle's Landing Restaurant...............9 B1
Food Fare.............................10 B1
Teen Planet...........................11 C1

TRANSPORT
Bahamas Ferries.......................(see 12)
Ferry Dock (Ferry to North
  Eleuthera).........................12 D2
Gas Station............................13 C1
Gemini Game Room & Snack Bar.....14 C1
Spanish Wells Yacht Haven.............15 C2

Bahamas for Rent (☎ 242-333-4080; www.bahamas vacationhomes.com; 13th St; r $850; P ✕ ✕) With not even a gate twixt you and the sea, and a stunning unspoilt beach, this is a pretty super option. The sliding-glass doors of this rental house let you make the most of this pretty little bay, and the modest property is clean and excellent value.

Eagle's Landing Restaurant (Main St; mains $4-14; ☺ breakfast, lunch & dinner) This big hall welcomes families with cheap sandwiches and burgers. The seating area is in front of the canteen, while the rest of the hall contains table games, an amusement arcade and pool tables.

Teen Planet (☎ 242-333-4001; Main St; mains $7-15; ☺ lunch & dinner) A very modern setup covers a few bases: downstairs is a café/bakery serving hot snacks such as burgers; upstairs is the theater in which you can call and book a movie at your own convenience. A great idea for getting your adolescents out of the place!

Food Fare (☎ 242-333-4675; Main St; ☺ 8am-5pm Mon-Fri, to 6pm Sat) This well-equipped supermarket contains a pharmacy and virtually all of your edible requirements.

In Gene's Bay there's parking, a phone booth and a **duty-free liquor store** (which should be called the Last Chance Saloon!).

Getting There & Around
For information on travel to North Eleuthera and Spanish Wells, see p182.

Government ferries run all day between Spanish Wells and the ferry dock at Gene's Bay ($5 per person if sharing or $10 for a ride as a sole passenger for the five-minute journey).

You can also charter a water taxi between Harbour Island and Spanish Wells (from $50 one way).

Spanish Wells Yacht Haven (☎ 242-333-4255; fax 242-333-4649; VHF Channel 16) has 40 slips and a Laundromat.

Gemini Game Room & Snack Bar (at Ferry Dock) rent out carts for $9/45 per hour/day. Many only spend an hour on the island in between ferries.

PREACHER'S CAVE
This large cave, about 2 miles east of Gene's Bay, is said to be where the Eleutheran adventurers found shelter after foundering in 1648. They made an altar here and surely prayed to be rescued. Some remnants of their belongings remain, and regular prayer meetings in the cavern keep their memories alive. The cave is fronted by a glorious beach, one of several beaches along the north coast.

CURRENT
Current may be the 'Oldest Settlement on the Island,' and some of the friendly townsfolk claim to also be descendants of Native Americans exiled here after a massacre at Cape Cod. While fishing is their industry, some are known for their basketware. Follow the western road for 5 miles at Lower Bogue's junction, and don't miss the lovely beach on the west side of town.

ELEUTHERA

The half-mile-long channel, Current Cut, separates North Eleuthera from Current Island. It is a popular dive and snorkel spot for very experienced swimmers who want to 'ride' the strong current.

Sandcastle Apartments (Map pp176-7; ☎ 242-335-3244; fax 242-393-0440; r $90; P ✖) has two very plain beachfront cottages a quarter-mile east of town; each contains a kitchen and sleeps three people. Bicycles may be rented ($5 per day). A small grocery store is nearby.

For information on travel to North Eleuthera and Current, see p182.

A taxi from North Eleuthera International Airport will cost $28 one-way.

GREGORY TOWN
This large settlement lies 25 miles north of Governor's Harbour and 5 miles south of the Glass Window. Here Eleuthera narrows down to a pencil-thin strip that separates the deep blue of the thundering Atlantic rollers from the placid, teal green shoals of the Bight of Eleuthera. A very uneven and narrow concrete bridge fills the gap on Queen's Hwy where the natural rock once arched. Do look out for other traffic, and if walking around, be aware; the cliffs are unstable and the pocked terrain is treacherous underfoot.

Gregory Town sits on a steep-sided cove, surrounded by small plots growing onions, peppers, cabbage, watermelons and other vegetables. Most famous as the center of pineapple farming, the industry is now so atrophied that local farmers have difficulty mustering a respectable supply of their usually large and succulent fruits to display at the annual Pineapple Festival. Gregory Town's young men have turned to lobstering, where the big bucks reside.

Gauldings Cay, 4 miles north of Gregory Town, is a splendid stretch of pure-white sand, while offshore the cay's waters are home to large communities of multihued sea anemones. The Cove Eleuthera (p186) offers a daily complimentary shuttle to Gauldings Cay for its guests.

Information
For emergencies call the **police** (Map pp176-7; ☎ 242-3325-5322, 919) or **Gregory Town Clinic** (Map pp176-7; ☎ 242-335-5108) which is down by the harbor, along with the **post office** (Map pp176-7; ☎ 242-335-5180).

Captain 2 (Map pp176-7; ☎ 242-335-5185) offers deep-sea fishing charters from $100 for three hours, and bonefishing for $200 for five hours.

Sleeping & Eating
Cocodimama Charming Resort (Map pp176-7; ☎ 242-332-3150; www.cocodimama.com; Queen's Hwy; r $210; P ✖ ✖) Some Italian style has definitely crept into the decor of these pretty fab beachside villas. Inside the brightly colored exteriors are rooms decorated with cool Italian tiles and rich Indonesian fur-

---

JUICY & SWEET: ELEUTHERA'S PINEAPPLE FESTIVAL

Throughout the 18th century, pineapple production blossomed in Eleuthera, and a local variety – the Eleutheran sugar loaf – earned recognition for Eleuthera and Gregory Town as an especially succulent fruit. In 1900 production peaked, and 7 million pineapples were exported, many heading for London's Convent Garden Market. Alas, they were eventually supplanted by fruit from Cuba, Jamaica and Hawaii. Eleuthera's pineapple farmers are now a dying breed. Some pineapples are still grown here, but raising pineapples is labor-intensive, requiring backbreaking work that has little appeal for young people.

In early June the town hosts the three-day Annual Eleuthera Pineapple Festival, highlighted by the Miss Teen Pineapple Princess Pageant and the Pineathelon, which is a swim-bike-run competition. There's also the Pineapple-on-a-Rope Eating Contest in which participants with hands tied behind their backs attempt to nibble a dangling pineapple; a basketball shootout; a kayak race; and the Saturday-night Junkanoo Rush, a street party offering music, dancing and some easy fun. You can find nonalcoholic pineapple smoothies and locally made pineapple rum at the Corner Bar, and the most wonderful juicy and fragrant pineapple tarts at **Thompson's Bakery** (☎ 242-335-5053; Johnson St; ✚ breakfast & lunch Mon-Sat).

Bahamas Ministry of Tourism (☎ 242-332-2142; fax 242-332-2480; www.bahamas.com; Governor's Harbour) is the place to go for more detailed information on this fine event.

niture. The attention to detail is excellent, and the off-season rates ($170) are particularly realistic. These lodgings and the small beach on which they sit are modest and perfect for a little getaway.

Cove Eleuthera (Map pp176-7; ☎ 242-335-5142, US ☎ 800-552-5960; www.thecoveeleuthera.com; Queen's Hwy; r standard/deluxe $195/345; P ☒ ☒ ☒) Just north of Gregory Town, this place is aptly named, with views over two coves and its own beach where the snorkeling is splendid (snorkel gear is provided), all fringed by 28 acres of vegetation. Each room is furnished in white rattan, with tile floors and private porch or deck. Facilities include kayaks, tennis courts and swinging hammocks. The Golden Grouper lounge and dining room serves very good Bahamian dishes and some choice fried chicken. A Saturday night buffet is very popular and is often accompanied by live music.

Elvina's Bar & Restaurant (Map pp176-7; ☎ 242-335-5032; Queen's Hwy) is a surfer-dude bar when they're in town, as well as being a quiet local bar with a pool table and occasional live music.

Thompson's Bakery (Map pp176-7; ☎ 242-335-5053; Johnson St; ☺ breakfast & lunch Mon-Sat) A reminder; don't forget the scrumptious pineapple tarts at this bakery.

Shopping

Island Made Gift Shop (Map pp176-7; ☎ 242-335-5369; Queen's Hwy) Worth a stop, this shop sells imaginative artworks, including island scenes painted on shells and driftwood, jewelry made from shells and glass, and some gorgeous handmade quilts using Bahamian batik prints.

Getting There & Around

Gregory Town is midway between the North Eleuthera and Governor's Harbour Airports.

Albury's Taxi (☎ 242-335-1370) and **Wendell's Taxi Service** (☎ 242-333-0165) both offer guided island tours.

GREGORY TOWN TO GOVERNOR'S HARBOUR

In the 25 miles between Gregory Town and Governor's Harbour – Eleuthera's main settlement – there are only two towns of any size: **Alice Town** (Map pp176-7), 7 miles south of Gregory Town and just south

of Hatchet Bay, the former center of an Angus cattle enterprise; and **James Cistern** (Map pp176-7), a picturesque albeit wind-battered waterfront hamlet 8 miles further south. The Governor's Harbour Airport is 3 miles south of James Cistern.

Waves kicked up by the various hurricanes have ravaged the road between Gregory Town and Governor's Harbour and you should look out for potholes here.

The Hatchet Bay Fest in Alice Town each August features dinghy races and partying.

Sights & Activities

Calling all surfers! **Surfer's Beach**, about 2 miles south of Gregory Town has some killer breaks rolling in from the Atlantic that you many want to ride. This 2-mile-long, lonesome, sugary beach lives up to its name, especially with southwest winds at low tide. The beach is reached by a horrendously potholed and rocky track from Queen's Hwy.

The half-mile-long **Hatchet Bay Cave** (turn south onto the dirt road near the three old silos) contains several chambers, which bear charcoal signatures dating back to the mid-19th century. Some harmless leaf-nosed bats reside within, as do stalactites and stalagmites – no touching! Bring a flashlight and rubber-soled shoes, as the going is slippery. There's a ladder to climb at one stage. You can hire a guide locally.

A bone-jarring dirt road leads north from James Cistern to **James Cistern Beach**, where waves sometimes reach 10ft with a brisk south wind. There's a shipwreck offshore, which is a good spot for snorkeling when the water is calm.

The couple who operate Surfer's Haven (below) also run **Bahamas Out-island Adventures**, offering kayaking and snorkeling excursions for $99. They offer overnight camping trips (adult/child $299/150). Trips can run from Nassau (for an additional $100/50 per adult/child).

Sleeping & Eating

Surfer's Haven (☎ 242-333-3282; www.bahamasadventures.com; d/upstairs apt $50/75; P ☒) This pretty blue building has sea views and is only a five-minute walk away from Surfer's Beach. Guestrooms here are cosy, clean and comfortable and all have access to the large open-air deck overlooking the tropical foliage and ocean. Rooms share a bathroom, while the

NORTH ELEUTHERA REGATTA

This brilliant three-day event, held every October, is one of the granddaddies of Bahamian sailing events and the highlight of the Eleutheran year, when islanders with their locally-built sloops descend for three days of racing. Ashore the action is just as lively, with Bahamian cooks and bands whipping up a storm, while everyone dances and parties hard. Special air and boat charters depart from Nassau. Contact the **Ministry of Youth & Culture** (☎ 242-322-3140) for more information.

apartment is self-contained with a kitchenette. Great for families.

Rainbow Inn (☎ /fax 242-335-0294; www.rainbowinn .com; Queen's Hwy; r $110; P 🗷 🗷 🗷) Attractive one-, two-, or three-bedroom octagonal villas have kitchenettes, ceiling fans and private decks facing onto a beach. The peaceful little resort has tennis courts, a small saltwater lap pool, snorkeling, fishing, and bicycles for hire. It also has an excellent restaurant, **Dolcevita Restaurant & Lounge** (🕑 breakfast, lunch & dinner Tue-Sat), furnished with varnished, rough-hewn tables and captain's chairs, and serving some pretty fab Bahamian food with a definite Italian slant. 'Dr Seabreeze' plays many Wednesday and Friday nights.

Juneek's Savoury Snacks (James Cistern) Craving pizza? Try this place, where outdoor clay ovens are still used. It also sells meat patties and ice cream.

For groceries, stop at **Big Rock General Store** 2 miles west of James Cistern.

GOVERNOR'S HARBOUR

This sleepy and amiable island capital surrounds an attractive broad harbor that is as still as the day is long. People live quietly here, until the Friday and Saturday Fish Fry kick off and the *goombay* beats drift across the harbor. The smell of frying chicken entices the populace along for a beer and a bite, and the stars shine overhead in the clear sky.

There are many faded remnants of past glory days here. During the 19th century, the harbor was filled with schooners shipping pineapples and citrus fruits to New York and New England, or unloading fineries for the wealthy merchants and their wives. The merchants' well-preserved old

white clapboard houses, many with ornate gingerbread gable trims, nestle on the hillside east of Queen's Hwy, where royal poincianas blaze vermilion in spring.

Information
Bahamas Tourist Office (☎ 242-332-2122; fax 242-332-2480; Queen's Hwy)
BaTelCo (☎ 242-332-2476; Haynes Ave) Atop the hill. There's a telephone booth here and another on Queen's Hwy.
First Caribbean International Bank (☎ 242-332-2300; Queen's Hwy; 🕑 9:30am-3pm Mon-Thu, to 4pm Fri) Has an ATM.
Government Medical Clinic (☎ 242-332-2774; Haynes Ave; 🕑 9am-5pm Mon-Fri)
Police station (☎ 242-332-2111; Queen's Hwy)
Post office (☎ 242-332-2060; Haynes Ave; 🕑 9am-4pm Mon-Fri)

Sights & Activities
A stroll along the harborfront passes **St Patrick's Anglican Church** and cemetery; the historic, pink **Commissioner's Office**; and the lovely old **Haynes Library** (1897).

There are some beautiful little beaches over the hill on the Atlantic shore, where the azure seas lazily drift onto pink sands and where you can easily while away a day or three…

Clearwater Dive Shop (☎ 242-332-2146; fax 242-332-2546) in the town center offers dive and snorkel trips.

Gladstone Petty (☎ 242-332-2280; Queen's Hwy) will take you reef- and bonefishing. He has an office downtown.

Sleeping
Laughing Bird Apartments (☎ 242-332-2012; ddavies@ batelnet.bs; Birdie Lane; r $80; P 🗷 🗷) These cozy one-bedroom studio apartments sit amid grounds full of hibiscus and palms. Each has a lounge-cum-bedroom and separate kitchen. Some have king-size beds. The great plus here is that the gardens face onto the sea and Town Beach which lie just over the road. Lie in a hammock and listen to the wind and wild birds.

Tuck-a-Way Hotel (☎ 242-322-2005; fax 242-322-2775; Graham St & Rolle Lane; r $80; P 🗷 🗷) These small, dark rooms and units benefit from their location in town, and are within walking distance of Town Beach. All come with TV, some with kitchenettes.

Duck Inn (☎ 242-332-2608; www.theduckinn.com; Queen's Hwy; d $110; P 🗷 🗷) A 200-year-old

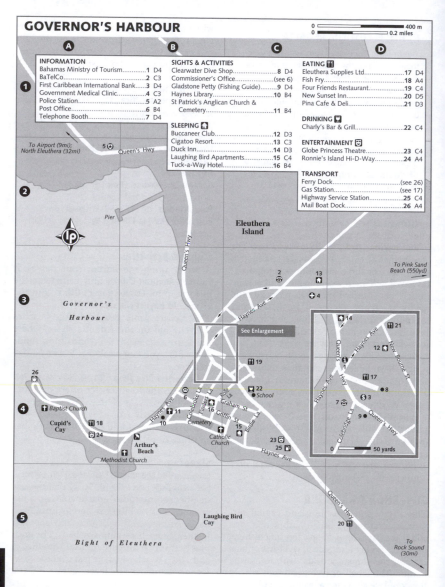

GOVERNOR'S HARBOUR

0 ————————— 400 m
0 ————————— 0.2 miles

INFORMATION
Bahamas Ministry of Tourism.............1 D4
BaTelCo...2 C3
First Caribbean International Bank....3 D4
Government Medical Clinic................4 C3
Police Station..................................5 A2
Post Office......................................6 B4
Telephone Booth.............................7 D4

SIGHTS & ACTIVITIES
Clearwater Dive Shop.......................8 D4
Commissioner's Office..................(see 6)
Gladstone Petty (Fishing Guide).......9 D4
Haynes Library...............................10 B4
St Patrick's Anglican Church &
Cemetery...................................11 B4

SLEEPING
Buccaneer Club.............................12 D3
Cigatoo Resort...............................13 C3
Duck Inn.......................................14 D3
Laughing Bird Apartments..............15 C4
Tuck-a-Way Hotel..........................16 B4

EATING
Eleuthera Supplies Ltd....................17 D4
Fish Fry...18 A4
Four Friends Restaurant..................19 C4
New Sunset Inn.............................20 D5
Pina Cafe & Deli............................21 D3

DRINKING
Charly's Bar & Grill.........................22 C4

ENTERTAINMENT
Globe Princess Theatre....................23 C4
Ronnie's Island Hi-D-Way................24 A4

TRANSPORT
Ferry Dock..................................(see 26)
Gas Station.................................(see 17)
Highway Service Station.................25 C4
Mail Boat Dock..............................26 A4

colonial complex set amid an orchid garden, incorporating the comfortable and fully equipped Hunnie Pot, Flora and Cupid's Cottage. Worth the trip alone, Cupid's Cottage overlooks the serene and beautiful bay waters. All three homely cottages are a delight, decked with orchids, personal knick-knacks and paperbacks, while the

kitchens have all mod cons. An excellent liquor store around the corner can supply you with most of your requirements, which should be consumed on the veranda at sunset. Cheers!

Cigatoo Resort (☎ 242-332-3060; www.choicehotels .com; Haynes Ave; r $100; P ☒ ☒ ☒) Sitting astride the top of a hill that overlooks the sea, this small hotel is clean and comfortable. The main building contains some lovely local art and a courtyard surrounds the pool. There's also an Italian restaurant, bar, tearoom and tennis courts.

Buccaneer Club (☎ 242-332-2000; fax 242-332-2888; New Bourne St; r $110; P ⊠ ⊠ ⊠) On the north side of town, this club has small yet tastefully appointed rooms with sliding glass doors opening onto a balcony. There's a small pool and a well-tended lawn.

Eating & Drinking

New Sunset Inn (☎ 242-332-2487; Queen's Hwy; mains $10-18; lunch & dinner) This friendly seaside bar and restaurant serves some of the best food in town. The walls are festooned with the works of local artists, and a tucked-away bar has a widescreen TV, great rums and friendly patrons.

Pina Cafe & Deli (☎ 242-332-3350; New Bourne St; mains $6-17; ☺ breakfast, lunch & dinner Mon-Sat) This is a cutie; an enticing little orange building with a grand outdoor deck, pretty garden and a range of homemade goodies. Breakfasts (from $3) and pizzas (from $6) are cheap. Daily freshly baked cookies and homemade jams will also help make you happy.

Four Friends Restaurant (☎ 242-332-3488; off Haynes St; mains $12-23; ☺ dinner Mon-Sat) Satisfy your hunger with a grand meal of mixed Bahamian and continental dishes such as rack of lamb. Monday, Wednesday and Friday buffets are very popular; book ahead.

Charly's Bar & Grill (☎ 242-332-3477; Queen's Hwy; mains $7-16; ☺ lunch & dinner) Watch for the blue light outside; when it's on, the bar is ready to open. It may not look much from the outside, but you know what they say about looks.

Eleuthera Supplies Limited (☎ 242-332-2728; ☺ 6:30am-7pm Mon-Sat, to 2:30pm Sun) The local supermarket.

Fish Fry (Cupid's Cay) On the dockside; starts at 7pm Friday and Saturday, but the music kicks off a little earlier.

Entertainment

Ronnie's Island Hi-D-Way (Cupid's Cay) A lively bar with a pool table and wide-screen TV, plus dancing on Friday and Saturday; don't even think of arriving before 10pm.

Globe Princess Theatre (☎ 242-332-2735; Queen's Hwy; admission adult/child $5.50/3) This town-center cinema shows movies at 8.15pm nightly, except Thursday.

BEACH HEDONISM

The Elusive Beaches of Eleuthera by Geoff & Vicky Wells is a little handbook that these two self-described 'beachologists' have compiled with sincere devotion to the art of beach-bumming. Every beach on the island is awarded scores for ease of access, privacy, swimming, diving and snorkeling, and shelling. Directions and a brief description of each of these little bits of paradise accompany the scorecards. Beg, borrow or steal one of these books when you arrive, or contact these clever people yourself; email Geoff and Vicky at elusive@batelnet.bs.

Getting There & Around

Please refer to p182 for flight, ferry and mailboat information to Eleuthera and Governor's Harbour.

Governor's Harbour is served by the Governor's Harbour Airport, about 10 miles north of town. Taxis from the airport to town are $25 one-way for two people.

Many enterprising individuals act both as taxi drivers and car-rental agencies. This means that it is often easier to book a car rental from the airport with a taxi ride to the airport when you depart. Car hire costs from around $70 per day.

To hire a taxi or rent a car, call:
Edgar Gardiner (☎ 242-332-266)
Tommy Pinder (☎ 242-332-2568)
Winsett Cooper (☎ 242-332-1592)

NORTH & SOUTH PALMETTO POINT

There are some happy retirees living 4 miles south of Governor's Harbour. North Palmetto Point enjoys a stunning 5-mile-long blushing pink beach and South Palmetto Point sits on a smaller beach and rocky shore with good bonefishing and snorkeling. There's a post office, clinic, pharmacy, grocery store and gas station. Fish stalls line South Palmetto beach, where there's a nice, little beach bar.

Sleeping & Eating

Tropical Dreams Motel Resort (Map pp176-7; ☎ 242-332-1632; www.bahamasvg.com/tropicaldream.html; Dry Hill Rd, North Palmetto Point; d per night/week $80/540; P ⊠ ⊠) These modern, clean and comfortable units with TV and kitchen facilities are a good mile from the beach, but are neat and a great budget option.

ELEUTHERA

Palmetto Shores Vacation Villas (Map pp176-7; ☎/fax 242-332-1305; psvacvillas@batelnet.bs; South Palmetto Point; r $110; P ✗ ✗) These modest and pleasant apartments are perfect for couples and have verandas that look out over a private beach. Water sport and car rentals can be arranged. This property was for sale at the time of research.

Unique Village Resort Hotel (Map pp176-7; ☎ 242-332-1830; www.uniquevillage.com; North Palmetto Point; r $130; P ✗ ✗ ✗) This small hotel offers attractively furnished rooms, two two-bedroom villas, and a one-bedroom apartment, all with ocean view, full kitchen, satellite TV and radio. There's a pleasant restaurant and bar with panoramic windows and an outside deck, plus grassy lawns with hammocks slung between palm trees. Nonguests are welcome to enjoy omelettes and fruit plates for breakfast, and Bahamian dishes (mains $7-25), plus steaks and fresh seafood at lunch and dinner.

Palmetto Point Lighthouse (Map pp176-7; US ☎/fax 561-395-0483; info@pinksandbeach.net) You can even rent a lighthouse! This fully-appointed three-bedroom home with king-size bed in the master bedroom also has a sliding glass door leading to a patio with a whirlpool. It rents for $1400 weekly in the low season, and $1680 in the high-season for four people.

Mate & Jenny's Restaurant & Bar (Map pp176-7; ☎ 242-332-1504; South Palmetto Point; mains $8-18; ☺ lunch & dinner) This place has a lot of character and cooks up some yummy pizzas as well as broiled fish and other Bahamian dishes. A jukebox and pool table add to the fun, as do their killer cocktails.

Tippy's Bar & Beach Restaurant (Map pp176-7; ☎ 242-332-3331; Banks Rd, North Palmetto Point Beach; mains $7-25; ☺ lunch & dinner) With a prime spot on this gorgeous beach, Tippy's offers up mouth-watering roasted vegetable ravioli and all manner of hot juicy pizzas; perfect after a hard day of lying in the sun.

Meryl's Bakery (North Palmetto) Buy bread and baked goods here. It's opposite the post office and police station.

Getting Around

Asa Bethel (☎/fax 242-332-1305; Palmetto Shores Vacation Villas, South Palmetto Point) rents cars, scooters as well as boats, as does **Arthur's Taxi** (☎ 242-332-2106).

For information on travel to North and South Palmetto Point, see p182.

SOUTH ELEUTHERA

Heading along the Queen's Hwy, the accumulated effects of a series of hurricanes and a downturn in tourism on this part of the island are sadly all too apparent. Nevertheless, the beaches down here are superb and remnants of days gone by will catch your eye and pique your curiosity.

WINDERMERE ISLAND

The near-destitute hamlet of **Savannah Sound** (Map pp176-7), which dates back to the 18th century, enjoys roaming goats and chickens among its tumbledown shacks and collapsed colonial-era buildings. The sound actually is good for bonefishing and nearby is **Ten Bay Beach** (Map pp176-7), another beauty that just calls out to you to abandon your life and live here for ever, padding along the soft sand and breathing in that clean sea air…

Secluded, broom-thin Windermere Island boasts a pristine blush-hued beach running the 4-mile Atlantic shore. It is speckled with snazzy homes reflecting its long-standing status as one of the most exclusive hideaways for the rich and famous. The chic Windermere Island Club, once the Bahamas' most fashionable resort, was a favorite of Lord Mountbatten and, later, Prince Charles and Princess Diana. Although the club is closed, the beach is still another made for fun and dreams.

The island is reached by a bridge straddling Savannah Sound (the turnoff from Queen's Hwy is 2 miles south of the village).

ROCK SOUND

The road south from Savannah Sound passes **Tarpum Bay**, a former pineapple-trading

---

OCEAN HOLE

This crater-like curiosity, along Fish Rd on the south edge of Rock Sound, is said to be bottomless. No one knows, but it is a 100yd-wide tidal blue hole populated by saltwater fish that move to and fro through subterranean sea tunnels. Throw some bread in and a surge of fish will head for the surface, taking great delight in a quick feed. Set off a rocky edge, it is also possible to descend some steps and hop in for a cool swim.

port, now a desolate place comprising some quaint old stone buildings, including **St Columbus Church**, and beaten-up clapboard houses. Bonefishing is good in Half Sound, south of Winding Bay.

Rock Sound is a small, charming village from where the original townsfolk set out on their prime occupation – wrecking. Hence the settlement's early name, Wreck Sound.

There are several historic buildings of note, plus the **Ocean Hole** (see boxed text, opposite) and, on the bay shore south of town, the **Blow Hole**, which erupts like a geyser during strong swells. Be sure to secure your car and belongings while you're out of sight having a look at these natural wonders.

Rock Sound famously comes alive each summer during the All-Eleuthera Regatta, one of the most vibrant let-your-hair-down affairs in the Bahamas, and the setting for all-out dinghy races. There are few beaches hereabouts.

Junkanoo traditionally begins at 5am on Boxing Day (December 26), when groups from the various settlements come together at Rock Sound.

For emergencies contact the **police** (☎ 242-334-2244) or try the **Government Medical Clinic** (☎ 242-334-2226; ⏱ 9am-1pm Mon-Fri). **Scotiabank** (☎ 242-334-2620; Queen's Hwy; ⏱ 9am-3pm Mon-Thu, to 4pm Fri) can help with the dollars!

A little north of Tarpum Bay, **Ingrahams Beach Inn** (☎ 242-334-4066; fax 242-334-2257; Tarpum Bay; r/apt $80/120; P ⊠) is a two-story building overlooking the sea and a lovely little beach. A gym, game room and dining room add to the facilities of this large and very well-maintained place. The rooms are spotless, simple but modern, and very good value. Car and bicycle rentals, and deep-sea fishing can also be arranged.

The most popular restaurant in Rock Sound is **Sammy's Place** (☎ 242-334-2121; P ⊠), which also has four rooms with satellite TV ($80). Everyone packs in for the

fritters and burgers. Cheese omelettes are grand for breakfast.

Take your pick among several down-home eateries serving Bahamian fare. Try the **Palm Garden Restaurant & Bar** or **Down Home Pizza**, and the **Haven Bakery** (☎ 242-334-2155). The **Marketplace Supermarket** is north of town, near the Shell gas station.

For information on travel to Eleuthera and Rock Sound, see p182.

Rock Sound Airport is 3 miles north of town. A taxi from the airport to Rock Sound settlement costs $14.

COTTON BAY TO ELEUTHERA POINT

Mile-long Cotton Bay, 6 miles south of Rock Sound, is favored by wealthy expats who own fancy villas above the shore. The homes are part of the Cotton Bay Club. Once beloved by hobnobbing socialites, the club has a troubled history and closed in 1995.

South of Cotton Bay, the island flares out in a lopsided, inverted 'T.' At Wemyss Bight, Queen's Hwy splits. One branch leads north 10 miles to Cape Eleuthera via Davis Harbour and the settlement of **Deep Creek**; the shore is lined by mangrove swamps. The beach here is lovely, and you can get a grand pizza at **D & N Pizza** in Davis Harbour.

The other branch heads towards **Bannerman** town, where a vastly deteriorating road and dirt track (for 4WD only) leads south to exquisite **Lighthouse Bay**. Offshore reefs and two small islands are good for snorkeling and scuba diving, but beware strong currents. A short trail leads up to the **East Point Lighthouse**, the southernmost point of Eleuthera.

On the Atlantic side of Eleuthera Point, hidden away behind sand dunes, is a dazzlingly beautiful 6 miles of rosy-pink beach, **Lighthouse Beach**, reckoned to be the best in Eleuthera. It really doesn't get much better than this – bring snorkel gear, a picnic and your soulmate.

ELEUTHERA

The Exumas

These islands are made for those who love nothing better than taking a boat off into the unknown, splashing in tranquil aquamarine waters or strolling across powder-soft beaches.

The Exumas comprises 365 islands: some of the cays are tiny dots, some are barren, and others luscious and fertile. Most are uninhabited – apart from sunbathing iguanas – but they all have glittering white sands and small harbors of emerald-green water.

This 100-mile-long necklace headed by Great Exuma and Little Exuma starts 40 miles southeast of Nassau. George Town is the chain's main town, on Great Exuma's Elizabeth Harbour. The small center is also a yachter's haven, and one of the Bahamas' main hubs for chartering boats for island-hopping. Jackie Onassis was once a regular, and the New England yachting crowd still has a penchant for the Exumas, especially for the annual Family Island Regatta.

Elegant Stocking Island has fine beaches and tranquil lagoons, shelters George Town from the Atlantic and is a beach-lounger's paradise. Those who want to follow in the fins of Jacques Cousteau can revel in the fish that flicker past pristine reefs, wrecks and blue holes, especially in the Exuma Cays Land & Sea Park, which protects birds, marine life and the endemic iguanas. Kayakers love these waters shared with dolphins, sharks and the occasional whale.

The vast flats west and south of the Exumas are bonefish habitat supreme, and great fishing lodges and friendly operators can be found in George and Rolle Towns.

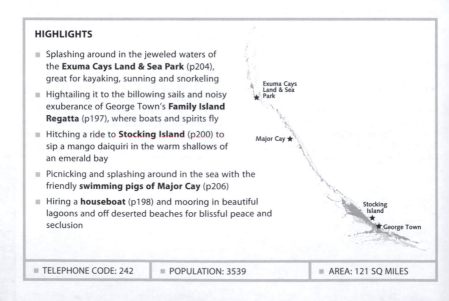

HIGHLIGHTS

- Splashing around in the jeweled waters of the **Exuma Cays Land & Sea Park** (p204), great for kayaking, sunning and snorkeling

- Hightailing it to the billowing sails and noisy exuberance of George Town's **Family Island Regatta** (p197), where boats and spirits fly

- Hitching a ride to **Stocking Island** (p200) to sip a mango daiquiri in the warm shallows of an emerald bay

- Picnicking and splashing around in the sea with the friendly **swimming pigs of Major Cay** (p206)

- Hiring a **houseboat** (p198) and mooring in beautiful lagoons and off deserted beaches for blissful peace and seclusion

Exuma Cays Land & Sea Park ★

Major Cay ★

Stocking Island ★

★ George Town

■ TELEPHONE CODE: 242	■ POPULATION: 3539	■ AREA: 121 SQ MILES

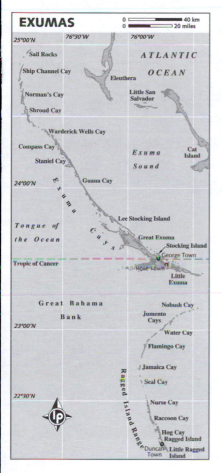

EXUMAS

History
During the 17th century, many residents of New Providence settled Great Exuma to escape ruthless buccaneers, and made a living as salt rakers.

Following the American Revolution, Loyalists under Lord Denys Rolle arrived with 140 slaves aboard a ship named the *Peace & Plenty*. Granted 7000 acres on which to plant cotton, Rolle's plantations blossomed until the chenille bug chewed through the cotton crop. The salt industry also evaporated, done in by more profitable operations on neighboring islands. In 1834, the year of emancipation, most Whites uprooted and left, while the newly freed slaves stayed and took over Rolle's land.

It was common back then for slaves to adopt the name of their master. Today every second person is a Rolle (locals, however, have a good grip on who their blood relatives are), and since the 1890s every Rolle has been permitted to build and farm on common land. Rolleville and Rolle Town, the two most important historic settlements on Great Exuma, are certainly worth a look. Although now claimed by bush, there are decrepit forts and ruined plantations lying scattered around in between the farming and fishing villages.

Getting There & Away
Most travelers to Exuma fly into the small Exuma International Airport, 6 miles north of George Town, or take the twice-weekly fast ferry from Nassau. Day trips to the cays from Nassau on super-zippy powerboats are also very popular. Expensive private boat charters and cheaper but slow mail boats round out the options.

The **Ettienne & Cephas** (from $50 for shorter trips, round-trip $140, 21hrs) mail boat departs Nassau on Tuesday for Staniel Cay, Farmer's Cay, Black Point, Little Farmer's Cay and Barreterre. Contact the **Dockmaster's Office** (☎ 242-393-1064) at Potter's Cay in Nassau for further details.

Getting Around
You'll need your own transport if you want to explore the islands outside George Town's immediate vicinity; rental agencies can be found at the airport. Affordable and more upmarket boats are also available for hire in George Town.

GREAT EXUMA

The main island in the chain, Great Exuma is the starting point for most people exploring the islands, and where boaters and yachties will call in for their supplies or to pick up mail.

GEORGE TOWN
pop 1071
George Town feels less like a convivial town in which to stay for a while, and more like a place to stock up on supplies, which is exactly what most visitors do, before heading off to explore the hundreds of gorgeous

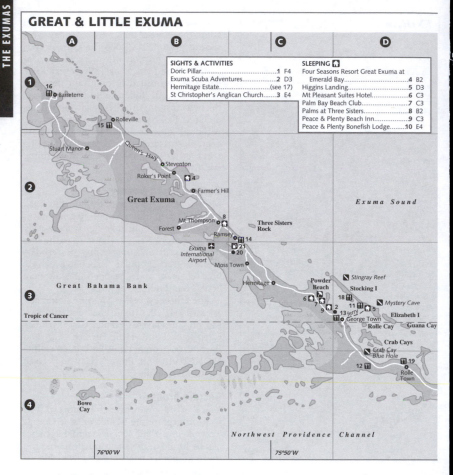

GREAT & LITTLE EXUMA

SIGHTS & ACTIVITIES
Doric Pillar.......................................1 F4	
Exuma Scuba Adventures...............2 D3	
Hermitage Estate..........................(see 17)	
St Christopher's Anglican Church.......3 E4	

SLEEPING
Four Seasons Resort Great Exuma at	
Emerald Bay...................................4 B2	
Higgins Landing..............................5 D3	
Mt Pleasant Suites Hotel..................6 C3	
Palm Bay Beach Club.......................7 C3	
Palms at Three Sisters......................8 B2	
Peace & Plenty Beach Inn.................9 C3	
Peace & Plenty Bonefish Lodge........10 E4	

cays and islands that make up this island chain. Queen's Hwy circles through town in one direction, leading past the shores of Lake Victoria and along the elegant length of Stocking Island, and into a conclave of a few stores, bank, cafés and dwellings that comprise George Town's small, dusty center.

Government Wharf is the focal point of most action, where townsfolk gather when the mail boat calls, fisherfolk return with their glistening catch and a myriad of visitors' boats are always on the move.

A night or two here will introduce you to some friendly locals, who will eagerly describe the amazing caverns and blue holes in the surrounding waters, as well as ensure

that you cross the Tropic of Cancer, which runs through town. The event of the year is April's Family Island Regatta, considered one of the Bahamas' best. Hundreds of islanders still make the annual pilgrimage to George Town's Elizabeth Harbour for this event, for which boatbuilders proudly ship in their handmade dinghies from other islands aboard the mail boats. During the regatta, the town is transformed into an outdoor party venue.

Victoria Lake is connected to Elizabeth Harbour by a 50yd-long channel. In the 1800s the British Navy used Elizabeth Harbour and Lake Victoria for refitting warships. The US Navy also had a small base here during WWII.

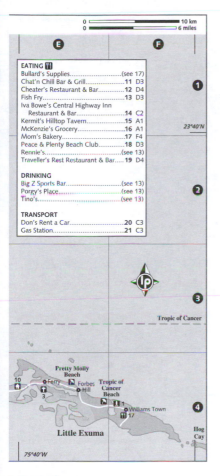

EATING
Bullard's Supplies...........................(see 17)
Chat'n Chill Bar & Grill...................**11** D3
Cheater's Restaurant & Bar.............**12** D4
Fish Fry..**13** D3
Iva Bowe's Central Highway Inn
  Restaurant & Bar.........................**14** C2
Kermit's Hilltop Tavern....................**15** A1
McKenzie's Grocery.........................**16** A1
Mom's Bakery................................**17** F4
Peace & Plenty Beach Club..............**18** D3
Rennie's.......................................(see 13)
Traveller's Rest Restaurant & Bar.....**19** D4

DRINKING
Big Z Sports Bar............................(see 13)
Porgy's Place................................(see 13)
Tino's..(see 13)

TRANSPORT
Don's Rent a Car...........................**20** C3
Gas Station...................................**21** C3

Information

The **Bahamas Ministry of Tourism** (242-336-2430; www.bahamas.com; Queen's Hwy) sits above Sam Grey's business on Queen's Hwy.

Scotiabank (242-336-2651; Queen's Hwy) is the town's one bank.

For all shopping needs and some good quality fruit and veg, head for the multifaceted **Exuma Markets** (242-336-2033; fax 242-336-2645; Queen's Hwy, George Town), which also has a fax and phone message service, and acts as an informal 'mail restante.'

Exuma Web Cafe (242-336-2562; Queen's Hwy, George Town; 8am-7:30pm Mon-Sat, 4:30-7:30pm Sun) charges around $10/18 per half-hour/hour.

The **post office** (242-347-3546; Queen's Hwy) is based at the big pink Government Administration Building, along with the **police** (242-336-2666, 919; Queen's Hwy). There is also a **Government Medical Clinic** (242-336-2088; Queen's Hwy).

Sights

A few buildings are of interest. **St Andrew's Anglican Church** (1802) gleams whitely on a hill above Lake Victoria, and opens for Sunday services (it's well worth the stroll to peek at the gravestones out back).

The pink and white neoclassical **Government Administration Building** (242-336-2600; Queen's Hwy; 9am-5pm Mon-Fri) accommodates everything: the post office, police station, customs and immigration, Ministry of Education, magistrates' court and jail.

Regatta Park is a scruffy piece of land in the center of George Town that fills with market stalls and partygoers during the annual regatta. The rest of the year, the park is home to a beaten-up old boat, *The Patsy*, which last raced in 1953.

The **Straw Market** (9am-5pm) sits on the edge of Regatta Park and sells a small range of straw bags and hats, some T-shirts and beachwear.

Activities

This is an excellent area for all water sports, especially boating of any kind, even for amateurs. Don't forget you can hire boats for exploring the wonderful Exuma Cays Land & Sea Park, see p200 for details.

DIVING & SNORKELING

The Exumas are replete with some fantastic snorkel and dive sites, including spectacular blue holes and caves, many of which have safety lines. Jacques Cousteau loved these sites, so it is a fair bet that you will too!

For great snorkel sites head for the schools of small and vibrant fish around **Bird Cay**; the odd-shaped **Duck Cay North**; **Duck Cay South**, a tiered reef that looks like an underwater wedding cake; and the shallow reefs of the **Three Sisters**.

Harbour Buoy Portside is a very active reef with lots of marine life, as is **Jolly Hall**, a favored hatchery for grunts and yellowtail snapper. **Loaded Barrel Reef** has plenty of fish species inhabiting its wide seabeds, as well as staghorn coral. **Harbour Buoy Starboard** is home to large brain corals, as are the shallow reefs of **Liz Lee Shoals**.

THE EXUMAS

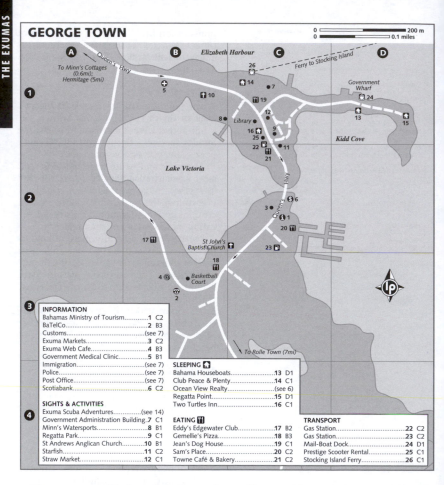

GEORGE TOWN

INFORMATION

Bahamas Ministry of Tourism	**1** C2
BaTelCo	**2** B3
Customs	(see 7)
Exuma Markets	**3** C2
Exuma Web Cafe	**4** B3
Government Medical Clinic	**5** B1
Immigration	(see 7)
Police	(see 7)
Post Office	(see 7)
Scotiabank	**6** C2

SIGHTS & ACTIVITIES

Exuma Scuba Adventures	(see 14)
Government Administration Building	**7** C1
Minn's Watersports	**8** B1
Regatta Park	**9** C1
St Andrews Anglican Church	**10** B1
Starfish	**11** C2
Straw Market	**12** C1

SLEEPING 🛏

Bahama Houseboats	**13** D1
Club Peace & Plenty	**14** C1
Ocean View Realty	(see 6)
Regatta Point	**15** D1
Two Turtles Inn	**16** C1

EATING 🍴

Eddy's Edgewater Club	**17** B2
Gemellie's Pizza	**18** B1
Jean's Dog House	**19** C1
Sam's Place	**20** C2
Towne Café & Bakery	**21** C2

TRANSPORT

Gas Station	**22** C2
Gas Station	**23** C2
Mail-Boat Dock	**24** D1
Prestige Scooter Rental	**25** C1
Stocking Island Ferry	**26** C1

There are some fabulous dive sites, and one of the easiest is **Stingray Reef** (Map pp194–5), where shallow waters are full of snapper, angelfish, grunts and stingrays.

Experienced daredevils may wish to try the **Angelfish Blue Hole**, a vertical shaft which starts at 30ft below the surface and falls to 90ft before leveling into a network of caves full of soft sponges and schooling angelfish. Another deep orifice, **Crab Cay Blue Hole** (Map pp194–5) is a 40ft-wide crevasse up to 90ft deep, with archways inhabited by lobsters, snappers and stingrays.

South of Stocking Island, access to Mystery Cave (p200) begins at 15ft below the surface and drops to 100ft, and is another one for the experienced.

You can either go it alone, or take kayaking and snorkeling trips with guides. For off-island adventure ideas and rates, contact **Captain Steven Cole** (☎ 242-554-2768) directly or through Minns Water Sports (p200).

Exuma Scuba Adventures (☎ 242-336-2893; www .dive-exuma.com; Club Peace & Plenty, Queen's Hwy) proffer two-tank dives ($75), one-tank night dives ($60) and three-tank dives including lunch on a deserted cay ($150). Snorkeling trips start at $25/10 per adult/child and gear-hire is also available ($25). An all-day snorkel trip with lunch on a deserted cay is $90.

Peace & Plenty Beach Club (☎ 242-336-2551; www.peaceandplenty.com; Stocking Island) will rent snorkel gear ($15 per day) and sailboards ($15/30 per half-day/day) to day-trippers.

KAYAKING

Starfish (☎ 242-336-3033; www.kayakbahamas.com; Queen's Hwy, George Town) present a variety of activities, including four-hour guided kayak trips ($60), Castaway Getaways trips ($125), which drop you off at a suitably remote spot with a two-person kayak, and three-hour guided Eco Boat tours (adult/child $55/44). Adventure packages start from $299 for three days, and include lodgings, kayak/bicycle hire, airport transfers and island tours. Kayaks can be hired for $40 per day, snorkel gear is $15 per day and camping gear (without sleeping bags) is $60 per day. Weekly rates are available on all rentals.

BONEFISHING & SPORTFISHING

There are some excellent bonefishing guides in the area, who can be contacted via the Bahamas Ministry of Tourism (p195), with average rates of about $300 per half-day or $400 to $500 per day. **Cooper's Charter Service** (☎ 242-336-2711) and the Peace & Plenty Bonefish Lodge (p202), around 3 miles south of Rolle Town, are renowned for their great guides. **Bandits Bonefishing Lodge & Pirate's Den** (☎ 242-358-8062; info@banditsbonefishing .com) offers angling ($400 per day) and has accommodation/fishing packages including 3 nights/2 days of fishing for $1450.

BIRD-WATCHING

It is not only the marine parks that are fabulous for living creatures. Bird-fanciers will jump for joy (quietly!) on the following islands that contain national bird reserves: Big Galliot, Channel and Flat Cays, Big and Little Darby Islands, and Guana, Goat, Betty, Pigeon, Cistern, Leaf, Harvey and Rocks Cays.

Tours

For an introduction to local plants and herbs, along with information on their uses, join up with **Bush Medicine Tours** (☎ 242-345-7044; prices upon booking, from around $35). You'll learn about remedies for all sorts of ailments, from burns to menstrual cramps and even infertility.

Festivals & Events

For information on the following festivals and other events contact the helpful staff of the Bahamas Ministry of Tourism (p195).
Family Island Regatta During the last week of April, visiting yachts congregate for this annual regatta in Elizabeth Harbour (see the boxed text, below). The premier regatta in the Bahamian islands, it's a general excuse for the hoi polloi to hobnob with the social elite, downing copious amounts of rum and beer and cheering on the sailboats whizzing along in the harbor.
Annual Bahamas Bonefish Bonanza One of the Bahamas' prime fishing tourneys, held in George Town in October.
Junkanoo Traditionally starts at 3am on December 26 (Boxing Day). The colorful and noisy festival builds beneath the stars as islanders take to the streets for an outpouring of bonhomie and carnivale.

FAMILY ISLAND REGATTA

The wildly festive, four-day Family Island Regatta has been held every April since 1953. The party really gets going the week before the regatta, when breweries and rum companies sponsor a host of daft and fun events as a buildup to the main event.

Around 50 Bahamian sailing vessels, all locally made and crewed, race in Elizabeth Harbour, and everyone within miles – landlubbers, yachties and far-flung Bahamians – arrives to cheer on the sloops. The boats race along with their tall sails billowing, spilling the odd drunken crew member as they go. For the islands' boatbuilders, it is a chance to see their lovingly-built vessels prove their master's craft.

Races are divided into five classes, including a junior class for youngsters. A hallmark of the races is the 'pry,' a long wooden plank jutting from the side of each dinghy and sloop. The crew – often as many as six or seven people – put their weight on it to keep the boat balanced as it zips along, typically in a stiff 30-knot breeze. Knowledge of the winds, currents and boat-handling is essential to winning.

The celebrated regatta is also an excuse for a party; sound systems are tweaked up and accompanied by a colorful and raucous Junkanoo band, while stalls sell cracked conch and fried chicken. Everyone chatters while they sip their favorite brew in the sunshine. The dancing starts as dusk falls, and the night's festivities begin…

Sleeping

Accommodation can be overpriced here. For good value your best bet is self-contained units or suites that start at around $130 per night. Check ahead, a few places ask up to $30 per day on top of the nightly rate for a variety of things such as cleaning.

The **Bahamas Ministry of Tourism** (www.bahamas .com) can help with details on guesthouses around the Exumas, or contact **Ocean View Realty** (☎ /fax 242-336-2443; Queen's Hwy).

Reserve lodgings well in advance at regatta time, as chances for last-minute accommodations are nil.

Bahama Houseboats (☎ 242-336-2628; www.baha mahouseboats.com; George Town; ⊠) Sleeping under the stars while moored on an uninhabited cay and surrounded by emerald seas; now that is a dream! Good little kitchens, as well as roof sundecks and comfortable furnishings make this a thoroughly enjoyable getaway-from-it-all option. Bathrooms have showers and flushing toilets, and there is also air-con and a fridge, microwave, toaster, coffee machine and barbecue. The boats come fully equipped with all linen and kitchenware. All you need to provide is food and your beverage of choice. This dream is an affordable reality, with 35ft one-bed houseboats (sleeping up to six people on convertible furniture) hiring at $315/1895 per night/week, and 43ft two-bed houseboats for $430/2600 per night/week. Rates drop outside of peak months.

Two Turtles Inn (☎ 242-336-2545, www.exumaba hamas.com/twoturtles.html; George Town; r $115; ⊠ ⊠) This renovated stone-and-timber lodge has 14 spacious and modern-style rooms with tiled floors, satellite TV and fresh furnishings. Some units come with small kitchenettes. A small on-site restaurant and patio-bar serves daily specials such as aromatic goat curry. Boats, scooters and dive equipment can also be hired through their offices.

Minns Cottages (☎ /fax 242-336-2033/2645; Queen's Hwy; r $135; Ⓟ ⊠ ⊠) Book ahead for these pristine, fully equipped and tasteful units just north of George Town. There are spacious modern rooms and facilities including an enclosed patio facing the sea (albeit from across the main road). The kitchens have coffeemakers, microwaves, ovens and fridges. The water is the only drawback, with a sulphuric smell and taste that declares its ecologically sound origins a little too brutally.

Regatta Point (☎ 242-336-2206; www.regattapoint bahamas.com; Regatta Point; d $148; Ⓟ ⊠ ⊠) The fabulous 360-degree sea views are well matched by spacious and classy waterfront units and apartments housed in an old plantation-style building. Boats can also be hired here ($80 per day).

Club Peace & Plenty (☎ 242-336-2551; www.peace andplenty.com; Elizabeth Harbour; r $160; Ⓟ ⊠ ⊠ ⊠) The rooms at this small hotel are modern if a little small and boxy. However, they are also cheerful and include a TV and balcony, and face either the small oval-shaped pool or Stocking Island. The staff are very friendly and helpful, and offer scuba diving and fishing by arrangement; snorkel gear and sailboards can be rented from Peace & Plenty Beach Club on Stocking Island.

Eating & Drinking

Jean's Dog House (mains $3-6; ☯ breakfast & lunch) A local institution, Jean serves great breakfast sandwiches, hotdogs and burgers from a converted school bus that parks at the town end of schoolhouse hill on weekdays.

Sam's Place (☎ 242-336-2579; upstairs at the Government Wharf; mains $5-9; ☯ breakfast, lunch & dinner) A steady stream of people go up and down these stairs all day long. This is the best takeout in town, serving breakfast dishes, burgers, chicken and salads. The hot sandwiches are a meal in themselves; the tuna and cheese is yummy and filling.

Towne Café & Bakery (☎ 242-336-2194; Queen's Hwy, George Town; mains $5-9; ☯ breakfast & lunch, closed Tue & Sun) This is the place for a Bahamian breakfast of boil' fish with onions and hot peppers, tuna-fish salad, or chicken souse with grits or mildly spiced johnnycake. Daily lunch specials include a great fried snapper.

Eddy's Edgewater Club (☎ 242-336-2050; Queen's Hwy; mains $8-15; ☯ lunch & dinner) On the south side of Lake Victoria, this friendly and informal restaurant and bar is known for the splendid Bahamian fare, such as steamed chicken, sautéed liver and onions, and a worthy pea soup with dumplings. Don't miss the rake 'n' scrape band, it pulls 'em in and everyone works up a sweat on the dance floor. Live music is normally on Saturday and Monday, although the bar is open nightly.

Gemellies Pizza (☎ 242-3336-3023; mains $8-15; Queen's Hwy, George Town; ☯ dinner) For those crying for some relief from fried fish and chicken dishes, obtain a takeout pizza here!

Mind you, they also serve, yup, fried fish and chicken.

Two Turtles Inn restaurant (☎ 242-336-2545, www .exumabahamas.com/twoturtles.html; George Town; mains $10-18; ☺ lunch & dinner) The air-con restaurant at Two Turtles Inn (opposite) is normally open for lunch and dinner daily; but call ahead, it does depend upon who's around. Schoolchildren get their hot lunches from here. This place is also hopping during the regatta frivolities.

Club Peace & Plenty (☎ 242-336-2551; www .peaceandplenty.com; Elizabeth Harbour; mains $12-30; ☺ breakfast, lunch & dinner) Breakfasts are good value and tasty while lunch and dinner are also popular, if not as good value. The menu includes dishes such as blackened mahimahi and baked chicken. Weekends in the tourist seasons bring live music and fun at the bar.

A choice of groceries and household goods can be found at the Exuma Markets (p195) in the town center, which opens daily from 8am to 5pm. The Fish Fry area (see p201), just north of George Town has great heaps of little eateries and is worth a visit.

Getting There & Away
AIR
Exuma International Airport is based at Moss Town, 6 miles north of George Town. For international flights to the Exumas and the Bahamas, please refer to p288.

These Bahamian airlines both fly between Nassau and Exuma International Airport.
Bahamasair (UP; Exuma International Airport ☎ 242-345-0035, Nassau ☎ 242-377-5505; www.bahamasair .com; hub Nassau) Flies between Nassau and George Town twice daily ($80 one-way).
Southern Air (Nassau ☎ 242-377-2014; www.southern aircharter.com; hub Nassau) Flies to Moss Town twice weekly from Nassau ($70 one-way) and between the Exumas and Long Island.

Quoted rates fares are one-way.

Route	Price	Frequency
Exumas International Airport – Nassau	$80	3 daily
Exumas International Airport – Deadmans Cay, Long Island	$60	2 weekly

BOAT
If traveling in your own boat, George Town is the official port of entry to the Exumas.

You'll need to call ahead to arrange clearance with **Customs** (☎ 242-345-0071) and **Immigration** (☎ 242-345-2569), both in the Government Administration Building on Queen's Hwy. You will also require a special sailing license for traveling around the islands.

Ferry
Bahamas Ferries (☎ 242-323-2166; www.bahamas ferries.com) travel every Monday and Wednesday from Nassau to George Town (adult/ child $90/50 one-way, 11 hours).

Mail Boat
Call the **Dockmaster's Office** (☎ 242-393-1064) at Potter's Cay in Nassau to confirm schedules, and for more contact and fare details.
Grand Master (☎ 242-393-1064) Departs Nassau for George Town (one-way $45/22.50 per adult/child, 12 hours) at 2pm Tuesday.
Sea Link (☎ 242-393-7457) Departs Nassau for George Town (one-way $50/30 per adult/child, 10 hours) at 7pm on Monday, Tuesday and Wednesday.

Day Trips from Nassau
The following trips depart from Nassau, and are very popular:
Powerboat Adventures (☎ 242-393-7116; www .powerboatadventures.com; Nassau, New Providence; adult/ child $190/130) offers a thrilling ride from Nassau as a powerboat zips you to Allan's Cays for snorkeling, then on to Ship Channel Cay for a nature hike and barbecue lunch on the beach.

Island World Adventures (☎ 242-363-3333; www .islandworldadventures.com; Nassau, New Providence; adult/child $175/120) offers daylong excursions on a high-powered speedboat from Paradise Island to Saddleback Cay's wonderful snorkeling and seven private beaches. Trips include lunch, an open bar, snorkeling gear and a stop at Leaf Cay.

Getting Around
Taxis await the arrival of flights and charge $28 to George Town. Two good car-rental agencies are also based at the airport.

BICYCLE, MOTORCYCLE & CAR HIRE
You will need your own transport if you want to explore the island outside George Town's immediate vicinity.
Don's Rent A Car (☎ 242-345-0112; Exuma International Airport; ☺ 7am-5pm Mon-Sun) rents excellent air-con vehicles from $65 per day.

Uptown Rent-a-Car (☎ 242-336-2822; uptownrent@ hotmail.com; George Town) has cars to rent from around $70 per day.

Prestige Scooter Rental (☎ 242-357-0066; Queen's Hwy, George Town) rents scooters from about $50 per day.

Starfish (p197) has bicycles for hire ($20/25 per half-day/day, inclusive of locks and helmets).

BOAT

To explore around the cays and Exuma Cays Land & Sea Park, you will need a boat of some kind. Some lodgings provide boats for hire, but the rates offered by **Minns Water Sports** (☎ 242-336-3483; info@mwsboats.com; George Town) are especially good. It rents out boats from $45/70 per half-day/day, but the rates are reduced for bookings over three days. The boats vary in size from 15ft to 22ft, and cash deposits are required.

BUS

Buses depart from and return to George Town daily via Emerald Bay ($3) and Rolleville ($5). Ask at the Bahamas Ministry of Tourism for a bus schedule.

FERRY

Ferries to Stocking Island depart the dock at **Club Peace & Plenty** (☎ 242-393-1064; round-trip $8, free for guests) at 10:30am and 1:30pm.

TAXI

Luther Rolle Taxis (☎ 242-345-5003) and **Leslie Dames** (☎ 242-357-0015) both run taxi services around the island.

STOCKING ISLAND & ROLLE CAY

Stocking Island is a 600-acre, pencil-thin island lined with beaches, about a mile offshore. It's rimmed by talcum-powder fine beaches and makes a fabulous day trip from George Town.

The best snorkel spots are located at the cuts between Stocking Island and Elizabeth Island and between Elizabeth Island and Guana Cay.

Rolle Cay is a smidgen-size isle midway between George Town and Stocking Island. **Mystery Cave** is a 400ft-deep blue hole on the Atlantic side and is said to be one of the few living intertidal stromatolite reefs in the world (the other major one is near Perth, Australia); a living fossil – dating back 3½

million years. Highborne Cay stromatolites are now being researched (see p203).

Peace & Plenty Beach Club (see below) will rent snorkel gear ($15 per day) and sailboards ($15/30 per half-day/day) to day-trippers as well as small sailboats and paddleboats ($25 per half-day).

The environmentally friendly **Higgins' Landing** (☎ 242-336-2460; www.higginslanding.com; Stocking Island; r $550; ☒ ☒) is the only accommodation on Stocking Island. Solar-powered and handsomely appointed cottages have comfortable furnishings and an informal ambience. Stepped down a small outcrop overlooking the sea, each cottage has a wide balcony and fantastic views. A bar and restaurant on the grounds stocks books and games. Rates include breakfast and dinner, transfers and water sports.

A spirited and affable outdoor bar, **Chat n Chill Bar & Grill** (☎ 242-336-2800; Stocking Island; mains $6-11; ☺ lunch & dinner) sits on the island's main beach and right at the water's edge, with customers' small boats and kayaks lined up alongside, their version of the pub 'car park.' The bar specialize in yummy mango, strawberry and banana daiquiris and really tasty grilled food. Chat n Chill's Sunday pig roast ($15) is one of the social highlights in George Town; call for pick up from Club Peace & Plenty dock, and rejoice in *the* perfect beach bar!

A talented cook has been making world-famous burgers for decades at **Peace & Plenty Beach Club** (☎ 242-336-2551; Stocking Island; mains $6-12; ☺ lunch) that both locals and traveling yachties return for again and again.

There are no roads on the island and access is by boat. Ferries to Stocking Island depart from the Club Peace & Plenty dock (☎ 242-393-1064; round-trip $8, free for guests; ☺ 10:30am & 1:30pm) on Elizabeth Harbour.

NORTH OF GEORGE TOWN

Queen's Hwy runs north of George Town through a string of small settlements with prim homes painted in Caribbean pastels and shaded by palms. Most are associated with plantation estates that now lie in ruins. Beautiful beaches line the shore.

A mile offshore opposite Mt Thompson sits **Three Sisters Rock**, a trio of craggy boulders rising from the sea. They're supposedly named for three sisters who each drowned herself here for the shame of bearing a child out of wedlock.

The historic settlement of **Rolleville**, 28 miles north of George Town, sits atop a hill at the northern end of Great Exuma. It's a poor village with many meager shacks and former slave homes, most in tumbledown condition, but it's brightened in late spring and early summer by African Flame Trees. The hamlet is the site of the Rolleville Regatta, held the first Monday in August. Several locals still make boats.

Sleeping

Palms at Three Sisters (☎ 242-358-4040, 800-688-4752; fax 242-358-4043; Mt Thompson; r $100; P ✕ ✕) This motel-style accommodations is a tad weary, but looks over a deserted, palm-lined beach in Mt Thompson. It has 12 large, air-con beachfront rooms and two cottages, all modestly but nicely furnished, with patios or balconies and satellite TV.

Mount Pleasant Suites Hotel (☎ 242-336-2690; fax 242-336-2964; Hooper's Bay; s/d $85/100; P ✕ ✕) These pristine and comfortably furnished units are excellent value, but lie 3 miles out of George Town, and there are no adjacent facilities. However, the units' balconies or patios overlook that glorious sea, and it is a 5-minute walk to the beach. A fully equipped kitchen, and satellite TV make this a popular holiday option. Book ahead by fax or writing to: PO Box EX-29019, George Town, Exumas.

Peace & Plenty Beach Inn (☎ 242-336-2250; www .peaceandplenty.com; George Town; r $170; P ✕ ✕ ☎) The rooms here are decidedly upmarket from those at its sibling, Club Peace & Plenty. The fresh and airy decor includes Italian tile floors, comfortable furniture and a private balcony in each room. An on-site bar hangs dreamily over the water, while its adjacent popular restaurant serves Bahamian and continental dishes (mains $18 to $35). Some water sports available for guests include scuba diving, snorkeling and Sunfish sailing. It's 1.5 miles from George Town.

Palm Bay Beach Club (☎ 242-336-2787; www.palm baybeachclub.com; Queen's Hwy; r $170; P ✕ ✕ ☎) This intimate place sits on a small beach and offers some fun at the weekends.

Four Seasons Resort Great Exuma at Emerald Bay (☎ 242-336-6989; www.emeraldbayresort.com; Queen's Hwy, Roker's Point; r $400-550; P ✕ ✕ ☐ ☎) This exclusive resort is a little iso-lated, but centers on a championship golf course designed by Greg Norman, and a dedicated kids' facility and pool will give mom and dad some long-desired peace. The resort complex features vacation town-house rentals and beachfront villas, all in plantation-style architecture, plus gourmet restaurants, a health and fitness club, and a full-service marina. A great beach, two oceanside pools and complimentary snor-keling, sailing, kayaking and sailboarding should keep everyone happy.

Eating & Drinking

There are a few bars up this way that serve food.

Iva Bowe's Central Highway Inn Restaurant & Bar (☎ 242-345-7014; Queen's Hwy, Ramsey; mains $8-25; ⏲ lunch & dinner Mon-Sat) Iva and her sons also run the adjacent gas station, but Iva is rightly more famous for her Bahamian seafood and shrimp dishes. Breakfast may also be avail-able, depending on who is around.

Kermit's Hilltop Tavern (☎ 242-345-6006; Queen's Hwy, Rolleville; mains $8-25; ⏲ lunch & dinner) This lively and popular bar has been going since the 1950s and is beloved of locals seeking good, authentic Bahamian dishes, curried mutton and fresh vegetables. Reservations are required for dinner. A seat at one of the rooftop tables with a marvelous view makes it well worth the drive. The tavern has open-air dancing and live music on weekends.

The **Fish Fry** area, down from Peace & Plenty Beach Inn, has a plethora of great little outdoor bars and takeouts housed in multicolored wooden huts that open at sun-set and weekends until late. **Rennie's** (☎ 5336 2300; ⏲ breakfast, lunch & dinner) makes wonderful banana, potato and corn bread, while **Porgy's Place** has a wide wooden deck perfect for sip-ping your sundowner beer. **Tino's** pulsates to the gentle rhythm of reggae and is a popular hangout of the local lads, while the **Big Z Sports Bar** has a lively mixed crowd and turns the reggae up a notch on a Friday night.

You can buy goods at **McKenzie's** grocery store in Barreterre.

Check in at Palm Bay Beach Club (see left) for some fun and music at the weekends.

Getting There & Around

There's a gas station opposite Iva Bowe's Central Hwy Inn (above) near Ramsey.

Ettienne & Cephas (around $50 for shorter trips, round-trip $140; 21hrs) mail boat departs Nassau on Tuesday for Staniel Cay, Farmer's Cay, Black Point, Little Farmer's Cay and Barreterre.

Kermit Rolle (☎ 242-345-6006) of Rolleville offers taxi tours.

Check with the **Bahamas Ministry of Tourism** (☎ 242-336-2430, www.bahamas.com; Queen's Hwy, George Town) for private minibus services.

SOUTH OF GEORGE TOWN

Follow the scenic views along Queen's Hwy until you reach **Rolle Town** (population 280). Despite its ramshackle appearance, the village, which produces fruit and vegetable crops (including onions, mangoes and bananas), is worth a stop to buy some fresh fruit as well as to see the fabulous view from its hillside setting.

Many of the decrepit sun-bleached pastel buildings and clapboard shacks date back over a century and have withstood storms and hurricanes. Goats graze freely and chickens roam with their broods in neat little fluffy lines alongside the road.

Try not to miss visiting a very evocative piece of local history at the Rolle Town Tombs. Here lie a few solitary 18th-century tombstones, one of which is shaped like a double bed with headboard and footboard and dated 1792. The plaque notes that the 26-year-old wife of a Scottish overseer, Captain Alexander McKay, slumbers there with her infant child. The poor man died the following year, said to be from a broken heart.

The Peace & Plenty Bonefish Lodge (below) is a well-known boy's club and carries a high reputation as one of the best fishing lodges in the Bahamas. It charges from $400 to $500 per day with boat, guide and tackle for two. The hotel has an intensive seven-day 'bonefish school' package each April and November, with 16 hours of instruction over four days. It's billed as 'the ultimate fly-fishing school challenge.'

Sleeping & Eating

Peace & Plenty Bonefish Lodge (☎ 242-345-5555; www.ppbonefishlodge.net; Queen's Hwy; d $252; mains $20-35; P ✕ ✕) Around 3 miles south of Rolle Town, this small attractive lodge overlooks the sea and a small beach. It is comfortable, friendly and beloved of fishing fans. A great bar is garnished with a rogue's gallery of

photos from successful fishing trips, while the restaurant will serve your catch, as well as seafood and steaks for dinner.

Cheaters Restaurant & Bar (☎ 242-336-2535; Queen's Hwy, South George Town; mains $8-25; ⌚ lunch & dinner Wed-Sat) Local fare served at this simple eatery draws a friendly Bahamian crowd. The air-con room is shady and refreshing, and the simple decor is a little sparse, but clean and certainly adequate for the yummy sides of peas and rice, coleslaw and macaroni (which alone makes it worth the trip). The bar livens up at night, but be warned: it is a fair drive from most lodgings.

Traveller's Rest Restaurant & Bar (Queen's Hwy, Rolle Town) This place is also popular. It has a pool table, satellite TV, and music and dancing.

LITTLE EXUMA

Little Exuma lies only around 10 miles from the Exuma International Airport, and is separated from the main isle by a 200yd bight; a bridge fills the gap.

A number of ongoing developments for private beachside dwellings have yet to encroach completely over some lovely beaches. A nice day can be spent here relaxing on the white sands and paddling around in the perfectly clear water.

Pretty Molly Beach is one of the loveliest beaches on the island, despite the sorrowful origin of its name – a slave killed herself one day by simply walking into the waves off this beach. The stark beauty of these shores is a fitting monument to her spirit, which is said to still walk alongside these waters.

FERRY TO WILLIAMS TOWN

Ferry is a small hillside settlement that lies immediately across the bridge from Great Exuma. A highlight is **St Christopher's Anglican Church**, a whitewashed chapel festooned with a bougainvillea bower. Supposedly it's the smallest church in the Bahamas.

Forbes Hill, 12 miles southeast of George Town, has a 100yd-wide scimitar of pure white sand with turquoise shallows cusped by tiny headlands. Idyllic! Two miles south of Forbes Hill a side road leads east to **Tropic of Cancer Beach**, another true stunner that runs south, unblemished, for several miles.

The southernmost settlement is **Williams Town** (population 300), populated predominantly by Kelsalls, descended from or named for the foremost Loyalist family that founded the settlement. The Kelsalls established a cotton plantation and sold salt drawn from nearby salt ponds. The brush-entangled ruins of the plantation home – **Hermitage Estate** – still stand amid pinkish brine ponds.

You can see locals dressing their fresh catch of fish and conch at the rickety wharf behind and just south of St Mary Magdalene's Church. North of town, on the bluff to the side of the road, you'll pass a tall **Doric pillar** transporting you (metaphorically) to ancient Greece. This column and a rusty cannon stand high above the rocky shore. The hulk of a ship lies dramatically on a white-sand beach fronting the village, within calling distance of the column meant to guide mariners.

Mom's Bakery in Williams Town is the place to stock up on rum cake, banana bread, coconut tarts and bread, while **Bullard's Supplies** is fine for basic groceries.

EXUMA CAYS

The cays begin at the barren Sail Rocks, 40 miles southeast of New Providence. Though they may seem alike, each has its own quirky character. Many are privately owned.

The cays offer a variety of extraordinary pleasures and experiences. A highlight of any visit is a snorkel or dive trip into Staniel Cay's Thunderball Grotto.

These waters are acclaimed as the 'finest cruising grounds in the Western Hemisphere.' *The Exuma Guide: A Cruising Guide to the Exuma Cays* by Stephen Pavlidis is a must-read for sailors.

Along with day trips to several of the cays from Nassau (see p80), or kayak and snorkel trips from George Town (see p197), you can always hire your own boat. Ask the **Bahamas Ministry of Tourism** (☎ 242-336-2430; www.bahamas.com; Queen's Hwy, George Town) or see recommendations under Boat, p200.

For details of the mail boat that visits some of the cays in this area from Nassau, see p193.

SHIP CHANNEL CAY & ALLAN'S CAYS

Long, narrow Ship Channel Cay is the northernmost cay after Sail Rocks, while

---

BOWE CAY IS FOR HIRE!

Any Robinson Crusoes out there fancy some time-out? This 220-acre cay is 10 miles around, has a lagoon ringed by mangroves, as well as walking trails and miles of white sandy beaches. Company consists of some friendly goats and sun-baking iguanas. Contact owners via www.bowecay.com.

Allan's Cays, immediately south, comprise about a dozen cays popular with boaters and fisherfolk. One of the prettiest is Leaf Cay, with a splendid beach and an endemic subspecies of iguana, the yellowish 'Bahamian dragon.' It can be visited by day trip from Nassau.

Yachters will find an exceptionally good anchorage at Leaf Cay.

HIGHBORNE CAY

This private cay, 2 miles south of Leaf Cay, is favored by yachies, who are permitted ashore if they are using the marina's facilities. The beach on the eastern side of the cay is one of the most beautiful in the Bahamas.

The **Highborne Cay Research Station** has recently been set up to research a year in the life of Bahamian stromatolites (living fossils) to see how they adapt to changing weather environments. For more information on stromatolites and Highborne Cay contact www.stromatolites.info.

The **Highborne Cay Marina** (☎ 242-355-1008; fax 242-355-1003, VHF channel 16; Nassau, New Providence) has a grocery store, pay phone and berths for yachts up to 130ft.

NORMAN'S CAY

One look at the stunning beaches and you'll understand why 4-mile-long Norman's Cay was once an idyllic hideaway for the wintering wealthy, and then a less salubrious crowd (see the boxed text, p205). The bonefishing here is said to be superb.

MacDuff's (☎ 242-357-8846; www.macduffs.com; r $230; ✉ 🐟) has four one-bedroom villas that will sleep 16 people in all. They are pleasantly decorated and come with an equipped kitchen. Water sports are offered, and food can be stocked by arrangement. The bar here is a popular lunch spot for yachties.

THE EXUMAS

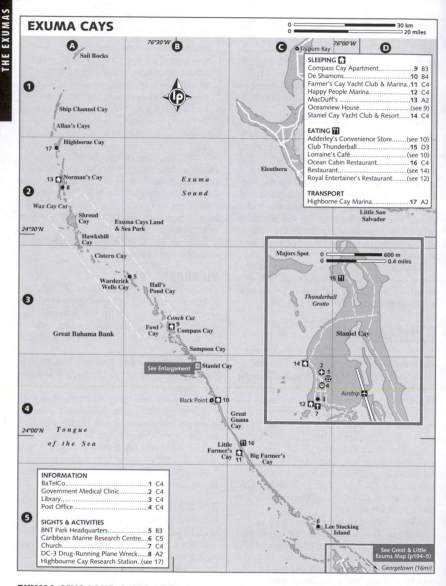

EXUMA CAYS

0 ——— 30 km
0 ——— 20 miles

SLEEPING
Compass Cay Apartment..................9 B3
De Shamons...................................10 B4
Farmer's Cay Yacht Club & Marina..11 C4
Happy People Marina.....................12 C4
MacDuff's.....................................13 A2
Oceanview House......................(see 9)
Staniel Cay Yacht Club & Resort......14 C4

EATING
Adderley's Convenience Store........(see 10)
Club Thunderball...........................15 D3
Lorraine's Café.............................(see 10)
Ocean Cabin Restaurant.................16 C4
Restaurant....................................(see 14)
Royal Entertainer's Restaurant........(see 12)

TRANSPORT
Highborne Cay Marina.....................17 A2

Sail Rocks

Ship Channel Cay

Allan's Cays

Highborne Cay
17

Norman's Cay
13
8

Exuma Sound

Tarpum Bay

Eleuthera

Little San Salvador

Wax Cay Cut

Shroud Cay

24°30'N

Hawksbill Cay

Exuma Cays Land & Sea Park

Cistern Cay

Warderick Wells Cay
5
Hall's Pond Cay

Great Bahama Bank

Conch Cut
Fowl Cay
9
Compass Cay

Sampson Cay

See Enlargement   Staniel Cay

Black Point   10

24°00'N   *Tongue of the Sea*

Great Guana Cay

Little Farmer's Cay
16
11
Big Farmer's Cay

Majors Spot
0 ——— 600 m
0 ——— 0.4 miles

15

Thunderball Grotto

Staniel Cay

14
2
1
4
Airstrip
3
12
7

6
Lee Stocking Island

See Great & Little Exuma Map (p194–5)

Georgetown (16mi)

INFORMATION
BaTelCo...1 C4
Government Medical Clinic...............2 C4
Library...3 C4
Post Office.......................................4 C4

SIGHTS & ACTIVITIES
BNT Park Headquarters.....................5 B3
Caribbean Marine Research Centre....6 C5
Church..7 C4
DC-3 Drug-Running Plane Wreck......8 A2
Highbourne Cay Research Station...(see 17)

EXUMA CAYS LAND & SEA PARK

The Bahamas has several jewels in its gorgeous turquoise crown, and this is one of them. An unspoilt underwater idyll teems with all sorts of fish and marine life that scarcely notice your presence as they dart through a labyrinth of vast caverns, down over walls, through blue holes and along

miles of reef that include pillar corals, where groupers and turtles swan lazily about.

The first marine 'replenishment nursery' in the world, the park consists of 112,640 acres or 175 sq miles of protected islands and surrounding seas, and was created in 1958. All fishing and collecting is banned. No marine or plant life, whether dead or alive, may be taken from here, including shells. Fish spawned in the park have now been proven to be breeding further afield and replenishing overfished areas, to everyone's delight.

The park runs 22 miles south from Wax Cay Cut (immediately south of Norman's Cay) to Conch Cut and Fowl Cay. It is 8 miles wide, extending 3½ miles east and west on each side of the islands. It has outstanding anchorages and even more outstanding dive sites.

On land, you may glimpse the Bahamian mockingbird, Bahamian banana quit, or the rare red-legged thrush. Seabirds abound, including terns, waders, and the elegant, long-tailed tropicbird, which nests in high bluffs. Land animals include curly-tailed and blue-tailed lizards, plump iguanas and endangered hutias that look like oversized guinea pigs.

Uninhabited **Hawksbill Cay**, ringed by stunning beaches, has marked nature trails that lead to the ruins of an old Loyalist plantation. **Little Hawksbill Cay** is a major nesting site for ospreys. **Warderick Wells Cay**, which has 4 miles of nature trails, is said to be haunted by the tormented spirits from a slave ship. **Shroud Cay** has 'Driftwood Village,' an ever-expanding piece of flotsam folk art. And the **Rocky Dundas**, two rocks in Conch Cut, has a cave full of stalactites and stalagmites.

Moriah Harbour Cay sits between Great and Little Exuma, and is comprised of beaches, sand dunes, mangrove creeks and sea-grass beds. This is another park for hikers, and for lovers of feathered creatures. Resident bird species include nighthawks, ospreys, oystercatchers and terns.

With no commercial development, the main cays in the park's vicinity are perfect for camping. There are no facilities, however, and you will need to take all food and water with you. The **Bahamas National Trust** (BNT; ☎ 242-359-1821; www.thebahamasnationaltrust.org; Warderick Wells Cay; ☉ 9am-noon & 3-5pm Mon-Fri, 9am-1pm Sat) has posted information leaflets on several cays; park access is free.

Apart from day tours to the park from Nassau or kayaking tours from George Town, your best bet is to hire a boat and camping gear from George Town and enjoy exploring this wonderful region in your own time. Otherwise access to the park is from Staniel Cay, where you might be able to hitch a ride with the park warden on his daily patrol. He monitors VHF channel 16 from the park headquarters at Warderick Wells Cay.

Boaters must anchor at Hog Cay at the south end of Warderick Wells Cay. Moorings cost from $15 daily, depending on your vessel's length. Call 'Exuma Park' on VHF 16 at least 24 hours in advance to check availability.

COMPASS & SAMPSON CAYS

These popular yachter's havens, south of the Exuma Cays Land & Sea Park, each boast a small harbor with a beach, beach-lined coves, and trails.

Two properties are up for rent, via an American-based website. **Compass Cay Apartment** (☎ US 540-721-9915; www.a1vacations.com; per week $1000; ✖ ✖) has two bedrooms, while Oceanview House is a three-bedroom house ($1750 per week). Both properties have a deck and complete kitchen.

CARLOS LEHDER RIVAS

In the 1970s most of Norman's Cay was purchased by Carlos Lehder Rivas, a founding member of the Medellin Cartel, the infamous and violent Colombian drug-smugglers. Lehder was well known for idolizing Hitler and labeled his drug packages with swastikas.

When he arrived in the Bahamas, Lehder brought in armed thugs, drove out most of the residents, and turned the cay into a landing strip for illegal cargoes. Cocaine was smuggled from Colombia, through the Bahamas and into the USA. An NBC documentary apparently blew the lid in 1983 and the authorities stepped in.

Lehder was prosecuted for drug-trafficking in 1987–88. He was convicted and sentenced to life plus 135 years in prison. He later struck a deal to testify in the drug-trafficking trial of former Panamanian leader Manuel Noriega. Lehder's whereabouts are a USA government secret, but it is widely believed that he is now under the States' witness protection scheme.

A DC-3 drug-running plane still lies rusting in Norman Cay's shallow water, having missed the runway during the period of Lehder's residence in the Bahamas.

THE EXUMAS

STANIEL CAY

pop 76

This tiny cay is the most sophisticated and visited settlement in the Exuma Cays and the main base from which to visit the Exuma Cays Land & Sea Park. The small, attractive village has all the necessities – grocery stores, post office, church and library (1776) – and the cay is lined with some lovely tranquil beaches on which to relax. The bonefishing is also supposed to be grand.

There is a BaTelCo station and several phonecard booths, plus **St Luke's Clinic** (☎ 242-355-2010), staffed by a nurse.

The **New Year's Day Regatta**, always fun, is when locally built dinghies compete for prizes, and the town beach celebrates the return of many local people and yachties for the festivities. The **Annual Staniel Cay Bonefish Tournament** in August is another big event that brings home the locals and makes big fish quiver in dismay.

Thunderball Grotto

This crystalline grotto, just northwest of the cay, is another Bahamian jewel. The exquisite cavern – lit by shafts of light pouring in from holes in the ceiling that sear through the water highlighting a myriad of darting fish – was named for the James Bond movie *Thunderball*, scenes from which were filmed here. So, too, were scenes from *Splash* and another 007 movie, *Never Say Never Again*. Although you swim in at low tide, the current is pretty strong – inexperienced swimmers may prefer to snorkel and swim elsewhere. Divers also love this spot.

Sleeping & Eating

The cay has two waterfront hotels that play to the boating crowd. For fully furnished holiday rentals contact the American-based agency www.a1vacations.com.

Staniel Cay Yacht Club & Resort (☎ 242-355-2024; www.stanielcay.com; r per day/week $148/945, mains $12-25; breakfast, lunch & dinner;) This is truly a place for lovers of perfect seafront views. Spacious verandas overlook the sea and create a feeling of total relaxation. There are cool and comfortable cottages (with kitchenettes) or suites (with kitchens) and great weekly rates. Use one of the resort's free Boston Whalers or Sunfish sailboats, take along the free scuba gear and go and visit gorgeous Major Cay. The restaurant here attracts the

yachting hoi polloi, and serves American- and Bahamian-style cuisine; book ahead. You can also order a boxed lunch for excursions (no pork sausages thank you).

Happy People Marina (☎ 242-355-2008; fax 242-355-2025; r $90-200; mains $10-28; breakfast, lunch & dinner;) Has eight air-con rooms with ceiling fans and a decor of rainbow pastels. Upstairs rooms boast marvelous views and have private bathrooms; those downstairs share bathrooms. Singer Jimmy Buffett drops in on occasion to play the Marina's Royal Entertainer's Restaurant, named as one of his favorite bars. Reservations are needed for dinner when lobster is added to the Bahamian menu. There is also a pool table and music at weekends.

Club Thunderball (☎ 242-355-2012; mains $10-20; lunch & dinner, closed Mon) This lively place is atop the bluff overlooking the Thunderball Grotto. It serves Bahamian food and has beach barbecues on Friday night (book a rib!), plus occasional pig roasts and a Super Bowl party in January. The club also features a pool table, satellite TV and dancing on weekends.

Several stores here sell groceries.

GREAT GUANA CAY

The largest of the Exuma Cays, 12-mile-long Great Guana Cay, also has the cays' largest settlement, **Black Point** (population 253), and has a reputation for not being the friendliest place. Facilities include an airstrip, post office, BaTelCo station and **Government Medical Clinic** (☎ 242-355-0007). An Emancipation Day Regatta is held here each August.

De Shamons (☎ 242-355-3009; Black Point; r $90) has four rooms with fridge over their restaurant. The restaurant specializes in freshly caught fish served in traditional Bahamian style. Ask about meals with bookings.

HAVE YOU SEEN THE LITTLE PIGGIES?

Only a short boat trip away from Staniel Cay, tiny Major Cay is a great place for a day of snorkeling and sunning. Don't forget a picnic for yourself and the friendly porcine population to enjoy! Yes, that's right, Major Cay has some famous swimming pigs that like nothing better than a plash, pat and a peanut-butter sandwich.

RAGGED ISLAND RANGE

Few visitors ever reach this crescent of a dozen or so isles and a score of small cays that lie about 25 miles south of Little Exuma. The chain begins with the Jumento Cays, arcs west and south for about 100 miles and ends with the largest isle, Ragged Island. During the 19th century the chains' flats were used for salt-crystal farming. Today they are virtually uninhabited.

Most of the cays here are windswept and barren, increasingly so to the south. The birdlife is varied and prolific. A lighthouse still stands on Flamingo Cay. Ragged Island has the only settlement, **Duncan Town** (population 70), where residents earn their living from fishing.

You will need to charter or hire your own boat to reach these islands. Ask the **Bahamas Ministry of Tourism** (☎ 242-336-2430; www.bahamas.com; Queen's Hwy, George Town) or see recommendations, p200).

Lorraine's Café (☎ 242-355-2201; ☽ breakfast) is recommended for inexpensive Bahamian fare and freshly baked bread and cookies. Call the day before to order breakfast.

Adderley's Convenience Store (☎ 242-358-8056; ☽ 7:30am-6pm) sells groceries.

LITTLE FARMER'S CAY

This cay is simply a stone's throw away from the southwest tip of Great Guana. It consists of a fairly small fishing village and bay. It hosts the annual **Farmer's Cay Festival & Regatta** in the first weekend of February as well as the spirited **Full Moon Beer Festival** in July.

Farmer's Cay Yacht Club & Marina (☎ /fax 242-355-4017; r $90; ☒) has three smallish rooms with TV. A fairly basic **restaurant** (mains $8-18; ☽ lunch & dinner) and bar also overlook the sea. Notice is needed for dinner.

Ocean Cabin Restaurant (☎ /fax 242-355-4006; mains $5-20; ☽ breakfast, lunch & dinner), a small, friendly bar in the hamlet, serves up meals and beers, and has regular barbecues during the winter season. The owners also run two cosy rental cottages on Dabba Hill (prices start at $130 per night).

Ettienne & Cephas (around $50 for shorter trips, round-trip $140; 21hrs) mail boat departs Nassau on Tuesday for Staniel Cay, Farmer's Cay, Black Point, Little Farmer's Cay and Barreterre.

LEE STOCKING ISLAND

About 5 miles north of Great Exuma, Lee Stocking has an airstrip and the **Caribbean Marine Research Centre** (☎ 242-345-6039; www.perryinstitute.org) This 100-acre scientific research facility is funded by grants from the US National Oceanic & Atmospheric Administration with the aim of researching underwater ecosystems and learning how to ensure the vitality of the reefs and aquatic life. Visitors are welcomed with short tours.

Cat & San Salvador Islands

Many Bahamians love these two islands because they represent a way of life that has existed in the Bahamas for hundreds of years. However, don't expect island idylls; these impoverished islands are different to other Family Islands. Their economic and cultural isolation is most apparent in Cat's decaying churches which would be kept pristine on most Family Islands regardless of the local economy's state.

Cat Island is barely touched by tourism, despite superb diving off the south shore where a 12-mile front contains a wealth of caves and coral canyons to explore. Climb the rock staircase hewn into the side of Como Hill by Father Jerome, the architect hermit, to see the little stone church that he built, and a spiritually reviving 360-degree view.

The boyhood home of Academy Award-winning actor Sir Sidney Poitier, Cat is also renowned for the continuing practice of obeah (a form of African-based ritual magic). San Salvadorians also still utilize bush medicine that derives from the first African slaves brought to the region.

'San Sal' is one of the best wall-dive destinations in the world. There are more than 40 dive sites within 30 minutes of shore, and more near Rum Cay and Conception Island. The island's waters are known for visibility up to 200ft; on special days it can exceed a miraculous 250ft!

The biggest event of the year is the Cat Island Regatta held on Emancipation Day (the first Monday in August). Scores of Cat Islanders return from afar, and sailboat races, dominoes tournaments and great rake 'n' scrape bands fill the island with a rare sense of fun.

HIGHLIGHTS

- Chat with islanders in Arthur's Town about Bahamian history and **obeah** (p212) in Cat Island and San Salvador
- Take a **guided walk** (p218) to learn about San Salvador's old plantations and bush medicine
- Experience a Cat Island sunrise, and the humbling work of Father Jerome's **Mt Alvernia Hermitage** (p210)
- Dive the pristine waters and numerous wall-dive sites of San Salvador (p217)
- Kick up your heels on a Friday night at the **Harlem Square Club** (p218) in Cockburn Town, San Salvador

Arthur's Town ★

Mt Alvernia ★

Cockburn Town ★

Vertical walls ★

■ TELEPHONE CODE: 242	■ POPULATION: 2576	■ AREA: 119 SQ MILES

CAT ISLAND

pop 1548

Here beats the heart of the traditional African-Bahamian culture. This 48 sq miles of remote island, south of Eleuthera and 130 miles southeast of Nassau, is an interesting

place to visit, but one that you have to dig deep to discover. There is no tourism infrastructure that hands the island's history and culture to you on a plate; non-Bahamian visitors are rare, and those who come here go to several diving resorts on the south coast.

A single road, Queen's Hwy, runs down the west shore, lined by plantation ruins

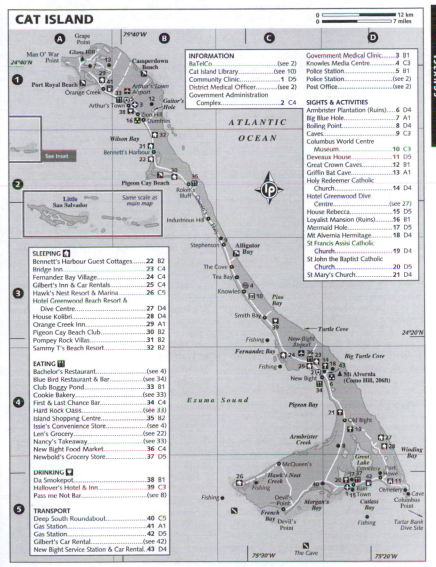

CAT ISLAND

0 ————— 12 km
0 ————— 7 miles

INFORMATION
BaTelCo...(see 2)
Cat Island Library....................(see 10)
Community Clinic..........................1 D5
District Medical Officer............(see 2)
Government Administration
  Complex..2 C4
Government Medical Clinic.......3 B1
Knowles Media Centre..............4 C3
Police Station.................................5 B1
Police Station.............................(see 2)
Post Office.................................(see 2)

SIGHTS & ACTIVITIES
Armbrister Plantation (Ruins)..... 6 D4
Big Blue Hole.................................7 A1
Boiling Point..................................8 D4
Caves...9 C3
Columbus World Centre
  Museum......................................10 C3
Deveaux House............................11 D5
Great Crown Caves....................12 B1
Griffin Bat Cave..........................13 A1
Holy Redeemer Catholic
  Church.......................................14 D4
Hotel Greenwood Dive
  Centre.....................................(see 27)
House Rebecca...........................15 D5
Loyalist Mansion (Ruins)..........16 B1
Mermaid Hole..............................17 D5
Mt Alvernia Hermitage.............18 D4
St Francis Assisi Catholic
  Church.......................................19 D4
St John the Baptist Catholic
  Church.......................................20 D5
St Mary's Church.......................21 D4

SLEEPING
Bennett's Harbour Guest Cottages.......22 B2
Bridge Inn.....................................23 C4
Fernandez Bay Village.................24 C4
Gilbert's Inn & Car Rentals.........25 C4
Hawk's Nest Resort & Marina...............26 C5
Hotel Greenwood Beach Resort &
  Dive Centre...............................27 D4
House Kolibri................................28 D4
Orange Creek Inn.........................29 A1
Pigeon Cay Beach Club................30 B2
Pompey Rock Villas......................31 B2
Sammy T's Beach Resort.............32 B2

EATING
Bachelor's Restaurant..........................(see 4)
Blue Bird Restaurant & Bar................(see 34)
Club Boggy Pond.........................33 B1
Cookie Bakery...........................(see 33)
First & Last Chance Bar.............34 C4
Hard Rock Oasis.......................(see 33)
Island Shopping Centre..............35 B2
Issie's Convenience Store.........(see 4)
Len's Grocery...........................(see 22)
Nancy's Takeaway....................(see 33)
New Bight Food Market..............36 C4
Newbold's Grocery Store............37 D5

DRINKING
Da Smokepot................................38 B1
Hallover's Hotel & Inn..................39 C3
Pass me Not Bar........................(see 8)

TRANSPORT
Deep South Roundabout..............40 C5
Gas Station...................................41 A1
Gas Station...................................42 D5
Gilbert's Car Rental...................(see 42)
New Bight Service Station & Car Rental..43 D4

ATLANTIC OCEAN

Exuma Sound

and ramshackle settlements where unemployment is rife, and goats wander amid fallen stone walls. Despite this, Cat Island is blessed with rolling hills and crowned by Como Hill (206ft) and its atmospheric hermitage, while the Atlantic or 'north' shore is crowned with miles of blush-colored beaches and dramatic cliffs.

Caves, blue holes, and freshwater lakes dot the island, known for a species of freshwater turtle or 'Peters,' which tragically are still eaten even though they are endangered. Also found here are harmless snakes, giant land crabs and bat-sized monarch moths (known locally as wealth-enhancing 'money bats').

The wall-diving accessed from the southwest coast is exceptional and there is some great hiking along old logging and plantation trails.

History

Following the American Revolution, Loyalists arrived with many African slaves and established around 40 cotton and cattle estates. Many homes still retain traditional African ovens for baking bread and teacakes, while the African culture of bush medicine and obeah are still powerful influences. Some of the islanders are said to be skilled witches, always happy to prescribe a homemade cure.

Since emancipation, things in a material sense haven't changed much for most of the population. Many depend upon selling their few tomatoes, onions, and pineapples (planted in limestone pot holes, where nutritious soils are aided by guano or bat excrement, gathered from caves for fertilizer) and on small stipends from the National Insurance Board.

Dangers & Annoyances

Many stretches of the roads are riddled with pot holes which can be a nasty surprise when driving. Some rental cars may be a little unreliable. There are no banks on Cat Island, and a limited choice of shops.

Getting There & Around

Most visitors fly into one of the two airports on Cat Island, while others arrive by mail boat. Taxis do meet the flights, but you will need a car to get around, so it's best to pre-book a rental car from the airport. Lodgings also provide free airport transfers.

SOUTH CAT ISLAND
New Bight

New Bight extends north to the tiny settlement of Smith Bay, where there's a **bat cave** amid the bush. A goat track leads from Smith Bay to **Pine Bay**, a good surf beach. Adventurous spirits can hike to **Turtle Cove**, a splendid cove on the Atlantic shore where marine turtles sometimes hang out.

New Bight originated as a free-slave settlement named Freetown. Much of the surrounding land has belonged to the Armbrister family since 1780.

There are several beautiful casuarina-lined beaches, including **Fernandez Bay**.

The **District Medical Officer** (☎ 242-342-3026) and **police** (☎ 242-342-3039) sit in the government administrative complex.

Father Jerome's **Mt Alvernia Hermitage** is a tiny blanched-stone church with a Gothic-style bell tower, small chapel, tiny cloister, and guest cell on Como Hill. Reached by a rock staircase on the hillside, the views from here are wonderful. A rough track to the hermitage, begins immediately south of the Government Administrative Complex on Queen's Hwy, north of the ruins of the old **Armbrister Plantation**.

The biggest happening of the year is August's **Cat Island Regatta**. Cat Islanders from far and wide head back to the island for the homemade sailboat races and land-based fun of Emancipation Day, while the four-day **Annual Rake 'n' Scrape Music Festival** in June is organized by Sidney Poitier's daughter, Pamela.

ACTIVITIES

There are several superb dive and snorkel sites down south at Morgan's Bay and Hawk's Nest Bay (p213) and . Dry Head, in shallow water close to shore here, also has prolific marine life.

Favored bonefishing spots include the flats of Joe's Sound Creek, a 20-minute boat ride south of Fernandez Bay, and Pigeon Creek, a 20-minute ride to the north.

Top Cat's Fishing Service (☎ 242-342-7003; Devil's Point) will tailor-make trips for you, priced accordingly.

Fernandez Bay Village (☎ 242-342-3043; www.fernandezbayvillage.com; Fernandez Bay) will arrange bonefishing (half-/full-day $195/280), bottom fishing (half-/full-day $250/400) and a short day fishing trip for children ($150).

FATHER JEROME *Christopher P Baker*

John Hawes – hermit and humanitarian – was born in England in 1876 to an upper-middle-class family. He was a visionary, prize-winning architect before entering theological college in 1901, preparing to becoming an Anglican minister.

Once ordained, he vowed to emulate the life of St Francis of Assisi and lived briefly as a tramp. In 1908 he came to the Bahamas and traveled around the islands to rebuild churches that had been destroyed by a hurricane, utilizing thick stone and Roman arches. Hawes offended local sensibilities, however, while preaching on Harbour Island. He asked the congregation why the Whites were sitting at the front and the Blacks at the back, when all men are created equal. 'The congregation nearly fainted with shock and I was rushed out of the church as quickly as possible,' Hawes recorded.

Between bouts of preaching, the eccentric Englishman worked as a mule driver in Canada, a fox terrier breeder, a cow puncher, and a sailor. In 1911 he converted to Catholicism and studied for the priesthood in Rome before moving to Australia to serve as a bush priest during the gold rush.

In 1939 Hawes came to Cat Island to live as a hermit and began work on his hermitage atop Como Hill, renamed Mt Alvernia after the site in Tuscany where St Francis received the wounds of the cross. Meanwhile, he lived in a cave amid snakes, tarantulas and crabs, and took unto himself the name Father Jerome.

He built four churches on Cat Island, as well as a medical clinic, convent, monastery, technical school, and other projects throughout the Bahamas, all featuring his trademark medievalist architectural motif, made of quarried rock.

Undoubtedly, locals regarded him as a saintly figure. Many climbed the monastery steps to ask for money 'in a state verging on destitution,' and none was denied. Locals of all denominations attended his sermons, although apparently he converted only five people to Catholicism.

He died in 1956 and was buried, as per his request, barefoot and without a casket in the cave that had once been his home.

You can also buy masks and snorkels here, while complimentary fins are leant to guests. A 13ft Boston Whaler can be hired at an hourly rate of $45.

SLEEPING & EATING

Gilbert's Inn & Car Rentals (☎ 242-342-3011; New Bight; s/d $80/95; P ⊠ ⊠) This two-story motel opposite the New Bight Food Market is very popular, so book ahead. Each spotless room has a bed with mirrored headboard (quite unnerving in the morning), good bathroom and TV. Car rentals are also possible.

Bridge Inn (☎ 242-342-3013; www.catislandbridge inn.com; r $88; P ⊠ ⊠) The gloomy rooms at this inn, just down the road from Gilbert's, are in need of maintenance and upgrading. Nevertheless, attractive native-stone walls and lofty wooden ceilings keep rooms cool, and come with a TV. A restaurant and bar serves Bahamian food and has a rocking jukebox.

Fernandez Bay Village (☎ 242-342-3043; www .fernandezbayvillage.com; Fernandez Bay; r $230; P ⊠) This quiet and attractive resort has fabulous beachside stone and timber rooms, with private open-air bathrooms overlooked by the sun and stars. An alfresco thatched bar and dining tables have a wonderful ocean backdrop and the offshore reefs are perfect for easy snorkeling. It offers free use of kayaks and canoes, while bicycles can be rented for $10 daily.

The **Blue Bird Restaurant & Bar** (☎ 242-342-3095), on Queen's Hwy near the Government adminstration complex, serves local fare, with mains from $8.

You can buy groceries from **Fernandez Bay Village** (☎ 242-342-3043) and at the well-stocked **New Bight Food Market** (☎ 242-342-3011).

The **Blue Restaurant & Bar** (☎ 242-342-3095) is a good place to play pool while the **First & Last Chance Bar** is known for its lively games of dominoes.

The modern **Hallover's Inn** has a pleasant bar with TV and pool table. The **Bridge Inn** sometimes hosts a local rake 'n' scrape band (percussion music made with household objects).

GETTING THERE & AWAY
Air
Please refer to p288 for information on international flights to the Bahamas.

Cat Island is served by two airports, **Arthur's Town Airport** (ATC; ☎ 242-354-2046), close to Arthur's Town, and **New Bight Airport** (TBI; ☎ 242-342-2016) at New Bight.

The following airlines fly between the Biminis and other Bahamian islands:

Bahamasair (UP; www.bahamasair.com) Freeport (☎ 242-352-8341); Nassau (☎ 242-377-5505) Hubs Freeport and Nassau.

Cat Island Air (☎ 242-377-3318; fax 242-377-3723) Hub Nassau.

Southern Air (☎ 242-367-2498; www.southernair charter.com) Hub Nassau; has flights from Deadman's Cay to Long Island.

Flights from Nassau to Cat Island ($75 one-way) operate twice weekly.

Boat
For mail boat information call the **Dockmaster's Office** (☎ 242-394-1237; Nassau) or check the **Bahamas Ministry of Tourism** (☎ 242-302-2034; www.bahamas.com) for updated information.

MV Lady Rosalind ($45 one way, 14 hrs) mail boat departs Nassau for Bennett's Harbour and Orange Creek on Thursday, returning on Saturday.

MV The Sea Hauler ($45 one-way, 12 hrs) mail boat departs Nassau for Smith Bay, Old Bight and New Bight on Tuesday, returning on Monday.

Marina
Many yachties hoist up in Fernandez Bay for food and water stores. Private boaters should check in with **Customs** (☎ 242-342-2016; fax 242-342-2041) in New Bight.

Hawk's Nest Resort & Marina (p214) has full service facilities, 28 slips, air-conditioned fish-cleaning sheds, accommodations and a private air-strip.

GETTING AROUND
Taxis do meet flights. Try **D&L Taxi Service** (☎ 242-354-5088; Wilson Bay). Your hotel will arrange a free airport pickup with advance notice. Car rental hire is about $90 per day. Insurance is not available.

Gilbert's Inn & Car Rental (☎ 242-342-3011; New Bight)

New Bight Service Station & Car Rental (☎ 242-342-3014)

Fernandez Bay Village (small boats per hr $45; captained larger boats per hr $90)

Old Bight
This slightly down-at-the-heels settlement straggles along the road for several miles. Plantation ruins lie to its east, shaded by trees festooned with Spanish moss.

Sitting on top of a little ridge beside the road is **St Francis Assisi Catholic Church**, a Father Jerome legacy. It has a Gothic facade topped by a cross and an engraving of St Francis with a flock of birds. Its interior has frescoes and sculptures. Mrs Burrows, across the road, has the key.

OBEAH   *Christopher P Baker*

Obeah is the practice of interacting with the spirit world. Part folklore, superstition, and magic ritual, it is deeply imbedded in the national psyche. Obeah (the word is Ashanti, from West Africa) was prohibited and severely suppressed by the Caribbean's colonial authorities.

The practice of obeah has diminished but still coexists alongside Christianity. Some faithful operate as 'balmists' who enact revenge or ensure successful romances. Firm believers sometimes heal, fall sick, or even die due to their faith in the power of obeah.

'Fixing' meanwhile is the deployment of a spell to protect property; it also means casting a spell or preventing a casting on or by other people. Many fixers ascribe their powers to God and place their 'fix' through directions 'derived' from the Bible.

Those trees with bottles dangling from them are not bearing strange tropical fruit – the bottles are spells to protect against thieves. Also stay clear of graveyards, which are littered with bottles for the spirits of the dead, who otherwise would bother the living for rum, according to local beliefs. Many houses, especially those north of New Bight, are also topped by spindles (like lightning rods) to ward off evil spirits.

On Cat Island the center of obeah is the Bight; on New Providence, it's the working-class area of Fox Hill, yet obeah is still legally banned, mostly due to pressure from the Baptist church.

Worth a visit, too, is **St Mary's Church**, fronted by an African flame tree. The church was a gift of the family of Blaney Balfour, the British governor who read the emancipation proclamation.

Armbrister Creek leads to a crystal-clear lake called 'Boiling Hole' that bubbles and churns under certain tidal conditions, fueling local fears that it is haunted by a monster. Baby sharks and rays can be seen cruising the sandy bottom. Birdlife also abounds in the mangrove estuary.

Don't ignore the wonderfully-named **Pass Me Not Bar** (242-342-4016; Queen's Hwy).

To explore the area, you can rent canoes at Fernandez Bay Village (p210).

Bain Town
The town lies along the shore south of the main road. There's a gas station east of town, halfway to Port Howe.

Look for **St John the Baptist Catholic Church**, another inspired Father Jerome creation, and **House Rebecca** built of local limestone and conch shells; owners Mr and Mrs Bain (242-342-5012) may invite you in to peek at the sitting room ceiling, made of 966 shells (they also offer accommodations).

Many believe that the 65ft-wide **Mermaid Hole** is inhabited by a mermaid. The lake is 10ft deep, but four holes in its bed lead into vast underwater chambers and passageways.

Newbold's Grocery Store lies just outside Bain Town.

Port Howe Area
The southeasternmost point of Cat Island, **Columbus Point**, lies 2 miles southeast of Port Howe at the south end of Churney Bay, but you will have to hike there from Port Howe. Cat Islanders cling to the belief – effectively debunked by recent evidence – that Columbus anchored here on October 12, 1492. Historians believe that 'Columba' (1495), the first Spanish settlement in the New World, was established to ship Lucayan Indians as slaves to Hispaniola.

Around 1670 a small group of English settlers arrived from Bermuda and established themselves here, earning a living as wreckers. Then, in 1783, 60 English Loyalists arrived here and established large nearby plantations.

Browse the **ruins** of some old fortresses and the **cemetery** on the west side of town.

The decrepit **Deveaux House** mansion was presented to Colonel Andrew Deveaux, who saved Nassau from Spanish occupation in 1783. Note the old slave quarters.

There's a **cave** worth exploring (it was once inhabited by Lucayan Indians, who left artifacts) and a **tidal geyser** in Churney Bay.

The diving off the south shore is superb; visit the **wall** which begins at 50ft and drops to 6000ft and **Tartar Bank**, covered by coral, sponges and sea fans. **Winding Bay** offers fabulous gorgonians and black coral.

Hotel Greenwood Beach Resort & Dive Centre offers one-/two-tank dives ($60/80), night dives ($65) and snorkeling (half-day $25), and hires out snorkel gear for $5.

There's good bonefishing in the bay off Port Howe, ask at the resort for recommended guides.

There's a **gas station** west of Port Howe, where you can rent a car from **Gilbert's Car Rental** in this area.

SLEEPING & EATING
Hotel Greenwood Beach Resort (242-342-3053; www.greenwoodbeachresort.com; Port Howe;) This isolated but affable resort lies on an 8-mile stretch of pink-sand beach. A bit tatty around the edges, it's great for families and divers, but not for those seeking a pristine idyll. Pleasant, light rooms are not screened (bring the mosquito spray), and facilities include a TV, lounge-cum-dining-room and bar (serving European and Bahamian fare) and dive shop. Kayaks and bicycles are complimentary for guests.

House Kolibri (/fax 242-342-305; Port Howe; weekly $1500;) This spacious three-bed house sits on a hill looking towards the ocean. Simple rooms are tiled and airy, although the furnishings are basic and pretty sparse.

Morgan's Bay to Hawk's Nest Creek
A badly potholed road leads west from the Deep South Roundabout, heading to **Devil's Point**, near **McQueen's** (founded in the 18th century by a Scottish loyalist, Alexander McQueen) and **Hawk's Nest**, a 15-mile drive from Deep South Roundabout.

There are several superb dive and snorkel sites locally including **Morgan's Bay**. **Dry Head**, close to shore has one of the healthiest and most-populated shallow reefs in the Bahamas. **Devil's Point** has large formations of elkhorn and staghorn, tube sponges, and brain coral, while the flats and inland tidal creeks at Hawk's Nest are crowded with bonefish.

Hawk's Nest Resort & Marina (☎ 242-342-7050; VHF Channel 16; www.hawks-nest.com; s/d $130/145; P ✕ ⧓ ⧓) This is a friendly and pristine resort, marina and dive operation. Spotless, cheerful and comfortable rooms all offer ocean views and patios. A bar and restaurant offers a range of pleasing dishes. Billiards, darts and movies occupy barflies, while ocean-side hammocks and the glorious beach keep everyone happy.

A private 1380yd hard-surface airstrip with tie-downs, deep-water marina with full services and some good packages make this a great option.

Contact the resort for tailor-made boating, fishing and diving trips; a top-notch small diving operation offers one-/two-tank dives ($60/80) and PADI Divemaster qualifications ($700), and hires snorkel ($5) and diving ($30) gear.

NORTH CAT ISLAND

The further north you explore, the more obvious is the poverty. Villages contain little more than dilapidated houses, shacks and hurricane-damaged buildings. Trees lie where they fell.

Knowles to Industrious Hill

Tumbledown slave-era homes dot the west shore and little boats lie upturned beneath spread-fingered palms.

Knowles, 8 miles north of New Bight, is the first of a half-dozen small settlements. There is the tiny **Columbus World Centre Museum** which tells the island history, **Holy Redeemer Catholic Church** and the **Cat Island Library**. The **Knowles Media Center** (☎ 242-342-6031) has Internet access, while **Bachelor's Restaurant** (☎ 242-342-6014; Knowles) is good for snacks.

The scenery is splendid at **Tea Bay** and the **Cove**. Endemic freshwater turtles inhabit the inland lakes and ponds, and there's a picturesque beach at **Alligator Bay**.

Issie's Convenient Store (☎ 242-342-6016) sells groceries.

Roker's Bluff

Also known as 'Zanicle,' Roker's Bluff was founded by Scottish settlers and many locals have Scottish surnames. A dirt road leads a mile northwest to beautiful **Pigeon Cay Beach**.

Pigeon Cay Beach Club (☎ 242-354-5084; www.pigeoncay-bahamas.com; r $140; P ✕ ⧓) Overlooking the beach, these self-contained charming cabanas have comfortable, colorful furnishings. An adjacent beach bar and barbecue is perfect for sunset dining. The club runs island tours ($60 to $100), fishing trips (half-day $250), rents Hobiecats (small boats) and dinghies (full-day $25). There are also snorkel gear, kayaks, bicycles and canoes for hire.

The **Island Shopping Centre** sells groceries and produce.

Bennett's Harbour

The settlement sprawls beneath blazing-colored flame trees that continue down to a picturesque sheltered **cove**, once favored by pirates and salt traders.

Little San Salvador island has a lagoon, placid iguanas and plenty of seabirds.

Sammy T's Beach Resort (☎ 242-354-6010; sam mytbahamas@direcway.com; r $225; P ✕ ⧓ ⧓) This classy, intimate resort has charming small cabanas with upmarket Caribbean furnishings and Bahamian artworks. Enjoy walk-off-the beach snorkeling, a beachside bar and seafood dishes. There are complimentary bicycles, kayaks and shuffle-boards.

Bennett's Harbour Guest Cottages (US ☎ 813-932-1152; per week $800; P ✕ ⧓) Ask locally about renting these attractive and affordable cottages made from coral limestone, stone and hardwood (retrieved from a sunken galleon). Cottages include romantic **Wilson Bay** which sits on a rock ledge overlooking the sea; perfect for those seeking a secluded hideaway. A van can be rented and boats are available.

Also recommended are the rooms at **Pompey Rock Villas** (☎ 242-354-6003; r $85; P ✕ ⧓) overlooking the shore.

You can buy foodstuffs at **Len's Grocery**.

See the Getting There & Away p212 for travel information.

Dumfries

Named by Scottish loyalist settlers, Dumfries sits on a salt lake separated from the sea by a drinking bar. A mile-long track leads from here to **Great Crown Caves**, a vast cave system, and a **loyalist mansion**, surrounded by stately silk cotton trees.

Gaitor's Hole is reached by a rough mile-long track running east from Dumfries. It

---

BEASTS IN THE BLUE HOLES *Christopher P Baker*

Many of Cat Island's saltwater blue holes are thought to be the home of awesome beasts, including an island equivalent of the Loch Ness Monster.

The monster of Big Blue Hole, just off Dickies Rd near Orange Creek, is said to have an appetite for horses. Hence some horses that die on Cat Island are tipped into the lake! (Objects are sucked out of blue holes by strong tidal flows through subterranean passages that link the holes to the sea. And though freshwater lakes are less feared, at least one – Mermaid Hole (p213) – is said to be the home of a mermaid; another has a no less seductive merman.

Although Cat Island fishermen will readily travel many miles offshore, many of these same men cannot, supposedly, be induced to travel even 50ft on these lakes.

---

is often a deep purple color, due to a dense bacterial population. Local folklore has a young island girl disappearing while visiting the hole to do laundry. Apparently she later reappeared; blissful and pregnant. Her father and brother in reprise, killed the hole's resident; the purported father. The girl later gave birth to a baby merman.

Arthur's Town

The island's second-largest settlement centers on Symonette Sq. The prim **St Andrews Anglican Church** (1870s) and other historic buildings project a faded grandeur.

The hamlet's claim to fame is that it was the boyhood home of Academy Award winner Sir Sidney Poitier.

There's a **Government Medical Clinic** (☎ 242-354-4050) and **police** (☎ 242-354-2046) here.

Arthur's Town hosts a **heritage festival** during the first weekend in May.

Cookie Bakery sells breads, pineapple and coconut tarts, plus burgers, fish and chips, and other snacks. For lunch and dinner also try **Nancy's Takeaway** (☎ 242-354-2024), **Da Smokepot** (☎ 242-354-2077) and **Hard Rock Oasis** (☎ 242-342-7050), while **Club Boggy Pond** (☎ 242-354-2215) has a pool table and TV.

Arthur's Town has a small airport. See Getting There & Away p212 for travel information.

Orange Creek

There's good bonefishing in the mouth of Orange Creek, where it spills onto a beach. Call **Willard Cleare** (☎ 242-354-4143), local bonefishing guide.

The turquoise waters offshore are superb snorkeling sites, with exquisite fan-coral formations.

From the head of Orange Creek, a trail leads west half a mile to the popular **Port Royal Beach**. Another leads north past **Oyster Lake** (good for spotting ducks and cormorants) and east to **Man O' War Point Beach**, also perfect for snorkeling.

A third track leads east from the head of Orange Creek to **Glass Hill** (162ft), where you'll have beautiful views.

Dickie's Rd runs east to **Griffin Bat Cave**, once home to slaves who built walls and windows into the entrance and to a series of blue holes.

Orange Creek Inn (☎ 242-354-4110; orangecreek inn@yahoo.com; r without/with air-con $70/80; P X R) Sitting above the creek and a good grocery store, this inn has spacious and well-maintained rooms. They are modestly furnished and a bit stuffy; some have kitchenettes and air-con. There's also a TV lounge and a laundry. You can hire cars here and there's a gas station in town.

SAN SALVADOR

pop 1028

Tiny San Salvador (nicknamed 'San Sal') 200 miles southeast of Nassau, is the nation's outermost island. This 12-mile speck is ringed by superb reefs, and over 40 dive sites lie within 30 minutes of the shore, with even more near Rum Cay and Conception Island. Divers rejoice in the crystalline water that gives visibility over an amazing 200ft, while 30 miles of gorgeous beaches are wonderful for walks and playing in the shallows.

Acres of mangroves and saltwater lakes give rise to some inaccessible areas inland that attract wildlife, mosquitos (unfortunately), and birds. It's a 1½-hour drive, or five-hour bicycle ride to circumnavigate the island along Queen's Hwy, which takes in Cockburn Town (p217) and United Estates

SAN SALVADOR

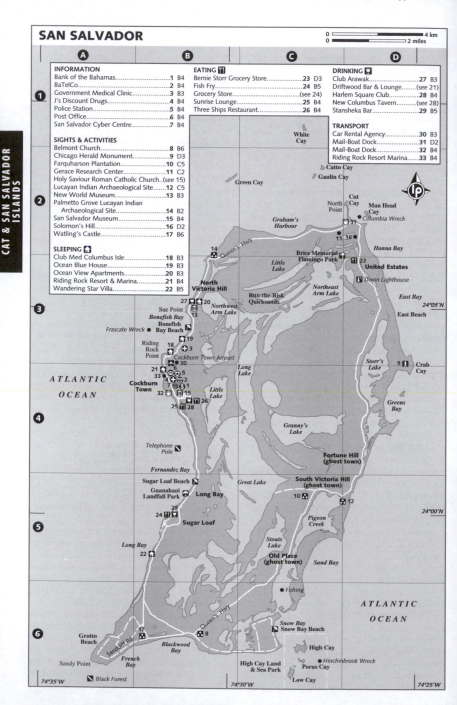

0 ——————— 4 km
0 ——————— 2 miles

CAT & SAN SALVADOR ISLANDS

INFORMATION
Bank of the Bahamas...........................1 B4
BaTelCo..2 B4
Government Medical Clinic..................3 B3
J's Discount Drugs..............................4 B4
Police Station......................................5 B4
Post Office..6 B4
San Salvador Cyber Centre................7 B4

SIGHTS & ACTIVITIES
Belmont Church...................................8 B6
Chicago Herald Monument.................9 D3
Farquharson Plantation.....................10 C5
Gerace Research Center....................11 C2
Holy Saviour Roman Catholic Church..(see 15)
Lucayan Indian Archaeological Site...12 C5
New World Museum..........................13 B3
Palmetto Grove Lucayan Indian
   Archaeological Site.......................14 B2
San Salvador Museum.......................15 B4
Solomon's Hill...................................16 D2
Watling's Castle.................................17 B6

SLEEPING
Club Med Columbus Isle....................18 B3
Ocean Blue House.............................19 B3
Ocean View Apartments....................20 B3
Riding Rock Resort & Marina............21 B4
Wandering Star Villa.........................22 B5

EATING
Bernie Storr Grocery Store................23 D3
Fish Fry...24 B5
Grocery Store..............................(see 24)
Sunrise Lounge.................................25 B4
Three Ships Restaurant.....................26 B4

DRINKING
Club Arawak.....................................27 B3
Driftwood Bar & Lounge..............(see 21)
Harlem Square Club.........................28 B4
New Columbus Tavern...............(see 28)
Stansheka Bar...................................29 B5

TRANSPORT
Car Rental Agency............................30 B3
Mail-Boat Dock................................31 D2
Mail-Boat Dock................................32 B4
Riding Rock Resort Marina...............33 B4

White Cay

Catto Cay

Green Cay

Gaulin Cay

North Point

Cut Cay

Man Head Cay

Columbia Wreck

Graham's Harbour

Hanna Bay

Brice Memorial Flamingo Park

United Estates

Dixon Lighthouse

Little Lake

Northeast Arm Lake

Run-the-Risk Quicksands

East Bay

24°05'N

East Beach

North Victoria Hill

Northwest Arm Lake

Suc Point

Bonefish Bay

Bonefish Bay Beach

Frascate Wreck

Riding Rock Point

Cockburn Town Airport

Long Lake

Storr's Lake

Crab Cay

ATLANTIC OCEAN

Cockburn Town

Little Lake

Greens Bay

Granny's Lake

Telephone Pole

Fernandez Bay

Fortune Hill (ghost town)

Sugar Loaf Beach

Great Lake

South Victoria Hill (ghost town)

Guanahani Landfall Park

Long Bay

Sugar Loaf

Pigeon Creek

24°00'N

Long Bay

Stouts Lake

Old Place (ghost town)

Sand Bay

Fishing

ATLANTIC OCEAN

Grotto Beach

Sandcliff Rd

Queen's Hwy

Blackwood Bay

Snow Bay
Snow Bay Beach

High Cay

Sandy Point

French Bay

High Cay Land & Sea Park

Hinchinbrook Wreck

Porus Cay

Black Forest

Low Cay

74°35'W

74°30'W

74°25'W

Queen's Hwy

(p219); the main villages. Decaying, abandoned settlements illustrate the economic hardships of inhabiting these islands.

San Sal offers excellent bird watching. Ospreys or 'chicken hawks' are everywhere. The cays off the north shore are favored by boobies and other seabirds. Egrets and herons pick for food in the brine pools. Besides diving and bird-watching, there's not much to do.

Rum Cay (p220), a small isle with beautiful beaches, lies 25 miles to San Salvador's southwest, while uninhabited Conception Island (p220) is a protected park northwest of Rum Cay.

History

San Salvador, meaning 'holy savior,' was bestowed by Christopher Columbus on the first land he sighted in 1492. There is little evidence to support the entrenched claim that Columbus first landed here, a fact accepted as religiously as was the belief Columbus set out to disprove, that the earth was flat.

Recent discoveries of Spanish artifacts are said to support the landfall claim, effectively debunked by *National Geographic* in 1986 which convincingly concluded that Columbus first landed at Samana Cay. However, in 1989 yachtsman Robin Knox-Johnson retraced Columbus' route using 15th-century instruments and ended up at…San Salvador. Take your pick!

Dangers & Annoyances

Industrial strength bug spray is in order at dusk and dawn, and a warning: beaches are infested with *no see 'ums,* the vicious sand flies so tiny that you never see them, but with appetites that would embarrass a fast-food chain. Try the mariners' solution; Avon Skin So Soft.

Also be careful if you explore the brush areas. There are quick sands as well as poisonwood and manchineel trees.

Getting There & Around

Most visitors fly into Cockburn Town Airport, a spit away from the town itself, while others arrive by mail boat. There are taxis, but you may avail yourself of airport transfers courtesy of your lodgings. Those planning to explore the island should collect a rental car at the airport.

COCKBURN TOWN

San Sal's major settlement and administrative center, midway down the west coast, is a motley affair comprising two parallel roads crisscrossed by five narrow lanes. Tumbledown stone cottages and clapboard shacks in faded pastels mingle with new, often stylish houses squatting in unkempt yards picked at by goats and cockerels.

A 12ft plastic iguana guards the entrance to town where locals gather under the 'Lazy Tree,' a gnarled almond tree whose shade is preferred for taking it easy.

Information

Bank of the Bahamas (☎ 242-331-2237;
🕒 9am-3pm Fri)
BaTelCo (☎ 242-331-2571)
Government Medical Clinic (☎ 242-331-2105;
🕒 9am-5:30pm Mon-Fri)
J's Discount Drugs (☎ 242-331-2570)
Police (☎ 242-331-2010) Also the island's emergency number.
Post office (☎ 242-331-2232)
San Salvador Cyber Centre (☎ 242-331-2925)

Sights & Activities

The small **San Salvador Museum,** housed in the old jail, has displays of Lucayan Indian remains and Columbus' conquest of the New World. Note the ceramic mural of Columbus. Ask for a key from the BaTelCo office.

The pretty pink **Holy Saviour Roman Catholic Church** (1992) was established by the Catholic Archdiocese of Nassau.

San Salvador has really fantastic diving; some of the best in the Bahamas. There are more than 20 miles of vertical walls, which begin as little as 40ft below the surface.

Try some of these dive sites; **Frascate**, a 261ft-long ship sunk in 1902 lies just 20ft down. Also **Rum Cay Wall**, which drops from 40ft to eternity. Nearby are remains of the **HMS Conqueror**, a 19th-century British steam-powered battleship. **Telephone Pole**, begins at 45ft. At 100ft a wall decorated with large purple sponges and plate coral is also attractive to large pelagics.

Snorkel sites include **Flower Gardens**, where scattered coral heads feature caves for exploring, and **Natural Bridges**, where a reef formation has natural arches. There's also **Sandy Point**, one of the best sites, and **Staghorn Reef**, where you'll find star and staghorn corals aplenty, as well as heaps of other marine life.

CAT & SAN SALVADOR ISLANDS

Riding Rock Resort & Marina (below) offer one-, two- and three-tank dives ($50/70/90), a special deal of 18 dives in six days ($360) and snorkeling ($20). This very well-reputed outfit is popular with divers.

Island Venture Fishing Charters (☎ 242-331-2306) run a deep-sea fishing trips (half-/full-day $500/800) for a maximum of four people.

Tours

Both lodgings listed below also offer tours, but head for Lagoon Tours first – they focus on the island's environment and beauty, and they seem to really know their stuff.

Lagoon Tours (☎ 242-359-4520; www.lagoontours bahamas.com) runs guided walks and combined hiking and kayaking tours with informed and enthusiastic guides. Try the fascinating trip that takes in bush-medicine plants, an old plantation and lake-kayaking ($70), a bird-watching leisure hike through Watling's Castle to spot thrush, warblers, osprey and herons (prices upon application), and lagoon tours ($80) with a peaceful boat-ride along beaches to beautiful lagoons and a visit to the iguanas of Low Cay.

Riding Rock Resort & Marina (below) offer excursions to the Exumas and the Low and High Cays to see iguanas and osprey.

Sleeping & Eating

Riding Rock Resort & Marina (☎ 242-331-2631; www.ridingrock.com; Cockburn Town; standard/ocean-view $114/140; P ⊠ ⊠ ⊠) This friendly and modern resort is loved by divers, and is very popular; book ahead! Sparkling white rooms with tiled floors are spotlessly clean and have either beach or poolside views. There's a nearby beach, tennis court, convivial beach-side bar and restaurant serving scrumptious Bahamian and US cuisine (advise ahead if you're vegetarian). Diving trips and tours are on offer, as are rental cars ($85) and bicycles (half-/full-day $6.50/10).

Wandering Star Villa (per week $990; P ⊠) Ask locally about renting this two-bedroom informal blue bungalow which sits right on the beach and sleeps four. It's pet-friendly and comes with all mod-cons (including music and bicycles); a real home away from home.

Club Med Columbus Isle (☎ 242-331-2000; www .come2clubmed.com/columbus_isle.htm; r per week $1665; P ⊠ ⊠ ⊠) This huge beachside resort is definitely geared towards French guests who want to party. The low-slung resort

displays exotic antique art and units have custom-fashioned furniture and mod-cons. Tennis courts, a fitness center, water sports and other recreational activities including diving trips are on offer, and there's much lively nocturnal entertainment.

Three Ships Restaurant (☎ 242-331-2787; mains $10-18; ☻ breakfast, lunch & dinner, closed Sun) This clean and tidy place serves boil' fish and grits for breakfast, along with meat and fish burgers.

Sunrise Lounge (Queen's Hwy) This place south of town also serves meat and fish burgers and fried chicken, as does the **Friday Fish Fry** (☎ 242-331-2051) at Long Bay and **New Columbus Tavern** (☎ 242-331-2788).

For nightlife, head to the **Driftwood Bar & Lounge** (located at Riding Rock Resort, left), exhibiting driftwood autographed by visitors from the '50s. Now visitors leave behind business cards and T-shirts. Another fave is the **Harlem Square Club** (☎ 242-331-2777), which serves traditional food, has rap and dance nights on weekends, and lots of clattering dominoes during the day.

Buy groceries at **Bernie Storr Grocery Store** (☎ 242-331-2512; United Estates).

Getting There & Away

AIR

See p288 for information on international flights to the Bahamas.

San Salvador is served by **Cockburn Town Airport** (ZSA; ☎ 242-331-2919), adjacent to town.

The following airlines fly between the Biminis and other Bahamian islands.

Bahamasair (UP; www.bahamasair.com) Freeport (☎ 242-352-8341); Nassau (☎ 242-377-5505) Hubs Freeport and Nassau.

Cat Island Air (☎ 242-377-3318; fax 242-377-3723); Hub Nassau.

Southern Air (☎ 242-367-2498; www.southernair charter.com) Hub Nassau.

Flights from Nassau to San Salvador Island ($80, one-way) operates three times a week.

BOAT

Call the **Dockmaster's Office** (☎ 242-394-1237, Nassau) and check the **Bahamas Ministry of Tourism** (☎ 242-302-2034; www.bahamas.com) for the latest schedules and prices.

MV Lady Francis ($45, 18 hours) mail boat departs Nassau for San Salvador and Rum Cay on Tuesday, returning on Sunday.

Marina

Boaters and pilots arriving from abroad must clear **Immigration** (☎ 242-331-2100) in Cockburn Town.

Riding Rock Resort & Marina (opposite) has 11 busy slips and facilities; book ahead.

Getting Around

Riding Rock Resort & Marina (opposite) provides complimentary transport to and from the airport for its guests, while Club Med Columbus Isle (opposite) charge $10.

Cars can be hired for about $80 per day, and the rental agencies are based in Cockburn Town. Riding Rock Resort & Marina hires bicycles for $6.50/10 per day and cars for $85 per day. For cars, also try **C&S Car Rental** (☎ 242-331-2714) and **D&W Rent-a-Car** (☎ 242-331-2184).

For taxi services, try **Livingstone Williams Taxis** (☎ 242-331-2025).

NORTHWEST COAST

The **Gerace Research Center** (☎ 242-331-2520; www.geraceresearchcenter.com; Graham's Harbour) primarily hosts scientific conferences and field courses for student groups. Scientists also run a coral reef monitoring project. Visitors are welcome.

Checkout the public and fab **Bonefish Bay Beach**, via North Victoria Hill, and the tiny **New World Museum**, displaying Lucayan Indian artifacts.

Graham's Harbour is good for swimming. A **Columbus Day Homecoming** and party is traditionally held here on Discovery Day (October 12) along with the annual **Columbus Bay Regatta**. The **Columbia**, wrecked in 1980, lies off North Point.

Elderhostel (US ☎ 877-426-8056; www.elderhostel.org) offers 12-day springtime geographical study trips of San Salvador for lively folks over 60 years old. Check with the organization for rates.

Earthwatch (US ☎ 978-461-0081; www.earthwatch.org) houses volunteers for its program to preserve San Sal's reef at the Gerace Research Center. It needs volunteer divers. You'll snorkel four or five hours daily and make observations about coral health. It has three trips annually (from $1895).

Cliff Fernandez (☎ 242-331-2676; ✗) rents out three modern air-con cottages. Or you can rent the three-bedroom **Ocean Blue House** (☎ /fax 242-331-2306; sansal.house@wanadoo.fr;

r per day/week $190/1170; P ✗ ✗) on a rocky perch about a mile north of Club Med. The house has an exquisitely decorated lounge with cathedral ceiling, a vast porch and a 19ft fishing boat (Floyd, the skipper, can take you fishing or lobstering).

Club Arawak, next to the New World Museum, serves the usual fried chicken and fish dishes and does double duty as the local nightspot.

NORTHEAST COAST

The east shore is lined with lonesome beaches, including the rosy-pink 5-mile-long **East Beach**.

In **United Estates** (locally called 'U-E'), look for the blue house, **Solomon's Hill**, decorated with dozens of plastic buoys.

U-E is pinned by the magnificent old **Dixon Lighthouse** (☽ 9am-noon & 2-5pm). From the balcony, there is a fabulous panoramic view of the entire island.

The weather-worn **Chicago Herald Monument** to Columbus stands at the south end of East Bay.

SOUTHEAST COAST

This area was once the center of cotton and citrus plantations. The most notable ruins are **Farquharson Plantation** (1820s).

Pigeon Creek is an 8-mile-long ecological treasure (baby sharks swim here) that opens to the ocean at **Snow Bay**. There's an unmarked **Lucayan Indian archaeological site** at the northern end of Pigeon Creek.

Don't miss breathtakingly beautiful **Snow Bay Beach** where you can be alone with the gentle lapping of the waves and the cry of sea birds. The road runs inland from the shore for most of the way, passing a series of smelly salt lakes.

High Cay Land & Sea Park protects High Cay, Porus Cay and Low Cay, which are important nesting sites for ospreys, boobies and other seabirds. Endangered iguanas also cling to Low Cay. The reefs have claimed several ships, notably the **Hinchinbrook** (1913), a wreck that is much favored by scuba divers.

SOUTHWEST COAST

Fernandez Bay and Long Bay are lined by beautiful **Sugar Loaf Beach** while the peninsula's leeward shore is fringed by beautiful **Grotto Beach** and several caves.

Founded by a Loyalist settler, and named for the pirate; **Watling's Castle** ruins sit atop a hill with good sea views.

There's a **grocery store** and the **Stansheka Bar** (Queen's Hwy) in Sugar Loaf, half a mile south of Guanahani Landfall Park.

RUM CAY

This 10-mile-long isle is lined by stunning beaches and the entire isle is fringed with coral. The **HMS Conqueror** (1861), a 101-gun British man o' war, sank in 30ft of water off Signal Point.

The only settlement is **Port Nelson.** The rest of the isle is a virtual wilderness of rolling hills browsed by feral cattle and donkeys.

There's a **post office**, **police station** (☎ 242-331-2807) and **BaTelCo office** (☎ 242-331-2871) in Port Nelson. For lodgings call Constable Ted Bain and Hermie at **Ocean View Restaurant** (☎ 242-331-2818), which is recommended for basic Bahamian fare. Call ahead on VHF Channel 16 for dinner reservations.

Two Sisters Take-A-Way sells fresh bread and chicken, and there's **Last Chance Convenience Store** (☎ 242-331-2806; King St). There is also **police** and **BalTelCo office** (☎ 242-331-2871).

See p218 for details of mail-boat stops at the cay.

CONCEPTION ISLAND

This 3-mile-long, uninhabited, speck on the map is rimmed with reefs. It is approximately 25 miles southeast of Cat Island and it's protected as the **Conception Island National Park** by the Bahamas National Trust (p74).

The island is an important nesting site for endangered green turtles as well as migratory seabirds, particularly boobies, which give their name to **Booby Cay**, east of the island.

Divers who enjoy deep dives will enjoy ferreting around the Black Forest Wreck spotting turtles, hammerhead sharks and eagle rays.

Southern Bahamas

Head for Long Island, the Crooked Island District and the Inaguas, and you will be surprised and delighted. There are clear sparkling seas, huge blue holes and perfect reefs for snorkeling and diving. Deserted beaches and striking azure bays invite days of splashing around in the sea, picnics and walks along sugar-soft sands. Vast scrub and forested lands entice all manner of birds, and occasional hikers and bird-watchers to wander in the wilderness.

The Crooked and Acklin Islands are renowned for Christopher Columbus' visit. He named Crooked the 'Fragrant Island,' where the aromas of herb and Cascarilla bark impregnate the air (and flavor Campari's liquor). Inagua's parklands are striking, with flying pink clouds of flamingos emerging at dusk and dawn. The age-old Bahamian industry of 'white gold' production is alive and well on this island, where huge hills of glittering salt are exported worldwide.

Long Island, the most developed and populated island of this group is dotted with pretty villages, which are accentuated by vivid flowering shrubs. Roadside schools fill with chattering, waving and giggling children during lesson breaks. Clusters of immaculate tiny Gothic churches gleam in the sunlight, marking settlements across the island.

This is a charming and happy place to visit and explore. Discover ancient Arawak drawings and blinking bats in a string of covert caves or the faded grandeur of old plantation ruins. Venture into genial local eateries and bars for a chat, beer and a bite of crispy fish, or down bumpy sideroads to those tranquil bays of pleasure.

SOUTHERN BAHAMAS

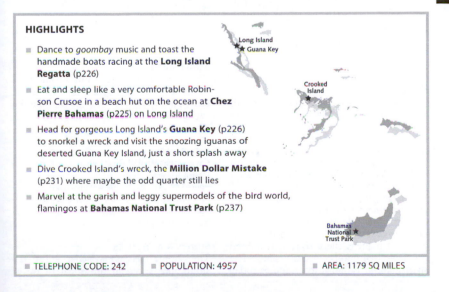

HIGHLIGHTS

- Dance to *goombay* music and toast the handmade boats racing at the **Long Island Regatta** (p226)

- Eat and sleep like a very comfortable Robinson Crusoe in a beach hut on the ocean at **Chez Pierre Bahamas** (p225) on Long Island

- Head for gorgeous Long Island's **Guana Key** (p226) to snorkel a wreck and visit the snoozing iguanas of deserted Guana Key Island, just a short splash away

- Dive Crooked Island's wreck, the **Million Dollar Mistake** (p231) where maybe the odd quarter still lies

- Marvel at the garish and leggy supermodels of the bird world, flamingos at **Bahamas National Trust Park** (p237)

Long Island
★ Guana Key

Crooked Island ★

Bahamas National ★ Trust Park

| ▪ TELEPHONE CODE: 242 | ▪ POPULATION: 4957 | ▪ AREA: 1179 SQ MILES |

LONG ISLAND

pop 2978

This is one of the prettiest Family Islands; a 2-mile wide narrow strip that stretches for 60 miles. Follow the solitary road, the Queen's Hwy past plantation ruins, stunning white and sky-blue Gothic churches, lush greenery, pretty villages brimming with bougainvillea and pastel-colored schoolyards full of curious and happy children.

You'll also come to a myriad of magnificent bays, blue holes, and miles and miles of beach. The island's inhabitants live in about 35 settlements, growing bananas and rows of corn, along with vegetables and pineapples. On the east shore, Atlantic rollers crash against dramatic cliffs and offshore reefs, while the west coast consists of a string of shallow bays. In late spring hundreds of yellow butterflies appear.

The northern tip of the island is heralded by a monument to Columbus, while caves that once were home to the Lucayans and pirates are now occupied by families of myopic bats.

This pristine diving paradise has untapped treasures, such as the newly discovered Neuritis Wall that drops off the Bahamas Banks, and the fast-paced action of Shark Reef is justifiably acclaimed. For those who prefer to eat fish rather than commune with them, the island also has top fishing year-round.

The highlight of the island's festivities is May's Long Island Regatta, held at Salt Pond.

History

The Lucayan Indian caves (they called this island Yuma) have yielded *duhos* (wooden seats) that archaeologists believe suggest chieftainship and ceremony, and *zemi* figurines bearing religious connotations. To the south, the island – Columbus' 'Fernandina' – ends at Cape Verde, where Columbus supposedly anchored on October 24, 1492.

A large percentage of Bahamians on the island are descendants of the 18th-century Loyalists. The colonists established a plantation system as viable as any in the archipelago. Uniquely, sheep-rearing remained profitable well into last century, and a few sheep remain. Farming, too, endures today

in large groves of bananas and rows of corn (especially around Deadman's Cay), in stock-rearing, and in cultivation of vegetables and pineapples in limestone potholes. You still can see wooden sailing dinghies being made by hand in fishing villages on the island.

Getting There & Away

Visitors fly to Stella Maris Airport at the northern end of the island or Deadman's Cay Airport in the middle, or take the mail boat from Nassau to Clarence Town, Deadman's Cay, Salt Pond and Seymours.

Getting Around

You'll need your own transport if you want to explore the island. Car hire companies are based at Deadman's Cay Airport (look left, right and up before crossing the plane's landing strip to reach the car rental places), and north of the island towards Stella Maris Resort & Marina. Car insurance is not generally on offer.

Remember when receiving directions that everyone here says 'up south' and 'down north,' the opposite of what you might expect.

NORTH LONG ISLAND

The north of the island is certainly worth exploring, from the Columbus Memorial to the vivid jade-colored seas which proffer great snorkeling and diving. Take insect spray – mosquitoes and sand flies up this end of the island get pretty hungry at dawn and dusk.

Stella Maris

The upscale residential community of Stella Maris stretches for about a mile along the coast amid palms and scrub. Dominating the area is the Stella Maris Resort Club & Marina (p224).

INFORMATION

Government Medical Clinic (☎ 242-338-8488) Located at Simms.
Police (☎ 242-338-2222; Stella Maris Airport)
Post office (☎ 242-338-2010; Stella Maris Airport)
Scotiabank (☎ 242-338-2057; ◷ 9:30am-1pm Mon-Thu, 9am-5pm Fri)

SIGHTS & ACTIVITIES

The remote **Columbus Memorial**, a 15ft-tall stone obelisk, sits at the northern tip of

LONG ISLAND

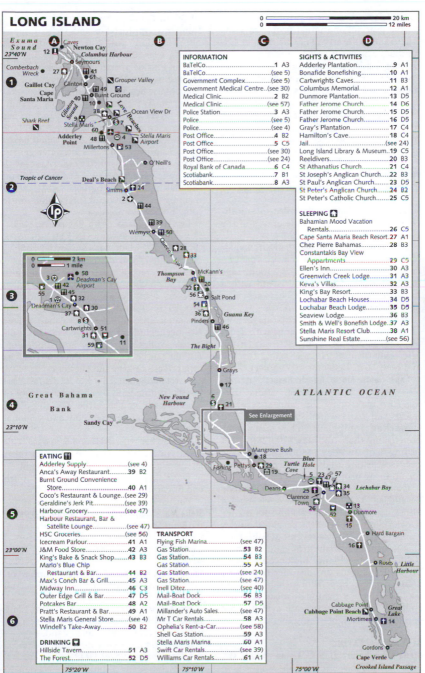

0 ──────── 20 km
0 ──────── 12 miles

SOUTHERN BAHAMAS

INFORMATION
BaTelCo.................................1 A3
BaTelCo................................(see 5)
Government Complex.............(see 5)
Government Medical Centre..(see 30)
Medical Clinic........................2 B2
Medical Clinic.......................(see 57)
Police Station.........................3 A3
Police...................................(see 5)
Police...................................(see 4)
Post Office.............................4 B2
Post Office.............................5 C5
Post Office...........................(see 30)
Post Office...........................(see 24)
Royal Bank of Canada.............6 C4
Scotiabank.............................7 B1
Scotiabank.............................8 A3

SIGHTS & ACTIVITIES
Adderley Plantation..................9 A1
Bonafide Bonefishing..............10 A1
Cartwrights Caves...................11 B3
Columbus Memorial................12 A1
Dunmore Plantation................13 D5
Father Jerome Church..............14 D6
Father Jerome Church..............15 D5
Father Jerome Church..............16 D5
Gray's Plantation...................(see 4)
Hamilton's Cave.....................17 C4
Jail......................................(see 24)
Long Island Library & Museum..19 C5
Reeldivers.............................20 B3
St Athanatius Church..............21 C4
St Joseph's Anglican Church....22 B3
St Paul's Anglican Church.......23 D5
St Peter's Anglican Church......24 B2
St Peter's Catholic Church.......25 C5

SLEEPING
Bahamian Mood Vacation
  Rentals...............................26 C5
Cape Santa Maria Beach Resort.27 A1
Chez Pierre Bahamas...............28 B3
Constantakis Bay View
  Appartments.......................29 C5
Ellen's Inn.............................30 A3
Greenwich Creek Lodge..........31 A3
Keva's Villas..........................32 A3
King's Bay Resort...................33 B3
Lochabar Beach Houses...........34 D5
Lochabar Beach Lodge............35 D5
Seaview Lodge.......................36 B3
Smith & Well's Bonefish Lodge.37 A3
Stella Maris Resort Club...........38 A1
Sunshine Real Estate..............(see 56)

EATING
Adderley Supply....................(see 4)
Anca's Away Restaurant.........39 B2
Burnt Ground Convenience
  Store.................................40 A1
Coco's Restaurant & Lounge..(see 29)
Geraldine's Jerk Pit................(see 39)
Harbour Grocery...................(see 47)
Harbour Restaurant, Bar &
  Satellite Lounge.................(see 47)
HSC Groceries.......................(see 56)
Icecream Parlour....................41 A1
J&M Food Store.....................42 A3
King's Bake & Snack Shop......43 B3
Marlo's Blue Chip
  Restaurant & Bar................44 B2
Max's Conch Bar & Grill.........45 A3
Midway Inn..........................46 C3
Outer Edge Grill & Bar...........47 D5
Potcakes Bar.........................48 A2
Pratt's Restaurant & Bar.........49 A1
Stella Maris General Store......(see 4)
Windell's Take-Away..............50 B2

DRINKING
Hillside Tavern......................51 A3
The Forest.............................52 D5

TRANSPORT
Flying Fish Marina.................(see 47)
Gas Station...........................53 B2
Gas Station...........................54 B3
Gas Station...........................55 A3
Gas Station..........................(see 24)
Gas Station..........................(see 47)
Inell Ditez............................(see 40)
Mail-Boat Dock.....................56 B3
Mail-Boat Dock.....................57 D5
Millander's Auto Sales...........(see 47)
Mr T Car Rentals...................58 A3
Ophelia's Rent-a-Car.............(see 58)
Shell Gas Station...................59 A3
Stella Maris Marina................60 A1
Swift Car Rentals..................(see 39)
Williams Car Rentals..............61 A1

Long Island, bearing a plaque dedicated to 'the peaceful aboriginal people of Long Island and to the arrival of Christopher Columbus.' The views and snorkeling around the headlands are stunning. Be careful on the mile-long rocky path that leads to the monument from Seymours.

The 3-mile-long **Galliot Cay** peninsula is linked to Long Island by a narrow spit with mangrove creeks, a gorgeous beach and turquoise shallows. Snorkeling is especially good at the reef gardens at the southern end.

The area's best beaches are the four pink-sand **Love Beaches** (the first has a shallow 'pool' perfect for small children). Head for Ocean View Dr.

The ruins of **Adderley Plantation** are smothered in vegetation, as are the graves in the slaves' cemetery.

At the shores of **Columbus Harbour**, a shallow bay lined with mangroves, you can cross the narrow tidal creek on a footbridge to reach **Newton Cay**, a small island with a beach on the Atlantic shore. There are caves around the headland to the north.

Stella Maris Resort Club & Marina (below) offers two-tank dives (without/with gear, $85/125) and resort courses (from $100). The resort also offers water-skiing for $40 and rents boats ($350 for a 27-footer).

Cape Santa Maria Beach Resort (☎ 242-338-5273; www.capesantamaria.com) offers diving (two-tank dives $85) and snorkeling ($45), and rents water sport, scuba and snorkeling equipment. They also offer bonefishing (half-/full-day $200/250), reef fishing (half-/full-day $450/600), as well as deep-sea fishing (half-/full-day $550/800) for up to six people.

Guided bonefishing is offered by **Bonafide Bonefishing** (☎ 242-338-2035; www.bonafidebonefishing.com; Queen's Hwy, Burnt Ground) and its owner 'Docky' Smith is one of the best local guides on the island, and has taken out John Grisham, Laurence Fishburne and Michael Keaton of novel and Hollywood fame. Fly-fishing lessons are on offer (per hour $60) as well as bonefishing (half-/full-day $300/350). A reef-fishing boat can be hired (full-day $475) and rates are available for snorkeling and sight-seeing tours.

SLEEPING & EATING
Stella Maris Resort Club & Marina (☎ 242-338-2051; www.stellamarisresort.com; Stella Maris; r $135;

$\boxed{P} \boxed{\times} \boxed{\times} \boxed{\text{R}}$) The ocean views are stunning from this comfortable and well-equipped old plantation, now a resort, dotted with palm groves and modern, breezy and delightful hillside apartments. The beach isn't the best but a cabana on the gorgeous Cape Santa Maria beach and shuttle service makes up for it. The relaxed and informal clubhouse serves a range of cuisines and the bar has some entertainment on each night. Free facilities include snorkel trips, small boats, bicycles, movies and lots of water sports. The resort hosts a Saturday night dance with live music, plus uses a cave as a nightclub on Monday night, with a barbecue and dancing to a rake 'n' scrape band (percussion music using household objects).

Cape Santa Maria Beach Resort (☎ 242-338-5273; www.capesantamaria.com; Cape Santa Maria; r $285; $\boxed{P} \boxed{\times} \boxed{\times} \boxed{\text{R}}$) Made for romancing couples of any age, these deluxe cottages are superb. Cool, restful and tropical they open to screened porches facing the beach. A wooden walkway leads to an airy and handsome two-tier restaurant and bar in gingerbread plantation style and offering vast views. Free facilities include catamarans, sailboats, sailboards, volleyball, diving, and snorkeling. Fishing can be arranged. The resort has its own private airstrip and charters.

Pratt's Restaurant & Bar (☎ 242-338-7051; Burnt Ground) To dine with locals and a cut-out of Miss Bacardi (you're warned) try this place; it serves Bahamian seafood and regional dishes.

Potcakes Bar (☎ 242-338-2018; Stella Maris) This place is next to the Stella Maris Marina. It has an upscale restaurant, and a bar by night.

There's an ice cream parlor at the north end of Glinton.

You can stock up your kitchen at the **Stella Maris General Store**, **Adderley Supply** or the **Burnt Ground Convenience Store** (Burnt Ground).

GETTING THERE & AWAY
Air
Please refer to p288 for information on international flights to the Bahamas and Long Island.

Stella Maris Airport serves north Long Island and **Deadman's Cay Airport** is best for the middle and south Long Island.

Bahamasair (UP; www.bahamasair.com; hubs Freeport & Nassau) Freeport (☎ 242-352-8341); Nassau (☎ 242-377-5505) has daily flights from Nassau to

Stella Maris and Deadman's Cay (both $85 one-way).

Stella Maris Resort Club & Marina (opposite) offers private plane charters for hotel guests only from January 5 to December 21. From Nassau, it costs $110 to fly one-way and, from Exema, it costs $80 one-way in conjunction with your hotel booking.

Boat

Please contact the **Dockmaster's Office** (☎ 242-393-1064) at Potter's Cay in Nassau to confirm mail-boat schedules. **Customs and Immigration** (☎ 242-338-2012).

MV Mia Dean ($45 one-way, 12hrs) sails from Nassau to Clarence Town on Tuesday.

MV Sherice M ($45 one-way, 15hrs) calls at Seymours weekly from Nassau, also stopping at Salt Pond and Deadman's Cay.

Stella Maris Resort Club & Marina (opposite) is an official port of entry, and has a full-service marina with boat yard and slips for boats up to 70 feet.

GETTING AROUND

Matthias Pratt (☎ 242-338-7051/7022) operates a minibus charter service. He charges about $150 for a ride for four people from Stella Maris to Clarence Town, in the southern part of the island. Matthias charges about $25 to drive four people from Stella Maris to the memorial.

Stella Maris Resort Club & Marina (opposite) rents cars for $75 a day plus mileage which can add up to well over $100 as Queen's Hwy runs 60 miles north to south. They also rent scooters (half-/full-day $30/46).

Williams Car Rentals (☎ 242-338-5002; Glinton) charges $65 daily, including unlimited mileage, and will deliver to Cape Santa Maria Beach Resort.

Inell Ditez, in Burnt Ground, rents scooters for $40 daily; there is also a simple **gas station** in Burnt Ground.

Stella Maris to Salt Pond

Queen's Hwy runs south from Stella Maris along the leeward shore. **Deal's Beach**, has fabulous snorkeling over a sea-fan garden. You can follow a road east from here to **O'Neill's**, a tiny hamlet with two beaches that also offer good snorkeling.

Simms, a quaint seaside hamlet about 10 miles south of Stella Maris, dates back to the plantation era. It is dominated by

well-kept **St Peter's Anglican Church**. The most endearing structure is a prim little **post office** and, nudging up behind it, an equally diminutive **jail** still bearing the sign 'HER MAJESTY'S PRISON.'

South of Simms, the road moves inland until it touches the shore again at **Thompson Bay**, about 5 miles further south. The bay is scenic, but far more spectacular is the one at **McKann's**, about half a mile east; turn east at the sign for King's Bay Resort.

SLEEPING & EATING

Chez Pierre Bahamas (☎ 242-338-8809; www.baha mahouseinn.com; Simms; d $130; P ⊠ ⊠ ⊟) Another hell-of-a-road leads you to this piece of heaven. A stretch of tucked-away beach contains chef Pierre's home, restaurant and dining room. There are also some modern and delightful wooden huts on stilts overlooking the ocean. Who needs mod-cons and TV? Dinner and breakfast for two are included in these excellent rates. Fall asleep after enjoying a delicious pasta dinner to the sound of the sea. Bliss. Hire cars and airport transfers can be arranged.

King's Bay Resort (☎ 242-338-8945; fax 242-338-8012; r $70; ☽ lunch & dinner) This rundown place enjoys a fabulous and breezy location atop the dunes on the Atlantic shore north of McKann's. There's a restaurant and bar serving Bahamian food.

Just past Simms, you can grab a bite to eat and drink at **Mario's Blue Chip Restaurant & Bar** (☎ 242-338-8106; ☽ lunch & dinner), the local hangout of choice that specializes in seafood platters. For spicy chicken, try the open-air **Geraldine's Jerk Pit** (☽ lunch & dinner), 2 miles further south. The air-conditioned **Anca's Away Restaurant** (☎ 242-338-8593; ☽ lunch & dinner), next door, serves steaks and seafood.

If hunger gets the better of you, check out either the very casual **Windell's Take-Away** or **King's Bake & Snack Shop** (☎ 242-338-8916; Queen's Hwy, McCann's; ☽ 7am-6pm), simply the best bakery on the island; Bahamians start trooping in here early to grab daily specials like yummy pineapple tarts, pumpkin bread and hot savory patties.

Swift Car Rentals (☎ 242-338-8533; Queen's Hwy, Simms) also rents cars (from $60 per day) from their garage situated north of Deadman's Cay.

Salt Pond

Twenty miles south of Stella Maris, Salt Pond is the main commercial node of the island, despite its diminutive size. A small lobster fleet is based here and a mail boat calls in weekly (see p225). There's a fish-processing plant, major supply store (Harding's Supply Store; HSC), and a gas station...about the only place on the island that's open on Sunday.

The **Royal Bank of Canada** (☎ 242-337-0100; 9am-1pm Thu, 9am-5pm Fri) is 3 miles south of Grays.

Just north of Salt Pond is **St Joseph's Anglican Church**, enjoying a sublime setting on a ridge above the beach and boneflats. Break out your camera!

Immediately north of HSC supply store (right), there is a road that leads east to the Atlantic shore and a headland with blush-pink beaches and a craggy, untouched shoreline. You can hike trails that lead south for several miles.

At Pinders, about 2 miles south of Salt Pond, another road (this one is in appalling condition) leads to **Guana Key**, a beautiful, well-protected, shallow bay; Guana Key Island is a short swim offshore. In good weather you are able to snorkel over the wreck of an old freighter in 15ft of water.

The highlight of the island's annual calendar is the **Long Island Regatta**, held at Salt Pond in mid-May. Sloops from throughout the islands compete during the festive four-day event.

ACTIVITIES

The snorkeling and diving here are simply superb. Divers should head for **Cape Santa Maria Ship's Graveyard** or **Grouper Valley** where thousands of these friendly (and possibly endangered) fish gather to spawn every November. There is also **Grouper Village**, where resident groupers and Brutus, a mammoth jewfish, expect to be fed. **Ocean Blue Hole**, a dramatic, ever-widening funnel, is worth seeing. Some like the adrenalin of feeding sharks at **Shark Reef** although this practice is now widely frowned upon.

Snorkers should head for **Coral Gardens** – Hawksbill turtles favor these awesome caves, overhangs, and valleys – and **Eagle Ray Reef** where rays flutter around guarded by a friendly grouper. **Flamingo Tongue Reef** and **Watermelon Beach** are both favored by countless species of corals and fish. Some very experienced divers have set up shop at Salt Pond, but they cover all the dive sites.

Reel Divers (☎ 242-338-0011; www.reeldivers.com; Salt Pond) have two-tank dives ($125), snorkel trips (3 hours $50), kayak/snorkeling trips (half-day $65) and underwater scooters ($35). Great-value dive-stay packages are also available with this professional friendly and highly recommended bunch.

SLEEPING & EATING

Seaview Lodge (☎ 242-333-0100; Salt Pond; r $90; P ⚡ ✕) For great value you don't need to go further than these modern, clean white and spacious apartments. Fully equipped kitchens and comfy living areas in these one- and two-bedroom lodgings make this a bargain for couples or families.

The **Midway Inn**, 3-miles south of Salt Pond at Pinders, has a fish-fry on Friday.

The large **HSC** (Harding's Supply Centre; ☎ 242-338-0333; Queen's Hwy) store is very well stocked.

SOUTH LONG ISLAND

There is a lot to see and enjoy down this end of the island, with caves, some gorgeous beaches, and supposedly the world's deepest blue hole (660ft) leading to a vast underwater cavern and magnificent cove. The soaring church spires of Clarence Town and the dazzling Lochabar Bay with another vast blue hole, white-sand beach and coral reefs put another little piece of heaven within your reach.

Deadman's Cay Area

Deadman's Cay is the site of another airport. There is no discernible center to the town, but Max's Conch Bar & Grill is the next best thing if you want friendly gossip and information.

INFORMATION

Public phone booths can be found in most villages and along Queen's Hwy.
Ambulance, fire, police (☎ 242-377-0999)
BaTelCo (☎ 242-337-1337; Deadman's Cay)
Government Medical Clinic (☎ 242-337-1222; Deadman's Cay)
Post office (☎ 242-337-1064; Deadman's Cay)
Scotiabank (☎ 242-338-2057; Deadman's Cay; 9am-1pm Mon-Thu, 9am-5pm Fri)

SIGHTS & ACTIVITIES

History buffs might enjoy the overgrown ruins of **Grays Plantation**, 2 miles north of Lower Deadman's Cay near Grays.

Lower Deadman's Cay is dominated by **St Athanatius Church**, which dates from 1929.

Cartwrights Caves, near the settlement of Cartwrights, immediately south of Deadman's Cay, were once used by Lucayan Indians. Harmless bats now live in the 150ft-long caves. They're on a private property, half a mile east of the main road. You'll see the sign. **Hamilton's Cave**, at the hamlet of Pettys, 4 miles southeast of Deadman's Cay, is 1500 feet long and is one of the largest caves in the Bahamas. It, too, contains bats, as well as stalactites, stalagmites, and a stone walkway with salt water on one side and fresh water on the other.

Reached from Queen's Hwy by a side road beginning at the Hillside Tavern, 1 mile south of Cartwrights, the fishing hamlet of **Mangrove Bush** is a center for traditional boatbuilding. Today the wooden vessels are built exclusively for racing regattas.

The **Long Island Library & Museum** in Pettys has a collection of photographs and artifacts (such as historic glass bottles) that chronicle the island's history and culture.

SLEEPING & EATING

There are also some fabulous rental properties on the island, just ask around or contact **Sunshine Real Estate** (☎ 242-338-0089; www .sunshine-real-estate.com; Salt Pond).

Ellen's Inn (☎ 242-337-1086; Queen's Hwy, Buckleys; s/d $75/90 P ⊠ ⊠) This little white bungalow is an immaculate and homely guesthouse. A guest lounge is comfortably furnished and even pastries and sweets are put out for guests. The guest kitchen makes this an affordable and good-value option. Rates are inclusive of taxes and Ellen also rents out cars for $60 per day.

Constantakis Bay View Apartments (☎ 242-337-0644; Pettys; r $70; P ⊠ ⊠) These attractive blue lodgings are again in a perfect location for a fisherman in need for bed, balcony and a beer. However, the comfortable kitchen, cable TV and two-bedroom also makes this ideal for a family looking for a quiet spot that overlooks the sea, although there is not really a beach here.

Keva's Villas (☎ 242-337-1054; Queen's Hwy, Deadman's Cay; r $70; P ⊠ ⊠) Within walking distance of Max's Conch Bar & Grill, these very plain but clean units are also good value, comfortable enough and owned by Mr T (who runs the car rentals; see below). Rates include taxes.

Smith & Wells Bonefish Lodge (☎ 242-337-1056; Queen's Hwy; r $65; P ⊠ ⊠) Sitting on the quiet edge of town, and adjacent to the water, this is the place for fishing fans who want nothing more than a simple but clean place to kip, somewhere to gut and store their fish, and a screened veranda for a beer in the evening.

Max's Conch Bar & Grill (☎ 242-337-0056; www .maxconchbar.com; Deadman's Cay; mains $6-12; ☯ lunch & dinner) THE hot spot in town, everything you need to know and want to share, you can do whilst sitting around this circular outdoor bar. A lively and convivial host is well-matched by his customers and family. Daily specials can satisfy the appetite while good humor is enriching.

Coco's Restaurant & Lounge (☎ 242-337-6242; Hamilton's) This is a nice place to stop, and serves daily specials of Bahamian dishes.

You can buy groceries at the **J&M Food Store** (☎ 242-337-1446), 400 yards north of the BaTelCo office. On Sunday when the entire island closes shop, you can buy basic foodstuffs at the Shell **gas station** south of Cartwright.

GETTING THERE & AROUND

For further information, please refer to Getting There & Away, p224.

Mr T Car Rentals (☎ 242-337-1054; Deadman's Cay Airport) rents good, reliable air-conditioned vehicles from $60 per day. Remember to look left, right and up, as you drive across the airport's runway to and from Mr T's residence!

Ophelia's Rent-A-Car (☎ 242-337-1042) is right next door to Mr T, and offers cars for the same rates.

Keep in mind that insurance is not on offer at car rental places.

Local taxis meet the planes, and Ellen's Inn can supply a taxi service, although it's more convenient to hire a car to get around.

Clarence Town Area

The peaceful harbor settlement of **Clarence Town** (population 1571) and its surrounds are perfect for those seeking some solitude, or a few quiet days living on a beach and

SOUTHERN BAHAMAS

pottering around. Long Island's administrative headquarters is very quiet, and has a lovely hillside setting that falls gently to the clear and sparkling waters of the town's small harbor.

INFORMATION
Government Medical Clinic (☎ 242-337-3333; 🕑 9am-3:30pm Mon-Fri) Located near the mail-boat dock.
Police (☎ 242-338-3919) Use this number for emergencies.
Post office (☎ 242-337-3030) On the north side of Clarence Town.

SIGHTS & ACTIVITIES
Even the spiritually unattached will be inspired by the simple beauty of the two churches that rise over the town; **St Paul's Anglican Church** and the sparkling white and blue **St Peter's Catholic Church**. Both were designed by Father Jerome, the enigmatic architect-hermit-cleric of Cat Island (see p211). The first was designed prior to, and the second after, his conversion to Catholicism. You can climb the ladders within one of its two medieval spires for a marvelous bird's-eye view.

Immediately east of town is **Lochabar Bay**, a stunning half-mile-wide, flask-shaped cove that funnels east to a vast **blue hole**. It is rimmed by a splendid and lonesome white-sand beach, surrounded on three sides by dense thickets of thatch palm and scrub. Coral reefs lie just offshore, with staghorn coral at 30ft.

The 2-mile wide **Turtle Cove** near Deans, has a fabulous beach and turquoise shallows. Its real treasure, however, lies to the southeast beyond a headland, where perhaps the world's deepest **blue hole** (660ft) leads to the world's eighth-largest underwater cavern. The neck of the aquamarine hole opens to a beautiful cove rimmed by gorgeous white sands. Magnificent! Bring a picnic.

The turnoff from Queen's Hwy is marked. Turtle Cove also can be reached by a shoreline trail from Mangrove Bush, north of Pettys.

The sound west of Deadman's Cay is superb for bonefishing.

SLEEPING & EATING
Bahamian Mood Vacation Rentals (☎ 242-337-0056; www.bahamianmood.com; Clarence Town; r U$100; P X X) This colorful two-story house contains four small units and a wrap-around

sundeck and has a startling white-sand beach on its doorstep. Each pristine white-and-navy apartment sleeps four, has comfortable furnishings and is just made for those who love solitude. Weekly and monthly rates are also excellent.

Lochabar Beach Lodge & Houses (☎ 242-337-0025, 242-337-6033; Clarence Town; r $130; P X X) This wonderfully lonesome and charming lodge is a mile away from town at Lochabar Bay. Spacious studio apartments and little villas have sponge-painted wooden walls, tile floors, a kitchenette, and wide French doors that open to a patio facing the bay, all with the beautiful white-sand beach just a step or two away. Weekly rates are good too. Highly recommended!

Greenwich Creek Lodge (☎ 242-337-6278; www.greenwichcreek.com; Clarence Town) One for the really serious bonefisherman, the lodge charges approximately $2500 per week for very comfortable accommodation, meals and bonefishing.

Outer Edge Grill & Bar (☎ 242-337-3445; Flying Fish Marina; mains $8-18; 🕑 breakfast, lunch & dinner Wed & Fri-Mon) Not a bad setting for this tiny outdoor harborside bar and restaurant. The food is quick and tasty, the rums are smooth and the atmosphere relaxing.

Harbour Restaurant, Bar & Satellite Lounge (☎ 242-337-3247; Lighthouse Point Rd; mains $7-20) Another popular place to eat and drink; it can get a bit smoky inside.

The Forest (☎ 242-337-3287; mains $7-18) This is a lurid-pink bar and restaurant that also doubles as the areas hotspot with live music and dancing at weekends. Checkout the great seashell bar.

You can stock up on groceries in town and at **Harbour Grocery** (☎ 242-337-3934).

GETTING THERE & AROUND
For information on getting to Long Island, please refer to Getting There & Away, p222.
Flying Fish Marina (☎ 242-337-3430; flyfishmarina@batelnet.bs; Lighthouse Point Rd, Clarence Town) has a 15-slip marina, provisions store, laundry, bathrooms and showers, plus accommodations for sailors, and a bar and food.
Millander's Auto Sales (☎ /fax 242-337-3227) rents cars for around $65 per day.

Dunmore to Cape Verde
The final 15-miles of the Queen's Hwy will take you past three exquisite **Father Jerome**

churches, whitewashed and painted in trademark blue, in **Dunmore**, **Hard Bargain**, and **Mortimers**.

Also just north of the church at Dunmore are the gates to some overgrown **plantation ruins,** named for a former governor of the Bahamas who had an estate producing sisal, cotton, and pineapples. You can follow a dirt track half a mile to the ruined hilltop mansion.

The road then passes turnoffs for shell-covered **Cabbage Point Beach**, some abandoned salt ponds and materially-desolated villages including the aptly-named Hard Bargain and quaint **Roses**, until it reaches **Gordons** settlement. From here you can hike the mile to **Cape Verde**, the island's southernmost point.

CROOKED ISLAND DISTRICT

pop 342
Crooked Island District consists of Crooked Island, Acklins Island, Long Cay, and outlying Samana and Plana Cays. These southerly islands are not developed for tourism, which is definitely part of their allure, but they are also not wealthy. Electricity still hasn't reached many areas and the island's descendants still fish, tend the land, and draw an income from stripping cascarilla bark and selling it to the manufacturers of Campari liquor (it is also used in medicines).

But other adventurers have arrived: Cubans and Haitians make the desperate run for a new life, and, not infrequently, drug-runners rush in aboard small planes to offload bales of cocaine.

A 50-mile barrier reef rings the entire island chain, offering drop-offs beginning at about 50ft and plunging to 3600ft in the Crooked Island Passage. Bring whatever you need, especially diving, snorkeling or fishing equipment. Make sure you pack mosquito repellent; in summer the mosquitoes are ferocious.

History
Recent evidence suggests that Columbus made Crooked Island his second New World landfall (he named it Santa María de la Con-

cepción after the Virgin Mary, although there is no mention made of this on the isle itself).

In the late 18th century the islands, like their northern neighbors, were settled by Loyalists from North America who attempted to develop a cotton industry. By the 1830s depleted soils, weevils, and emancipation of the slave-labor workforce doomed the plantations forever. The white landowners left. The black laborers remained and turned to subsistence fishing and farming.

Getting There & Around
Visitors mainly fly into the main airfield just east of Colonel Hill, and Pittstown Point Landing has its own 2000ft airstrip. A weekly mail boat also brings people from Nassau.

A small passenger ferry runs between Cove Point, Crooked Island, and Lovely Bay, Acklins Island, twice daily. Other than that you may be able to rent a car from a resident. Ask your hosts for suggestions and bear in mind that the daily rate is $80 to $90 per day on some of the other islands. Likewise ask your hosts about organizing a boat trip to Long Cay.

CROOKED ISLAND
Spring on Crooked Island releases dozens of fluttering, vividly colored butterflies, which tentatively explore scrub and dense pockets of woodland, while herons, ospreys, egrets, mockingbirds, finches, wild canaries, hummingbirds, and flamingos swoop over briny lagoons and swamps. There is also a rugged shoreline with deep inlets, sounds and many lovely beaches on this isle. The island lies about 250 miles southeast of Nassau.

One main road runs along the north shore and leads to Landrail Point and Colonel Hill, the island's main villages which run on farming and fishing, a number of generators and a lot of faith. About 60% of the islanders are Seventh-Day Adventists (the rest are Baptists and Presbyterians), and a devout lot they are, too! From Friday sundown to Saturday sundown, the island comes to a virtual halt.

Colonel Hill Area
pop 240
The only major settlement of **Colonel Hill** flanks a hill midway along the north coast. The scrub-covered plain below slopes down

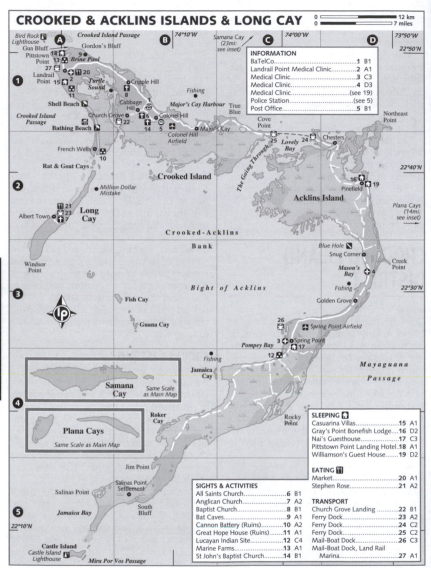

CROOKED & ACKLINS ISLANDS & LONG CAY

INFORMATION	
BaTelCo	**1** B1
Landrail Point Medical Clinic	**2** A1
Medical Clinic	**3** C3
Medical Clinic	**4** D3
Medical Clinic	(see 19)
Police Station	(see 5)
Post Office	**5** B1

SLEEPING	
Casuarina Villas	**15** A1
Gray's Point Bonefish Lodge	**16** D2
Nai's Guesthouse	**17** C3
Pittstown Point Landing Hotel	**18** A1
Williamson's Guest House	**19** D2

EATING	
Market	**20** A1
Stephen Rose	**21** A2

SIGHTS & ACTIVITIES	
All Saints Church	**6** B1
Anglican Church	**7** A2
Baptist Church	**8** B1
Bat Caves	**9** A1
Cannon Battery (Ruins)	**10** A2
Great Hope House (Ruins)	**11** A1
Lucayan Indian Site	**12** C4
Marine Farms	**13** A1
St John's Baptist Church	**14** B1

TRANSPORT	
Church Grove Landing	**22** B1
Ferry Dock	**23** A2
Ferry Dock	**24** C2
Ferry Dock	**25** C2
Mail-Boat Dock	**26** C3
Mail-Boat Dock, Land Rail Marina	**27** A1

SOUTHERN BAHAMAS

to a beach-rimmed bay. The village comprises a few dozen ramshackle clapboard huts, emancipation-era houses, and pastel-painted modern concrete homes. The only building of note is **St John's Baptist Church**, atop the hill.

The road leads northwest 1½ miles to the lime-green **All Saints Church**, surrounded by African flame trees in Cabbage Hill, and the small **Baptist church**, fronted by a tiny bell tower in Cripple Hill.

There are no banks in the Crooked Island District. The **post office** (☎ 242-344-2526), beside the **police** (☎ 242-344-2599) in the administration building in Colonel Hill, may provide basic banking transactions.

The **BaTelCo office** (☎ 242-344-2590) is in Church Grove and the medical clinic is in **Landrail Point Community Clinic** (fax 242-344-2345).

A few eateries and very basic guesthouses exist here, but visitors mainly head for Landrail Point.

You can buy groceries at the **Cabbage Hill Supermarket**.

GETTING THERE & AWAY

The main airfield is 1½ miles east of Colonel Hill, and Pittstown Point Landing has its own 2000ft airstrip.

Bahamasair (UP; www.bahamasair.com; hubs Freeport & Nassau) Freeport (☎ 242-352-8341); Nassau (☎ 242-377-5505) flies between Nassau and Colonel Hill twice weekly ($105 one-way), also stopping at Acklins Island.

Contact the **Potter's Cay Dockmaster's Office** (☎ 242-393-1064) in Nassau for mail-boat departure times.

MV United Star ($70 one-way, 18hrs) sails from Nassau weekly, stopping at Acklins Island and Long Cay.

GETTING AROUND

Car rentals are organized on a haphazard basis, and may not be possible, but ask around when booking accommodations or when you arrive.

A small passenger ferry runs between Church Grove Landing, Crooked Island, and Lovely Bay, Acklins Island, twice daily.

Ask at the **Land Rail Marina** (☎ 242-344-2676; Landrail Point) to see if any boats will take you to Long Cay (about $130, 30 minutes) or on sightseeing trips.

Landrail Point Area

This hamlet, 9 miles northwest of Colonel Hill, has a teeny harbor, a wealth of adjacent natural sights and most of the fun. The mail boat calls here, and a sandy 4WD track leads north 1½ miles to Pittstown Point, the northwestern tip of the island.

Crooked's most impressive site is a small, coral-encrusted, sand-edged cay a mile offshore from Pittstown Point. It is pinned by a stately 115ft-tall **Bird Rock Lighthouse** (1876), erected to guide ships through the treacherous Crooked Island Passage. The cay is a prime nesting colony for snowy white terns and tropical birds, and is a five-minute boat ride from Pittstown Point.

Bat Caves lie 100yd inland from the shore, near Gordon's Bluff near Gordon's Beach. They're easily explored, the walking is level and there are stalactites in the depths.

Brine Pool is a lagoon, stretching from Landrail Point north to Pittstown Point, along whose shore several expats have built modest homes, and seabirds, ospreys and sometimes flamingos flock.

Marine Farms, a salt farm on an island in the midst of the pond, began life as a cotton plantation and a Spanish or British fort that is said to have managed a firefight with US warships in the War of 1812. Cannons still can be seen lying amid the ruins and salt pans. **Great Hope House**, about a mile south of Landrail Point, was once the centerpiece of a 19th-century plantation.

The lovely **Shell Beach** and **Bathing Beach** stretch south from Landrail Point for 7 miles to **French Wells**. Snorkeling is divine, with fabulous coral heads just below the water. Alas, sharks are often present.

For bonefishing guides, ask at **Pittstown Point Landings Hotel** (☎ 242-344-2507; www.pittstownpointlandings.com). Rates vary from (half-day $200-400, full-day $500-700) for up to six people. Also try **Elton 'Bonefish Shakey' McKinney** (☎ 242-344-2507) and **Derrick Ingraham** (☎ 242-556-8769; half-/full-day $200/450).

Ask if the ferry can drop you off at the old Landing's Point ferry stop. The Captain may oblige.

SLEEPING & EATING

Pittstown Point Landings Hotel (☎ 242-344-2507; www.pittstownpointlandings.com; Landrail Point; s/d $105/115; P ⊠ ✹ ▣) The main lodge once housed the Bahamas' first post office, and now houses a nice little library, bar and restaurant (most guests take a meal-plan

---

A MILLION DOLLAR MISTAKE

This famous **plane wreck** is in 12ft of water about 50yd offshore Long Cay. The plane was on a drug run when it crashed at sea. Locals found a suitcase containing about $1,000,000. It was handed to an official from Nassau who, it seems, pocketed the money and went on to live the life of Riley. Nowadays divers hoping for any crumbs of this hoard will find no money but a wealth of fish and marine-life instead.

SOUTHERN BAHAMAS

option) decorated with fishermen's nets. The rooms are shaded by coconut palms and decorated in tropical pastels and face onto to a splendid beach.

Diving, snorkeling, fishing, and volleyball, bicycle, and boat rental are on offer.

Casuarina Villas (☎ 242-344-2197; Landrail Point; $90-130) As well as leading diving expeditions, the owner of these beachfront cottages can organize car rental for guests. The villas come with full kitchen facilities and a deck, and are located around 1 mile from Landrail Point.

There's a local market in Landrail Point.

Colonel Hill to Cove Point

Follow the north shore to **Major's Cay**, a hamlet facing turquoise-jade waters rimmed by a narrow yet splendid beach. Further east, the road becomes a narrow track leading to **Cove Point**, 12 miles east of Major's Cay. There's nothing here but a tiny concrete wharf where the ferry departs for Acklins Island.

LONG CAY

This small island is separated by a mile-wide channel from Crooked Island. Columbus, it seems, landed here on October 19, 1492. The explorer named the island Isabela after the Spanish queen who funded his jaunts to the New World.

The island was later known as Fortune Island and once boasted thriving sponging

and salt industries. Flamingos wade in the bight on the south side of the island and an endemic subspecies of iguana inhabits two tiny cays – Fish Cay and Guana Cay – that lie 7 and 10 miles southeast of Long Cay.

In the 19th century **Albert Town**, also called Windsor and the island's only settlement, was the main base in the archipelago for transatlantic mail and freight ships hiring and dropping off stevedores, or 'coast crew.' Wild goats have taken over the ruins, though the largest **Anglican church** south of Nassau still stands.

Stephen Rose (☎ 242-344-3011) has a small grocery store and acts as a bonefishing guide.

ACKLINS ISLAND

pop 435

Another place for those seeking a true outpost is the undeveloped 45-mile-long Acklins Island, separated from Crooked Island by a shallow passage called 'The Going Through.' Reefs lie offshore to the east and there are fabulous and lonesome beaches along the shores. Flamingos also inhabit the briny flats. Hiking fans should head for the hilly and rugged north and east coasts.

The main settlement is **Spring Point**, midway down the west coast. Public electricity arrived in 1998, although plenty of homes still use a small generator. To bathe, most

---

COLUMBUS STOOD HERE

No one (except perhaps residents of the Turks and Caicos) disputes that Columbus' first landfall in the New World in 1492 was in the Bahamas. But the question of which island he landed on has aroused considerable controversy. Nine first landfalls have been proposed, although, incredibly, no one had taken into account 'dead reckoning' – the cumulative effect of current and leeway (wind-caused slippage) on a vessel's course – in tracing the route of the round-bottomed fleet.

In November 1986, following five years of extensive study by Joseph Judge and a team of scholarly interests under the aegis of the National Geographic Society, *National Geographic* magazine announced that it had solved the 'grandest of all geographic mysteries.' Judge ordered a new translation of the Columbus diaries, drew the first-ever track of the log, then input all the variables into a computer to adjust for leeway, current, and magnetic variation, and traveled to the islands to find actual evidence. Judge's team also was the first to track Columbus' course using the Spanish league (2.82 nautical miles), not the English league (2.5 nautical miles) previously used. Presto! The exact landing spot turns out to be latitude 23¼°09'00"N and longitude 73¼°29'13"W…the island of Samana Cay.

If the claim is true, the *Niña*, *Pinta*, and *Santa María* anchored on Samana's southwest side, at a spot where the reef opens. Columbus explored inside the reef in a rowboat and recorded the features of the island that he named San Salvador.

locals scoop water from barrels, while their earnings come from fishing and beating bark for Campari.

Information

There is a **Government Medical Clinic** (☎ 242-344-3615) at Spring Point, plus a nurse in Mason's Bay (☎ 242-344-3628) and a **BaTelCo** (☎ 242-344-3536) office at Spring Point.

Sights & Activities

A partially excavated **Lucayan Indian site** along the shore of Pompey Bay, immediately south of Spring Point, may have been the largest Lucayan settlement in the Bahamas. The only other site of interest is the remote **Castle Island Lighthouse** (1867) at the southern tip of the island.

The annual **Acklins Homecoming & Regatta** is held during the first weekend of August.

The bonefishing is as good as it gets, as the Bight of Acklins has more than 1000 sq miles of knee-deep water. Most hotels can arrange fishing trips.

Sleeping & Eating

Nai's Guesthouse (☎ 242-344-3089; r $65) Nai's has four rooms and offers meals by appointment. Its restaurant has a bar with pool table and TV, and music keeps things humming along.

Gray's Point Bonefish Lodge (☎ 242-344-3210; r $65) This is another simple guesthouse in Pinefield.

Williamson's Guest House (☎ 242-344-3210) This family also rents rooms.

Head to Spring Point and Cabbage Hill for groceries.

Getting There & Around

Please refer to the Getting There & Away, p231, for flight and boat information on getting to the island.

The airfield is immediately northeast of Spring Point.

The government operates a passenger ferry from Cove Point (Crooked Island) to Lovely Bay, 3 miles west of Chesters, twice daily except Sunday ($7 one-way). The mail boat dock lies north of Spring Point.

SAMANA CAY

This uninhabited cay still fits Columbus' description: 'quite large…flat…green…with many waters and white cliffs facing south.'

Archaeological digs led by the National Geographic Society have found 10 **Lucayan sites** (plus a Spanish earthenware vessel) and an ancient causeway of conch shells.

PLANA CAYS

This string of small cays, beginning 15 miles east of Acklins Island, is a protected reserve for endangered great iguanas and estimated hutias (which resemble a guinea pig); the Bahamas' only endemic mammal. No dogs are allowed ashore.

INAGUAS & MAYAGUANA

This group consists of three islands; Great Inagua (the southernmost Bahamian island) is famous for a vast flamingo sanctuary and salt industry, it also lies a spit away from Cuba and Haiti, and a long 325 miles from Nassau. Little Inagua is a diminutive isle to its northeast, while Mayaguana can rightfully be called one of the most lonesome of all

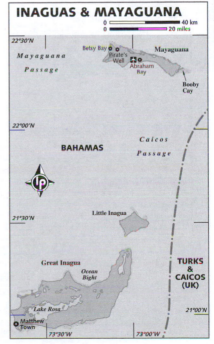

Bahamian islands, lying just 50 miles north-west of Providenciales (Turks and Caicos).

Half of Great Inagua lies within Bahamas National Trust Park and therefore much of the island is only accessible with some arduous trekking through brush, with vast acres of exceedingly briny lakes where wild boars, horses and donkeys roam (the latter two outnumber humans by five-to-one). If this matches your sense of adventure then you're in for some excitement! You will be made welcome by local Bahamians and the birdlife, including some rare feathered-beauties and the hemisphere's largest flock of West Indian flamingos, is fabulous.

The islands are hot; the mosquitoes are overwhelming. However the islands are free

of mainstream tourists and the air-kissing set, only occasional fellow bird- and nature-lovers ever appear in these parts.

History

Great Inagua's human settlement was financed and supported by salt. 'Crystal farming' was began in the late 18th century. The island became a major salt exporter (as told in *Great Inagua* by Margery O Erickson).

Great Inagua's southernmost position also makes it a prime piece of real estate for drug-runners heading in from Colombia and other drug-producing nations. So many islanders profited from the drug trade in the 1980s that when a policeman became overzealous, locals burned down the police

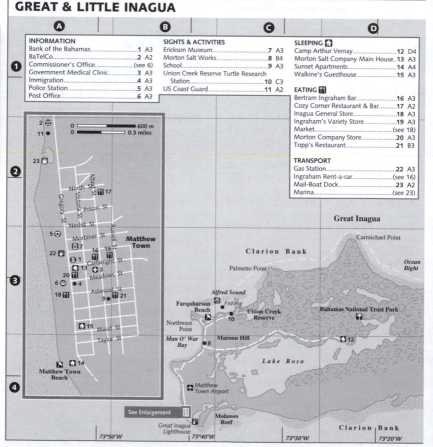

station and took him hostage. The Drug Enforcement Administration now have a permanent presence on the islands.

Getting There & Around
Most visitors fly into Great Inagua or Mayaguana. Others catch the weekly mail boat from Nassau.

You'll need your own transport if you want to explore the islands. Car hire companies are based at Matthew Town. Car insurance is not generally on offer.

GREAT & LITTLE INAGUA
pop 951
With salt traders and birds the most recognizable visitors, not many realized that

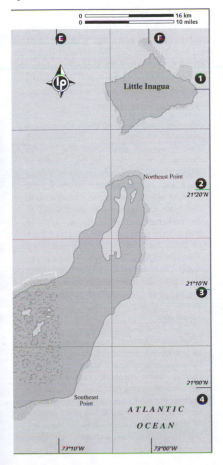

novelist Ian Fleming also visited the islands in the 1950s. He thought Great Inagua quite strange, with its lake 'only a couple of feet deep and the color of a corpse.' Thus it became the home of Dr No, the villain of the first James Bond film.

Great Inagua is 35 miles east to west and 20 miles north to south at its widest. Uninhabited Little Inagua lies to the northeast.

Matthew Town is the only settlement and is also a center for the Morton Salt Company, who produces nearly a million pounds of salt here annually. Also likely to make you thirsty is the knowledge that the islands have no potable water supply; water currently is shipped in and distributed by truck.

Sport fishing and scuba-diving fans will enjoy these pristine waters but will need their own gear.

Matthew Town
pop 452
The white gold of former years is still a regular income for most of the town's folk, while others get by on fishing and farming. The faded bungalows and old two-story whitewashed houses with green shuttered windows make up the town center along with a few shops and bars and the island commissioner's office, topped by a clock tower. There's a small beach to the south, with shade trees and picnic benches.

INFORMATION
Public telephone booths are scattered around town.

Bank of the Bahamas (☎ 242-339-1264; Ground fl, commissioner's office, Gregory St; 🕑 9:30am-2pm Mon-Thu, 9:30am-5:30pm Fri)

BaTelco office (☎ 242-339-2002; Matthew Town)

Government Medical Clinic (☎ 242-339-1249, 242-339-1226 after 5:30pm; Victoria St)

Police station (☎ 242-339-1444, 919; Gregory St)

Post office (☎ 242-339-1248; Ground fl, commissioner's office, Gregory St)

SIGHTS & ACTIVITIES
The small **Erickson Museum** (☎ 242-339-1863; Gregory St; 🕑 9am-1pm & 3-6pm Mon-Fri, 9am-1pm Sat) contains profiles on salt production and native fauna, including flamingos. Ask the librarian to open it for you.

The **Great Inagua Lighthouse** (☎ 242-339-1370; Southwest Point) is one of four kerosene lighthouses in the country that that must be wound by hand every 1½ hours throughout the night.

A good place for snorkeling is **Alfred Sound**, at the end of the road north of town, where bonefishing also is said to be excellent.

SLEEPING & EATING

Great Inagua is a bit of a culinary wasteland and there is little seafood or vegetables, but at least there's no shortage of salt. Cash is preferred here.

Morton Salt Company Main House (☎ 242-339-1267; Gregory St; d $70-90; P ✗ 🏠) This endearing and well-maintained little two-story guesthouse sits in the town, albeit across from a noisy power plant. Three rooms have their own bathrooms, and all are very clean and adequately furnished. Gideon's Bibles can occupy you in the toilets!

Walkine's Guesthouse (☎ 242-339-1612; cnr Gregory & Maud Sts; r $80-90) A more modern option is this guesthouse with five well-maintained rooms, all with crisp, attractive decor, neat bathrooms, and modern furniture, including TVs.

Sunset Apartments (☎ 242-339-1362; r $120) In the south end of town, and sitting right on the water, these units are cheerful and nicely furnished with tiles and rattan furniture. It is only a five-minute walk to the nearest beach.

Cozy Corner Restaurant & Bar (☎ 242-339-1440; North St; mains $7-18; 🕑 lunch & dinner) Your best bet on the island; enjoy some boiled fish, fried chicken and burgers or have a drink and a game of pool.

Topps Restaurant (☎ 242-339-1465) in town and **Bertram Ingraham Bar** (☎ 242-339-1659; Kortwright St) both sell the liquid stuff we all enjoy so much.

Inagua General Store (☎ 242-339-1460; Gregory St) and **Ingrahams Variety Store** (☎ 242-339-1232; Cartwright St) are useful stores, while a market is held intermittently by the beach.

GETTING THERE & AROUND

For international flights to the Bahamas please refer to p288.

Matthew Town Airport (☎ 242-339-1680) is 2 miles north of town.

Bahamasair (UP; www.bahamasair.com; hubs Freeport & Nassau) Freeport (☎ 242-352-8341); Nassau (☎ 242-377-5505) flies from Nassau to Matthew Town

Inagua, and Mayaguana ($111 one-way, three times a week).

For boat schedules and departure times, call the **Dockmaster's office** (☎ 242-393-1064) on Potter's Cay in Nassau.

MV Trans-Cargo II ($70 one way; 24hrs) sails from Nassau weekly to Inagua and Mayanagua.

Matthew Town Harbour (☎ 242-339-1427) has slips and fuel, and you can 'enter' the island at **Immigration** (☎ 242-339-1234; Gregory St). There is also a US Coast Guard.

For car rentals call **Ingraham Rent-a-Car** (☎ 242-339-1667) or **Henry Nixon** (☎ 242-339-1616; Victoria St). There is a gas station on Gregory Street.

Ingraham's Variety Store (☎ 242-339-1232; Cartwright St) rents bicycles out at $12 per day.

North of Matthew Town

About 4 miles past Matthew Town, the dirt road passes between the southernmost of part the Morton Salt Works' salt pans; the pans are contained by dikes that connect them to equally briny natural lakes. Further

---

FLAMING FLAMINGOS

The West Indian (or roseate) flamingo is restricted to Great Inagua, the Turks and Caicos, Bonaire, portions of the Yucatán Peninsula, and Cuba. Around 60,000 of these leggy birds inhabit 12-mile-long Lake Rosa in the Bahamas National Trust Park. In season (November through June) the birds can be seen in great flocks in the park, most magnificently, taking off en masse in a pink blizzard. The birds mate in December and January and nest from February to April. They migrate annually to Cuba. There are other rare birds to entice even the most jaded bird-watcher, including the reddish egret. Each spring a **bird count** is undertaken. You're welcome to volunteer.

Flamingos have started to repopulate neighboring islands, a sure sign of success, as the birds have been hunted ruthlessly for meat and milliners' stores during the past 200 years. Locals still have a taste for flamingo steak (the flesh is said to taste like partridge) and occasionally shoot the birds for meat, despite a $1000 fine and a penalty of three months' imprisonment. Hogs are the birds' other main enemy.

north, the dirt road passes sporadic beaches, the ruins of an old sisal plantation, and an abandoned loyalist settlement.

The road finishes at **Farquharson Beach**, a protected bay and a prime snorkeling and bonefishing spot where the abandoned US Aerostat station is located. A turnoff here leads east – inland – to the Union Creek Reserve (see right).

The **Morton Salt Works** are the second-largest solar **saline plant** in the hemisphere; comprising 34,000 acres of reservoirs and salt pans surrounding a cleaning, storage, and bulk-freight loading facility.

Each pan is 'harvested' once a year between March and June, and its salt is transported and washed. The soggy crystals then are stacked into huge mountains to dry in the sun. Each pile of salt contains crystals of a specific size and shape; the different grades of salt are each intended for a different purpose.

The company's **managing director** (☎ 242-339-1811) is normally happy to organize a tour to show you around.

Bahamas National Trust Park

This 287-sq-mile national park protects the world's largest breeding colony of West Indian (or roseate) flamingos and has been in operation since 1963. Drought-resistant scrub, bonsai forests and vast acres of deceased, leafless trees indicate the effects of the briny waters. However, the super-salty soup teems with brine shrimp and larval brine flies, foods favored by flamingos and a parade of other waders. Dominating the park is Lake Rosa, a precious mirror reflecting the antics of roseate spoonbills, endemic reddish pink egrets, avocets, cormorants, tricolored Louisiana herons, and flamingos.

Sometimes you can see flamingos in the brine pools on the edge of the Morton Salt Works, outside the park boundary. But the large flocks are within the park, far from traffic and other disturbances. The best times to visit are early morning and late evening.

There are also burrowing owls, Bahamian pintails, endemic Bahamian woodstar hummingbirds, brown pelicans, stripe-headed tanagers, American kestrels and endangered Bahama parrots.

Before you arrive, contact the **Bahamas National Trust** (BNT; ☎ 242-393-1317; Nassau, New

Providence) to make reservations, buy a day pass ($25) or book a tour ($50 for four adults, including tip). Taking in the salt works, tours are run by **Henry Nixon** (☎ 242-339-1616; fax 242-339-1850; VHF Channel 16), the BNT warden on Inagua. All visitors must be accompanied by a warden and passes have to be bought in advance.

Hawksbill turtles also come ashore to nest and freshwater turtles inhabit ponds on these isles. **Union Creek Reserve**, lies at Bahamas National Trust Park's northwest corner and encompasses tidal creeks and beach where sea turtles – notably green turtles – feed and come ashore to nest. The sanctuary is the only natural feeding ground in the Caribbean region and mid-Americas where sea turtles are not hunted or exploited in any way. The BNT is working in conjunction with the US-based **Caribbean Conservation Corporation & Sea Turtle Survival League** (US ☎ 800-678-7853, 352-373-6441; www.cccturtle.org) to protect the turtles.

The cactus-covered limestone ridge of **Maroon Hill** is a good vantage point for spying the location of flamingos, which usually can be seen in the brine ponds immediately to the west.

Camp Arthur Vernay (☎ 242-339-1616; fax 242-339-1850; VHF Channel 16; dm per person $30) The plain bunkhouse sleeps nine and has two shared showers with cold and lukewarm water and an outdoor kitchen. Take your own food, but the BNT warden Henry Nixon may cook for you on request; be prepared to tip extra.

Little Inagua

This 30-sq-mile island, 5 miles northeast of Great Inagua, is uninhabited, despite its relatively rich soils, which support a dense stand of Cuban royal palm and sizeable populations of wild burros and goats. Several bird species and marine turtles also nest here.

MAYAGUANA
pop 251

The silent beaches, rugged and rocky shores, and unspoilt reefs entice occasional boaters to this 25-mile-long isle that is barely 6 miles wide, and is located 65 miles from Great Inagua. Some fantastic snorkeling can be enjoyed here and **Booby Cay**, offshore, is an important nesting site for seabirds.

Abraham Bay, on the south coast, is the largest of three small settlements on the island. Roads northwest lead to the other settlements: **Pirate's Well** and **Betsy Bay**. Electricity and a full telephone service arrived here only in 1997, despite the US Air Force's missile-tracking station (now defunct) that was here during NASA's Apollo and Mercury programs.

Probably your bet on the island, **Reggie's Guest House & Lounge** (☎ 242-422-0131; Abraham's Bay; r $150) can offer breakfast, dinner and fishing excursions. While the beachside restaurant and bar, **Buccaneers' Rest** (☎ 242-339-3605; Pirate's Well; r $130), offers 16 simple rooms in its little single-story yellow building.

Brook's, **Brown's**, and **Farrington's** are all tiny grocery stores open daily.

Most visitors fly here, but it's possible to catch the weekly ferry from Nassau. The airfield is 2 miles west of Abraham Bay.

Ask at the grocery stores about water-taxi services.

Turks & Caicos

Caicos Islands

These islands, headed by Providenciales (or 'Provo'), have pristine resorts dotted with palm trees, perfect beaches lined with honey-brown sunbathers and warm, glistening shallows.

At night wine and wafts of garlic accompany the chatter from intimate alfresco restaurants, and people stroll under the stars to lively bars where the music has a *goombay* beat. Belongers mix with visitors at karaoke nights, where hilarity and talent are shown in equal measures.

The Caicos chain arcs through West Caicos, Providenciales, North Caicos, Middle Caicos, East Caicos and South Caicos. The rocky landscape of Middle Caicos has created some picturesque coves and private beaches overlooked by a range of cute cottages perfect for solitude, while lush North Caicos produces a range of exotic sweet fruits and fantastic conditions for biking and hiking. West Caicos has small sandy beaches and a historic plantation, while the East and South Caicos celebrate their undisturbed inhabitants; flocks of leggy flamingos and sleepy wild donkeys.

The islands, despite their different characters, share a common bond; magically warm and soothing jade seas that soak away the stresses of modern living. While there are any number of wonderful diving experiences around the Caicos Islands, snorkeling is also an easy option with some reefs just a short swim off the beach.

The tiny cays sprayed around the main islands are made for day trips. Visit some docile and friendly rock iguanas, wander white shores looking for shells and sand dollars, cycle through tiny villages or just sit and stare at that incredibly beautiful and wide blue horizon.

HIGHLIGHTS

- Heading out for a boisterous night of bingo or exuberant karaoke at a **Turtle Cove** (p249) nightspot
- Meeting Curious, an iguana who belts across the sand like Michael Jordan when thrown an edible morsel, on **Little Water Cay** (p252)
- Biking around lush **North Caicos** (p253) spotting gangly flamingos and predatory ospreys
- Melting into a chocolate soufflé under the stars at romantic Grace's Cottage restaurant, **Grace Bay** (p249)
- Swimming with docile stingrays as they glide through the shallows of **French Cay** (p252)

■ TELEPHONE CODE: 649	■ POPULATION: 13,302	■ AREA: 178 SQ MILES

CAICOS ISLANDS

History

From something as simple as an ancient paddle and a few cave drawings, historians have observed that Lucayan Indians simultaneously inhabited the Turks, Caicos and Bahamian islands, and were therefore the earliest known inhabitants of the region. These two countries also share a history of mining 'white gold' or salt, which in the Turks and Caicos proved highly viable until the 1950s.

The Caicos Islands were 'discovered' by seven millionaires (including Teddy Roosevelt III and a couple of DuPonts) in the early 1960s – they leased land from the British government, built a small airstrip for their private planes, and constructed a deepwater anchorage for their yachts and those of

friends escaping the rigors of US East Coast winters. By the 1970s, Providenciales was the near-private domain of a group of wealthy escape artists from long-john climates.

Around the same time, Count Ferdinand Czernin, son of the last prime minister of the Austro–Hungarian Empire, planned a Walden Pond–like resort on tiny Pine Cay, which later became the exclusive Meridian Club. This development was followed by Club Med, which opened its doors on Provo in 1984, and with this the Turks and Caicos started to boom. In the blink of an eye, the islands, which previously had no electricity, acquired satellite TV.

Today finance, tourism and fishing generate most income but the islands cannot

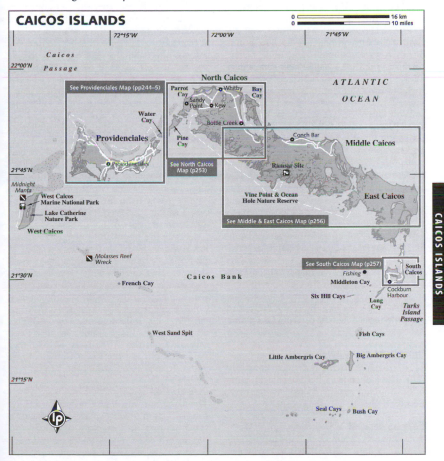

survive without British aid, despite continuing calls for independence.

National Parks

Nature lovers will enjoy exploring this region. There are more than 30 protected national parks, sanctuaries, nature reserves and historical sites, run by the **Turks & Caicos National Parks** (p44).

The **Turks & Caicos National Trust** (☎ 649-941-5710; tc.nattrust@tciway.tc; PO Box 540, Providenciales, Caicos) has established two underwater snorkeling trails off Provo's Smith's and Bight Reefs. It has initiated countrywide studies of bird populations, and in 1999 gained international funding to manage the Ramsar wetlands in North, Middle and East Caicos. See the Environment chapter (p44) for more information and contact details.

Providenciales has the **Northwest Point Marine National Park**, whose inland saline ponds attract roseate spoonbills and other waterfowl, and the **Chalk Sound National Park**, a cay-studded lagoon. **Princess Alexandra National Park** includes the shore and offshore reefs along Grace Bay and the cays northeast of Provo.

West Caicos has the **West Caicos Marine National Park**, and **Lake Catherine Nature Reserve**, a breeding ground for flamingos, ospreys and water birds.

The North, Middle and East Caicos share the **Ramsar Site**. The **Middle Caicos Reserve & Trail System** is part of this park, and incorporates a marsh and intertidal wetlands; a breeding site and nursery for waterfowl, lobster, conch and fish. Middle Caicos also has the **Conch Bar Caves National Park**, an extensive cave system, and the **Vine Point & Ocean Hole Nature Reserve**.

North Caicos enjoys the **Three Mary Cays National Park** and **East Bay Islands National Park**, both favored by seabirds.

South Caicos has two parks; the **Admiral Cockburn Land & Sea Park** with coral reefs, and the **Belle Sound & Admiral Cockburn Cays Nature Reserve**.

Getting There & Away

Most travelers to the Caicos Islands fly into Providenciales International Airport in downtown Providenciales. For information on flights to the islands, see (p251).

Getting Around

You will need your own transport if you want to explore the main island outside of Providenciales' main tourist centers. You can rent cars, scooters and bicycles. Some public buses run infrequently on limited routes.

Scheduled flights depart to the other Caicos islands regularly. Otherwise a plethora of trips, charters and tours depart daily to the islands and their cays from Turtle Cove and the Leeward Marinas (see Tours, p247).

PROVIDENCIALES

pop 8851

As recently as 1964, the island of Providenciales (colloquially called 'Provo') did not have a single wheeled vehicle. Provo is now the most developed island of the Turks and Caicos Islands and tourism is booming.

Provo's iconic beach, the sugar-white **Grace Bay Beach** with its extraordinary aquamarine waters, begins east of Turtle Cove and stretches along the north shore's 5-mile-long Grace Bay to Leeward Marina. White flamingos often alight on the beaches and golf courses at sunrise, while tourism sleeps.

A wealth of resort hotels and residential developments are expanding along the beach and the whole north shore at a rate of knots. This is especially so now that seven-story buildings are permitted on the seafront, both saddening and infuriating Belongers.

East of Provo, the entire north shore and offshore waters are within the protected Princess Alexandra National Park. The south shore is a series of connecting lakes and sounds. Away from the beaches, Provo's appeal lies in its western rugged hills and ridges, and national parks.

Despite the boom in tourism, Provo still has a quiet charm that makes the place a pleasure to explore, and the Belongers are a delight to chat and joke with. The island's tiny cays and surrounding pockets of sparkling sea are visually and sensually stunning. These can be easily reached by chartered boat or excursion, while miles and miles of coral reefs lie temptingly close to shore. Smith's Reef, offshore from the Turtle Cove Marina, and the beach outside the Coral Gardens hotel both offer highly rewarding snorkeling.

Orientation

The main four-lane highway, Leeward Hwy, runs east from downtown along the island's spine, ending at Heaving Down Rock on the eastern coast. A coastal highway, Grace Bay Rd, parallels Grace Bay.

A separate coast road runs northwest from downtown to Blue Hills and Wheeland settlements, beyond which it continues to Northwest Point. This potholed and corrugated road has been slightly improved, but take care when driving. Another very potholed route is South Dock Rd, which runs from South Dock to Sapodilla and Taylor Bays, and along the peninsula that passes Silly Cay.

Information
BOOKSTORES
Most resort boutiques sell a small supply of books and magazines.
Unicorn Bookstore (☎ 649-941-5458; IGA Graceway Mall, Leeward Hwy) Has a large selection including local publications, some great books and maps on the Turks and Caicos, newspapers and magazines.

EMERGENCY
Ambulance & Emergencies (☎ 911)
Fire (☎ 649-946-4444)
Police (☎ 649-946-4259; Old Airport Rd)

MEDICAL SERVICES
Associated Medical Practices Clinic (☎ 649-946-4242; Leeward Hwy) Clinic with several private doctors; has a recompression chamber.
Provo Discount Pharmacy (☎ 649-946-4844; Central Square Plaza, Leeward Hwy; ☻ 8am–10pm)

MONEY
First Caribbean International Bank (☎ 649-946-4245; Butterfield Sq, Leeward Hwy)
Scotiabank (☎ 649-946-4750; Cherokee Rd) Has a 24hr ATM.
Western Union (☎ 649-946-5484; Butterfield Sq, Leeward Hwy)

POST & COMMUNICATIONS
There are public phone booths at several roadside locations. Dial ☎ 111 to place credit-card calls.
DHL Worldwide Express (☎ 649-946-4352; Butterfield Sq, Leeward Hwy)
Federal Express (FedEx; ☎ 649-946-4682; www.fedex.com; Center Complex, Leeward Hwy)
Post office (☎ 649-946-4676; Old Airport Rd; ☻ 8am–noon & 2-4pm Mon-Thu, 8am-12:30pm & 2-5:30pm Fri) Next to the police station.

TOURIST INFORMATION
Tourist information booth (Arrivals Hall, Providenciales International Airport)

Tourist office (☎ 649-946-4970; www.turksandcaicostourism.com; Stubbs Diamond Plaza; ☻ 9am-5pm Mon-Fri)

Sights
Attractions for sightseers are rather slim downtown, but history buffs might check out the ruins of **Cheshire Hall** (Leeward Hwy), a 1790s plantation house constructed by British Loyalists.

A rugged road leads from the settlement of Wheeland (a 4WD might be more comfortable), northwest of downtown, to **Malcolm Roads**, a superb two-mile-long beach good for snorkeling and popular with locals on weekends. Following this arduous, windy, hilly, rocky track, you're soon amid cacti, with views over the inland saline lakes.

Another dirt road leads from Crystal Bay Resorts, northwest of Wheeland, to **Northwest Point**. From here you can walk east to a lighthouse. It's a desperate drive, with deep sand

---

JOJO: A NATIONAL TREASURE

JoJo is a wonderful ambassador for marine life who well and truly holds the hearts of Turks and Caicos islanders. For more than two decades this 7ft bottlenose male dolphin has cruised the waters off Provo and North Caicos on his own, abandoning or deserted by his fellow dolphins. He actively seeks out human contact and has built a close relationship with a handler appointed and paid for by the state.

When he first appeared, he was shy and limited his human contact to following or playing in the bow waves of boats, but he now often appears when people are in the water to join in the fun. JoJo even crossed the Turks Island Passage and hung around Grand Turk for a month some years ago.

Recognized as a national treasure by the Ministry of Natural Resources, JoJo's handler studies his behavior and looks out for him as part of the **JoJo Dolphins Project** (☎ 649-941-5617; www.marinewildlife.org; PO Box 153, Providenciales, Caicos).

JoJo, as with any wild dolphin, interprets an attempt to touch him as an aggressive act, and will react to defend himself, so please bear this in mind if you're lucky enough to experience his playfulness and companionship for a while.

PROVIDENCIALES

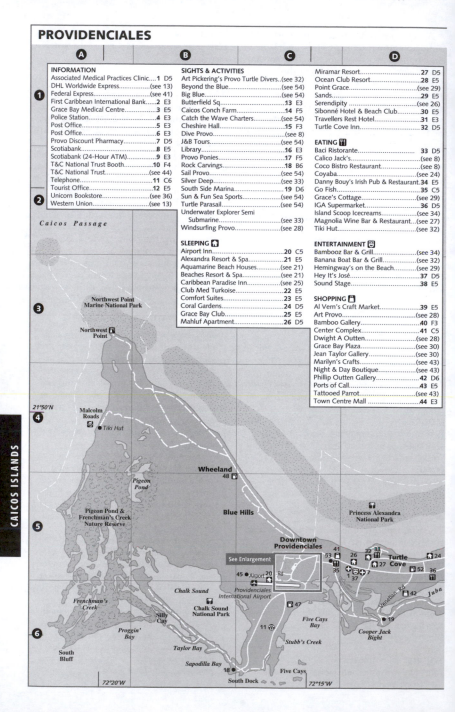

INFORMATION
Associated Medical Practices Clinic.....**1** D5
DHL Worldwide Express..................(see 13)
Federal Express...........................(see 41)
First Caribbean International Bank......**2** E3
Grace Bay Medical Centre................**3** E5
Police Station.............................**4** E3
Post Office................................**5** E3
Post Office................................**6** E3
Provo Discount Pharmacy................**7** D5
Scotiabank................................**8** E5
Scotiabank (24-Hour ATM)...............**9** E3
T&C National Trust Booth...............**10** F4
T&C National Trust.......................(see 44)
Telephone................................**11** C6
Tourist Office.............................**12** E5
Unicorn Bookstore.......................(see 36)
Western Union...........................(see 13)

SIGHTS & ACTIVITIES
Art Pickering's Provo Turtle Divers..(see 32)
Beyond the Blue.........................(see 54)
Big Blue..................................(see 54)
Butterfield Sq............................**13** E3
Caicos Conch Farm.......................**14** F5
Catch the Wave Charters...............(see 54)
Cheshire Hall.............................**15** F3
Dive Provo...............................(see 8)
J&B Tours................................(see 54)
Library...................................**16** E3
Provo Ponies............................**17** F5
Rock Carvings...........................**18** B6
Sail Provo................................(see 54)
Silver Deep..............................(see 33)
South Side Marina.......................**19** D6
Sun & Fun Sea Sports...................(see 54)
Turtle Parasail...........................(see 54)
Underwater Explorer Semi
　Submarine.............................(see 33)
Windsurfing Provo......................(see 28)

SLEEPING
Airport Inn...............................**20** C5
Alexandra Resort & Spa.................**21** E5
Aquamarine Beach Houses..............(see 21)
Beaches Resort & Spa...................(see 21)
Caribbean Paradise Inn..................(see 25)
Club Med Turkoise......................**22** E5
Comfort Suites..........................**23** E5
Coral Gardens...........................**24** D5
Grace Bay Club..........................**25** E5
Mahluf Apartment.......................**26** D5

Miramar Resort..........................**27** D5
Ocean Club Resort.......................**28** E5
Point Grace..............................(see 29)
Sands....................................**29** E5
Serendipity..............................(see 26)
Sibonné Hotel & Beach Club............**30** E5
Travellers Rest Hotel.....................**31** E3
Turtle Cove Inn..........................**32** D5

EATING
Baci Ristorante..........................**33** D5
Calico Jack's............................(see 8)
Coco Bistro Restaurant.................(see 8)
Coyaba..................................(see 24)
Danny Bouy's Irish Pub & Restaurant.**34** E5
Go Fish..................................**35** E5
Grace's Cottage.........................(see 29)
IGA Supermarket........................**36** D5
Island Scoop Icecreams.................(see 34)
Magnolia Wine Bar & Restaurant...(see 27)
Tiki Hut.................................(see 32)

ENTERTAINMENT
Bambooz Bar & Grill....................(see 34)
Banana Boat Bar & Grill.................(see 32)
Hemingway's on the Beach............(see 29)
Hey It's José.............................**37** D5
Sound Stage............................**38** E5

SHOPPING
Al Vern's Craft Market...................**39** E5
Art Provo................................(see 28)
Bamboo Gallery.........................**40** F3
Center Complex..........................**41** C5
Dwight A Outten.........................(see 28)
Grace Bay Plaza.........................(see 30)
Jean Taylor Gallery......................(see 30)
Marilyn's Crafts.........................(see 43)
Night & Day Boutique...................(see 43)
Phillip Outten Gallery...................**42** D6
Ports of Call.............................**43** E5
Tattooed Parrot.........................(see 43)
Town Centre Mall **44** E3

CAICOS ISLANDS

Caicos Passage

Northwest Point
Marine National Park

Northwest
Point

21°50'N

Malcolm
Roads
● Tiki Hut

Wheeland
48

Pigeon
Pond

Blue Hills

Pigeon Pond &
Frenchman's Creek
Nature Reserve

Princess Alexandra
National Park

Downtown
Providenciales
See Enlargement

41　32 33
53　26　27
35　　7
1　37

Turtle
Cove

24
52　36
42　Juba

45 ● Airport 20 Rd
Providenciales
International Airport

47

Chalk Sound

Frenchman's
Creek

Chalk Sound
National Park

Silly
Cay

11

Five Cays
Bay

19
Cooper Jack
Bight

Proggin'
Bay

Stubb's Creek

South
Bluff

Taylor Bay

Sapodilla Bay
18 ●
72°20'W　　South Dock　　72°15'W

Five Cays

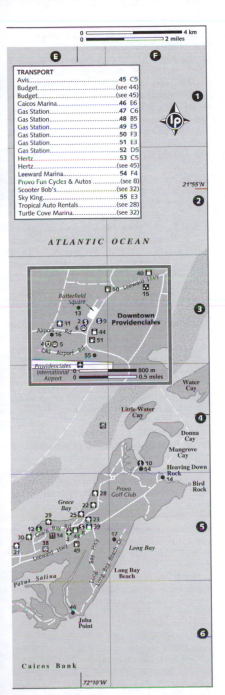

and potholes, and you shouldn't attempt it unless you have courage and a large 4WD.

Protecting reefs off Provo's west shore, Northwest Point Marine National Park encompasses several saline lakes that attract breeding and migrant waterfowl. The largest is Pigeon Pond, inland. This part of the park is the **Pigeon Pond & Frenchman's Creek Nature Reserve**. Other ponds – notably **Northwest Point Pond** and **Frenchman's Creek** – encompass tidal flats and mangrove swamps along the west coast, attracting fish and fowl in large numbers. You'll have to hike to get here, and come equipped with food and water.

CHALK SOUND NATIONAL PARK

The waters of this 3-mile-long bay, 2 miles southwest of downtown, define 'turquoise.' The color is uniform: a vast, unrippled, electric-blue carpet eerily and magnificently studded with countless tiny islets.

A slender peninsula separates the sound from the sea. The peninsula is scalloped with beach-lined bays, notably **Sapodilla Bay**. A potholed road runs along the peninsula; although it is accessible, drive carefully! Unfortunately large vacation homes along both sides of the peninsula clip the views and hinders public access from the roads to the water and beaches.

At the far eastern end of the Sapodilla Bay peninsula, a rocky hilltop boasts **rock carvings**, dating back to 1844. The slabs are intricately carved with Roman lettering that records the names of sailors shipwrecked here and the dates of their sojourns. The carvings are reached via a rocky trail that begins 200yd east of the Mariner Hotel; it leads uphill to the summit, which offers wonderful views over the island and Chalk Sound.

CAICOS CONCH FARM

Located near the northeastern tip of Provo, **Caicos Conch Farm** (☎ 649-946-5643/5330; fax 649-946-5849; tour adult/child $6/3; ⓨ 9am-4pm Mon-Fri, 9am-2pm Sat) claims to be 'the world's only conch farm.' This place is a little creepy and is basically a battery-farm of the critters. Nonetheless, the farm is striving to protect the Caribbean queen conch from extinction by raising the mollusks commercially for export and local use. On a 20-minute tour, you can learn how conchs are grown from eggs to adults.

Activities

DIVING

All the dive operators offer a range of dive and snorkel options, from introductory 'resort courses' to PADI certification ($350 to $395). Most offer free hotel pick-ups and drop-offs. Dive sites include most Caicos islands and cays. For further snorkeling options, see right.

Art Pickering's Provo Turtle Divers (☎ 649-946-4232; www.provoturtledivers.com; Turtle Cove Marina) is a popular outfit offering two-tank and night dives ($95/65). Tailored trips to French Cay and West Caicos are also popular. This company also has facilities at the Ocean Club Resort (p248).

Big Blue (☎ 649-946-5034; www.bigblue.tc; Leeward Marina) runs a large range of diving trips and courses, including a useful refresher course for $125. Two-tank dives are $135 and the diving packages are good value (four days of two-tank dives costs $485).

Dive Provo (☎ 649-946-5040; www.diveprovo.com; Ports of Call, Grace Bay Rd) has two-tank dives ($100) and night dives ($71) at sites around the island, plus photo and video services.

SPORTFISHING & BONEFISHING

A plethora of boat charters and trips can be arranged from Leeward and Turtle Cove Marinas. Try the following operators.

Catch the Wave Charters (☎ 649-941-3047; catchthewave@tciway.tc; Leeward Marina) runs a heap of chartered trips, from $400/800 per half day/full day for three fishing fans, and cruisers from $500/1050 per half/full day for up to eight people. Yummy luxury lobster and wine picnics, and barbecues, can be provided.

Bonefish Unlimited (☎ 649-946-4874; www.provo.net/bonefish) is run by veteran bonefishing guide Captain Barr Gardiner. Call to arrange a tailored half- or full-day fishing trip.

Silver Deep (☎ 649-946-5612; www.silverdeep.com; Turtle Cove Marina) specializes in fishing excursions, but also runs a number of day trips to other Caicos islands and cays. Prices upon application.

J&B Tours (see right) has bonefishing excursions for $240/450 per half/full day.

Beyond the Blue (☎ 649-231-1703; www.beyondtheblue.com; Leeward Marina, Providenciales) will take you on fishing excursions to Belle Sound, South Caicos and design itineraries to suit your requirements.

BOAT EXCURSIONS & SNORKELING

There are plenty of operators offering snorkeling trips to the cays. The following are some renowned and popular choices.

J&B Tours (☎ 649-946-5047; www.jbtours.com; Leeward Marina) is a friendly team who runs great, affordable trips to suit all tastes, budgets and ages. A half-day trip (adult/child $35/20) takes in a snorkel and visit to Little Water Cay's protected iguanas; ask to meet the iguana aptly named Curious. Also on offer is a romantic island getaway ($225 per couple), glow-worm cruise (adult/child $60/40), power-boat charters (from $675), deep-sea fishing charters (from $150 per person) and waterskiing ($60).

Sail Provo (☎ 649-946-4783; www.sailprovo.com; Leeward Marina) offers half-day ($58) and full-day ($108) snorkeling excursions to Little Water Cay aboard 48- to 52ft catamarans. It also offers sunset cruises ($58) and private charters.

Undersea Explorer Semi Submarine (☎ 649-231-0006; www.caicostours.com; Turtle Cove Marina; adult/child $40/30) will take you on a cruise to the reef in a boat with a glass observatory. The observatory, located 5ft below the waves, was developed for Australia's Great Barrier Reef. Private charters are also on offer.

Scooter Bob's (☎ 649-946-4684; scooter@provo.net; Turtle Cove Marina Plaza) Rents snorkel gear for $10 per day.

WATER SPORTS & BOAT RENTALS

Turtle Parasail (☎ 649-941-0643; Leeward Marina) offers parasailing ($70) and banana-boat rides ($25).

Windsurfing Provo (☎ 649-241-1687; windpro@tciway.tc; Ocean Club Resort) offers windsurfing for $25 per hour, as well as lessons for beginners. Sailing is $35/20/90 per hour/additional hour/day, or rent kayaks for $15 per hour. Motor boats can be rented for $70/110/190 per two hours/one day/two days.

Sun & Fun Seasports (☎ 649-946-5724; Leeward Marina) rents jet skis ($90/240/300 per hour/one day/two days) and jet boats ($160/300/400 per hour/one day/two days), for two to eight people.

Parasail 500ft above the ocean for $70 (a minimum weight applicable for children) at **Captain Marvin's Watersports** (☎ 649-231-0643; www.captainmarvinsparasail.com), or take a banana-boat ride ($25).

OTHER ACTIVITIES

Club Med Turkoise (p248) is noted for its tennis facilities, but you'll find similar tennis facilities at most resorts.

Phillip Outten (☎ 649-941-3610; phillipoutten@ tciway.tc; Venetian Rd, off Leeward Hwy), one of the island's noted artists (p250) and a really nice guy, offers horseback rides along the beach ($60 per 1½ hours).

Provo Ponies (☎ 649-241-6350; Long Bay; from $70) also offers rides along quiet hill roads, canals and beaches.

Tours

Big Blue (☎ 649-946-5034; www.bigblue.tc; Leeward Marina) Runs cycling eco-adventure and kayak tours on North Caicos ($60), plus diving trips and courses (opposite).
J&B Tours (☎ 649-946-5047; jill@jbtours.com; Leeward Marina) Offers an 'Island Exploration' tour combining historical and scenic sites with snorkeling (including the Marifax wreck), plus picnic and free drinks ($119; children $70). Also runs fishing and boat trips (opposite).
Ocean Outback (☎ 649-941-5810, 649-231-0824; www .provo.net/oceanoutback/oceanoutbackhome.html) Runs a great-value full-day 'Outback Adventure Cruise' (adult/child $90/40) that takes in a pirates' cave (with 200-year-old carvings), and includes snorkeling, visits to secluded beaches and a barbecue lunch with unlimited drinks. Boat rentals and private charters are available along with glow-worm cruises. Island drop-offs and live-aboard diving (all inclusive board and meals plus access to dive sites) are also on offer.

Festivals & Events

The archipelago's biggest bash is held on Provo each July and August. The **Provo Summer Festival** features regattas, float parades, partying and a 'Miss Turks & Caicos Beauty Pageant' that garners noisy input from everyone. These lively events are spread over a week around Emancipation Day.

The **Turks & Caicos International Billfish Tournament** and the **Invitational Billfish Tournament** are held in July; the two events comprise the Turks & Caicos Billfish Challenge.

A **Culture Night** is held in mid-May.

Sleeping

Much of the accommodation on Provo is quite pricey, but the hotels, resorts, villas and condominium resorts along Grace Bay Beach are of very good quality. Several dozen fab villas are available for rent along Chalk Sound and the Sapodilla peninsula. Cheaper efficiency apartments are in lovely spots along Turtle Cove and the northwestern

beaches. Browse these websites for some alternative rentals; www.wherewhenhow.com and www.provo.net. Also check the hotels' websites listed here for discounts.

DOWNTOWN & TURTLE COVE

Airport Inn (☎ 649-941-3514; fax 649-941-3281; Airport Plaza; r $65-75; ✕ ✕) A perfect option if you're in transit between islands, this small inn is at the airport and has rooms with modern decor, cable TV and phone; some have kitchenettes. It offers special rates for airline crew, free rides to the beach, plus 15% off car-rental rates for guests.

Turtle Cove Inn (☎ 649-946-4203; www.turtlecoveho tel.com; Turtle Cove Marina; d $85; P ✕ ✕ ✕) Don't pay any extra here for rooms that overlook the marina, it's not worth it. Although this place is a bit tired and the pool is tiny, it is a good budget option (ask about specials), set in the centre of Turtle Cove's small bar and restaurant strip. Rooms have cable TV and phone. There are also some excellent dive packages available, too. Ask about rates.

Travellers Rest Hotel (☎ 649-946-4927; www .travelersresthotel.com; Airport Rd, downtown Provo; r $100; P ✕ ✕ ✕) This neat and spacious hotel is good for those jumping on a plane. It's two minutes away from the airport, and you can take the complimentary shuttles that run between the airport and Princess Alexander National Park's 12-mile-long beach.

Miramar Resort (☎ 649-946-4240; www.miramar resort.tc; Turtle Cove; d $120; P ✕ ✕ ✕) Set on a hill above the Turtle Cove Marina, it is a steep walk up from the area's bars and restaurants. The 6-acre site has a pleasant Mediterranean air about it, and the rooms are spacious, attractive and airy, with great views. All rooms come with fridge, cable TV, phone and Internet connection. The resort has a pool, gym, tennis court, wine bar and fairly gloomy restaurant. Diving packages are on offer.

Mahluf Apartment (☎ 649-946-4989; www.silk road.tc; Turtle Cove; apt $150; P ✕ ✕) This modern, light apartment, with a fab L-shaped pool and clear ocean views, is close to the night life of Turtle Cove. It's located in the lower level of a private home and a five-night minimum stay is required.

GRACE BAY & EAST PROVIDENCIALES
Midrange
Caribbean Paradise Inn (☎ 649-946-5022; www.para dise.tc; Grace Bay; r $140; P ✕ ✕ ✕) At Paradise

Inn's heart is a small, attractive pool fringed by bougainvillea. There's a bar in a canopied patio, where buffet breakfasts are served. Rooms have rattan furnishings, terracotta-tiled floors, king-size beds, light that pours in through French windows opening onto wide balconies. It's only 300yd from the beach.

Comfort Suites (☎ 649-946-8888; www.comfort suitestci.com; Grace Bay; r $150; P X X 🖳 🖳) This comfortable, friendly and amazingly efficient hotel is a great deal. The location is central to Grace Bay's restaurants and bars, but it's a fifteen-minute walk to the beach. The rooms are cheerful and roomy, and furnished with sofas, refrigerator, coffeemaker, cable TV, in-room safe and ceiling fans. A complimentary breakfast of croissant and *pain au chocolat* (chocolate croissant) is served in the courtyard alongside the lively outdoor bar and small swimming pool. Good dive packages should also be checked out.

Sibonné Hotel & Beach Club (☎ 649-946-5547; www.sibonne.com; Grace Bay; r $175; P X X 🖳) This small and romantic inn sits on the beach and has comfortable rooms set around a garden strewn with hammocks and palm trees. A fabulous restaurant and bar sit adjacent to the freshwater pool and overlook the beach. The renowned Bay Bistro serves a delicious grilled vegetable and brie tart, and desserts involve lots of chocolate wickedness. What else do you need other than elasticized clothes? Dive and golf packages are offered, and regular specials bring this place within a midrange budget.

Other beachside recommendations include **Alexandra Resort & Spa** (☎ 649-946-5807; www.alexandraresort.com; Grace Bay; r $140; P X X 🖳) for its great views, children's activities and bubbling spa and the **Aquamarine Beach Houses** (☎ 649-941-5690; www.aquamarinebeachhou ses.com; Grace Bay; r $145; P X X 🖳), which has stunning views over Grace Bay and a white and light decor.

Top End
Ocean Club Resort (☎ 649-946-5880; www.oceanclub resorts.com; r $225; P X X 🖳) The first-class condos here are set in beautifully manicured grounds with shaded hammocks slung between the palms, a swim-up bar, fitness room and a night-lit tennis court. The resort also runs a dive operation.

Sands (☎ 649-941-5199; www.thesandresort.com; Grace Bay; d $225; P X X 🖳) This beachside

resort is quiet and has modern rental condos plus it's blessed with the convivial Hemingway's Bar & Restaurant (p250); the cocktails and mango-and-shrimp salad are delicious.

Coral Gardens (☎ 649-941-3713; www.coralgardens .com; Grace Bay; d $300; P X X 🖳 🖳) Has huge, well-lit two-bedroom suites with king-size beds and wrap-around plate-glass windows. The hotel sits on the beach and has the Whitehouse Reef directly offshore; great for easy snorkeling. You will need transport to get around as it's away from the action.

Also recommended:

Beaches Resort & Spa (☎ 649-946-8000; www .beaches.com; Grace Bay; r $350; P X X 🖳 🖳) A popular all-inclusive 45-acre resort preferred by families; there's a great kid's club on site.

Club Med Turkoise (☎ 649-946-5500; www.clubmed .com; r per person $190; X X 🖳) This 70-acre all-inclusive adult-only resort is beloved of single thirty-somethings who want to play hard.

Point Grace (☎ 649-946-5096; www.pointgrace.com; r $600; P X X 🖳 🖳)There's real class and luxury at this boutique hotel.

Grace Bay Club (☎ 649-946-5757; www.gracebayclub .com; r $650; P X X 🖳 🖳) A lush 5-acre world centered around an Andalusian-style mansion and a plaza with fountain, waterfall and real burping frogs.

WEST PROVIDENCIALES
Serendipity (☎ 649-946-4787; www.serendipity.tc; Babalua Beach; apt per week $800) This pristine, modern and airy one-bedroom, self-contained apartment is on the lower level of a private home that sits on a ridge overlooking the ocean. The views are fabulous, although it's a 15-minute walk from the beach.

Eating & Drinking
There are French influences aplenty in the Provo restaurants, and this doesn't just mean lots of cream and butter sauces. Subtle flavorings and fresh combinations create some imaginative menus.

The northwestern shore has some good Bahamian takeouts; vegetarians are well catered for.

DOWNTOWN & TURTLE COVE
Tiki Hut (☎ 649-941-5341; Turtle Cove Inn; mains $10-25; 🕒 breakfast, lunch & dinner, closed Sun) Adjacent to Turtle Cove Marina, this is a good place for breakfast, but an even better place for Wednesday night's $10 barbecue; a 13-year tradition that packs out the place. Chicken,

ribs or steaks are served with sautéed vegetables, and with garlic-mashed potatoes so creamy they would make an Irishman cry. Buckets of beer at $20 are guzzled by this happy crowd. Don't miss out!

Baci Ristorante (☎ 649-941-3044; Harbour Towne Plaza, Turtle Cove; mains $10-27; Tue-Fri, dinner only Sat & Sun) This classy place has terracotta-tiled floors and wrought-iron furnishings, plus a bougainvillea-shaded patio. It serves some truly grand grub; blackened snapper with lemon sauce, penne with vodka-chicken and the luscious chocolate pâté with crème anglaise and fruit coulis.

Magnolia Winebar & Restaurant (☎ 649-946-4240; www.miramarresort.tc; Miramar Resort, Turtle Cove; mains $12-28; lunch & dinner) The restaurant offers a view over Turtle Cove, a selection of mainly French wines and specializes in Asian-Caribbean cuisine, such as sesame seared tuna with wok-fried veggies, baby bok choy, and coconut wasabi with mashed potato.

Go Fish (☎ 649-941-4646; Centre Mews, Leeward Hwy; breakfast & lunch) Offers fish specials to eat in or takeout. Also has herb roast chicken.

IGA Supermarket (☎ 649-941-5000; Graceway Plaza, Leeward Hwy; 7am-10pm) For deli foods, great fresh fruit and veg, vegetarian soya dishes and all other foodstuffs, head for the region's best and largest food store.

GRACE BAY & EAST PROVIDENCIALES
Many of the resort hotels also have fabulous restaurants and some lively and fun bars that are open to nonguests.

There's a heap of great informal eateries at the Ports of Call plaza and along Grace Bay Rd, within a five-minute walk of the Comfort Suites, all with vegetarian dishes on the menu.

Island Scoop Icecreams (☎ 649-241-4230; Grace Bay Plaza, Grace Bay Rd; ice cream $3; 10am-9pm) A couple of very smart cookies are selling heaps of this lush and creamy ice cream, gelato and sorbets to outlets around the island. Try the wonderful mango gelato; it's magic!

Calico Jack's (☎ 649-946-5120; upstairs, Ports of Call plaza; mains $8-20; dinner Sun-Fri) This lively bar and restaurant is known for its gazpacho ($5) and yummy great-value pizzas. Friday nights it is the place to be; on the outdoor deck carousing with the band and fun-loving residents.

Danny Buoy's Irish Pub & Restaurant (☎ 649-946-5921; Grace Bay Rd; mains $9-15; lunch & dinner)

A Celt set up this pub, and did a genuinely good job on it. Walk in and see the polished wooden bar, draft beers and row of behind-shined barstools, and you would swear that you're in a misty part of boggy Ireland. That is, apart from the Becks beer and a menu that would please an English country lord no end; bangers and mash with baked beans, fish and chips – oh, simple joys. Live music and quiz nights add to the fun.

Coyaba (☎ 649-941-3713; Coral Gardens, Grace Bay; mains $18-35; lunch & dinner) This place offers elegant dining under a canopy at a lovely beachside spot. Highlights feature such dishes as Atlantic salmon wrapped in filo and stuffed with goat cheese, anise, lobster mushroom, saffron and vanilla: yum!

Coco Bistro Restaurant (☎ 649-946-5369; Ports of Call plaza, Grace Bay Rd; mains $25-30; lunch & dinner) The combined tropical and rustic style of Coco Bistro is obviously French, as is the influence on the menu. Surrounded by abundant Haitian art, choose from fresh indoor dining, or the alfresco option on a palm-shaded patio. Creative dishes include mussels in curry and hurricane ginger shrimp.

Grace's Cottage (☎ 649-946-8147; www.pointgrace .com; Point Grace; mains $26-35; lunch & dinner) Possibly the finest dining in Caicos. There's an old wood-lined bar and intimate tables clothed in crisp white linen set among flowering shrubs in an outdoor courtyard. The superb dishes are unpretentious and delicious; gorgonzola and broccoli soup, grilled mango with lemon and orange duck, and chocolate soufflé. A romantic and very special meal is enhanced by professional and friendly staff.

Entertainment
Banana Boat Bar & Grill (☎ 649-941-5706; mains $15-18; lunch & dinner) This atmospheric and gaily painted place, adjoining Turtle Cove Marina, serves good grilled dishes, burgers and Bahamian cooking. And the nightlife here is brilliant: Thursday is CD night (bring your own, and preferably not Leonard Cohen or The Wiggles); Friday is a live calypso or reggae band; Saturday is karaoke, with renditions sung to much mirth and commentary; and Sunday night is bingo, with jackpots of up to $15,000! The latter is a raucous event that could possibly be the best night in town.

Calico Jack's (☎ 649-946-5120; upstairs, Ports of Call plaza) This place gets packed on a Friday

CAICOS ISLANDS

night, with live calypso, reggae and soca bands playing on the outdoor deck. Regulars also recommend the pizza restaurant.

Bambooz Bar & Grill (☎ 649-946-8146; Salt Mills Plaza, Grace Bay Rd; mains $9-18; ⏱ dinner) *The* hot spot: Thursday night karaoke brings in the heavyweight political and religious hoi-polloi, as well as some serious crooners to belt out their favorites (country-and-western ballads go down a storm). The action starts around 9pm and on weekends continues until the early hours.

Hemingway's on the Beach (☎ 649-946-5199; Sands Resort, Grace Bay) This great little bar serves some multihued cocktails and tasty plates of food, while also celebrating the sunset with regular live music.

Hey It's José (☎ 649-946-4812; Central Square Plaza, Leeward Hwy) The free movies on Saturday night from 9pm pull in the crowds, as do the half-price Margaritas at happy hour (which in Provo normally lasts two hours).

DANCE CLUBS

Most of the upscale resorts in Grace Bay have dance clubs, including Beaches Resort & Spa and Club Med Turkoise who welcome nonguests with a paid entry fee (both places charge $30).

Sound Stage (Grace Bay, Leeward Hwy; ⏱ 4pm-midnight Mon, 4pm-2am Fri & Sat, 1-9pm Sun) This is the best nightspot (if you ignore the poker machines indoors), with a great outdoor bar and dance club fringed by palm trees and ocean views. A mix of DJ nights, live bands and jazz evenings keeps everyone happy. Comedy nights are also planned. There's a choice of varied, tasty buffet dishes (mains $18 to $45). Tight security keeps out the rougher crowds, and a strict dress-code applies – smart casual and no beanies (knitted skullcaps).

Shopping

A large selection of beachy items, casual clothing, and batiks is offered at **Tattooed Par-**

COLORFUL MEMORIES

Art fans will love the range of original and affordable artworks on sale in Provo. Some are sold in local stores and hotel reception areas from $15 for an original oil or acrylic painting! Many of these artworks are copies of original Haitian paintings, but are still talented depictions in their own right. Make sure you hunt out the truly talented Turks and Caicos stars, including the following headline acts/galleries.

■ **Anna Bourne** The North Caicos Art Society in Whitby (North Caicos) sponsor local art, emphasizing silkscreen painting. Bourne, who lives on Provo, is perhaps the leading artist in the genre; she paints on silk with French dyes.

■ **Dwight A Outten** (☎ 649-941-4545; www.artprovo.com; Art Provo, Ocean Club Plaza) Love of nature and all things Caicos obviously flows in the blood, for Dwight's flamingos, indigenous birds and island houses are similarly as catching, and arguably as good as the paintings of his Rastafarian cousin Phillip Outten.

■ **Jean Taylor Gallery** (☎ 5649-231-2708; Grace Bay Plaza, Grace Bay Rd) The gallery opens on demand only, but Taylor's unique vision of Bahamian life and humor also can be seen at Art Provo in Ocean Club Plaza.

■ **Phillip Outten Gallery** (☎ 649-941-3610; phillipoutten@tciway.tc; Venetian Rd, off Leeward Hwy) Some people consider genial Rastafarian Phillip Outten the leading artist in the Turks and Caicos. His home – gaily painted in Rasta colors – is his gallery, and he always welcomes visitors. His best paintings are of the animals and nature he so obviously relishes.

Al Vern's Craft Market sits on the side of Turquoise Rd, and is a collection of small huts selling local paintings and crafts. You will also find some wonderful metal carvings depicting a range of scenes: underwater mermaids and mermen entwined with fish and seaweed; school buses full of cheerful kids; and cycling Rastafarians. The artists use metal cut from old car wrecks, which is then painted and varnished.

Bamboo Gallery (☎ 649-946-4748; www.provo.net/bamboo; Market Place, Leeward Hwy) and **Art Provo** (☎ 649-941-4545; www.artprovo.com; Ocean Club Plaza) are two fabulous galleries that sell many leading and local artists' vibrant works.

rot (☎ 649-946-5829), Marilyn's Crafts, and the Night & Day Boutique, all in the Ports of Call plaza.

Getting There & Around
AIR
For information on flights to and from the Turks and Caicos Islands, see p291.

There are no buses from Providenciales International Airport. A taxi to Grace Bay costs $16 one-way for two people; each extra person costs $5. Some resorts have their own minibus transfers.

The following airlines fly between the Turks and Caicos Islands.

Air Turks & Caicos (www.airturksandcaicos.com) Grand Turk (☎ 649-946-2709); Provo (☎ 649-946-4181); Salt Cay (☎ 649-946-6900) Flies between the Caicos, Grand Turk and Salt Cay.

Sky King Airlines (☎ 649-941-5464; www.skyking.tc) Flies between Provo, Grand Turk and South Caicos. Also to the Bahamas, Cuba, Jamaica, Dominican Republic and Haiti.

Turks & Caicos Airways Provo (☎ 649-946-2709); Grand Turk (☎ 649-946-2709); Sth Caicos (☎ 649-946-3279); Mid Caicos (☎ 649-946-6136); Nth Caicos (☎ 649-946-7246); Salt Cay (☎ 649-946-6928; fax 649-946-4483) Flies between Provo and other Caicos Islands, Salt Cay and Grand Turk.

The following prices are for one-way flights from Provo.

Destination	Price	Frequency
Grand Turk	$75	several daily
Mid Caicos	$45	4 weekly
Nth Caicos	$35	several daily
Salt Cay	$55	several daily
Sth Caicos	$65	several daily

BICYCLE
Provo Fun Cycles & Autos and Scooter Bob's (see right) rent mountain bikes.

BOAT
A plethora of boat charters and trips can be arranged to the islands and cays from Leeward and Turtle Cove Marinas. See p247.

Caicos Marina (☎ 649-946-5416; VHF Ch16) Has a few slips and basic facilities.

Leeward Marina (☎ 649-946-5553; VHF Ch 16) At the eastern end of the island, has limited services and dockside berths only.

South Side Marina (☎ 649-946-3508; VHF Ch 16) Has a few slips.

Turtle Cove Marina (☎ 649-941-3781; fax 649-941-5782; VHF Ch16) Has more than 100 deep-water slips plus full services and accommodations.

CAR, MOTORCYCLE & SCOOTER
Mandatory insurance costs $14 and a one-off government tax is also payable. Most rental companies offer free drop-off and pick-up. The local companies are very good, and can be cheaper than the internationals. Rental drivers may be required to have a minimum age of 25 years.

Hertz (☎ 649-941-3910; mystique@tciway.tc), **Avis** (☎ 649-946-4705; www.avistci.com) and **Budget** (☎ 649-946-4079) are at the airport. Hertz also has an outlet at Southern Shores Centre, and Budget has an outlet at Town Centre Mall, both on Leeward Hwy.

Provo Fun Cycles & Autos (☎ 649-946-5868; provofuncycles@tciway.tc; Ports of Call plaza) based across the street from Comfort Suites, is friendly and helpful. It rents good compact cars and jeeps from $45 per day, scooters for $42, and rents mountain bikes for $15 per day.

Scooter Bob's (☎ 649-946-4684, scooter@provo.net; Turtle Cove Marina Plaza) rents cars and jeeps from $60 per day, motorbikes from $50 per day, and rents mountain bikes for $15 per day.

Tropical Auto Rentals (☎ 649-946-5300; tropical@tciway.tc; Ocean Club Plaza, Grace Bay) charges from $65 for compacts and $76 for jeep hire.

PUBLIC TRANSPORT
Sporadic buses run routes to some of the settlements out of town. A public minibus runs along Leeward Hwy; it also runs southwest as far as South Dock and Sapodilla Bay ($2). Ask at the tourist office for schedules.

TAXI
There are several taxi companies that mainly use minivans. Many congregate around the main hotels' entrances, and are quick to respond to a call. You can call VHF Channel 06 for the dispatcher, or contact the following companies.

Nell's Taxi Service (☎ 649-941-3228)
Provo Taxi & Bus Group (☎ 649-946-5481)

WEST CAICOS
This island is renowned for its fabulous diving, and attracts many dive operators from Provo. West Caicos was a successful sisal plantation in the 1800s, complete with railroad tracks and a small township. Inland,

Lake Catherine is a nature reserve that attracts flamingos, ospreys, ducks and waders. On the coast, the small, sandy beaches make perfect picnic spots.

The island is 6 miles southwest of Provo, and was undergoing private development at the time of writing, which may limit access.

However the sea remains a public domain. Molasses Reef harbors the remains of the oldest known shipwreck in the western hemisphere, dating from 1513. The reefs off the west shore are protected within West Caicos Marine National Park. Other prime dive sites include Elephant Ear Canyon, named for the resident 95ft sponges – the biggest found in the Turks and Caicos. One 10ft-wide monster masks a cave. There's also the Magic Mushroom: a sand chute leads to a precipice where sponges and black coral anchor the coral buttresses and nervous lobsters pack the cracks.

There's no scheduled transport to West Caicos. To get there, you'll need to hire a boat or take a diving tour. See Diving, p246

FRENCH CAY

This tiny cay, about 15 miles due south of Provo, is an uninhabited wildlife sanctuary protecting more than 2000 nesting and migrating species of birds, including frigate birds and ospreys. Stingrays gather in the seas to give birth, and nurse sharks are also drawn here during summer to breed. You will need a permit to visit the cay.

The French pirate L'Olonnois hid here while he preyed on Spanish galleons.

Art Pickering's Provo Turtle Divers makes this trip, see p246 for details. Trips include swimming and snorkeling with the friendly sharks in summer, and with stingrays year-round.

CAYS EAST OF PROVIDENCIALES
Little Water Cay

This small cay within the Princess Alexandra National Park is a sanctuary for endangered and very cute Turks and Caicos rock iguanas, as well as graceful ospreys. Many official and unofficial operators bring out visitors (around $55 for a half-day trip from Provo), who must each buy a $5 permit and be accompanied by an official guide.

The guides will handfeed some of these little critters who can run like the wind when food or danger is in sight. One of the guides'

favorite iguanas named 'Curious' normally checks out visitors. He also outruns and outwits larger iguanas to reach any food in the offing. Show these creatures due respect; iguanas live for up to forty years, and are a lot more successful at monogamous relationships than humans, managing it for life.

The 170yd-long **North Shore Trail** leads from the beach to a shallow mangrove estuary where you can learn about this vital ecosystem. A lookout deck offers views over a pond and large osprey nest. Iguanas frequently forage along the 225yd-long **South Shore Trail**, which passes through a lush coastal coppice and also has a lookout deck. You are requested to stay to the trails to avoid trampling the iguanas' burrows and the ecologically sensitive plants.

Pine Cay

Two miles northeast of Provo, this idyllic little isle isn't really for most travelers, unless you really want to spoil yourself, or just happen to be a wealthy mega-star. This 800-acre private cay only welcomes guests by prior arrangement. Seasonal residents include a few little-known characters; Bill Cosby, Denzel Washington and Jimmy Buffett, who has a passion for bonefishing here.

The cay is so far out that it doesn't take note of daylight saving time, thereby constituting its own little time zone. About two-thirds of the island is set aside as a nature preserve, accessed by 9 miles of nature trails. There are semitame iguanas and 120 species of birds, including white-tailed tropic birds.

A fabulous beach runs almost the full length of the west shore. At its northern end, **Sand Dollar Point**, you can wade out 400yd in knee-deep water and search for the eponymous shells. A 70ft wreck lies partially submerged a stone's throw from shore, with a cannon on the seabed. Snorkeling is superb at the **Aquarium**, a cove on the east shore of Pine Cay, with two anemone-covered coral arms embracing a sandy floor – the anemones pulse like little translucent green hearts. Pine Cay has a packed-sand airstrip.

All-inclusive packages and a ban on guest phones and pagers appeal to travelers with a taste for luxurious and unpretentious isolation at **Meridian Club** (US ☎ 1-203-602-0300; www .meridianclub.com; d per week $4,555; ✗ ✗ ✗). One-bed cabañas are tucked amid sand dunes, each with lounge, kitchen and screened porch fronting the beach. Rooms are austere, with neither telephones nor TVs. There's also a tennis court, sailboats, sailboards and bicycles, and boating tours on the fancy launch, with crew decked out in yachting whites. Two children per family (aged four to 17) enjoy complimentary stays.

Fort George Cay

This tiny cay, just north of Pine Cay, is a national historic site as it's home to the remains of an 18th-century British fort built to protect the Caicos Islands from attack. Divers and snorkelers can inspect barnacle-encrusted cannons lying on the bottom of the ocean. The site is protected within Fort George Land & Sea National Park.

Dellis Cay

Next north in the necklace of cays, Dellis is locally called Shell Island, and is another regular stop for tour operators. Enjoy a stroll, swim and the gorgeous 360-degree views. Thanks to a mix of tide patterns and current, there's a wealth of shells here. However no shells may be removed from the isle.

Parrot Cay

This private cay, west of North Caicos, is said to have been the lair of pirates Calico Jack and vicious Anne Bonney in the 1720s. The only treasure today is a deluxe resort once owned by a Kuwaiti shah and the scintillating 3-mile-long beach. Bring bug spray.

The boat to parrot cay leaves by demand from Leeward Marina on Provo. To arrange a ride, you call ahead to Parrot Cay club.

Parrot Cay (☎ 649-946-7788; www.besthotelsresorts.com/parrotcay.htm; r $590; ✗ ☒ ☒) This upmarket place, with lots of white and Indonesian furnishings, is favored by air-kissing celebrities such as Donatella Versace. You can cool off in the infinity pool and relax in the super-deluxe Asian spa. Ancient Eastern treatments, yoga packages and the week-long healing Como Shambhla Retreat encourage mind-over-material-matter thoughts.

NORTH CAICOS
pop 2075
Little-visited North Caicos appeals to eco-tourists. Paved roads make scooters and bicycles a great way to get around. There are

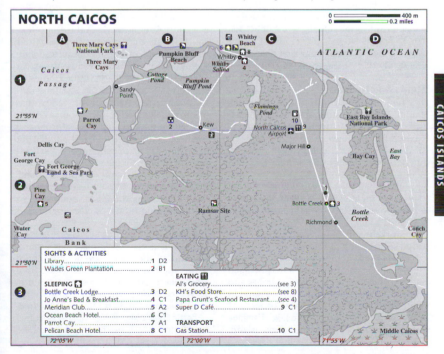

four small settlements; tiny Sandy Point and Kew, and larger Whitby and Bottle Creek.

Kew is located near the island's center with a fresh-water sinkhole, and Bottle Creek is on a breezy coastal bluff 2 miles south of the airport.

North Caicos gets more rainfall than other islands and hence has more lush vegetation. Traditionally the bread basket of the island chain, in the last century it was also the seat of government for these islands. Farms evolved in colonial times and sloops were built to transport crops to the other islands. Mangoes, oranges, and other fruits and vegetables still thrive beside sea grapes and sugar apples.

North Caicos hosts the **Festarama Festival** each July. This annual regatta includes beach parties, while October's **North Caicos Extravaganza** features a Junkanoo carnival (a street 'Carnivale' with parades, costumes and *goombay* music).

Information

There's a post office in Kew, and Bottle Creek has a small public library. A fax and email service is available in the office of Papa Grunt's Seafood Restaurant. For emergencies contact the **police** (Bottle Creek ☎ 649-946-7116; Kew ☎ 649-946-7261), or call ☎ 911. There are also two **government medical clinics** (Bottle Creek ☎ 649-946-7194; Kew ☎ 649-946-7397).

Sights & Activities

The Kew area has several historic ruins, including the interesting **Wades Green Plantation**, granted to a British Loyalist by King George III. The owners struggled to grow sisal and Sea Island cotton until drought, hurricanes and bugs drove them out. The plantation lasted a mere 25 years; the owners abandoned their slaves and left.

Beaches include **Pumpkin Bluff**, **Horsestable** and the lovely deserted **Whitby Beach**. Pumpkin Bluff beach is especially beautiful and the snorkeling is good, with a foundered cargo ship adding to the allure.

Cottage Pond, a 150ft-deep blue hole on the northwest coast, attracts waterfowl such as West Indian whistling ducks, grebes and waders. Bellfield Landing Pond, Pumpkin Bluff Pond and Dick Hill Creek attract flamingos, as does a large brine lake, **Flamingo Pond**, which floods the center of the island. The ponds are protected as individual nature reserves and the gangly birds strut around.

A series of small cays off the northeast shore are protected within **East Bay Islands National Park**, and a trio of cays to the northwest form **Three Mary Cays National Park**, another flamingo sanctuary and an osprey nesting site. The snorkeling is good at Three Mary Cays National Park and further west at Sandy Point Beach.

Vast bonefish flats extend east of the island. The entire south shore is encompassed by the **Ramsar Site** sanctuary, which is comprised of a vast series of marsh and intertidal wetlands. It extends to East Caicos, and protects an important breeding site and nursery for waterfowl, lobster, conch and fish. The creeks are full of schooling bonefish and tarpon.

Sleeping & Eating

The best website displaying the North Caicos' accommodations and rentals is www.tcimall.tc.

Jo Anne's Bed & Breakfast (☎ 649-946-7184; www.tcimall.tc/joannesbnb/index.htm; Whitby; r $80; ⊠) This modest accommodation option has an adjoining restaurant and the beach is a short walk away. Jo Anne also offers a courtesy van service. More comfortable villas ($200) and two-room oceanfront suites with kitchen ($110) are also available.

Pelican Beach Hotel (☎ 649-946-7112; www.pelicanbeach.tc; Whitby; r $145; ⊠ ⊠) Spacious, modestly furnished oceanfront rooms have wood-paneled walls, tiled floors, and patios with lounge chairs. The bathrooms are small but enhanced by hand-painted motifs. There are no telephones or TVs. Breakfasts, sandwich lunches and dinner meals are prepared on request, while a friendly little bar and restaurant serves good local dishes including the freshest of grilled fish with the ubiquitous peas 'n' rice (mains around $12 to $25).

Ocean Beach Hotel (☎ 649-946-7113; Whitby; s/d $115/130) This nice little place has a homey feel and all the rooms are beachfront with patios. Rattan furniture adds to the bright atmosphere. An on-site restaurant and bar serves meals on request. Fishing charters are available, and children under 12 stay free.

Bottle Creek Lodge (winter ☎ 649-946-7080, summer ☎ 410-968-2214; www.bottlecreeklodge.com; Bottle Creek; r per six nights $960) A small, modern-style eco-lodge perched on a ridge on the north-eastern side of Flamingo Pond. It's simple and airy, and features modest furnishings. All rooms face the sea and prevailing trade winds. Complimentary kayaks, bikes, snorkel gear and fishing rods are supplied.

Papa Grunt's Seafood Restaurant (☎ 649-946-7113; mains $6-28; 🕒 breakfast, lunch & dinner; 🖳) Dinners are by reservation at Jo Anne's no-frills diner (which adjoins her B&B). Here seafood dishes rule, although other fare includes pizza, sandwiches and burgers.

Super D Café (☎ 649-946-7528) For traditional Caicos fare head for Super D Café at the airport.

You can buy produce and groceries at KH's Food Store in Whitby and at Al's Grocery in Bottle Creek.

Getting There & Around

For information on flights to and from the island, see p251.

A taxi from the airport to Whitby costs $10 one-way. Mac of **M&M Tours** (☎ 649-946-7338) offers island tours for $30 per hour. You won't need more than three hours to see the entire island.

Many boat and diving operators listed under Activities (p246) go to North Caicos (and also have kayaking and cycling).

You can hire bicycles at Whitby Plaza for $20 per day.

Car rental costs around $80 per day. Try the following options. They deliver to your location:

Gardiners (☎ 649-946-7141)
Old Nick (☎ 649-946-7280)

MIDDLE CAICOS

pop 437

The largest of the Caicos islands (48 sq miles) retains evidence of pre-Columbian Lucayans: around 38 of their dwelling sites have been discovered here, many of which have been excavated by archaeologists.

The fishermen and farmers in the tiny hamlets of Conch Bar, Bambarra and Lorimers give visitors a warm welcome. Bambarra was named for people from the Bombarras tribe of the Niger River, who were shipwrecked here in 1842 when a slavetrader ran aground.

The southern half of the island is composed of vast intertidal swamplands. Offshore, **Vine Point & Ocean Hole Nature Reserve** protects a

---

> **HIKING THE ISLAND: MIDDLE CAICOS RESERVE & TRAIL SYSTEM**
>
> Many of the growing ecotourism operations will take you on an adventure where you'll use your feet or a bicycle to experience the beauty of these islands. However, you may want to organize this trip yourself.
>
> Miles of beaches, large freshwater lakes and lavish pine forests can be accessed by 10 miles of trails along the north coast, created in conjunction with the Turks & Caicos National Trust as part of the Ramsar Site. One trail leads from Mudjen Harbour Beach to join the historic Crossing Over Trail that leads from Middle to North Caicos. En route, it passes the ruins of several Loyalist cotton plantations, as well as brine pools favored by cranes and flamingos. Signs at regular intervals point out highlights of the trek.
>
> The north coast is dramatically scenic, with long beaches and scalloped bays beside rugged limestone cliffs. Mudjen Harbour Beach features a huge amphitheater carved from the raw limestone bluffs. Here, the long unfurling of turquoise waves is broken by pretty Dragon Cay, connected to the shore by a sand spit and surrounded by placid sea pools; perfect for soaking your feet in after a trek.

---

frigate-bird breeding colony, plus a 210ft-deep, 400yd-wide marine blue hole favored as a hangout by turtles and sharks. Kayak, dive or snorkel here; you'll have a ball.

The **Conch Bar Caves National Park** protects 15 miles of underground caverns. Some have lagoons and stalactites and stalagmites, and most are home to colonies of bats. The caves were used as sacred sanctuaries by the Lucayan Indians, who left petroglyphs on the walls. The most notable Lucayan site is the **Armstrong Pond Village Historical Site**.

The island hosts the **Middle Caicos Expo** each August.

Contact the operators listed under Activities, p246, for diving and boat trips from Provo to Middle Caicos.

Sleeping & Eating

Budget rates can really only be achieved by sharing rental accommodation.

Crosswinds (☎ 828-479-1056; www.crosswindstci .com; per week $900; ❎) Also close to the little

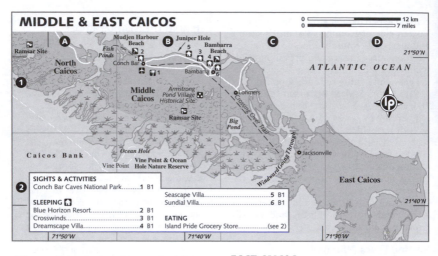

MIDDLE & EAST CAICOS

SIGHTS & ACTIVITIES	
Conch Bar Caves National Park.........1 B1	Seascape Villa.........................5 B1
	Sundial Villa............................6 B1
SLEEPING	
Blue Horizon Resort.........................2 B1	EATING
Crosswinds.......................................3 B1	Island Pride Grocery Store.............(see 2)
Dreamscape Villa............................4 B1	

village of Bambarra, this two-bed house sits on stilts, with views of the surrounding bush and ocean in the distance. There's a modern kitchen, and the cool and spacious open-plan living is enhanced by the simple, white rattan furniture.

Sundial Villas (☎ 604-576-9369; www.sundialvillas .com; r per night/week $150/1050) This colorful and cheerful two-bed villa close to Bambarra has comfy appeal, with a great family room, kitchen and screened veranda. Perfect for families, additional joys (simple ones are always the best) include a bread machine, dried herbs, spices and use of the houseowner's private thatched tiki hut on the adjacent beach. Get out the Jackie Collins novel and watch your kids splash in the sea. Bliss.

Blue Horizon Resort (☎ 649-946-6141; www.bhres ort.com; r $185; ✗ ✗) This residential and vacation community in pretty Mudjen Harbour overlooks Dragon Cay and has stunning views of the ocean. Set in 50 acres, it has attractive blue-and-white rental cottages with porches, full modern kitchens and a TV.

Also recommended is the spacious three-bedroom **Dreamscape Villa** (☎ 649-946-6175; www. middlecaicos.com; r per week $1700; ✗ ✗) at stunning Bambarra Beach (priced for four adults). **Seascape Villa** (per week $1850; ✗ ✗), also priced for four adults, is a three-bedroom home with sea views, cathedral ceiling, flowering shrubs and a screened-in porch.

Groceries can be bought at the Island Pride Grocery Store.

For flight information, see p251.

EAST CAICOS

The least-visited island of the chain is often labeled 'uninhabited,' although there is an impoverished settlement of Haitians. It's also home to small herds of wild cattle and flocks of flamingos flaunting their neon-pink liveries. Neverending miles of beaches are perfect for the adventurous beachcomber.

With no air service; East Caicos can be reached only by boat.

SOUTH CAICOS

pop 1939

After the salt industry passed on, lobster- and conch-fishing long provided this arid island, 22 miles west of Grand Turk, with a reasonably healthy income. However this industry has also experienced problems and many islanders have drifted to Provo in the last decade.

Cockburn Harbour, the only settlement, is perfect to launch across the 40-mile-wide Caicos Bank in search of bonefish. In addition birdwatchers may flock here (sorry) to see the flamingos that inhabit the vast *salinas* (salt ponds) on the northeast edge of the harbor; dozens of flamingos are resident year-round. However it is divers who will really bubble with joy. A reef and wall run the length of the east coast, meaning both 20ft and wall dives offer fabulous marine-life encounters.

In town, withdraw money from the **First Caribbean International Bank** (☎ 649-946-3268; fax 649-946-3388; Lee St).

CAICOS ISLANDS

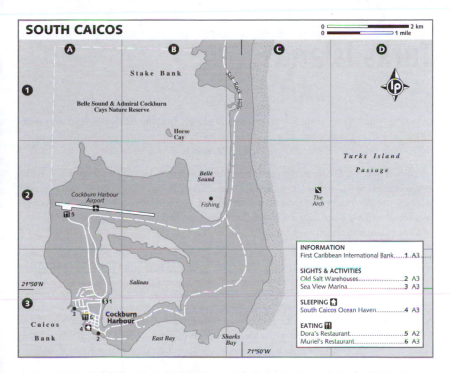

Most historic buildings are at the southeast end of town, centered on the old **Wesleyan church** with its tall spire. By its lonesome atop Tucker's Hill at the south end of town is the **old commissioner's house**.

Much of the island is within the **Belle Sound & Admiral Cockburn Cays Nature Reserve**. It encompasses the **Sail Rock Hills**, a ridge extending along the panhandle and rising to 178ft. The hills offer spectacular views east over the Turks Island Passage and west over **Belle Sound**, a vast turquoise bay opening to the flats of the Caicos Bank. The reserve extends west for several miles to protect the mangroves and bonefish flats, and also extends windward to protect the offshore coral reefs.

South Caicos is known for its wall-diving, plus you're sure to see plenty of pelagic animals, including eagle rays, Atlantic rays,

blacktip sharks, and the highlight, humpback whales in January and February. Boat and diving operators based in Providenciales make this trip (see p246); contact them for details.

Sitting over the ocean at the edge of town, the comfortable rooms at **South Caicos Ocean Haven** (☎ 649-946-3444; r $120; ✗ ✗ ✗) have cable TV and refrigerators. The meals here are also tasty and filling. Keep in mind that meal reservations are required for nonguests.

Other good spots to eat include **Muriel's Restaurant** (☎ 649-946-3535; Graham St; mains $6-20; ✗ breakfast, lunch & dinner) and **Dora's Restaurant** (☎ 649-946-3247; Airport; mains $7-22; ✗ breakfast, lunch & dinner), which serves a great lobster sandwich.

The airport is about a mile north of town. See p251 for flight information.

CAICOS ISLANDS

Turks Islands

Days simply drift by on these traditional, sleepy islands. Daylight hours are filled with snorkeling and diving, and quiet villages occasionally burst into activity when fishing boats return with bright silver fish and gleaming pink conch.

Quiet evenings are spent sipping spiced rum on wooden decks against a backdrop of milky turquoise seas and pink skies. In beachside bars, expats, Belongers and bureaucrats engage in noisy debate about development and cruise-ship plans for their island, while fishermen recall days when the ocean's now-barren shallows were lined with conch, and fish filled the waves close to shore.

The Turks group includes Grand Turk and its southern neighbor, Salt Cay, and several tiny cays. The islands lie east of the Caicos, separated by the 22-mile-wide Turks Island Passage.

Divers head for Salt Cay and the stunning reef wall that is a few hundred yards off Grand Turk. It stretches the island's length before plunging more than 8000ft into a deep blue chasm. Nature lovers enjoy the arrival of rare green and hawksbill turtles, which come ashore to lay their eggs. Bird-watchers delight in the variety of birds that can be seen at Gibb's, Penniston, Long, and Martin Alonza Pinzon Cays, known as the Grand Turk Cays Land & Sea Park.

The ocean's depths, full of colorful life and velvety darkness, envelop birthing humpback whales. The quiet awe of a dive with these creatures will never be forgotten.

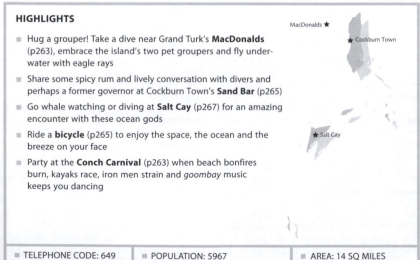

HIGHLIGHTS

MacDonalds ★
★ Cockburn Town

- Hug a grouper! Take a dive near Grand Turk's **MacDonalds** (p263), embrace the island's two pet groupers and fly underwater with eagle rays
- Share some spicy rum and lively conversation with divers and perhaps a former governor at Cockburn Town's **Sand Bar** (p265)
- Go whale watching or diving at **Salt Cay** (p267) for an amazing encounter with these ocean gods
- Ride a **bicycle** (p265) to enjoy the space, the ocean and the breeze on your face
- Party at the **Conch Carnival** (p263) when beach bonfires burn, kayaks race, iron men strain and *goombay* music keeps you dancing

★ Salt Cay

■ TELEPHONE CODE: 649	■ POPULATION: 5967	■ AREA: 14 SQ MILES

TURKS ISLANDS

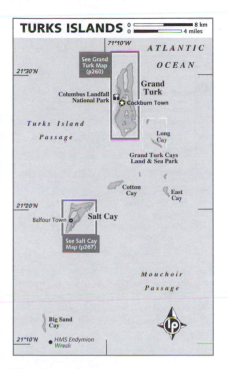

TURKS ISLANDS

0 ___ 8 km
0 ___ 4 miles

71°10'W

ATLANTIC

OCEAN

21°30'N

See Grand
Turk Map
(p260)

**Grand
Turk**

Columbus Landfall
National Park

Cockburn Town

Turks Island

Passage

Long
Cay

**Grand Turk Cays
Land & Sea Park**

Cotton
Cay

East
Cay

21°20'N

Balfour Town

Salt Cay

See Salt Cay
Map (p267)

Mouchoir

Passage

Big Sand
Cay

21°10'N   HMS Endymion
Wreck

National Parks

Native flora and fauna are protected within 33 areas set aside as national parks, nature reserves, sanctuaries, and sites of historical interest under the aegis of Turks & Caicos Islands National Parks.

The Turks and Caicos National Trust has established an underwater snorkeling trail off Grand Turk and initiated countrywide studies of bird populations. See the Environment chapter (p44) for more information and contact details.

Columbus Landfall National Park covers the Western shore and coral reefs off Cockburn Town; the ocean deep begins within 400yd of shore and the marine life here is extraordinary.

South Creek National Park incorporates the mangroves and wetlands along Grand Turk's south shore, and is home to migrating shorebirds and waders.

Grand Turk Cays Land & Sea Park, off the southeast shore, consists of Gibb's, Penniston, Long, and Martin Alonza Pinzon Cays. It contains important nesting sites for seabirds, as well as abundant iguanas and Turk's Head cacti. The marine life also includes pelagics, stingrays, sea mammals and fish.

History

The Lucayan Indians paddled their way to Grand Turk, the Caicos and the Bahamian islands at the turn of the 9th century. From these early days the Turks and Caicos and the Bahamas shared a similar history. Locals claim that the islands were Christopher Columbus' first landfall in 1492. Experts, however, have debunked the theory.

The Turks and Caicos relied upon salt export, which was the backbone of the British colony until the 1950s. Today finance, tourism, and fishing create most income, but the islands can't survive without British aid.

Relations between the islanders and their British-appointed governors have been strained since 1996, when the incumbent governor suggested that government and police corruption had turned the islands into a haven for drug trafficking. These comments appeared in the *Offshore Finance Annual*, and opponents accused the governor of harming investment. Growing opposition threatened to spill over into civil unrest. The issue created a resurgence in calls for independence, which still continue today.

Getting There & Away

Most travelers to the Turks Islands fly into Grand Turk's International Airport (via Providenciales or Nassau in New Providence, the Bahamas), a few miles from Cockburn Town.

A CONFUSED CREST

Artists were asked to submit a design for the territory's colonial crest in 1860. The selected design showed a schooner in the background and two men in the foreground raking heaps of salt, or 'white gold.' It was a typical and relevant island scene of the 19th century.

Unfortunately, the London flag maker hired to complete the job assumed that the salt heaps were igloos and added entrances to the white mounds.

The flag was finally updated in 1967 to include a new crest, depicting the country's indigenous spiny lobster, queen conch, and Turk's Head cactus.

TURKS ISLANDS

Getting Around

You'll need your own transportation if you want to explore the island outside of Cockburn Town, where you can rent a car or bicycle. In town you can walk around easily, but bicycles are also available for rent.

There is a twice-daily flight and a twice-weekly ferry to Salt Cay, where most people use bicycles, golf carts or their legs to get around.

GRAND TURK

Donkeys, horses and chickens ramble in tatty, contented groups on Grand Turk's winding roads. The narrow, sleepy streets are lined with houses from the early 1800s with overhanging creaking balconies, faded paint and swathes of brilliant scarlet bougainvillea; while leafy trees cast dappled shade over passing bicycles carrying Belongers, who smile while asking 'How are you today?'

Grand Turk is a charming, offbeat gem with a rare sense of innocence. At just 6½ miles long and 1½ miles across at its widest, this small island is centered on sleepy Cockburn Town, which, amazingly, has been the administrative and political capital of the archipelago for more than 400 years.

Limestone cliffs rise along the north and east shores, and unspoilt beaches line the island with South, Governor's and Corktree Beaches the clear winners, while inland there are caves once used by Lucayans. Many Belongers and expats live in more modern homes in the eastern 'suburbs,' where the land rises to Colonel Murray's Hill.

The island's middle is dominated by several *salinas,* or salt ponds, which nowadays attract birds and mosquitoes rather than those working to extract pure salt. Salt, or 'white gold,' was the island's most important export until the industry collapsed in 1962. The entrancing groups of wandering horses and donkeys on the islands are actually descendants of the beasts of burden that worked on the salt plantations back in the 17th century, carrying 25lb bags of salt from the ponds to the warehouses and docks. When salt production was halted the creatures were set free to roam as they pleased.

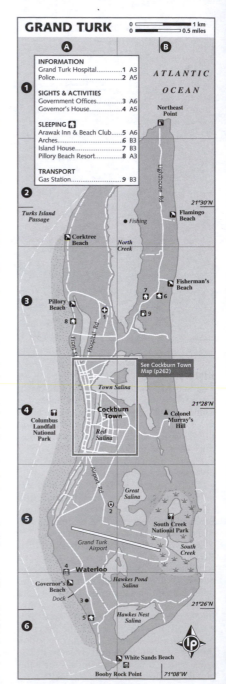

COCKBURN TOWN

pop 5525

This charming business center consists of a bank, a few shops, the post office, some government buildings and a museum. You would never guess that this was the nation's capital; the faded colonial buildings and empty streets are the antithesis of Provo's sophisticated allure. Yet visitors find themselves easily adjusting to a slow and relaxed pace that matches this dozing and amiable backwater. Old warehouses built of limestone and two-tiered wooden buildings with shuttered windows elongate the town along the coastline. On the edges of town live the less-affluent Belongers. A few hotels and expat holiday homes are beginning to sprout here.

Orientation

The heart of town is sandwiched between the ocean and the salt pond named Red Salina. Front St runs one way, along the waterfront, then narrows and becomes Duke St three blocks south of the government plaza.

Pond St runs parallel 50yd to the east, along Red Salina. To the north Pond St divides: Hospital St runs north to the hospital and Lighthouse Rd runs northeast to the lighthouse at Northeast Point. Lighthouse Rd then divides to follow the waterfront to Governor's Beach and the dock, and run southeast to the airport.

Information

Businesses and government offices close at 3pm on Friday. Some businesses open 9am to 1pm on Saturday. Public phones can be found at most central places.

Cable & Wireless (☎ 649-946-2200; cwtci@tciway.tc; Front St; 🖳)

Emergency (ambulance, fire, police ☎ 911)

Federal Express (☎ 649-231-6097; mobile office)

First Caribbean International Bank (☎ 649-946-2831; Front St)

General Post Office (☎ 649-946-1334; Front St)

Grand Turk Hospital (☎ 649-946-2333; Hospital Rd)

Police (☎ 649-946-2299)

Scotiabank (☎ 649-946-2507; Front St)

Turks & Caicos Islands Tourist Board (☎ 649-946-2321; www.turksandcaicostourism.com; Front St)

Sights

The Turks & Caicos Island Tourist Board hands out free Heritage Walk pamphlets.

FRONT STREET

Many waterfront government buildings are weathered but still retain a faded glory, notably the handsome **General Post Office**. Here the **Philatelic Bureau** displays scores of the beautiful stamps for which the Turks and Caicos are justly famous.

A small grassed plaza contains the **Columbus Monument** which claims cheekily and confidently that the explorer landed here on October 12, 1492.

Important historic buildings further north include little **St Mary's Anglican Church**, **St Thomas Anglican Church**, the pink-faced **Victoria Public Library**, **Oddfellows Lodge** and the battered **Masonic Lodge**.

The excellent **Turks & Caicos National Museum** (☎ 649-946-2160; www.tcmuseum.org; Front St; nonresidents $5; 🕑 9am-4pm Mon-Fri, 9am-6pm Wed, 9am-1pm Sat) displays shell tools, beads, stamps, locks and greenstone *celts* (tools) dug up from the past. Other sections are devoted to the salt industry and life on the coral reef. Its central exhibit is the remains from the Molasses Reef, the oldest authenticated shipwreck in the Americas, whose hull is shown alongside the world's largest collection of wrought-iron breech-loading cannon. A gallery upstairs has an incredible, lifelike 3D underwater display; a natural history gallery with displays on local wildlife; and a room devoted to the pre-Columbian Taino culture, featuring a Taino paddle – one of only two ever found – dating to AD 1100. Tours are given at 2pm weekdays upon request.

DUKE STREET

South of downtown's main area, Duke St is lined by stone walls behind which a few mansions have been turned into rakish inns, notably the old Turk's Head Inn (sadly it belongs to a film production company and is being used for shoots in made-for-TV B-movies) and the Salt Raker Inn. Equally disappointing is the barren reef off Duke Street's beach, which is void of marine life.

AROUND TOWN

North of town, the island divides like a tuning fork, with the prongs separated by North Creek. A 2-mile-long lagoon opens to the sea via a pencil-thin mouth. **Flamingo Beach** (Map p260) and **Fisherman's Beach** (Map p260) run south from Northeast Point; seaweed and choppy waters detract from swimming.

COCKBURN TOWN

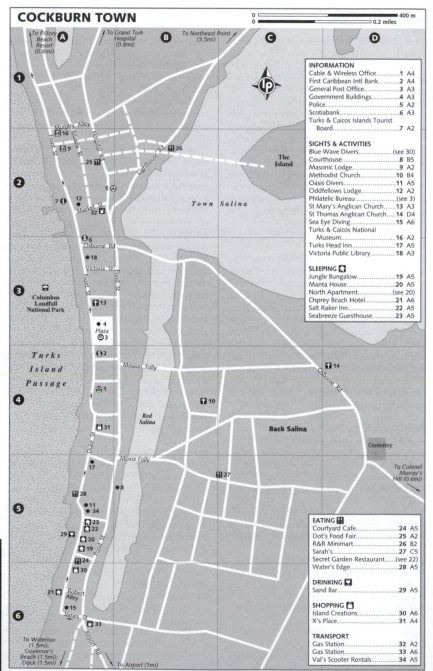

0 ———————— 400 m
0 ———————— 0.2 miles

To Pillory
Beach
Resort
(0.8mi)

To Grand Turk
Hospital
(0.8mi)

To Northeast Point
(3.5mi)

**The
Island**

Town Salina

Murphy Alley

Front St

Middle Rd

Hospital Rd

Lighthouse Rd

Market St

Osborne Rd

Victoria St

Pond St

*Turks
Island
Passage*

**Columbus
Landfall
National Park**

Mission Folly

*Red
Salina*

Moxie Folly

Duke St

Osborne Rd

Back Salina

Cemetery

To Colonel
Murray's
Hill (0.6mi)

Robert
Alley

James St

Airport Rd

To Waterloo
(1.5mi);
Governor's
Beach (1.5mi);
Dock (1.5mi)

To Airport (1mi)

INFORMATION
Cable & Wireless Office............1 A4
First Caribbean Intl Bank...........2 A4
General Post Office...................3 A3
Government Buildings...............4 A3
Police......................................5 A2
Scotiabank...............................6 A3
Turks & Caicos Islands Tourist
    Board..................................7 A2

SIGHTS & ACTIVITIES
Blue Wave Divers.................(see 30)
Courthouse...............................8 B5
Masonic Lodge..........................9 A2
Methodist Church....................10 B4
Oasis Divers...........................11 A2
Oddfellows Lodge...................12 A2
Philatelic Bureau.................(see 3)
St Mary's Anglican Church......13 A3
St Thomas Anglican Church.....14 D4
Sea Eye Diving........................15 A6
Turks & Caicos National
    Museum...............................16 A2
Turks Head Inn.......................17 A5
Victoria Public Library............18 A3

SLEEPING
Jungle Bungalow....................19 A5
Manta House..........................20 A5
North Apartment................(see 20)
Osprey Beach Hotel................21 A6
Salt Raker Inn........................22 A5
Seabreeze Guesthouse...........23 A5

EATING
Courtyard Cafe.......................24 A5
Dot's Food Fair.......................25 A2
R&R Minimart.........................26 B2
Sarah's...................................27 C5
Secret Garden Restaurant......(see 22)
Water's Edge..........................28 A5

DRINKING
Sand Bar.................................29 A5

SHOPPING
Island Creations......................30 A6
X's Place.................................31 A4

TRANSPORT
Gas Station.............................32 A2
Gas Station.............................33 A6
Val's Scooter Rentals..............34 A5

TURKS ISLANDS

A century-old cast-iron **lighthouse** blinks myopically from Northeast Point, while nearby **Corktree Beach** (Map p260) and **Pillory Beach** (Map p260) are great for bathing.

The government dock is at Waterloo, 1½ miles south of Cockburn Town. Also here is lovely, pine-shaded **Governor's Beach** (Map p260), a popular picnic and party spot for Belongers. Unfortunately plans for cruise-ship stops may informally 'sequester' this part of the island.

Grand Turk's other highlights are the official **Governor's residence** (1815; Map p260) at Waterloo; a grand old dame of a house that was built the year of the famous battle for which the village is named. The island's dock is here, as is the US missile-tracking station where John Glenn was debriefed in 1962 when he splashed down off Grand Turk.

Dirt roads lead south to **White Sands Beach** (Map p260) for snorkelers, and east to three prime **bird-watching spots**: Hawkes Pond Salina, Hawkes Nest Salina, and South Creek National Park, which protects the mangroves and wetlands along the island's southeast shore.

Activities

Local divers have compiled dive-site maps that list over 23 superb pristine wall-dive sites. These will show you anything you desire to see. Also extraordinary are night dives, when the coral glows as if embedded with huge luminescent gemstones. Some have mentioned Black Forest, where five types of black coral cling to an undercut festooned with sponges; Macdonalds, a coral arch where all sorts of fish, from giant friendly groupers to angelfish, hang out; and the Tunnels, where sand chutes slope down to the entrance of twin tunnels that drop to 100ft and emerge in a sponge theme park.

There are a number of diving outfits (also offering snorkel trips) in Cockburn and Salt Cay, testament to how many of the locals and visitors make the most of these fabulous coral reefs.

DIVING & SNORKELING
Oasis Divers (☎ 649-946-1128; www.oasisdivers.com; Duke St) offers two-tank dives ($70), popular night dives ($40) and equipment rentals for reasonable rates. Packages and special excursions include the wonderful Gibb's Cay and hand-feeding stingrays ($50 plus

diving rates). Trips to dive close to breeding humpback whales (when in season), and to explore the 18th-century wreck off Salt Cay certainly should be considered!

The small outfit **Sea Eye Diving** (☎ 649-946-2432; www.seaeyediving.com; Duke St) also offers a trip to Gibbs Cay ($50), two-tank dives ($60) and night dives ($45).

Multitalented Mitch Rollins, the dive operator at **Blue Water Divers** (☎ 649-945-1226; www.grandturkscuba.com; Island Creations, Duke St), also sings and plays guitar at the Salt Raker Inn at night. He offers a full range of dives including two-tank dives ($70) and night dives ($45).

SPORTFISHING
You can charter a boat for fishing from **Dutchie's** (☎ 649-946-2244; Airport Rd) for between $300 and $400 daily.

Festivals & Events
The island hosts a **Spring Garden Festival** each April. The merriment of the **Conch Carnival** in June is in no doubt. Four days of fun include treasure hunts, kayak relays, iron dive-master competitions and much dancing and partying. The **Queen's Official Birthday Celebration** features the police marching band playing with jingoistic fervor.

Cultural and musical events occur in May, August, September and November. These include the **Ripshaw Music Festival**, when Turks and Caicos rake 'n' scrape musicians gather to out-rake and out-scrape each other with much exuberance.

The annual **Grand Turk Game Fishing Tournament** is held at the end of July or in early August. The annual **Turks & Caicos International Billfish Tournament** is held each July.

There's a **Cactus Fest** in August, plus a weeklong carnival with reggae music and general festivities.

December has a **marathon** run that tests the physical mettle of all competitors, the usual joyous occasions and an annual **Christmas Tree Lighting Ceremony**.

Sleeping
There are a number of rental houses both downtown and around the island that are particularly great for families. Most of the expat businesses also manage rentals for absent owners, so just ask around, and check the websites listed in the Directory (p270).

TURKS ISLANDS

COCKBURN TOWN

Manta House (☎ 649-946-111; www.grandturk-manta house.com; Duke St; s/d $70/75; ✗ ✗) This lovely little guesthouse is an idyllic old wooden single-story home with polished wood floors, romantic Caribbean pastels and tasteful decor. A complimentary continental breakfast, small shared living room, fridge and back garden help make this a superb place to stay, budget price or not. With uninterrupted sea views from the front yard, the cottage is also just across the road from a tiny beach and the Sand Bar.

Jungle Bungalow (☎ 649-946-111; www.grandturk-mantahouse.com; Duke St; r per week incl breakfast $995; ✗ ✗) Adjacent to the Manta House, this equally charming place has a more romantic edge, and is made for glamorous couples on a midrange budget. The simple but elegant decor incorporates animal prints, polished wood floors and a white sofa. You can also lounge in the back garden and relish the sea views from your doorstep.

Seabreeze Guesthouse (☎ 649-946-1594; www.sea breeze.tc; Duke St; r per week $1400; ✗ ✗) This amiable and attractive blue-and-white house sits in the lovely, leafy part of Duke St, and is a five-minute walk away from restaurants, bars and the town beach. A top-story balcony spans the front of the house, with hammocks conveniently hung to watch life go by from. Three bedrooms make this a good-value option for sharing couples or a large family, as do the barbecue, bicycles, cable TV and DVD/CD player. Beach towels and other necessary linen are provided.

Salt Raker Inn (☎ 649-946-2260; www.saltraker.com; Duke St; r per week $85-110; ✗ ✗) This 150-year-old former home of a Bermudian shipwright has been turned into an intimate, oceanfront inn. The Caribbean charm and friendly atmosphere compensate for the Inn's worn appearance (there are different rates for renovated and unrenovated rooms). All rooms have ceiling fans, fridges, and verandas. Upstairs suites have an ocean-view balcony with hammocks. The informal Secret Garden Restaurant (see opposite) is set in a quaint patio.

North Bungalow (☎ 649-946-111; www.grandturk-mantahouse.com; Duke St; r per week incl breakfast $1300; ✗ ✗) The third of the super Manta House lodgings is made for small families. Polished wood floors gleam throughout the lodgings and the raised kitchen and additional space make it an appealing proposition. The

attractive and comfortable living room is perfect for lounging after a hard day's diving or sand-castle production on the beach. TVs can be supplied upon request. Use of the back garden and that view lend even more allure!

Osprey Beach Hotel (☎ 649-946-2666; www.osprey beachhotel.com; r $160; ✗ ✗ ✗) This hotel has a great seafront position at the leafy end of Duke St, and the rooms are cool, spotlessly clean and spacious. Standard suites come with a well-equipped kitchen, while deluxe rooms have more upmarket decor. All rooms are oceanfront and equipped with a phone, a coffee maker, cable TV and a private little balcony. It is only a short walk to the eateries and bars down the street, although the hotel's seafront alfresco restaurant is perfect for a quiet meal and restful glass of something cool; enjoy the killer key lime pie! Dive and meal-plan package rates include taxes, and it is cheaper to book directly with the hotel.

AROUND COCKBURN TOWN

Island House (Map p260; ☎ 649-946-1519; www.island house-tci.com; Grand Turk; d $90; P ✗ ✗ ✗) Book ahead to beat the regulars for small suites in this attractive and soothing Mediterranean-style whitewashed villa set on the crest of a hill. Prior bookings also receive discounted rates. Comfortable and spotless rooms include contemporary kitchens, en suites, cable TV and balconies with hammocks. Rates include free use of utility vehicles and airport transfers. Beaches are a 10-minute drive from this tranquil, friendly and great value place.

Arches (Map p260; ☎ 649-946-2941; www.grandturk arches.com; r $180; P ✗ ✗ ✗) Another fabulous place, just up the road from Island House, enjoys a breezy ridgetop setting with views over the Atlantic. Four immaculate, spacious, self-contained apartments have been lovingly decorated in white and blue and offer the feel of a modern apartment. Great for families, but you will need a car to get around.

Pillory Beach Resort (Map p260; ☎ 649-946-2135; N Front St; s/d per 3 nights $450/600; P ✗ ✗ ✗) This pristine and attractive beachside resort offers modern and bright rooms, each with two double beds, telephone, cable TV and ocean-view balcony. A guest-only dive operation and top-class restaurant serving food with European influences makes this an enticing option. The stretch of wonderful beach that lines this resort should appeal to families as well as lounging couples. Some great dive packages are on offer.

Arawak Inn & Beach Club (Map p260; ☎ 649-946-2277; fax 649-946 2279; r $180; P ⊠ ⊠ ⊡) This gleaming yellow and white place is a couple of miles south of town on a secluded and gorgeous strip of beach.

Eating & Drinking

Secret Garden Restaurant (☎ 649-946-2260; www .saltraker.com; Duke St; mains $15-26) The French owner's influences are obvious in the menu of this alfresco restaurant. Try the garlic chicken breast, the Saltraker Plate, lobster or the day's catch, plus splendid desserts such as cherry pie with ice cream. Live music, thanks to Mitch Rollins, creates a sing-along atmosphere.

Courtyard Café (☎ 649-946-2666; Duke St; mains $5-15; ☺ breakfast & lunch) This friendly café serves the best breakfasts in town. The all-in ome-lettes are tasty and filling, and light lunches can be enjoyed in a shady courtyard. Waf-fles, cinnamon rolls, and bagels and cream cheese are other breakfast staples.

Water's Edge (☎ 649-946-1680; Duke St; mains $6-24; ☺ breakfast, lunch & dinner; ⊡) This informal restaurant and bar has the best location in town, and makes the most of it. A wooden deck overlooks the beach and is the per-fect location for a yummy crab salad, cajun snapper and cocktails.

Sand Bar (☎ 649-946-1111; Duke St; ☺ noon-1am) This small but vibrant alfresco bar attracts an eclectic crowd of ex-governors, ani-mated lawyers and innocent passersby en-ticed in to sip killer rum cocktails and chat the evening away. Others happily consume bar food on the beachside deck.

Groceries can be bought from **Dot's Food Fair** (Hospital Rd), **R&R Minimart** (Lighthouse Rd; ☺ 8:30am-1pm, 4-9pm Mon-Sat) and **Sarah's** (off Moxey Rd; ☺ 7:30am-6:30pm Mon-Sat).

Shopping

Island Creations (☎ 649-946-1594; Duke St; ☺ 8am-5pm) Down the south end of Duke St, this small store sells some beautiful hand-dyed silk slips, T-shirts and dresses. Ceramic pic-tures and other enticements show a love of color and an upbeat feel.

X's Place (☎ 649-946-1299; Duke St; ☺ 9:30am-sundown Mon-Sat) This is a trove of Haitian art, antiques, antique maps drawn by hand, and carved items.

Getting There & Away
AIR

Refer to the Transportation chapter (p292) for information on international flights to/from the Turks and Caicos.

The following airlines fly between the Turks and Caicos Islands.

Air Turks & Caicos (www.airturksandcaicos.com) Grand Turk (☎ 649-946-2709); Provo (☎ 649-946-4181); Salt Cay (☎ 649-946-6900) Flies between the Caicos, Grand Turk and Salt Cay.

Sky King Airlines (☎ 649-941-5464; fax 649-941-5127; www.skyking.tc) Flies between Provo, Grand Turk and South Caicos. Also to the Bahamas, Cuba, Jamaica, Dominican Republic and Haiti.

Turks & Caicos Airways Provo (☎ 649-946-4255); Grand Turk (☎ 649-946-2709); Sth Caicos (☎ 649-946-3279); Mid Caicos (☎ 649-946-6136); Nth Caicos (☎ 649-946-7246); Salt Cay (☎ 649-946-6928, fax 649-946-4483) Flies between Provo, other Caicos Islands, Salt Cay and Grand Turks.

The prices quoted are for one-way flights.

Route	Price	Frequency
Grand Turk–Provo	$75	several daily
Grand Turk–Salt Cay	$35	2 daily
Grand Turk–Mid Caicos	$112	3 weekly
Grand Turk–Sth Caicos	$65	3 daily
Grand Turk–Nth Caicos	$105	several daily

BOAT

A ferry runs biweekly from Grand Turk to Salt Cay ($12 round-trip). Contact **Salt Cay Charters** (☎ 649-231-6663; piratequeen3@hotmail .com). Whale-watching boat trips with this company cost $75.

A government ferry runs from the South Dock on Grand Turk on Monday, Wednes-day and Friday afternoons ($12 round-trip). Call the **Harbormaster** (☎ 649-946-2325) in Grand Turk for information.

Flamingo Cove Marina (☎ 649-946-2227; VHF Channel 16) has a few slips and basic facilities.

Getting Around
TO/FROM THE AIRPORT

Taxis meet incoming flights and cost $7 to Cockburn Town. There are no buses, but prebooked hire cars will meet your plane.

BICYCLE

You can rent a bicycle at **Sea Eye Diving** (☎ 649-946-2432; Duke St) for $15 per day.

TURKS ISLANDS

CARS & SCOOTERS

You're hardly likely to need a car in town, but pay attention anyway to the one-way system along Duke and Front Sts.

You will need a car or scooter to explore further afield. In this case be aware that groups of donkeys, horses, dogs and chickens are likely to stroll at will on and off the roads, so drive slowly, especially around bends!

Cars are available for $80 about day. You can hire air-con cars from the following.

Ed-Rico's Rent-a-Car (☎ 649-946-1744, 649-946-1042; seacair@tciway.tc; Churchill Bldg, Front St) Will do airport pickup/drop offs.

Tony's Car Rental (☎ 649-231-1806; Grand Turk Airport, Airport Rd)

Val's Scooter Rentals (☎ 649-946-1022, 649-946-1022; per day $40; Duke St) Near Water's Edge restaurant.

TAXI

Several locals run taxis on Grand Turk. Ask at your hotel or restaurant for recommendations. If you hire a taxi for an island tour, be sure to negotiate the fare beforehand.

GRAND TURK CAYS LAND & SEA PARK

Gibb's, Penniston, Long, and Martin Alonza Pinzon Cays make up this small park (Map p259) southeast of Grand Turk. It protects important nesting sites for seabirds and there are also large numbers of Turk's Head cacti. Penniston is an important nesting site for frigate birds, and boobies and noddy and sooty terns abound on Gibb's. The terns come to Gibb's each May and June to breed (the females lay a single egg in a thick carpet of cactus spines); human visitation is discouraged during these months. Long Cay is a separate sanctuary with a population of iguanas.

There's no scheduled transportation; you'll need to rent a boat and guide in Cockburn Town. However, dive and tour operators in Provo (see p246) and Grand Turk (see p263) offer trips.

SALT CAY

pop 339

This lovely little spot on the Turks Passage is barely 3 miles across, but is rich in nature, the highlight of which is the annual visit of the graceful and gentle humpback whales. The deep waters that surround this cay are perfect breeding grounds for whales, and the lucky people who visit at this time may witness some real miracles. Boats set out from Grand Turk and the cay for both whale-watchers and divers to relish this experience.

The cay is 8 miles southwest of Grand Turk, has only 12 cars and plenty of sandy beaches. Donkeys and wild cattle outnumber human inhabitants, as do iguanas. Simple island living that appeals to so many, and is often unattainable, can be found here.

Divers have known about this cay and the wonderful diving here for decades, hence the comparatively great range of lodgings, bars and eateries that center around the main settlement, historic Balfour Town. This attractive place has some lovely old plantation two-story homes with wide verandas and jalousied windows. Many of these have been renovated and offer lodgings with character, class and comfort.

Big Sand Cay, 8 miles south of Salt Cay, is a haven for diminishing numbers of green and hawksbill turtles, which come ashore to lay their eggs in the sand.

The modern history of the archipelago began here in the 17th century, when Bermudian salt traders settled and a salt industry began. They made ponds linked to the sea by canals and sluice gates and built windmills to control water flow. Salt Cay was once the world's largest producer of salt. In the industry's heyday, over 100 vessels a year departed the isle for the US, bulging with 'white gold.' Nominations by Unesco to make this cay a World Heritage site as 'a time capsule from the days when Salt was King' are not surprising. It could be a museum of industrial archeology, with its decrepit windmills, sheds, and *salinas*, now smelly and scummed with wind-whipped froth.

Information

Salt Cay has a **post office** (☎ 649-946-6985; 8am-12:30pm & 2-4pm Mon-Thu, 8am-3:30pm Fri). There's a small **clinic** (☎ 649-946-6970) with two nurses; a doctor visits once every two weeks. You can contact the **police** (☎ 649-946-6929).

The **Fun in the Sun Festival** is held in Balfour Town in Salt Cay each June.

Sights

The most noteworthy attraction is the splendidly preserved **White House** in north Balfour

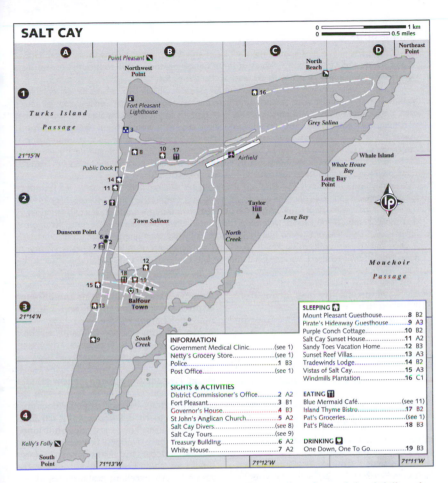

SALT CAY

INFORMATION
Government Medical Clinic..............(see 1)
Netty's Grocery Store......................(see 1)
Police..1 B3
Post Office......................................(see 1)

SIGHTS & ACTIVITIES
District Commissioner's Office.........2 A2
Fort Pleasant....................................3 B1
Governor's House..............................4 B3
St John's Anglican Church...............5 A2
Salt Cay Divers..............................(see 8)
Salt Cay Tours...............................(see 9)
Treasury Building.............................6 A2
White House.....................................7 A2

SLEEPING
Mount Pleasant Guesthouse..............8 B2
Pirate's Hideaway Guesthouse...........9 A3
Purple Conch Cottage....................10 B2
Salt Cay Sunset House....................11 A2
Sandy Toes Vacation Home............12 B3
Sunset Reef Villas...........................13 A3
Tradewinds Lodge...........................14 B2
Vistas of Salt Cay...........................15 A3
Windmills Plantation......................16 C1

EATING
Blue Mermaid Café.......................(see 11)
Island Thyme Bistro.......................17 B2
Pat's Groceries...............................(see 1)
Pat's Place.......................................18 B3

DRINKING
One Down, One To Go....................19 B3

Town, a salt merchant's stately manor with a stepped (Bermudian) stone roof and chimney. It is still owned by the Harriott family, who built the house in 1835 from stone brought here as ballast. Next door is the old wooden **Treasury Building**, where salt workers once collected their pay. Nearby are **St John's Anglican Church** and the **District Commissioner's Office**, housing the old jail.

Rusting 18th-century cannon sit atop **Fort Pleasant**, about 400yd north of Mt Pleasant Guest House.

Activities

Choice dive sites include Wanda Lust, known for its plankton-rich waters that attract whales and eagle rays; Kelly's Folly, a rolling coral garden with hawksbill turtles, morays, and parrotfish; and HMS *Endymion* (Map p259), a never-salvaged, 18th-century British warship bristling with cannon and massive anchors in a coral canyon just 25ft down. The wreck is south of Big Sand Cay and the sea mound here has swim-throughs. There's also the Northwest Wall, plunging from 50ft to 120ft and covered with corals, and Point Pleasant, a shallow cove crowded with coral heads topped with elkhorn.

Salt Cay Divers (☎ 649-946-6906; www.saltcaydivers.tc) is a well-established outfit with two boats. It offers two-tank dives for $80 and a number of excellent dive/stay packages. From January to March the whales are in town, and seven-night packages include

TURKS ISLANDS

MARINE GODS

Salt Cay is perhaps the best spot in the Caribbean and West Indian regions to see humpback whales during the winter months. Scores of these gentle creatures arrive to breed in the warm waters of the Silver and Mouchoir Banks, east and south of Salt Cay.

Although a sheltered environment is important for pregnant whales, baby whales have a very thin blubber layer; the warmer water temperatures here may be needed for their survival. You will see each mother with only one newborn, as whales give birth to only one baby at a time.

A humpback whale may eat up to a ton of food a day, so it would also be safe to presume that this location supports the humpback's vast appetite for krill! It is believed that a humpback can probably stay underwater for as long as 35 minutes, although the average time may only be 10 to 15 minutes in the West Indies. This means that you should definitely be able to enjoy some privileged sights of these graceful and gentle colossi.

You may also be honored enough to hear the whales singing. Male humpbacks are famous for their songs, a sound that no-one who hears it will ever forget. The songs are probably part of the whales' mating rituals and are used in the declaration of territories. Initially scientists thought that these 20-minute-long songs were repeated continually, rather like a bird's song. Yet upon further research it was discovered that their evocative hymns change every year.

Dive and charter outfits in Cockburn Town and Salt Cay both organize whale-watching and diving trips (for Cockburn Town, see p263 and for Salt Cay, see p267).

---

whale watching and five days' diving from $1090 – excellent value.

Oasis Divers (Map p262; ☎ 649-946-1128; www .oasisdivers.com; Duke St) offers whale-watching trips ($50) as well as an HMS *Endymion* wreck trip ($75) from Grand Turk. Diving on these excursions costs extra; a prepaid two-tank dive is $70. Gear rental is also possible from these friendly guys.

Salt Cay Charters (☎ 649-231-6663; piratequeen3@ hotmail.com) offers whale-watching boat trips that start around $75. It also offers a range of motor water sports and boats for charter (prices upon application).

Salt Cay Tours (☎ 649-946-6904; Pirate's Hideaway Guesthouse, Victoria St, Salt Cay) will take you on a tour of the island's historical landmarks and good bird-watching spots (see the useful website www.turksandcaicosbirdwatch ing.com). It also rents out bicycles and kayaks. The rates vary and will be supplied upon application.

Sleeping & Eating

There are also several great vacation cottages and houses to rent that range from simple stone cottages to brand-new modern villas. Check the Turks and Caicos websites, www.tcimall.tc, www.turksandcaicostour ism.com and www.saltcay.org for listings.

Refreshing breezes will help keep you free of pesky mosquitoes, and lodgings require little cooling other than an open

window or two. Note that if air-conditioning is provided and you use it, you will normally be charged for the electricity.

Most lodgings have restaurants and bars that are also open to nonguests.

MIDRANGE

Mount Pleasant Guest House (☎ 649-946-6927; mtpleasantinfo@yahoo.com; Balfour Town; r $105; ✖ ✖) This timber-beamed, unpretentious gem dates back to 1830, when it was a salt merchant's house. The seven air-conditioned rooms all have wooden floors, lively tropical pastel decor, and heaps of charm. Hammocks are slung between shade trees in the grounds. An excellent restaurant and bar also keeps you very well fed and watered (try the superb seafood, carrot cake and homemade sherry trifle) and bicycles are provided for guests. Dive packages are available.

Tradewinds Lodge (☎ 649-946-6906; www.trade winds.tc; Victoria St, Balfour Town; r $145; ✖ ✖) This modern and light beachside property offers weekly packages. All rooms are bright, spotlessly clean and comfortably furnished. They have well-fitted kitchens or kitchenettes, a screened patio and ocean views. Dining is also available on an outdoor deck, perfect for sunbathing and whale watching. Bicycles and a barbecue are also available for guests.

Pirate's Hideaway Guesthouse (☎ 649-946-6909; www.saltcay.tc; Victoria St, Salt Cay; r $120; ✖ ✖) This

Hansel-and-Gretel-style B&B abounds in stained glass, Haitian art, and murals on a pirate theme. Hardwood floors, nautical-themed bathrooms (plus shell-lined tubs), and tropical decor add to the character of these comfy rooms. A bar and restaurant have an outdoor deck which overlooks the sea, and is lit at night with flaming torches.

Salt Cay Sunset House & Blue Mermaid Cafe (☎ /fax 649-946-6942; Balfour Town; r $140; ✕ ✕) This lovingly-restored plantation house sits on the beach.

Some great rentals also exist; try the cute whitewashed old stone **Purple Conch Cottage** (www.saltcay.org; $100), which looks directly out over the beach, or **Sandy Toes Vacation Home** (☎ 649-946-6906; www.saltcay.org; apt per week $1200; ✕ ✕), a fresh and comfortable house that contains two tasteful and bright apartments. Facilities include a golf cart. **Vistas of Salt Cay** (☎ 649-946-6906; www.saltcay.org; r per week $1000-1200; ✕ ✕) is close to the beach, and offers use of bicycles or a golf-cart.

TOP END

Windmills Plantation (☎ 649-946-6962; www.saltcay site.com; d with/without meals $495/375; ✕ ✕ ✕) This small deluxe resort in a stunning beachside location about 1½ miles north-east of Balfour Town is a replica of an 18th-century colonial plantation. Eight classic and elegant suites have hand-carved four-poster beds, lanterns and terra-cotta-tiled floors. Each ground-floor room also has a private outdoor courtyard and plunge pool. It has its own restaurant and bar (the owners of this resort pride themselves on their Caribbean cuisine), and diving packages are available. Not one for children.

Sunset Reef Villas (☎ 649-946-6901; www.sun setreef.com; Balfour Town; d per week $1300; ✕ ✕) Pleasant and simple one- and two-bedroom modern beachside villas come with all the mod-cons, including TV, video, CD, stereo, washing machine and fully equipped kitchen. An outdoor grill on a deck with hammocks helps provide the island ambience. You can rent a golf cart for $50 per day, and a bicycle for $40 per week. Snorkel gear is $10/50 per day/week.

Island Thyme Bistro (☎ 649-946-6977; mains $10-23; ✕ lunch & dinner Thu-Tue) Either eat alfresco in the sheltered Coconut Room, or indoors where a bar serves some wicked cocktails. Bahamian and American fare with a special twist is popular with many. Picnics can also be made with advance notice.

Pat's Place (mains $6-17; ✕ breakfast, lunch & dinner) Serves great island dishes, especially tasty steamed fish.

Groceries can be bought at **Netty's Grocery Store** and at **Pat's Groceries**. Knock at their houses if the stores are closed.

Entertainment

Locals gather to play dominoes at the One Down, One to Go bar. It has a large-screen TV, a pool table, darts, a pool and dancing. The bars at the Mount Pleasant Guest House and Pirate's Hideaway Guesthouse are alternative venues, and a tad more sophisticated.

Getting There & Around

AIR

Please refer to the Transportation chapter (p292) for information on international flights to/from the Turks Islands.

For flights between the Turks and Caicos Islands, including Salt Cay, please refer to the Getting There & Away section in Cockburn Town (p265).

One of the island's two taxis will inevitably show up after the driver sees the plane land at the Salt Cay Airfield.

BICYCLE

Many lodgings provide free bicycles for guests. You can rent a bicycle from Pirate's Hideaway Guesthouse on Salt Cay for around $10 per day and from Sunset Reef Villas for $40 per week.

BOAT

A ferry runs biweekly from Grand Turk to Salt Cay ($12 round-trip; 45 minutes). Contact **Salt Cay Charters** (☎ 649-231-6663; pirate queen3@hotmail.com). Whale-watching boat trips with this operator cost $75.

A government ferry runs from the South Dock on Grand Turk Monday, Wednesday and Friday afternoons ($12 round-trip). Call the **harbormaster** in Grand Turk (☎ 649-946-2325) for information.

GOLF CARTS

Everyone uses golf carts to traverse the island. Many lodgings offer free carts, or they can be hired from Pirate's Hideaway Guesthouse on Salt Cay from around $40 per day and from Sunset Reef Villas for $50 per day.

TURKS ISLANDS

Directory

CONTENTS

ACCOMMODATIONS

With a fantastic range of cheerful little cottages, welcoming inns, stylish condos, excellent hotels and all-inclusive resorts, the Bahamian, Turks and Caicos Islands cater for most tastes, if not for all budgets! You may come across some very scary and often unjustified high rates when checking out accommodation, as many hotels of similar price vary dramatically in ambience and value.

Room taxes can be around 12% and, to add insult to injury, surcharges can hike up your bill by another 10% to 30%. These miscellaneous charges will be described as an energy surcharge, a 'resort levy,' or a per-diem fee for housekeeping service. The housekeeping service charge is legal, but the energy tab is left over from the oil crisis days of the mid-'70s and is definitely illegitimate. Check whether the service charges and taxes are per room or per person (even couples and children sharing rooms can sometimes be charged individually). Charges may also be added for credit-card payments.

Most hotels also have a price system tiered into peak- and low-season rates. Low or off season (summer) is usually mid-April to mid-December; high or peak season (winter) is the remainder of the year, when hotel prices increase by 25% to 50% or more.

Now for the good news: the off-season (or summer) encompasses many months of great weather, and during this time virtually all accommodation rates drop anywhere from 25% to 60%. During these times even the top-end hotels are usually looking to fill their rooms and may be affordable. So although this region is pricey, it is possible to find value-for-money lodgings and even some great bargains.

Even during peak times, many of the quieter accommodations offer some amazing specials. Your best bet is to contact the hotels directly by telephone and via their websites. These discounts and special website offers can save up to 30% on the book price and many need to be booked online.

Additionally, small guesthouses, hotels or units where Bahamians stay when they're on holiday are normally advertised in local newspapers or in grocery stores.

Similarly, diving and fishing fans should check out the very good-value diving and fishing packages on many islands.

Rental properties shared by at least four people can also bring the rates down a fair bit, and there are some really terrific self-contained condos, apartments and villas in which to stay, especially on the cays.

Rates

The listings in the sleeping sections of this guidebook come in three broad categories of 'budget', 'midrange' and 'top end'. We haven't included either taxes or hotel surcharges in our listings, unless they are included in the rates, which we have indicated. Rates for all budgets are generally for two people. In high season, decent budget rooms are around $65 to $80 a night, but a few bargains can be found. Midrange hotels will usually cost $110 to $180 (with $120 to

PRACTICALITIES

Newspapers

- Daily New Providence newspapers include the morning's *Nassau Guardian* and the afternoon's *Tribune* as well as the *Bahama Journal*. The tabloids *Punch* and *Confidential Source* are published weekly. Grand Bahama has the daily *Freeport News* and twice-monthly *Freeport Times*. Abaconians read the weekly *Abaconian* and *Abaco Journal*.

- There are two newspapers in the Turks and Caicos: the biweekly *Free Press* and the weekly *Turks and Caicos News*.

Magazines

- A number of free magazines on the Bahamas are published locally. *Island Scene* is the official magazine of the Bahamas; also look for *Destination Bahamas* and *Getaway Magazine*.

- The Turks and Caicos has the free *Times of the Islands*, *Where, When, How: Turks & Caicos Islands*, the monthly *Discover Turks & Caicos* and the evocatively named quarterly *S3 Sand Sea Serenity*.

Radio & TV

- The government-owned Bahamas Broadcasting Corporation operates TV Channel 13 (ZNS) and radio stations ZNS-1, ZNS-2, ZNS-FM and ZNS-3. Commercial radio stations include Love 97FM, More 94.9FM and Jamz 100FM. Most hotels also offer American cable TV.

- The official Turks and Caicos government radio station is Radio Turks and Caicos (106FM) on Grand Turk. There are several private stations. For contemporary light rock, try 92.5FM. You'll find country and western on 90.5FM, easy-listening music on 89.3FM, and classical music on 89.9FM. WPRT at 88.7FM is a religious and public announcement channel, as is WIV at 96.7FM. Multichannel satellite TV is received from the US and Canada. The islands have one private TV station.

Video Systems

- VHS is the standard, and tapes can be bought in photo supply shops but prices are significantly higher than you may be used to in North America or Europe.

Electricity

- Hotels operate on 110v (60 cycles), as in the USA and Canada. Plug sockets are two- or three-pin US standard.

Weights & Measures

- The British Imperial and metric systems are both in use. Liquids are generally measured in pints, quarts and gallons, and weight in grams, ounces and pounds.

$150 being the average). Upscale resorts will cost from $180 to $500 per night as a standard, and above that, the stars are the limit.

Prices in the guidebook refer to room only, or European Plan (EP). Some hotels will quote rates as Continental Plan (CP; room and breakfast), Modified American Plan (MAP; room plus breakfast and dinner) or American Plan (AP; room plus all-inclusive meals).

Accommodation Websites

Aside from the ones listed below, check out the Internet Resources section on p14 to find useful accommodation links.

Abaco Real Estate Agency (www.abacobahamas.com)
Bahama Houseboats (www.bahamahouseboats.com)
Island Dreams Rentals (www.islanddreamrentals.com)
Prestigious Properties (www.prestigiousproperties.com)
Provo.net (www.provo.net)
Rent-a-Home International (www.rentavilla.com)

DIRECTORY

Turks & Caicos Real Estate Association (www
.tcirealestate.com) Lists all the real-estate agencies,
most of which will arrange rental properties.
Turks & Caicos Realty (www.tcrealty.com)
VHR Worldwide (www.hideaways.com)
Abaco Bahamas Homepage (www.oii.net) Contains
Abaco boat rental and accommodation information.

Camping

The Bahamas does not encourage campers.
Camping on the beaches is illegal and there
are no official campsites, even in wilderness
areas. However, many land and sea parks
contain cays that are perfect for pitching
a tent. Do check which cays are the best
for camping with the park operators (see
Environment, p37) as some cays may be
out of bounds as they contain nesting or
breeding species. A few charter companies
and activity operators will rent out basic
camping equipment, but don't count on
finding rental gear easily.

Guesthouses

These are the accommodations of choice for
Bahamians when traveling. Usually they're
small, no-frills, family-run properties. Standards and prices vary enormously. Some are
exquisite, with a live-in owner who provides
breakfast and sometimes dinner onsite.
Some are self-contained apartments, while
others are indistinguishable from hotels
or motels. In New Providence the *Nassau
Guardian* and *Tribune* newspapers list guesthouses under 'Guesthouse' and 'Boarding
Accommodation' headings in their classified-
ad sections. On other islands check both the
local newspapers and grocery stores.

Homestays & Home Exchanges

Try contacting the following organizations
to see if there are any suitable homestays.
You gain access to the database upon pay-
ing a fee.
Homestay Finder (www.homestayfinder.com)
World Homestays (www.worldhomestays.com)

Another option is to exchange homes with a
family in the Bahamas. These private organizations have databases on available homes
around the world. Again, you gain access to
the database upon paying a fee.
HomeExchange.com (www.homeexchange.com)
Homelink International (www.homelink.org.uk)
Intervac (www.intervac-online.com)

Hotels

Bahamian hotels run the gamut, but it is un-
wise to rely solely on a hotel's brochure or
promotional literature. The following associ-
ations do not represent all hoteliers and other
accommodation owners and tourism service
providers on the islands, but can help with
information on their members' properties.
Bahamas Hotel Association (☎ 242-322-8381; fax
242-326-5346; W Bay St, Nassau)
Turks & Caicos Hotel Association (☎ 649-941-5787;
www.tcimall.tc/tcresorts; Ports of Call, Providence)

Rental Accommodations

The Bahamian, Turks and Caicos Islands and
their cays have great private cottages, apartments, condos and houses available for rent.
These properties range from modest units
at $850 to lavish villas at $12,000 and more
per week. Affordable, charming one- or two-
bedroom cottages rent from $1,400 and three-
bedroom houses from $1,800 per week. Rates
can fall as much as 30% in summer (May to
November). Check the websites listed earlier
or the links to real-estate agencies from the
websites listed on p14. Also try the classified-
ad sections of *Caribbean Travel & Life* (www
.caribbeantravelmag.com) and *Islands* (www
.islands.com) magazines.

Many condos are attached to resort hotels to which you have access. These self-
contained, fully furnished apartments are
normally timeshare properties with a fully
equipped kitchen (some have only a kitchenette), and some will also have their own
swimming pool, tennis court or boat jetty
or all three. Check for incidentals costs.

Resorts

All-inclusive resorts are cash-free, village
resorts or self-contained hotels; you pay a
set price and (theoretically) nothing more
once you set foot inside. Take care when
choosing a resort. Many properties have
jumped onto the 'all-inclusive' bandwagon
for marketing purposes. In reality you'll
have to pay for booze and some extras, such
as scuba-diving. Check carefully for hidden
charges for water sports, laundry, and other
activities or services not included in the
price. Rates begin at about $230 per day.

ACTIVITIES

The Bahamas and Turks and Caicos Islands
have a range of sports and special-interest

activities for those who get a bit restless after lying around on a beach for an hour or two. Anything to do with these gloriously warm and brilliantly colored seas is a particular delight, and easy to arrange. The island chapters have more specific information, including details on sites of particular interest for each activity and contact information for local activity tour-operators.

Bicycling

Few people explore the islands by bicycle, but the relative flatness of the islands would seem to be ideal for biking. Many hotels and concessions rent bicycles ($12 to $20 per day). Some places have mountain bikes, but most have heavy single-gear beach cruisers, which are definitely *not* for touring.

Grand Bahama hosts the Tour de Freeport 100-mile road race in spring.

Bird-Watching

The Bahamas and Turks and Caicos Islands are heaven for bird-watchers (see Environment p38). More than two dozen reserves in the Bahamas protect more than 230 bird species, including West Indian flamingos and Bahama parrots.

The **Bahamas National Trust** (Map pp66-7; ☎ 242-393-1317; fax 242-393-4978; Village Rd, Nassau; ⓧ 9am-5pm Mon-Fri) offers guided bird-watching walks regularly and has information on the wonderful species that visit or live on these isles.

A list of all the Bahamian Wild Bird Reserves is obtainable from the **Department of Agriculture** (☎ 242-325-7413; fax 242-325-3960; Levy Bldg, E Bay St, Nassau).

Also contact the **Bahamas Ornothology Group** (☎ 242-393-1317) for news on further bird-watching activities.

In the Turks and Caicos, the **Department of Environment & Coastal Resources** (Grand Turk ☎ 649-946-2855; fax 649-946-1895; ccr@tciway.tc; Providenciales ☎ 649-946-4017; fax 649-941-3063; South Caicos ☎ /fax 649-946-3306) administers 23 national parks and nature reserves.

For information on the Ramsar wetlands in North, Middle and East Caicos, contact **Turks & Caicos National Trust** (TCNT; ☎ 649-941-5710; tc.nattrust@tciway.tc; PO Box 540, Providenciales, Caicos).

Boating & Sailing

With more than 3000 islands and cays scattered over 100,000 sq miles of ocean, the region is a boater's dream. Indispensable guidebooks are the *2004 Yachtsman's Guide to The Bahamas and Turks & Caicos*, edited by Tom Daly, and *Explorer Chartbook: Far Bahamas*, *Explorer Chartbook: Near Bahamas* and *Explorer Chartbook: Exumas*, written by Monty and Sara Lewis. These give details on cruising permits and customs regulations, plus a list of designated ports of entry.

Favored areas in the Bahamas are the protected waters of the Sea of Abaco (between Great Abaco and the Abaco Cays) and Exuma Sound and Exuma Cays Land & Sea Park. Both are good for beginning sailors, as the waters are shallow and sheltered, and land is always within sight.

The Turks and Caicos also offer excellent boating and sailing opportunities.

BOAT CHARTERS

Experienced sailors and novices can charter sailboats, yachts and cruisers by the day or week. Most marinas offer boats with a skipper and crew, as well as 'bareboat' vessels on which you're your own skipper. You'll need to be a certified sailor to charter bareboat; usually you'll have to demonstrate proficiency before being able to sail away. All boats are stocked with linens and other supplies.

Charters can be arranged at most major hotels or by calling a local charter company. Many individuals offer sportfishing, but will happily take you exploring, diving and snorkeling. They charge anything from $350 to $500 per half-day, $600 to $1000 per day.

In the Turks and Caicos chartered trips range from $400/$700 per half-day/full day and cruisers from $500/$1050 per half/full day for up to eight people.

Bareboat charters are usually by the week; prices begin at $1200, depending on size. Crewed charters often cost about double that. Skippers can be hired for about $400 a day. See Activities sections in the island chapters for details on local charter companies.

Most resorts provide small sailboats called Sunfish, either as part of the hotel package rate or for an hourly rental fee. You also can rent motorboats, from small fry such as Boston Whalers to giant luxury cruisers with price tags to match, from local marinas.

BOAT EXCURSIONS

Boat excursions for all sorts of activities abound, whether your thing is fishing, sailing, kayaking, sightseeing or simply lazing on a boat sipping rum punch while someone else does all the hard work.

Fast-ferry trips from Nassau are a cheap and fast way to get to a few of the Family Islands, and a great day out. Tickets start from $75 one way.

Day excursions are priced from about $85 to $180 depending upon your activities.

Caving

The islands are honeycombed with dozens of limestone caverns, many only partially explored and mapped. In some, Lucayan Indian petroglyphs add to the allure. Many caves are also roosts for harmless bats. Use extreme caution if you're exploring without a guide.

Grand Bahama has the world's longest cave system in Lucayan National Park. Permits are required to dive these caves, while sightseeing adventure excursions are available. The Turks and Caicos also have plenty of caves, notably Conch Bar Caves National Park on Middle Caicos, a 15-mile-long system full of stalactites and stalagmites. A few tour operators offer day-long cave excursions here. Refer to the islands' Activities sections for operators details.

Also see the Blue Holes boxed text on p49 for a different type of caving.

Diving & Snorkeling

These are the region's headline acts. The range of sites means that both novice and experienced divers and snorkelers can enjoy these waters and their exotic occupants. See the Activities sections in each island chapter, plus the Diving chapter (p45), for details on key dive and snorkel sites and local operators.

It's possible to walk off a beach on the islands and be within yards of precious living coral teeming with fish. There is a range of operators that will take snorkelers out to a variety of sites. You may be reminded by the captains not to touch the coral. Don't take offence, as a mere tap with your fins is enough to kill whole sections of the reef, which then has the domino effect of wiping out the area's marine and fish life.

If you intend to do a lot of snorkeling or diving, it is worth bringing your own mask, snorkel and fins, otherwise it is $10 per day to hire the equipment.

DIVING ORGANIZATIONS

The following organizations are good to know:

Divers Alert Network (DAN; US ☎ 919-684-2948; www.diversalertnetwork.org; Peter B Bennett Center, 6 W Colony Place, Durham, NC 27705, USA) Offers divers' health insurance, covering evacuation and emergency treatment.

National Association of Underwater Instructors (NAUI; US ☎ 813-628-6284; www.naui.org; 1232 Tech Blvd, Tampa, FL 33619-2667, USA)

Professional Association of Diving Instructors (PADI; US ☎ 949-858-7234; www.padi.com; 30151 Tomas St, Rancho Santa Margarita, CA 92688-2125, USA)

RECOMPRESSION CHAMBERS

There are two of these in the Bahamas.

Club Med Columbus Isle resort (☎ 242-331-2000; www.clubmed.com; San Salvador)

Underwater Explorers Society (UNEXSO; ☎ 242-373-1244; www.unexso.com; Port Lucaya Marina, Freeport, Grand Bahama)

In Turks and Caicos, there is a recompression chamber at **Associated Medical Practices Clinic** (☎ 649-946-4242; Leeward Hwy) on Provo.

Dolphin Encounters

There are several outfits across the Bahamas that offer swimming with dolphins; details are included in the islands' Activities sections. Some high-profile international organizations point out the detrimental effects that these encounters have on the mammals and their lifespans. For more information please refer to the boxed text on dolphins in captivity (p81).

On North Bimini, operators can take you out to meet wild dolphins.

The protected inshore waters of the Sea of Abaco immediately southeast of Marsh Harbour are also home to a resident population of about 100 bottlenose dolphins.

Fishing

Very strict regulations are in place, and marine and sea parks are off-limits to all fishing fans, so check with the relevant authorities.

These regions host major annual fishing tournaments (often held from April to June), from big-game contests for serious contenders to laidback, family-oriented contests. Check the tourism websites such as www.bahamas.com and www.turksandcaicostourism.com for details. Also, see the Bamahas Billfish Championship boxed text on p152.

SPORTFISHING

As fans of Ernest Hemingway realize, the archipelago's ocean waters are a pelagic playpen for schools of marlin, dolphin fish, wahoo and tuna. And reef or bottom fishing for snapper or yellowtail is plentiful.

In the Bahamas, fishing is strictly regulated. Visiting boaters must have a permit for sportfishing ($20 per trip or $150 yearly for up to six reels). Boats with more than six reels are charged $10,000 yearly. No foreign vessels may fish commercially. You can get a permit at your port of entry or in advance from the **Department of Fisheries** (☎ 242-393-1014; PO Box N-3028, E Bay St, Nassau), who can offer current fishing regulations. The capture, possession or molestation of coral, turtles and marine mammals is forbidden, as is long-line, spear and net fishing. Other restrictions exist.

The Turks and Caicos lie on a major route for migrating Atlantic blue marlin, which cross in massive numbers from June to August. All the other game fish of the Bahamas can be caught here, too. Provo has several marinas where fishing boats can be chartered. Prices are similar to those in the Bahamas and a permit is required. No spearfishing (including Hawaiian slings) or scuba gear is allowed, nor may visiting vessels take conch or lobster. Information on regulations can be obtained from the **Department of Environment & Coastal Resources** (Grand Turk ☎ 649-946-2855; fax 649-946-1895; ccr@tciway.tc; Providenciales ☎ 649-946-4017; fax 649-941-3063; South Caicos ☎ /fax 649-946-3306)

BONEFISHING

The gin-clear waters of the sandbanks that shelve the perimeters of most islands are made for battles with the bonefish: pound for pound, one of the world's fighting champions. Related to the herring, it's named for its complex skeleton, and makes for bony eating. Many lodges are devoted to bonefishing and there are local bonefishing guides on all islands. Bait and tackle are sold and rods rented at many fishing lodges.

The Bahamas gets the fanfare for bonefishing, but the Turks and Caicos give it a run for its money. There are 2000 sq miles of flats between Grand Turk and Provo!

CHARTER & GUIDE RATES

Dozens of commercial operators offer sportfishing charters, and will charge from $350 to $500 per half-day, $600 to $1000 per day (in the Turks and Caicos chartered trips range from $400/$700 per half-day/full day) with bait and tackle provided. You usually take your own food and drinks. Most charter boats require a 50% deposit (if you cancel, you should do so at least 24 hours before departure to avoid losing your deposit). Some operators keep half the catch. Discuss terms with the skipper before setting out.

FISHING TOURS

Several companies offer fishing tours to the Bahamas. Aside from those in the island chapters, try the following:
Angler Adventure (US ☎ 813-754-3737; www.anglers adventures.com; PO Box 872, Old Lyme, CT 06371, USA)
Fishing International (US ☎ 800-950-4242; www .fishinginternational.com; 1825 Fourth St, Santa Rosa, CA 95404, USA)
Frontiers International (UK ☎ 44-1285-741-341, US ☎ 800-245-1950; www.frontiersinternational.net; UK Tithe Barn, Barnsley Park, Barnsley, Cirencester GL7 5EG, UK; US PO Box 959, Wexford, PA 15090-0595, USA)

Hiking

A few wildlife reserves have tracks, while several islands have tracks originally cut by lumber companies.

Always carry plenty of water and insect repellent, especially in summer, plus a small first-aid kit when hiking in remote places. Rarely will you be far from a settlement. The limestone terrain is too treacherous to permit you to walk off the track safely, as thick vegetation hides sinkholes and crevasses. Be especially wary of clifftops, which are often undercut and can give way easily.

A few tour operators offer a mix of kayaking, snorkeling and hiking tours in Grand Bahama's Lucayan National Park (p118). In the Abacos, Abaco Outback (p151) has guided hiking in Abaco National Park, and Earth Village (p83) has walking tours of the New Providence's central coppice forest. See those island chapters for more details.

There are hunters in Great Abaco's and Andros' backcountry seeking wild boar. Beware! Consider hiring a hunter as a guide.

Cat Island has some of the best hiking. The Fernandez Bay Village resort (p210) is a good starting point; the owners can provide maps and even a guide, if required.

On Great Inagua, trails lead into Bahamas National Trust Park (p237), a semi-arid, rugged landscape with fabulous bird-watching.

In the Turks and Caicos, the Middle Caicos Reserve & Trail System (p255) has 10 miles of trails along the north coast. On Provo you can follow dirt tracks along the east and west shores to Northwest Point Marine National Park (p245).

Kayaking

Miles and miles of creeks and flats provide wonderful entrances to the redolent world of the mangroves and wetlands of Grand Bahama and the Family Islands.

Many hotels and resorts rent kayaks or provide free use for guests. And several tour operators are now introducing kayaking as an organized activity.

Guided excursions are offered in the Caicos, Abacos and Grand Bahama. See the island chapters for contact information. The Exuma Cays Land & Sea Park (p204) is a particularly good destination for kayaking.

Water Sports, Surfing & Windsurfing

Most resort hotels either include water sports in their rates or offer them as extras. On offer are all kinds of beach and water sport, such as parasailing, waterskiing, and windsurfing. Typical rates are as follows: sailboards are $20 per hour; jet skiing $50 for 30 minutes; for a 15-minute banana boat ride $30 per person; parasailing is $70 per hour; windsurfing is $25 per hour; sailing is $90 per day and kayaks rent for $15 per hour.

For surfers seeking the ultimate wave, look elsewhere. There are a few spots on the Bahamas' east coasts, however, where surfers can find decent Atlantic waves, notably Surfer's Beach on Eleuthera and, most importantly, Garbanzo Reef off Elbow Cay (Abacos). Winter months are best.

Virtually the entire east side of the chain is fringed by an offshore barrier reef onto which the waves break, making surfing dangerous far out. The trade winds, however, continue to blow inside the barrier reef, so the placid stretches inside the reef are perfect for windsurfing (in the absence of other coral).

Resorts and concessionaires rent equipment on the main beaches of New Providence and Grand Bahama. Many hotels have free sailboard use for guests. The Romora Bay Dive Shop (p178) on Harbour Island, Eleuthera, is a good bet for windsurfing.

The Bahamas Windsurfing Championship is held in January in Freeport.

The Turks and Caicos islands are virgin territory for surfers but superbly suited to windsurfing. On Provo, Grace Bay is a fabulous location for windsurfing, with the consistent trade winds behind you.

On Grand Turk you may see windsurfers whizzing along the waters of North Creek.

BUSINESS HOURS
Bahamas

In Nassau and on Grand Bahama some banks close at 2pm and reopen from 3pm to 5pm on Friday, when they can be very busy. In the Family Islands, bank hours vary widely. Usually local banks are open only one or two days a week for two or three hours. A few local banks open 9am to noon on Saturday.

Few businesses and stores open on Sunday, outside of the tourist centers. In the Family Islands many stores and businesses will close for lunch during the week. Most restaurants and cafés in the tourist centers open seven days a week. The following hours should be regarded as a general guide.

Banks (9am-3pm Mon-Thu, 9am-5pm Fri)
Government offices (9am-5pm Mon-Fri)
Private businesses (9am-5pm Mon-Fri)
Shops (Fri, 9-10am-5pm Sat)
Post offices (9am-5pm Mon-Fri, 9am-noon Sat)
Restaurants (breakfast 6am-9am; lunch noon-2pm, dinner 6-9pm)
Tourist information (9am-5pm Mon-Fri)

Turks & Caicos Islands
Government offices (9am-4pm Mon-Thu, 9am-3pm Fri)
Private offices and businesses (8:30am-5pm Mon-Fri)
Banks (9am-3pm Mon-Thu, 9am-5pm Fri)
Post Offices (9am-4pm)

CHILDREN

These islands chase the family traveler aggressively, and the larger hotels compete by having children's facilities. Most hotels will have a babysitter, while most larger resorts, such as Atlantis, with its Discovery Channel Camp, cater to families and have a range of activities and amenities for children. These features are covered in this guide's listings.

The best kids' clubs are found in resorts on Nassau, New Providence, Freeport and Lucaya in Grand Bahama, and Caicos in the Turks and Caicos Islands. Yet many other hotels do have a wealth of sea sports and activities on offer and actually do enjoy having children around.

Most hotels also offer free accommodations or greatly reduced rates for children staying in their parents' rooms (a child is usually defined as being 12 years or younger, but some classify those 16 or younger as children). Rental villas and apartments are also good options for families.

It's a good idea to prearrange necessities such as cribs, babysitters and baby food. Stores sell formula and disposable diapers, but there's not a huge range to choose from, and the prices are high. These problems are exacerbated in the Family Islands, Caicos Islands and less populated cays.

Many of the car-rental agencies can supply safety seats, but you should book these ahead.

Bahamas Ministry of Tourism (☎ 242-322-7500; www.bahamas.com) has a very popular and well-organized program, Children-to-Children, which links visiting children with local kids. The program is in operation on many of the Bahamian islands and encourages the children to participate in activities together. The aim is for children to gain an understanding about each other's lives; a fabulous idea.

Bahamian kids play basketball with a passion. The islands' patron saint is Mychal Thompson, a Los Angeles Lakers player from Harbour Island; the first Bahamian to make it to the NBA. Most towns have a small court with makeshift stands for fellow fans.

Travel with Children, by Cathy Lanigan and Lonely Planet co-founder Maureen Wheeler, gives you the lowdown on preparing for family travel, as well as basic health advice.

For encouragement, you might also check out Nancy Jeffrey's *Bahamas – Out Island Odyssey*, her tale of traveling through the islands with two teenage sons and an infant.

A note of caution: you do not see mothers nursing their babies or changing diapers in public, either in the Bahamas or the Turks and Caicos Islands. You will probably cause offence if you do either of these inappropriately.

CLIMATE CHARTS

In general, the Bahamas is balmy year-round, with cooling, near-constant trade winds blowing by day from the east. The so-called rainy season extends from late May

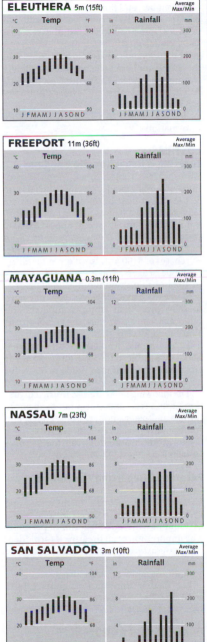

to November, and humidity in the northern islands is relatively high year-round, but declines from northwest to southeast across the archipelago.

The Turks and Caicos' climate is similar to that of the southern Bahamas, though slightly warmer and drier. The hottest months are August to November and average humidity is 35%.

Refer to When to Go on p13 for more information.

CUSTOMS
Entering & Departing the Bahamas

All baggage is subject to a customs inspection, and Bahamian customs officials are serious about their business. All visitors are expected to fill a Baggage Declaration Form.

Individuals are allowed to import $10,000 cash, plus 50 cigars, 200 cigarettes or 1lb of tobacco, plus 1 quart of spirits free of charge. Purchases of $100 are also allowed for all arriving passengers. You are allowed to bring in a reasonable amount of personal belongings free of charge. However, you may need to show proof that laptop computers and other expensive items are for personal use. You should declare these upon arrival.

Excess items deemed to be imported goods are subject to 35% duty (25% for clothing). The tariff is as much as 300% for certain items.

The following items are also restricted: firearms, drugs (except prescription medicines), flowers and plants, honey, fruits, coffee, and meats and vegetables (unless canned).

For more information, call the **Bahamas Customs Department** (☎ 242-325-6550).

Entering & Departing the Turks & Caicos

Visitors may each bring in duty free one carton of cigarettes or 50 cigars, one bottle of liquor or wine, and 50 grams of perfume. The importation of all firearms is forbidden, except upon written authorization from the Commissioner of Police. Spear guns, drugs and pornography are also illegal.

For further information, contact **Turks and Caicos Customs** (Grand Turk ☎ 649-946-2801, Provo ☎ 649-946-4241).

DANGERS AND ANNOYANCES

The most you will probably have to worry about on the islands are mosquitoes and 'no see ums' (sandflies), which contrary to most expectations do not confine their human-munching to dawn and dusk, and in the case of sandflies, only to the beach. Do not be shy about applying mosquito repellent and covering up at night to prevent the sandflies' powerful bites. Invisible crowds of these little pests will otherwise leave you spottier than a leopard and itchier than a dog's bottom. The Bahamian chemists sell a pink calamine-style lotion that soothes the itching a bit.

Another threat in the Turks and Caicos, and some of the Family Islands, may be the roving bands of donkeys and horses. Dogs and chickens also tend to wander off, so although all these creatures are pretty wary of vehicles, take care on the roads nonetheless.

Natural Hazards

Many of the reefs and beaches across the region have dangerous undertows and currents, so do take care.

Public warnings will be issued if a hurricane is due to come ashore. In the event of a hurricane, seek shelter in the sturdiest structure you can find. (For more on hurricane seasons see p37).

The manchineel tree, which grows along the Bahamian shoreline, produces small, applelike green fruits. Don't eat them – they're highly poisonous! The sap is also irritating. Take care not to sit beneath the tree, as even raindrops running off the leaves onto your skin can cause blisters.

Human Hazards

Most Bahamians are extremely law-abiding citizens and their tolerance of thieves and criminals is extremely low. The Turks and Caicos Islands are also relatively crime-free and are therefore a joy to explore.

Nassau is a distinct exception, where shootings and violent robberies are frequent…with most murders and crimes related to the drug trade. They occur overwhelmingly in the low-income area south of downtown and to a lesser degree in parts of Freetown on Grand Bahama. Even the mellow Family Islands have seen noticeable increases in crime levels in recent years, notably in Marsh Harbour, Abacos.

However, most crime against travelers is petty opportunistic theft, so take sensible precautions with your valuables.

DISABLED TRAVELERS

Disabled travelers will need to plan their vacation carefully, as few allowances have been made for them in either the Bahamas or the Turks and Caicos, although the Bahamas is slightly better equipped.

New construction codes mandate ramps and parking spots for disabled people at shopping plazas and other select sites. Larger hotels are beginning to introduce features such as Braille instructions and chimes for elevators, bathrooms with grab bars, and ramps. However, only the most recent structures in Nassau and, to a lesser degree, Freeport have adopted these features.

The tourism boards can provide a list of hotels with wheelchair ramps, as can the **Bahamas Council for the Handicapped** (☎ 242-322-4260; Commonwealth Blvd, Elizabeth Estates, Nassau) and the **Bahamas Association for the Physically Disabled** (☎ 242-322-2393; fax 242-322-7984; Dolphin Dr, Nassau, PO Box N-4252, Nassau). The latter can also hire out a van and portable ramps for those with wheelchairs.

EMBASSIES & CONSULATES

There are no foreign embassies or consulates in the Turks and Caicos. Contact the relevant officials in Nassau, New Providence.

Bahamian Embassies & Consulates

Canada Ottawa (☎ 613-232-1724; ottawa-mission@bahighco.com; 50 O'Connor St, Suite 1313, Ottawa, ON K1P 6L2, Canada)
China Hong Kong (☎ 852-2147-0202; fax-852-2893-3917; Suite 704-5 A Sino Plaza 7F, 255-257 Gloucester Rd, Causeway Bay, Hong Kong, Republic of China)
UK London (☎ 207-408-4488; fax 207-499-9937; 10 Chesterfield St, London W1X 8AH, England)
USA Washington DC (☎ 202-319-2660; bahemb@aol.doc; 2220 Massachusetts Ave NW, Washington, DC 20008, USA); Florida (☎ 305-373-6295; fax 305-373-6312; Bahamas Consulate General, 25 SE 2nd Ave, Suite 818, Miami, FL 33131, USA)

Turks & Caicos Embassies & Consulates

As a British crown colony, the Turks and Caicos are represented via British embassies and consulates abroad. There are also British Consulate-Generals in many US cities.
Australia Canberra (☎ 02-6270-6666; fax 02-6237-3236; British High Commission, Commonwealth Ave, ACT 2600, Australia)
Canada Montreal (☎ 514-866-5863; montreal@britainincanada.org; Consulate-General, 1000 De La Gauchetiere St W, suite 4200, Montreal, Quebec H3b 4W5, Canada)
France Paris (☎ 144-51-3100; fax 144-51-4127; British Embassy, 35, rue du Faubourg St Honoré, 75383 Paris Cedex 08, France)
USA San Francisco (☎ 415-617-1300; fax 415-434-2018; British Consulate General, 1 Sansome St, Suite 850, San Francisco, CA 94104, USA); Washington DC (☎ 202-588-7800; British Embassy, 3100 Massachusetts Ave NW, Washington, DC 20008, USA)

Embassies & Consulates in the Bahamas

Most countries are represented by honorary consuls, individuals appointed to represent the respective country.
Canada (Map pp66–7; ☎ 242-393-2123/4; fax 252-393-1305; Shirley St Plaza, Nassau)
UK (Map p69; ☎ 242-325-7471; 242-323-3871; www.britishhighcommission.gov.uk/bahamas; Bitco Bldg, E St, Nassau)
USA (Map p69; ☎ 242-322-1181/2/3; fax 242-328-7838; www.usemb.state.gov/nassau; Mosmar Bldg, Queen St, Nassau)

FESTIVALS & EVENTS
Bahamas

No traditional African festivals were kept in the Bahamas, but several folk festivals evolved from the brief slave era, notably Junkanoo (p34) and Emancipation Day. Nassau and Freeport in Grand Bahama host a midyear Junkanoo in June, while other islands also host a summer 'Goombay Festival.'

Most events run on a predictable schedule. Many annual events occur at the cusp of months, so the specific month may vary from year to year. For more information contact the **Bahamas Ministry of Tourism** (☎ 242-322-7500; www.bahamas.com; Welcome Centre, Festival Place, Prince George Wharf, Nassau; ⊙ 9am-5pm Mon-Sat, Sun if cruise-ship in port).

There's a wealth of festivals in the Family Islands involving bonefishing championships, as well as cultural and sporting celebrations. Information for these can be found through the Bahamas Ministry of Tourism websites and via visitor information centers. The more famous regattas, the Family Island Regatta in the Exumas (April) and the Long Island Regatta (May), are fabulous fun; locally made sailing craft compete for prizes and partying abounds.

Most Family Island towns also celebrate 'homecomings,' the absolute heart of the

Bahamian social scene, when family members return from Nassau, other islands or the US. Usually these homecomings are associated with national holidays so that participants can stretch the festivities for three to five days.

January

Polar Bear Swim A beach party culminates in some crazy fun: people swimming in the sea among giant ice cubes off Nassau.

New Year's Day The Junkanoo parade on Bay Street in Nassau is a great visual and musical spectacle.

Staniel Cay New Year's Day Cruising Regatta Craft from all over speed around Exumas cays.

Nassau Classic Car Festival A parade of polished classics and proud owners through Nassau.

Supreme Court Opening This formal ceremony opens the annual session of the Bahamas Supreme Court, accompanied by the Royal Bahamas Police Force Band.

February

George Town Cruising Regatta More than 500 yachts visit for a week of fun and partying at this fabulous sailing regatta.

March

Bacardi Rum Cup Two days of sailing competitions and notes of encouragement from the Royal Bahamas Police Force Band in Nassau.

Freeport Rugby Club Annual Easter Rugby Festival Grand Bahama hosts 15 of the world's top rugby teams, as players from as far afield as Argentina and Wales gather to tussle for the grand prize.

Hope Town Heritage Day Abaco has a day of fun for all the family.

April

Family Island Regatta This four-day extravaganza of sailboat races and general merry-making is a highlight of the Bahamian social calendar. It takes place in George Town (Great Exuma), and thousands fly in for the lively social scene, which includes beauty pageants, cooking demonstrations, and plenty of drinking and dancing.

May

Bimini Festival A popular sportfishing tournament is the highlight of this festival in mid-May, featuring barbecues, cookouts and general merriment.

Bahamas Heritage Festival A cultural event with lots of traditional music, food and fun.

Long Island Sailing Regatta More than 40 locally built sailing sloops, representing each of the major Bahamian islands, compete for prizes. Onshore rake 'n' scrape bands, sporting activities and Bahamian food keep it lively.

June

Annual Eleuthera Pineapple Festival This annual festival, held in early June in Gregory Town (Eleuthera), combines four days of music, games and festivities with cooking contests, 'best pineapple' contests, beauty pageants and the highlight – the crowning of the young Pineapple Queen.

Bahamas Boating Flings Each June through mid-August, a lead boat guides a flotilla of yachts and other craft from Fort Lauderdale into the Biminis.

Goombay Summer Festival Nassau hosts a midyear Junkanoo parade, with round-the-clock festivities for summertime visitors.

Rake 'n' Scrape Music Festival A four-day annual event held in June. It's organized by Sidney Poitier's daughter, Pamela.

July

Independence Day A public holiday across the Bahamas with parades, celebrations and festivities.

Beer Festival During full moon in this month, Exuma consumes beer and pizza; what a great excuse!

August

Emancipation Day Held the first Monday in August to commemorate the emancipation of slaves in 1834 across the islands.

Cat Island Regatta Held on Emancipation Day, this is the biggest event of the year on Cat Island, where sailboat races, dominoes tournament and rake 'n' scrape music are all the rage.

Great Abaco Triathlon Athletes descend on Marsh Harbour to test their mettle, with a children's triathlon and Sprintman race.

September

Bahamas Atlantis Superboat Challenge Life is never so fast in Nassau as in late September during this annual professional powerboat race.

October

Annual Grand Bahama Triathlon Watch and wonder as superhumans compete in a 1½-mile swim, 15-mile bike race and 3-mile run.

Great Bahamas Seafood Festival The Arawak Cay Seafood Market in Nassau is the setting for this annual four-day culinary and cultural extravaganza, featuring concerts, Junkanoo and plenty of food.

International Cultural Weekend Bahamians celebrate unity with a weekend of float parades, food fests, arts and crafts displays and concerts in Nassau.

North Eleuthera Sailing Regatta This three-day racing pageant features scores of locally built sloops vying for the championship while onshore festivities are roaring.

November
Annual Grand Bahama Conchman Triathlon More than 200 athletes gather in Freeport to compete in swimming, bicycling and running, while others party.
Andros Community Awareness Week Androsians celebrate their Bahamian dishes, music, Junkanoo, dance and stories.
Bahamas Wahoo Tournament Hosted by the Bimini Big Game Fishing Club, this game is for fishing fans.
All Abaco Sailing Regatta Boats and Bahamian fun on the water and land.

December
Christmas Concert Under the Stars Green Turtle Cay (Abacos) has a grand open-air concert of traditional Christmas music and performances.
Annual Christmas Day Parade Bimini hosts a 5am parade with music and festivities.
Plymouth Historical Weekend Residents of Green Turtle Cay celebrate their Loyalist heritage with musical concerts, theater, art exhibit and barbecues.
Junkanoo The national street party of the year starts in the early hours of Boxing Day across the isles; don't miss the parades and partying!

Turks & Caicos
These islands do not miss out on festivities, with many local events taking place. Cultural and musical events occur in May, August, September and November including the Ripshaw Music Festival, when Turks and Caicos rake 'n' scrape musicians gather in Grand Turk to outrake and scrape each other with much exuberance and entertainment.

For more information contact **Turks and Caicos Tourism** (☎ 649-946-4970; www.turksandcaicostourism.com; Stubbs Diamond Plaza, Providenciales).

May
Regatta on South Caicos The oldest and most playful festival held on the islands.
Culture Night Held on Provo to make up for all the regatta's partying; well you have to pay your dues!

June
Conch Carnival on Grand Turk Conch-fritter eating contests, dancing, island music and the Grand Turk Iron Divemaster competition, finished off with beach bonfires.
Fun in the Sun Festival Held in Salt Cay.

July
Provo Day 'Summer Festival' Miss Turks and Caicos is crowned in Provo amid much chatter and hollering, alongside regattas, parades and partying. These lively events are spread over a week around Emancipation Day.

Turks & Caicos International Billfish Tournament Incorporates the Invitational Billfish Tournament. One for those who get excited by discussing the intricacies of bait.
Festarama Festival North Caicos has fun; this annual regatta includes beach parties.

August
Ripsaw Music Festival on Grand Turk Rake 'n' scrape musicians have noisy fun.
Cactus Fest A week-long carnival on Grand Turk with reggae music and general festivities.

September
Cultural Week Island culture is relived and celebrated throughout the islands.
Middle Caicos Expo Held every year, with a bit of everything.

October
North Caicos Extravaganza These festivities feature a Junkanoo rush.

December
Marathon A run that tests the physical mettle of all competitors on Grand Turk.
Christmas Tree Lighting Ceremony Many of the islands enjoy this event.

FOOD & DRINK
For a full explanation of local cuisine and drinks, please refer to the Food and Drink chapter (p55). Listings are categorized into 'budget' (anything up to $10), 'midrange' (mains averaging $12 to $23) and 'top end' (mains around and over $23).

GAY & LESBIAN TRAVELERS
Gay travelers need to be discreet in either Bahamas or the Turks and Caicos Islands. Most Bahamian gays and lesbians are still in the closet, and the nation has draconian laws against homosexual activity, which is punishable by prison terms. Laws are strictly enforced; sadly any public expressions of affection between gays may well bring trouble.

Please refer to the boxed text on p62 as this information, both social and legal, basically applies across the whole region.

HOLIDAYS
You may also want to check out the 'When to Go' section on p13 when planning your trip.

Bahamas

Bahamian national holidays that fall on Saturday or Sunday are usually observed on the following Monday.

New Year's Day January 1
Good Friday Friday before Easter
Easter Monday Monday after Easter
Whit Monday Seven weeks after Easter
Labour Day First Friday in June
Independence Day July 10
Emancipation Day First Monday in August
Discovery Day October 12
Christmas Day December 25
Boxing Day December 26

Turks & Caicos

The following national holidays are recognized in this region.

New Year's Day January 1
Commonwealth Day March 13
Good Friday Friday before Easter
Easter Monday Monday after Easter
National Heroes' Day May 29
Her Majesty the Queen's Official Birthday June 14 (or nearest weekday)
Emancipation Day August 1
National Youth Day September 26
Columbus Day October 13
International Human Rights Day October 24
Christmas Day December 25
Boxing Day December 26

INSURANCE

A travel insurance policy to cover theft, loss and medical problems is worth organizing for your trip. There is a wide variety of policies available, so check the small print.

Some policies specifically exclude 'dangerous activities' (eg motorcycling, rock climbing, canoeing, scuba-diving and even hiking). If you're planning on doing any of those activities, be sure to hunt down the right policy to cover yourself.

You may prefer a policy that pays doctors or hospitals directly rather than requiring you to pay on the spot and claim later. If you have to claim later make sure you keep all documentation. Some policies ask you to call back (reverse charges) to a center in your home country where an immediate assessment of your problem is made.

Check that the policy covers ambulances or an emergency flight home.

For health insurance information see p296; for car insurance see p294.

INTERNET ACCESS

A few of the midrange and most of the top-end accommodations in the Bahamas and Turks and Caicos Islands have Internet connections in the guest rooms. Some hotels also offer the use or 'hire' of a computer.

Internet connections will accept the standard laptop jacks, while plugs accept the standard USA/Canadian two or three-pin plugs. You will require a local ISP provider's dial-up number however, which can be arranged through your home ISP operator.

If you do not have a laptop, you will not be completely bereft. Internet cafés exist in most tourist centers, and in some of the larger towns in both the Bahamas and the Turks and Caicos. The quality of connections is normally pretty good across the board, but expect to pay from $10 for 15 minutes.

For a list of useful websites please refer to p14.

LEGAL MATTERS

Marijuana (ganja) and cocaine are prevalent in the Bahamas and in the Turks and Caicos, which are used as a transshipment point for drug traffic into North America and Europe. At some stage, you may be approached by hustlers selling drugs.

Possession and use of drugs and the 'facilitation of drug trafficking' in these islands are strictly illegal and penalties are severe. The islands are swarming with US Drug Enforcement agents, and purchasing drugs is a risky business. Foreigners do not receive special consideration if caught and Bahamian prisons are notoriously nasty places.

MONEY

The Bahamian dollar is linked one-to-one with the US dollar, so you can use US currency everywhere. Note the only bank permitted to exchange amounts of more than BS$70 is the Central Bank of the Bahamas on Market St in Nassau. It's a good idea to spend all your Bahamian dollars before you leave. Major commercial banks maintain branches throughout the islands, although in the Family Islands they are thin on the ground. Most hotels and car-rental companies will take credit cards on the Family Islands, but do have some ready cash just in case.

The Turks and Caicos are unique: a British-dependent territory with the US dollar as its official currency. The treasury also issues a Turks and Caicos crown and quarter. There are no currency restrictions on the amount of money that visitors can bring in.

ATMs
Automated teller machine (ATM) cards are a good way to obtain incidental cash. There are ATMs in the leading tourist centers and at many (but not all) banks around the islands. Most machines accept Visa, MasterCard and American Express via international networks such as Cirrus and Visa/PLUS.

Credit Cards
Major credit cards are widely accepted throughout the Bahamas, Provo and Grand Turk as well as the bigger hotels on the Turks and Caicos islands. Credit cards are not widely accepted for general transactions in the more remote Family Islands or Turks and Caicos Islands. Elsewhere you may need to operate on a cash-only basis. You can use your credit card to get cash advances at most commercial banks. Companies that accept credit cards may add an additional charge of up to 5%.

Foreign currency can be changed at banks in Provo and Grand Turk, which can also issue credit-card advances and operate ATMs.

Traveler's Checks
These are widely accepted throughout the Bahamas and Turks and Caicos except on more remote Family Islands, although some hotels, restaurants and exchange bureaus charge a hefty fee for cashing traveler's checks. They are accepted in the Caicos and Grand Turk but you may be charged a transaction fee of 5%.

To report lost American Express traveler's checks in the Bahamas, contact **Destinations** (☎ 242-322-2931; 303 Shirley St, Nassau).

POST
Mail from the islands is slow. Airmail to North America usually takes about 10 days. Allow about four weeks for mail to Europe, Australia and New Zealand.

Postcards to the UK, US, or Canada cost $0.55. Airmail letters cost $0.65 per half-ounce to the US and Canada; $0.70 to the UK and Europe; and $0.90 to Africa, Asia, or Australasia.

Express mail services are listed in the Yellow Pages. Note that 24-hour service is not usually guaranteed from the Family or Turks and outlying Caicos Islands, as the express-mail services tend to rely on air-charter services.

You can have mail addressed to you 'Poste Restante' care of 'The General Post Office,' East Hill St, Nassau, The Bahamas. Mail should be marked 'To be collected from the General Delivery desk.' All correspondence is retained for three weeks.

TELEPHONE
Hotel telephone rates are expensive across the region and should be avoided when possible. Many hotels also charge for an unanswered call after the receiving phone has rung five times.

Most US toll-free numbers can't be accessed from the Bahamas or Turks and Caicos. Usually you must dial ☎ 1-880, plus the last seven digits of the number.

Bahamas
The government-owned **Bahamas Telecommunications Corporation** (☎ 242-302-7000; John F Kennedy Dr, Nassau), or BaTelCo, has an office on most Bahamian islands. Even the smallest settlement usually has at least one public phone.

The Bahamian country code is ☎ 242. You need to dial this when making inter-island calls. To call the Bahamas from the US and Canada, dial ☎ 1-242. From elsewhere, dial your country's international access code + ☎ 242 + the local number.

MOBILE PHONES
You can travel with your own cellular phone in the Bahamas, but you may be charged a customs fee upon entry (which is refunded when you leave). Your phone will not function on BaTelCo's cellular system unless you rent temporary use of a 'roaming' cellular line.

DOMESTIC CALLS
Local calls are free of charge, although hotels will charge you between $0.75 to $1 per call.
Current Time & Temperature ☎ 917
Directory Assistance ☎ 916
Interisland calls ☎ 1-242 followed by the seven-digit local number

DIRECTORY

International Operator Assistance ☎ 0
Weather by Phone ☎ 915

INTERNATIONAL CALLS

Many Bahamian phone booths and all BaTelCo offices permit direct dial to overseas numbers. It is far cheaper to call direct from a phone booth than to call from your hotel via operator-assisted calls. Assisted calls to the USA cost around $1.80 per three-minute minimum, then $0.90 per minute. Calls to Canada cost around $1.30, then $1.30 per minute, to Europe it costs $2.90, then $2.15 per minute while calls to Australia and New Zealand are just frightening.

Many national companies offer a service for their subscribers, issuing international charge cards and a code number. Costs for calling home are then billed directly to your home number. The following companies provide such cards.

AT&T USA Direct (☎ 1-800-225-5288)
British Telecom (☎ 0-800-345-144)
Canada Direct (☎ 1-800-389-0004)
MCI (☎ 1-800-888-8000)
Sprint (☎ 1-800-389-2111)
Telstra Australia (☎ 1-800-038-000)

PHONECARDS

The majority of Bahamian public telephones accept only prepaid phonecards issued by **BaTelCo** (☎ 242-302-7827), available at stores and other accredited outlets near phone card booths. The cards are sold in denominations of $5, $10, $20 and $50.

Turks & Caicos Islands

Cable & Wireless (☎ 1800-804-2994) operates a digital network from its offices in Grand Turk and Provo. Direct dial is standard.

Public phone booths are located throughout the islands. Many booths require phonecards, issued in denominations of $5, $10, and $15.

Hotels will charge you $1 per local call, and some also charge for unanswered calls after the receiving phone has rung five times.

The Turks and Caicos country code is ☎ 649. To call from North America, dial ☎ 1-649 + the local number. From elsewhere, dial your country's international access code + the local number For interisland calls, dial the seven-digit local number.

Directory Assistance (☎ 118)
Local operator (☎ 0)
International Operator Assistance (☎ 115)

MOBILE PHONES

American mobiles can work here, as long as you register with Cable & Wireless call roaming. Mobiles can also be rented from around $10 per day.

PHONECARDS

Phonecards are issued in denominations of $5, $10 and $15 and can be bought from Cable & Wireless outlets and also shops and delis.

You can also bill calls to your American Express, Discover, Visa or MasterCard by dialing ☎ 1-800-744-7777 on any touchtone phone and giving the operator your card details (there's a one-minute minimum).

SHOPPING

Most prices are fixed, and bargaining is less of a common practice than it is on Caribbean islands. Feel free to bargain, however, at straw markets and crafts stalls.

Bahamas
DUTY-FREE GOODS

The two main resort towns, Nassau and Freeport, and major settlements have a wide choice of duty-free stores stocked with perfumes, Cuban cigars, Italian leathers, Colombian emeralds, plus china, crystal, gold, silverware, linens, watches, and silks. Many items can be bought at up to 30% below US or European retail prices.

Paying by credit card is best, as this protects you if the item is defective (some card companies provide buyers' insurance).

Fine handmade cigars from Cuba are all the rage in the Bahamas. Nassau and Freeport boast well-stocked tobacco shops dedicated to cigar lovers.

ARTS & CRAFTS

The Bahamas is well known for its busy straw markets, as Bahamian weavers were among the first in the Caribbean region to take their skills to commercial heights. You'll find crafts stores virtually everywhere, selling baskets, bags, mats, dolls and hats woven from the top fronds of coconut palms. Much of the straw-work for sale in Nassau is actually imported from Taiwan and the Orient (even if it has 'Made in Bahamas' stitched across the front in blazing colors)!

Also look for Androsia batik, brightly colored, handmade, authentically Bahamian material.

There are dozens of art galleries throughout the chain. The Abacos are particularly blessed, for here reside some of the islands' most famous artists; originals by collector-name artists can be had for a relative steal.

Turks & Caicos

The handcrafted plait-and-sew style of straw weaving survives. Handmade rag rugs and baskets are a great buy. The art scene is also pretty lively on Provo; you can pick up some splendid Haitian art for a few dollars as well as a some excellent local art works. And you can stock up on Cuban cigars.

TOURIST INFORMATION
Bahamas Visitor Centres

Abacos (☎ 242-367-3067; Queen Elizabeth Dr, Marsh Harbour; www.go-abacos.com)

Andros (☎ 242-368-2286; Andros Town Airport, Fresh Creek)

Eleuthera Governor's Harbour (☎ 242-332-2142; Queen's Hwy) Harbour Island (☎ 242-333-2621; Bay St)

Exumas (☎ 242-336-2430; Queen's Hwy, George Town)

Freeport (☎ 242-352-8044; www.grand-bahama.com; International Bazaar)

Nassau Welcome Centre (☎ 242-323-3182, 322 7680; Prince George Dock) Airport Arrivals Terminal (☎ 242-377-6806; www.bahamas.com)

Bahamas Tourism Offices Abroad

The **Bahamas Ministry of Tourism** (☎ 800-422-4262; www.bahamas.com) has a central information office in the US that sends out literature. There are also regional offices across the USA and in other countries that can also help with information.

Also in the US is the **Bahama Out Islands Promotion Board** (US ☎ 954-475-8315; www.boipb .com; 1200 South Pine Island Rd, Suite 750, Plantation, FL 33324, USA).

Canada (☎ 416-968-2999; bmotca@bahamas.com; 121 Bloor St E, No 1101, Toronto, Ontario, M4W 3M5, Canada)

France (☎ 01-45-26-62-62; info@bahamas-tourisme.fr; 113-115 rue du Cherche Midi, 75006 Paris, France)

Italy (☎ 2-48194390-2; info@vertexic.com; Corso Magenta 54, 20123 Milano, Italy)

UK (☎ 44-20-7355-0800; info@bahamas.co.uk; Bahamas House, 10 Chesterfield St, London W1J 5JL, UK)

USA California (☎ 800-439-6993 or 310-312-9544; gjohnson@bahamas.com; 11400 W Olympic Blvd, suite 204, Los Angeles, CA 90064, USA; Florida (☎ 954-236-9292; bmotfl@bahamas.com; 1200 S Pine Island Rd, Suite 750, Plantation, FL 33324, USA) Illinois (☎ 773-693-1500; bmotch@bahamas.com; 8600 W Bryn Mawr Ave, No 820, Chicago, IL 60631, USA) New York (☎ 212-758-2777; bmotny@bahamas.com; 150 E 52nd St, 28th fl, New York, NY 10022, USA)

Additional Bahamas websites include the following.

www.bahamasnet.com
www.bahamas-on-line.com
www.caribbeanaviation.com
www.cruisecritic.com
www.interknowledge.com/bahamas
www.thenassauguardian.com
www.thinkbahamas.org

Turks & Caicos Visitor Centers

Cockburn Town (☎ 649-946-2321; www.turksandcaicostourism.com; tci.tourism@tciway.tc; Front St, Cockburn Town, Grand Turk)

Providenciales Providenciales Airport (☎ 649-941-5496; www.turksandcaicostourism.com) Stubbs Diamond Plaza (☎ 649-946-4970; Providenciales)

Turks & Caicos Tourism Offices Abroad

USA (☎ 800-241-0824; tcitrsm@bellsouth.net; 2715 E Oakland Pk Blvd, Suite 101, Ft Lauderdale FL33306, USA)

Canada (☎ 613-332-6470; rwilson@northcom.net; 29620 Hwy 62N RR#2, Bancroft, Ontario K0L 1L0, Canada)

UK (☎ 0180-350-1000; fax 0181-350-1011; 66 Abbey Rd, Bush Hill Pk, Enfield, Middlesex EN12RQ, England, UK)

Additional Turks and Caicos websites:
www.northcaicos.tc
www.wherewhenhow.com
www.tcisearch.com
www.milk.tciway.tc

VISAS
Bahamas

Canadians and citizens of the UK and Commonwealth countries may enter the Bahamas without a passport or visa for up to three weeks. For longer stays, a passport is required. However, UK citizens need to show a passport to re-enter their home country. Changes to the law in effect from 31 December 2005 mean US citizens and all visitors are now required to have a passport or 'other secure, accepted document' to enter or re-enter the USA from the Caribbean. Onward tickets will also be required.

Visitors from most European countries, Turkey and Israel require passports but no visas for stays up to three months. Citizens of most Central and South American countries, including Mexico, require passports but no visas for stays up to 14 days. Visas are required for longer stays.

Citizens of the following countries require passports and visas for stays of any duration: Dominican Republic, Haiti, South Africa and all communist countries. Citizens of all other countries should check current entry requirements with the nearest Bahamian embassy. For any enquiries about extended stays or work (there are strict legal regulations about foreigners seeking work in the Bahamas) check with the **Ministry of Labour & Immigration Department** (☎ 242-322-7530; fax 242-326-0977; PO Box N-831, E Hill St, Nassau).

Turks & Caicos

US citizens need proof of citizenship (a valid passport, voter's registration card or birth certificate) and photo identification to enter the Turks and Caicos. Changes to the law in effect from 31 December 2005 mean US citizens and all visitors are required to have a passport or 'other secure, accepted document' to enter or re-enter the USA from the Caribbean. No visas are required for citizens of the US, Canada, UK and Commonwealth countries, Ireland and most Western European countries. Citizens of most other countries require visas, which can be obtained from British embassies, High Commissions or consulates abroad.

Proof of onward transportation or tickets are required upon entry.

For information on work, residence, or stays longer than three months, contact the **Turks and Caicos Immigration Department** (☎ 649-946-2929; fax 649-946-2924; South Base, Grand Turk, Turks and Caicos, BWI).

WOMEN TRAVELERS

It is unusual for women to travel alone in the Caribbean and West Indies, and you will be asked on many occasions by curious men and women about your husband's whereabouts. This is a friendly enquiry, and it is often easier to reply that you are meeting up somewhere or that he is working, rather than get into the whole discussion about free choice.

There is no doubt that these amiable locals will be concerned about your welfare. Although single women have little to fear in either the Bahamas or the Turks and Caicos, and cases of sexual assault are very, very rare, there is always the exception that proves the rule. Enjoy the warmth of their trepidation, take obvious precautions at night, and dress appropriately; you'll *never* see a Bahamian or Turks and Caicos woman in shorts, let alone a bikini top, around town.

Women's Crisis Centre (☎ 242-328-0922; Shirley St, Nassau) can assist in an emergency or if you need emotional support, while the **Women's Health & Diagnostic Centre** (☎ 242-322-6440; 1st Terr, Collins Ave, Nassau) and **Women's Health** (☎ 242-328-6636; Collins Ave, Nassau) are useful resources.

Transportation

CONTENTS

GETTING THERE & AWAY

With the Bahamas consisting of some 700 islands and 2000 cays spread over a 100,000-sq-mile radius and the Turks and Caicos having a further 40-odd islands and cays to explore, this is not exactly a simple one flight in and another flight out set of islands. But isn't that part of the region's charms? Private boat–owners certainly believe so.

Nearly all the region's major international traffic flows through Nassau, New Providence. The main forms of transport are scheduled flights and cruise liners. From Nassau, local carriers, a few ferries and the slower mail boats reach most inhabited islands and cays.

The skies are opening up, however, and it is now possible to take direct flights from the USA and Europe to a few of the other Bahamian islands and Providenciales in the Caicos.

THINGS CHANGE

The information in this chapter is particularly vulnerable to change. Check directly with the airline or a travel agent to make sure you understand how a fare (and ticket you may buy) works and be aware of the security requirements for international travel. Shop carefully. The details given in this chapter should be regarded as pointers and are not a substitute for your own careful, up-to-date research.

BAHAMAS
Entering the Bahamas

All baggage is subject to customs inspection, and Bahamian customs officials take this business seriously. All visitors must complete a Baggage Declaration Form.

Individuals are allowed to import $10,000 cash, plus 50 cigars, 200 cigarettes, or 1lb of tobacco, plus 1 quart of spirits free of charge. Purchases totaling $100 are also allowed for all arriving passengers. You are allowed to bring in a reasonable amount of personal belongings free of charge. However, you may need to show proof that laptop computers and other expensive items are for personal use. You should declare these upon arrival.

Excess items deemed to be imported goods are generally subject to 35% duty. The tariff is 25% for clothing and increases to 300% for certain items.

The following items are also restricted: firearms, drugs (except prescription medicines), flowers and plants, honey, fruits, coffee, and meats and vegetables (unless canned).

For further information, contact the **Bahamas Customs Department** (☎ 242-325-6550).

PASSPORT

Changes to the law in effect from 31 December 2005 mean US citizens and all visitors are now required to have a passport or 'other secure, accepted document' to enter or re-enter the United States from the Caribbean. Onward tickets will also be required.

Visitors from most European countries, Turkey and Israel require passports but no visas for stays of up to three months. Citizens of most Central and South American countries, including Mexico, require passports but no visas for stays of up to 14 days. Visas are required for longer stays.

Citizens of the following countries require passports and visas for stays of any duration: Dominican Republic, Haiti, South Africa, and all communist countries. Citizens of all other countries should check current entry requirements with the nearest Bahamian embassy. For information about extended stays or work (there are strict regulations for foreigners seeking work in the Bahamas) check with the **Ministry of Labor & Immigration**

Department (☎ 242-322-7530; fax 242-326-0977; PO Box N-831, E Hill St, Nassau).

Air

AIRPORTS & AIRLINES

The Bahamas has six international airports, including two major hubs at Nassau and Freeport.

Exuma International Airport (GGT; ☎ 242-345-00095) Located in George Town, Exuma.

Freeport International Airport (FPO; ☎ 242-352-6020) Located in Freeport, Grand Bahama.

Marsh Harbour International Airport (MHH; ☎ 242-367-3039) Located in Marsh Harbour, Abacos.

Moss Town Exuma International Airport (MWX; ☎ 242-345-0030) Located in Moss Town, Exuma.

Nassau International Airport (NAS; ☎ 242-377-7281) Located in Nassau, New Providence.

North Eleuthera International Airport (ELH; ☎ 242-335-1242) Located in North Eleuthera.

Airlines Flying To & From the Bahamas

The Bahamas is well served by flights from North America and Europe. Its proximity to Florida means regular, relatively inexpensive flights from Miami, Fort Lauderdale and Orlando, as well as other east coast gateways. Nassau is less than three hours' flying time from the northeast USA and about 30 minutes by jet from Miami.

The national airline of the Bahamas, **Bahamasair** (☎ 242-377-5505, Freeport ☎ 242-352-8341; www.bahamasair.com) has an unblemished safety record and the pilots have an excellent reputation (see www.airsafe.com for details). However, delays and lost luggage are regular occurrences. Bahamians say 'If you have time to spare, fly Bahamasair.' You are warned.

The following major international airlines have offices at Nassau Airport.

Air Canada (AC; ☎ 1-888-247-2262, 242-377-8220; www.aircanada.ca; hubs Toronto & Montréal)

Air Jamaica (JM; ☎ 1-800-523-5585, 242-377-3301; www.airjamaica.com; hub Montego Bay)

Air Sunshine (YI; ☎ 1-800-327-8900, 954-434-8900; www.airsunshine.com; hub Fort Lauderdale)

American Airlines/American Eagle (AA; ☎ 1-800-433-7300, 242-377-2355; www.aa.com; hubs New York, Newark, Miami & Orlando)

Bahamasair (UP; ☎ 242-377-5505, Freeport ☎ 242-352-8341; www.bahamasair.com; hubs Nassau & Freeport, Miami, Orlando & Fort Lauderdale)

British Airways (BA; ☎ 1-800-247-9297, 242-377-2338; www.british-airways.com; hubs Heathrow & Gatwick)

Chalk's Ocean Airways (OP; ☎ 1-800-424-2557, 242-363-3114; www.flychalks.com; hubs Atlantis Heliport, Paradise Island nr Nassau, Fort Lauderdale & Miami)

Continental Connection/Gulfstream International (3M; ☎ 1-800-231-0856, 242-394-6019; www.gulfstreamair.com; Star Plaza, Mackey St, Nassau; hubs Miami, Fort Lauderdale & West Palm Beach)

Delta Air Lines/Comair (DL; ☎ 1-800-241-4141, 242-377-7774, 800-354-9822; www.delta.com; hubs New York, Orlando, Cincinnati & Atlanta)

Island Express (3Z; ☎ 954-359-0380; www.abacotoday.com/islandexpress; hub Fort Lauderdale)

Laker Airways (7Z; ☎ 242-352-3389; Freeport International Airport; hub Freeport)

US Airways/US Air Express (US; ☎ 1-800-622-1015, 242-377-8886; www.usair.com; hubs New York & Miami)

Charter Airlines

Charter flights are available throughout the Bahamas and Turks and Caicos. Some of the major charter companies flying in this region:

Cherokee Air (☎ 242-367-3450; www.cherokeeair.com; hub Marsh Harbour, Abaco)

Lynx (☎ 954-772-9808; www.lynxair.com; hub Fort Lauderdale)

Professional Air Charters (☎ 888-938-9508; www.professionalaircharters.com; hub Fort Lauderdale)

Twin Air Airways (☎ 954-359-8266; www.flytwinair.com; hub Fort Lauderdale Jet Centre)

Yellow Taxi–Charter (☎ 888-935-5694; www.flyyellowairtaxi.com; hub Fort Lauderdale Jet Centre)

TICKETS

As an alternative to booking directly with airlines, there is a plethora of web-based companies selling flights, and you can sometimes find bargain fares this way. Some websites are listed below:

Airbrokers (www.airbrokers.com) A US company specializing in cheap tickets.

Cheap Flights (www.chepflight.com) A very informative site with specials, airline info and flight searches mainly from the USA and UK.

Cheap Tickets (www.cheaptickets.com) Discount flight specialists.

Expedia (www.expedia.co.uk) A UK-based company listing major airlines; the earlier you book the better.

Flight Centre (www.flightcentre.co.uk, www.flightcentre.com.au) One of the largest and cheapest travel agents in the UK and Australia.

Hotwire (www.hotwire.com) Bookings from the US only, some cheap last-minute deals.

Last Minute (www.lastminute.com) One of the better sites for last-minute deals including hotels.

Orbitz (www.orbitz.com) Cheap deals when flying from the USA.
Priceline (www.priceline.com) A name-your-own-price site.
STA Travel (www.sta-travel.com) Prominent in international student travel, but you don't have to be a student to use the site.
Travel (www.travel.com.au) Reputable online flight-bookers from New Zealand and Australia.
Travelocity (www.travelocity.com) A US site that allows you to search fares to and from practically anywhere.

The following table includes prices for one-way tickets on popular routes.

Route	Price	Frequency
Biminis–Fort Lauderdale	$117	3 daily
Freeport–Miami	$267	3 daily
Freeport–New York	$674	3 daily
George Town–Fort Lauderdale	$167	3 weekly
Governor's Harbour–Fort Lauderdale	$164	4 weekly
Marsh Harbour–Fort Lauderdale	$186	3 daily
Marsh Harbour–Miami	$186	1 daily
Marsh Harbour–West Palm Beach	$186	2 daily
Nassau–London	$919	2 weekly
Nassau–Miami	$185	5 daily
Nassau–Montego Bay	$333	5 weekly
Nassau–Montréal	$540	1 weekly
Nassau–Provo, Caicos	$216	2 weekly
Nassau–Toronto	$540	1 daily
New Bight–Fort Lauderdale	$217	4 weekly
North Eleuthera–Miami	$196	2 daily
Treasure Cay–Miami	$188	1 daily
Treasure Cay Beach–Fort Lauderdale	$186	2 daily

AUSTRALIA & NEW ZEALAND
Flight Centre Australia (☎ 131-600; www.flightcentre.com.au) New Zealand (☎ 1800-243-544; www.flightcentre.co.nz)
STA Travel Australia (☎ 1300-360-960; www.statravel.com.au) New Zealand (☎ 1800-874-773; www.statravel.co.nz)
Thor Travel Australia (☎ 1800-801-119; www.thorworldtravel.com)

CANADA & THE USA
Air Brokers International (☎ 1800-883-3273; www.airbrokers.com)
Airtech (☎ 1877-247-8324; www.airtech.com)
Airtreks Inc (☎ 1800-350-0612; www.airtreks.com)
Skylinks US (☎ 1800-247-6659; www.skylinkus.com)
STA Travel (☎ 1800-777-0112; www.statravel.com)

Travac (☎ 1800-872-8800; www.thetravelsite.com)
Travel Cuts (☎ 800-667-2887; www.travelcuts.com)

CONTINENTAL EUROPE
France
OTU Voyages (☎ 0820-817-817; www.otu.fr)
Voyageurs du Monde (☎ 01-42-86-1600; www.vdm.com)

Germany
Just Travel (☎ 089-747-3330; www.justtravel.de)
STA Travel (☎ 01805-456-422; www.statravel.de)

Italy
CTS Viaggi (☎ 06-462-0431)
Passagi (☎ 06-474-0923)

Netherlands
Airfair (☎ 020-620-5121; www.airfair.nl)
NBBS Reizen (☎ 0900-10-20-300; www.mytravel.nl)

THE UK & IRELAND
Bridge the World (☎ 0870-444-7474; www.b-t-w.co.uk)
Dive Worldwide (☎ 1794-389-372; www.diveworldwide.com)
Flight Centre (☎ 0870-890-8099; www.flightcentre.co.uk)
Flightbookers (☎ 0870-010-7000; www.ebookers.com)
STA Travel (☎ 0870-160-0599; www.statravel.co.uk)
Trailfinders (☎ 020-7938-3939; www.trailfinders.co.uk)

Sea
CRUISE SHIPS
If you just want a short taste of the Bahamas, consider visiting by cruise ship. The Bahamas is by far the most popular port of call in the Caribbean region.

Cruise experiences vary vastly according to the cruise company and individual ship you choose. One person's sugar may be another's poison. For example, some passengers may wish to avoid the cruise liners now trotting out old rock bands such as REO Speedwagon or Foreigner for 'rock-nights,' while other travelers may whip out their snakeskin boots and shoulder pads, do a combover, and just get on down. *Caveat emptor!*

Cruise Line International Association (www.cruising.org) is a handy resource. Most cruises that call in the Bahamas depart from Florida and, less frequently, from New York.

Immigration and customs formalities are handled by the cruise companies upon arrival in port.

Some major cruise lines include the following:

Cape Canaveral Cruise Line (☎ 321-783-4052, 800-910-7447; www.capecanaveral.com)

Carnival Cruise Lines (☎ 305-599-2200, 800-327-9501; www.carnival.com)

Celebrity Cruises (☎ 305-358-7325, 800-437-3111; www.celebrity.com)

Costa Cruises (☎ 305-358-7325, 800-462-6782; www.costacruises.com)

Crystal Cruises (☎ 310-785-9300, 800-446-6620; www.crystalcruises.com)

Discovery Cruise Line (☎ 800-866-8687, 800-937-4477; www.discoverycruise.com)

Disney Cruise Line (☎ 407-566-3500, 800-511-8444; http://disneycruise.disney.go.com/dcl/en_US/home)

Dolphin Cruise Lines (☎ 305-358-5122; www.dolphincruise.com)

Holland America Line (☎ 206-281-3535, 800-426-0327; www.hollandamerica.com)

Norwegian Cruise Line (NCL; ☎ 305-436-4000, 800-327-7030; www.ncl.com)

Premier Cruises (☎ 305-358-5122, 800-990-7770; www.premiercruises.com)

Princess Cruises (☎ 310-553-1770, 800-421-0522; www.princess.com)

Royal Caribbean Cruise Lines (☎ 305-379-4731, 800-327-6700; www.royalcaribbean.com)

FERRIES
Discovery Cruise (☎ 1800-937-4477; www.discoverycruise.com) runs daily between Fort Lauderdale and Freeport, Grand Bahama ($129). It leaves Fort Lauderdale at 7:45am, returning at 10pm. Rates include three main meals. There's a Las Vegas–style casino on board.

FREIGHTERS
Gone are the good ol' days when travelers could easily buy passage aboard the banana freighters that plied between the Caribbean and North America and Europe, but it's not impossible. Try the following for some helpful information on traveling by freighter.

Ford's Freighter Travel Guide & Waterways of the World by **Judith Howard** (☎ 818-701-7414; 19448 Londelius St, Northridge, CA 91324, USA) lists freighters that carry passengers. The **Freight & Cruise Travel Association** (TravlTips; www.travltips.com) has a website that lists freight ships that take passengers.

Windjammer Barefoot Cruises (☎ 305-672-6453, 800-327-2601; www.windjammer.com) has a 13-day cruise from Freeport to Trinidad ($1,475) aboard the *Amazing Grace,* a 'workhorse'

vessel supplying the company's clipper ships in the Caribbean (none of which sail to the Bahamas). It has elegant cabins and charm. It stops at Nassau, Little San Salvador, Conception Island, Little Inagua and the Plana Cays, plus Grand Turk and Providenciales.

YACHTS
The sheltered waters of the 750-mile-long archipelago attract thousands of yachters each year. Winds and currents favor the passage south. Sailing conditions are at their best in summer, though you should keep fully abreast of weather reports, as summer is hurricane season.

Customs
You must clear customs and immigration upon arrival in the Bahamas. For details of each port's marinas, see the destination chapters. Your crew and guests will each need either a passport or birth certificate (a driver's license is not proof of citizenship). You'll need to clear customs again upon arrival at *each* island. It's a hassle, but the Bahamas' drug problem is such that you should be sympathetic to this policy. Anticipate the possibility of being boarded and searched by the US or Bahamian coast guard.

Details of official requirements are given in the *Yachtsman's Guide to The Bahamas including Turks & Caicos* (see opposite).

Specified marinas on each island are designated ports of entry (you may not enter at any other place):

Abacos Green Turtle Cay, Treasure Cay, Marsh Harbour, Spanish Cay, Walker's Cay.

Andros Congo Town, Fresh Creek, San Andros.

Berry Islands Chub Cay, Great Harbour Cay.

Biminis Alice Town, South Bimini, Cat Cay.

Cat Island Smith's Bay, New Bight, Bennett's Harbour.

Eleuthera Governor's Harbour, Harbour Island, North Eleuthera, Rock Sound, Spanish Wells.

Exumas George Town, Moss Town.

Grand Bahama Freeport Harbour, Port Lucaya Marina, Old Bahamas Bay Marina (West End).

Great Inagua Matthew Town.

Long Island Stella Maris.

Mayaguana Abraham's Bay.

New Providence Nassau (any yacht basin).

San Salvador Cockburn Town.

Permits
You'll require the regular documentation for foreign travel (see p287). There is a $150

charge for each foreign pleasure vessel under 30ft, and a $300 charge for vessels longer than 30ft with up to four passengers. Each additional person must pay $15. These charges cover customs and immigration services as well as fishing and cruising permits.

You must have a separate import permit for any pets on board. Contact the **Department of Agriculture** (☎ 242-325-7413; fax 242-325-3960; Levy Bldg, E Bay St, Nassau) for information.

Maps, Charts & Guidebooks

You'll need accurate maps and charts for any voyage through the Bahamas and Turks and Caicos' reef-infested waters. British Admiralty charts, US Defense Mapping Agency charts, and Imray yachting charts are all accurate. You can order them in advance from **Bluewater Books & Charts** (US ☎ 1-954-763-6533, 1-800-942-2583; www.bluewaterweb.com).

No sailor should set out without the excellent *Yachtsman's Guide to The Bahamas including Turks & Caicos* ($40). It provides detailed descriptions of just about every possible anchorage in the archipelago, and lists information on marinas throughout the islands as well as other invaluable information. Small sketch charts are *not* intended for use in navigation. It's available at bookstores and marinas in the Bahamas or by mail from **Tropic Isle Publishers** (US ☎ 305-893-4277; PO Box 610938, N Miami, FL 33261, USA).

Likewise, refer to the splendid *Bahamas Cruising Guide* by Mathew Wilson, which is available at good bookstores, and Julius Wilensky's *Cruising Guide to the Abacos and the Northern Bahamas* ($20). These and many other regional boating guides can be ordered from **White Sound Press** (US ☎ 386-423-7880; www.wspress.com).

Waterproof Charts (☎ 800-423-9026; www.waterproofcharts.com) publishes a series of large-scale waterproof sectional charts of the Bahamas. The charts mostly show physical features and are of limited use as travel maps. Larger-scale (11in by 17in) versions of the charts can be ordered; they're highly detailed and durable. A complete set of eight charts covers the Bahamas and Turks and Caicos ($160).

US government charts of the region can be ordered through most marine stores, as can detailed charts from **National Oceanic & Atmospheric Administration** (NOAA; ☎ 301-436-6829; www.nws.noaa.gov).

Crewing

Crewing aboard a yacht destined for the Bahamas from North America or the Caribbean is a popular way of getting to the islands. Check the bulletin boards of marinas: often you'll find notes advertising for crew or you can leave one of your own.

TURKS & CAICOS
Entering the Turks & Caicos

Visitors may each bring in duty free one carton of cigarettes or 50 cigars, one bottle of liquor or wine and 50g of perfume. The importation of all firearms is forbidden, except upon written authorization from the Commissioner of Police. Having spear guns, drugs and pornography with you is also illegal.

For further information, contact **Turks and Caicos Customs** (Grand Turk ☎ 649-946-2801; Provo ☎ 649-946-4241).

PASSPORT

Changes to the law in 2005 mean US citizens and all visitors are now required to have a passport or 'other secure, accepted document' to enter or re-enter the United States from the Caribbean. Everyone else including UK citizens also need a valid passport. No visas are required for citizens of the US, Canada, the UK and Commonwealth countries, Ireland, and most Western European countries. Citizens of most other countries require visas, which can be obtained from British embassies, High Commissions or consulates abroad (see p279).

Proof of onward transportation or tickets are required upon entry.

For information on work, residency or stays longer than three months, contact the **Turks and Caicos Immigration Department** (☎ 649-946-2929; fax 649-946-2924; South Base, Grand Turk, Turks & Caicos, BWI).

Air
AIRPORTS & AIRLINES

There are three airports handling international traffic to Grand Turk and Provo, but most international flights arrive at Provo. Other islands have local airstrips.

Grand Turk International Airport (GDT; ☎ 649-946-2233)

Providenciales International Airport, Caicos (PLS; ☎ 649-941-5670)

South Caicos International Airport (XSC; ☎ 649-946-4255)

The national carrier is **Air Turks and Caicos** (QW; ☎ 649-941-5481; www.airturksandcaicos.com; hub Caicos). It has a very good safety record and flies to Miami and Nassau.

Airlines Flying To and From the Turks & Caicos

Air Canada (AC; ☎ 649-941-3136; www.aircanada.com; hub Toronto)

Air Jamaica (JM; ☎ 1-800-523-5585; www.airjamaica .com; hub Montego Bay)

American Airlines/American Eagle (AA; ☎ 649-946-4948; www.aa.com; hubs New York & Miami)

Bahamasair (UP; ☎ 649-941-3136; www.bahamasair .com; hub Nassau)

British Airways (BA; ☎ 1-800-247-9297, 649-946-4420; www.british-airways.com; hubs Heathrow & Gatwick)

Delta Air Lines/Comair (DL; ☎ 1-800-221-1212; www .delta.com; hubs La Guardia New York & Boston)

US Airways/US Air Express (US; ☎ 1-800-622-1015; www.usair.com; hubs Philadelphia & New York)

TICKETS

See p288 for a list of online travel agencies. The fares below are one way.

Route	Price	Frequency
Providenciales–Atlanta	$449	1 daily
Providenciales–Boston	$431	1 weekly
Providenciales–Cap Haitien	$140	4 daily
Providenciales–Charlotte	$473	1 daily
Providenciales–Cuba	$380	2 weekly
Providenciales–Heathrow	$952	2 weekly
Providenciales–Miami	$371	2 daily
Providenciales–Montego Bay	$343	4 weekly
Providenciales–Nassau	$216	2 weekly
Providenciales–New York	$416	1 daily
Providenciales–Puerto Plaza	$179	2 daily
Providenciales–Toronto	$813	2 weekly

SEA
CRUISE SHIPS

The major cruise lines bypass the Turks and Caicos, although this may change in the future – the government has been talking of building a cruise-ship terminal on East Caicos.

At the time of going to press, a couple of cruise companies provided regular cruises to these islands: **American Canadian Caribbean Line** (☎ 0800-556-7450; www.accl-sm allships.com) as well as **Windjammer Barefoot Cruises** (☎ 305-672-6453, 800-327-2601; www.wind jammer.com).

FREIGHTERS

A comfortable passenger-carrying freighter departs from Grand Bahama to drop off supplies at Nassau, Little San Salvador, Conception Island, Little Inagua and the Plana Cays, plus Grand Turk and Providenciales. See p290 for details of this trip and some other useful information sources on freighter travel.

YACHTS

Yachters are permitted seven days in the islands, after which they must obtain a cruising permit good for three months. See the island chapters for marina details.

If traveling in your own boat, you must clear customs and immigration. Contact details for these officials are listed in destination chapters.

Many of the approaches and landfalls lie within protected areas where anchoring is strictly controlled (moorings within such areas are for dive boats only, although visiting yachts can moor while diving). No firearms may be brought into the Turks and Caicos (you must surrender them for the duration of your stay). No conch or lobster may be taken and fishing in national sea parks is forbidden.

The latest regulations can be obtained from the **Department of Environment & Coastal Resources** (Grand Turk ☎ 649-946-2855; fax 649-946-1895; ccr@tciway.tc; Providenciales ☎ 649-946-4017; fax 649-941-3063; South Caicos ☎ /fax 649-946-3306).

Contact **Wavey Line Publishing** (www.wavey linepublishing.com) to obtain a copy of *Turks & Caicos Islands Overall*, a series of navigational charts of the Turks and Caicos ($28 each). Nautical charts are sold in the Turks and Caicos at the Unicorn Bookstore (p243) on Provo. See Maps, Charts & Guidebooks (p291) for some other excellent reference materials.

Boaters and yachties should use VHF channel 16 (and VHF 09 or 13 in an emergency) for communications.

GETTING AROUND

Perusing a map, you may be tempted to think that island-hopping down the chain is easy. But unless you have your own boat or plane, it isn't. Interisland air travel is centered on Nassau. Getting between the islands without constantly backtracking is a bit of a feat. Even the mail boats are Nassau-centric.

BAHAMAS
Air
AIRLINES IN THE BAHAMAS

Interisland flights offer the only quick and convenient way to travel within the Bahamas, and islanders ride airplanes like Londoners use buses. You don't save any money by booking interisland tickets for the Bahamas in advance.

The scene is dominated by **Bahamasair** (UP; ☎ 242-377-5505, Freeport ☎ 242-352-8341; www .bahamasair.com; hubs Nassau & Freeport). The airline runs on a hub-and-spoke system: Nassau's the main hub. If you island-hop a lot, you'll feel like a yo-yo and may need to stay in Nassau between flights. Budget accordingly.

There are several airlines operating in the Bahamas.

Abaco Air (☎ 242-367-2266; www.abacoaviationcentre .com/abacoair; hub Marsh Harbour)

Caribbean Aviation (☎ 242-377-3317; caribairline@ yahoo.com; hub Nassau)

Cat Island Air (☎ 242-377-3318; fax 242-377-3723; hub Nassau)

Flamingo Air Charter Services (☎ 242-377-0354; www.flamingoair.com; hub Nassau)

Major's Air Services (☎ 242-352-5778; www.thebaha masguide.com/majorair; hubs Grand Bahama & Eleuthera)

Southern Air (☎ 242-367-2498; www.southernair charter.com; hub Nassau)

Western Air (☎ 242-329-4000; fax 242-329-3167; hub Andros & Nassau)

Tickets

Refer to the destination chapters for relevant interisland flight information. The table below includes prices for one-way fares for connections to Nassau.

Route	Price	Frequency
Nassau–Abacos	$81	3 daily
Nassau–Andros	$68	2 daily
Nassau–Biminis	$85	2 daily
Nassau–Cat Island	$75	2 daily
Nassau–Crooked	$105	2 weekly
Nassau–Eleuthera	$69	2 daily
Nassau–Exumas	$81	3 daily
Nassau–Grand Bahama	$85	6 daily
Nassau–Inagua	$111	3 weekly
Nassau–Long Island	$85	1 daily
Nassau–San Salvador	$80	3 weekly

CHARTER FLIGHTS

See p288 for a list of the region's major charter airlines.

Bicycle

Cycling is a cheap, convenient, healthy, environmentally sound and above all fun way to travel. Major resort hotels rent bicycles for $20 a day. Unfortunately, the bikes are heavy, have only one gear and are virtually guaranteed to give you a sore bum.

Boat
BOAT EXCURSIONS

There are a myriad of boat excursions on offer covering activities such as watersports, sightseeing, pleasure cruises, snorkeling and diving. Refer to the destination chapters for further information.

FERRY & WATER TAXI

The only ferry operator in the islands is **Bahamas Ferries** (☎ 242-323-2166/8; www.baha masferries.com), which runs a high-speed ferry linking Nassau, Andros, Abacos, Eleuthera and the Exumas.

Water taxis ply between Nassau and Paradise Island. Several other offshore islands and their neighboring cays are served by private water taxis.

Government-run water taxis link islands that are a short distance apart, such as North Bimini and South Bimini; Mangrove Cay and South Andros; and Crooked and Acklins Islands.

MAIL BOAT

Around 30 mail boats sail under government contract to most inhabited islands. They regularly depart Potter's Cay for Grand Bahama and all the Family Islands. Traditionally sailing overnight, boat journeys last between five and 24 hours. You can call the **Dockmaster's Office** (☎ 242-394-1237) and check with the **Bahamas Ministry of Tourism** (☎ 242-322-7500; www.bahamas.com) for the latest schedules and prices.

Car & Motorcycle

Bahamians are generally very cautious and civilized drivers. Main roads are normally in good condition, but minor roads are often indented with deep potholes. Believe any Bahamian who warns you that a road is in bad condition.

TRANSPORTATION

TRANSPORTATION

DRIVER'S LICENSE
To rent a car you must be 21 (some companies rent only to those 25 or older) and must have a current license for your home country or state. Visitors can drive using their home license for up to three months.

FUEL
Esso, Shell and Texaco maintain gas (petrol) stations on most islands. Gas stations are usually open from 8am to about 7pm. Some close on Sunday. In Nassau and Freeport you'll find stations open 24 hours a day. Gasoline costs $3.50 per US gallon. Credit cards are accepted in major settlements; elsewhere, it's cash only.

HIRE
Several major international car-rental companies have outlets in Nassau and Freeport, as do smaller local firms. In the Family Islands there are some very good local agencies. Ask your hotel for recommendations, or look for display boards at the airport. Local companies may not offer insurance.

You usually rent for 24-hour periods with rates starting at $70. Rates start from around $80 in Nassau, and from $60 on the smaller islands.

Golf carts can be rented on the smaller islands and cays for $40 per day.

INSURANCE
Damage-waiver insurance is $15 a day. On many Family Islands, however, no insurance is on offer at all.

ROAD RULES
Always drive on the left-hand side of the road. At traffic circles (roundabouts), remember to circle in a clockwise direction, entering to the left. You must give way to traffic already in the circle. It is compulsory to wear a helmet when riding a motorcycle or scooter.

Hitchhiking
Hitching is never entirely safe anywhere, and we don't recommend it. Travelers who do decide to hitch should understand that they are taking a small but potentially serious risk. Those who choose to hitch will be safer if they travel in pairs, and let someone know where they are planning to go. Hitchhiking by locals is fairly prevalent (and legal) in the Bahamas, especially in the Family Islands.

Local Transportation
BUS
Nassau and Freeport have dozens of jitney buses (private minibuses) licensed to operate on set routes.

There is no public transportation on the Family Islands or at airports (the taxi drivers' union is too powerful). Few hotels are allowed to run a transfer service for guests.

TAXI
There's no shortage of licensed taxis in Nassau and Freeport, where they can be hailed on the streets. Taxis are also the main form of local transportation in the Family Islands, where they meet all incoming planes.

All taxi operators are licensed. Taxi fares are fixed by the government based on distance. Rates are usually for two people, with each additional person charged a flat-rate of $3. Fixed rates have been established from airports and cruise terminals to specific hotels and major destinations. These rates should be shown in the taxi. However, you should be aware of some crafty scams in Nassau and Freeport, where an unscrupulous driver may attempt to charge additional people the same rate as the first and second passengers.

TURKS & CAICOS
Air
AIRLINES IN THE TURKS & CAICOS
Both scheduled local carriers have excellent safety records:

Air Turks & Caicos (JY; ☎ 649-941-5481; www.airturks andcaicos.com; hub Providenciales)

Skyking (RU; ☎ 649-941-5464; www.skyking.tc; hub Provenciales)

Tickets
The two local carriers fly between the following islands in the Turks and Caicos region. The following are sample prices for one-way fares.

Route	Price	Frequency
Grand Turk–Salt Cay	$25	2 daily
Providenciales–Grand Turk	$70	11 daily
Providenciales–Sth Caicos	$65	3 daily
Providenciales–Middle Caicos	$40	1 daily
Providenciales–Nth Caicos	$30	2 daily

Charter planes are available on most islands for private hire.

Bicycle

Cycling is an inexpensive and great way to travel. Bicycles can be rented at many hotels and concessions for about $20 per day.

Boat

BOAT EXCURSIONS

Most trips depart from the marinas in Provo (Providenciales). They cover the full gamut of pleasure cruises, watersports and sightseeing. Snorkeling and diving trips are offered on every island and operators will normally include any special wishes in their itineraries. Please refer to the destination chapters for specific trip details.

FERRY & WATER TAXI

A ferry normally runs biweekly from Grand Turk to Salt Cay ($12 round trip). Book ahead with **Salt Cay Charters** (☎ 649-231-6663; piratequeen3@hotmail.com). Whale-watching trips with this company cost $75.

Car, Motorcycle & Scooter

Because local transportation is limited, renting a car makes sense if you plan to explore Provo or Grand Turk. Provo does have a few atrocious, potholed, rocky and dusty roads, although many are now paved.

DRIVER'S LICENSE

To rent a car for up to three months, citizens of the USA, Canada, the UK and Commonwealth countries are required to have a valid driver's license from their home country. Everyone else requires an International Driving Permit. You must obtain this permit before you arrive in the Turks and Caicos.

FUEL

Gas stations are plentiful and usually open from 8am to 7pm. Some close on Sunday. Gasoline costs $3.50 per US gallon. Credit cards are accepted in major settlements. Elsewhere, you'll need to pay cash.

HIRE

Car rentals are available from $80 per day. Otherwise, stick to taxis for one-off trips or bicycles for scooting around locally. A government tax of $15 per rental on cars and $8 on scooter rentals is levied. Please refer to island destinations for rental companies.

INSURANCE

Mandatory insurance costs $15 per day.

ROAD RULES

Driving is on the left-hand side of the road. At traffic circles (roundabouts), remember to circle in a clockwise direction, entering to the left. You must give way to traffic already in the circle. Speed limits in the Turks and Caicos are 20mph in settlements and 40mph on main highways.

Hitchhiking

Hitchhiking is legal in the Turks and Caicos islands. However, only locals heading to and from work normally use their thumbs.

Local Transportation

BUS

Public bus services are limited to a few jitney routes in Provo. For regular routes, check with the **Turks & Caicos Tourist Board** (Providenciales Airport ☎ 649-941-5496, 649-946-4970; www.turksandcaicostourism.com; Stubbs Diamond Plaza, Providenciales).

TAXI

Taxis are available on all the inhabited islands. Most are minivans. They're a good bet for touring; most taxi drivers double as guides. Be sure to negotiate an agreeable price before setting out.

TRANSPORTATION

Health David Goldberg MD

Prevention is the key to staying healthy while abroad. Travelers who receive the recommended vaccines and follow common-sense precautions usually come away with nothing more than a little diarrhea.

From the medical standpoint, the Bahamas and Turks and Caicos are usually safe as long as you're pretty careful about what you eat and drink. The most common travel-related diseases, such as dysentery and hepatitis, are acquired by consumption of contaminated food and water. Mosquito-borne illnesses are not a significant concern here, except during outbreaks of dengue fever.

BEFORE YOU GO

Bring medications in their original containers, clearly labeled. A signed, dated letter from your physician describing all medical conditions and medications, including generic names, is also a good idea. If carrying syringes or needles, be sure to have a physician's letter documenting their medical necessity.

INSURANCE

If your health insurance does not cover you for medical expenses abroad, consider supplemental insurance. Check the Subway section of the **Lonely Planet website** (www.lonelyplanet.com/travel_links) for more information. US travelers can find a list of medical evacuation and travel insurance companies on the **US State Department website** (http://travel.state.gov). Find out in advance if your insurance plan will make payments directly to providers or reimburse you later for overseas health expenditures.

RECOMMENDED VACCINATIONS

No vaccinations are required to enter the Bahamas or Turks and Caicos. However, a yellow fever vaccination certificate is required for travelers arriving within seven days of traveling in many central African and South American countries. See www.mdtravelhealth.com for a current list of infected areas. Vaccination protection lasts 10 years.

MEDICAL CHECKLIST

- acetaminophen/paracetamol (Tylenol) or aspirin
- adhesive or paper tape
- antibacterial ointment (eg Bactroban) for cuts and abrasions
- antibiotics
- antidiarrheal drugs (eg loperamide)
- antihistamines (for hay fever and allergic reactions)
- anti-inflammatory drugs (eg ibuprofen)
- bandages, gauze and gauze rolls
- DEET-containing insect repellent for the skin
- iodine tablets (for water purification)
- oral rehydration salts
- permethrin-containing insect spray for clothing, tents and bed nets
- pocketknife
- scissors, safety pins and tweezers
- steroid cream or cortisone (for poison ivy and other allergic rashes)
- sunblock
- syringes and sterile needles
- thermometer

INTERNET RESOURCES

There is a wealth of travel health advice on the Internet. The **Lonely Planet website** (www.lonelyplanet.com) is a good place to start. The **World Health Organization** (www.who.int/ith/) publishes a superb book called *International Travel and Health,* which is revised annually and is available online at no cost. Another website of general interest is **MD Travel Health** (www.mdtravelhealth.com), which offers travel health recommendations for every country, updated daily, also at no cost.

It's usually a good idea to consult your government's travel health website before departure, if one is available.

Australia (www.smartraveller.gov.au)
Canada (www.hc-sc.gc.ca/english)
UK (www.doh.gov.uk/traveladvice)
USA (www.cdc.gov/travel)

FURTHER READING
If you're traveling with children, Lonely Planet's *Travel with Children* may be useful. *ABC of Healthy Travel* by E Walker et al, and *Medicine for the Outdoors* by Paul S Auerbach, are other valuable resources.

IN TRANSIT

DEEP VEIN THROMBOSIS (DVT)
Blood clots may form in the legs during plane flights, chiefly because of prolonged immobility. The longer the flight, the greater the risk. Though most blood clots are reabsorbed uneventfully, some may break off and travel through the blood vessels to the lungs, where they could cause life-threatening complications.

The chief symptom of DVT is swelling or pain in the foot, ankle or calf, usually but not always on just one side. When a blood clot travels to the lungs, it may cause chest pain and difficulty in breathing. Travelers with any of these symptoms should immediately seek medical attention.

To prevent the development of DVT on long flights, you should walk about the cabin, perform isometric compressions of the leg muscles (ie contract the leg muscles while sitting), drink plenty of fluids and avoid alcohol and tobacco.

JET LAG & MOTION SICKNESS
Jet lag is common when crossing more than five time zones, and is characterized by insomnia, fatigue, malaise or nausea. To avoid jet lag, try drinking plenty of fluids (nonalcoholic) and eating light meals. Upon arrival, get exposure to natural sunlight and readjust your schedule (for meals, sleep etc) as soon as possible.

Antihistamines such as dimenhydrinate (Dramamine) and meclizine (Antivert, Bonine) are usually the first choice for treating motion sickness. Their main side effect is drowsiness. A herbal alternative is ginger, which works like a charm for some people.

IN THE BAHAMAS & TURKS & CAICOS

AVAILABILITY & COST OF HEALTH CARE
High-quality medical care is usually available, but expensive, in Nassau and Freeport in the Bahamas. Medical care is limited elsewhere. Bahamian doctors and hospitals expect payment in cash, regardless of whether you have travel health insurance. If you develop a life-threatening medical problem, you'll probably want to be evacuated to a country with state-of-the-art medical care. Since this may cost tens of thousands of dollars, be sure you have insurance to cover this before you depart (see opposite).

Many pharmacies are well supplied, but important medications may not be consistently available. Be sure to bring along enough supplies of all prescription drugs.

Medical facilities are limited in the Turks and Caicos. There is a small public hospital on Grand Turk and a private clinic on Provo, which has a hyperbaric chamber. Most serious medical problems require medical evacuation by air from the Turks and Caicos to the US.

INFECTIOUS DISEASES
Dengue Fever
Dengue fever is a viral infection found throughout the Caribbean. Dengue is transmitted by aedes mosquitoes, which bite mostly during the daytime and are usually found close to human habitations, often indoors. They breed primarily in artificial water containers, such as jars, barrels, cans, cisterns, metal drums, plastic containers and discarded tires. As a result, dengue is especially common in densely populated, urban environments.

Dengue usually causes flu-like symptoms, including fever, muscle aches, joint pains, headaches, nausea and vomiting, often followed by a rash. The body aches may be quite uncomfortable, but most cases resolve uneventfully in a few days. Severe cases usually occur in children under age 15 who are experiencing their second dengue infection.

There is no treatment for dengue fever except to take analgesics such as acetaminophen or paracetamol (Tylenol) and drink plenty of fluids. Severe cases may require hospitalization for intravenous fluids and supportive care. There is no vaccine. The cornerstone of prevention is insect-protection measures, described on opposite.

Hepatitis A

Hepatitis A is the second most common travel-related infection (after travelers' diarrhea). It occurs throughout the Caribbean, particularly in the northern islands. Hepatitis A is a viral infection of the liver that is usually acquired by ingestion of contaminated water, food or ice, though it may also be acquired by direct contact with infected persons. The illness occurs throughout the world, but the incidence is higher in developing nations. Symptoms may include fever, malaise, jaundice, nausea, vomiting and abdominal pain. Most cases resolve without complications, though hepatitis A occasionally causes severe liver damage. There is no treatment.

The vaccine for hepatitis A is extremely safe and highly effective. If you get a booster six to 12 months later, it lasts for at least 10 years. You really should get it before you go to any developing nation. Because the safety of hepatitis A vaccine has not been established for pregnant women or children under age two, they should instead be given a gamma globulin injection.

Hepatitis B

Like hepatitis A, hepatitis B is a liver infection that occurs worldwide but is more common in developing nations. Unlike hepatitis A, the disease is usually acquired by sexual contact or by exposure to infected blood, generally through blood transfusions or contaminated needles. The vaccine is recommended only for long-term travelers (on the road more than six months) who expect to live in rural areas or have close physical contact with locals. Additionally, the vaccine is recommended for anyone who anticipates sexual contact with the local inhabitants or

a possible need for medical, dental or other treatments while abroad, especially if a need for transfusions or injections is expected.

Hepatitis B vaccine is safe and highly effective. However, a total of three injections are necessary to establish full immunity. Several countries added the hepatitis B vaccine to the list of routine childhood immunizations in the 1980s, so many young adults are already protected.

HIV/AIDS

HIV/AIDS has been reported in all Caribbean countries. More than 2% of all adults in the Caribbean carry HIV, which makes it the second-worst-affected region in the world, after sub-Saharan Africa. The highest prevalence is reported in the Bahamas, Haiti and Trinidad and Tobago. In the Caribbean, most cases are related to heterosexual contacts, especially with sex workers. Be sure to use condoms for all sexual encounters. If you think you might visit a piercing or tattoo parlor, or if you have a medical condition that might require an injection, make certain you bring along your own sterile needles.

Typhoid Fever

Typhoid is uncommon on most of the Caribbean islands, except Haiti, which has reported a number of typhoid outbreaks.

Typhoid fever is caused by ingestion of food or water contaminated by a species of salmonella known as *Salmonella typhi*. Fever occurs in virtually all cases. Other symptoms may include headache, malaise, muscle aches, dizziness, loss of appetite, nausea and abdominal pain. Either diarrhea or constipation may occur. Possible complications include intestinal perforation, intestinal bleeding, confusion, delirium or (rarely) coma.

Typhoid vaccine is recommended for all travelers to Haiti, and for travelers to the other islands who expect to stay in rural areas for an extended period or who may consume potentially contaminated food or water. Typhoid vaccine is usually given orally, but is also available as an injection. Neither vaccine is approved for use in children under age two. If you get typhoid fever, the drug of choice is usually a quinolone antibiotic such as ciprofloxacin (Cipro) or levofloxacin (Levaquin), which many travelers carry for treatment of travelers' diarrhea.

Yellow Fever

There is no yellow fever on the Bahamas or Turks and Caicos, but they require proof of yellow fever vaccination if you're arriving there from a yellow-fever-infected country in Africa or the Americas.

Yellow fever vaccine is provided only in approved yellow fever vaccination centers, which provide validated international certificates of vaccination ('yellow booklets'). The vaccine should be given at least 10 days before any potential exposure to yellow fever and remains effective for approximately 10 years. Reactions to the vaccine are generally mild and may include headaches, muscle aches, low-grade fevers or discomfort at the injection site. Severe, life-threatening reactions have been described but are extremely rare. In general, the risk of becoming ill from the vaccine is far less than the risk of becoming ill from yellow fever, and you're strongly encouraged to get the vaccine.

TRAVELERS' DIARRHEA

To prevent diarrhea, avoid tap water unless it has been boiled, filtered or chemically disinfected (with iodine tablets); eat fresh fruits or vegetables only if cooked or peeled; be wary of dairy products that might contain unpasteurized milk; and be highly selective when eating food from street vendors.

If you develop diarrhea, be sure to drink plenty of fluid, preferably an oral rehydration solution containing lots of salt and sugar. A few loose stools don't require treatment, but if you start having more than four or five stools a day, you should start taking an antibiotic (usually a quinolone drug) and an antidiarrheal agent (such as loperamide). If diarrhea is bloody or persists for more than 72 hours or is accompanied by fever, shaking chills or severe abdominal pain, you should seek medical attention.

ENVIRONMENTAL HAZARDS
Animal Bites

Do not attempt to pet, handle or feed any animal, with the exception of domestic animals known to be free of any infectious disease. Most animal injuries are directly related to a person's attempt to touch or feed the animal.

Any bite or scratch by a mammal, including bats, should be promptly and thoroughly cleansed with large amounts of soap and water, then an antiseptic such as iodine or alcohol should be applied. The local health authorities should be contacted immediately regarding possible postexposure rabies treatment, whether or not you've been immunized against rabies. It may also be advisable to start an antibiotic, since wounds caused by animal bites and scratches frequently become infected. One of the newer quinolones, such as levofloxacin (Levaquin), which many travelers carry in case of diarrhea, would be an appropriate choice.

Mosquito Bites

To prevent mosquito bites, wear long sleeves, long pants, hats and shoes (rather than sandals). Bring along a good insect repellent, preferably one containing DEET, which should be applied to exposed skin and clothing but not to eyes, mouth, cuts, wounds or irritated skin. In general, adults and children over 12 should use preparations containing 25% to 35% DEET, which usually lasts about six hours. Children between two and 12 years of age should use preparations containing no more than 10% DEET, applied sparingly, which will usually last about three hours. Products containing lower concentrations of DEET are as effective, but for shorter periods of time. Neurological toxicity has been reported from DEET, especially in children, but appears to be extremely uncommon and generally related to overuse. Compounds containing DEET should not be used on children under the age of two.

Insect repellents containing certain botanical products, including eucalyptus oil and soybean oil, are effective but last only 1½ to two hours. Repellents containing DEET are preferable for areas where there is a high risk of malaria, dengue fever or yellow fever. Products based on citronella are not effective.

For additional protection, you can apply permethrin to clothing, shoes, tents and bed nets. Permethrin treatments are safe and remain effective for at least two weeks, even when items are laundered. Permethrin should not be applied directly to skin.

Don't sleep with the window open unless there is a screen. If sleeping outdoors or in accommodations that allow entry of mosquitoes, use a bed net, preferably treated with permethrin, with edges tucked in under the mattress. The mesh size should be less

HEALTH

than 0.6in (1.5mm). If the sleeping area is not otherwise protected, use a mosquito coil, which will fill the room with insecticide through the night. Wristbands impregnated with repellent are not effective.

Sun

To protect yourself from excessive sun exposure, you should stay out of the midday sun, wear sunglasses and a wide-brimmed sun hat, and apply sunscreen with SPF 15 or higher, with both UVA and UVB protection. Sunscreen should be generously applied to all exposed parts of the body approximately 30 minutes before sun exposure and should be reapplied after swimming or vigorous activity. Travelers should also drink plenty of fluids and avoid strenuous exercise when the temperature is high.

Water

Tap water is safe to drink in the Bahamas and Turks and Caicos.

CHILDREN & PREGNANT WOMEN

In general, it's safe for children and pregnant women to go to the Bahamas and Turks and Caicos. When traveling with children, make sure they're up to date on all routine immunizations. It's sometimes appropriate to give children some of their vaccines a little early before visiting a developing nation. You should discuss this with your pediatrician. If pregnant, you should bear in mind that should a complication such as premature labor develop while you're on the islands, the quality of medical care may not be comparable to that in your home country.

Since the yellow fever vaccine is not recommended for pregnant women or children less than nine months old, these travelers, if arriving from a country with yellow fever, should obtain a waiver letter, preferably written on letterhead stationary and bearing the stamp used by official immunization centers to validate the international certificate of vaccination.

HEALTH

Glossary

English, the official language and that of business and daily life, is spoken by everyone but a handful of Haitian immigrants, who speak their own Creole. Many words in the region's lexicon are carryovers from the early English colonial days. You may, for example, be served a drink in a 'goblet.' Other words have been passed down from Africa, such as *bo-bo* (fool) and *nyam* (to eat).

'True-true' Bahamians normally speak both Bahamian Standard English (BSE) and their own distinct island patois, a musical Caribbean dialect with its own rhythm and cadence. Though there are variances among the islands and between Blacks and Whites, all sectors of Bahamian society understand patois, the language of the street.

The official language of the Turks and Caicos Islands is English. The local islanders' distinct dialect bears much resemblance to the Bahamian dialect. The Haitians speak their own French-based Creole patois.

All is well? – How are you today?

Bahama Mama – rum, fruit juice and coffee liqueur cocktail
Bahama parrot – endangered indigenous species of parrot
bangers and mash – a meal of sausages and mashed potatoes, usually served with baked beans
blockade running – avoiding the blockade during the American Civil War by traveling through the Bahamas to supply the Confederates
bo-bo – a fool or idiot
bound – constipated

cascating – being sick or vomiting
chile – a child or youngster
conch – large endangered marine snail, the flesh of which is a popular staple of Bahamian diet
Conchy Joes – Loyalist descendants
cook-outs – meals cooked outside, normally a social gathering with music

dress down to a fowl feather – to get dressed respectably eg for church services

fillymingo – flamingo
Fish Fry – a collection of informal bars and takeouts, prime party spots at weekends

fishenin – fishing
flim – movie, film

goblet – a glass, such as a goblet of beer
Gombay – otherwise called 'Junkanoo' is a fruit drink, popular with children
goombay – island music derived from the days of slavery
Goombay Smash – a classic Bahamian rum cocktail
Guava Duff – traditional Bahamian dessert made from guava jelly and sponge
go spillygatin' – going out to party
grits – a tapioca-like side dish (made of potato)
Gussy Mae – term of affection for a woman with an ample posterior

Hey man – typical colloquial and cordial greeting

jerk – peppery seasoning used in Jamaican cooking
Junkanoo – Boxing Day street carnival with parades, costumes and *goombay* music
johnnycakes – sweet bread or drop-scones made with shortening, fried or baked

Kalik – award-winning, locally brewed Bahamian beer

Loyalists – American colonists who supported British royalty during the US Revolution

man – friend
mash up – smashed up, such as a car after it has been in an accident
montell – a rogue; a person (typically a man) who is befriending people for their wealth
Moon Juice – alcoholic drink made with fresh coconut water and rum

no see ums – aggressive and invisible sandflies, whose bites will leave you itching for days
nyam – to eat or to consume

obeah – African-based practice; communicating with spirits

peas 'n' rice – commonplace side dish of boiled or fried rice and kidney beans
peas 'n' rice boungy – a woman with an ample posterior
pinas – pineapples
Pineathelon – a triathlon, run as part of the Pineapple Festival on the island of Eleuthera
plantain – banana variety and side dish that tastes like squash

GLOSSARY

potcake – mongrel dog, fed food from the bottom of pots
pudin de pan – bread pudding, a traditional English dessert

rake 'n' scrape – music made with household objects used as percussion
rat – wrath
rigging and chatting – a cornerstone of religious celebrations, much like a call and answer sermon
rum – local alcohol made from molasses, which comes in many flavors and strengths
Rum Cream – chilled drink made with rum, cream, custard and spices

sapodilla – fruit often made into custard and ice cream
seed-pods – a shaker that can be used as a popular musical instrument
slippy dick – a slipped disc
souse – a stew made from fish, goat and mutton often utilizing offal
soursop – also known as custard apple, a sweet and musky fruit used in ice cream

spiny lobster – the traditional Caribbean lobster, very popular
steak and kidney pud' – pastry-topped pie, made with kidney and steak; a traditional English dish
strongbark – tree with brilliantly colored white flowers, sometimes called the butterfly tree

T'anks – thank you
Ting – Jamaica's exported grapefruit carbonated drink, very tasty
tot – though
t'ree – three
true-true – definitely correct or real and genuine
Turks Head – local dark brewed beer made in the Turks and Caicos Islands

What happ'nin? – How are you? What has happened to you lately?
Who yo daddy is? – Where are you from?
wining – an intimate and common form of dancing across the Caribbean and West Indies

Behind the Scenes

THIS BOOK

This third edition of *Bahamas, Turks & Caicos* was researched and written by Jill Kirby except for the Diving chapter, which was prepared by Jean-Bernard Carillet, and the Health chapter, which was adapted for this region from material by Dr David Goldberg. The previous two editions of *Bahamas, Turks & Caicos* were researched and written by Christopher P Baker.

THANKS from the Author

My appreciation is manifold for Christopher Baker's inspiring initial work on this guide. Thanks also to Commissioning Editor Kathleen Munnelly, Managing Cartographer Alison Lyall, fellow author Jean-Bernard Carillet as well as Dr David Goldberg.

Also, much gratitude goes to (in Caicos) Wayne Garland and staff of the Comfort Suites, Dinesh Rampersaud of J&B Tours, staff of the Unicorn Bookstore, Chad, Ana and Bazile of Provo Fun Cycles & Autos; (in Nassau) thanks to Vernetta Roker at the Holiday Inn Junkanoo Beach Hotel, Paolo Garzaroli of Graycliff Hotel & Restaurant and Renea Knowles of Nassau & Paradise Island's Promotions Board; and (in Exumas) thanks to Godfrey Minns, Alvin Demeritte and Kay Turnquest of Bahama Houseboats as well as Nyoka Deveaux of the Bahamas Ministry of Tourism.

A toast to new friends: (in Long Island) Jean Pierce and Kris Newman of Reel Divers, Lynn Faulkner and Lucy Wells of Seaview Lodge; (in Eleuthera) John and Kay Duckworth of the Duck Inn; and (in Provo) Sandra Forbes.

Thank you, Cynthia & Norman Kirby, for your visit, the Bahamian dubloon and your love. While at my side, and in my heart John Allen made this journey possible and joyful. With love and gratitude for all your help on the road and at home; this one's for you, John.

CREDITS
Commissioning Editor: Kathleen Munnelly
Coordinating Editor: Melissa Faulkner
Coordinating Cartographer: Helen Rowley
Coordinating Layout Designer: Kaitlin Beckett
Managing Cartographer: Alison Lyall
Assisting Editors: Sasha Baskett, Kate Evans, Emma Gilmour, Carly Hall, Charlotte Harrison, Trent Holden, Katie Lynch, Charlotte Orr, Gary Walsh & Kate Whitfield
Cover Designer: Pepi Bluck
Project Manager: Ray Thomson

Thanks to Yvonne Bischofberger, Piotr Czajkowski, Sally Darmody, Martin Heng, Laura Jane, Adriana Mammarella, Fabrice Rocher, Lachlan Ross and Celia Wood

THANKS from Lonely Planet
Many thanks to the following travelers who used the last edition and wrote to us with helpful hints, useful advice and interesting anecdotes.

A Elaine Abel, Sonya Alvino, Erica Anderson **B** Jere Bacharach, Dawn Bays, Mohammed Bilal, Simon Blakemore, Kim Boyer, Eden Brower

---

THE LONELY PLANET STORY

The story begins with a classic travel adventure: Tony and Maureen Wheeler's 1972 journey across Europe and Asia to Australia. There was no useful information about the overland trail then, so Tony and Maureen published the first Lonely Planet guidebook to meet a growing need.

From a kitchen table, Lonely Planet has grown to become the largest independent travel publisher in the world, with offices in Melbourne (Australia), Oakland (USA) and London (UK). Today Lonely Planet guidebooks cover the globe. There is an ever-growing list of books and information in a variety of media. Some things haven't changed. The main aim is still to make it possible for adventurous travelers to get out there – to explore and better understand the world.

At Lonely Planet we believe travelers can make a positive contribution to the countries they visit – if they respect their host communities and spend their money wisely. Every year 5% of company profit is donated to charities around the world.

C Iku Collins, SJ Connerty-Smith, Peter Courtney **E** Shinann Earnshaw, Emefe Efe **F** Alison & Hank Fitzgerald, Sunita Foley **G** Kris Gerhardt, Ulli Gnigler **H** Tony Hartnett, Glenn Havelock, Judy Haywood, John Heneghan, Eric Henriksen, Tommy Huynh **J** Christi Jolly, Nick Jones, Rosemary Jones **K** Katrina Kernodle, Dennis F King, Connie Kuhn **M** Karen Marty, Guy Massey, BA McGraal **P** PJ Pace, Ron Pagliaro, Dianne Palmer **R** Cornelia Reschke, Marilyn Rigden **S** Vivek Sharma, Tracey Shelmerdine, Jonathan Sibert, Julia Smith, Randi Somers, Lisa Strachan, Bruce Stuart **T** Kevin Tearle **W** Gustaf Wachtmeister, Dan Webb, Fred Westwood, John White **Y** Robert Youker

ACKNOWLEDGMENTS

Many thanks to the following for the use of their content:

Globe on back cover © Mountain High Maps 1993 Digital Wisdom, Inc.

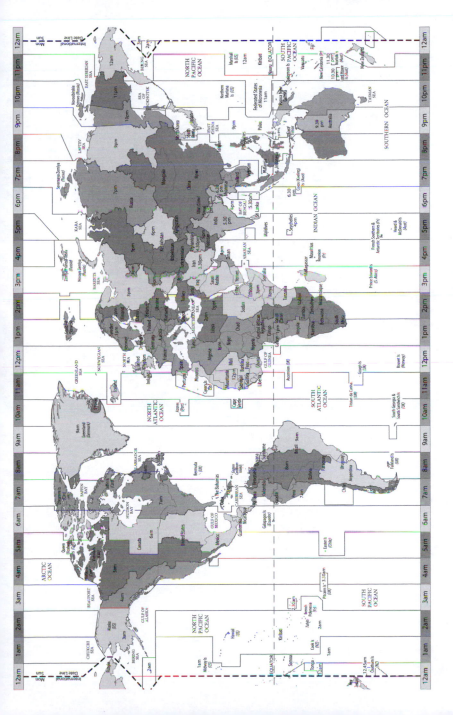

Index

000 Map pages
000 Location of color photographs

MAP LEGEND
ROUTES

Primary Road	Unsealed Road
Secondary Road	One-Way Street
Tertiary Road	Steps
Lane	Walking Trail

TRANSPORT

Ferry

HYDROGRAPHY

River, Creek	Reef
Mangrove	Water

BOUNDARIES

International	Marine Park

AREA FEATURES

Airport	Land
Beach	Park
Building	Rocks
Cemetery, Christian	Sports

POPULATION

CAPITAL (NATIONAL)	Small City
CAPITAL (PROVINCE)	Medium City
Large City	Town, Village

SYMBOLS

Sights/Activities
Beach
Castle, Fort
Christian
Diving
Kayaking
Monument
Museum, Gallery
Point of Interest
Ramsar Site
Ruin
Surfing
Snorkeling
Trail Head

Eating
Eating
Drinking
Drinking
Café
Entertainment
Entertainment
Shopping
Shopping
Sleeping
Sleeping
Transport
Airport, Airfield
Bus Station
Gas Station

Information
Bank, ATM
Embassy/Consulate
Hospital, Medical
Information
Internet Facilities
Police Station
Post Office
Telephone
Toilets
Geographic
Lighthouse
Mountain
National Park

LONELY PLANET OFFICES

Australia
Head Office
Locked Bag 1, Footscray, Victoria 3011
☎ 03 8379 8000, fax 03 8379 8111
talk2us@lonelyplanet.com.au

USA
150 Linden St, Oakland, CA 94607
☎ 510 893 8555, toll free 800 275 8555
fax 510 893 8572, info@lonelyplanet.com

UK
72–82 Rosebery Ave,
Clerkenwell, London EC1R 4RW
☎ 020 7841 9000, fax 020 7841 9001
go@lonelyplanet.co.uk

Published by Lonely Planet Publications Pty Ltd
ABN 36 005 607 983

© Lonely Planet 2005

© photographers as indicated 2005

Cover photographs: Harbour Island, Bahamas, Scott Barrow, Inc./ Photolibrary.com (front); Sailboats on the beach, Mark & Audrey Gibson/Lonely Planet Images (back). Many of the images in this guide are available for licensing from Lonely Planet Images: www .lonelyplanetimages.com

Printed through The Bookmaker International Ltd.
Printed in China